the ART&SOUL of BAKING

To our customers, for whom baking is a passion!
They constantly remind us of the joy and
pleasure in the art and soul of baking and have
made us a destination for the tools of their trade.

the ART & SOUL of BAKING

Sur La Table
with Cindy Mushet

FOREWORD BY Alice Medrich
PHOTOGRAPHY BY Maren Caruso

Andrews McMeel
Publishing, LLC

Kansas City

The Art and Soul of Baking © 2008 by Sur La Table, Inc. All rights reserved. Printed in China. No part of this book may be used or reproduced in any manner whatsoever without written permission except in the case of reprints in the context of reviews. For information, write Andrews McMeel Publishing, LLC, an Andrews McMeel Universal company, 1130 Walnut Street, Kansas City, Missouri 64106.

08 09 10 11 12 SDB 10 9 8 7 6 5 4 3 2 1

Library of Congress Cataloging-in-Publication Data:
Mushet, Cindy, 1960-
  The art and soul of baking / Cindy Mushet.—1st ed.
    p. cm.
  ISBN-13: 978-0-7407-7334-1
  ISBN-10: 0-7407-7334-8
  1. Baking. I. Sur La Table (Firm) II. Title. III. Title: Art and soul of baking.

TX765.M87 2008
641.8'15—dc22

2008008232

www.andrewsmcmeel.com
www.surlatable.com

Design: Vertigo Design NYC
Food Stylist: Kim Konecny
Prop Stylist: Kerrie Sherrell Walsh

ATTENTION: SCHOOLS AND BUSINESSES
Andrews McMeel books are available at quantity discounts with bulk purchase for educational, business, or sales promotional use. For information, please write to: Special Sales Department, Andrews McMeel Publishing, LLC, 1130 Walnut Street, Kansas City, Missouri 64106.

Contents

FOREWORD
by Alice Medrich

NEARLY TWENTY YEARS AGO, I demonstrated a simple French chocolate torte recipe from my first book, *Cocolat*, at a small table in a tiny cookware shop on the Seattle waterfront. The original Sur La Table store was cramped and crowded with people, and a serious *batterie de cuisine* filled the shelves from the worn, wooden floor right up to the ceiling. Or so I remember it. Sur La Table was the only store in America that evoked, for me, the venerable and iconic chef's emporium, Dehillerin, adjacent to the original Les Halles in the center of Paris, where I'd bought my first copper bowl and balloon whisk.

When additional Sur La Table stores opened, I taught countless classes across the country in their new kitchens. I met avid home cooks and talented professionals in every location. And I bought beautiful cookware without going to Paris! Many years and six cookbooks later, I am grateful that I had the opportunity to become acquainted with my readers, hone my recipes, and improve my teaching skills.

Cindy Mushet, in her own words, came of age as a pastry chef and baker in Berkeley, buying chocolate truffles in my shop (every couple of days she says!), and reading, tasting, and devouring classes at Tante Marie's Cooking School in San Francisco where she learned from a panoply of the best American bakers and chefs. Our paths crossed as early members of the first chapter of the Baker's Dozen, and as Cindy worked in restaurants, bakeries, and test kitchens; started her own baking business; taught; and wrote.

A talented, accomplished baker, and a dedicated teacher, Cindy brings her expertise to this comprehensive but clear and accessible new baking book. Cindy's voice and authority spring from her own hands-on experience as a tinkerer and tester who always wants to know why, and from her formal training and study. She is, thus, a superb and empowering teacher who relates to the beginner as well as the seasoned baker. *The Art and Soul of Baking* is loaded with information yet remarkably down-to-earth, personal, clear, well organized, and simple to navigate. Recipes are easy to follow; separate sidebars handle the "whys" with just the right amount of science, and include invaluable professional insights and tips.

In each chapter you'll find basic recipes that every baker needs, as well as more inspiring contemporary variations and new twists. You'll also learn the importance of accuracy and good technique while acquiring the knowledge and confidence to improvise and create! Tips and primers abound on subjects from custards to meringues, to plating and decorating, plus essential troubleshooting tactics to cope with curdled or soupy buttercream or misbehaving ganache; then it's onward to making stencils, spinning sugar, and all the stuff of bakers' dreams.

Prosaic as it may seem, I am glad that ingredient quantities expressed in traditional cup and spoon measurements are also given in weights. I hope that Cindy's passionate argument for the scale will persuade home bakers that weighing ingredients produces more consistently delectable results, streamlines the work, and reduces cleanup. Regardless, the book's two essential double-page charts should be photocopied and hung inside a cupboard door for easy reference: the first converts measures to weights and the second is a handy guide to pan sizes and volumes.

The Art and Soul of Baking is a joyous invitation to the world of butter, sugar, flour, eggs, and chocolate: an inspired guide to the practice of baking today. It is a wonderful addition to any cook's library.

Introduction

WELCOME TO THE WORLD OF BAKING, where the tantalizing aromas of chocolate, vanilla, butter, and cinnamon fill the air and tempt the palate. With today's hectic schedules, it's truly a gift to take the time to bake something from scratch, whether it's as simple as a welcome-home cookie or as ambitious as homemade croissants. The process of baking is soothing and satisfying on many levels: The ingredients smell wonderful, mixing and kneading are hypnotic and relaxing, decorating is creative and fun, and the enthusiastic reactions of friends and family after they have tasted something fresh from the oven are heartwarming. It's this sharing and sense of accomplishment that brings bakers back to the kitchen again and again.

But for some, the baking process can seem daunting and the techniques involved less than intuitive. It can be frustrating when things go wrong, often with no clear reason why. This book is here to help. In addition to its many mouthwatering recipes, *The Art and Soul of Baking* is also a tool for learning about the ingredients and techniques in baking—knowledge that will improve your skills and enrich your experiences no matter what your level of expertise.

At the beginning of each chapter, you'll find a primer that describes in detail the style of baked goods within the chapter, as well as a review of the ingredients, techniques, and, yes, even the science you need to know for success with the recipes that follow. For example, if you've never made bread before, you'll learn why the flour you choose is key, why kneading is important, and how to tell when you've kneaded or risen the dough long enough. You'll learn what a starter is, the differences between *poolish* and *biga,* and how to use them for maximum flavor in your bread.

One of the best things about having a professional baker guide you through the book is the inside information you'll glean along the way . . . the tips, techniques, and tidbits of knowledge that can make a huge difference in the fine points of a recipe. Many of these tips, known as *truc* in the industry, are included in the primers and recipe instructions, while others are found throughout the book under the heading "What the Pros Know." They relate specifically to the recipe at hand, and give you greater insight into a technique or ingredient in the recipe, options for improvisation, or the food science behind its success. It's like having a pastry chef next to you in the kitchen, encouraging and empowering you to become a better baker.

The recipes in each chapter span a range of levels, from simple to more advanced. But no matter which recipe you choose, the thorough, step-by-step instructions will take you by the hand and guide you to baking success. Each recipe includes a list of equipment so you know in advance exactly what you need to complete each step. There are also helpful "Getting Ahead" notes, with ideas on which steps can be completed in advance. This advice is particularly relevant for entertaining and fitting baking into a busy schedule. Additionally, you'll find suggestions on the best way to store the finished baked good, and how long it will keep. Many recipes are followed by variations that offer fun twists such as using a different pan, adding a new flavoring, or substituting a different fruit to expand your baking repertoire.

Before you begin baking though, take the time to read through the first two chapters. They will help you organize your mind, your kitchen, and your approach to baking, resulting in better baked goods on your very first try. Chapter 1 is dedicated to setting up your baking kitchen. Here you'll learn some great tips for organizing your kitchen like a professional, which will help make your time in the kitchen more enjoyable. All the baking equipment you'll need is explained, from cake pans to *bannetons* to rolling pins, with recommendations on everything from the type of metal in the pans you buy to the most often used size of pans and equipment, and even substitution suggestions for equipment you don't have on hand. You'll learn how to make sure your oven is accurate, a tip that can improve your baking before you mix your first batter.

Chapter 1 will also teach you how to measure accurately with dry and liquid measuring cups, which is the key to baking success. Moreover, you'll learn why professionals love to weigh their ingredients, and how a simple digital scale can revolutionize your baking at home. Included is an easy reference chart that converts cup measurements to weights for all the most commonly used baking ingredients, including flours, sugars, nuts, and chocolate. This allows you to weigh ingredients for any recipe you like, whether it's in this book or not. A second chart makes substituting baking pans a breeze, and is a handy reference when you're ready to bake and suddenly find you don't have the right size pan.

Chapter 2 is where you begin to think like a pastry chef. It covers all the ingredients used in recipes from this book, with special emphasis on the seven main baking components: flour, sugar, eggs, butter and other dairy products, leaveners, chocolate, and vanilla. You'll learn how to choose, store, and use your ingredients properly. In addition, you'll learn how and why these ingredients work, both independently and when combined, which will boost your confidence and ensure success when creating the pastries you love. For instance, why can't baking powder and baking soda be used interchangeably? Why is room temperature butter often a problem in cake batters? What do those percentages on the front of chocolate bars mean? Why can't milk chocolate be substituted for dark chocolate?

The information contained in chapter 2 is what professional bakers know, and what students attending *patisserie* school learn in class. A bit of food science in language you can understand is a boon to those who've always wanted to know why some recipes work and others fail, and it's one of the key components of this book. After all, each baked good is like a little chemistry experiment. And chemistry is based on ratios. What is a recipe, then, but a list of ingredient ratios and the method on how to blend them?

Don't worry, this doesn't mean you need to be a scientist to make a cake. You simply need a good recipe and someone to explain what matters and why—information that is easily found in these pages. For instance, baking powder added in the correct amount will cause cake batter to rise; add too much and the cake will fall. Warm liquid awakens yeast and encourages them to start the bread-rising process, but liquid that is too hot kills yeast and dooms bread from the start. Air beaten into egg whites makes soufflés rise, but those same egg whites beaten too long result in a leaden batter that won't cross the rim of the dish. Armed with the information in chapter 2 and the primers throughout the book, any recipe you make will look and taste its best.

Once you've got an overview of the basics, you'll feel confident delving into the recipe chapters (chapters 3 through 13), which are the very heart of this book and full of recipes you'll want to make again and again. If the aroma of baking bread makes you weak in the knees, begin your baking journey with yeast breads, which are the focus in chapter 3. Here you'll learn about the different types of bread dough, what starters are, and

how they make a difference, as well as a foolproof method for determining when bread is finished baking. Try your hand at Rustic Thyme and Olive Bread, Pizza Dough, Cinnamon-Currant Bread, or Maple-Pecan Sticky Buns.

Chapter 4 ventures into territory that intimidates many home bakers as well as aspiring professionals—the layered doughs such as puff pastry, croissant, and Danish. Once you've read the primer, though, you'll understand how the multiple layers are created, and the landmines to avoid in the process. Follow the recipes patiently and you'll find yourself turning out flaky, blistered croissants that rival those in France, and puff pastry creations that put store-bought varieties to shame. Chapter 5 covers quick breads and provides great tips on these fast, easy pastries for everyday baking, including muffins, scones, biscuits, and popovers.

Chapter 6 explores pies, turnovers, and dumplings, and begins by taking the intimidation out of classic pie dough, and putting a crisp, flaky, golden pie crust firmly within your grasp. You'll also learn how to roll dough easily, make a decorative edge, and weave a beautiful lattice. Fruit pie thickeners and the technique of prebaking pie crusts are explained as well. Soon you'll be turning out All-American Apple Pie, Peach-Gingerbread Dumplings, and Herbed Chicken Pot Pie with ease. Tarts are the subject of chapter 7. These low-profile French beauties use simple crusts that are virtually foolproof to delicious effect in recipes that range from a chewy hazelnut and caramel Baci Tart with Frangelico Cream to a luscious Malted Milk Chocolate Tart, and a simple Apricot-Cherry Galette with Almond Cream. And if you love fruit desserts, then chapter 8 will be dog-eared with favorites. These recipes are easy to make so they're great for beginners, and result in some of the best-loved desserts of all, including Apple-Cranberry Crisp with Oatmeal Topping, Peach–Vanilla Bean Cobbler with Sugar Crunch Lattice, and Gingerbread Shortcakes with Caramelized Apples and Cider Sabayon. Chapter 9 explores cookies and includes plenty of tips, such as how to portion so all the cookies bake in the same amount of time, how to prevent spreading, and how to have fresh-baked treats in less than 15 minutes, whether you make Chocolate Chip Cookies (with two kinds of chocolate) or Peanut Butter Thumbprints with Peanut Caramel.

Chapter 10 offers cakes for every occasion. The primer guides you through the types of cakes, the science behind their success, and the methods used to produce them. If you've ever had trouble with heavy butter cakes or less-than-airy sponge cakes, this chapter will answer your questions and give you the confidence you need to eschew cake mixes forever. Recipes include favorites, such as Classic Yellow Layer Cake, which is perfect for a birthday party, and continue through a host of tempting titles like Tangerine–Poppy Seed Chiffon Cake and Flourless Chocolate Cake with Crème Fraîche Topping. In chapter 11, you'll learn about velvety custards, with plenty of advice on everything from how to prevent cheesecakes from cracking to creating the perfect burnt sugar topping on crème brûlée. For a delicious twist on tried-and-true favorites, try Bananas Foster Bread Pudding, Citrus–Goat Cheese Cheesecake, or White Chocolate–Lime Crème Caramel. Chapter 12 celebrates the role of eggs in desserts with easy insights into soufflés, meringues, and pâte à choux, which are all entirely reliant upon eggs for their drama and texture. You'll learn how to dispense with tricky paper soufflé collars, and what makes soufflés fall (it's not what you think). Learn why meringues bead and weep, and how to add flavor without deflating the airy foam. Discover the science behind the simple, hollow puffs known as *pâte à choux*, and get some advice on piping the sticky dough. You'll love the recipe for Raspberry Soufflés with Hidden Chocolate Truffles, the ethereal Pavlovas with Honey-Lavender Cream and Poached Strawberries, and the addictive Dulce de Leche Éclairs with Milk Chocolate Glaze.

Chapter 13 contains all the basic recipes and finishing techniques you need to add creativity and spark to your pastries. Here you'll find a bevy of luscious frostings ranging from classic Silky Vanilla Buttercream to soft and tangy Cream Cheese Frosting to sensuously rich Dark Chocolate Ganache, each followed by variations to give you flavoring ideas and ignite the fire of dessert improvisation. You'll also find tips on pairing frostings with cakes for optimum flavor and texture. On those special occasions when you want to go the extra mile, serve your pastry with a sauce, such as Fresh Raspberry Sauce, Honeyed Yogurt, or Orange Sabayon Cream. The classic Vanilla Custard Sauce can be flavored to match any pastry and is wonderful in combination with other sauces. You'll find instructions on how to create beautiful sauce designs, sugared flowers, chocolate decorations, and spun sugar sure to wow your guests (and nobody needs to know how easy and fun it all is). For the ultimate treat, you'll learn how to use gold and silver leaf for a striking garnish, and how to accent or "paint" desserts with shimmering luster dust.

The title of this book, *The Art and Soul of Baking*, speaks to the love of craft felt by those with a passion for baking. The art is technique and the soul is that intangible quality the baker gives to each loaf of bread or pastry created by hand. Whether you're new to the kitchen or baking is a familiar old friend, the guidance and recipes in *The Art and Soul of Baking* will not only make everything you bake look and taste better, they will also improve the quality of your time spent in the kitchen. Have fun, enjoy the process, and when you're done, sit back and lick the spatula every once in a while.

There are few things more soothing than the aroma of baking bread on a rainy day, or the sweet scent of cookies after a long day at school. Baking involves all of the senses—touch, taste, sight, scent, and even sound (ever hear bread crust crackle as it cools?). Your senses tell you when cookies are done, when caramel is the right color, when dough feels soft and supple. Details count. Well-made equipment and attention to measuring techniques are as important as the gentle folding of batter or fingertips schooled in pie dough.

The equipment you use for baking need not be expensive, extensive, or even necessarily new, but as with any endeavor, your tools can make the task at hand a pleasure or a chore. Whether you choose to begin baking breads, cakes, or cookies, your measuring technique, equipment, and ingredients will determine to a great extent the quality of your efforts. For proof, you need only look to your own profession, taking a close look at the equipment and "ingredients" that make the work easier and more efficient, resulting in a job well done. The baking profession is just the same. Oh, you can make a great cake with a warped cake pan, worn-out mixer, and wildly fluctuating oven, but it's much more difficult than it need be, and could likely result in disaster. Where's the pleasure in that? You're likely to love baking if your time in the kitchen is a good experience. Within this chapter is some of the most important information you need to make baking a true pleasure.

Organizing Your Work Area

Professional bakers work in a kitchen that is organized and stocked for maximum efficiency, and while keeping comfort in mind, the home baker can incorporate some of the same ideas to make baking more pleasurable. Keep everything in as tight a work area as possible, so you're not walking all over the kitchen to find ingredients and equipment. Though professional kitchens can seem large and cavernous (most are not), individual workstations are usually quite small to keep movement efficient, so you needn't feel you're at a disadvantage if your kitchen is not spacious.

Keep flour and sugar in airtight containers on the counter where you measure and blend your ingredients, preferably near your mixer. More obscure ingredients can be tucked away somewhere, but always use sturdy airtight containers, so the ingredients are in good condition when you need them—there's nothing worse than finding moths in your cake flour or spilled cocoa powder when you're in the middle of a baking session. Have some of the most popular sweet spices nearby, such as cinnamon, ginger, cloves, allspice, and cardamom.

Keep all your baking tools together, so you don't have to run around looking for them just to whip up a batch of cookies. Have your measuring cups (dry and liquid) and spoons within easy reach. If you bake often, a crock full of the utensils used specifically for baking is handy on the counter, but if space is limited, store them in an airtight box tucked into a closet or under your bed. Many ingredients in the baking kitchen, such as butter, eggs, cream, and chocolate, readily absorb flavors, so it's better to keep some utensils separate. Have a couple of silicone or rubber spatulas of various sizes dedicated specifically to baking, so you're not stirring chocolate with a garlic-scented tool. Ditto with soft bristle pastry brushes and wooden utensils, since they retain odors no matter how often or how well they are washed. For stirring, a flat-edged wooden spatula is great for custard sauces and puddings. And two brushes are really all you need—a smaller one for wet mixtures and a larger one for brushing flour from dough.

Keep a stack of mixing bowls in an easily accessible spot, since many baking recipes require two or more. Stainless-steel bowls are great because they don't absorb odors or fat, are easy to clean, and are virtually unbreakable. And you'll definitely want a supply of parchment paper on hand, precut to the size of the pans you use most often. You can purchase precut rounds at fine cooking stores, but it's easy to cut a stack of them yourself while watching TV. In baking, as in life, it's often the little things that count, and having parchment in ready-to-use condition and equipment within arm's reach means you can relax and focus on the more creative and engaging aspects of the task at hand.

Ensuring Oven Accuracy

There is no tool more fundamental to baking than your oven. Most people assume that their ovens are accurate, but the reality is that many home ovens are off by at least 25° to 50°F, sometimes up to 100°F, even when brand new! It doesn't matter if your oven is inaccurate, so long as you know. You can always adjust the temperature to correct any inconsistencies. It's when you don't realize your oven is hotter or cooler than indicated on the dial that your time and efforts are wasted. Too high a temperature and your pastries burn on the outside before the inside is cooked. Ensuring that your oven is accurate is one of the easiest ways to immediately improve your baking: Purchase an alcohol-based oven thermometer (the type with the glass tube) and test your oven regularly.

TESTING YOUR OVEN

Adjust an oven rack to the center position and set the thermometer in the center of the rack—this is key. Many people push the thermometer to the side or back of the oven where the temperature is hotter because of the metal oven walls. You want to test the temperature where you will bake your breads and pastries—in the center.

Set the oven to 350°F and allow time for it to fully heat. Many ovens will beep to let you know when they have reached the set temperature, often in as few as 5 to 10 minutes. Don't believe it. Allow at least 20 to 30 minutes for the oven to reach the temperature you set. Then quickly open the door and read the thermometer. If the temperature is lower or higher than the

temperature you set, make a note of it and remember to adjust for this each time you bake. If the thermometer reads 325°F, set the oven 25°F higher than the temperature you want (375°F in this case). If the thermometer reads 375°F, set the oven 25°F lower, 325°F in this case. If it is inaccurate by 75°F or more, consider having a new oven thermostat installed.

Once you've tested the oven, you can leave the thermometer in the oven, or let it cool and store it in a drawer until you test again, in a month or so. If you leave it in the oven, be sure to remove it when heating the oven to a temperature over 450°F, or when roasting chicken or meats, as the grease splattered on the thermometer will obscure the reading.

Measuring 101

Aside from your oven, nothing can influence the outcome of your breads and pastries more than measuring. Baking is chemistry, and chemistry depends on ratios. The amount of flour in relation to butter, liquid, and leavener in a recipe is crucial to successful baking. There's an age-old divide between cooks and bakers, and it revolves around this specific point. The stereotypes are that cooks are intuitive, open-minded souls who cook by the seat of their pants, whereas bakers are precise and controlling slaves to recipes, carefully measuring every ingredient. While there's a bit of truth in those stereotypes, it is because bakers need to be more precise, and that is because of chemistry.

In cooking, you can throw in a bit of this and a handful of that, tasting and tasting as you go along, making corrections throughout the process. Not so in baking. Once the ingredients are mixed and put in the pan, there's no more fixing or correcting. If the cake falls, there's nothing you can do except try to hide it under frosting. Nobody wants to invest time, energy, and money in making something that is disappointing. Stereotypes aside, anybody can bake, and bake well. And the best way to ensure that you'll have successful baked goods is to measure accurately. Each recipe in this book gives measurements in both volume (cups and tablespoons) and weights. Home cooks are more comfortable with measuring by volume, but did you know that there's a whole technique to it?

MEASURING BY VOLUME

Buy high-quality measuring cups and spoons. They'll last the rest of your life, and you can be assured of their accuracy. A schoolteacher we know purchased ten sets of colorful plastic measuring cups and spoons at a popular superstore to teach cooking in her classroom, then experienced disaster after disaster until she compared them to her home set of measuring tools. She found the inexpensive tools were woefully inaccurate. They seemed like

what the
pros
know   An oven temperature that is too low will cause your batters and doughs to melt before they set, resulting in greasy, undercooked pastries.

a bargain until she added up the cost of all the ruined food, not to mention the disappointed children. You'll need a nesting set of four dry measuring cups, a set of four measuring spoons, and two liquid measuring cups (see page 8 for buying tips).

Take your time. Remember the old carpenter's adage, "measure twice, cut once." Precision matters. You don't have to measure twice, but do be careful that you have the correct measuring cup for the task at hand, and that you are certain of the amount to be measured. This is especially important when doubling or halving a recipe—it's easy to lose track if you're doing the math in your head. If you want to adjust recipes upward or downward, write the adjustments in pencil in the margin of the recipe, next to the original measurements. This way, if you get distracted by kids, dogs, or the news, you will still bake a delicous cake.

HOW TO MEASURE LIQUIDS

Liquid measuring cups are glass or clear plastic, have a pour spout, and feature plenty of extra headroom above the highest marking, so they can be filled to that measure without spilling over. Remember the meniscus line from science class? It's the curved surface line of water and is the reason you shouldn't measure liquids in dry measuring cups—to fill the cup completely, the meniscus line would have to rise above the rim of the cup, and since that is impossible, the liquid will spill over, leaving less than a full cup.

To properly measure liquids, set the liquid measuring cup on a flat surface, pour in the liquid, and lean over to gauge the accuracy at eye level. Then make the necessary adjustments, always rechecking at eye level. (Some newer models of liquid measuring cups are marked in an innovative manner on the inside of the cup to alleviate the need for bending over.) When measuring small amounts of liquid in measuring spoons, simply fill them to the top edge of the spoon and add it to the recipe. Because every recipe that uses measuring spoons is aware of their shortfall when measuring liquids, the meniscus line issue has already been taken into account. Besides, with the liquids measured in these small amounts, a tiny bit more or less doesn't really matter (not so with the dry ingredients like baking powder and baking soda, but those are easy to measure accurately in spoons).

HOW TO MEASURE FLOUR AND OTHER DRY INGREDIENTS

Dry measuring cups are made of metal or plastic and come in nesting sets of four, containing one of each of the following: 1 cup, ½ cup, ⅓ cup, and ¼ cup. Occasionally, there may be extra cups included in a set, measuring ⅔ cup or ¾ cup, but all you really need are the basic four. To properly measure dry ingredients, it's important to carefully watch the wording of each ingredient. Is the cocoa sifted? Are the dried apricots packed? Firmly or loosely? If the recipe asks you to pack the brown sugar, press it into the cup tightly. If the confectioners' sugar is lightly spooned into the cup,

do so until it mounds over the rim, then gently sweep the edge of a knife or a spatula across the top to level the sugar flush with the rim of the cup.

It's especially important to pay attention to the modifier when measuring flour. These entries in an ingredient list result in two separate amounts:

1 cup flour, sifted
1 cup sifted flour

In the first entry, the flour is scooped into the cup and leveled flush with the rim (resulting in a weight of 5 ounces per cup), then sifted after it has been measured. In the second, the flour is sifted before measuring, resulting in a weight of 3¾ ounces per cup.

To measure a sifted ingredient, place the measuring cup on a piece of parchment paper and sift the flour over the cup until it fills the cup and is slightly mounded over the rim. Use the straight edge of a knife or a spatula to gently scrape off the mounded excess, leveling the flour with the rim of the measuring cup. This leveling technique is the reason you shouldn't measure dry ingredients in a liquid measuring cup—you can't level it at the top edge, so you end up shaking the cup to level the contents, compacting them in the process and throwing off the measurement. If a recipe asks you to "lightly spoon and level," do just that, spooning the flour into the cup, mounding and leveling as described above. If the recipe asks you to measure by the "dip and sweep" method, first loosen the flour in the bag or container slightly by gently "stirring" it with the handle of a wooden spoon. Then dip the measuring cup into the flour, lift it out with flour mounded above the rim and level it off as described. Use this same dip and sweep method with measuring spoons, mounding them and then scraping off the excess until the ingredient is level with the rim of the spoon.

Sifting aerates flour particles, separating them slightly, resulting in a "light" cup of flour. Lightly spooned flour results in a "medium" cup of flour. The dip-and-sweep method results in the most amount of flour in a cup, and is the heaviest. Never pack flour or any other ingredient unless the recipe specifically requests that you do so. If a recipe doesn't indicate which of these methods to use, default to dip and sweep (unless it's an older recipe, pre-1960; then assume flour should be sifted).

The recipes in this book use the following volume measurements for the four basic dry ingredients in baking:

**Unbleached all-purpose flour, dip and sweep,
5 ounces per cup**

**Cake flour, always sifted before measuring,
3½ ounces per cup**

Granulated sugar, dip and sweep, 7 ounces per cup

Firmly packed brown sugar, 8 ounces per cup

MEASURING BY WEIGHT

The advice above will help you with volume measuring, but here's the most foolproof path to success: Put aside the dry measuring cups, purchase a digital scale, and start weighing. If one thing can improve your baking, beginning with your first pan of brownies, it's a scale. You don't need a big, professional scale; in fact, a slim, digital one that slips easily out of sight when not in use is perfect for all your home baking. (For more on choosing a scale, see page 8.) Not only is weighing more accurate and efficient, but there is less to clean as well. Using a scale is especially helpful when ingredients need to be sifted. Sifting flour into a measuring cup is a messy proposition. When using a scale, you simply add the weight of a cup of sifted flour to the bowl, then sift it later as you add it to the batter. No mess to clean! You love it already, right?

Professional bakers always weigh their ingredients (known as *scaling*), both for precision and to ensure the consistency of their baked goods. After all, a bakery can't have chocolate chip cookies that are flat one day (too little flour) and puffy the next (too much flour), or the endless permutations that might occur with a staff of bakers each using a different volume measuring technique. As you've just learned, a "cup" of flour can weigh as little as 3¾ ounces when sifted, all the way up to 6 ounces when packed into the measuring cup. Multiply that times 3 if a recipe has 3 cups of flour, and you can see how, depending on the measuring method, a cake can have either a weak structure (not enough flour) or a dry texture (too much flour). Now imagine a bakery, where the 3 cups of flour becomes 150 cups of flour, and the multiplied skewing of the recipe becomes an expensive nightmare. Weighing completely eliminates problems caused by volume measurement inconsistencies.

HOW TO USE A DIGITAL SCALE

Set the scale in front of you and turn it on. Place a bowl on top. Notice the handy tare button on the instrument panel, which, when pressed, resets the scale to zero, so that the weight next registered will just be that of your ingredient; you won't have to subtract the weight of the bowl. So, with your bowl in place, press the tare button to reset the scale to zero. Now you are ready to weigh your first ingredient.

Start with the dry ingredients, adding the largest amount first—usually the flour. Pour or spoon it into the bowl until the scale registers the correct weight. Press the tare button again. The scale will reset to zero and you can then add the next ingredient. You can keep adding/weighing ingredients in the same bowl, as long as they are mixed together in the recipe (for instance, flour, cocoa, baking soda, and salt are usually combined for chocolate cakes). Once you've finished weighing, blend or sift according to your recipe. You're done!

When measuring liquid ingredients, you can either weigh them or simply use a liquid measuring cup—both are perfectly acceptable. If you want to weigh your liquids, please note that there is often a difference between "fluid ounces" and actual weights. The term "fluid ounces" refers to volume—the measuring lines marked on a liquid measuring cup. The line at ½ cup reads 4 ounces, which is the weight of water at that line. But many liquids are heavier than water. For instance, ½ cup of maple syrup is 4 fluid ounces when measured in a cup. But it actually weighs 5¾ ounces. Since liquid reliably fills a measuring cup exactly the same every time, you will have great success measuring your liquids by volume at home. Professionals, however, often need to measure amounts greater than even the largest liquid measuring cup, so for them, weighing on a scale is preferable. Each recipe here gives you the option of measuring liquids by volume (½ cup) or weight (5¾ ounces), so you can choose the method that works for you.

WEIGHING INGREDIENTS FOR OTHER RECIPES

You can weigh ingredients for recipes outside this book—even if those recipes don't list a weight alternative, only volume—by consulting the Volume and Weight Equivalents chart on pages 6–7. Just be sure to check the introductory section of other baking books or magazines so you know how they are measuring (do they sift flour, or dip and sweep it?). Then use the corresponding weight from the conversion table when scaling your ingredients. If a book or magazine states a particular weight for a flour measurement, say a 4-ounce cup of dip and sweep flour, use their weight when making their recipe. Again, as mentioned above, if you are using older recipes—like those handed down from your grandmother—you should assume that the flour was sifted, which was standard procedure in "the old days."

Equipment

Sur La Table built its reputation on high-quality equipment for the home kitchen, purveying tools that not only perform well and last a lifetime, but are also aesthetically pleasing. A gleaming porcelain baking dish with clean lines and artful details is a thing of beauty. Tools like a well-made whisk, a wooden spatula, or a rolling pin have a timeless appeal that give a kitchen roots and a sense of comfort. You don't need a battery of equipment to bake well (though that can be fun), but do choose each piece carefully, for your tools and pans can dramatically increase the quality of your breads and pastries and make your time spent in the kitchen a true pleasure.

Volume and Weight Equivalents (Rounded to the nearest ¼ ounce)

INGREDIENT	OUNCES PER CUP
DRY INGREDIENTS	
Flour, unbleached all-purpose (dip and sweep)*	5
Flour, unbleached all-purpose (lightly spooned)	4½
Flour, unbleached all-purpose (sifted)	3¾
Flour, cake (dip and sweep)	4½
Flour, cake (lightly spooned)	4
Flour, cake (sifted)*	3½
Flour, bread (dip and sweep)*	5
Flour, bread (lightly spooned)	4½
Flour, Southern, self-rising (dip and sweep)*	5
Flour, Southern, self-rising (lightly spooned)	4½
Flour, whole wheat (dip and sweep)*	5
Flour, whole wheat (lightly spooned)	4½
Cocoa powder, natural (lightly spooned)*	3
Cocoa powder, natural (sifted)	2¾
Cocoa powder, Dutch process (lightly spooned)*	4
Cocoa powder, Dutch process (sifted)	3¾
Cocoa nibs	4
Chocolate chips	7
Mini chocolate chips	6½
Malted milk powder	3
Dry buttermilk powder (lightly spooned)	4¾
Oats, old-fashioned rolled	3
Oats, quick-cooking	3½
Sugar, granulated or superfine (dip and sweep)*	7
Sugar, confectioners' (lightly spooned)	4
Sugar, confectioners' (sifted)	3
Sugar, light or dark brown (packed)	8
Sugar, Demerara	7½
Sugar, Hawaiian washed raw; sanding; turbinado	8
Sugar, large crystal	8¾
Sugar, maple	5
LIQUID SWEETENERS / SYRUPS	
Honey	11¾
Corn syrup, light	11½
Maple syrup	11½
Molasses	11¼
LIQUIDS/DAIRY	
Milk, heavy cream, buttermilk, sour cream	8
Crème fraîche, yogurt	8
Mascarpone	8½
Sweetened condensed milk	10½

NOTE: *Some ingredients are not listed on this chart because they are used in such small quantities that it is more efficient to use a measuring spoon when measuring. They include baking powder, baking soda, salt, and spices, among others.*

INGREDIENT	OUNCES PER CUP
LIQUIDS/DAIRY (CON'T)	
Dulce de leche	11
Cream cheese	9
Clear fruit juices (not nectars) such as lemon, orange, lime, apple, pomegranate, etc.	8
Apricot jam	10¾
Seedless raspberry jam	10
EGGS	
1 large, in shell	2
1 large, out of shell	1¾
FATS	
Butter	8
Olive oil, canola oil, safflower oil	7½
Shortening	6¾
DRIED FRUIT	
Apricots, California (packed)	5
Apricots, Turkish (packed)	6¾
Cherries	5
Cranberries	4
Currants	5
Figs, Black Mission (packed)	6
Raisins	5
NUTS	
Almonds, raw, whole	5¼
Almonds, raw, slivered	4½
Almonds, raw, coarsely chopped	4½
Almonds, sliced	3
Almond paste	10
Hazelnuts, raw, whole	4¾
Hazelnuts, raw, coarsely chopped	4¾
Macadamias, raw, whole	5
Macadamias, raw, chopped	4½
Peanuts, raw whole	5½
Peanuts, raw, chopped	5
Pecans, raw, whole	4
Pecans, raw, pieces or coarsely chopped	4
Pistachios, raw, whole	4¼
Pistachios, raw, coarsely chopped	4½
Walnuts, raw, halves	3½
Walnuts, raw, pieces or coarsely chopped	4¼
Peanut butter, smooth	16½
Coconut, sweetened shredded (packed)	3½
Coconut, dried unsweetened	2¼

*indicates the method of measuring and its corresponding weight for ingredients used in this book when alternative measurements are also given. For example, though flour may be measured several ways, the * next to the dip-and-sweep method indicates that this is the standard for the recipes in this book.

THERMOMETERS

Thermometers, like ovens, can be inaccurate, and it's best to know up front. To test an instant-read or a candy thermometer's accuracy, immerse the tip in boiling water, but don't let it touch the bottom or side of the pan. At sea level, the thermometer should read 212°F. If it is higher or lower by a few degrees, you can still use it, but you'll need to make a note of the discrepancy and keep it in mind when taking the temperature of sugar syrups or baked goods. For instance, if your thermometer is 5°F low (that is, it registered 207°F in boiling water), and you need to cook a sugar syrup to 240°F, then the thermometer will register 235°F when the syrup is at the proper temperature. If it is 5°F high (that is, it registered 217°F in boiling water), and you need to cook a syrup to 240°F, then the thermometer will register 245°F when finished.

Oven thermometers are difficult to test for accuracy, which is why it's best to purchase the glass tube, alcohol-based type. These are reliably accurate for a lifetime (unless the glass breaks, of course).

CANDY THERMOMETER

Great for cooking sugar syrups, candy thermometers are marked in increments of 2°F and are used when precision is neces- sary. They are left in the liquid while it cooks (as opposed to the instant-read variety) and you can watch the heat increase as the alcohol (or mercury) slowly creeps up the numbers. When a recipe calls for a candy thermometer, don't substitute an instant- read, unless it's the type with a wire that runs to a separate dis- play unit, and you are careful to keep the tip of the metal probe from resting on the side or bottom of the cooking pan.

INSTANT-READ THERMOMETER

These are great for taking a quick temperature reading of breads, pastries, and other foods. Insert the thermometer so the area about 1 inch from the tip is in the center of the product being measured. It will take just a few seconds for the temperature to register. Digital thermometers are more precise and easy to read than the round dial style.

OVEN THERMOMETER

A must-have for anyone who wants to improve the quality of their baked goods immediately is an oven thermometer that ensures that your oven is always at the accurate baking temperature. Look for the alcohol (or mercury) glass tube models; they're the most accurate and can last a lifetime. The only time they are inaccurate is when the oven temperature is hotter than they can register or when the glass tube is broken. (For more on using this style of thermometer, see page 3.)

MEASURING EQUIPMENT

MEASURING SPOONS

The best measuring spoons are made of durable stainless steel and have straight rims to allow easy leveling of ingredients. Oval or rectangular spoons fit into spice jars whereas round will not. The set should include ¼ teaspoon, ½ teaspoon, 1 teaspoon, and 1 tablespoon. Some sets also include ⅛ teaspoon, ¾ teaspoon, and ½ tablespoon. Having two sets is useful so you don't have to wash and dry a spoon you may need for measuring multiple ingredients.

DRY MEASURING CUPS

Most dry measuring cup sets include ¼ cup, ⅓ cup, ½ cup, and 1 cup. The cups should be made of sturdy stainless steel or plastic and have straight edges to allow for easy leveling. Having two sets is useful so you don't have to wash and dry a cup you may need for measuring multiple ingredients. Check the capacity of your dry measuring cup with the help of a scale. One cup of granulated sugar should weigh 7 ounces.

LIQUID MEASURING CUPS

These are made of glass or transparent plastic so you can see through the cup for accurate measuring. Liquid measuring cups are available in many sizes but a 1-cup and a 4-cup will serve the needs of most home bakers. Check the capacity of your liquid measuring cups with the help of a scale. One cup of water should weigh 8 ounces.

SCALES

As previously mentioned, most professional bakers prefer to weigh ingredients, called *scaling,* rather than measure by volume. Scaling is more accurate and is easier than scooping ingredients into measuring cups and then adding them to the mixing bowl; you can weigh ingredients one after another in the same bowl (see "Measuring 101," page 3). However, the recipes in this book provide both volume and weight measures.

Thin, battery-powered digital scales are affordable, easy to use, and slip into a cupboard for storage. Most can weigh in both metric and U.S./Imperial units. Look for a model that measures in ¼-ounce increments, has a tare button, and waits at least 3 or 4 minutes after being used before automatically shutting off. Choose one that can measure at least 4 pounds and up to 10, depending on your baking needs.

MIXING EQUIPMENT

BOWLS

A home baker needs at least one small, one medium, and one large mixing bowl, though two of each would be better. A very small and an extra-large bowl are also useful. Sets of graduated sizes are widely available in a variety of materials. Stainless-steel bowls, the most versatile, are inexpensive, lightweight, dishwasher safe, and nearly indestructible; they're a great choice for almost any kitchen job. Stainless steel cannot be put in the microwave, however. Glass and ceramic bowls are heavy, thick, and breakable, making them unsuitable as all-purpose mixing bowls, but work well for fermenting yeasted doughs. Plastic bowls are unsuitable for most baking purposes as they retain odors and fat, which get into the pores of the plastic and are difficult to remove completely.

STAND MIXER

Worth every penny if you love to bake, a stand mixer can quickly and easily mix batters, knead bread doughs, and whip egg whites. They also leave your hands free to tend to other tasks. The mixer should come with a whisk, a dough hook, a paddle (flat beater), and one bowl. If possible, buy an extra bowl, which comes in handy when you have a batter that requires egg whites to be whipped separately, or you need to make several batters or frostings and don't want to wash in the middle. Stand mixers come in capacities from 4-quart to 7-quart. The smaller models will serve most home baking needs beautifully. If you like to regularly double or triple cookies or bread recipes, you'll want a larger-capacity mixer.

HAND MIXER

A hand mixer can perform nearly any beating and whipping task that a stand mixer can, except for bread doughs. These are less expensive, easy to use, and take up less kitchen space than a stand mixer. Buy a powerful model with large beaters and at least 3 speeds. Keep in mind that many recipes are written for a stand mixer, which is quite powerful, so when substituting a hand mixer, you'll need a few extra minutes of beating to reach each stage in a recipe.

FOOD PROCESSOR

A food processor makes quick work of chopping or grinding nuts and pureeing fruit. You can use it to mix some batters and doughs, but be careful not to overprocess. Choose a powerful model with a 1½- to 2-quart capacity.

BAKING PANS

MATERIALS

Baking pans are made of a variety of materials, from aluminum to glass, all of which conduct heat slightly differently. Heat conduction refers to how quickly the pan heats up and cools down.

ALUMINUM PANS Aluminum is the best conductor of heat in bakeware, and professionals prefer it. Aluminum pans heat quickly, creating appealing brown crusts; then they hold the heat steadily for even baking and cool down quickly once removed from the oven. Some aluminum pans are coated with a layer of stainless steel for beauty and cleaning efficiency. They're fine to use, but bakeware that is exclusively stainless steel (no aluminum core) is not recommended.

GLASS AND CERAMIC PANS Although they don't conduct heat as well, they're very attractive and great for baking desserts such as fruit crisps, cobblers and crumbles, bread pudding, and baklava. Glass pie pans can be very helpful in judging the doneness of a crust.

NONSTICK PANS The nonstick coating on these pans is good for helping release cakes and breads after baking, though you will still need to prepare the pan as directed in the recipe's instructions to guarantee easy removal. Be careful not to cut cakes and breads in nonstick pans, or you can scrape off some of the nonstick finish with the metal blade. For best baking results, make sure the material under the coating is aluminum or an aluminum blend.

DARK OR BLACK PANS Dark pans absorb and retain heat well, which can cause edges and crusts to brown—or burn—more quickly than desired. If baking with dark pans, watch very carefully and note that pastries may be done sooner than the recipe indicates.

FLEXIBLE SILICONE BAKING PANS Very popular for their easy-release qualities, these come in standard shapes and a whole array of fanciful and unusual forms. They are popular with professionals for shaping ice cream, sorbet, and other frozen desserts, as well as for assembling miniature cakes and mousse-layered pastries. These pans are a real boon for baking cakes and pastries that are difficult to remove from traditional pans (think fruitcake, madeleine cookies, *canelles,* and more). For best release results, manufacturers recommend you always prepare their pans with a thin coating of butter or oil and a dusting of flour. Even when prepared in this manner, the crust of some baked goods will remain in the pan when unmolded, resulting in pale, though nicely baked, pastries. And keep in mind that you will need two baking pans instead of one, since you'll need a baking sheet underneath the floppy silicone pans to keep them stable and level during baking.

PAN SIZE AND SHAPE

The diameter of a baking pan (for instance, a 9-inch cake or tart pan or an 8 by 8-inch pan) is measured across the top of the pan from the inside of one edge to the inside of the other. Always use the pan size specified in the recipe, or your results may be less than desired. If your pan is just slightly smaller or larger than the one called for, you can still use it as long as you understand that the batter or baked good in a smaller pan will take a little longer to cook because it will be in a deeper layer, and vice versa. The Baking Pan Volume chart (pages 12–13) can help you in choosing alternate pans when it's necessary to substitute.

LOAF PANS These are classics in the American kitchen, used for yeast breads and quick breads. They come in many sizes, but the two most useful are a 9 by 5 by 2½-inch for larger loaves, and an 8½ by 4½ by 2½-inch for slightly smaller loaves. Be sure to use the one specified in the recipe, for although they seem quite similar, there is a 2-cup volume difference between them. Batter baked in a pan that is too small may overflow, while that baked in a pan that is too large will be flat, rather than beautifully domed on top.

MUFFIN PANS Ranging in size from mini to jumbo, muffin pans are used for muffins and cupcakes, but can also be used to make popovers, dinner rolls, sweet and savory tartlets, and individual brownies.

COOKIE AND BAKING SHEETS Cookie sheets are rimless, while baking sheets have raised edges, usually ½- to 1-inch high. Professionals use heavy-duty aluminum baking sheets (known as half-sheet pans) for everything. They are a good, all-purpose size of 12 by 17 inches, do not warp, and are used throughout this book. Cookie sheets are useful when you want to slide cookies baked on a sheet of parchment onto a cooling rack while still attached to the parchment (no edge to damage the cookies). If you need a rimless baking sheet and don't own one, you can improvise by flipping a baking sheet upside down and baking on the inverted surface. Some cookie sheets are insulated, containing a layer of air in the center, which prevents cookies and pastries from overbrowning on the bottom, and sometimes prevents them from browning at all. If you love deeply browned, caramelized bottom crusts, don't use insulated pans.

CAKE PANS

LAYER CAKE PANS Whether round or square, cake layer pans come in a range of sizes, though 8- and 9-inch pans are standard for most home recipes. The best cake pans are about 2 inches deep and are made of aluminum, though there are also 3-inch-deep pans available that are used for tall cakes and layers for wedding cakes. While aluminum pans serve all purposes, some people prefer nonstick pans. As long as the core of the pan is aluminum,

these pans will work well for most baking. However, do not bake sponge cakes in nonstick pans (for they will not rise as fully as they should—for more on this, see page 303). Make sure the pans you buy have perfectly straight sides, not flared, which makes layering and frosting much easier. A large, rectangular 9 by 13 by 2-inch baking pan is commonly used for making single or double layer sheet cakes, bar cookies, and brownies.

SPRINGFORM CAKE PANS These are usually round, with a removable side that is clipped in place on the bottom of the pan. Springform pans are used for cheesecakes, streusel-topped cake, or other cakes that would be damaged by turning them upside down to remove them from the pan. Look for heavy-duty pans that clip tightly. Cheaper pans bend and warp easily, and once there is a gap between the side piece and the bottom, the pan is useless.

TUBE PANS A tube conducts heat through the center of the deep tube pan, which insures that the cake bakes evenly. Tube pans come in a multitude of shapes and sizes, though Bundt and angel food are two of the most common.

The round-bottomed, fluted Bundt pan is a classic, and cakes baked in it are beautiful when unmolded. Nordic Ware originated the Bundt pan, and now it and other companies make a plethora of beautifully carved tube and decorative pans. There are several sizes of the pan available, with 8- to 12-cup capacities. There are individual- and miniature-sized versions of the pan as well, similar to a muffin pan, that hold 6 or 12 individual-serving cakes. To ensure complete and easy removal of the cake, always prepare the pan by generously coating with butter or oil and a dusting of flour, cocoa powder, or fine, dry bread crumbs, tapping out any excess.

An angel food pan is a very tall, aluminum tube pan. If you like angel food cake, you'll want to invest in one, as your cake will never turn out quite right when baked in a different type of pan. Do not buy nonstick angel food cake pans or your cake will not rise properly.

PIE AND TART PANS

PIE PANS Most of the recipes in this book call for a 9-inch pie pan, found in every supermarket and cookware store across the country. But be forewarned, there is a big difference between types of 9-inch pans. Although they all measure 9 inches across the top, their depths are dramatically different. A foil pan holds 3 to 3½ cups; a glass Pyrex pan, aluminum pan, or tinned steel pan holds 4 cups; and a deep-dish pie pan or fluted edge pie pan such as Emile Henry, holds 6 cups. The recipes in this book were tested using a Pyrex pan, which is considered a standard. If you use a foil pan, you'll want to reduce the filling amount by one-third or you'll have some left over, and if you bake with deep-dish pie pans or Emile Henry pans, you'll want to increase the filling by one-third to one-half so that you have enough to fill the pie plate.

As for the virtues of each, the Pyrex pan allows you to see when the crust is perfectly browned, which is helpful when you begin baking. The Emile Henry earthenware or ceramic pans require a bit longer baking, but create a beautifully crisp crust and look attractive on the table. Foil pie plates are cheap and disposable, good for gatherings when you don't want to worry about retrieving your pan at the end. Aluminum pans brown beautifully and are lightweight, while tinned steel, although it doesn't brown quite as well, has a shiny, modern look on the table. If you have a black or very dark pie pan, watch carefully, as your pie may be done earlier than the recipe states.

TART PANS The most common type of tart pan is a shiny, tin-lined, removable-bottom pan with a fluted edge about 1 inch tall. It comes in a range of sizes, from individual (4 inches) to bakery-size (12 inches or larger) and in shapes from round to rectangular, though the most commonly used is a 9½-inch round pan. You can also find tartlet pans in myriad sizes and styles that are great for buffets, teas, and other occasions when a tiny all-to-yourself dessert is just right. Be careful when moving filled tart pans; hold them by the sides, rather than the removable bottom—the fluted ring may wind up dangling around your arm like an oversized bracelet, especially painful when the pan is hot out of the oven.

Ceramic tart pans are a beautiful choice when you want to present your tart in its baking pan, though the tart may need to bake longer than the recipe specifies due to the poor heat conductivity of ceramic.

FLAN RINGS A metal ring with no fluting around the sides, a flan ring is set on a baking sheet lined with parchment paper or a silicone mat and then filled. The baking sheet, which needs to be perfectly flat and heavy-duty, serves as the pan bottom. The simple, straight sides of flan rings lend a clean, modern look to the finished tart. Flan rings have become more widely available, so you might want to give one a try. Be sure to let your tart cool completely on the baking sheet before using a large spatula or cake lifter to move it onto a serving plate, as the pastry is more fragile when warm.

CERAMIC BAKING DISHES

ROUND OR RECTANGULAR DISHES Both round and rectangular baking dishes are perfect for baking fruit crisps, cobblers, crumbles, and bread puddings because they go from oven to table beautifully. Look for 6-cup ceramic dishes for the recipes in this book, available in a whole range of colors and styles.

SOUFFLÉ DISHES Deep, straight-sided, round baking dishes with ridges decorating the sides, soufflé dishes range in size from large (7½ cups to 8 cups) to miniature (¼ cup). A soufflé will always rise properly if baked in a dish of this design. Small, individual soufflé dishes are often called ramekins and may also be used to bake bread pudding or individual crisps and cobblers or to hold measured ingredients while prepping. While ceramic is widely available, soufflé dishes and ramekins may also be found in materials such as glass, porcelain, and earthenware, and in a wide range of beautiful colors.

CUSTARD CUPS Custard cups are 6-ounce ceramic or glass cups, usually with flared sides, made for baking custards, though they can be used for other desserts as well. Six-ounce ramekins (individual soufflé dishes) may be used in their place.

OTHER KITCHEN EQUIPMENT

BAKING STONE

This large, flat stone is placed on the bottom of the oven (or the bottom shelf if your oven has an electric element on the bottom) to mimic the heat of a brick or stone oven. Used for baking pizzas and artisanal breads, it must be preheated for an hour. It can be stored in the oven or removed after baking. (For more on baking stones, see page 70.)

BANNETON

A *banneton* is a woven basket, sometimes lined with cloth, that is dusted with flour and used for proofing bread just before it goes into the oven. The ridges of the basket imprint their pattern on the dough as it rises, creating a beautiful, decorative pattern on the bread's surface.

BENCH SCRAPER

Also called a board scraper, dough scraper, or pastry scraper, this tool is basically a flat metal blade measuring about 6 by 3 inches, with a rounded handle across the top. It's used to scrape flour and dough bits from the pastry board and is handy for transferring pastry or bread doughs from one place to another. Its blade neatly cuts pastry, cookie, or bread dough into pieces.

BOWL SCRAPER

This small, flexible plastic scraper is rounded on one edge and flat on the other. The rounded edge is used to get every last bit of batter, dough, or frosting out of a mixing bowl. The flat edge can be used to clean your work surface, spread and level batters in pans and perform other little tasks around the kitchen.

CAKE LIFTER

This handy tool, with a wide stainless-steel surface, is reminiscent of a small pizza peel, and while thin enough to slip under a cake, is also strong enough to lift it and move it from counter to serving platter or wherever you desire. You can also use the lifter to move tart shells (filled or not), shaped Danish or puff pastry dough, and more. To improvise a cake lifter, use the bottom of a removable-bottom tart pan.

CARDBOARD CAKE ROUNDS

These corrugated rounds (also known as cake circles) are what professionals use to build cakes on or to slip under individual cake layers to move them around. To improvise a cake cardboard, use the bottom of a removable-bottom tart pan. Cakes assembled on cardboards are easy to lift and tilt for pressing nuts or chocolate into the sides. They also make frosting and decorating much easier than working on a plate (no need for paper tucked under

Baking Pan Volumes

This chart covers some of the most commonly used baking pans and dishes and the volumes they hold. It is helpful if you don't have the specific pan called for in a recipe and want to substitute another pan. Choose a pan that has the same volume capacity as the one the recipe calls for. Note that a dramatic change in the height of the pan can cause problems. If the pan is too short, your batter or filling may spill over, and if the pan is too tall, your pastry will not brown as well and the sides of a cake will be higher than the center.

PAN DIMENSIONS (INCHES)	PAN SHAPE AND TYPE	CAPACITY
2¼ by 4 by 1¼	loaf pan, mini	⅔ cup
8½ by 4½ by 2½	loaf pan	6 cups
9 by 5 by 3	loaf pan	8 cups
1¾ by ¾	muffin cup, mini	2 tablespoons
2¾ by 1⅜	muffin cup, standard	scant ½ cup
3⅜ by 1¾	muffin cup, jumbo	⅞ cup*
8 by 1½	cake pan, round	4 cups
8 by 2	cake pan, round	6 cups
9 by 1½	cake pan, round	6 cups
9 by 1¾	cake pan, round	7½ cups
9 by 2	cake pan, round	8 cups
9 by 3	cake pan, round	13 cups
10 by 2	cake pan, round	11 cups
8 by 8 by 1½	cake pan, square	6 cups
8 by 8 by 2	cake pan, square	8 cups
9 by 9 by 1½	cake pan, square	8 cups
9 by 9 by 2	cake pan, square	10 cups
6 by 3	springform pan	4 cups
7 by 2½	springform pan	5½ cups
8 by 2	springform pan	6 cups
8½ by 2½	springform pan	7½ cups
9½ by 2½	springform pan	9 cups
8 by 3	springform pan	10 cups

* ⅞ cup = 1 cup minus 2 tablespoons

the cake to keep the plate clean while you're frosting the cake).

To lift a frosted cake assembled on a cardboard without damaging the sides, slip the tip of a paring knife under the cardboard, lift the cake slightly at an angle, and slip your hand underneath to finish lifting it. The finished cake can then be placed on a serving plate, or on a second, larger cardboard (also known as the presentation cardboard) that is coated with glassine, a grease-proof coating, or a doily. Attach the first cardboard to the presentation one with several loops of tape to hold it in place. To set the cake onto the presentation cardboard, rest one edge of the cake in a place at an angle. Slip the tip of a paring knife under the lifted edge, remove your hand from under the cake, and gently use the knife to lower it. Pretty cardboards are also great for bringing cakes and other pastries to parties or school, since you never have to worry about retrieving your platter.

CHEESECLOTH

This light cotton gauze is used to contain ingredients that you wish to remain separate from the rest of the mixture. For example, small, hard spices used to flavor a liquid with poaching fruit would be wrapped in cheesecloth to prevent them from getting caught in the fruit and possibly eaten (ouch!). It may also be used to strain liquids, although not in this book. It is sold in supermarkets and cookware stores.

PAN DIMENSIONS (INCHES)	PAN SHAPE AND TYPE	CAPACITY
9½ by 2½	springform pan	10 cups
9 by 3	springform pan	11 cups
10 by 2½	springform pan	12 cups
1¾ by 4	Bundt cup, mini	1 cup
6½ by 3½	Bundt pan	5½ cups
7½ by 3	Bundt pan	6 cups
8½ by 3½	Bundt pan	7 cups
9 by 3	Bundt pan	9 cups
10 by 3½	Bundt pan	12 cups
7½ by 3	tube pan	6 cups
10 by 4	tube pan	16 cups
8½ by 3½	Kugelhopf pan	9 cups
8 by 1½	pie pan	4 cups
9 by 1	pie pan, foil	3– 3½ cups
9 by 1½	pie pan, Pyrex	4 cups
9 by 2	pie pan, Emile Henry fluted	6 cups
10 by 1½	pie pan	6½ cups
9½ by 2	pie pan, deep-dish glass	7 cups
2½ by ¾	tartlet pan, mini	2 tablespoons
9 by 1	tart pan, fluted, removable-bottom	4 cups
9½ by 1½	tart pan, round, fluted ceramic	4 cups
6-½ by 1	gratin dish, round	1½ cups
7 by 11 by 2	baking pan, rectangular	6 cups
9 by 13 by 2	baking pan, rectangular	12 cups
13 by 9 by 3	baking pan, rectangular	14 cups
3¼ by 2	soufflé dish	⅔ cup
3¾ by 1⅞	soufflé dish	1 cup
7½ by 3¼	soufflé dish	7½ cups
3¼ by 1¾	custard cup	¾ cup

NOTE: The volume capacity for each pan was measured by filling the pan to the rim with water.

CHERRY PITTER

Also used to pit olives, this small, handheld tool easily extracts the pits from cherries. Available in stainless steel, aluminum, or plastic. If you love to bake with cherries in season, you'll want to look for a large-capacity cherry pitter. It is a clear plastic box with a spring-loaded pitting mechanism on top, which makes quick work of a pile of fresh cherries.

CITRUS ZESTER

A citrus zester is a small tool with fine, tiny, sharp-edged holes at one end. It is used to remove the zest, the highly colored outer portion of citrus skin, in long even strips without including any of the bitter white pith underneath.

COOKIE PRESS

Used to pipe beautifully shaped cookies, a cookie press has a long, hollow tube that is filled with cookie dough, and a plunger that pushes the dough out through a decorative plate fitted into the end. Traditionally hand-operated, there is now an electric model available that makes piping cookies a breeze. If you don't have a cookie press, you can make pretty cookies using a pastry bag fitted with a large star tip.

COOLING RACKS

Made of heavy wire or steel with small ridges, or feet, to hold the rack off the counter, cooling racks allow air to circulate all around the pan or a freestanding cake or cookies, cooling them faster and more efficiently. Setting a pan on a rack also cuts down on condensation between the bottom of the pan and the baked item within.

DOUBLE BOILER

Designed to melt chocolate and cook foods that need very gentle heat, a double boiler is a set of two pans nested together, with enough room in the bottom pan for an inch or two of water. The top pan should never touch the water below. The water is brought to a simmer and the second pan, filled with the ingredient to be cooked or melted, is fitted into the first. A double boiler can be improvised with a medium saucepan coupled with a medium bowl that fits about halfway inside the pan.

DOUGH DOCKER (OR DOUGH PRICKER)

A rolling cylinder covered with spikes, the docker is used to poke holes in various pastry doughs (such as pie dough and puff pastry) to prevent the pastry from rising unevenly, or much at all (as is the case with napoleons). To improvise a docker, use a couple of forks.

GRATERS

Graters are available in many varieties. A box grater is the most versatile. It is free-standing and can have 4 or 6 sides, each side having different sizes of holes for grating. It's easy to use but cum-bersome to store and clean. Flat graters are easier to store and clean but have only one grating surface so you will need to buy several sizes. The Microplane, or rasp-style zester, is a flat grater that grates food into very fine pieces. The Microplane is perfect for grating citrus zest, fresh ginger, hard cheeses, chocolate, and whole nutmeg.

You can also use a nutmeg grater for grating nutmeg. Freshly grated nutmeg is far more flavorful and aromatic than ground nutmeg. Nutmeg graters have a very fine, curved cutting surface and often have a little compartment at one end for storing the nutmeg. Spring-loaded models resemble pepper grinders. Load the nutmeg into the grinder, screw on the top—which presses the nutmeg against the cutting blade—and turn the handle for freshly grated nutmeg.

ICE CREAM SCOOPS

These handy scoops (known as dishers or portion scoops to professionals) are made of stainless steel and come in a wide range of sizes. They ensure portion consistency and keep scooping neat (no drips when filling muffin or cupcake liners). Some scoops have a number etched on the side or end that signifies to professionals how many scoops of that particular size are in a gallon ("#20" means 20 scoops per gallon). Scoop sizes range from chocolate-truffle size up to a giant ½ cup size, good for jumbo muffins or monster cookies. Look for heavy-duty scoops and squeeze the mechanism a few times to make sure the sliding metal band that moves between the food and the scoop works smoothly.

JUICER

Whether you choose an electric model, a bright-colored, hand-powered Mexican juicer, or a simple reamer, a juicer makes quick work of extracting all the juice from a piece of citrus fruit. Electric models are the most efficient, extracting the maximum amount of juice from each piece of fruit. If you like to make lemon bars, lemon meringue tarts, and other juice-based desserts, you'll want to invest in an electric model. For small amounts of juice, a Mexican juicer is quick and easy to clean, essentially turning each citrus half inside out, while forcing the juice through well-placed holes in the device. These come in sizes (and colors) to match the width of limes, lemons, and oranges, though the lemon-sized juicer does a good job on all types of citrus (except for very large oranges, and grapefruits). An old-fashioned wooden or stainless-steel reamer also gets the juicing job done, although it requires a bit more elbow grease and the inevitable fishing out of seeds that drop into the juice.

KNIVES

Well-made knives are a pleasure to hold and work with and are an investment that will last the rest of your life. Try several brands and sizes at the cookware store and see which one fits your hands and your needs. Buy the best you can afford and keep them sharp by using a sharpening steel whenever they begin to feel dull. Get them professionally sharpened every few months to a year to keep their edges sharp and safe (dull knives are much more dangerous than sharp ones, since you have to use more force to cut). For baking you'll need a paring knife, a chef's knife, and a serrated (or bread) knife with a 10- to 12-inch blade. The jagged edge of the serrated knife is especially important for slicing breads, some cakes, and other pastries whose crumb would be squashed and/or torn by a straight-edged knife. Wash and dry by hand after every use—do not put them in the dishwasher. Keep them in a knife sleeve (a plastic edge protector) if they are in a drawer with other utensils, or store them in knife block to safeguard the blades.

LAME

This French tool, which features a curved razor blade attached to a plastic handle, is used to slash the top of bread just before it enters the oven. The slashing allows the bread to expand fully and adds a beautiful pattern to the top of the crust. A very sharp serrated knife may be used as a substitute.

OVEN MITTS

Crucial to protect hands from hot pans, oven mitts are available in a range of materials and lengths. Try them on and buy a pair that fits well—too large and you'll be smashing or denting cookies, cakes, and pastries as you remove them from the oven. If cloth, look for mitts that are as thick and as heat-resistant as possible. Silicone oven mitts can withstand high heat and are thin, but can be inflexible and awkward, so test them in the store by trying them on and moving around several pans.

PARCHMENT PAPER

The baker's kitchen would be incomplete without parchment paper. Coated with silicone, it's used constantly for lining pans and shaping into cones for piping chocolate. Nearly everything releases from parchment, which means no more worrying about whether the cake or brownies will come out in one piece. Plus, it makes cleanup a breeze. Purchase high-quality parchment paper, as some "baking papers" without silicone stick unmercifully. If yours is sticking, it's not true parchment paper.

PASTRY BAGS AND TIPS

Available in polyester, nylon, plastic-lined canvas, and disposable plastic, cone-shaped pastry bags are used with pastry tips to pipe decorative borders of frosting and to portion soufflé batter, meringues, *pâte à choux*, even cookie dough. Two or three bags of various sizes are handy to have on hand. Buy at least a 12- to 14-inch bag, as smaller ones hold very little and will need to be refilled constantly. Wash the pastry bags in hot, soapy water and dry completely (try slipping it over a wine bottle to dry) before storing, or they may mold. For very small amounts of melted

chocolate, buy an 8-inch disposable bag or use a small resealable plastic bag, squeezing the chocolate into one corner and snipping a small hole for piping.

Pastry tips, available in a vast array of sizes and designs, are stainless steel or chrome-plated tips that shape a filling or frosting as it's pushed from the bag onto a surface. All tips are designed to fit into the narrow opening at the bottom of a pastry bag. If you want to change tips for different designs while you're working, buy a coupler (a plastic ring with an insert for the bag); these allow you to change tips without cleaning the bag. Always wash the tips thoroughly with soap and water after use and dry them immediately to prevent rust. One way to dry them is to set them on baking sheet in a low oven (or turned off but still warm oven) for 15 minutes to dry. (For instructions on filling a pastry bag, see page 309.)

PASTRY BLENDER

An arc of metal wires or thin steel blades attached at both ends to a handle, a pastry blender is handy for cutting butter into biscuit or pie dough. Choose one that is comfortable in your hand.

PASTRY BOARD

A large slab of polished marble with small rubber feet to prevent slipping, this board can be chilled to help keep pastry dough at a cool temperature while you are rolling it. If yours won't fit into your refrigerator for chilling, put a bag of ice on it while you prepare the pastry, then just wipe it dry before you begin rolling.

PASTRY BRUSHES

These small brushes are used to brush flour from dough during rolling and to apply egg wash or glaze. The bristles should be soft and flexible, preferably natural (or boar), although nylon is fine if it's soft—stiff bristles can tear dough. Silicone brushes are becoming more popular as the bristles become thinner and finer. A 1-inch-wide brush is good for applying egg wash and jam glaze, while a 3- to 4-inch-wide brush is ideal for brushing flour from pie dough, layered dough, scones, and biscuits. Plan on dedicating one of each type to your "pastry-only" equipment, for brushes retain odors and will transfer that garlic or onion aroma to your baked goods. Immediately after use, always wash wet or gooey brushes with hot soapy water and air-dry. Floured brushes only need shaking out. Do not soak brushes in water as the wood will swell and crack.

PEELER

Vegetable peelers are used to remove the skins of fruit and vegetables or to make Parmesan shavings or chocolate curls. Choose one that is comfortable in your hand and has a sharp blade. Replace the peeler when the blade dulls. A serrated peeler is handy for peeling thin-skinned, delicate fruits such as tomatoes, peaches, and plums.

PIE WEIGHTS

Ceramic or metal beads about the size of marbles, these are used in prebaking, or blind baking, pie and tart shells. The raw shell is lined with foil, then filled with the weights and baked. The weights hold the pastry flat and help it keep its shape. (For more on prebaking, see page 175.) After baking, remove pie weights from the shell by lifting them out with the foil and let them cool completely, then store. While you could substitute dried beans or rice, pie weights will last forever and do not smell burned after repeated use.

PIZZA PEEL

A large, flat sheet of wood or aluminum with a long handle, a pizza peel is used to transfer pizzas and rustic breads into and out of the oven.

PLASTIC SQUEEZE BOTTLE

A plastic bottle with about a 2-cup capacity and a cone-shaped screw top can be filled with chocolate sauce, custard sauce, or other dessert sauces and used to make sauce patterns on dessert plates. If you enjoy creating patterns, you'll want two or three of these.

POPOVER PAN

Used to make tall, dramatic popovers, this pan consists of 12 deep metal wells attached by thin metal rails. If the model you purchase is not nonstick, you'll need to grease it well before every use until it takes on the deep, brown finish and nonstick properties that are the signs of a seasoned pan. A muffin pan may be substituted, though the finished popovers will not be as tall.

PROPANE OR BUTANE TORCH

Whether the torch is large (such as the kind at hardware stores) or small (such as the kind at cookware stores), a propane or butane torch has many uses in the baking kitchen. Pastry chefs use it for everything from browning meringues on pies to warming the outside of a pan in order to remove a mousse. The torch is used most frequently for caramelizing sugar on top of custard for the ever-popular dessert crème brulee. When shopping for a propane or butane torch, look for a model that feels good in your hand, and that has an automatic lighting attachment (if possible), which will light the torch with the flick of a switch. Also, be sure it comes with 8 to 10 minutes of running fuel, so you won't run out while caramelizing custards for a dinner party.

ROLLING PINS

This will become you best friend when rolling out all kinds of doughs. There are two basic styles of rolling pins—dowel and ball bearing. With either type, be sure to try it out on the counter at the cookware shop so you get a feel for its handles and rolling ability. Pins must suit their user, and everyone has his or her favorite. Take good care of your pin and it will be an heirloom. Never submerge it in water or place it in the dishwasher. Wooden pins will swell and crack, and the water can cause the ball-bearing mechanism inside the pin to rust, preventing it from rolling smoothly. When finished using your rolling pin, simply wipe it down with a warm, damp cloth.

The dowel rolling pin was Julia Child's favorite, and indeed the French love this pin, which is a single piece of rounded wood. Some have tapered ends, while others are long and straight. To use one, place your hands in the center of the pin and roll from the fingertips to the palm of the hand and back again. Many bakers feel they have more control and can "feel" the dough more closely with this type of pin.

Bal-bearing pins have a long barrel in the center—of wood, marble, silicone-coated metal, plastic, or even glass—that moves separately from the handles. The handles are key, for they will bear your weight and should fit your hands and feel comfortable. The barrel should roll smoothly and easily, even when you're pressing on the handles firmly. A heavy barrel is best in this model, as its weight helps to roll the dough more quickly. Buy the longest pin you feel comfortable with, for it will serve you well in every possible pastry situation.

RULER

An 18-inch clear plastic ruler makes measuring and portioning a breeze, provides a neat, straight cutting edge, and is easy to wash.

SCISSORS

Choose a sturdy, rustproof set of kitchen scissors and they will last for years. Use to trim the overhang from a double-crust pie, cut parchment paper, and perform a thousand other tasks.

SILICONE BAKING MATS

Nonstick silicone mats are made of woven silicone fibers and nothing, absolutely nothing, in the kitchen sticks to them. Buy the thinnest you can find, as thicker ones can insulate baked goods and keep them from browning (though they are terrific for candy making). They come in sizes that fit standard baking sheets, as well as rounds cut to fit cake pans. They last for many years and eliminate the need to line pans with parchment paper. Clean them by wiping with a warm, damp cloth or washing in soapy water. Dry thoroughly and store flat on an extra baking sheet, or roll into a cylinder and secure with a rubber band or large paper clip. Do not fold, as it stresses the fibers and eventually the mats will fray. Do not cut on the baking mats or you'll create holes that cannot be repaired.

SPATULAS, ICING

STRAIGHT These spatulas have a long, thin, flexible, rectangular metal blade with a rounded tip that is set into a wooden, plastic, or metal handle. Used most often for spreading frostings over the tops and sides of cakes, they can also be used for applying chocolate glazes on cakes, spreading batters in pans, releasing baked goods from the sides of pans, and moving cookies or small pastries from one point to another. Sizes available range from mini (4-inch blade) to large (14-inch blade). The mini size and an 8- to 10-inch size are the ones most useful for the home baker.

OFFSET These spatulas are identical to straight spatulas, except for a bend in the blade adjacent to the handle, which then straightens out again. They come in the same variety of sizes and handle materials as straight spatulas, and may be used in the same manner. Pastry chefs love offset spatulas because they allow them to spread evenly while keeping their fingers away from the frosting, batter, and edges of pans. Some people prefer offset spatulas to the straight spatulas and use them exclusively. A mini offset spatula is indispensable in the kitchen for spreading batters inside cake pans (and many other uses), and is highly recommended.

SPATULAS, RUBBER OR SILICONE

A long handle connected to a flat or cupped rubber or silicone blade, these are used in the pastry kitchen to scrape down mixing bowls, stir batters, and remove every last scrap of batter or dough, as well as many other uses. Rubber spatulas have mostly been replaced in cookware stores with silicone spatulas, which are easier to clean and much more heat resistant (they don't melt when in contact with a hot pan or molten sugar). Silicone spatulas are available in a number of colors and sizes and are heat resistant up to 400°F, and some even higher (follow manufacturer's instructions). You'll want at least one for savory foods and two for sweets (so you don't stir your cake batter with a spatula that smells like last night's meat sauce). You should have one spatula with the largest blade possible for folding batters and scraping down bowls, and a second spatula with a smaller blade for fitting into tight spaces.

SPOONS

Wooden spoons can withstand heat and won't scratch nonstick surfaces but can absorb food odors and discolor, so be sure to keep one for sweet foods and one for savory. Metal withstands heat and won't discolor or absorb food odors but can scratch non-stick surfaces—and, because it conducts heat, can become too hot to hold when left in the pan. Nylon is heat resistant to 400°F and safe for nonstick surfaces (follow manufacturer's instructions). Plastic melts in contact with heat and absorbs odors and is not the best choice for a cook's spoon.

STRAIGHT-SIDED TUB

Tall, translucent, or clear plastic tubs, either round or rectangular, are used by professionals for rising bread dough. This style of container makes it especially easy to tell when dough has doubled in size. These tubs are available in any warehouse-style store that caters to food industry professionals. A bowl may be used in its place.

STRAINER

Also known as a sieve, this is a metal mesh "bowl" used to strain liquids and to sift flour and other dry ingredients. The mesh ranges from very fine (for straining fruit purees) to coarse (for larger-particle ingredients). It's nice to have one of each. Always dry strainers immediately after washing, as they may rust. A *chinois,* a long, conical strainer with very fine mesh, is used mainly by professionals for sauce making (straining purees and custard sauces). A fine-mesh strainer will serve the same purpose for home bakers.

STRAWBERRY HULLER

This small, U-shaped piece of metal or plastic with serrated ends makes short work of removing the green hull from the top of a strawberry without damaging the delicate fruit. Simply insert the end on either side of the hull, pinch them together, and twist.

TIMERS

If you've ever forgotten cookies in the oven, you'll appreciate the value of a timer. Digital timers are good for the accuracy and bonus features they offer. Some even start counting upward once the timer stops ringing, so if you were outside and didn't hear it, you'll know how much time has passed since the timer went off.

WIRE WHISKS

You'll need at least one sauce whisk and one balloon whisk. A sauce whisk is long and narrow, meant to blend mixtures and whisk out any lumps without incorporating a lot of air. Its narrow, tapered shape helps it fit into the corners of the pan. A round, fat balloon whisk is designed to add air to mixtures. It should have a long handle and lots of thin wires to incorporate air using fewer strokes; use to whip egg whites or cream. If you want to go beyond the basics, a flat whisk is useful for stirring small quantities and for gently folding ingredients into delicate batters. A mini whisk comes in handy for small tasks like making an egg glaze.

The ingredients you choose directly influence the quality of your baked goods, for they will not transform during baking. Poor-quality butter and flavorings will not mutate to produce an extraordinary cake; what goes in, comes out. Good baking results from attention to detail, including ingredients. So just like a pastry chef, you should use the best possible ingredients, including high-quality extracts and oils, fresh nuts and fruits, good flour, and sweet, creamy butter.

Despite its reputation for being complicated and difficult, the world of baking is relatively simple when it comes to ingredients: The same ones are used over and over again. It is the technique used and the ratio of ingredients that produce all the dazzling different forms, from bread to cake to custard. With that in mind, it's relatively simple to become familiar with those limited ingredients. Here are the ones used throughout this book. Bear in mind that the storage suggestions are only broad guidelines—how well your ingredients keep depends on how fresh they were when you bought them. Trust your senses, especially when it comes to produce: if something still seems crisp and firm, it's fine; if it's limp and sad, throw it out.

This chapter not only defines the ingredients used in baking and how to choose and store them, it also explores how and why these same ingredients, when combined with others, work together to produce a particular texture, crumb, or flavor in your pastry. Some professional bakers and pastry chefs learn about food science in culinary school and others acquire their knowledge through years of hands-on work in the business. But when you bake only occasionally, the whole process can seem mysterious, from the way ingredients are measured to the different types of flour. Here you'll learn the *how* and *why* behind the ingredients and the techniques used to combine them, which will make you a more comfortable and confident baker each time you enter your kitchen.

The first part of this chapter covers the eight main ingredients used in baking—flour, sugar, eggs, butter, other dairy, leaveners, chocolate, and vanilla—and explains what they are, how they work, and why they are important. From these eight

foods you can produce nearly every recipe in this book. The food science here is key to understanding how baking works.

How you purchase, store, measure, and combine these ingredients can result in crisp cookies, a tender cake, a rustic bread ... or a complete failure. If you keep the information in this chapter in mind, you'll achieve success in the pastry kitchen.

The second part of the chapter covers the remaining ingredients used throughout the book, from fruits to nuts to cheeses, and from liqueurs to spices. Whether they are the stars, like peaches in peach pie, or supporting players, like almond extract in a tart filling, these are the ingredients that add vitality and flavor to your baking. Knowing how to choose fruit, toast nuts, and differentiate between coriander and cardamom makes baking fun, because the elements in this part of the chapter are often what are used to express your creativity in the kitchen.

The Eight Main Ingredients in Baking

Flour

Flour is the most important structural ingredient in baking, and the type and quality you use will have a profound impact on your baked goods. White flour used in baking is derived from wheat. The two basic categories of wheat are hard wheat and soft wheat. Hard wheat contains a higher protein content than soft wheat, and is often labeled as bread flour and used for baked goods that need a strong, flexible structure. Soft wheat has less protein and more starch and is often labeled as cake or pastry flour and used in products that need less structure and a very tender crumb. Hard and soft wheats are blended to produce all-purpose flour, and each flour company has its own proprietary ratio for this flour.

Why is protein content important? Protein, when combined with liquid and mixed or kneaded, creates gluten, a web of strong, yet flexible, strands that give breads and pastries their structure. It is the very backbone of baked goods. But not all baked goods need the same kind of structure. Bread needs a stronger, stretchier network of gluten, whereas cakes require very little.

HOW FLOUR IS MADE

The wheat berry, or wheat kernel, consists of a hard brown outer coating known as bran, and inside is a small nutrient and oil-filled germ, or seed, and the endosperm, the bulk of the wheat kernel. White flour is the finely ground and sifted endosperm. To make white flour, the entire wheat berry is repeatedly crushed, ground and sifted to remove the bran and germ, resulting in a silky soft white flour. Whole wheat flour, on the other hand, has the bran and germ left in, giving it a brown color, sweet, nutty flavor, higher nutritional and fiber content, and gritty texture. Whole wheat flour presents two problems for the baker when used instead of white flour. First, it has a shorter shelf life because the germ has natural oils, which turn rancid quickly. Second, the sharp edges of the bran cut through lengthening strands of gluten during kneading, shortening them and diminishing the structure that allows breads and pastries to rise and expand, resulting in dense, heavy products. This is why most baked goods are made using white flour.

TYPES OF FLOUR

With rows of flour in the supermarket, how do you know which one to choose for your recipe? The amount of protein present in each is the main clue to its use. Hint: To figure out the protein content of any flour, divide the number of protein grams per serving by the number of total grams in a serving. Let's look at some of the most common types of flour.

CAKE FLOUR With just 5 to 7 percent protein, silky white cake flour's low protein produces a very tender, fine crumb. It is essential for light and lovely angel food, chiffon, and other sponge or foam cakes. Because it has so little protein, it is nearly impossible to toughen the crumb by overmixing and overdeveloping the gluten. Sift cake flour when measuring, since it is so finely milled that it clumps easily. Find it in the baking aisle of the supermarket and in the bulk section of many stores.

PASTRY FLOUR With only 7 to 9 percent protein, pastry flour is particularly useful for making pie crusts. It has enough protein to create the gluten needed to hold the structure of a pie, but not so much that a little exuberant mixing will make it tough. However, pastry flour is not called for in this book because it has become increasingly difficult to find and you can make great pie dough without it.

If you want to try pastry flour, the best place to look is in the bulk section of a natural foods store. To substitute pastry flour for all-purpose flour, simply use the same quantity of flour as the recipe states. Be aware that you may need less liquid in the recipe, because pastry flour does not absorb as much liquid as all-purpose flour.

SELF-RISING FLOUR With 7 to 11 percent protein, self-rising flour, which is popular in the southern United States and England, is a low- to medium-protein flour (similar to pastry or all-purpose flour) that contains 1½ teaspoons of baking powder and ½ teaspoon of salt per cup of flour. Use it only in recipes calling for self-rising flour.

ALL-PURPOSE FLOUR With anywhere from 7 to 12 percent protein, all-purpose flour is an example of the axiom "jack of all trades, master of none." Is it the best flour for cakes, pies, pastries, and breads? No. But it's the one type of flour that can be used, with some success, to make each of those things. Note that while cake, pastry, and bread flours have reliable, consistent attributes for specific purposes, all-purpose flour does not. All-purpose flour is a blend of flours, and each company has its own trademark style and protein content for its all-purpose flour. Bleached all-purpose flours tend to have low protein content and we recommend you stay away from them; bleaching strips the flour of flavor and some people even say they can detect a chemical flavor (see more on this on next page). For the best results with the recipes in this book, use a national brand of unbleached all-purpose flour, such as Gold Medal, which has a protein content of 10 to 11 percent and is available in virtually every supermarket in the country.

Unless the recipe specifically asks you to, don't sift all-purpose flour when you measure, as that will throw off the ratio of ingredients (a cup of sifted flour is lighter than a cup of unsifted flour). Most bags of flour state that the flour has been sifted at the factory. Maybe so, but by the time it reaches your home, it's been compacted again. If a recipe asks for sifted flour, then you'll need to sift, but in most cases, all-purpose flour is measured by the dip-and-sweep method (see "Measuring 101," page 3) rather than the sifting method.

BREAD FLOUR High-protein bread flour is 12 to 14 percent protein. It is great for making bread because the prodigious amount of gluten it yields enables bread and yeasted pastries to expand dramatically yet still hold their shape, especially free-form loaves baked without pans. Bread flour is almost never bleached, letting

Bleached versus unbleached flours: When flour is milled and allowed to rest for a few weeks, it oxidizes naturally, turning a lighter shade of creamy beige. As you might imagine, huge flour companies don't have the time or storage space to allow all that flour to sit around until it reaches the right color, so they whiten the flour after the milling is complete, using either chlorine gas, chlorine dioxide, or benzoyl peroxide to speed the process along. Some also use potassium bromate, which is banned in numerous countries as a carcinogen, although it is still approved for use here (though in California, bags must contain a warning label). Elsewhere, you must contact the manufacturer to find out whether it uses potassium bromate.

Bleached cake flour has its place in the world of baking—besides helping the gluten network to set quickly, it also increases a flour's ability to absorb liquid—but the notion that snowy white flour is somehow superior is a fallacy left from a time in history when millers could produce only small amounts of white flour, so it was expensive and went to the wealthy. The truth is, unbleached flour has a superior flavor (bleached flours often have a detectable bitterness), is kinder to the environment, and is certainly better for our bodies.

the flavor of the wheat shine through. It may contain some additives such as malted barley flour to aid in fermentation and prolong shelf life.

Storing: All flour should be stored airtight in a cool, dry location. Flour dries out quickly after opening, which means your dough or batter may require more liquid than the recipe states, wreaking havoc with ratios. White flours will keep for up to 9 months, whereas whole wheat flour will only last a few months because the oil in the germ goes rancid quickly. Refrigerating the flour (for up to 6 months) or freezing it (for up to 12 months) will significantly extend its shelf life.

MEASURING FLOUR

Problems with measuring flour are the cause of many baking failures. Before you measure your first cup, read "Measuring 101" on page 3.

HOW GLUTEN WORKS

Most flour used in baking is derived from wheat (as opposed to rye or corn), for only wheat contains the two proteins—glutenin and gliadin—that, when combined with liquid and mixed or kneaded, produce gluten, the structural backbone of most baked goods. Once the proteins in flour are hydrated and the mixing or kneading begins, they begin to form tangled strands (when your dough comes together in a rough mass, that's what's happening on the

molecular level). As kneading continues, the proteins straighten out and bond with one another, creating long, less twisted chains of protein. These chains become quite strong as you work them—strong enough to be stretched, yet tight enough to spring back after stretching. This complex network of gluten strands is elastic as well, able to expand with the lift of powerful leaveners such as yeast, baking powder, baking soda, air, and steam. Gluten lets the dough expand to its fullest potential and provides structure by holding it in place when the proteins harden, or coagulate, from the heat of the oven. This prevents the pastry or bread from collapsing when you remove it to cool.

GUIDING GLUTEN DEVELOPMENT Some factors can interfere with (or control, depending on your point of view) gluten development. Each of the following techniques can be used to change the texture and structure of a recipe.

- **Choose a different flour.** For instance, if your bread dough is slack or your quick bread collapses, use a flour with a higher protein content, resulting in more gluten.
- **Knead the dough more (or less).** If bread dough is not kneaded well after the liquid is added, very little gluten will form, and you'll have a dense, heavy loaf. But when you're making pie dough, you must be careful not to overmix it, or the gluten will be too developed and your dough will be tough.
- **Control the water.** Protein molecules need to hydrate before they can begin to form gluten. If a recipe contains little or no liquid, you won't get much gluten—exactly what you want for crisp, crumbly streusel-style toppings for fruit crisps. But too much liquid can weaken the gluten as well, diluting the proteins and affecting their ability to bond tightly and strengthen. You can observe this in a loaf of Italian ciabatta (or "slipper bread"). This bread is made with a very wet dough that resembles pancake batter. The plentiful water overwhelms the strands of gluten, and the dough doesn't have enough structure to rise or form a regular crumb, resulting in a flat bread with large holes in the chewy crumb. When it comes to water and dough, as with Goldilocks and the three bears, "just right" is what you're after here: The amount of water in the dough must suit what you're trying to bake.
- **Adjust the temperature of the liquid.** Warm liquid hydrates proteins more quickly than does cold. Cold liquid can be used to delay gluten formation, which is one of the reasons it is used in making pie dough (the other reason is to keep the butter cold and firm).
- **Vary the amount of fat.** Fats interfere with gluten formation and development because they coat the strands of proteins like a raincoat, preventing them from absorbing the liquid they need to fully hydrate. If they can't hydrate, they can't bond to

form gluten; in other words, they are "shortened." Shortened baked goods are very delicate—think of shortbread cookies, with their buttery crumbliness, and you'll realize where it got its name.

- **Play with sugar amounts.** Because it is hygroscopic (water-attracting), sugar steals water from the proteins, which then can't hydrate and form gluten.
- **Add or subtract flavoring ingredients.** Sometimes other ingredients in a dough or batter can interfere with the bonding and lengthening of gluten strands, either by cutting through them—as is the case with the sharp edges of bran in whole wheat flour—or by their mere physical presence. For example, nuts, cheese, chocolate chips, dried fruit, and sesame seeds can all get in the way of the lengthening process and disrupt the formation of gluten.

OTHER ROLES OF FLOUR IN BAKING

Like proteins, the starch in flour adds structure as well. Starch is an especially vital component of cake flour. Cake flour has very little protein, and yet cakes made with it still manage to hold their shape—even very tall ones like chiffon and angel food cake—because of the flour's high starch content. Cake flour is always bleached with chlorine, which changes the starch and allows it to hold more liquid than it otherwise would. The bleaching process also lowers the pH of the flour, making it more acidic. This higher acidity allows the starch to set, or harden, at a lower temperature than other flours. When the cake bakes, the starch in the flour swells and thickens the batter, lifting the cake high in the pan; then the acidity kicks in to set the structure quickly, resulting in firm yet tender cakes.

Flour can also be used to thicken fruit-pie fillings and custards cooked on top of the stove, such as pastry cream and chocolate pudding. It also adds a subtle undertone of flavor to everything and a small amount of nutritional value as well, although some flours have more nutrients than others. Flour dusted on the counter keeps dough from sticking as it's being rolled or kneaded, and is a decorative element when sifted over bread dough just before slashing and baking.

Sugar

In this book, "sugar" means white granulated sugar and its relations. Liquid sugars such as honey, molasses, maple syrup, and corn syrup are used less frequently in home baking and are explained later in this chapter.

Sugar is refined from either sugarcane (a tropical, bamboo-like grass) or sugar beets (varieties of beets with a high sugar content), which both produce table sugar that is nearly pure sucrose. Beet sugar contains more natural impurities, which aren't harmful

to eat, but can cause a sugar mixture to crystallize. Although they are considered chemically identical, many professional bakers prefer pure cane sugar to beet sugar, especially when making frostings and candies.

HOW SUGAR IS MADE

To make sugar, sugarcane or sugar beets are chopped until they release as much liquid as possible. The juice is then combined with lime and carbon dioxide, which trap impurities in the juice that are then filtered out. The purified juice is heated, and as it concentrates, its sugars crystallize. The mixture is then centrifuged, removing the uncrystallized liquid that remains, which is molasses. The crystals that remain are then washed, heated, liquified, and centrifuged at least once more. When as many impurities as possible have been removed through this process, the liquid sugar is then usually bleached and purified. Finally, it is recrystallized again, dried, sifted, and transferred into bags for sale.

TYPES OF SUGAR

GRANULATED SUGAR Also called *table sugar* and *fine sugar,* granulated sugar is the most common form of sugar. Don't confuse it with superfine sugar (below), although you can substitute one for the other.

SUPERFINE SUGAR This is also known as *caster* or *bar sugar* because it's used by bartenders, who appreciate its ability to dissolve almost instantly in liquid. Superfine sugar is simply very finely ground granulated sugar. It is more expensive than table sugar, and comes in 1-pound boxes or in larger bags marketed as "Baker's Sugar."

Bakers do love the fine granules of this sugar for the tight-grained crumb it lends to cakes. You can make your own superfine sugar by whirling granulated sugar in the food processor for 60 seconds. You can substitute superfine sugar for granulated sugar one to one. The smaller crystals of superfine sugar do pack together more tightly when poured or spooned into a measuring cup, but the difference is so small as to be negligible.

CONFECTIONERS' SUGAR Confectioners' sugar (also called *powdered sugar*) is granulated sugar pulverized into powder and blended with about 3 percent cornstarch. This prevents it from clumping or liquefying. The granules are so fine in confectioners' sugar that, were a drying agent like cornstarch not added, they could easily bond with moisture in the air and then stick together into a hard lump. Do not substitute confectioners' sugar for granulated sugar in baking.

BROWN SUGAR Brown sugar is simply granulated sugar with molasses added. The type and intensity of molasses added determines whether the sugar will be light brown or dark brown. Dark brown has a slightly stronger molasses flavor, although the

pros

Brown sugar hardens quickly when left exposed to the air, resulting in hard, unusable lumps of sugar. If this happens, you can resuscitate the sugar by slipping a brown sugar softener (it looks like a clay teddy bear) soaked briefly in water into the container of hardened sugar. A damp, wrung-out paper towel will serve the same purpose. Close the lid tightly, or wrap the mixture airtight, and the next morning the sugar will be soft again. Some people advocate adding a slice of fresh apple to the mixture overnight, and that will work, too, but if you forget to take it out, you could wind up with an unpleasant surprise two weeks later when you open your brown sugar and find a piece of molded fruit.

two can be used interchangeably in most recipes. If you're out of brown sugar, you can make your own by substituting granulated sugar and adding a tablespoon of light, unsulfured molasses for each cup of sugar. Since brown sugar is moist and doesn't flow, it is always measured by packing it tightly into the measuring cup.

TYPES OF SPECIALTY AND DECORATIVE SUGARS

MAPLE SUGAR Bursting with the flavor of maple syrup, maple sugar is syrup that has been dried and then crystallized into powdery, taupe granules. It can be sprinkled over cakes or quick breads before baking, or onto hot cereal or toast. Roll cookies in it for a crispy layer of maple flavor, or use it to sweeten and flavor cookies by substituting it for the granulated sugar in the recipe.

COARSE, SANDING, AND LARGE-CRYSTAL SUGAR These sugars have larger crystals than granulated sugar, and they provide a sparkling finish to baked goods because they don't melt in the oven. They are more expensive than regular sugar because the sugar must be very pure to form the large crystals. Sometimes these sugars are colored, for an added decorative affect. Don't substitute large-crystal sugar for granulated sugar in recipe formulas.

TURBINADO SUGAR This is a light brown, large-crystal sugar with a slight molasses flavor. Turbinado sugar is sometimes sold as "Sugar in the Raw" or "Hawaiian Washed Raw Sugar." Although minimally refined and still containing some molasses, it is purified and sterilized to remove bacteria or mold, so it's not actually raw. It cannot be substituted for brown sugar.

DEMERARA SUGAR A large-crystal turbinado popular in England for use in tea (it's great on hot cereal). It was originally produced in the Demerara district of Guyana. It is most often used in syrups and as a dusting on top of desserts before baking. Like turbinado, it should not be substituted for brown sugar in recipe fomulas.

MUSCOVADO OR BARBADOS SUGAR Made at one time in Barbados, muscovado is another minimally refined sugar but, instead of being crunchy, it has a fine grain and a soft, moist texture like brown sugar. It is available in light and dark versions, and can be substituted for brown sugar in recipes.

Storing: Store all sugars in airtight containers to avoid spillage or contamination, and to prevent soft brown sugars from hardening.

THE ROLES OF SUGAR IN BAKING

Beyond sweetening anything it touches, sugar performs several additional, and very important, jobs in the pastry kitchen: tenderizing, adding moisture, and leavening.

TENDERIZING Sugar tenderizes breads and pastries by interfering with gluten formation. Its presence in shortbread cookies, shortcrust for tarts, and crumble toppings influences the delicate crumb of these pastries. Sugar's hygroscopic (liquid-absorbing) quality robs the flour of much of the water required for gluten development. (Remember that gluten is the long-stranded protein that makes it possible for bread to rise and hold its structure, but too much can toughen cookies and tart crusts.) Sugar also tenderizes by both slowing down protein coagulation in eggs, resulting in velvety custards, and starch gelatinization in flour, helping to give cakes a soft and tender crumb.

ADDING MOISTURE Because of its water-attracting nature, sugar increases the moisture in breads and pastries and helps prevent them from drying out (getting stale). Conversely, sugar can also make baked goods crisp when it crystallizes on their surfaces.

LEAVENING When butter and sugar are beaten together, or creamed, the sharp edges of the sugar crystals cut into the butter, forming little air pockets—thousands and thousands of them.

The chemical leavener (baking powder or baking soda) and the heat of the oven increase the size of those bubbles, causing the cake to rise. Sugar also delays the setting, or gelatinization, of starches in the batter, allowing more time for the cake to rise and resulting in a lighter, more open crumb.

OTHER SUPPORTING ROLES Sugar moistens and stabilizes egg foams, especially meringue. It also provides food for yeast so that the natural leavener can do its job, for as the yeast feed, they produce CO_2 bubbles, which get trapped in the gluten network and cause the bread to rise. Sugar lends a caramel flavor when baked at a high temperature, and contributes additional flavors depending on the type of sugar added (brown sugar, honey, turbinado, maple syrup, etc.). When added at high levels, sugar "steals" or binds all the water, preventing microbial growth (think of jams and jellies or candied orange peel) and increasing the shelf life of sweetened breads and pastries.

TURNING SUGAR INTO CARAMEL

One of the most wonderful transformations in the pastry kitchen is that of plain table sugar into golden brown, bittersweet caramel. Pastry chefs love caramel (who doesn't?) because its sultry taste enhances nearly everything it touches with big, bold, luscious flavor. Caramelized sugar has many particular uses, not the least of which is caramel sauce, that velvety, golden brown nectar that can be used to grace nearly any dessert. Caramel may seem intimidating to the novice, but a few tips will lead you to success on your first try.

HOW TO MAKE CARAMEL There are two methods for making caramel: the dry method and the wet method. The dry method involves sugar in a saucepan over medium heat and lots of stirring. As the sugar melts, it immediately caramelizes. There is always some crystallization with this process, resulting in a few residual lumps and some brown specks in the final caramel, which can unnerve home bakers. The wet method incorporates water to dissolve the sugar, slowing down the whole process to a more reasonable pace, and ensuring a smooth, clear caramel. This is the method used here.

To make caramel, gather all the utensils and ingredients you will need and have them at arm's reach. Once the sugar begins to brown, it can burn in a matter of seconds and you don't want to be running around the kitchen looking for a whisk at the crucial moment. Don't answer the phone or watch TV—you need to focus. Keep a bowl of ice water nearby in case the caramel splatters on you—it is very hot and will cause immediate blistering. Place a white plate, a measuring cup filled with hot water, and a wooden, metal, or silicone spoon next to the stove. You'll use these to test the color of the caramel.

Use a heavy saucepan with a light interior so you'll be able to gauge the color of the sugar. Do not use tin-lined copper, as caramel will melt the tin. The pan should be a larger size than you think you need, because when you add liquid to the caramel (such as cream for caramel sauce), it rises up in the pan and boils vigorously.

To caramelize a cup of sugar, pour ⅓ to ½ cup of water into the saucepan. You may use as much water as you like, for it is simply there to dissolve the sugar. Keep in mind, though, that the sugar won't progress in the cooking process until all of the water has evaporated, so the more water you add, the longer the process takes. Add corn syrup or cream of tartar (see "A Few Notes on Crystallization" below). Sprinkle the sugar slowly over the water and set the pan over medium-low heat. Warm, stirring frequently, until the sugar has dissolved and the liquid is clear. Set the spoon into the measuring cup of hot water and don't stir again until the end. Stirring can cause crystallization or introduce microscopic debris that results in crystallization.

Once the liquid is clear, turn the heat to medium-high and cook, without stirring, until the sugar begins to turn golden around the edges. Swirl the pan gently to distribute the color and to ensure that the sugar cooks evenly. (All pans and stoves have hot spots, so this will help prevent any one spot in the pan from darkening too quickly.) Test the sugar with the spoon, dipping it into the sugar, pulling out a tiny bit and dripping it on the plate. Continue testing every 5 to 10 seconds, until the correct color is reached.

Why the plate? Sugar always looks darker in the pan than it really is, because you are looking through several layers of sugar. A drop on a white plate reveals the true color. The tendency is to undercook caramel. You want it dark enough so it ceases to be simply

tips for success A Few Notes on Crystallization

Sugar crystallizes easily, and once you've melted the granulated sugar crystals, you don't want them to recrystallize. Crystallized sugar looks like damp, white sand. Any speck of debris in the sugar syrup can cause a crystal to form, and once one forms, chains of crystals link together until your pan is filled with a chunky, sugary mess. Sugar is inexpen-sive and you can throw the batch out and start over, but time is precious.

There are a couple of things you can do to avoid crystallization. Make sure your pan and utensils are very clean. Add light corn syrup (1 tablespoon per cup of sugar) or cream of tartar (⅛ teaspoon per cup of sugar) to the sugar. Light corn syrup is an invert sugar, just different enough in chemical structure from table sugar to interfere with the formation and linking of crystals. Cream of tartar, an acid, accomplishes the same thing by turning some of the table sugar into invert sugar. These two "insurance policies" against crystallization may be added even when the recipe doesn't specifically ask for them.

sweet and takes on an edge of bitterness that balances the remaining sweetness. As caramelization begins, the sugar will appear clear with a yellow tinge. As it continues, the color progresses from light yellow to light amber to dark amber (yes, the color of prehistoric sap with insects preserved in it) to golden brown, then dark reddish brown, and finally black. You want to avoid black sugar. Unless the recipe specifies otherwise, cook the caramel to dark amber or golden brown for fullest flavor, or reddish brown if you want the darkest, most complex flavor. Keep in mind that caramel will continue to cook and darken in color, even when you turn off the heat.

Once the sugar has reached the desired color, you need to immediately stop the cooking. To do this you can add some liquid to the caramel, or put the pan in an ice bath. If adding liquid, do so all at once. Be careful here, as the liquid will cause the caramel to rise in the pan and sputter—you may want to wear an oven mitt on the hand adding the liquid. The caramel won't react as violently if the liquid is warm, so first heat it gently and keep it on the stove. Stir or whisk the caramel to finish blending it with the liquid. If the liquid was warm or hot, there won't be any hard spots. If the liquid was cold, you'll have some bits of hardened caramel in the pan. Should this happen, return the pan to low heat and stir slowly until the hardened bits melt again. Don't taste the caramel until it has cooled for a while or you'll burn your tongue!

If you are not going to add a liquid to the caramel, either have an ice bath nearby into which you can plunge the bottom of the pan to stop the cooking, or remove the pan from the heat a few seconds early, before the correct color is reached. Gently swirl and watch until it reaches the correct color, then use the caramel as desired.

Cleanup: Don't try to scrub the caramel pan and utensils clean (a sure exercise in frustration). Simply fill the pan with water, add the utensils, bring everything to a boil, and cook for 5 minutes. Then pour the water down the drain. Usually, this is enough to remove all the caramel. If there is still some remaining, repeat the procedure.

Eggs

The world of cakes and pastries would not be possible without eggs, and they hold a place of prime importance alongside flour. Most baking recipes call for large eggs, that is, eggs that weigh about 2 ounces each (in the shell). The egg white weighs about 1 ounce, while the yolk weighs about ⅔ ounce. Egg size is determined by the weight per dozen eggs and ranges from jumbo (30 ounce per dozen) to extra large (27 ounces) to large (24 ounces) to medium (21 ounces) to small (18 ounces) and peewee (15 ounces). Though you may certainly use a size of egg other than large when baking, you'll need to take the difference in size into account and make adjustments accordingly.

Egg shells range in color from white to brown to green and beyond, but the color of the shell does not affect the nutritional content or quality of the egg. It simply reflects the type of chicken that laid the egg. Within the shell is the albumen (egg white), the yolk, and the chalazae cords. These twisted cords of egg white center the yolk and hold it in place and, except for custards, do not need to be removed or worried about before using an egg in baking.

Eggs are graded by the USDA, and the grades, ranging from AA to A to B, are a determination of quality, not nutrition. Grade AA eggs have a firm, thick white, a round, high and centered yolk, and a clean, unbroken shell. They are the type recommended for all your baking and cooking needs. Lower grades may be slightly misshapen, or have thin yolks or whites, but are not dangerous in any way, and may be used for baking and eating as well.

Egg cartons sport many confusing labels these days, such as free-range or pasture-raised or omega-3. Conventional egg-laying operations keep the hens confined in small cages their entire life. Free-range, pasture-raised, free-roaming, and cage-free eggs theoretically come from chickens that are allowed the space to walk about, peck, and stretch their wings if they want, but there is no third-party verification of such egg carton labels. And just because they're given the room, doesn't mean they take advantage of it. They aren't like dogs, yearning to run free, and their natural tendency is to stay within a close distance to their nesting area. Certified humane and certified organic labels do require third-party verification, and both allow the chickens free range. In addition, the certified organic chickens are fed an all-vegetarian diet free of antibiotics and pesticides.

Fertile eggs are those laid by hens who live with roosters. The label of natural on an egg carton has no industry regulations attached to it and may be used indiscriminately. Omega-3 eggs are produced by feeding hens a diet rich in flaxseed (which is a good source of omega-3 fatty acids), and the eggs they produce also contain a significantly higher amount of omega-3 than other eggs (about 100 to 200 mg, which is 3 to 6 times more than a normal egg).

Some eggs undergo a pasteurization process while still in their shells, rendering the egg safe from salmonella bacteria. Others are dried and powdered, resulting in a shelf-stable egg white powder sometimes called meringue powder. This powder needs to be reconstituted with water before being whipped or otherwise used in dessert making or general cooking.

SEPARATING EGGS

When separating eggs, it is very important to keep the egg whites free from any of the fat-laden yolks, because fat will prevent the whites from whipping properly. It is easiest to separate eggs while they are cold from the refrigerator, since room temperature yolks puncture easily. Place three small bowls in a line. Crack an egg by striking it firmly on the counter, then hold it over the center bowl and gently pull it apart, allowing the white to fall into the bowl, while the yolk nestles in one of the shell halves. Pass the yolk back and forth between the two shell halves, avoiding any sharp edges that could puncture the yolk, while separating any remaining white from the yolk. Place the yolk in the bowl to the right. Transfer the white in the center bowl to the bowl on the left. Continue separating as many eggs as needed. This method ensures that if you do puncture a yolk and contaminate the white in the center bowl, you have only ruined one egg white, rather than the entire batch. If a little egg yolk drips into the white, you may be able to retrieve it. Use a clean piece of egg shell as a scoop and put it next to the piece of yolk—it should glide right into your scoop.

EGG SAFETY

It is important to take egg safety into consideration these days. Salmonella, a bacteria present in the intestines of hens, can be found on the shell or even inside of eggs. Salmonella can cause illness, and the elderly, young children, and those with compromised immune systems are especially susceptible. Since there is no way to tell whether the bacteria are present, it's best to be careful in every circumstance, which is why recipes in this book always heat eggs that are not fully cooked (such as those for sabayon and buttercream) to 160°F, which is the instant-kill temperature for the salmonella bacteria.

Keep cross-contamination in mind when working with raw eggs, and wipe up any spills with hot soapy water, wash your hands, and never reuse equipment that has come in contact with raw eggs before washing it thoroughly. And if you are heating eggs to 160°F, be careful to wash the tip of the thermometer with hot water before reinserting it into the eggs to test a second or third time during the heating process.

Once your cooked egg product is finished, eat it or chill it quickly, as eggs are an excellent breeding ground for bacteria. This is why custard sauce, pastry cream, sabayon cream, and the like should be chilled in an ice bath and then refrigerated once they are cooled.

Storing: Eggs should be kept refrigerated at a temperature less than 40°F at all times. An egg left at room temperature ages as much in 1 day as a full week in the refrigerator. When kept at the proper temperature, fresh eggs will easily last a month past the date on the carton.

ROOM TEMERATURE EGGS

Many baking recipes call for room temperature eggs. The best way to bring eggs to room temperature safely is to place them, still in their shells, in a large bowl and cover them with plenty of hot tap water (not boiling water). Wait 5 minutes, then drain the water (see page 302). Your eggs are now warm enough to be considered room temperature. If you need to separate eggs, do it while the eggs are cold from the refrigerator, as this is when it is easiest to detach the yolk from the white. Room temperature yolks are tender and puncture easily, contaminating your whites with their fat (which can prevent whites from whipping properly).

THE ROLES OF EGGS IN BAKING

Eggs are the chameleons of the baking world. They can make one pastry soft and tender, like sabayon cream, and another tough and dry, as when too many egg whites in a cake batter toughen and dry the cake because of the extra protein. Although the yolk is full of flavorful fat, eggs are similar to flour because they provide structure in pastries. However, egg proteins are not as strong as a gluten network; they coagulate at a lower temperature, so they hold the dough in place until the proteins in the gluten have a chance to set. Angel food cake is a good example of this. This ability to add structure can also be seen in custards. As the eggs heat up, the custard thickens (such as lemon curd or custard sauce) and may even set completely, as is the case with baked custards like crème brulee or crème caramel.

Eggs have an amazing ability to hold air bubbles, so they often act as a support to the real leavener that works with them, which is air. That is, the egg itself doesn't make the cake rise, but the air bubbles trapped within the egg's structure expand in the heat of the oven, causing the baked good to rise. This quality is especially important with foam or sponge cakes such as chiffon, genoise, and angel food. Eggs' ability to hold air bubbles also helps to aerate mixtures like chocolate mousse and sabayon, both of which would be heavy and uninteresting without their fluffy texture.

Eggs—especially the yolks—are emulsifiers. The yolk contains a natural emulsifier called *lecithin,* which is especially good at bringing disparate ingredients together, such as fat and liquid, and keeping them in blended suspension. Lecithin works its magic behind the scenes, allowing the egg itself to take the credit. It creates the satiny texture we love in certain foods like French (custard) ice cream, cake batters, and buttercreams.

Eggs also contribute flavor to baked goods—their own, of course, but they also carry and enhance other flavors in a pastry. They add an appealing golden color to doughs and batters, and when used as a wash on top of breads, they dry to a rich, shiny brown. An egg wash (a light glaze of whole egg, sometimes mixed with a small amount of water, milk, or cream) is also the perfect glue to attach decorative seeds to the outside of breads, or large-crystal sugars to the outside of cookies and pastries.

Many home bakers believe that eggs are responsible for the moist texture of breads and pastries, and then reach the logical conclusion that if their cake is dry, they should add another egg. While it is true that eggs are mostly moisture themselves, that doesn't necessarily mean they'll make a cake moist. Eggs are also full of protein, a toughener, which easily overwhelms any moistness the yolk's fat may have added. Instead, if a cake is dry, try reducing or changing the flour, adding more liquid (milk, etc.) or even additional fat (butter or oil) to the formula.

Butter

Butter imparts a unique flavor unmatched by that of any other fat, and it is the preferred fat in this book. Part of the reason for butter's popularity, much like chocolate's, is its melting point, which is slightly below our body temperature. This gives pastries baked with butter a literally melt-in-your-mouth quality.

Certainly there are many concerns about excessive fat and calories in this day and age. Homemade baked goods should be enjoyed to their fullest. If you're concerned about fat intake, cut a smaller slice and give any tempting leftovers to friends and neighbors.

HOW BUTTER IS MADE

While we harbor a romantic notion of a farm wife making butter in a wooden churn, it is now a large-scale process. To make butter, cream is first pasteurized and cooled. Then coloring is added (natural yellow annatto). Coloring is added because many years ago butter had different colors in the winter and summer, due to the cow's feed. Dried grains in the winter led to pale-colored butter, whereas green grass in the spring and summer resulted in a pleasantly yellow butter with a slightly different, more appealing flavor. This butter was the best, and when butter-making went large-scale, coloring was added to make "spring butter" all year long.

Once the coloring is added, the cream is churned, first thickening to whipped cream. Then the fat begins to clump into larger and larger pieces, while the remaining liquid—buttermilk—is drained away. The butter clumps are washed and kneaded (and salt is added, if desired) to form the smooth blocks we buy in the store.

BUTTER GRADES

Butter adds a wonderful flavor and mouthfeel to baked goods that no other fat can match. This is why the recipes in this book use butter rather than shortening or margarine. Whipped butter and butter/oil blends should not be substituted for stick, or solid, butter in recipes.

Butter in this country must contain 80 percent milk fat and 16 percent or more water and milk solids (proteins, lactose, and minerals). Grade AA has the mildest, sweetest flavor and Grade A has a stronger, slightly acidic flavor. Grade B has the strongest, most acidic flavor, and tastes more like cultured butter (see below). The higher the water content, the softer the butter and the less fat available for your recipe; therefore, the best butters for baking contain the least water. Premium brands usually have less water. Cold

butter should be hard to the touch; if yours is pliable, it contains too much water. Switch to another, higher-quality brand.

TYPES OF BUTTER

SALTED VERSUS UNSALTED Pastry chefs always use unsalted butter in their baking, and you should, too. First of all, there is no industry standard for the amount of salt in a pound of butter, so there's no real way for you to know how much salt you're adding to your recipe when using salted butter. In most cases, if you use salted butter, your pastry will end up tasting too salty. Second, salt is a preservative, so unsalted butter has a small sales window, which means the supermarket stock is constantly replenished with fresh butter; the salted stuff hangs around longer and may not be as fresh. The downside is that unsalted butter also goes rancid more quickly than salted, so store it properly (below 40°F in the refrigerator) and use it within a few weeks of its stamped date or freeze it for longer storage. If you decide to use salted butter, omit any salt the recipe calls for.

CULTURED BUTTER This style of butter can now increasingly be found in specialty markets and even in some supermarkets. Cultured butter, sometimes marketed as "European-style," is made from sour cream and has a pronounced sour flavor, and usually a higher fat content, too—from 84 to 88 percent. Some chefs love it for the acidity it adds to baked goods, and its nutty flavor can be divine with good bread. Although popular in France and other European countries, it is an acquired taste for most Americans, much like crème fraîche was when it first began to appear on dessert menus across the country. You can substitute unsalted cultured butter for standard unsalted butter in baking, keeping in mind that there will be a distinct flavor difference and an additional level of acidity.

Storing: Always refrigerate butter well wrapped or in a resealable plastic bag, as it absorbs flavors quickly. Use unsalted butter within 1 month, or freeze it wrapped in plastic and slipped inside a resealable plastic bag for up to 4 months.

PLASTICITY AND ROOM-TEMPERATURE BUTTER

A *plastic* texture in butter is a professional term that describes the narrow range of temperatures at which butter is soft enough to manipulate, but firm enough to hold its shape. Butter is plastic between 65° and 68°F. This temperature is vital to the success of many pastries. The problem is that many recipes refer to this range of temperatures as "room temperature," when, in fact, room temperature is often a much higher temperature, especially during the summer! Butter at 85°F performs very differently than butter at 65°F, and pastries can turn out heavy or even fail if the butter is too warm. In this way, plasticity is key to the texture of many baked goods. Plastic butter is flexible enough to expand and fill with air bubbles during the creaming process, yet stable enough to hold them in suspension. Plasticity also allows the creation of the little air pockets that form flakes in pie dough and the thin sheets of butter that separate long layers of dough, resulting in hundreds of layers in puff pastry.

When a recipe calls for softened butter, remove it from the refrigerator 35 to 45 minutes before use so the butter has enough time to warm to between 65° and 68°F.

If you're in a hurry, slice the butter into pieces and separate the pieces on a plate, which will speed their warming. In some instances, such as during creaming, you may be able to use the butter straight from the refrigerator (see below).

CREAMING BUTTER AND SUGAR

This technique lightens batters and is the basis for leavening in any recipe where it appears, such as those for cakes, quick breads, and cookies. Let's look at butter cakes (pound cakes). These cakes rely on creaming for their leavening. This may seem strange, since the batters also contain baking powder, baking soda, or a combination of the two. But these chemical leaveners only make existing bubbles in the batter larger—they don't create new bubbles themselves. This means the batter must be filled with thousands of tiny air bubbles, or the cake will end up dense, heavy and unappealing.

Begin the creaming process with butter that is between 65° and 68°F. Butter that is too cold (and therefore not elastic enough to hold bubbles) or too warm (and too soft to keep bubbles in suspension) will create a cake that lacks a fine crumb and light, open texture. If your butter is soft, squishy, or separated, measure some new butter.

Say you forgot to take the butter out of the refrigerator to warm it up before creaming. This is one instance when you can use butter straight from the refrigerator, although the process will take a little longer.

Cut the cold butter into tablespoon-size pieces, put it in the mixing bowl with the sugar, and begin beating. Start off on a low speed so the butter pieces don't fly out of the bowl, and increase the speed as the butter softens and smoothes out.

It will take a couple of minutes longer for the mixture to become fully creamed, but you'll be able to make a cake batter in record time. This works because the friction generated by the sugar crystals and the motion of the paddle attachment will warm the butter up. Note: If you use a hand mixer, be sure the motor and beaters are powerful enough to mix cold butter. A stand mixer with a paddle attachment handles it well.

THE CREAMING METHOD FOR CAKES The creaming method for cakes is discussed in detail in "Butter Cakes" on page 301.

THE CREAMING METHOD FOR COOKIES AND TART DOUGH While the creaming method always includes the same steps, it is slightly different for cakes than it is for cookies and tart dough. Cakes need to rise dramatically and have an open, tender crumb, so the maximum number of air bubbles is necessary. However, cookies are much smaller, with little rise, and tart dough is similarly thin.

For these pastries, the butter and sugar are creamed for only for a couple of minutes, or until the mixture is smooth.

Too many air bubbles can cause problems. Cookies have no pan sides to hold them in place, like cakes, so if there are too many air bubbles, the cookies rise dramatically, but because they do not have pan sides guiding their rise, they spread outward, creating flat, crispy cookies.

Tart doughs don't usually contain leaveners, but too much air can cause a coarse texture and make the dough stick in the pan.

BUTTER SUBSTITUTES

Vegetable shortening and margarine do not appear in this book's recipes; each recipe was specifically designed with butter in mind. Substituting another fat will result in a pastry different from the one described. Shortening and margarine were developed as "improvements" on butter and lard because they were cheaper, stiffer, and have a higher melting point, which makes them more plastic and easy to work with when making creamed cake batter, pie crust, and layered dough such as croissant and puff pastry.

Shortening is an especially hard fat because it contains 100 percent fat, rather than the 80 percent of butter and margarine.

tips for success A Word about Oils in Baking

Oils differ from butter because they are liquid rather than solid, and are 100 percent fat rather than 80 percent.

Oil is derived from plants and seeds rather than animal fats. Baked goods made with oil instead of butter are softer, denser, and more tender because of the higher fat content and the oil's inability to hold vast numbers of air bubbles in suspension. This lack of air bubbles results in reduced leavening, since chemical leaveners rely upon bubbles in the batter to create their rise. When choosing oils for baking, use a neutral-flavored oil such as canola, corn, or safflower.

It has no flavor (except when it is rancid) and has such a high melting point that it doesn't melt fully in the mouth, leaving behind an unpleasant, waxy coating on the palate. In addition, those shortenings that contain trans fats are a health concern.

While it's true that butter requires more attention because it must be worked with while it is between 65° and 68°F, the flavor, color, and texture it adds to baked goods is incomparable. Never use whipped, light, or low-fat butters, or blends of butter and margarine in your baking, because they won't perform the same as butter and your recipe may fail.

THE ROLES OF BUTTER IN BAKING

TENDERIZING Fats coat the proteins in flour like a raincoat, preventing them from hydrating and bonding to form gluten, so cakes, quick breads, cookies, pie and tart doughs, and layered doughs become tender and toothsome. The protein strands that do manage to form gluten are short, hence the names *shortbread* cookie and *shortcrust* tart dough. The softer the fat, the softer the pastry, for it can coat the protein strands more thoroughly, so oil produces softer baked goods than butter (but in most cases, oil cannot be substituted for butter). Too much fat can cause problems, though, creating baked goods that are greasy, crumbly, mealy, or simply collapse from lack of structure, or gluten.

MOISTENING Butter also adds moistness to doughs and batters, aiding in mouthfeel and storage qualities.

GIVING AND ENHANCING FLAVOR Need it be said (again) that butter adds exceptional, milk-sweet flavor that is the benchmark of good pastries? Also, fats are terrific carriers of flavors, and without them, food tastes flat. Not only does butter add flavor, but it enhances the flavors of the ingredients blended with it, such as spices, zests, extracts—even the flour and eggs.

AIDING IN LEAVENING While butter is not a leavener itself, it does hold air bubbles in suspension (through the creaming process) so that chemical leaveners and the heat of the oven can work their magic by enlarging the size of the bubbles. The water and air trapped in butter help separate the layers and form the flakes so characteristic of layered pastries and pie doughs. During baking, the butterfat melts and flavors the dough, while the water turns to steam and the air expands, pushing against the dough on top and creating a space between the two layers that is known as a *flake*. As long as the butter is kept cold and plastic during the mixing and rolling process, and is well chilled before baking, the layering works beautifully. But if the butter is too warm during mixing or rolling, it will blend into the dough, rather than separating it. If it is too warm when it enters the oven, the butter melts long before the proteins and starches in the dough set. Either situation results in few layers and a heavy, greasy dough.

ADDING COLOR Butter gives a beautiful yellow hue to baked goods and also contributes to Maillard browning on the surface of pastries and breads. The Maillard reaction is when a combination of sugars, carbohydrates, and amino acids work together with the heat of the oven to produce a beautiful brown crust filled with complex flavors.

GIVING MOUTHFEEL Butter adds a sensuous mouthfeel to sauces and icings as well as baked goods. What would buttercream be without butter? And both butter and oil contribute to the release qualities of breads and pastries, allowing them to be removed from baking pans relatively easily.

Other Dairy Products

All dairy products consist of water and fat, milk sugar (also called *lactose*), proteins, and natural salts. Often, recipes will ask for dairy products to be at room temperature (such as some cakes), or even lightly warmed (such as some yeast breads). Measure first, then allow 35 to 40 minutes for dairy products to reach room temperature.

Or, heat until tepid in a small saucepan or in the microwave. Be careful not to overheat, though, or you could dramatically affect the bread or pastry. For instance, milk that is too hot can kill yeast before bread dough has even begun. And buttermilk that is too hot can melt the creamed butter and sugar in a cake batter, destroying the suspended air bubbles and ruining the texture of the cake. When in doubt, slightly cool is better than too warm.

MILK

Milk is nature's food for the young, and the slightly sweet product of dairy cows is full of nutrition, including complete proteins. Whole milk is the standard in baking, although you could substitute goat's or even sheep's milk in its place. Whole milk (containing about 3 percent fat) is the best to use in baking, since recipes developed with milk require a certain level of milk fat. You can substitute 2 percent milk, if you like, but if you decrease the fat any more, your baked good will suffer in tenderness. Milk is usually pasteurized (to remove any harmful bacteria) and homogenized, a process that evenly suspends the fat molecules in the liquid.

BUTTERMILK

Originally, buttermilk was the watery liquid left after butter had been churned from heavy cream. Today, buttermilk is made by adding lactic acid bacteria to low-fat or nonfat milk, culturing it for a tangy flavor. It adds a wonderful, homey flavor to baked goods and is almost always paired with baking soda, which neutralizes some of its acidity. Most bakers prefer fresh buttermilk but also keep a container of dried buttermilk powder in the pantry for spur-of-the-moment baking. You don't need to reconstitute the dried buttermilk to use it—to replace 1 cup of buttermilk, simply add ¼ cup of buttermilk powder to the dry ingredients and 1 cup of water to the liquid ingredients. Dry milk powder has had all of the liquid removed and can be kept on the shelf for at least a year. In a pinch, you can substitute 1 cup of milk combined with 1 tablespoon of lemon juice or cider vinegar for buttermilk.

YOGURT

Yogurt is milk—whole, low-fat, or nonfat—that has been cultured with friendly bacteria, then allowed to sour and thicken. Plain yogurt is the only type that should be used in baking, where it can be substituted for buttermilk. Thicker, Greek-style yogurts may be substituted for sour cream, though they have a lower fat content. In addition, whole milk yogurt is the best choice for baking, though low-fat may be substituted.

CREAM

Heavy whipping cream is an important member of the pastry team. It has between 36 and 40 percent milk fat and the best flavor and whipping qualities of any of the creams. Not only does it make any sauce or filling more flavorful and sensuously smooth, it whips beautifully and holds its shape for hours. Buy the best heavy cream you can, as the cream's flavor is integral to many desserts.

Always buy cream that is pasteurized but not ultra-pasteurized (often labeled "UHT," for ultra-high temperature). Ultra-pasteurized cream has been heated to a much higher temperature than required for simple pasteurization; this extends the shelf life considerably, but also kills nearly all the flavor, leaving it with an odd, cooked taste that is especially evident in simple preparations like whipped cream. It is also harder to whip UHT cream to a fluffy softness, and it breaks down more quickly.

Professional chefs and pastry chefs use a type of heavy whipping cream known as "manufacturing cream," which contains at least 40 percent milk fat and is thick and rich right out of the container. It is never ultra-pasteurized, whips quickly and perfectly, and makes every preparation smooth and creamy. You can often find it in warehouse stores that attract a food-service clientele, and some specialty markets. It is well worth finding.

To whip cream, buy cream with the highest milk fat content possible for the best flavor and stability (more fat helps cream hold its shape when whipped). If you want the cream to whip as quickly as possible, chill the whisk and bowl in the freezer for at least 10 minutes before whipping. Don't use presweetened whipping cream or canned pressurized whipped cream in your baking, as they are full of preservatives and flavorings that will adversely affect the texture and flavor of your pastries.

Other types of cream are available and sometimes used in the pastry kitchen:

HALF-AND-HALF A blend of half milk and half cream, with 10 to 12 percent milk fat, half-and-half cannot be whipped, but may be used for custards.

LIGHT CREAM Usually used for coffee, light cream has 18 to 25 percent milk fat and cannot be whipped. It is not used in the pastry kitchen.

LIGHT WHIPPING CREAM Also simply labeled whipping cream, this has 30 to 36 percent milk fat. It can whip, but is not as flavorful or stable as heavy whipping cream, and is better used in sauces, custards, and fillings.

CRÈME FRAÎCHE

The French version of sour cream, crème fraîche is luxuriously rich, with a mellow, nutty flavor. It is available in cheese shops and in the dairy section of specialty markets and many supermarkets. It is also very easy to make at home, as long as you have access to cream that is not ultra-pasteurized (see above). For recipe, see page 420.

SOUR CREAM

Thick, white, cultured light cream with a bright acidic flavor and a milk fat content of 18 percent, sour cream adds a tangy flavor to baked goods and can be used in recipes in place of yogurt. You can also use it instead of buttermilk, but you will need to thin it to a pouring consistency with a little water. Otherwise the recipe may not have enough liquid, resulting in a dry texture. Do not substitute low-fat or nonfat sour cream in baking.

THE ROLES OF DAIRY PRODUCTS IN BAKING

Cakes, quick breads, and yeast breads have a finer, softer crumb when made with dairy products. Milkfat means their crusts are softer too, and staling is slower. Yeast breads also benefit from the sugars in dairy products: Lactose, a sugar, is food for the yeast in bread and therefore encourages fermentation. The natural proteins and milk sugars in dairy products combine with oven heat to produce the Maillard reaction (see page 32), resulting in beautiful brown crusts with complex flavors. Dairy products also add liquid to recipes, which hydrates the proteins in flour and results in the gluten development necessary for proper structure. As with butter and oil, the fats in dairy products both enhance and distribute the flavors in baked goods. Many dairy products, such as buttermilk, sour cream, or yogurt, also add their own flavor. Milk and cream are vital to the body and texture of both baked and stovetop custards as well as frozen desserts such as ice cream.

And, of course, cream serves not only as an ingredient in baked goods, but as a filling, frosting, and accompaniment as well.

Leaveners

Leaveners make breads and pastries rise. There are three types of leaveners in baking: biological (yeast), chemical (baking powder and baking soda), and physical (air and steam).

YEAST—THE BIOLOGICAL LEAVENER

HOW YEAST WORKS

Yeast are the microscopic, single-cell living organisms that make bread rise. They feed on the sugars in the starch of the flour and then multiply. The by-products of their feeding—carbon dioxide and alcohol—are what create the breads we love. As the yeast expel carbon dioxide, the bubbles of gas are caught in the dough's gluten web, causing the dough to expand, or rise. The alcohol adds flavor to the bread, but only when it is present in small quantities. When too much alcohol builds up in the dough—for example, when dough has been left unattended for too long—the pronounced alcohol flavor can ruin the bread with an unpleasant, overfermented taste.

Yeast, like all living things, need four things to survive—warmth, moisture, food, and oxygen. Warmth is provided in several ways. Warm liquid is often used to wake up, or activate, the yeast, and the mixing and kneading processes generate additional warmth. The final warmth, the oven's heat, results in a feeding frenzy—the last burst of energy that propels the loaf upward (known as *oven spring*).

Yeast can survive and function in the cold (after all, they survive storage in the refrigerator and freezer), but they don't work very efficiently in cold dough. This can be used to advantage. Many artisan bread makers deliberately use cold water and refrigerate the dough to slow down the feeding, or fermentation, of the yeast, so that they get a long, slow rise—resulting in optimum flavor and texture in hearth breads.

Yeast absorb the moisture they need to survive from the liquid in the dough, they feed on the sugars in the starch of the flour, and they become oxygenated during mixing and kneading, when air is forced into the dough. As they use up the available oxygen, the rate at which they eat and multiply slows down. This is why bread dough is "punched down"—to expel some of the carbon dioxide and incorporate new oxygen, so the yeast can continue their feeding cycle, adding more flavor to the bread. Once the yeast is actively feeding, the dough rises higher and higher until one of several things happens to the yeast: they run out of food; they run out of oxygen; or they are killed in the heat of the oven.

WHERE YEAST COMES FROM

Yeast is in the air around us and can be found on the surface of many fruits and grains. Early bread bakers "captured" these wild yeasts in flour and water batters exposed to the air, known as *starters*. San Francisco sourdough was developed from just such a starter. However, not all yeasts are desirable in bread making, and many wild yeasts are fragile. Luckily, we now have commercial yeast, which is made from reliable, strong strains of yeast. These yeasts are "grown" on pools of food in a controlled, hygienic facility.

TYPES OF YEAST

FRESH OR COMPRESSED YEAST To make fresh yeast, the organisms are harvested from the pools mentioned above and then compressed to remove excess water, though some remains to keep the yeast active.

It is shaped into blocks resembling clay, and must be kept refrigerated. Fresh yeast used to be available in the dairy section of nearly every supermarket, but with the decrease in home bread baking, it is now very difficult to find.

A local bakery will often sell you some if you ask. Professional bakers love this yeast, because it's easy to use and requires no activation with warm water. To use fresh yeast, simply whisk it into the liquid portion of the recipe to dissolve the lumps and proceed with the recipe.

Storing: Keep fresh yeast in an airtight container in the refrigerator for 1 to 2 weeks. If it shows signs of drying, cut off the affected portion and use the remaining moist yeast. If the yeast has molded, discard immediately.

ACTIVE DRY YEAST Dried yeast is cultivated in the same manner as fresh yeast, but the cells are sprayed into a drier, which eliminates most of the water (more than 90 percent) and kills about a quarter of the yeast cells. While this does reduce the number available to rise dough, the dead cells actually contribute important flavor components and elasticity to bread. Each granule of dried yeast is actually a tiny little clump of thousands of yeast cells.

Active dry yeast is the type most familiar to home bakers. The small dried granules of yeast have been available in premeasured packets for generations. Each packet weighs ¼ ounce and contains 2¼ teaspoons of yeast.

The yeast needs to be activated by soaking it in warm liquid, usually water, before combining it with the remaining ingredients. The water needs to be warm enough to awaken the yeast, but not so hot that it kills them.

Yeast dies around 140°F, so it's best to keep the temperature of the liquid well below that, 110° to 115°F, which feels comfortably warm, not hot. Our average body temperature is 98.6°F, so this temperature range will not feel very hot to the skin. Many home bakers are doomed from the start when they activate their yeast with boiling water (212°F) or exceedingly hot tap water. You might want to test the water with an instant-read thermometer until you get the feel for the level of warmth that is needed.

If you add a pinch of sugar to the activating liquid, the yeast will begin to feed immediately upon awakening, and you'll see a foam form on top of the liquid, letting you know they are ready to make bread (without the sugar, you won't necessarily see dramatic activity).

INSTANT YEAST Instant yeast is made in the same way as active dry yeast, but the cells are dried more gently, preserving more of them. The clumps of yeast are broken into much smaller granules as well. The result is that instant yeast activates quickly and rises dough much more rapidly.

Instant yeast is the new kid on the block. Smaller granules, fewer dead cells per packet, and no need to activate in advance have made this a popular option with both home and commercial bakers. The yeast granules are simply added to the dry ingredients before combining with the liquid.

Instant yeast is often sold in packages marked "rapid rise," "perfect rise," "quick rise," or "bread machine yeast." It does not actually work faster, but because there are more granules in each measurement, if you use the same amount of instant as active dry yeast, the dough will definitely rise faster. We suggest using a slightly smaller amount, as a slower rise develops better flavor and texture.

Though there is no need to activate instant yeast, you might want to do anyway, just to get the party started.

This can be helpful when cold liquid is used to create artisan breads. Set aside ¼ cup of the liquid, warm it up, and activate the instant yeast. Otherwise, it can take quite a while for the yeast to begin multiplying, which is great for flavor, but not so great for a busy home baker's schedule.

Storing: Both instant and active dry yeast should be kept in airtight containers in the refrigerator or freezer for maximum shelf life.

SUBSTITUTING TYPES OF YEAST

The recipes in this book offer the option of using either active dry or instant yeast, the two most commonly available types of yeast. They should not be substituted one for one, as their strength is slightly different.

Each recipe gives a measurement for both active dry and instant yeast, but if you wish to adapt any recipes outside this book to use a different type of yeast, these guidelines will help:

- **For each teaspoon of active dry yeast, use ¾ teaspoon instant yeast (or multiply the weight of the active dry yeast by .75).**
- **For each teaspoon of instant yeast, use 1¼ teaspoons active dry yeast (or multiply the weight of the instant yeast by 1.25).**
- **For each ounce of fresh yeast, use 2¼ teaspoons active dry yeast or 1½ teaspoons instant yeast. To substitute fresh yeast for active dry or instant, use twice as much fresh.**

CHEMICAL LEAVENERS

Although yeast has been used since ancient times, the more recently developed baking powder and baking soda, formulated and perfected over the past 200 years, are the leaveners most familiar to home bakers. As long as they are fresh and stored properly, they reliably and predictably rise cakes, cookies, quick breads, muffins, and scones.

Many home bakers believe that baking powder and baking soda are interchangeable, and this is the cause of many failed baking projects. Although the results of their chemical reaction are similar, the two leaveners react differently with individual ingredients and are difficult to substitute for each other. Let's take a closer look.

HOW CHEMICAL LEAVENERS WORK

Most people assume that baking powder and baking soda create the carbon dioxide bubbles that expand in the heat of the oven, causing baked goods to rise. This belief may have something to do with all of those vinegar- and baking soda–powered rockets made in science classes.

When the vinegar is combined with baking soda, it looks as though bubbles are created, but that is not what actually happens.

tips for success Why Measuring Matters

Chemical leaveners need to be measured precisely.

Remember, baking is chemistry, and the ratio of leavener to liquid to flour is a careful chemical balance. Although it is a common notion that too much leavener will cause a cake to rise out of its pan, perhaps even the oven (as is often shown in cartoons), in fact the opposite is true. Too much chemical leavener causes the air bubbles in the batter to expand dramatically. They get too big, bump into each other, and pop. The result of too much leavening is a cake with either a depression in the center or, in extreme circumstances, one that completely collapses.

You can test the viability of your baking soda by stirring ½ teaspoon into a couple tablespoons of vinegar or lemon juice. If it bubbles and fizzes, it's fine. If not, buy a new box.

Test your baking powder by stirring ½ teaspoon into a couple of tablespoons of hot water—if it bubbles and fizzes, it's good.

The air bubbles already exist in the vinegar. The baking soda, activated by the water and acid in vinegar, gives off carbon dioxide, which enlarges the bubbles.

The reaction is similar in baked goods. This means you must first fill the batter or dough with air bubbles to create the texture you want. This is why creaming butter and sugar properly is so important to the texture and rise of cakes. If you don't create a million air bubbles, the few that are there will result in an uneven, coarse texture, rather than the fine, tight-grained crumb produced from lots of tiny bubbles. You can see the difference vividly when comparing a butter cake (made by the creaming method) with muffins (made by the muffin method).

In creaming, the sugar cuts into the butter and each sugar granule forms a little air bubble, resulting in a miniaturized version of Bubble Wrap, full of evenly sized, regularly placed air cells.

In the muffin method, the butter is melted, blended with the rest of the liquid ingredients, and gently stirred into the dry ingredients. The naturally occurring air bubbles in melted butter aren't nearly as numerous as those in a creamed batter, and the air bubbles are certainly not all the same size. The baking soda or baking powder in the recipe works to expand this irregular network, producing the coarse, uneven texture typical of muffins.

TYPES OF CHEMICAL LEAVENERS

BAKING SODA (SODIUM BICARBONATE) This leavener is activated by liquid and acid—in fact, often the liquid is also an acid. Examples of acidic liquids include buttermilk, sour cream, yogurt, and lemon or lime juice; other acidic ingredients are molasses, honey, natural cocoa powder, and brown sugar.

Baking soda begins to leaven the batter as soon as it is moistened, so it's important that you get your batter into the oven as quickly as possible. If you wait too long, the carbon dioxide bubbles will already have expanded to their fullest potential and begun their decline before your batter even reaches the oven, resulting in a reduced rise and heavy texture. In addition to leavening, baking soda also neutralizes acidity, reducing the pronounced acidic flavor of ingredients like buttermilk and sour cream.

Measure baking soda carefully. If you use too much, your baked good many not only fall (see "Why Measuring Matters," page 35), but will also have an unpleasant chemical flavor. If you've ever brushed your teeth with baking soda, you'll recognize its bitter, slightly salty presence immediately.

Storing: If stored airtight, baking soda has a shelf life of 6 to 9 months (check the date on the box). If exposed to moisture, even in the air, it quickly loses its ability to leaven, so don't leave the box standing open on your shelf—keep it in a resealable plastic bag.

BAKING POWDER Baking powder is a combination of baking soda, two additional acids (usually monocalcium phosphate and sodium aluminum sulphate, for you chemistry majors), and a bit of cornstarch to absorb moisture and keep the acids dry during storage. One of the acids activates the baking soda as soon as the mixture is combined with liquid. The second acid doesn't activate until it is heated. This is why baking powder is usually labeled "double acting." Because the acids needed for activation are already present in the leavener, baking powder is often used in recipes that do not contain acidic ingredients.

Although it doesn't need additional acid, baking powder still needs moisture to activate. The advantage that baking powder has over baking soda is the second, heat-activated acid, which allows the professional and home baker a little extra time. Remember that batters using baking soda must be baked immediately, before the reaction dissipates. Batters with baking powder don't require the same urgency. In fact, muffin, scone, and cookie batters using baking powder may be held overnight before baking (don't try this with cakes, as they have a much more delicate structure). They will not rise as high as they would have if baked immediately—after all, the first reaction caused by moisture has already faded—but they will still rise to an acceptable height. Cookie dough may even be frozen for several months and still perform well in the oven, since cookies need only a tiny bit of rise to create their texture.

Storing: When stored airtight, baking powder can last up to a year.

Are baking soda and baking powder interchangeable? Yes and no. Baking soda is four times as strong as baking powder; 1 teaspoon of baking powder will rise a cup of flour, but you only need ¼ teaspoon of baking soda for the same effect. (Note that this ratio is only a guideline, and you may find it tweaked in some recipes to achieve a certain texture.) Can you use this information to substitute one for another? Yes. Is it an exact science? No. You have to take into account that a recipe with baking powder is usually missing the acid needed to activate baking soda, and a recipe with baking soda may be much too acidic in tandem with baking powder (soda neutralizes some of the acidity). Substituting can be done, but it usually takes a bit of fine-tuning before the recipe works as desired. Why complicate life further? It's much easier to simply use the leavener called for in the original recipe.

Some recipes call for both baking soda and baking powder. They are combined when the baking soda is used to neutralize acidity but cannot provide all the leavening needed for the desired texture, so the job of extra leavening falls to the baking powder. This works especially well for acidic doughs that need to sit overnight. The baking soda takes care of the acidity, and in the morning, when the baking soda is exhausted, the powder will activate in the heat of the oven.

THE OTHER ROLES OF CHEMICAL LEAVENERS

Leaveners tenderize a baking dough. As the air bubbles expand, they stretch the gluten network into thin strands, which are much more tender than thick ones (think soft versus chewy). They also contribute to the crumb of a bread or pastry, making it fine and delicate (many bubbles) or coarse and craggy (fewer bubbles). Baking soda neutralizes acidity in recipes, mellowing a harsh component to a pleasant tang. Baking soda also adds color to baked goods by elevating the pH, which aids in browning—in fact, many commercially produced items contain baking soda not so much for leavening as for the appealing golden brown color it encourages.

PHYSICAL LEAVENERS

Air and steam are the oft-forgotten workhorses in baking. Rarely are they mentioned but, without them, most baked goods would be flat and heavy. The incorporation of air is vital to the leavening of baked goods. The expansion that occurs when water turns to steam is another powerful leavener.

AIR

Chemical leaveners would not be able to raise a baked good without the presence of air bubbles. Air is already present in most of the ingredients used in baking, such as butter and other dairy products, liquids, eggs, liquid sweeteners, nut butters, and fruit, to name a few. Air is also deliberately incorporated when you cream butter and sugar, whip egg whites to firm peaks, or knead bread dough.

The texture of the final product is determined by whether these air bubbles, or cells, are large and irregular or small and fine. How do they attain their numbers and sizes? Remember, leaveners do nothing more than increase the size of already existing air cells. The leavener—yeast, baking powder, baking soda—fills the air cells with carbon dioxide and expands them. It cannot change the texture that has been predetermined by the air cells. If there are many tiny cells, the resulting crumb is fine and delicate.

If the air cells are few and irregular, the texture is coarse. If there are too many air cells (from overbeating), the cell walls of the bubbles will be stretched too thin when they expand. Sometimes these fragile cells will collapse at the bottom of the pastry under the weight of the rest of the baked good, and a line of dense, uncooked-looking batter or dough forms—a sure sign of overmixing.

STEAM

Whenever a moist ingredient—such as butter, water, milk, or eggs—is heated, steam is formed. Since moisture exists in all baked goods, steam is at work in everything you bake. It leavens exponentially, increasing in volume over 1,500 times as it changes from water to steam. This power is especially evident in high-moisture pastries like pâte à choux (cream puff dough), popovers, and sponge cakes, all of which are baked in a hot oven and rely on steam for much of their rise.

Chocolate

HOW CHOCOLATE IS MADE

Chocolate's botanical name, *Theobroma cacao,* aptly describes this favorite of pastry ingredients—*Theobroma* translates as "food of the gods." It is made from the football-size and -shaped cocoa pods that grow directly out of the trunk of the tropical cacao tree. The pods are harvested, split open, and the beans inside are removed and fermented in their surrounding pulp to bring out their fullest flavor. This step is very important to the flavor of fine-quality chocolate, for just as poorly handled grapes cannot produce fine wine, unripe and/or improperly fermented beans cannot produce good chocolate.

Fermentation does not result in beans that taste of chocolate as we know it, but the flavoring compounds developed during fermentation will emerge during the roasting and blending processes at the factory. If fermentation is cut short, there is no chance that the chocolate will be of good quality.

Once fermented, the beans are then dried. The best beans are dried in the sun, often spread on the ground and turned over daily to expose all sides. As you can imagine, tropical weather is not always cooperative during the drying process. Too much rain and the beans won't dry properly and will develop mold. Sometimes, to avoid this issue, the beans are dried over fires, which results in a undesirable smoky flavor that translates directly to the chocolate. Chocolate made with such beans is called *hammy* by professionals.

When the beans are thoroughly dried, they are bagged for sale. Dried cacao beans are about the size of large lima beans. When they arrive at the chocolate factory, the beans are roasted to bring out their fullest flavor. Each variety of bean is roasted separately because each requires a slightly different roasting time to highlight its flavor components. Most chocolate is a blend of varieties, but they are not mixed indiscriminately—every chocolate maker has unique, proprietary blends.

After roasting, the beans are cracked open and the nibs, or meat of the bean, are removed and separated from the hard outer shell. Roasted nibs, similar in texture and bitterness to coffee beans, have a deeply enchanting chocolate flavor. You can find these roasted cocoa nibs for sale in gourmet and specialty stores and some supermarkets, and they can be a wonderful addition to pastries (see Chocolate Cocoa–Nib Shortbread Cookies, page 281, and Cream Puffs with Cocoa Nib Cream, page 402). Avoid raw nibs in your baking for they are not as crisp or flavorful.

The various types of roasted nibs are blended (in a top-secret formula) to a specific flavor profile, then crushed. The heat generated by the friction of crushing liquefies the fat within the nibs, known as cocoa butter.

The melted cocoa butter coats the ground dark chocolate solids, causing the mixture to form a paste known as *chocolate liquor*. (The term *liquor* has nothing to do with alcohol; it's an industry term to describe unsweetened chocolate.)

What happens next depends on the goal of the chocolate maker. If the goal is unsweetened baking chocolate, the liquor is formed into bars at this point and sold. If the goal is cocoa powder, the liquor enters a hydraulic press, which separates nearly all of the cream-colored cocoa butter from the dark solids. The dark solids, when ground and sifted, become cocoa powder. If the goal is a bar of chocolate, the chocolate liquor is blended with sugar, vanilla (or vanillin, an imitation vanilla extract), and lecithin (an emulsifier) to produce semisweet or bittersweet chocolate. Milk and white chocolate also contain dried milk solids or condensed milk (more about this on page 40). Sometimes extra cocoa butter is added, contributing to a smooth texture and increasing the fluidity of the final chocolate when melted, which is especially important when the chocolate is used for coating truffles and candies.

Cocoa butter is also responsible for the wonderful mouth-feel of chocolate, since it melts at our body temperature. This body-melting asset makes cocoa butter extremely valuable to the cosmetics industry, where it is included in formulas for lotions and beauty products.

Some chocolate companies remove all the cocoa butter from the crushed nibs and sell it to the beauty industry. They then replace the cocoa butter with hydrogenated vegetable oils or other substitutes, producing "chocolate" that does not have the proper flavor, texture, or melting properties for pastries and baking.

Always check the ingredient label to make sure the semisweet or bittersweet chocolate you are using is real, pure chocolate, consisting of chocolate liquor (sometimes called *cocoa mass*) and cocoa butter, in addition to sugar, vanilla, and lecithin.

Once the chocolate is blended, the mixture is then transferred to a conching machine, where it is "kneaded," or rolled, for at least several hours, and, for some high-quality chocolates, up to 2 or even 3 days. Conching aerates the chocolate and reduces particle size, making it smoother and more luxurious.

Tempering comes next. This is a process of warming and cooling the chocolate to encourage the formation of a particularly stable crystal within the chocolate's structure—one that, when cooled, results in chocolate that has a glossy finish, a clean snap when broken, and contracts upon cooling for easy removal from molds.

After tempering, the chocolate is poured into bar molds, then cooled and wrapped for sale.

Storing: All chocolates should be wrapped well and kept in a dark, cool location (60° to 75°F). Chocolate quickly absorbs odors, so be sure to keep it away from onions, garlic, and a musty cupboard. Stored properly, unsweetened, semisweet, and bittersweet chocolates have a shelf life of at least a year and up to 3 years. Milk and white chocolates turn rancid quickly because they contain milk solids, so store them properly and use the milk chocolate within 5 months; the white chocolate within 3 months. For longer storage, wrap milk or white chocolate in plastic, seal it in a resealable plastic freezer bag, and freeze for up to 9 months. Thaw completely, still inside the bag, before use.

CHOCOLATE BLOOM During storage or delivery, chocolate may develop whitish streaks or blotches on its surface. This is known in the industry as *bloom*, and there are two types. Fat bloom is the most common and is caused by too much heat. When the temperature of chocolate rises above 90°F, some of the cocoa butter separates and floats to the surface of the chocolate, then recrystallizes upon cooling, forming streaks of creamy-colored cocoa butter. At this point the chocolate is said to be "out of temper." The chocolate is still perfectly good for eating or baking—it just doesn't look as pretty. Fat bloom can happen in the back of a delivery truck, on a loading dock, or in a hot car on the way home. Any time you melt chocolate at home, chocolate bloom will occur upon cooling unless the product is refrigerated (such as chocolate curls and shapes, page 428), or the chocolate is blended with another fat, such as cream for ganache or butter for frosting.

None of the recipes in this book require tempered chocolate, which is used mostly for dipping candies that will be stored at room temperature for several days at a time, and whose finish should be beautifully glossy. If you want to make dipped candies, you can skip the tempering and still avoid bloom by keeping the candies refrigerated in an airtight container until an hour or so before serving—or by dipping them in confectionary coating instead of real chocolate.

A second type of bloom is known as *sugar bloom*. This occurs when water is introduced to the surface of the chocolate, usually as a result of condensation on chocolate that has been stored in the refrigerator or freezer.

When the water droplets form, sugar in the chocolate underneath dissolves into the water. Once the droplets evaporate, the sugar recrystallizes, resulting in a streaked surface with slightly gritty sugar crystals.

It can still be used for eating and baking, as long as you know that the sugar bloom occurred after you purchased the chocolate. But if you buy chocolate that already has this gritty sugar bloom, return it, as water can also introduce bacteria to the chocolate and make it spoil.

TYPES OF CHOCOLATE

UNSWEETENED CHOCOLATE Unsweetened chocolate is pure (99 percent) chocolate liquor (or cacao), with no sugar added, though an emulsifier is usually included. Sometimes called *bitter chocolate* (not to be confused with bittersweet, below) or *baking chocolate,* it is usually equal parts chocolate solids and cocoa butter.

SEMISWEET AND BITTERSWEET CHOCOLATE Semisweet and bittersweet chocolates are the most widely used types of chocolate in baking. (Milk and white chocolate are used much less frequently because of their tendency to scorch at low temperatures.) To produce semisweet or bittersweet chocolate, the chocolate liquor is blended with sugar, vanilla, and lecithin (an emulsifier).

The difference between semisweet and bittersweet chocolate is not clear-cut in the United States. In Europe, where the nomenclature began, regulations require that semisweet chocolate has more sugar and less chocolate liquor (unsweetened chocolate) than bittersweet. Bittersweet is exactly as its name implies: darker, more bitter, with less sugar and more chocolate liquor. In the United States, however, there are no such labeling regulations, and one company's semisweet may be stronger and less sweet than another company's bittersweet. To differentiate, one must taste the chocolates or check the label for an indication of chocolate liquor or cacao content. By law, semisweet or bittersweet chocolates must be at least 35 percent cacao, although most baking chocolates are at least 50 percent. The remaining 50 percent is almost all sugar.

Chocolate manufacturers are starting to label their retail bars with the percentage of cacao (this percentage has always been included on wholesale bars for pastry chefs). Keep in mind that 50 percent cacao is about average for most supermarket dark chocolates. In general, a low percentage, around 50 percent, means a sweeter, milder chocolate, while a higher percentage indicates a darker, more intense chocolate flavor. Some bittersweet chocolates are as high as 85 percent cacao—compare that to the 99 percent cacao in unsweetened chocolate and you'll see just how intense that chocolate must be!

The percentage has nothing to do with quality, however, so beware; just because a bar boasts a high percentage does not mean it is also high quality. Taste is your final determiner, though some brands have justifiably good reputations. If you love the extra-dark, high-percentage chocolates and want to use them in your baking, be aware that their lack of sugar and extra chocolate solids may cause problems in recipes that were developed using the average 50 percent chocolates. (See "Baking with High-Percentage Chocolate" on page 42.)

VARIETAL CHOCOLATE Varietal chocolate is semisweet or bittersweet chocolate that contains only one type of cacao bean.

Most dark chocolates are a blend of varietals from around the world. Blending results in a more complex flavor profile and allows manufacturers to adjust for the fact that cacao is a third-world agricultural crop, the quality and quantity of which can fluctuate wildly from year to year. Since consumers (home bakers and professionals) expect each type of chocolate from a manufacturer to have a particular flavor and texture profile, the factory can consistently attain these attributes each year by blending cacao "to taste."

A varietal chocolate can still contain beans from around the world, but they must all be the same variety of cacao bean. Varietal chocolates can be interesting or forgettable, depending on the type and quality of bean.

Certainly, sampling varietal chocolates is educational, since you can really taste the flavor characteristics of that particular bean and begin to detect its presence in blended chocolates.

SINGLE ORIGIN OR CRU CHOCOLATE Sometimes labeled "single estate" or "plantation bar," this is a varietal chocolate made with cacao beans from only one growing area, region, or plantation. This style of chocolate can be very educational for pinpointing specific flavors inherent in a type of cacao bean, but they can take some getting used to. While they can be exciting, they can also seem one-dimensional and uninteresting, since our palates are used to a blend of beans and a mixture of flavor notes. Single-origin chocolates are definitely worth trying, and will broaden your experience with dark chocolate.

MILK CHOCOLATE Milk chocolate must contain at least 10 to 15 percent cacao, so compared to dark chocolate its flavor is quite muted and the bar is very sweet. It also has dry milk powder added for that wonderfully creamy flavor we love (Cadbury contains condensed milk instead of powder). The high percentage of sugar and the added milk solids make it nearly impossible to substitute milk chocolate for dark chocolate in recipes (unless, for example, it is added as chips or chunks to cookies).

Some chocolate makers are starting to offer "dark milk chocolate," milk chocolate with a higher percentage of chocolate liquor—some as much as 41 percent—adding a deep chocolate flavor to the milky sweetness. These new chocolates combine the best of both worlds, and you are encouraged to seek them out.

They're great for eating out of hand and for using as chips and additions to cakes, quick breads, cookies, and other pastries.

WHITE CHOCOLATE The classification of white chocolate is a relatively new one. For years, any chocolate that did not contain dark chocolate solids could not legally be called chocolate. Not anymore! Real white chocolate—that which contains cocoa butter as the main fat—is now a proud member of the chocolate label family. It consists of only cocoa butter (20 percent minimum), dry milk powder (14 percent), sugar (55 percent maximum), vanilla, and lecithin. Without any of the chocolate solids, it is a very sweet chocolate, but can be superb when paired with an ingredient that is very tart or bitter.

When purchasing white chocolate, check the ingredient list to make sure the main fat contained in the bar is cocoa butter. Avoid bars listing alternative fats such as hydrogenated vegetable oil or palm kernel oil, for they are not true white chocolate. A good sign is a creamy color rather than a stark white color.

COUVERTURE CHOCOLATE This high-quality chocolate used by pastry chefs and fine chocolate shops has an extra measure of cocoa butter added during manufacturing. More cocoa butter results in more fluidity when melted, which is especially important when you're dipping pastries or candies in chocolate. The extra fluidity allows the melted chocolate to flow quickly over the candy or pastry, resulting in a thin, crisp shell, the mark of a true professional.

CONFECTIONARY COATING CHOCOLATES Sometimes called *summer coating* or *compound chocolate,* these "chocolates" are often used in home candy making. They come in a rainbow of colors and do not need to be tempered—once melted and used for molding or dipping, the chocolate cools into a shiny finish. They are not real chocolate; their cocoa butter has been replaced by other fats, usually soybean, cottonseed, or palm kernel oil. They are, however, quick and easy to use, and are great for children to work with. They should be stored just like real chocolate, as described on page 39, and will last for up to 6 months.

CHOCOLATE CHIPS Chocolate chips are available in dark, milk, and white chocolate, and fall into one of two categories: imitation and real. Most chocolate chips are not real chocolate. Their cocoa butter has been replaced with hydrogenated oil so they hold their shape in the oven and are inexpensive to produce. Although they are fine in cookies and such, they should not be used as a substitute for real chocolate when baking (for instance, in a flourless chocolate cake). Other chocolate chips are real chocolate, and you can quickly discern the difference by checking the ingredient list on the package. Real chocolate chips come in the classic shape as well as in chunks or flattened rounds, and they add a burst of pure chocolate flavor to your pastries. You can also make your own chips by chopping good-quality chocolate into the size you desire and using it in place of store-bought chips. Chips should be stored according to the kind of chocolate used in their manufacture; for storage instructions, see the individual entries above.

COCOA POWDER: NATURAL VERSUS DUTCH PROCESS Cocoa powder is made when the chocolate liquor is put into a hydraulic press, yielding cocoa butter and nearly fat-free chocolate solids. When ground and sifted, the solids become cocoa powder.

NATURAL COCOA POWDER Also known as *non-alkalized cocoa powder* (and often simply labeled "cocoa powder"), this style may contain from 10 to 12 percent up to 22 to 24 percent cocoa butter and is the classic American-style cocoa powder—medium brown in color, and bitter in flavor. It's great for brownies and old-fashioned chocolate cakes. Some canisters or boxes of cocoa powder may bear the marking "10/12" or "22/24"—this simply denotes how much cocoa butter is left in the powder.

Be sure to buy pure cocoa powder for baking, not sweetened chocolate drink mixes. If you're not sure what type of cocoa powder is in the box, look at the ingredient list—if it reads cocoa, cocoa powder, or unsweetened cocoa powder, you have natural cocoa powder. If it reads "cocoa powder processed with alkali," you have Dutch-process cocoa powder (see below). Natural cocoa powder is very acidic and is nearly always paired with baking

tips for success How to Get the Most Cocoa Flavor

The best way to heighten the flavor of cocoa powder is to blend it with boiling water before adding it to the recipe. This technique appears in some recipes, and you can adapt it for use in recipes that don't call for it, too. While this step is not always possible, it can often be done in cakes and other recipes that have liquids added to the batter.

Heat the liquid in the recipe to boiling, then add it to the cocoa powder a little at a time, whisking or stirring constantly to smooth out any lumps. Allow the mixture to cool completely before using it in the recipe.

soda as a leavener. The soda also helps to mellow, or neutralize, the acidity in the powder.

DUTCH-PROCESS COCOA POWDER Popular in Europe and becoming increasingly popular in this country, Dutch-process cocoa powder is also known as *alkalized cocoa powder*. The powder has been processed with an alkali (similar to baking soda), which neutralizes its acidity, softens its flavor, and changes the color to a beautifully dark, sometimes red-tinged, brown. This process was invented in Holland (hence the name *Dutch-process*) in the early 1800s by Conrad Van Houten in an attempt to reduce the harsh acidity of cocoa.

Dutch-process cocoa powder usually contains 22 to 24 percent cocoa butter, which results in a more pronounced chocolate flavor (fat carries and enhances flavor). Note that the darker color of Dutch-process cocoa powder does not necessarily mean better flavor (although many professionals prefer it), and highly Dutched or alkalized cocoa powder, sometimes called *black cocoa,* is left with little true chocolate flavor, and is used mainly to give baked goods an almost black color (Oreos contain just such a cocoa).

The acidity of Dutch-process cocoa powder has already been neutralized with alkali during processing, so it is nearly always paired with baking powder as a leavener. If you're not sure what type of cocoa powder is in the box or package, read the ingredient list. It should say "cocoa processed with alkali," or some variation of this wording. If there is no mention of alkali, the cocoa inside is natural or non alkalized.

Which cocoa powder is the best? Natural and Dutch-process cocoa powders may be used interchangeably as long as there is no leavening in the recipe. You can use the one you like best when making chocolate pudding, shortbread, hot cocoa, or other recipes that have no chemical leaveners in the ingredient list. However, if a recipe calls for baking powder or baking soda, be sure to use the cocoa specified. If you mismatch cocoa powder and leavening, the texture and flavor of your pastry will suffer and the recipe may even fail, though this is much more exaggerated in the tall open crumb of a cake than in a little cookie.

Sometimes a recipe ingredient list will simply ask for "cocoa powder." If it is an American book, you can safely assume the writer means natural cocoa powder. Recipes that require Dutch-

tips for success Baking with High-Percentage Chocolate

If you love the darker, more intense chocolates that have a high percentage of cacao (60 percent or more)—you'll no doubt want to use them in your baking. More cacao and the resulting decrease in sugar adds wonderful flavor. These chocolates can cause problems, however. As the percentage increases, it doesn't automatically signify a corresponding increase in chocolate liquor, which is equal parts dark chocolate solids and cocoa butter, but instead a larger amount of chocolate solids, and a lesser amount of cocoa butter. Since dark chocolate solids can be thought of as cocoa powder, when you bake with high-percentage chocolates, you are essentially adding a measure of cocoa powder to any recipe you make. At the same time, you are removing sugar, and sugar adds moisture in addition to sweetness to baked goods.

Since most recipes have been developed based on the texture and flavor of 50 percent cacao chocolate, using a high-percentage chocolate—with its extra cocoa powder and reduced sugar—can literally be a recipe for disaster, producing a disappointingly dry pastry.

Each chocolate recipe in this book has a note stating the highest-percentage chocolate that may be used successfully with that particular recipe. If the note suggests a maximum of 60 percent cacao, you can use any dark chocolate you want, as long as the percentage does not exceed 60 percent. If you like 50 percent, use that. But once you exceed the maximum, you'll likely have problems with dryness, texture, and baking times (since there is less moisture in the batter, baked goods with high-percentage chocolate bake more quickly).

High-percentage chocolates can also cause problems with ganache. This emulsion of chocolate and cream relies on a balance between chocolate solids and liquid. The chocolate solids soak up liquid quite dramatically (think of making hot cocoa and stirring the milk into the cocoa powder). Since high-percentage chocolates have more chocolate solids, they need more liquid to create the soft, silky texture of ganache. If there is not enough liquid, the ganache "breaks," or separates, and looks like a greasy mess.

To save the broken ganache, simply stir in extra cream, a tablespoon or two at a time, until the mixture is smooth again. Even if the ganache doesn't break, you'll want to add a few extra tablespoons of cream to a high-percentage ganache or it may be too thick and firm upon cooling.

process cocoa will always mention it by name. If you are still unsure, you can look at the leavener in the recipe for a clue as to which type of cocoa powder would be best. As stated above, natural cocoa is usually paired with baking soda, while Dutch-process teams with baking powder.

Storing: Kept airtight in a cool, dark location (just like dark chocolate), both types of cocoa powder will last for at least a year.

HOW TO CHOP CHOCOLATE

If you buy chocolate already in small chunks, *pistoles* (small round pieces), or other small portions, you don't need to chop them any further for melting. This time-saving form is often how professionals purchase chocolate.

If you have bar chocolate, a serrated knife is the most efficient tool for chopping. Make sure your cutting board is dry and odor-free. Start at a corner of the bar and work backward, moving the knife back ¼ inch after each cut so that you're essentially "shaving" the bar. Once you lose the point of the corner, turn the bar and begin again at another corner. Continue turning the bar until it is completely shaved or chopped. Any leftover chopped chocolate may be stored in an airtight container and used for a future recipe. In fact, it's often worth it to purchase large bars of chocolate, spend some time chopping them, and then keep the chocolate ready to go in the cupboard. Not only is good-quality chocolate less expensive in larger quantities, having chopped chocolate on hand saves a step in the baking process, making life easier.

HOW TO MELT CHOCOLATE

Always chop the chocolate into small pieces before melting it. Large chunks take much longer to melt, and because they melt unevenly, some of the chocolate could scorch before the rest is ready.

You must melt chocolate gently (no boiling water underneath!) and carefully, as it scorches easily. Dark chocolate begins to burn at 120°F, which is only about 20°F hotter than our body temperature! Milk and white chocolate start to deteriorate at an even lower temperature, at about 110°F. Scorched chocolate may look fine, but its flavor will be damaged, and it will cause an unpleasant drying sensation in your mouth, like a very tannic wine. Badly scorched chocolate will form tiny lumps that will not melt, as though you've added sand, and eventually will separate.

Chocolate must be stirred frequently while melting because it holds its shape, even when fully melted. Unless you stir, breaking the shape of the chocolate pieces, you may not realize the chocolate has melted and could scorch it by continuing to heat it.

TO MELT CHOCOLATE IN A DOUBLE BOILER Transfer the chopped chocolate to the top section of a double boiler and set aside. Pour an inch or two of water into the lower, saucepan portion and bring to a rolling boil over high heat. Turn off the heat

and set the chocolate over the steaming water. Since chocolate melts at our body temperature, steaming water is plenty hot enough to melt chocolate quickly and safely. Let the chocolate melt for 3 minutes; then stir gently with a dry, odor-free silicone or rubber spatula until all the chocolate has melted and is smooth and fluid. Remove the chocolate from the heat and use as directed. Note: Some recipes melt chocolate over boiling or simmering water, but not only is this unnecessary for the relatively small amounts of chocolate melted by the home baker, it can also quickly scorch the chocolate if left unattended for even a short time. If you are going to melt a large amount, say 3 pounds of chocolate, you may want a low simmer underneath, but be sure to stir constantly and remove it from the heat as soon as it is melted.

TO MELT CHOCOLATE IN A MICROWAVE OVEN Transfer the chopped chocolate to a microwave-safe bowl or container. Heat at 50 percent power for 40 seconds. Remove and stir. Continue to heat and stir every 20 seconds until the chocolate is melted, smooth, and fluid.

SEIZED CHOCOLATE When a tiny amount of water is added to melted chocolate, it thickens and becomes grainy, a development known as *seizing.* This can happen if the cutting surface, the bowl, or the knife used to cut the chocolate was damp, if the bowl or spatula used to melt and stir the chocolate was damp, or if a bit of water or steam from the double boiler dripped into the chocolate. No matter the cause, seized chocolate is now ruined for its original intended use. It can be saved, however, for another use — ganache or chocolate sauce.

For ganache, add an equal amount of warm cream to the thickened mass of dark chocolate (for milk chocolate or white ganache, see page 413) and stir until it smoothes out. Use as desired or refrigerate for up to 1 week. It's great as a tart filling, a cake filling or frosting, or for making truffles.

For sauce, add cream and/or other liquid, stirring constantly, until a saucelike consistency is achieved.

HOW TO SAFELY ADD LIQUID TO CHOCOLATE After learning about seizing, many home bakers are afraid to add any liquid at all to chocolate. Don't be. A tiny bit of liquid is a disaster, but enough liquid is no problem at all. For every 2 ounces of chocolate, you can add 1 tablespoon of liquid with no fear of seizing (most recipes use even more liquid). If you are working with a high-percentage chocolate (for instance, dark chocolate that is more than 60 percent chocolate liquor or *cacao*), you'll want to add 1½ tablespoons of liquid for every 2 ounces. Be sure to warm the liquid first, as cold can cause the chocolate to harden upon contact.

Vanilla

The most essential flavoring in the pastry kitchen, real vanilla has an exquisite floral fragrance that is prized by pastry chefs and home bakers everywhere. The vanilla bean is actually the fruit of a climbing orchid vine, *Vanilla planifolia* or *Vanilla tahitensis,* and these two produce the only edible fruits in the vast orchid family. While *Vanilla planifolia* is native to the New World, it is now cultivated in Madagascar, Costa Rica, Guyana, and many other tropical locales to supply the worldwide demand for vanilla. Vanilla is the second most expensive spice because of the labor and time invested in growing, harvesting, and curing each bean.

The flowers of the vanilla orchid open and die within just a few hours, so they must be pollinated by hand to ensure that the fruit sets. The fruit, or beans, which resemble very long green beans hanging from the vine, need to mature for about 9 months before they are harvested. They are then blanched and/or heated and dried in the sun day after day until they shrink to a quarter of their original length. This long growing and curing process is responsible for the many complex flavor notes in vanilla. Vanilla is available in several forms.

VANILLA BEANS

There are only two types of vanilla beans, although there are vast differences in flavors among beans throughout the world due to soil, growing, and curing conditions—in this way, vanilla beans are very similar to chocolate or wine.

The Mexican vanilla orchid, *Vanilla planifolia,* produces the "original" bean, and is native to the Gulf of Mexico and Central America. It is called a *Bourbon bean* when it is grown anywhere else in the world, such as Madagascar, India, China, and other tropical locales, although it is sometimes referred to simply as a Madagascar bean. (Bourbon vanilla has nothing to do with Kentucky whiskey, but is named for the Bourbon kings of France, who once controlled the island of Reunion, a major producer of the beans.)

The Tahitian vanilla orchid, *Vanilla tahitensis,* was originally *planifolia* when brought to Tahiti, but mutated into a new type of vanilla and was eventually given its own species name. Pastry chefs love Tahitian beans, which are shorter, thicker, moister, very floral, and much more expensive than Bourbon vanilla beans. They may be substituted one to one with Bourbon beans, although the flavor will be quite different. Whichever beans you buy, they should be moist and flexible, shiny, oily, and very fragrant.

SPLITTING A VANILLA BEAN Many recipes call for splitting and seeding a vanilla bean. To do this, lay the bean on a work surface. Use the tip of a paring knife to cut the bean in half lengthwise. Turn the knife over and use the dull side to scrape out the thousands of tiny, specklike vanilla seeds inside the bean. Add the seeds to the recipe. Most of the time, you will add the pod as well.

REUSING A VANILLA BEAN Just because a bean has steeped in liquid doesn't mean it is spent. Whole beans may be rinsed, allowed to dry, stored, and reused one time. If the bean has been split and scraped, or if you just don't want to steep it again, rinse it, dry it and grind it in the food processor with some sugar to make vanilla sugar (at right). Use vanilla sugar in place of plain sugar in baking recipes, coffee, tea, and anywhere you'd like a whisper of vanilla fragrance and flavor.

Storing: Keep vanilla beans in an airtight container in a cool, dark cupboard, where they will last for several years. If your vanilla beans become hard and dry, don't worry. They will plump up and release their flavor when soaked in hot liquid. Don't refrigerate beans, as they will harden and crystallize. Sometimes vanillin crystals form on the outside of the bean, giving it a whitish cast—this is not mold, but an indicator of flavorful, good-quality beans. If you're not sure, look closely—mold is fuzzy and dull, whereas crystals look like, well, crystals and are almost iridescent in the sunlight. If a bean is mildewed or moldy, throw it away.

VANILLA EXTRACT

Made by combining vanilla beans and alcohol, the vanilla flavor is eventually extracted into the alcohol, which is then blended with water and sugar. Pure vanilla extract is regulated by the FDA and must contain 35 percent alcohol (the alcohol burns off during cooking and baking). Fine extract makers will list right on the label the variety of vanilla bean used to make the extract. Bourbon vanilla extract is not made of Kentucky whiskey, but is extracted from Bourbon vanilla beans, described above. If you don't want even a tiny amount of alcohol, look for "pure natural vanilla," a non-alcohol, glycerin-based flavoring found in natural foods stores, and use it the same way you would extract.

If using extract instead of a vanilla bean, substitute 2 to 3 teaspoons of pure vanilla extract in place of each vanilla bean in a recipe. Avoid imitation vanilla, which has none of the complexity of the original. Cheap vanilla sold to tourists in other countries is not pure vanilla extract, no matter what the label says, and may contain chemicals long outlawed in this country. Real vanilla extract is pricey, regardless of where you buy it, and always contains 35 percent alcohol. If not, throw it out.

VANILLA PASTE

A recent innovation in the vanilla industry, vanilla bean paste is a combination of pure vanilla extract blended with water, sugar, seeds from the vanilla bean, and a natural thickener. It is a viscous liquid, thicker than extract, and can be substituted one to one for vanilla extract. The advantage to the paste is purely visual—thousands of tiny black vanilla bean seeds give the illusion that a real bean was used to make the sweet—which, in a roundabout way, is true. The seeds, however, are devoid of flavor

Vanilla Sugar

MAKES 2 CUPS This is a snap to assemble and adds instant zing to anything you're making. It's wonderful to use in place of plain sugar whenever you want a hint of vanilla—in your coffee or tea for example—or when making cookies, custards, tarts…

INGREDIENTS

½ moist, pliable vanilla bean

2 cups (14 ounces) sugar

EQUIPMENT

Food Processor Fitted with a Metal Blade, Medium-Mesh Strainer

1 Cut the bean into small pieces and place in the food processor with the sugar. Process for 20 to 30 seconds, until very finely ground.

2 Strain the mixture through the strainer to remove any large pieces of pod, then transfer to an airtight container and store at room temperature indefinitely.

"Has Bean" Vanilla Sugar

When you have finished using a vanilla bean to make a custard or other dessert, rinse it well and set it on a paper towel to dry for several days. When completely dry, break or cut it into pieces and use it in place of the "fresh" vanilla bean above. As you continue to use vanilla beans, pour the old vanilla sugar into the processor, adding a little additional sugar for extra volume, so the vanilla flavor keeps getting more and more intense.

when added to the paste, having given their essence to another preparation in the factory. They are pretty, though, and give desserts and sauces a distinctly homemade look.

Storing: Store both vanilla extract and paste in a cool, dark cupboard at room temperature, where they will keep for several years.

Other Ingredients Used in Baking

While the first eight ingredients discussed in this chapter are those most commonly used in baking, the ones reviewed here are the pastry chef's choice for adding vitality and excitement to breads and pastries. Spices, extracts, fruits, nuts, cheeses, wines, and liqueurs give baked goods personality and panache. Note that this is not an exhaustive list—instead, the ingredients here reflect those used in recipes throughout this book.

ALLSPICE Contrary to popular belief, allspice is not a blend of many spices, but instead is the dried, unripe berry of a tree in the myrtle family that is native to Latin America and the West Indies. Its flavor combines notes of cinnamon, cloves, and nutmeg.

ALMOND EXTRACT The oil of bitter almonds is blended with alcohol to make this intensely flavorful extract. Always buy pure almond extract, never imitation.

ALMONDS This most versatile of nuts is a member of the rose family, related to peaches, nectarines, plums, and cherries, which explains its special affinity for these fruits. Almonds are a popular addition to many desserts and breads and are available in several forms.

NATURAL VERSUS BLANCHED ALMONDS Natural almonds are still in their skins, whereas blanched almonds have been dunked in boiling water, then slipped out of their skins. You can use these two interchangeably as long as you understand that the natural almonds will always add flecks of brown to whatever they are mixed into, while blanched almonds have a clean off-white appearance. Almond skins have good flavor, so this book rarely calls for blanched almonds.

SLICED VERSUS SLIVERED ALMONDS Sliced almonds are thin, flat ovals of nut and are available either natural, with the skin forming a brown edge on each slice, or blanched. Slivered nuts resemble little matchsticks and are always cut from blanched almonds.

Storing: Store almonds airtight in a cool, dry location at room temperature for up to 3 months. Because nuts are rich in oils, they go rancid quickly. For longer storage, keep airtight in the refrigerator for up to 5 months, or the freezer for up to 9 months.

TOASTING ALMONDS Toasting almonds crisps the meat and brings out its full flavor. Toast on a baking sheet, spread out in a single layer, in a 350°F oven until fragrant and hot to the touch, 7 to 9 minutes for whole almonds, 5 to 7 minutes for sliced or slivered almonds.

ALMOND MEAL This is very finely ground almonds, either blanched or natural; also sometimes referred to as almond flour. You can make your own at home by grinding almonds in the food processor, but it is impossible to get them as fine and powdery as meal that you can purchase.

ALMOND PASTE VERSUS MARZIPAN Almond paste is almonds that are ground and blended with sugar to form a flavorful paste used as an ingredient in cakes, cookies, and fillings. Marzipan, a ready to eat confection, is much sweeter, with a higher ratio of sugar to nuts, and includes liquid sugar as well, which makes the marzipan more pliable. It is used mainly for covering cakes or molding into fanciful fruits, flowers, and other decorations. Do not substitute marzipan for almond paste (or the other way around) because of the great differences in their sugar content. **Storing:** Unopened, almond paste and marzipan may be stored at room temperature (note date on packaging). Once opened, wrap the leftovers tightly in plastic and refrigerate for up to 6 months.

AMARETTI Translated as "little bitter things," amaretti are highly flavorful and crispy Italian cookies made with both almonds and almond extract, tasting strongly of the bitter almonds (or in some cases the bitter almond–flavored apricot kernels) used to make the extract. They are often sold in red tins, wrapped in colorful paper.

AMARETTO Amaretto is an Italian almond liquor. The best, Amaretto di Saronno, has a refreshingly clean flavor of almonds that is extracted from the tiny bitter almond–flavored kernel inside apricot pits. Another good brand is Lazzaroni Amarello, made by the same company that produces the red tins of amaretti cookies.

ANISE Licorice is the flavor of this ancient spice, which is a member of the parsley family. It is most often available as seeds, which are used whole or ground in a spice grinder as needed.

APPLES To a pastry chef, apples fall into one of two categories— eating apples and baking apples. Eating apples are quite sweet and juicy but, unfortunately, are usually not able to maintain those qualities in a baked item, often collapsing into applesauce when fully cooked. Baking apples have strong flavor and are generally a bit drier in texture, holding their shape beautifully even with prolonged cooking in a pie. The best baking apples in the supermarket are Granny Smith, Pippin, and Fuji, but every baker has a favorite, so feel free to experiment. Explore local possibilities at farmers' markets, where you may find "antique" or heirloom varieties of apples that are grown in small quantities and do not ship well; sometimes they are less than beautiful. These apples are usually far superior to anything you can find in a supermarket. Apple season begins in late summer and continues until the last variety is picked sometime in November. **Storing:** Refrigerate apples in a plastic bag until needed.

APRICOTS

FRESH APRICOTS These luscious, orange-fleshed fruit stubbornly refuse to be extended beyond their short growing season, so enjoy them when they are fresh and at their best, May through August. When baking with apricots, it's best if the fruit is slightly underripe, so it doesn't disintegrate in the heat of the oven. Look for fruit that has a beautiful orange color and gives slightly when pressed at the stem end. While there are a number of apricot varieties, the queen of all is the Blenheim, or Royal, apricot, which appear in market toward the end of June and stay through much of July. Blenheims have a perfect balance of sweet and tart, which makes them ideal for baking. **Storing:** Store fresh apricots in the refrigerator for up to 1 week after purchase.

DRIED APRICOTS There are two types of dried apricots— California and Turkish. If you have the option, always choose California apricots, which are often the Blenheim variety and have an intense tart-sweet flavor; the Turkish variety is merely sweet and offers none of the complexity of the California variety. The fun thing about Turkish apricots is that they are dried whole (as opposed to the California apricots, which are halved before drying), which means the center where the pit used to be is the perfect spot for inserting a bit of chocolate ganache or other flavorful surprise. See Dried Fruit, page 50, for more purchasing information and how to store.

BAKING POWDER see Leaveners, page 34

BAKING SODA see Leaveners, page 34

BANANA LIQUEUR Tasting intensely of ripe bananas, this yellow liqueur adds great flavor to classic Bananas Foster, or to any recipe where you want a punch of sweet banana flavor tempered with a bite of alcohol.

BANANAS These lunchbox favorites are great in desserts as well. When you want the slices to hold up in a banana cream pie or for sautéing, choose bananas that are fully yellow, with just a few black specks on the skin. Very ripe bananas, those that are very mottled or completely black, are perfect for mashing and adding to cakes, quick breads, bread pudding, and even cookie batters. Most bananas are purchased green and should be ripened at room temperature (refrigeration delays ripening while turning the skins completely black). **Storing:** If you have very ripe bananas but no time to use them, refrigerate for several days, or throw them into a resealable plastic freezer bag and freeze for up to 3 months.

BASIL A fresh herb belonging to the *Labiatae* family, basil has flat leaves and a wonderful aroma usually associated with Italian cooking (it is the main ingredient in pesto). It lends a bright summer flavor to savory baking, and is sometimes used in desserts as well.

BLACKBERRIES Big, plump, glossy purple-black berries that resemble raspberries on steroids, blackberries are great in pies, crisps, and cobblers, as well as stirred into cake and quick bread batters. The darker the color, the sweeter the flavor.

Before buying, always check the container for any sign of leakage or molding. To use, pour the blackberries onto a baking sheet and sort through them to pick out and discard any moldy berries or debris. Do not wash or they will absorb water and turn to mush. If you feel you absolutely must wash them, do so just before use, rinsing them in cold water and immediately patting them dry with paper towels. **Storing:** Refrigerate and use within a day or two of purchase.

BLUEBERRIES These small, round berries are grown on bushes and are harvested during the summer months. Before buying, always check the container for any sign of leakage or molding. Just before use, pour the berries onto a baking sheet and pick through them, removing any stems or debris that you find. Transfer them to a strainer and rinse under cold water. Pat dry with paper towels. If you use frozen blueberries, be sure to add them to the batter while still frozen. Thawed berries lose quite a bit of juice, and it will turn the batter purple. **Storing:** Refrigerate and use within 3 to 4 days of purchase.

BUTTER see page 29

BUTTERMILK see Other Dairy Products, page 32

CAKE FLOUR see Flour, page 20

CALVADOS Calvados is an apple brandy distilled from apple cider and aged in oak casks. It is often added to desserts containing apples, to add another layer—subtle and sophisticated—of apple flavor.

CARDAMOM This aromatic member of the ginger family is a tropical spice native to Ceylon and south India. It has a lovely, complex flavor of citrus blended with flowers, mint, and ginger. Popular in Scandinavia, the Middle East, and India, it is a prominent flavor of Indian spiced tea (*masala chai*). Cardamom is costly—in third place behind saffron and vanilla beans—because it needs to be harvested five or six times a year entirely by hand. It is available in several forms: seeds ground into a powder; whole seeds, used for infusing flavor into tea or custards; and whole pods, full of the small black seeds. If you buy pods, look for green ones, as the white pods have been bleached and are much less flavorful.

CHEESE

BLUE CHEESE Flavorful blue cheese may be aged from 1 month to 1 year, crumbly or creamy, mild or sharp, but always ribboned with veins of flavorful blue mold. Some of the most famous blue cheeses are English Stilton, French Roquefort, and Italian Gorgonzola. Ask for a taste and choose one you'd love to use in your baking. **Storing:** Refrigerate, wrapped well in parchment or waxed paper and placed inside an airtight container, until needed.

CREAM CHEESE A white, soft, tangy cow's milk cheese, cream cheese is used to make smooth, rich, dense icings and cheesecake. The high fat content (nearly 90 percent) of cream cheese is what gives cheesecake and cream cheese icing that wonderful melt-in-your-mouth richness. Do not substitute low-fat, nonfat, or whipped cream cheese in baking, for they will dramatically compromise the flavor and texture of your pastries. **Storing:** Keep refrigerated, and wrap any leftovers tightly in plastic wrap, mark the box's expiration date on the wrapping, and refrigerate them until needed.

FETA A white cheese traditionally made from sheep's or goat's milk and cured in brine. Today, this cheese is often made from cow's milk. It has a crumbly texture and sharp, salty flavor. **Storing:** Store airtight in the refrigerator.

FROMAGE BLANC A soft, very fresh goat's milk or cow's milk cheese with a lightly acidic flavor and a fluffy, ricotta-like texture. Available at cheese shops and the cheese department of specialty grocery stores and some supermarkets. **Storing:** Keep refrigerated and use within 3 to 5 days of purchase.

MASCARPONE A fresh, thick, sensuously rich cow's milk cheese from Italy, most famously known for its inclusion in tiramisù. It has a soft, creamy texture and resembles triple-cream cheese in density, with a fat content of nearly 90 percent. Fabulous with fruit, chocolate, caramel, and just about anything else. Be cautious when mixing or whipping mascarpone, for it can become grainy, just like over-whipped cream. If this happens, stir in a few tablespoons of cream, just until it smoothes out again. **Storing:** Keep mascarpone refrigerated and use while it is cold—room temperature mascarpone breaks easily and cannot be repaired.

RICOTTA A fresh cheese with moist, soft curds and a mild, sweet, milky flavor, ricotta was originally produced in Italy. The name translates as "recooked," because it is made with the whey left over from making other cheeses. The whey is reheated to form curds again. Ricotta is made from whole or low-fat milk whey; for the best flavor and texture, always use whole-milk ricotta in your baking. **Storing:** Keep refrigerated and use any leftovers within 5 days.

CHERRIES
FRESH CHERRIES These have a very short season, beginning in late spring and ending in mid-summer. Among the sweet cherries are varieties such as Burlat, Rainier, Queen Anne, and Bing. Sour cherries such as Morello and Montmorency are fabulous for pies. Since cherries are almost always sold loose, take the time to pick through the bin and find the best specimens. They should be firm, plump, and shiny, with stems that are still moist and pliable. **Storing:** Refrigerate in a plastic produce or resealable plastic bag and use within 4 days of purchase. Wash and pat dry before use.

DRIED CHERRIES Both sweet and sour cherries are available in dried form. The sweet ones are rather uninteresting. Dried sour cherries, however, are a bright hit of summer flavor that enlivens everything from bread to cookies to cakes and scones. Anywhere you might use raisins, you can substitute dried sour cherries. **Storing:** Store in an airtight container at room temperature for up to 6 months.

CHIVES A fresh green herb that resembles a thin reed, chives are a member of the onion family and impart a wonderful mild onion flavor to all manner of savory baked goods, from tarts, to muffins, to cheesecakes.

CHOCOLATE see page 37

CILANTRO A fresh green herb with flat rounded leaves that are feathery around the edges, cilantro has a delightful, pungent flavor that is often associated with Mexican food, although it is also popular in China and India.

CINNAMON This much-loved spice is one of the oldest used by mankind. True cinnamon is actually the bark of a tree (*Cinnamomum zeylanicum*) that is a member of the laurel family, native to Ceylon and India. The bark is peeled off the tree and fermented briefly, then the outer layer is scraped off and the lighter inner layer is left to dry for several days. It curls during drying, resulting in shaggy rolls that are thin and brittle. It is often sold in the United States as Mexican cinnamon. Cassia, a related spice that is also the bark of a laurel species (*Cinnamomum cassia*) is not true cinnamon, but is the one most familiar to Americans. The outer bark is not removed, creating thicker sheets that are much darker in color and curl into individual scrolls as they dry.

CITRUS OILS High-quality citrus oils are made from the essential oils in the skin of lemons, limes, oranges, and tangerines, and have a very intense, clean, and pure flavor. These oils can be found in cookware stores, gourmet stores, and some supermarkets. **Storing:** Once opened, store the citrus oil at room temperature for several months. For longer storage, keep refrigerated.

CLOVES This spice, used since ancient times, is the dried flower bud of a tree in the myrtle family. Its name comes from the French *clou* ("nail"). The rich, deep flavor of cloves is a comforting presence in gingerbread, pumpkin pie, and many wintertime baked goods, although it must be used sparingly or it can quickly become overwhelming. Cloves may be purchased whole or ground. Whole cloves do not soften during cooking, so always remember to remove them before serving.

COCOA POWDER see Chocolate, page 41

COCONUT The fruit of the coconut palm, a native of Asia, was a star on *Gilligan's Island,* where marooned shipmates used them to construct nearly every household item imaginable, with comical results. If you aren't adept at working with fresh coconuts, don't worry. Prepared coconut is quite easy to find, and is the type used for recipes in this book.

SWEETENED SHREDDED OR FLAKED COCONUT Found in the baking aisle of the supermarket, this moist, sweet coconut is easy to use, but lacks flavor. To give it a boost, toast the coconut on a baking sheet in a 350°F oven for 7 to 8 minutes, stirring halfway through, until it's lightly speckled with golden brown. **Storing:** Keep airtight in a cool, dry location for up to 6 months.

DRIED UNSWEETENED SHREDDED COCONUT More brittle and finely shredded than sweetened coconut, this variety can be found most often in the bulk sections of natural food stores, and occasionally in supermarkets as well.

It may be toasted or not, according to the directions above, depending on the needs of your recipe. **Storing:** Keep airtight in a cool, dry location for up to 1 year.

COCONUT MILK This is not, as many think, the watery liquid in the center of a fresh coconut (that liquid is called coconut juice, coconut water, or sometimes green coconut water). Coconut milk is produced by shredding the meat of a fresh coconut, mixing it with an equal amount of hot water, then squeezing until dry. The milky, opaque liquid that streams out, full of the fat and flavor of the coconut, is coconut milk. Good-quality coconut milk is available in cans in the Asian section of the supermarket.

Most canned coconut milks separate during storage into a layer of very thick fat over a layer of thin, watery liquid. Stir them together before measuring if you will not be using the whole can. Do not substitute low-fat or nonfat coconut milk in baking—most of the flavor is in the fat, and without it, your pastry will not have the intensity of coconut flavor you desire. **Storing:** Store unopened cans at room temperature. Once opened, any leftovers should be transferred to a storage container, refrigerated, and used within 2 to 3 days.

COCONUT CREAM Similar to coconut milk, but produced from a ratio of 4 parts coconut to 1 part water, resulting in a very thick, very flavorful liquid. **Storing:** Same as for coconut milk.

CREAM OF COCONUT Used mainly for preparing tropical mixed drinks such as piña colada, this is coconut cream blended with lots of sugar, preservatives, and emulsifiers. It is available in cans in the liquor section of the supermarket. It doesn't taste very good on its own, but blends well with other ingredients and adds strong coconut flavor to some pastries and icings. **Storing:** Same as for coconut milk; use within 1 week of opening.

COOKING OIL SPRAY There is a wide range of sprays used to coat pans during cooking, and many sprays can be adapted to coat baking pans as well. High-heat canola spray, such as Spectrum brand, which is available in natural food stores and some supermarkets, is the best since it performs well with prolonged heat in the oven, and is nearly flavorless. Sprays with flour are not recommended, because the flour often clogs the spraying mechanism. Many supermarket brands have strong flavors and are often rancid, and can impart these qualities to the surface of your baked good. Always remove the cap and smell the spray before purchasing.

CORIANDER SEEDS Native to southern Europe and the Mediterranean, coriander is a member of the parsley family. Coriander seeds are the dried ripe fruit of this herb. Ground coriander loses its flavor quickly, so it's best to buy it whole and grind it with a spice grinder or coffee mill when you need it.

CORN SYRUP This liquid sweetener is made from cornstarch treated with an enzyme that converts the starch to the sugars glucose and maltose. Commercial corn syrup is a combination of glucose, high-fructose corn syrup (fructose being a super-sweet refinement of glucose), water, salt, and vanilla. It is not as sweet as sugar, but like sugar, it is hygroscopic and bonds with water, helping to keep baked goods moist. It will last for several years. It is used in caramel and candy making to prevent crystallization of the cooking sugar. For more on this, see "A Few Notes on Crystallization," page 26.

CORNMEAL Made by grinding dried corn kernels, cornmeal is available in several textures, depending upon how finely it is ground: corn flour (the finest grind), as well as fine, medium, and coarse meal (also known as polenta). Most cornmeal available in this country has had the perishable germ removed, which allows it to last longer. Stone-ground cornmeal has the nutrient-rich germ intact but a shorter shelf life, for the germ contains oil that will go rancid. **Storing:** Without the germ, cornmeal keeps for at least 1 year when stored airtight in a cool, dark location. Stone-ground cornmeal can be stored the same way, but only for 4 to 6 months; you can also freeze it for up to a year.

TOASTING CORNMEAL Toasting cornmeal intensifies its sweet, nutty flavor, adding a whole new dimension to favorites like corn bread. Place a dry skillet (not nonstick) over high heat. When hot, add the cornmeal and toss or stir frequently until it is very fragrant and has a golden toasted look (it should not brown), 4 to 5 minutes. Remove from the heat and pour onto a baking sheet or plate to cool completely before using.

CORNSTARCH The powdered starch made from corn kernels, cornstarch is used as a thickener in fruit desserts such as pies, crisps, and cobblers. Its clear, shiny gel allows the beauty of the fruit to shine through. It is also used to thicken custards cooked on the stovetop, such as pastry cream and chocolate pudding. You must be cautious, though, when cooking with cornstarch, for when cooked too long, it loses its thickening ability. Bring it to a boil to fully thicken, but keep the boiling short. If boiled longer than a minute or two, the starch granules swell too much and burst, releasing the liquid they had absorbed, resulting in a soupy pudding. **Storing:** Keep cornstarch airtight in a cool, dry cupboard for up to 1 year.

CRANBERRIES

FRESH CRANBERRIES The appearance of this native American fruit in the supermarket is a sure sign that fall has arrived. Cranberries are grown in huge, shallow bogs and are harvested by raking the red fruits off the surface of the water. Their intense flavor and bright red color make them a natural for desserts, providing a tart counterpoint to the sweetness. Look for fresh berries that are red, plump, and shiny. Before using, pour the contents of the bag onto a baking sheet and pick through the berries, discarding any shriveled or molded berries or debris, then rinse under cold water and pat dry with paper towels. **Storing:** Cranberries keep well in the refrigerator for at least 2 to 3 weeks and may be frozen for up to 1 year.

DRIED CRANBERRIES These tart little red nuggets are readily available in the supermarket. They are almost always sweetened before packaging, and some even have flavorings such as orange added. For the recipes in this book, use sweetened dried cranberries without any extra flavorings. They may be used wherever you might use raisins. **Storing:** Store in an airtight container at room temperature for up to 6 months.

CREAM see Other Dairy Products, page 32

CREAM OF COCONUT see Coconut, page 48

CREAM OF TARTAR The powdered crystals of tartaric acid, which form on the inside of wine barrels during grape fermentation, cream of tartar is sold in the spice section of the supermarket. It's one of the main components in baking powder, and its acidity is also often used to stabilize whipped egg whites and to prevent sugar from crystallizing during caramel or candy making.

CRÈME FRAÎCHE see Other Dairy Products, page 33

CUMIN The dried seedlike fruit of a member of the parsley family, native to Egypt and the eastern Mediterranean, cumin is used widely around the world. In this country we most often associate its wonderful, earthy fragrance with Mexican or Indian cooking, and its presence in baked goods provides a link to those cuisines. Cumin can be bought whole or ground into powder.

DATES The fruit of the date palm tree has been cultivated since ancient times in the Middle East and North Africa, and thrives in California's Coachella Valley (best known for the star-studded

city of Palm Springs). Though there are many varieties of dates, one of the best by far is the Medjool, a large, soft, mahogany-colored date with wrinkled skin and a rich and chewy interior. Another is Barhi, a soft, plump, caramel-like date. They can often be found in the produce section of the supermarket. **Storing:** Store in an airtight container at cool room temperature for a few weeks. For longer storage, refrigerate for up to 1 year.

If a whitish bloom appears on the surface, do not be alarmed; it's only sugar crystals. They won't affect the flavor, but if you are concerned about the appearance of the fruit, wipe them off with a damp cloth.

DECORATIVE SUGAR see Sugar, page 24

DESSICANT Silica gel, which absorbs moisture, is the most readily available dessicant. It is used when storing pastries or garnishes that are especially prone to absorbing moisture yet need to be kept crisp and dry, such as caramel decorations or thin, crispy tuile cookies. Silica gel is placed into an airtight storage container with the items to be kept dry (do not let the gel come in contact with the food). Silica gel may be used over and over again, and is available at craft and floral supply stores.

DRIED FRUIT This winter staple of the seasonal pastry kitchen has long taken a backseat to fresh fruit, but is now making a strong comeback as people appreciate the intense flavors, soft texture, and easy availability of high-quality dried fruit. And for those who like to support local growers and eat sustainably, dried fruit is an excellent way to taste a bit of summer during the long winter months.

It's best to purchase dried fruit from the bulk section of a natural foods store, where you can see and feel the quality of the fruit. If you are purchasing packaged fruit, always bend or squeeze the fruit through the packaging to make sure it is soft and pliable, as rock-hard fruit is difficult and frustrating to work with. If the fruit is a bit harder than you like, soften it up by pouring boiling water to cover, then submerging it by setting a plate on top. Let it sit for 5 to 10 minutes, then drain off the water, pat the fruit dry, and cool before continuing with the recipe.

In general, unsulfured dried fruit has a much better flavor than those that have been treated with chemicals to retain their natural colors. Many bakers do use sulfured apricots, however, because their bright orange color is a vibrant addition to many winter desserts. **Storing:** Keep any leftover dried fruit in an airtight container or resealable plastic bag in a cool, dark cupboard, where it will keep for 3 to 6 months.

For specific types of dried fruit, see the separate entries in this glossary.

DULCE DE LECHE This thick, rich, caramel-colored cream is made by boiling down cow's or goat's milk with a bit of sugar until it is deeply browned and full of complex caramel flavors.

It can be used to flavor all kinds of desserts, from puddings to cakes to cookies, and is found canned in the Latin American section of the supermarket or in Latin American markets. **Storing:** Once opened, transfer any leftovers to an airtight container, then refrigerate and use within a month. (But you may not be able to resist eating it by the spoonful straight from the container.)

EARL GREY TEA Earl Grey is a classic black tea flavored with the oil of the bergamot orange, a member of the citrus family grown in the Mediterranean for the fragrant oil in its skin.

Loose-leaf tea is higher quality than tea in prepackaged bags, and is available in bulk at tea shops and many coffeehouses. It is a wonderful partner to dark chocolate in desserts, and can also be used to infuse custards.

EGGS see page 27

ESPRESSO POWDER For a deep, rich coffee flavor, high-quality espresso powder dissolved in a small amount of warm water can provide a pure, deep coffee flavor that rivals the best coffee extract. Pastry chefs love the crisp flavor of Medaglia d'Oro from Italy, available in small bottles in Italian markets, specialty and gourmet markets, and some supermarkets.

FENNEL SEEDS Another relative of the parsley family (along with cumin and coriander), fennel seed is the dried fruit of the feathery fennel plant and has a pronounced licorice flavor. (This is not the same plant that produces fennel bulbs, though they are related.) Fennel is rarely found ground, but you can grind it easily with a spice or coffee grinder.

FIGS Luscious, jammy, and sweet, the fig is one of the great culinary gifts of late summer. Though their skins range in hue from brown to purple to green to black, and their interiors from pale pink to rose to deep salmon, all figs share a classic voluptuous curviness, and when ripe they are meltingly soft, with a slight raggedness about the neck attesting to their readiness. The best-known variety, the Black Mission fig, was brought to California in the eighteenth century by Franciscan friars from Mexico, who in turn had received it from Spanish missionaries. There are over six hundred varieties worldwide, with their names almost always corresponding in some manner to the color of their skins.

FRESH FIGS Whatever the variety, figs are best when allowed to ripen on the tree. Choose figs that are soft and dry, with a slight wrinkling or near splitting of the skin, indicating their ripeness. **Storing:** Keep at room temperature for best flavor and use within 2 days of purchase.

DRIED FIGS The dried Black Mission fig is especially good for baking, as it is generally moister and has a more tender skin than other varieties. See Dried Fruit, page 50, for purchasing and storage information.

FLOUR see page 20

FRAMBOISE Framboise is a clear brandy distilled from fresh raspberries, with a strong flavor and fragrance of the berries. It is used to give an added layer of flavor to raspberry desserts.

FRANGELICO An intense hazelnut liquor from Italy, Frangelico was first made by monastery monks to raise funds for their living and ministering expenses. It adds terrific flavor to hazelnut and chocolate desserts.

FROMAGE BLANC see Cheese, page 47

GINGER Ginger is the rhizome—the thick, tuberous underground stem, or "hand" as it is often called—of a tall herb native to southern Asia. It has long been used in dried, powdered form in baked goods such as gingerbread. Now other forms of ginger have become increasingly popular in the pastry kitchen as well.

FRESH GINGER There is nothing like the floral zing of fresh ginger in desserts. Look for smooth skin with no wrinkling (a sign of drying out) or mold. To efficiently peel off the thin skin, use the rounded tip of a spoon. For grated ginger, use a Microplane zester, which makes quick work of the task and catches most of the fibrous ginger "hairs" in its fine openings. **Storing:** Store in a plastic bag in the refrigerator for up to 3 weeks, depending upon freshness when purchased.

CANDIED OR CRYSTALLIZED GINGER The two terms that describe ginger cooked in sugar syrup are used interchangeably, but they're not exactly the same. Technically, candied ginger is naked, whereas crystallized ginger sports a crunchy sugar coating. Several forms of both sugared gingers are available in stores—slices, chunks, or small "chips." All are tender and sweet, with a spicy heat that tempers sweetness and adds a bit of excitement to many desserts.

STEM GINGER IN SYRUP These are larger chunks of ginger cooked and jarred in sugar syrup. The pieces of stem ginger may be patted dry, chopped, and used like candied or crystallized ginger in baking. The syrup is also very flavorful and can be brushed over cakes, added to dessert sauces, stirred into sparkling water, and myriad other uses.

Sometimes large pieces of candied ginger are quite fibrous. To make these usable, cut the ginger into small pieces to reduce the length of their stringy fibers inside—and buy another brand next time.

Storing: Store candied ginger airtight at cool room temperature for 6 to 8 months. Stem ginger in syrup should be refrigerated after opening, where it will keep for months.

GOLD LEAF A sparkle of real gold makes any dessert special, and culinary grade (22 to 24 carat) gold leaf is now easily available to the home baker in small retail portions. For details on how to use gold leaf in decorating special-occasion desserts, see page 436. Always work with gold leaf in a draft-free area, for even a small breeze can quickly disintegrate the gold or blow it onto the counter or floor.

SHEETS Tissue-thin rectangular gold leaf sheets can be broken into "petals" (see below) or small individual pieces with the tip of a paring knife, or may be used a sheet at a time for a bold, dramatic presence on a cake or other pastry.

PETALS Sheets of gold leaf are broken into small irregular pieces to make petals. They are generally used one or two at a time, to decorate an individual dessert or portion, though they may be clustered or strewn over the top of a dessert as well. They are sold in a small box with holes in the top, so you can shake the petals out over your dessert for decoration. You can also remove the box top and use a pair of tweezers or the tip of a paring knife to place the petals exactly where we you want them.

POWDERED Ground into a fine powder, powdered gold is great for sprinkling over desserts, or any time you want a fine shimmer of gold.

Storing: Store gold leaf, petals, and powder at room temperature in a cool, dry location, where it will keep indefinitely.

HAWAIIAN WASHED RAW SUGAR see Sugar, page 24

HAZELNUTS Also known as *filberts,* hazelnuts have a long history, originating in China more than 4,500 years ago. Although Turkey is the world's largest producer of hazelnuts, nearly all of the nuts we buy in this country are grown in Oregon.

The small, round nut has a distinctively sweet and earthy flavor, one that figures prominently in many Italian desserts, as well as an addictive Italian import—Nutella, the Italian "peanut butter" of ground hazelnuts and chocolate. Specialty and gourmet markets and the bulk section of natural foods stores are your best bet for finding this distinctive and delicious nut.

Purchase hazelnuts from a shop that has a high turnover. Skinned hazelnuts, long available to the professional, are occasionally available in specialty markets—if you find them, purchase a couple of bags and freeze them for future use. **Storing:** At room temperature they will keep for 3 to 4 months, but eventually they will turn rancid. To prolong their freshness, store them airtight in the refrigerator (6 months) or the freezer (1 year).

TOASTING HAZELNUTS Toast raw hazelnuts on a baking sheet in a 350°F oven for 8 to 10 minutes. Cool completely before using them in a recipe.

SKINNING HAZELNUTS The skins of Turkish hazelnuts can be quite bitter, but the skins of our domestic hazelnuts are usually mild in flavor. Taste one and decide for yourself. If the skins are mild, you may want to forgo the extra step of removing their skins. If you want to skin the nuts, toast them on a baking sheet in a 350°F oven for 10 to 14 minutes, until the skins begin to split and come away from the nuts. Transfer the hot nuts to a clean kitchen towel and wrap them tightly inside it—the steam will help loosen the skins. After 3 to 4 minutes, rub the nuts vigorously inside the towel to remove as much of the skins as possible. Depending on the variety, you may be able to remove some of the skin, but sometimes very little rubs off. Don't worry; the remaining skin will add flavor and color to your baking.

HONEY Bees make this complex liquid sweetener from the nectar of flowers. The type of flower greatly influences the flavor of the honey, though the honey rarely tastes like the flowers. Some honeys are sweet and floral, like orange blossom honey; some are quite bitter, like chestnut honey; and some are fascinating mixtures of a variety of flowers, such as wildflower honey. If all you've ever tasted is the honey in the plastic bear from the supermarket, it's time to expand your palate. There are many varietal honeys (honeys derived from a single plant source) all over the country—and the world—and they are truly a taste of *terroir,* captured and interpreted by bees. There is lavender honey from the south of France, buckwheat honey from California, and tupelo honey from Florida. Next time you're at the farmers' market, look for the honey table; every region has its share of beekeepers who delight in introducing customers to the flavor nuances of their particular honey varietals. **Storing:** Honey may be stored in a cool, dark cupboard practically indefinitely. Many honeys are filtered, to prevent crystallization, so they stay fluid for a long time. If your honey crystallizes, simply set the container in a small pot of hot water and the crystals will melt. Some honeys, especially those mass-produced or with high water content, are pasteurized to prevent the fermentation of yeast spores, which would spoil the honey.

KUMQUATS A diminutive fruit resembling a miniature oblong orange, kumquats are actually in a genus separate from other citrus. And unlike citrus, the sweet and flavorful skin is the real star of kumquats, while the inside is quite tart although edible (seeds and all). Kumquats are available from November through spring. Choose fruits that are bright orange, firm, plump, and shiny. **Storing:** Store kumquats in a plastic bag in the refrigerator, where they will keep for several weeks.

LAVENDER An herb prized for its fragrant purple flowers, lavender is a highly aromatic member of the mint family, and its oil is added to countless soaps and perfumes.

Dried lavender flowers are the most common form used by pastry chefs. The fragrant buds are infused into custards and whipped cream, or ground with sugar to make lavender sugar. Always buy lavender that has been grown specifically for eating, as the lavender available in flower shops and craft stores has been treated with chemicals that can be dangerous if ingested. Specialty and gourmet markets and natural foods stores are the best places to find dried lavender. **Storing:** Stored airtight in a cool, dark cupboard, dried lavender will last for 1 year.

LEMONS Sunshine-colored lemon brings a bright acidic flavor to everything it touches, and the pastry kitchen is unimaginable without it. The most common varieties in the supermarket are the Eureka and the Lisbon, and they are practically identical in color and acidity. They are available year-round, although their season is winter through early summer.

A third variety, the intoxicating Meyer lemon, has become more available over the past 15 years, and if you see them, give them a try. Discovered in China in 1908 by Frank Meyer while on an expedition to find new agricultural possibilities for the U.S. government, these thin-skinned, yolk-colored lemons are the result of a cross with a mandarin at some point in history, giving them their characteristic color, floral fragrance, and fruity yet tart flavor. Meyer lemons are in season from fall into early spring, with some available during the summer, as well.

Whatever the variety, choose lemons that are firm, feel heavy for their size, and have small pores (an indication of juiciness). **Storing:** Store in a plastic bag in the refrigerator for up to 3 weeks.

LIMES The most acidic member of the citrus family, limes add a shot of lively flavor to pies, tarts, fruit desserts, ice creams,

and more. Supermarket limes are the Tahiti lime, also known as the Persian or Bearss lime, and are round, deep green fruit. Ripe limes are yellow, but they can be difficult to tell from lemons, so growers pick the limes while they are still green, then gas them to preserve the familiar green color. They are in season all year long. Mexican limes, also called Key limes, are quite small, with a leathery skin that is green mottled with yellow. The juice is very tart, with a distinctive spicy flavor well-loved in margaritas and mojitos, curd, and—of course—Key lime pie. Choose limes that are firm, feel heavy for their size, and have small pores (an indication of juiciness). **Storing:** Keep in a plastic bag in the refrigerator for up to 3 weeks.

LIMONCELLO Limoncello is a sweetened, lemon-infused alcohol from the Amalfi coast of Italy. It adds a bracing hit of lemon to desserts and their sauces, or wherever a touch of lemon is needed.

LUSTER DUST Luster dust is edible mineral dust with a fine, sparkly finish. It is available in myriad colors and is used to create beautiful, glittering color on wedding cakes and other special-occasion cakes. To use luster dust, see the instructions on page 436.

MACADAMIA NUTS Native to Australia, these large, round, creamy-beige nuts full of buttery flavor are now grown on huge plantations in Hawaii. They are expensive, but worth the investment for baking. They pair exceptionally well with tropical fruits and flavors. Look for roasted, unsalted macadamias in specialty markets and natural foods stores.

If you can only find the salted variety, simply pour them into a strainer, rinse the salt off with cold water, and dry on a baking pan in a 200°F for 20 to 30 minutes, until the moisture has evaporated. Cool completely before using in a recipe. **Storing:** Because of their high fat content, macadamias turn rancid quickly, so use them within several weeks. For longer storage, transfer them to an airtight container or resealable plastic bag and refrigerate for up to 3 months or freeze for up to 1 year.

MALTED MILK POWDER An old-fashioned drink powder used to flavor milk and give the kids some nutrition as well, malted milk powder has a wonderful malty flavor that is excellent with chocolate. The most common brand, Ovaltine, is available in most supermarkets. For best results, be sure to use the original style (yellow label) and not the chocolate one.

MAPLE SYRUP The gathering and refining of maple tree sap into syrup has been practiced for longer than recorded history.

When the sap warms in the spring and begins to flow through the tree, it is collected and cooked down to the proper *brix,* or density. It takes 30 to 40 gallons of sap to produce 1 gallon of maple syrup.

The grading of maple syrup is determined mainly by color, and has nothing to do with the quality of the syrup. Grade A light amber is considered to be the best tasting, and is usually made from the first runs of sap. Medium amber and dark amber are progressively more robust in flavor. Grades B and C are very dark, concentrated, and intensely flavored, and are the best types to use for all your baking. Do not substitute imitation-maple pancake syrup, which is truly a pale imitation of the real thing.

MAPLE SUGAR see Sugar, page 24

MARSALA Marsala is a fortified white wine from Sicily. To fortify a wine, brandy is added to halt the fermentation process and make the wine shelf stable. **Storing:** Fortified wines (including port) may be kept at room temperature, with the top firmly secured, for at least a year.

MASCARPONE see Cheese, page 47

MOLASSES A by-product of sugar refining, molasses is a thick, dark, bitter syrup most commonly used in gingerbread cakes and cookies. It is available in three grades, related directly to the three refining stages of sugar making. Any of the grades may be sulfured or unsulfured, depending upon the manufacturer; unsulfured has a cleaner flavor. You may use any grade you like for baking, depending upon the strength and intensity of molasses flavor desired. Light molasses, also known as *Barbados molasses,* is the lightest in color and flavor and is a product of the first stage of refinement. This is the grade used most often in baking.

Dark molasses is darker, stronger in flavor, and a product of the second stage. Blackstrap molasses is the very dark (almost black), bitter syrup left after the third and final refining. **Storing:** Store opened bottles of molasses with the lid screwed on firmly, in a cool, dark cupboard. They will keep for at least 1 year.

NECTARINES Named after the drink consumed by ancient Greek gods, nectarines are one of the most popular summer stone fruits. In essence, the nectarine is a fuzzless peach; the two fruits are very closely related, although nectarines have a stronger flavor, thinner skin, and are less prone to bruising during shipping. They can be substituted for peaches in baking recipes.

Nectarines are in season June through September and are available in both yellow- and white-fleshed varieties. Look for nectarines that have a yellow or orange background color (creamy white for white nectarines). Green is an indication that they were picked too soon and will never ripen to the luscious juiciness for which they are famous. Choose fruits that are plump and firm, but yield to gentle pressure at the blossom end. To bring out their sweetness, let them sit on the counter for a day or two. **Storing:** Refrigerate and use within a day or two of purchase.

NUTMEG Native to Indonesia, the nutmeg tree (*Myristica fragrans*) produces two separate spices, nutmeg and mace.

The fruit of the tree, which resembles an apricot, splits open when ripe, exposing a seed encased in a red, netlike substance. The "net" is mace; the seed is the nutmeg. Mace is always ground once dried. Nutmeg is available either whole or ground. **Storing:** Whole nutmegs may be stored, airtight, and grated finely as needed, for several years. The warm, spicy aroma of freshly grated nutmeg is well worth the few seconds of work.

ORANGE BLOSSOM WATER Distilled from the blossoms of the bergamot (or Seville) orange tree, potent orange blossom water is used in the cooking and baking of the eastern Mediterranean. Orange blossom water can be found in some supermarkets, specialty grocers, and markets catering to a Middle Eastern or Mediterranean clientele. **Storing:** After opening orange blossom water, it can be kept at room temperature for at least 1 year.

ORANGES The most popular member of the citrus family, the orange is indigenous to China and began its travels around the world thanks to Arab traders. Oranges are available year round, though they are at their peak during the winter months. Valencia oranges are considered the best variety for juice, while the seedless navels—Washington is the most popular variety—are great for eating out of hand or slicing for desserts. The zest of oranges is a common dessert ingredient, perfuming everything with bright citrus flavor.

Blood oranges have become quite popular in the last 10 years, with flesh that ranges from rosy orange to deep burgundy and a flavor that combines the rich sweetness of orange juice with deep berry undertones and a sprightly nip of acidity. Whatever the variety, choose oranges that are firm, feel heavy for their size, and have small pores (an indication of juiciness). **Storing:** Keep in a plastic bag in the refrigerator for up to 3 weeks.

PASSION FRUIT Small globes with a hard, deep purple shell, passion fruits are filled with a thin, juicy pulp that is vibrant orange, very acidic (think lemon or lime), and intoxicatingly floral and tropical. The dramatic black seeds suspended in the pulp are entirely edible, though they are often strained out in dessert making. Passion fruits are grown all over the world and can be found year-round. Choose fruit that is heavy for its size. A ripe passion fruit is quite wrinkled, but should not have any brown spots or mold. If you only find smooth round fruits, leave them at room temperature until they have wrinkled. **Storing:** Keep ripe passion fruits in a plastic bag in the refrigerator for up to a week.

PEACHES A member of the rose family (along with nectarines, apricots, plums, apples, and pears), the peach is certainly the queen of summer fruits, with juicy, highly perfumed flesh. The best peach is a tree-ripened peach, but because they do not travel well, they are often picked and shipped unripe. Peaches are in season from May through late September. Look for fruit with a creamy background color and no greenness. Keep in mind that the blush of redness on the skin, although beautiful, has nothing to do with ripeness or the quality of the fruit. Choose peaches that are plump and firm, but yield to gentle pressure at the blossom end. To bring out their sweetness, let them sit on the counter for a day or two. **Storing:** Refrigerate peaches and use within a day or two of purchase.

PEELING PEACHES Most of the fuzz associated with peach skin has been bred out of modern varieties, but if you have an heirloom variety of peach, or simply don't want the skins in your dessert, you'll need to remove their peels. If the peaches are fairly firm, you can peel them simply by using a sharp, serrated peeler (the type designed to peel tomatoes) to gently remove the skin. If the skin is tenacious, the fruit is too ripe to peel by hand, or you don't own a serrated peeler, you'll need to dip the peaches in boiling water to loosen the skins. To do this, place a bowl of ice water nearby, and bring a large saucepan of water to boil. Use the tip of a knife to cut a small x in the rounded end of each peach. Use a slotted spoon to gently lower the peaches, two at a time, into the boiling water. Cook for about 1 minute, then remove the peaches with the slotted spoon and check to see if you can pull back the skin easily at the x. If so, transfer the peaches to the ice water and continue with the remaining peaches. If the skin won't peel, put the peaches back into the boiling water and check again every 30 seconds until the skin has loosened. Then transfer them to the ice water. When the peaches have cooled, remove them from the ice bath and peel off the skins. Cut the peaches in half and remove the pits.

PEANUTS Technically not a nut, peanuts are a member of the legume family, like beans and lentils, although they are used in the same manner as nuts. Peanuts are cultivated extensively in the South, where they grow underground. The "nuts" are actually the seeds of the plant, encased in distinctively shaped and easily opened pods. Although usually roasted and salted (or boiled raw in the South) for snacking, unsalted nuts—raw or roasted—can be found for baking purposes. If you can only find the salted variety, simply pour the shelled nuts into a strainer, rinse the salt off with cold water, and dry on a baking pan in a 200°F for 15 to 20 minutes, until the moisture has evaporated. Cool completely before using in a recipe.

Peanut butter is just peanuts ground to a thick paste. Natural varieties contain only peanuts; commercial peanut butters are about 10 percent sugar, with salt and stabilizers mixed in as well. **Storing:** Store peanuts airtight at room temperature for 3 to 4 months. Eventually they will turn rancid, so, to prolong their freshness, store them in the refrigerator (6 months) or the freezer (1 year). Commercial peanut butter may be stored at room temperature for up to 6 months, or in the refrigerator for up to a year. Natural peanut butter should be refrigerated after opening and will keep for up to a year. Always bring refrigerated peanut butter to room temperature before using for cooking, or it will be too thick and hard to blend with other ingredients.

PEARS Another member of the extensive rose family, pears are related to apples and their meltingly fragrant flesh can be enjoyed in many of the same preparations. Asian pears, which are round, crisp, juicy, and sweet, are great for eating out of hand, but of little use in most dessert making. European pears are best for desserts and include varieties such as Bosc, Anjou, and Winter Nelis (good for poaching, roasting, and baking); Bartlett, Comice, and French Butter (great for eating out of hand); and small pears like the miniature Seckel (for baking or eating).

Pears are picked when underripe, for if they ripen on the tree, they become mushy. Choose firm, hard pears and ripen them at room temperature, until they are fragrant and yield to gentle pressure at the stem end. **Storing:** Once ripe, keep pears in the refrigerator for up to 5 days.

PECANS Native to North America, pecans are a sweet nut with a soft texture that is grown through the Southern states and into the Southwest. They are particularly prized in Southern desserts such as pecan pie, although their beautiful oval appearance and luscious caramel-like undertones have made them a popular choice in pastry and candy kitchens all across the country. They are available in halves, which are striking but expensive, and in pieces. **Storing:** Keep airtight at room temperature for 2 to 3 months. Eventually they will turn rancid, so, to prolong their freshness, store in the refrigerator (up to 6 months) or the freezer (up to 1 year).

TOASTING PECANS This crisps the meat and brings out their full flavor. Toast on a baking sheet in a 350°F oven for 7 to 9 minutes, until fragrant and hot to the touch. Transfer to a plate to cool completely before using.

PEPPER, BLACK The dried berry of the pepper vine (including the dark outer hull), black pepper is native to South India. The berries are picked while still green and allowed to ferment for a few days. They are then dried until they are black or dark brown. For best flavor, purchase whole black peppercorns and grind them with a pepper grinder as needed. Preground black pepper rarely has much flavor.

PHYLLO A flaky, paper-thin dough from the Eastern Mediterranean, phyllo is used for pastries throughout the Mediterranean and the Middle East. In Turkey, where it most likely originated, it is called *yufka; phyllo* is the Greek word.

SHEET PHYLLO These paper-thin sheets of dough are used to make many types of Greek and Middle Eastern dishes and desserts, of which baklava is the most famous. Although still made by hand in traditional homes and shops, phyllo is more often mechanically rolled or extruded. For more on how to use phyllo, see page 107. **Storing:** Keep frozen. Unused thawed phyllo may be wrapped tightly in plastic wrap and returned to the refrigerator where it will keep for at least 2 to 3 weeks. Do not refreeze.

SHREDDED PHYLLO Also known as *kataifi,* shredded phyllo resembles shredded wheat or vermicelli in texture, and is made from a thin, batterlike mixture that is tossed onto a hot griddle from a device resembling a potato ricer. Just as the strands set, they are scooped off and packaged.

Where sheet phyllo is thin and delicate, prone to cracking and tearing, shredded phyllo is flexible, wiry, and virtually indestructible. You can thaw it at room temperature with no ill effects, unlike sheet phyllo. It is, however, much harder to find, although if you shop in a market that has an eastern Mediterranean clientele, it will almost certainly be in the frozen section next to the sheet phyllo. **Storing:** Keep frozen until a couple of hours before you need it. Thaw on the counter. Unused shredded phyllo may be wrapped in plastic and refrigerated for a couple of weeks, or refrozen in a resealable plastic freezer bag.

PINEAPPLE A symbol of hospitality, sweet and utterly satisfying, the pineapple is most closely associated with carefree vacations in Hawaii. They are native to Central and South America and arrived in Hawaii in the late 1700s with Captain James Cook. Since then, Hawaii has become the largest grower of pineapples in the world, known for its premium fruit. Many people believe that if a leaf comes away easily from the center of the crown when pulled, the pineapple is ripe, but this isn't an accurate test. Instead, look for a fruit that feels heavy for its size and has a strong, sweet aroma, since pineapples don't ripen much after picking. A new variety, called *Gold* or *Extra-Sweet,* has an almost candylike sweetness and is almost always of very high quality. **Storing:** Keep ripe pineapples in the refrigerator for up to 5 days after purchase.

PISTACHIOS Native to Turkey, these small, green, tender nuts are popular throughout the Middle East and the Mediterranean for both snacking and desserts. Pistachios grown in this region are usually of very high quality, with a gorgeous, almost neon green color and sweet flavor. Most pistachios available in this country, though, are grown in California and are the Kerman variety, named for the major city at the center of Iran's largest pistachio-producing region. Be sure to buy raw, shelled, unsalted pistachios for baking and avoid any that have been dyed an artificial red. **Storing:** Pistachios have a high oil content and will keep in an airtight container at room temperature for several weeks to a few months, but they are best stored in the refrigerator (4 to 6 months) or the freezer (9 to 12 months).

TOASTING PISTACHIOS Toast on a baking sheet in a 350°F oven for 6 to 8 minutes—long enough to crisp the meat and bring out the flavor but not so long as to turn the green color to brown. Transfer to a plate to cool completely before using.

PLUMS Most commercial plums fall into one of two categories, European or Japanese. European plums, also known as *prune plums,* are the "blue" varieties that are either blue or purple in color, usually freestone and ultra-sweet. You can occasionally find them fresh at farmers' markets and in the specialty fruit section of the produce department during summer, but the majority of the crop is dried and sold as prunes (or "dried plums" as they are sometimes marketed). Japanese plums span a range of hues and shapes and offer a nice balance of acidic skin and sweet flesh, great for eating or baking. They are in season from May through October, with succeeding varieties ripening every week or so. Some varieties to try include Santa Rosa, Elephant Heart, Casselman, and Wickson. Choose fruit that feels heavy for its size, smells fragrant, and yields to gentle pressure at the blossom end. Once picked, they do not ripen any further, so be sure to taste before purchasing. Their flesh can be softened by closing them in a paper bag at room temperature for a few days. **Storing:** Keep in the refrigerator in a plastic or paper bag for up to 5 days.

POIRE WILLIAMS Poire Williams is a clear brandy distilled from fresh Bartlett pears. It is, of course, a welcome accent in any dessert that features pears.

POPPY SEEDS The dried, diminutive seeds of the poppy flower (yes, the one that produces opium) add texture and flavor to baked goods and are especially popular in the baking of Germany and Scandinavia. Don't worry; the seeds have no narcotic effects. **Storing:** Poppy seeds are high in oil and turn rancid very quickly when left at room temperature, so should be stored in an airtight container or resealable plastic bag in the freezer, where they will keep for 6 to 8 months.

PUMPKIN The only American pumpkin suitable for use in desserts is the sugar pumpkin, much smaller (2 to 3 pounds) and more flavorful than the giant jack-o'-lantern varieties. Sugar, or pie, pumpkins can be found in the produce section during the fall season. To use, cut the pumpkin in half across its equator, scoop out the seeds, and roast the halves, cut sides down, on a baking sheet in a 400°F oven until tender when pierced with the tip of a paring knife, about 45 to 60 minutes. Cool and scoop out the flesh, discarding the skin, then puree in a food processor or blender until smooth.

Canned pumpkin (with no added spices) is a good substitute, and in fact most people are accustomed to its strong, concentrated flavor and prefer it to fresh. It is generally made from a mixture of squash varieties and cooked down to evaporate much of the water present in the flesh, hence the thickness and strong flavor. Be sure to use solid-pack pumpkin and not canned pumpkin pie filling. **Storing:** Refrigerate leftover pumpkin, covered, and use within 3 days; you can also freeze it for up to 1 month.

QUINCES Native to Iran and the Caspian region, the quince is an ancient fruit with a long history in both sweet and savory dishes. A relative of the apple, it was once popular in early America, and is currently making a comeback thanks to food lovers across the nation.

Quinces can be found in supermarkets during the late fall and winter, usually in the specialty fruit section of the produce department. The varieties in this country are inedible in their raw state, and they take a while to cook, but in the end you are rewarded with gorgeous deep red or pink slices and a flavor that is a combination of apple, pear, citrus, pineapple, and ginger.

Quinces are round or oblong and, when ripe, have yellow skin that is tinged with green and covered with a downy fuzz.

When buying quinces, choose fruit that is firm and heavy and relatively free of blemishes, though it is common for them to have a few small brown spots, for they bruise easily. They have a sweet fragrance, and if they are green, you can ripen them in a bowl on the table—they make a lovely centerpiece that doubles as an air freshener. Once they are fully yellow and fragrant, refrigerate them. Quinces have very hard flesh, so use a sharp knife and work firmly yet carefully when cutting. **Storing:** Once ripe, store in a paper bag in the refrigerator for up to 2 weeks.

RASPBERRIES It's hard to imagine the pastry kitchen without these jewel-like red berries. They are used in sauces and garnishes and everything in between. Although they are available in the market all year long, they are a summer fruit and at their best from late spring through early fall. Those shipped in from far away during the winter never live up to their rosy red promise, so it's best to enjoy them in season. If the berries will be added to a batter or turned into sauce, frozen berries are a good source during the winter.

Before buying, always check the berry container for any sign of leakage or molding. To use, pour the raspberries onto a baking sheet and sort through them to pick out and discard any moldy berries or debris. Do not wash them or they will absorb water and turn to mush. If you feel you absolutely must wash them, do so just before use, rinsing them in cold water and immediately patting them dry with paper towels. **Storing:** Keep refrigerated and use within a day or two of purchase.

RHUBARB While technically a vegetable (it resembles rosy celery stalks), rhubarb is used mainly in desserts because its highly acidic flesh is best when prepared with sugar. In early America, it was so popular in baking that people referred to it as *pie plant*. It is in season during the spring and summer months, though it can often be found in the market year-round, thanks to hothouses. Choose firm stalks with no brown spots or mold. Never use rhubarb leaves, for they contain oxalic acid in dangerous amounts. **Storing:** Refrigerate in a plastic bag for up to 5 days after purchase.

ROSEMARY A resinous green herb, rosemary belongs to the *Labiatae* family, along with basil, lavender, mint, and thyme. Rosemary has the strongest flavor of the bunch and a distinctive earthy pine fragrance. Its woody stems are sometimes used as skewers for food, and the small, thin, pointed leaves are quite tough, so be sure to chop them thoroughly. Because of its strong flavor, use it judiciously or rosemary can easily overwhelm any baked good it is supposed to be enhancing.

ROSE WATER Distilled from the most fragrant of roses—often the damask rose—rose water is an ancient flavoring in the countries of the eastern Mediterranean. Rose water can be found in some supermarkets, specialty grocers, and markets catering to a Middle Eastern or Mediterranean clientele. **Storing:** After opening, rose water can be stored at room temperature for at least 1 year.

RUM Distilled from fermented sugarcane juice—sometimes with molasses included—rum is a good match for fruits, nuts, and chocolate. Full-flavored dark rum is the best type to use in baking.

SAGE A fresh green herb with an elongated pointed leaf, sage is muted in color and textured rather than smooth. It has a musky flavor that enhances many soups and stews, and is often used in corn breads and dressing at Thanksgiving.

SALT There are a large variety of salts on the market these days, but whatever type you use for baking, the texture must be very fine or the salt will not disperse evenly in the dough or batter. In addition, large crystals may not dissolve entirely, resulting in pockets of salty crunchiness. Kosher salt is particularly good for baking, because it is free of any chemical additives, but before measuring you should grind it into powder, either in a salt grinder or in a coffee/spice grinder. All coarse salts can be ground this way. Fine granules of sea salt are also a good choice. Regular table salt is the standard type used in baking recipes, and it will work just fine in all the recipes here; however, it does contain a number of additives that can lend a chemical or bitter taste to food.

SESAME SEEDS Native to the Mediterranean, sesame seeds were pressed and used for cooking oil and medicine by the ancient Egyptians. They were introduced to America in the seventeenth century by African slaves, who called them *benne,* and are currently grown throughout the South. The seeds have a unique, nutty flavor, and are available hulled (creamy white and best for baking) or unhulled (red, yellow, brown, and black). **Storing:** Sesame seeds have a high oil content, so they turn rancid quickly. Store in an airtight container or resealable plastic bag in the freezer for 6 to 8 months.

TOASTING SESAME SEEDS Place a dry (not nonstick) skillet over medium heat. When the pan is hot, add the sesame seeds and cook, stirring frequently, until they are lightly browned, 2 to 3 minutes. They will not brown evenly, but will be a mixture of beige and brown. Pour immediately onto a plate or baking sheet to cool completely before using.

SILVER LEAF Silver leaf, tissue-thin sheets of pounded silver, should be pure silver and culinary grade when used in dessert garnishing. See Gold Leaf on page 52 for information on how to use and store silver leaf. It is also available in petal and powder forms.

SOUR CREAM see Other Dairy Products, page 32

STRAWBERRIES Cultivated since ancient times, these shiny red berries with jaunty green tops are by far the country's favorite berry. And what's not to like? They are beautiful, fragrant, sweet, and are as delicious out of hand as they are in dessert. Their season runs from May through September, although they can be found in markets year-round.

There are fields in California that now produce strawberries all year, but these berries are never as sweet and luscious as in their traditional season. Look for berries that are shiny, plump, and red from top to bottom, the darker the better—white shoulders indicate they were picked before fully ripe, and will not have the sweet flavor you crave. The best-looking berries are always on the top, so turn the container over and examine the rest of the fruit, looking for ripeness, moisture, and/or mold. Wild strawberries, also called *fraises des bois,* are tiny, elongated and highly perfumed. If you can find them, buy them and savor each one. Strawberries deteriorate quickly and are best eaten within a day or two of purchase (if you can wait that long). **Storing:** Keep in their basket in the refrigerator for 1 or 2 days. If the basket shows signs of moisture, turn the berries out onto a paper towel–lined plate, cover with another towel, and return to the refrigerator.

SUGAR see page 24

SWEETENED CONDENSED MILK Invented by Gail Borden in the 1800s, this thick, golden, canned dairy product is a combination of whole milk and sugar (about 40 percent sugar), reduced until 60 percent of the water has been evaporated. The result is a very sweet, lightly caramel-flavored, thickened milk that is popular in some puddings, candies, and cakes. Evaporated milk, while it is also reduced until 60 percent of its water is gone, has no added sugar, so the two cannot be substituted for each other. **Storing:** Store unopened cans at room temperature. Once opened, any leftovers should be transferred to a storage container, refrigerated, and used within 3 to 5 days.

TANGERINES Tangerines are the most popular members of the mandarin group of citrus, which features fruit with loose, easy-to-peel skins and easy-to-separate segments. Their juice is a lovely blend of rich sweetness with a touch of tart acidity, and they can be used in any preparation that calls for orange juice. As with most citrus, look for fruit that feels heavy for its size and has small pores (an indication of juiciness). **Storing:** Unless you'll be consuming the fruit within a few days, tangerines are best stored in a plastic bag in the refrigerator, where they will keep for a week or more.

TAPIOCA FLOUR A powdered form of tapioca—a starch extracted from the root of the cassava plant—tapioca flour is used as a thickener for fruit pies, cobblers, crisps, and such. Like cornstarch, it has twice the thickening ability of wheat flour, and produces a natural-looking gel, neither cloudy like wheat flour nor shiny like cornstarch. It can be found in natural food stores and some specialty markets. Do not substitute quick-cooking or pearl tapioca for tapioca flour—the resulting texture will be quite different.

THYME A fresh green herb with tiny round leaves on long thin stems, thyme is popular in French cooking, especially in Provence, where it grows wild. Its friendly, earthy fragrance makes it a good ingredient in many savory baked goods, from tarts to breads. The leaves can be a bit tough, so make sure you chop them before adding the herb to your dough or filling.

WALNUTS California is the largest producer of flavorful walnuts, growing over 90 percent of the world's supply. Most of them are the English, or Persian variety, which has a strong, earthy flavor tempered with a buttery sweetness that is especially welcome in desserts and breads. Walnuts can quickly turn bitter and unpalatable, though, so buy them from shops that have a high turnover, preferably a bulk section where you can test one for freshness. Be sure to buy raw, shelled, unsalted walnuts for baking. They are available as halves and pieces. If you've ever tried to crack walnuts and remove the nuts intact, you'll appreciate the high price of walnut halves. **Storing:** Walnuts have a tendency to turn rancid quickly, so although they will keep in an airtight container at room temperature for up to a few months, they are best stored in the refrigerator (4 to 6 months) or the freezer (9 to 12 months) until needed.

TOASTING WALNUTS Toast on a baking sheet in a 350°F oven for 7 to 9 minutes, until the meat is crisp and the aroma is strong. Transfer to a plate to cool completely before using.

WHITE CHOCOLATE see Chocolate, page 37

YEAST see Leaveners, page 34

YOGURT see Other Dairy Products, page 32

It is fitting to begin this baking book with breads, since they are the seed from which all other baking has evolved. Bread has sustained humans for literally thousands of years, and surely this has something to do with the universally joyful reaction we all have to the warm, yeasty aroma of baking bread. Just look at the line outside a favorite neighborhood bakery on weekend mornings, the tantalizing scents of freshly baked breads and pastries drawing people in. The bread renaissance that took root in this country nearly 30 years ago has been blossoming ever since. It seems that every large city, and many a small one, has a wonderful bread bakery manned by a skilled artisan dedicated to his or her craft, turning out loaves rich in integrity and flavor.

"Well," you might think, "if that's true, why make bread at home?" And the answer is . . . for the sheer joy of it. Bread making is such a pleasurable experience. The earthy, pungent smell of yeast. The silky, slightly sticky feeling of the dough. The satisfaction of pushing and shaping dough into loaves. The knowledge that bread is alive, full of living organisms that create complex flavors and connect us to ancient civilizations. Added bonuses include the mouth-watering aromas that fill the house as the loaves bake, and the love and appreciation from friends and family, amazed that you took the time to bake bread from scratch.

A Primer on Breads

Bread is forgiving and resilient, so it's a good place to begin if you're new to baking. And if you already love to bake, it's a good place to hone your skills, for, as many a professional bread baker can attest, the quest for truly great bread is addictive and consuming. Bread baking is not difficult—let's face it, people were making bread and cooking it on rocks 2,000 years ago, using unrefined flour and unpredictable yeast. As always, an understanding of the ingredients and how they work together will shed light on a subject that can be mysterious. Let's take a look at the main ingredients in bread and then explore the best way to combine them for the ultimate artisanal loaf at home.

THE BUILDING BLOCKS OF BREAD

Flour is responsible for the structure of bread, as well as some of its flavor and its beautifully browned crust. There are several types of flour to choose from.

FLOUR

WHEAT FLOUR Wheat is the only grain that has ample supplies of glutenin and gliaden, the two proteins needed to form gluten. These two proteins, when combined with liquid and exercised by stirring and kneading, form gluten strands. The strands link together and become longer and stronger as kneading continues. The web of gluten that develops is like a flexible fishing net woven throughout a loaf of bread. This net traps the little bubbles of carbon dioxide given off by the feeding yeast and expands as the bubbles proliferate, allowing the bread to rise.

Without a strong network of flexible gluten strands, bread cannot rise properly, so it is important to choose a flour that contains high levels of these two proteins. Bread flour has the optimum percentage of protein (12 to 14 percent), but you can also find high levels of protein in unbleached all-purpose flour (Gold Medal, King Arthur, and Pillsbury are all good choices). The recipes here can be made using either bread flour or unbleached all-purpose flour. Do not use bleached all-purpose flour, as it contributes little flavor and may not contain enough protein to form sufficient gluten strands for bread development and expansion. Pastry flour, cake flour, and low-protein Southern flour have even less protein and are to be avoided in bread making, though they can be wonderful in pastries and cakes. Store your flour airtight and use it within a year—it makes a difference.

SPECIALTY FLOURS Other grains, such as corn, rye, buckwheat, oat, and spelt, may contain some amount of the two vital proteins, but not enough of them to form the gluten network. Perhaps surprisingly, whole wheat flour is among these specialty flours. While it has the proteins necessary for gluten development, it also contains the bran portion of the wheat kernel, responsible for the health benefits and brown color of whole wheat flour. The ground bran has sharp, jagged edges that cut into the strands of gluten during kneading, preventing them from lengthening. If you've ever tried to make whole wheat bread with all whole wheat flour, you'll know what this means—the result is a leaden brick.

Breads made with specialty flours always have some bread flour or unbleached all-purpose flour to ensure formation of a baseline structure that will allow the bread to rise, yet still retain the flavor and health benefits of the specialty flour. Store specialty flours airtight in the freezer to prolong their short shelf life.

YEAST

Yeast are the microscopic, single-cell living organisms that make bread rise. Feeding on the sugars in the starch of the flour, the yeast multiply. The by-products of their feeding—carbon dioxide and alcohol—create the breads we love. Bubbles of carbon dioxide are caught in the gluten web, causing the dough to expand. The alcohol adds flavor to the bread, but, if the dough is left unattended for too long, too much alcohol can develop, causing a pronounced alcohol flavor that ruins the bread.

There are several types of yeast available, and they are explored in depth on page 34. If you are new to bread baking, you'll want to read this section before you proceed, to learn about the varieties and how to work with each one for optimal results.

tips for success   Converting Yeast in Recipes

The recipes in this chapter offer the option of using either active dry or instant yeast, though the measurements are slightly different. If you need to convert any of your existing recipes, these conversion guidelines will help:

For each teaspoon of active dry yeast: Use ¾ teaspoon instant yeast (or multiply the weight of the active dry yeast by .75).

For each teaspoon of instant yeast: Use 1¼ teaspoons active dry yeast (or multiply the weight of the instant yeast by 1.25).

LIQUID

Water is the most commonly used liquid in breads, and quality matters. Most tap water is fine, but it's a good idea to know your water—if it is heavily chlorinated, use bottled water. The minerals in water can affect the dough as well. Very hard water (lots of minerals) will slow down the fermentation of your dough, whereas very soft water (a low mineral content) can make dough soft and sticky. In most cases, though, plain tap water will produce delicious bread.

Sometimes milk or buttermilk is used in bread, contributing flavor, fat (which softens the crumb), and sugar, resulting in a lovely browned crust. Both of these liquids serve to strengthen the gluten network as well. Eggs are sometimes added to doughs to enrich them, and they certainly add color and flavor to any baked good. Yolks in particular, with their fat and lecithin, add more color, flavor, and textural benefits than whites, which can make bread dry. Breads made with whole eggs often also contain milk, sugar, and butter or oil—all or any of which make up for the drying effects of the whites.

SALT

Bread made without salt is strangely flavorless, so don't leave it out. Salt not only enhances flavor, it also slows down the fermentation process, and a long, slow rise results in better flavor. Salt is hygroscopic, which means it attracts and bonds with water, so salt helps bread stay soft and fresh longer by retaining moisture. Fine sea salt or iodized table salt will work in the recipes in this book. Salts with larger crystals don't pack tightly or dissolve quickly, so if you wish to use them be sure to grind them first.

SUGAR

Many recipes call for adding sugar to the warm water that activates yeast. Yeast love to eat sugar, so adding a pinch of sugar starts the feeding frenzy immediately and proves that the yeast are alive and working. Sugar also adds sweetness to bread doughs, and, because it is hygroscopic (attracts and bonds with moisture), it keeps them from getting stale. But too much sugar in a recipe will rob some of the liquid needed for the formation of gluten, resulting in less gluten and a weak structure.

TYPES OF BREAD

There are many ways to categorize the great variety of breads available. Two classifications are particularly descriptive and useful when referring to bread at home. The first classifies breads by their fat, or richness. Bread made with milk, butter, oil, and sometimes sugar is known as **enriched dough**, whereas bread made with little or no fat, such as baguettes and many hearth breads, is known as **lean dough**.

The second classification refers to the method used to make the bread. For **straight dough**, the ingredients are mixed all at once. For **pre-ferment dough**, part of the dough is begun ahead of time and fermented, then added to the final dough. The most well-known type of pre-ferment is sourdough starter. Since there are several types of pre-ferments, let's take a closer look at each one and how they differ from one another.

PRE-FERMENTS

Pre-ferments are jump-starts for bread dough. They involve mixing flour, water, and yeast and allowing the mixture to ferment for several hours, days, or weeks, developing flavor in the process. The pre-ferment is then added to the dough during the mixing stage, imparting a level of flavor that would not be possible in a straight dough. Sometimes pre-ferments are grouped under the umbrella name of *starter* or *sponge,* but professional bakers know that each type of pre-ferment represents a very specific ratio of water to flour to yeast, as well as fermentation time.

PÂTE FERMENTÉE French for "fermented dough" or "old dough," pâte fermentée refers to a piece of dough that is saved from a previous batch that has been through its first fermentation. Unless you bake bread every day, you probably won't have a piece of old dough lying around, so some recipes will have you create new "old dough" specifically for that recipe. Old dough is firm, just like bread dough.

BIGA This is a saltless Italian pre-ferment that also has the firm consistency of bread dough, but is made specifically for the dough at hand rather than being cut from an earlier batch of dough. It is usually made 4 to 8 hours ahead, but may be refrigerated for up to 3 days before use. The absence of salt allows the yeast to feed freely, since salt slows the fermentation process.

POOLISH Saltless like *biga*, *poolish* is a wet pre-ferment, resembling pancake batter, and is made from equal weights of flour and water. The yeast feed more quickly with no salt and plenty of liquid, so poolish is used either the same day or within 24 hours.

SPONGE Though similar to *poolish* in that it is often made from equal weights of flour and water, a sponge includes more yeast; in fact, nearly all the yeast for the intended bread are included in the sponge. Because of the extra yeast, the sponge ferments quickly and is ready for use within a few hours.

STARTER Also called sourdough starter, this pre-ferment is made by capturing wild yeast in a mixture of flour and water. Wild yeast, present in the air around us and on the skins of many organically grown foods, are quickly attracted to the batterlike food source of a starter. Starters may be kept alive and fermenting for weeks, months, years, even centuries. This is done by feeding or refreshing the starter: When part of the starter is used for bread (or discarded), equal amounts of flour and water are added to the existing starter, providing a new food source for the remaining yeast.

Biga (Doughlike)   *Poolish* (Batterlike)

HOW TO MAKE BREAD

Ingredients and rising times may vary, but the steps to making a loaf of bread are reliably predictable. The steps below do not include a pre-ferment, which by definition is made before the dough is begun.

MEASURING THE INGREDIENTS

A scale is the best way to measure for any baking, and this is certainly true in bread making. Too much flour will result in a tough, dry dough. If you don't have a scale, follow the measuring guidelines on page 3.

MIXING THE DOUGH

Activate the yeast first, if necessary, with warm liquid. Then add the remaining ingredients and mix on low speed or stir by hand until the dough comes together and begins to develop gluten, 3 to 4 minutes with a mixer.

Although the recipes in this chapter refer to a stand mixer, you can certainly make bread by hand. Use a large bowl and a sturdy wooden spoon or spatula to stir the ingredients together. Once a rough dough has formed, turn it out of the bowl onto a work surface (lightly dusted with flour if the dough is very sticky) and knead by hand for 2 to 3 minutes. To do this, use the heels of your hands to push the dough away from you firmly, but not roughly or with too much pressure. The goal is to exercise the dough by gently bouncing or rubbing it against the counter, not to tear it. Fold the dough in half toward yourself, then rotate the dough clockwise one quarter turn. Repeat the pushing, folding and rotating for several minutes.

LETTING THE DOUGH REST

Professional bakers let the dough rest for 20 minutes to allow it to fully hydrate before the bulk of the kneading occurs. This rest, called the *autolyse,* improves the elasticity and flavor of the dough, and prevents it from overheating during a long kneading time. The autolyse gives the proteins in the flour time to fully hydrate. Once kneading begins again, gluten is developed quickly, and the "windowpane" is achieved in just a few short minutes. For the autolyse, cover the bowl with plastic wrap or a damp lint-free cotton towel during the autolyse. If you're in a hurry, you can skip this step.

KNEADING THE DOUGH

Kneading develops the gluten strands, lengthening and strengthening them into the network of gluten that is necessary for a good rise. You can do this step by hand, although a machine is helpful here, as hand-kneading the bread can be tiring and you might be tempted to stop before enough gluten has developed. In addition, most people tend to add extra flour while hand-kneading to keep the dough from sticking to their hands and countertop. But sticky doughs make the best bread, and the addition of extra flour can result in a dry, tough loaf. Regardless of the kneading method you choose, be careful you don't knead for too long. Over-kneading can over-oxidize the dough, adversely affecting its flavor. It can also overheat the dough and cause fermentation to occur more quickly than desired. When the dough looks smooth and elastic, stop kneading and check for gluten development.

HOW DO YOU TELL WHEN YOU'VE KNEADED ENOUGH?

A couple of methods can be used to test for gluten development. Professionals "pull a gluten windowpane," and you can, too (see page 67). This method won't work with dough that has lots of specialty grains, seeds, or fruit, because they will cause the dough to tear even if it has been kneaded long enough. To test such a dough, press firmly into the dough with the palm of your hand. If the impression fills quickly when you remove your hand and the dough is very stretchy and resilient, you're probably done.

LETTING THE DOUGH RISE (FERMENTATION OR FIRST RISE)

During rising, or fermentation, the yeast feed on the starches in the flour and produce carbon dioxide and alcohol as by-products. The carbon dioxide bubbles get trapped in the gluten network and the dough increases in volume. This rise develops flavor and gluten elasticity.

Transfer the dough to a tub or bowl that has been lightly oiled with vegetable oil or high-heat canola-oil spray. The thin layer of grease allows the dough to expand easily and fully. The top of the dough is usually lightly oiled as well, to prevent a skin from forming, which would impair expansion. It's helpful to use a straight-sided translucent

Pulling a Gluten Windowpane

Pinch off a small piece of dough. Stretch it between your fingers slowly and consistently, turning it for an even pull. If the gluten is fully developed, you'll be able to stretch it a couple of inches into a thin, translucent membrane with visible strands of gluten. If the dough tears easily, you'll need to knead longer.

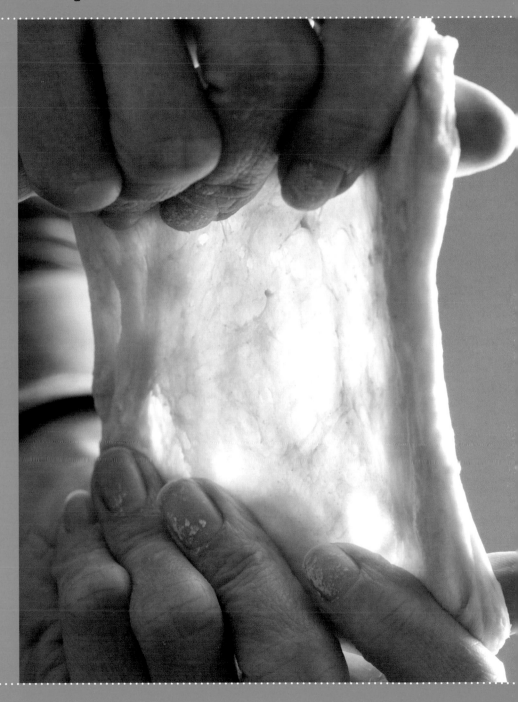

plastic tub and mark the beginning level of the dough on the outside with a pen, pencil, or piece of tape. This type of container makes it easy to tell when the dough has doubled (see below). You can also rise the bread in a bowl, although the doubling is a bit harder to define in a sloping container. Gently poke a finger into the dough—if the hole doesn't refill, it's probably finished rising.

Rising times may vary. If your kitchen is quite cool, it will take longer for the dough to rise. This is not necessarily a bad thing, for a long, slow rise develops the best flavor and texture in breads. If your kitchen is quite warm, the dough will rise quickly. The optimum temperature for dough fermentation is around 75°F, so keep this in mind as you make your dough and plan your schedule.

PUNCHING DOWN THE DOUGH

Punching down is not the violent action you might imagine, but instead a gentle releasing of some of the carbon dioxide built up in the bread. Turn the dough out of the tub or bowl onto a work surface lightly dusted with flour and press it down firmly to expel some of the gas. You might be tempted to knead the dough to release the gas, but the next step is shaping and you want the gluten to be relaxed, so resist the temptation.

Underrisen   Perfectly Risen

DIVIDING AND SHAPING THE DOUGH

If you are making rolls or more than one loaf, portion the dough with a bench scraper or a chef's knife. It's most precise to weigh each portion on a scale to ensure they are all the same size and will bake in the same amount of time, but if you don't have a scale, you can estimate the portions.

Shaping a loaf is all about creating tension. The dough must be taut so it keeps its shape as it rises. If the dough is slack, when it rises it will take on the shape of a blob, rather than the shape you wish. To create surface tension, you need to tighten the dough at the bottom of the loaf. Be sure your work surface is free of flour—the dough needs to slightly grab the surface rather than slipping across it.

To shape a round loaf or roll, press the dough into a flattened disk, then grab the edges and draw them up into the center, pinching all the edges together where they meet. Flip the dough over so the smooth side is up. Cup your hands around the dough and create extra tension by gently pulling the dough downward and tucking it under. Move the dough in a small circle between your cupped hands, passing it back and forth, and gently tucking around the edges to create extra tension. This takes some practice, but even if it's not perfect the first couple of times, a free-form loaf is simply that—not perfect.

Overrisen

To shape a rectangular loaf, press the dough into a flattened rectangle whose long sides are a couple of inches shorter than the long sides of the bread pan. Arrange the dough so a long side is parallel to the edge of your work surface. Fold the long side opposite you up into the center of the rectangle. Fold the long side nearest you into the center. Use the heel of your hand to press the two edges together. Turn the dough 90 degrees. Roll the short side opposite you toward the center, and with each roll press your thumbs into the crease to seal it and to create tension on the outside of the dough. When you reach the bottom edge closest to you, use your fingers to pinch the final seam closed. The dough should be the same length as your baking pan. If it is short, gently roll it back and forth on your work surface, pressing slightly to elongate the dough. If it is long, squeeze the dough together slightly to shorten it, and tuck the ends under if necessary. Always place the dough in the pan seam side down.

During the shaping process, if the gluten becomes too activated and the dough begins to "fight" you, refusing to take the shape you want, you'll need to allow some time for the dough to relax. Cover it loosely with plastic wrap or a damp lint-free cotton towel and let it rest for 10 to 20 minutes, then try again.

PROOFING THE DOUGH (SECOND RISE)

Once the dough is shaped and transferred to the baking pan or peel, it needs to rise, or ferment, again. Cover the shaped dough loosely (it needs room to expand) with plastic wrap or a damp lint-free towel and let it rise until not quite doubled in size. Just slightly under-proofing the dough means there is plenty of yeast activity left to provide a dramatic *oven spring,* the baker's term for the last burst of growth that occurs within the first few minutes of oven time. If the loaf is very under-proofed, there will be too much activity in the oven and some of the inside dough will burst through the crust, causing a crack or seam to open, usually at the side of

Preheat the oven 50°F hotter than the recipe states, then reduce the temperature once you've added the bread and closed the door. This makes up for the heat loss caused by the open door.

If you are using a baking stone, preheat to the temperature stated in the recipe. The stone retains heat so well it is unnecessary to compensate for heat loss caused by an open oven door.

the loaf. Conversely, if the loaf is overproofed, it will not rise or brown in the oven and will taste of alcohol. Usually, even the act of moving the overproofed loaf into the oven will cause it to collapse and flatten. If this happens, punch down the loaf, reshape it, and proof again. Although the flavor will be slightly compromised, the loaf will be saved. Note: You can only save it once, and this works best if the dough is overproofed by no more than 30 to 45 minutes. If the dough has been forgotten for hours, it's hopeless.

HOW TO TELL WHEN A LOAF IS SUFFICIENTLY PROOFED Basically, it will look like it took a deep breath. Professional bakers test their breads with the thumb test. At the side of the loaf, gently press your thumb about ¼ inch into the dough and remove it. The hole should fill up slowly. If it springs back quickly, the dough needs to be proofed longer. If it doesn't spring back at all, the dough is probably fully proofed, or even slightly overproofed. If you touch the dough and it collapses, it is definitely overproofed. Reshape and proof again.

GLAZING AND SLASHING THE LOAF

Some loaves are glazed before baking, wheareas others look better when left as they are or dusted lightly with flour. A thin film of egg wash adds shine to the crust as well as a deeper golden brown color. If a decorative coat of seeds is sprinkled over the surface, the glaze also acts as glue. Be gentle when brushing on the glaze so you don't deflate the dough. When a glaze is applied, it is always done before any slashing so there is a striking contrast in color between the surface of the bread and the inside of the slashes.

Slashing is not necessary, but is both decorative and functional. In the first few minutes of baking, as bread rises dramatically, slashes allow the bread to expand in a predetermined manner. As the bread rises, the slashes open in the oven, resulting in a beautiful pattern on top of the loaf. You can express your artistic creativity here, for there is no set pattern of slashes. You may slash bread with a *lame* (a French tool with a curved razor blade attached to a handle), razor blade, X-acto knife, paring knife, or serrated knife. Just be sure that whatever you use is very sharp; you don't want to tear or deflate the loaf. For most loaves, ¼-inch-deep slashes are sufficient; ½ inch is as deep as you want to go.

BAKING THE LOAF

Allow plenty of time for your oven to preheat. Using an oven thermometer (page 8) helps ensure your oven is accurate. Bread can be baked in pans, or in free-form shapes on a parchment- or silicone-lined baking sheet.

USING A BAKING STONE If you are baking free-form loaves or pizza, a baking or pizza stone is highly recommended (page 11). Purchase the thickest one you can find; it will hold heat better. The stone simulates a hearth oven, radiating heat to create a beautifully dry and crispy crust. When using a baking stone, allow at least 30 minutes, and preferably 1 hour, for the stone to fully preheat. Position the stone on the bottom of the oven, unless there is an electric heating element or gas vents (neither of those should be covered), in which case you should place the stone on the lowest oven rack. Proof your bread or pizza on a semolina or flour-dusted pizza peel for easy transfer to the stone.

If you don't have a pizza peel, turn a baking sheet upside down, line it with parchment paper, and proof on this, sliding the parchment paper and bread off the baking sheet and onto the stone. You can leave the parchment paper attached until the bread is finished baking. Be sure to use professional-quality parchment paper, as anything less may burn in the high heats required for pizza and artisan loaves. If transferring a loaf of bread from a peel or pan is too intimidating, you can also simply bake your bread on a baking sheet lined with parchment paper or a silicone mat, setting the pan directly on the baking stone.

USING STEAM Many artisan breads benefit from steam during the first few minutes of baking. The steam keeps the crust moist and flexible, allowing the bread to expand fully. Professional bread ovens have steam injectors that release steam with the push of a button, but home bakers use other methods. One option is to fill a spray bottle with water and mist the loaf before it goes into the oven (do not mist loaves that have been dusted with flour as they will get gummy). The other option is to heat an empty heavy-duty baking sheet or pan near the top of the oven. When you set the bread in the oven, toss a handful of ice cubes or pour ½ cup of tap water into the hot pan and quickly close the door. Either will turn to steam almost immediately, filling the oven with the moisture needed. Be careful to cover the glass on the open oven door with a towel while you are adding the ice or water—if any drips onto the glass, it may crack.

HOW TO TELL WHEN BREAD IS DONE Many recipes suggest you thump the bottom of the loaf, listening for a hollow sound. Unless you bake every day, this technique is less than accurate. An instant-read thermometer is foolproof. Rich, butter and egg–laden breads are finished when their internal temperatures register 185° to 190°F, whereas leaner, crisper breads are finished at 200° to 205°F. To test the bread, remove it from the oven and close the door. If it's baked without a pan, put on oven mitts, flip the bread upside down, and insert the probe into the bottom of the loaf—you don't want to damage the attractive surface. The tip of the probe should be angled so it is near the center of the bread, as this is the last area to cook through. Wait for the temperature to register, then return the loaf to the oven or transfer it to a cooling rack. Test breads baked in a pan by inserting the probe just above the edge of the pan, angled downward into the center of the loaf.

COOLING THE LOAF

Always cool bread on a rack so air can circulate around it evenly. Sandwich-style loaves may be left in their baking pans until cool enough to handle. If the sides seem a bit soft, return the bread to the oven for 5 to 8 minutes, without the baking pan, to crisp them.

STORING BREAD

In the best of all worlds, bread would be eaten the same day it was baked. Realistically speaking, there are going to be leftovers. Since bread begins to stale almost as soon as it is removed from the oven, the key is to keep the loaf from drying out. Plastic is the best material to retain moisture but ruins the crispy crust we all love. A paper bag or breadbox is better for the crust and fine for the first day or two, but the crumb dries out quickly. Since it's easier to crisp a crust than reintroduce moisture to the crumb, plastic is the better solution. Put the loaf in a resealable plastic bag or wrap it tightly in plastic wrap. Reheat the bread as described in each recipe. Or you can slice all the leftovers at once and then group the slices in serving sizes (2 to 4 slices) and wrap in plastic. Once all the slices have been portioned and wrapped, put the portions in a resealable plastic freezer bag and freeze. This makes it easy to pull out only what you need for the day.

OLD-FASHIONED WHITE LOAF

MAKES 1 LOAF Mass-produced sandwich bread has given white bread an undeserved bad reputation. The homemade version is a whole different species. Real white bread has a soft but sturdy crumb that is perfect for sandwiches or toast, and a neutral flavor that encourages you to pair it with just about anything. This is a fun bread to make with kids because the silky-smooth dough is easy to mix and knead, even by hand. For a real treat, make the sweet monkey bread variation and watch them go wild. The cheddar-mustard variation is fabulous with all kinds of meat and makes an over-the-top grilled cheese sandwich.

INGREDIENTS

¼ cup (2 ounces) warm water (110° to 115°F)

1 teaspoon sugar

1 tablespoon active dry yeast, or 2¼ teaspoons instant yeast

1 cup (8 ounces) warm whole milk (110° to 115°F)

2 tablespoons (1 ounce) unsalted butter, melted

3 cups (15 ounces) bread flour or unbleached all-purpose flour

1½ teaspoons salt

1 egg, lightly beaten

EQUIPMENT

Small Bowl, Whisk, Medium Bowl, Stand Mixer Fitted with a Dough Hook Attachment, 10- to 12-inch Straight-Sided Translucent Plastic Tub or Mixing Bowl, Bowl Scraper, 9 by 5-inch Loaf Pan, Small Pastry Brush, Instant-Read Thermometer, Cooling Rack, Serrated Knife

1 MIX, REST, AND KNEAD THE DOUGH: Place the water, sugar, and yeast in the small bowl and whisk to blend. Allow the mixture to sit for 10 minutes, or until the yeast is activated and foamy or bubbling. In the medium bowl, whisk together the warm milk and melted butter.

2 Place the flour and salt in the bowl of the stand mixer. Mix for 1 minute on medium speed to blend. Add the yeast mixture and milk mixture and mix on medium speed just until the dough comes together, 2 to 3 minutes. Cover the bowl with plastic wrap or a damp lint-free cotton towel and let the dough rest for 20 minutes to allow it to fully hydrate before further kneading. Turn the speed to medium-low and continue to knead until the dough is firm, elastic, and smooth, 3 to 6 minutes. (To mix by hand, mix the flour and salt in a large bowl, add the yeast mixture and milk mixture, and mix until a dough forms. Turn the dough out onto a work surface and knead until firm, elastic, and smooth, about 8 to 10 minutes.)

3 RISE THE DOUGH (FIRST RISE): Lightly oil the tub or bowl, scrape the dough into the tub, and lightly coat the surface of the dough with a little oil. Cover the bowl with plastic wrap or a damp lint-free cotton towel and let the dough rise until doubled, 45 to 60 minutes (longer if the room is cold). If you are using a tub, be sure to mark the starting level of the dough with a pencil or piece of tape so it's easy to tell when the dough has doubled.

GETTING AHEAD The dough can be prepared through Step 5 and chilled overnight. To do this, allow the dough to rise until it is ⅔ up the sides of the pan. Cover loosely with plastic and refrigerate overnight. The next day, let the bread sit at room temperature for 1 hour, or until the dough has risen ½ to 1 inch above the rim of the pan, before baking. It may take a few extra minutes to bake—take the internal temperature with an instant-read thermometer to be sure it is cooked through.

4 PUNCH DOWN AND SHAPE THE LOAF: Turn the dough out onto a lightly floured work surface. Press down on the dough firmly to expel some of the air bubbles, but don't knead the dough again or it will be too springy and difficult to shape (if this happens, simply cover the dough with plastic wrap or a damp lint-free cotton towel and let it rest for 10 to 15 minutes to give the gluten some time to relax). Shape the dough according to the directions on page 69. Lightly coat the loaf pan with melted butter, or a high-heat canola oil spray. Place the dough, seam side down, in the pan.

5 PROOF THE DOUGH (SECOND RISE): Lightly oil the top of the dough to keep it moist. Cover the pan loosely with plastic wrap or a damp lint-free cotton towel and allow the dough to rise again until its top is ½ to 1 inch above the rim of the pan, 45 to 60 minutes.

6 GLAZE AND BAKE THE BREAD: Preheat the oven to 400°F and position an oven rack in the center. Brush the top of the loaf with a thin film of the beaten egg. Bake for 35 to 40 minutes, until the bread is golden brown and the internal temperature registers 200°F on an instant-read thermometer. Transfer to a rack to cool completely. Slice with the serrated knife.

STORING Wrap the bread in plastic and keep at room temperature for 3 to 4 days. For longer storage, double-wrap in plastic and freeze for up to 1 month. To reheat frozen bread, thaw on the counter for 1½ hours, or until it reaches room temperature, then unwrap and heat in a 400°F oven for 10 to 15 minutes, until the crumb is warmed and the crust is crisped.

Monkey Bread
Although this pull-apart bread is a kid favorite, adults are just as delighted by its sweet presence at the table.

Prepare the dough as directed through Step 3. Turn the dough out onto your work surface and press on it firmly to expel all the air bubbles. Using a pair of kitchen scissors or a bench scraper, cut the dough into pieces about the size of fresh cherries.

In a small saucepan over low heat, melt 1 stick (4 ounces) of unsalted butter until it is liquid but not too hot to the touch and pour into a bowl. In a separate medium bowl, stir together 1¼ cups (8¾ ounces) sugar and 4 teaspoons ground cinnamon.

Working with a few balls of dough at a time, coat them in the melted butter and then roll them in the cinnamon-sugar. Set the balls next to each other in the prepared loaf pan, filling one layer with dough before stacking the remaining balls on top. When all the dough has been coated and added to the pan, gently press it into an even layer. Cover the pan with plastic wrap or a lint-free cotton towel and proof. Omit the egg glaze, and bake for about 40 minutes at 375°F instead of 400°F to keep the sugar from burning. The bread should be golden brown and register 200°F on an instant-read thermometer.

Cheddar Cheese-Mustard Loaf
Grate 4 ounces of sharp cheddar cheese using the large holes of a box grater. Toss the cheese with 1 tablespoon of flour and set aside. Add 3 tablespoons Dijon mustard to the dough along with the milk mixture in Step 2. Knead the dough for about 5 minutes. Add the floured cheese to the dough and knead for 2 or 3 minutes longer. If the dough is very sticky, add a tablespoon or two of flour, but it should be tacky to the touch. Follow the recipe as directed above but bake at 375°F instead of 400°F for about 40 minutes, until the bread is golden brown and registers 200°F on an instant-read thermometer.

RUSTIC OLIVE AND THYME BREAD

MAKES 2 LOAVES Dense and chewy, studded with olives and fragrant with thyme, this bread is a perfect match for the bright flavors of summer. It pairs deliciously with roasted red peppers, eggplant, and grilled lamb or chicken. The poolish, a type of pre-ferment, gives it a wonderful, slightly sour note. Leftover bread can be toasted and spread with young goat cheese to use as croutons in a mixed green salad.

INGREDIENTS

POOLISH (PRE-FERMENT)

1 cup (8 ounces) warm water

½ teaspoon active dry yeast, or generous ¼ teaspoon instant yeast

1 cup (5 ounces) bread flour or unbleached all-purpose flour

DOUGH

½ cup (4 ounces) warm water

1 teaspoon sugar

1½ teaspoons active dry yeast, or 1⅛ teaspoons instant yeast

3 cups (15 ounces) bread flour or unbleached all-purpose flour

1½ teaspoons salt

2 tablespoons olive oil

1 tablespoon plus 1 teaspoon finely chopped fresh thyme

1 cup (4 ounces) pitted and coarsely chopped olives, such as Kalamata

EQUIPMENT

Medium Bowl, Whisk, Stand Mixer Fitted with a Dough Hook Attachment, 10- to 12-inch Straight-Sided Translucent Plastic Tub or Mixing Bowl, Bowl Scraper, Two Bannetons (Bread Baskets, Optional), Baking Sheet, Parchment Paper or a Silicone Mat, Small Pastry Brush, Lame or Razor or Chef's Knife, Instant-Read Thermometer, Cooling Rack, Serrated Knife

1 **MAKE THE *POOLISH*:** Pour the water into a medium bowl and whisk in the yeast. Let the mixture stand for 10 minutes, or until the yeast is activated and looks creamy. Stir in the flour and mix until no patches of dry flour remain. Cover the bowl with plastic wrap and set aside for 4 to 6 hours (or up to 12 hours) at room temperature, or 24 hours in the refrigerator.

2 **MIX, REST, AND KNEAD THE DOUGH:** Pour the warm water into the bowl of the stand mixer. Add the sugar and yeast, whisk by hand to blend, and allow the mixture to sit for 10 minutes, or until the yeast is activated and foamy or bubbling. Add the *poolish* and whisk by hand to blend well. Add the flour, salt, olive oil, thyme, and olives. Knead the dough on low speed until it comes together in a cohesive mass, about 3 or 4 minutes. Cover the bowl with plastic wrap or a damp lint-free cotton towel and let the dough rest for 20 minutes to allow it to fully hydrate before further kneading. Turn the mixer to medium-low and continue to knead until the dough is firm, elastic, and smooth, 3 to 6 minutes.

3 **RISE THE DOUGH (FIRST RISE):** Lightly oil the tub or bowl, scrape the dough into the tub, and lightly coat the surface of the dough with a little oil. Cover the bowl tightly with plastic wrap and let the dough rise until doubled, 1½ to 2 hours (longer if the room is cold). If you are using a tub, be sure to mark the starting level of the dough with a pencil or piece of tape so it's easy to tell when the dough has doubled.

4 **PUNCH DOWN, DIVIDE, AND SHAPE THE LOAF:** Turn the dough out onto a lightly floured work surface. Press down on the dough firmly to expel some of the air bubbles, but don't knead the dough again or it will be too springy and difficult to shape (if this happens, simply cover the dough with plastic wrap or a damp lint-free cotton towel and

Kalamata olives have a big, meaty presence in bread, adding a substantial burst of salty flavor to every bite. Feel free to use whatever olives you like, as long as they are not the sliced, canned variety. Some bakers prefer dry-cured olives to avoid having excess brine taint the flavor and color of the dough. If you use brined olives, pat them dry with paper towels. Whether you buy the olives pitted or pit them yourself, double-check for pits by gently squeezing each olive before you chop it to ensure no one breaks a tooth while enjoying your handiwork.

GETTING AHEAD **The *poolish* can be made up to 24 hours in advance and kept in the refrigerator, covered. The dough can be prepared and risen through Step 5 and refrigerated overnight before baking. To do this, let the loaves rise until they are slightly less than doubled in size, cover loosely with plastic wrap, and refrigerate overnight. The next day, let the dough sit at room temperature for 1 hour before baking. It may take a few extra minutes to bake—take the internal temperature with an instant-read thermometer to be sure they are cooked through.**

let it rest for 10 to 15 minutes to give the gluten some time to relax). Divide the dough in half and shape into two round, taut loaves according to the directions on page 69.

5 PROOF THE DOUGH (SECOND RISE): Dust the *bannetons* generously with flour and set the loaves in them with their seam sides facing up. If not using *bannetons,* line the baking sheet with parchment paper or a silicone mat and place the loaves on the sheet about 5 inches apart, seam sides down. Brush the loaves lightly with oil. Cover loosely with plastic wrap or a lint-free cotton towel. Allow the loaves to rise until they are almost doubled in size and look like they have taken a deep breath, 45 to 60 minutes.

6 BAKE THE BREAD: Preheat the oven to 425°F and position a rack in the lower third of the oven. If using *bannetons,* gently turn the loaves out directly onto the prepared baking sheet, about 5 inches apart. Be careful not to deflate the dough as you do this, and don't try to move the loaves around once they are on the baking sheet as they may collapse. Slash a pattern into the top of the dough with a *lame,* razor blade, or chef's knife. Bake for 25 to 30 minutes, until their internal temperature registers 200°F on an instant-read thermometer. Transfer to a rack to cool completely. Slice with a serrated knife.

STORING **Olive and thyme bread will keep at room temperature, uncovered, for 2 days. Cover any cut areas with a piece of plastic wrap. For longer storage, double-wrap in plastic and freeze for up to 1 month. Thaw on the counter for 2 hours, or until it reaches room temperature; then unwrap and reheat in a 400°F oven for 10 to 15 minutes, until the crumb is warmed and the crust is crisped.**

PIZZA DOUGH

MAKES 1 POUND, 12 OUNCES OF DOUGH, ENOUGH FOR 2 (12-INCH) PIZZAS OR 4 (7- TO 8-INCH) PIZZAS

Pizza is a hands-down favorite anytime, anywhere. And while you can get good pizza when eating out, truly great pizza is much easier to find at home, mostly because you can top it exactly the way you want. This dough is a good starting point for your creations and can be stored in the refrigerator for 24 hours or frozen for up to 1 month. If you like lots of toppings, roll the crust a bit thicker so it can support their weight and moisture. If you like a thin crust, keep your toppings spare and packed with flavor. To help the dough slide onto the pizza stone, dust your pizza peel with semolina. If you don't have semolina, cornmeal will work, but it burns more quickly.

INGREDIENTS

¼ cup (2 ounces) warm water (110° to 115°F)

2¼ teaspoons active dry yeast, or
1¾ teaspoons instant yeast

1 cup (8 ounces) water

3 tablespoons (1½ ounces) olive oil,
plus 1 tablespoon for brushing

3¼ cups (16¼ ounces) bread flour
or unbleached all-purpose flour

1½ teaspoons salt

Semolina or cornmeal

EQUIPMENT

Stand Mixer Fitted with a Dough Hook Attachment, Whisk, 10- to 12-inch Straight-Sided Translucent Plastic Tub or Mixing Bowl, Bowl Scraper, Baking or Pizza Stone, Rolling Pin (Optional), Pastry Brush, Pizza Peel, or Baking Sheet, Parchment Paper, Large Metal Spatula or Cake Lifter (Optional), Pizza Cutter or Chef's Knife

1 MIX, REST, AND KNEAD THE DOUGH: Pour the warm water into the bowl of the stand mixer. Add the yeast, whisk by hand to blend, and allow the mixture to sit for 5 to 10 minutes, until the yeast is activated and looks creamy. Add the 1 cup water and the 3 tablespoons olive oil and whisk by hand to blend. Add the flour and salt. Knead the dough on low speed for 2 minutes, or until it comes together in a cohesive mass. Cover the bowl with plastic wrap or a damp lint-free cotton towel and let the dough rest for 20 minutes to allow it to fully hydrate before further kneading. Turn the mixer to medium-low and continue to knead until the dough is firm, elastic, and smooth, 3 to 6 minutes.

2 RISE THE DOUGH: Lightly oil the tub or bowl, scrape the dough into the tub, and lightly coat the surface of the dough with a little oil. Cover tightly with plastic wrap and let the dough rise at room temperature until doubled, 45 to 60 minutes (longer if the room is cold). If you are using a tub, be sure to mark the starting level of the dough with a pencil or piece of tape so it's easy to tell when the dough has doubled.

3 PREPARE THE OVEN: Place the baking or pizza stone in the oven. Preheat the oven to 500°F. Be sure to allow 30 minutes to 1 hour for the stone to fully heat.

4 DIVIDE AND SHAPE THE DOUGH: Turn the dough out onto a lightly floured work surface. Press down on the dough firmly to expel some of the air bubbles, but don't

The dough for these pizzas freezes so well you'll never have to order delivery pizza again. Just follow the steps in "Getting Ahead" and, with a few pantry basics, you can have your favorite pizza any time. It's even better if cooked on a pizza stone, which simulates a hearth oven, blasting the bottom of the pizza with an enormous amount of heat, cooking it quickly, crisping it beautifully, and creating the crust you've always dreamed of.

GETTING AHEAD **Pizza dough may be prepared a day ahead through Step 4: Expel the air bubbles as described, then portion and shape into 2 to 4 round, taut balls according to the directions on page 69. To refrigerate for up to 24 hours, dust a baking sheet lightly with flour, transfer the dough balls to the sheet, placing them about 3 inches apart, and cover the sheet with plastic wrap. The next day, let the dough sit at room temperature for 15 to 20 minutes before stretching the dough into a pizza.**

To freeze for up to 1 month, put each dough ball in a quart-size resealable plastic freezer bag, squeeze out as much air as possible, and seal tightly. To thaw, transfer to the refrigerator the day before you want to make pizza, or simply remove from the freezer and let thaw on the counter.

knead the dough again or it will be too springy and difficult to shape (if this happens, simply cover the dough with plastic wrap or a damp lint-free cotton towel and let it rest for 10 to 15 minutes to give the gluten some time to relax). Divide the dough in half (or quarters if making smaller individual pizzas). At this point, you can refrigerate or freeze all or some of the dough (see "Getting Ahead," at left).

5 Dust the top of the dough lightly with flour, then press down with your fingers (or use a rolling pin) to flatten the dough into a disk about 12 inches in diameter. Alternatively, slip your hands, knuckles up, under the dough and lift it up, then gently stretch the dough by pulling your fists apart. Rotate the dough a little each time you pull so the dough is stretched into an even circle. Brush any excess flour from the surface and underside of the dough.

6 TOP THE PIZZA: Dust the pizza peel with semolina and set the dough round in the center of the peel (if you are using a baking sheet, center the round on a piece of parchment paper on the sheet). You can use the pizza recipes in this book, or apply the toppings of your choice, leaving a ½-inch border at the edges. The toppings should be in a fairly thin layer. Otherwise they will weigh down the dough and make it soggy.

7 BAKE THE PIZZA: Shake the peel or sheet forward and back to make sure the pizza is loose enough to slide. If it's stuck, use a spatula to lift up the dough and toss a bit of semolina underneath. Once the pizza moves freely, gently shake the peel or sheet until the pizza is at the very front edge. Open the oven door and set the front edge of the peel at the back of the baking stone. With a quick jerk, remove the peel and allow the pizza to settle on the stone. Bake for 7 to 9 minutes, until the dough is golden brown at the edges and across the bottom (use a metal spatula to lift the pizza slightly to check). Slip the peel under the pizza to remove it from the oven (or use a large metal spatula or a cake lifter) and transfer to a cutting board. Brush the edge of the pizza with the 1 tablespoon olive oil to give the golden crust a beautiful shine. Use a pizza cutter or chef's knife to cut the pizza into 8 wedges and serve immediately.

STORING **Pizza is best when served immediately after it is baked. Leftovers should be wrapped in plastic and refrigerated for up to 3 days. Reheat, unwrapped, in a 450°F oven for 5 to 6 minutes, until hot and crisp.**

Pizza Margherita

MAKES 1 (12-INCH) PIZZA

INGREDIENTS

½ recipe Pizza Dough (page 77), prepared through Step 5

¼ cup (2 ounces) tomato sauce

6 ounces fresh mozzarella cheese, chilled (or ¾ cup [3 oz] of packaged, pregrated cheese)

4 large leaves fresh basil, coarsely chopped

EQUIPMENT

Serrated Knife or Box Grater

1 Spread the tomato sauce over the pizza dough, leaving a ½-inch border. Slice the mozzarella as thinly as possible (at least ¼-inch thin—a serrated knife works well here), or grate with a box grater. Arrange the cheese evenly over the sauce.

2 Bake the pizza according to Step 7 of the Pizza Dough recipe. Scatter the basil over the top and serve immediately.

Caramelized Onion and Blue Cheese Pizza

MAKES 1 (12-INCH) PIZZA

INGREDIENTS

½ recipe Pizza Dough (page 77), prepared through Step 5

2 medium onions, sliced ¼ inch thick

2 tablespoons (1 ounce) olive oil, plus more for brushing

2 ounces blue cheese

EQUIPMENT

10-inch Sauté Pan, Pastry Brush

1 In the sauté pan, cook the onions in the olive oil for 20 to 30 minutes over medium-high heat, until soft and golden brown in color. Cool to room temperature. Brush the center of the pizza dough lightly with olive oil. Spread the cooled onions over the crust, leaving a ½-inch border. Crumble the blue cheese evenly over the top.

2 Bake the pizza according to Step 7 of the Pizza Dough recipe. Serve immediately.

Pizza with Herb Salad and Lemon-Shallot Vinaigrette

MAKES 1 (12-INCH) PIZZA

INGREDIENTS

½ recipe Pizza Dough (page 77), prepared through Step 5

½ large shallot, very finely chopped

1 tablespoon freshly squeezed lemon juice

¼ teaspoon Dijon mustard

2 tablespoons (1 ounce) olive oil

Pinch salt and pepper

1 cup (1 ounce) packed arugula, baby spinach, or mixed greens

⅓ cup (¼ ounce) Italian parsley, leaves only

10 leaves basil, coarsely chopped

3 ounces fontina cheese, grated

EQUIPMENT

Small Bowl, Whisk, Medium Bowl

1 Make the vinaigrette and salad: In a small bowl, whisk together the shallot, lemon juice, and mustard. Whisk in the olive oil and season to taste with salt and pepper. In a medium bowl, toss the arugula, parsley, and basil together until thoroughly mixed.

2 Spread the fontina evenly over the pizza dough, leaving a ½-inch border. Bake the pizza according to Step 7 of the Pizza Dough recipe.

3 Toss the salad with the vinaigrette until all the leaves are evenly coated. Cover the pizza with the salad and serve immediately.

PESTO ROLLS

MAKES 8 (4-OUNCE) ROLLS These plump green rolls, heady with the fragrance of basil and garlic, are the perfect partner to a salad of juicy tomatoes and fresh, soft mozzarella. They also make mighty fine hamburger buns. Leftover rolls become irresistible croutons when cubed, sautéed in a little olive oil, and sprinkled with Parmesan cheese. The traditional pine nuts or walnuts have been left out of the pesto, but feel free to add a few tablespoons if you like.

INGREDIENTS

2 cups (1½ ounces) loosely packed fresh basil leaves

¼ cup (2 ounces) olive oil

¼ cup (1 ounce) freshly grated Parmesan cheese

4 cloves garlic, thinly sliced

¼ cup (2 ounces) olive oil

½ teaspoon plus 1½ teaspoons salt

1 cup (8 ounces) warm water (110° to 115°F)

1 tablespoon active dry yeast, or 2¼ teaspoons instant yeast

3¼ cups (16¼ ounces) bread flour or unbleached all-purpose flour

EQUIPMENT

Food Processor Fitted with a Metal Blade, Stand Mixer Fitted with a Dough Hook Attachment, Whisk, Bowl Scraper, 10- to 12-inch Straight-Sided Translucent Plastic Tub or Mixing Bowl, Baking Sheet, Parchment Paper or a Silicone Mat, Baking or Pizza Stone, Lame or Razor or Sharp Scissors, Instant-Read Thermometer, Cooling Rack

1 MAKE THE PESTO: Combine the basil, olive oil, Parmesan, garlic, and ½ teaspoon salt in the bowl of the food processor and process until very finely chopped and paste-like.

2 MIX, REST, AND KNEAD THE DOUGH: Place the warm water in the bowl of the stand mixer and sprinkle the yeast over the top. By hand, whisk in ¼ cup of the flour. Let the mixture sit for 10 minutes, or until the yeast is activated and looks foamy. Add the pesto and whisk by hand until well blended. Add the remaining 3 cups flour and the 1½ teaspoons salt. Attach the dough hook and blend on low until the dough begins to come together and form a cohesive mass, about 2 to 3 minutes. Cover the bowl with plastic wrap or a damp lint-free cotton towel and let the dough rest for 20 minutes to allow it to fully hydrate before further kneading. Scrape down the sides of the bowl and turn the dough over so everything gets mixed evenly. Knead on low speed until the dough is firm, elastic, and smooth, 3 to 6 minutes.

3 RISE THE DOUGH (FIRST RISE): Lightly oil the tub or bowl, scrape the dough into the tub, and brush the surface of the dough with a little oil. Cover tightly with plastic wrap and let the dough rise until doubled, about 1 hour (longer if the room is cold). If you are using a tub, be sure to mark the starting level of the dough with a pencil or piece of tape so it's easy to tell when the dough has doubled.

4 PUNCH DOWN, DIVIDE, AND SHAPE THE ROLLS: Turn the dough out onto a work surface. Press down on the dough firmly to expel some of the air bubbles, but don't knead the dough again or it will be too springy and difficult to shape (if this happens, simply cover the dough with plastic wrap or a damp lint-free cotton towel and let it rest for 10 to 15 minutes to give the gluten some time to relax). Divide the dough into 8 equal pieces (about

GETTING AHEAD **The dough can be prepared ahead through Step 4 and refrigerated overnight. To do this, let the rolls rise until they are slightly less than doubled in size, cover loosely with plastic wrap, and refrigerate overnight. The next day, let the rolls sit at room temperature for 35 minutes before baking. They may take a few extra minutes to bake—take the internal temperature to be sure they are cooked through.**

The rolls can be baked early in the day and reheated in a 400°F oven for 6 to 7 minutes. Store, uncovered, at room temperature for 1 day. They can also be baked ahead and frozen for 1 month. To freeze, let the rolls cool completely, then wrap them in plastic wrap and place inside a resealable plastic freezer bag. Thaw the rolls, spread apart on a baking sheet, at room temperature for 1½ hours, then reheat as directed above to crisp the crust and warm the center.

3¾ ounces each) and shape each one into a taut, round ball according to the directions on page 69. Place the rolls on the prepared baking sheet about 3 inches apart.

5 PROOF THE DOUGH (SECOND RISE): Cover the rolls loosely with plastic wrap or a damp lint-free cotton towel and let rise until almost doubled in size, 35 to 45 minutes. They should look like they took a deep breath and should pass the thumb test (page 70).

6 PREPARE THE OVEN: Place a baking or pizza stone in the oven. Preheat the oven to 400°F. Be sure to allow 30 minutes to 1 hour for the stone to fully heat.

7 BAKE THE ROLLS: Remove the plastic wrap or towel and dust the top of the rolls lightly with a sprinkling of flour—don't go crazy here or you'll have a mouthful of flour. Use the *lame,* razor, or the tip of a pair of kitchen scissors to make a decorative slash or two in the top of each roll. Immediately place the pan in the oven on the baking stone or baking sheet. Bake for 15 to 18 minutes, until cooked through and the internal temperature registers 200°F on an instant-read thermometer. Transfer to a cooling rack. Serve warm or at room temperature.

HERBED FOUGASSE

MAKES 1 LARGE LOAF This Provençal bread is rustic, flavorful, and ready for a party. The large loaf (nearly the size of a baking sheet) feeds a small crowd, and the unique leaf pattern cut into the bread before baking gives it a striking presence. Feel free to change the herbs, or add some chopped olives, walnuts, or cheese. The olive oil in the dough crisps the crust and adds an irresistible chewiness to the crumb.

INGREDIENTS

BIGA (PRE-FERMENT)

½ cup (4 ounces) warm water (110° to 115°F)

¼ teaspoon active dry yeast, or generous ⅛ teaspoon instant yeast

1 cup minus 1 tablespoon (4½ ounces) bread flour or unbleached all-purpose flour

DOUGH

½ cup (4 ounces) warm water (110° to 115°F)

½ teaspoon active dry yeast, or generous ¼ teaspoon instant yeast

2 tablespoons (1 ounce) olive oil

1¼ cups plus 1 tablespoon (7 ounces) bread flour or unbleached all-purpose flour

1½ teaspoons finely chopped fresh rosemary

1 teaspoon finely chopped fresh thyme

½ teaspoon salt

1 tablespoon olive oil

½ to 1 teaspoon kosher salt or coarse sea salt

1 teaspoon finely chopped mixture of fresh rosemary and thyme

EQUIPMENT

Medium Bowl, Whisk, Stand Mixer Fitted with a Paddle Attachment, 10- to 12-inch Straight-Sided Translucent Plastic Tub or Mixing Bowl, Bowl Scraper, Baking Sheet, Parchment Paper, Paring Knife or Lame or Bench Scraper, Baking or Pizza Stone (Optional), Pastry Brush, Instant-Read Thermometer, Cooling Rack, Serrated Knife (Optional)

1 MAKE THE *BIGA*: Pour the warm water into the medium bowl and whisk in the yeast. Let the mixture stand for 10 minutes, or until the yeast is activated and looks creamy. Stir in the flour and mix until it forms a rough dough. Turn onto a work surface and knead until smooth and elastic. Return to the bowl, cover with plastic wrap, and set aside for 4 to 6 hours (or up to 12 hours) at room temperature, or 24 hours in the refrigerator.

2 MIX, REST, AND KNEAD THE DOUGH: Pour the warm water into the bowl of the stand mixer. Add the yeast, whisk by hand to blend, and let the mixture stand until the yeast is activated and looks creamy, 5 to 10 minutes. Add the *biga* and the olive oil and mix on low speed for 1 minute. Add the flour, rosemary, thyme, and salt. Knead the dough on low speed until it comes together in a cohesive mass, about 2 to 3 minutes. Cover the bowl with plastic wrap or a damp lint-free cotton towel and let the dough rest for 20 minutes to allow it to fully hydrate before further kneading. Turn the mixer to medium-low and continue to knead until the dough is firm, elastic, and smooth, 4 to 6 minutes.

3 RISE THE DOUGH (FIRST RISE): Lightly oil the tub or bowl, scrape the dough into the tub, and lightly coat the surface of the dough with a little oil. Cover tightly with plastic wrap and let the dough rise until doubled in size, 1½ to 2 hours (longer if the room is cold). If you are using a tub, be sure to mark the starting level of the dough with a pencil or piece of tape so it's easy to tell when the dough has doubled.

4 PUNCH DOWN AND SHAPE THE DOUGH: Turn the dough out onto a lightly floured work surface. Press down on the dough firmly to expel some of the air bubbles, but don't knead the dough again or it will be too springy and difficult to shape (if this happens, simply cover the dough with plastic wrap or a lint-free cotton towel and let it rest for 10 to 15

GETTING AHEAD **The** *biga* **can**
be made 24 hours in advance and
kept, covered, in the refrigerator. The
dough can be prepared through Step
5 and refrigerated overnight before
baking. To do this, let the loaf rise for
15 minutes, then cover loosely with
plastic wrap, and refrigerate overnight.
The next day, let the bread sit at room
temperature for 20 minutes before
baking. It may take a few extra minutes
to bake—take the internal temperature
to be sure it is cooked through.

minutes to give the gluten some time to relax). Transfer the dough to the prepared baking sheet. If you will be using a baking or pizza stone to bake the bread, place the parchment paper and dough on the bottom of the baking sheet so you can slide them easily onto the stone. Press the dough into a large half circle that is about 12 inches across the flat bottom, 11 inches tall at the peak of the circle, and about ⅜ inch thick. Let the dough rest, covered with plastic wrap or a lint-free cotton towel, for 10 to 15 minutes. To make the design in the dough, use a very sharp paring knife or a *lame* (you don't want to pull or drag the dough) to make a slit down the center, then two or three slits at an angle on each side of the center so they resemble the veins in a leaf. Each slit should go all the way through the dough to the baking sheet. Gently stretch each slit so the cut edges are about 1½ inches apart, making decorative holes in the dough.

5 PROOF THE DOUGH (SECOND RISE): Cover the dough loosely with plastic wrap or a damp lint-free cotton towel. Allow the dough to rise until it is almost doubled in size and looks like it has taken a deep breath, 30 to 40 minutes.

6 PREPARE THE OVEN: Place a baking or pizza stone in the oven. Preheat the oven to 425°F. Be sure to allow 30 minutes to 1 hour for the stone to fully heat.

7 BAKE THE BREAD: Dimple the dough by gently pressing your fingertips into the dough about ¼ inch deep, taking care that you don't deflate the dough by pressing too vigorously or making too many indentations. Gently brush the surface of the dough with the olive oil. Sprinkle the salt and chopped herbs evenly over the top. Bake for 20 to 25 minutes, until the bread is golden brown and the internal temperature registers 200°F on an instant-read thermometer. Transfer to a rack and cool completely. Slice the bread with a serrated knife or simply let guests tear off pieces.

STORING **The** *fougasse* **will keep at room temperature, uncovered, for 2 days. Cover any**
cut areas with plastic wrap. For longer storage, double-wrap in plastic and freeze for up to 1
month. Thaw on the counter for 2 hours, or until room temperature. Place the thawed bread
in a 400°F oven for 10 to 15 minutes, until the crumb is warmed and the crust is crisped.

Moroccan-Spiced Fougasse Omit the rosemary and thyme both in and
on top of the dough. Add 1½ teaspoons Moroccan Spice Blend to the dough (page 136).

NINE-GRAIN WHOLE WHEAT HARVEST BREAD

MAKES 1 ROUND LOAF Whole wheat bread has many health advantages, but the best reason for making this loaf is because it tastes so good. Wholesale flour supply companies always offer several grain mixes to professional bakers; good-quality hot cereal mixes from the health food store are an excellent substitute. We particularly like the nine-grain version, but if you find a six-grain cereal, it will work just as well. Add a handful of additional sunflower, flax, or sesame seeds, if you like, for extra flavor and texture. Be sure to let the cereal mixture cool to room temperature—if it is too hot it will kill the yeast.

INGREDIENTS

½ cup (3 ounces) 9-grain hot cereal mix (not instant)

½ cup (4 ounces) boiling water

1 cup plus 2 tablespoons (9 ounces) warm water (110° to 115°F)

1 teaspoon sugar

1 tablespoon active dry yeast, or 2¼ teaspoons instant yeast

¼ cup (3 ounces) honey

2¾ cups (14 ounces) bread flour or unbleached all-purpose flour

¾ cup (4 ounces) whole wheat flour

1 teaspoon salt

EQUIPMENT

Medium Bowl, Stand Mixer Fitted with a Dough Hook Attachment, Whisk, 10- to 12-inch Straight-Sided Translucent Plastic Tub or Mixing Bowl, Bowl Scraper, Pizza Peel, or Baking Sheet, Parchment Paper, Baking or Pizza Stone, Lame or Razor or Chef's Knife, Instant-Read Thermometer, Serrated Knife

1 MAKE THE CEREAL MIX: Pour the cereal into the medium bowl. Add the boiling water and stir to blend. Let the mixture sit for 20 minutes or refrigerate overnight (bring the mixture to room temperature before continuing).

2 MIX, REST, AND KNEAD THE DOUGH: Pour the warm water into the bowl of the stand mixer. Add the sugar and yeast and whisk by hand to blend. Let sit for 10 minutes, or until the yeast is activated and foamy or bubbling. Add the cooled cereal, honey, bread flour, whole wheat flour, and salt. Knead the dough on low speed for 2 to 3 minutes. Cover the bowl with plastic wrap or a damp lint-free cotton towel and let the dough rest for 20 minutes to allow it to fully hydrate before further kneading. Turn the mixer to medium-low and continue to knead until the dough is firm and elastic, 4 to 7 minutes.

3 RISE THE DOUGH (FIRST RISE): Lightly oil the tub or bowl, scrape the dough into the tub, and lightly coat the surface of the dough with a little oil. Cover with plastic wrap or a damp lint-free cotton towel and let the dough rise until doubled in size, 35 to 45 minutes (longer if the room is cold). If you are using a tub, be sure to mark the starting level of the dough with a pencil or piece of tape so it's easy to tell when the dough has doubled.

4 PUNCH DOWN AND SHAPE THE DOUGH: Turn the dough out onto a lightly floured work surface. Press down on the dough firmly to expel some of the air bubbles, but don't knead the dough again or it will be too springy and difficult to shape (if this happens, simply cover the dough with plastic wrap or a damp lint-free cotton towel and let it rest for 10 to 15 minutes to give the gluten some time to relax). Shape into a round, taut loaf

according to the directions on page 69. If you are using a baking or pizza stone, transfer the loaf to the semolina-dusted pizza peel, or form a makeshift peel by lining the bottom of a baking sheet with parchment paper. If you are not using a baking stone, transfer the loaf to the center of a parchment-lined baking pan.

5 PROOF THE DOUGH (SECOND RISE): Lightly cover the dough with plastic wrap or a damp lint-free cotton towel and allow to rise until it is almost doubled and looks like it has taken a deep breath, 20 to 30 minutes.

6 PREPARE THE OVEN: Place the baking or pizza stone in the oven. Preheat the oven to 400°F. Be sure to allow 30 minutes to 1 hour for the stone to fully heat.

7 BAKE THE LOAF: Dust the top lightly with flour—don't go crazy here or you'll have a mouthful of flour. Slash a pattern in the top of the dough with a *lame,* razor blade, or chef's knife. If the dough is on a pizza peel, transfer to the baking stone; if on a baking sheet, simply set the baking sheet on the baking stone or oven rack. Bake for 40 minutes, or until the loaf is golden brown and the internal temperature registers 190°F on an instant-read thermometer. Transfer to a rack and cool completely. Slice with a serrated knife.

STORING **The bread will keep at room temperature, wrapped in plastic, for 3 to 4 days. For longer storage, double-wrap in plastic and freeze for up to 1 month. To thaw, place on the counter for 2 hours, or until it reaches room temperature. Reheat the unwrapped thawed bread in a 400°F oven for 10 to 15 minutes, until the crumb is warmed and the crust is crisped.**

RAISIN, ROSEMARY, AND CINNAMON FOCACCIA

MAKES 1 BAKING SHEET, OR TWENTY 3 BY 3-INCH SQUARES **If you think the combination of raisins and rosemary sounds strange, one taste will convince you that it is a match made in heaven, and is especially welcome at breakfast. Don't worry, it's not necessary to get up at 4:00 a.m. for warm breakfast bread–the dough can be made the day before and refrigerated. In the morning, all you have to do is pop it in the oven. If you like, serve with a bit of mascarpone or your favorite jam and a good cup of coffee. Leftovers can be frozen for reheating another day. They're delicious split, toasted under the broiler, and spread with butter or cream cheese. Or, cut leftovers into cubes, dry them out, and use them to make a stuffing that would be especially nice with roasted pork loin.**

INGREDIENTS

2 cups (10 ounces) plump, sweet raisins

2¼ cups (18 ounces) warm whole milk (110° to 115°F)

1 teaspoon sugar

1 tablespoon active dry yeast, or 2¼ teaspoons instant yeast

5 cups (25 ounces) bread flour or unbleached all-purpose flour

3 tablespoons (1½ ounces) olive oil, plus additional for brushing

2 bunches fresh rosemary, leaves removed and very finely chopped (about ⅓ cup)

1½ teaspoons ground cinnamon

1 teaspoon salt

2 to 3 tablespoons sanding sugar or turbinado sugar

EQUIPMENT

Medium Saucepan and Colander and Baking Sheet, Whisk, Stand Mixer with Paddle and Dough Hook Attachments, Bowl Scraper, 10- to 12-inch Straight-Sided Translucent Plastic Tub or Mixing Bowl, 17 by 12-inch Baking Sheet with ½-inch Sides, Pastry Brush, Baking or Pizza Stone, Instant-Read Thermometer, Cooling Rack, Serrated Knife

1 TO PLUMP THE RAISINS IF THEY SEEM DRY (IF NOT, CONTINUE TO NEXT STEP): Place the raisins in the medium saucepan with water to cover. Bring the water to a boil, then turn off the heat, cover the pan, and let the raisins sit for 5 minutes. Drain the raisins in the colander set in the sink and shake off any excess water. Spread the raisins on the baking sheet and let cool.

2 MIX AND KNEAD THE DOUGH: Combine the warmed milk and sugar in the bowl of a stand mixer and sprinkle the yeast over the top. Whisk in ¼ cup of the flour by hand. Let the mixture sit for 10 minutes, or until the yeast is activated and foamy or bubbling. Whisk in another 2 cups of flour, or enough that the dough resembles a thick pancake batter. Attach the paddle attachment and mix on low speed for 4 minutes.

3 Add the raisins, olive oil, rosemary, cinnamon, and salt to the dough, attach the dough hook, and knead on low until well blended. Add the remaining 2¾ cups flour and knead for 2 minutes. Scrape down the sides of the bowl and turn the dough over in the bowl so everything is mixed evenly. Continue to knead for 2 minutes longer. Don't worry if the dough sticks to the side of the bowl—the extra moisture gives the crumb an open and chewy texture that is the signature of a good focaccia.

what the
pros
know

Using milk in this focaccia instead of the usual water results in a crumb that is softer and more suited to a breakfast bread. The fat in the milk coats the gluten strands, shortening them and creating a more tender dough. In addition, the natural sugars in milk combine with the fat to create a beautiful golden brown crust.

GETTING AHEAD **The dough can be prepared 1 day ahead through Step 6 with the following adjustment: Brush with olive oil and let the dough rise for 20 minutes, then refrigerate, covered with plastic wrap. The dough will continue to rise slowly overnight and will be nearly doubled in size by morning. The next day, let the bread sit at room temperature for 30 minutes before baking. Brush the top with additional oil, dimple the dough, and sprinkle with sugar. It may take a few extra minutes to bake—take the internal temperature to be sure it is cooked through.**

4 RISE THE DOUGH (FIRST RISE): Lightly oil the tub or bowl, scrape the dough into the tub, and lightly coat the surface of the dough with a little oil. Cover with plastic wrap or a damp lint-free cotton towel and let the dough rise until doubled in size, 1 to 1½ hours. If you are using a tub, be sure to mark the starting level of the dough with a pencil or piece of tape so it's easy to tell when the dough has doubled.

5 PUNCH DOWN AND SHAPE THE DOUGH: Scrape the risen dough onto the prepared baking sheet. Lightly oil your hands and press down on the dough firmly to expel some of the air bubbles, but don't knead the dough again. Begin to push and gently stretch the dough into an even layer in the pan. To stretch the dough into the corners of the pan, slip your hand under the dough and pull gently from the center of the dough toward the corner. As you reach the corner, grip the dough and gently shake it up and down as you pull outward—this will help to stretch the dough while preventing it from tearing. Repeat until the dough is in an even layer filling the pan all the way into the corners. You may not be able to stretch it into the corners on the first try. If the dough begins to pull back and resist the stretching, brush the top with a little olive oil, set the pan aside for 10 minutes, and then try again.

6 PROOF THE DOUGH (SECOND RISE): Brush the top of the dough with a little olive oil and cover the pan with plastic wrap. Let the dough rise until it is almost doubled in size (it will look quite puffy and bubbly).

7 PREPARE THE OVEN: Place a baking or pizza stone in the oven. Preheat the oven to 375°F. Be sure to allow 30 minutes to 1 hour for the stone to fully heat.

8 BAKE THE FOCACCIA: Remove the plastic wrap. Dimple the dough by gently pressing your fingertips into the dough, about ½-inch deep, taking care that you don't deflate the dough by pressing too vigorously or making too many indentations.

9 Sprinkle the dough with the sanding sugar. Bake for 30 to 35 minutes, until the bread is a deep golden brown and cooked through. The internal temperature should register 200°F on an instant-read thermometer. Transfer to a cooling rack and immediately brush the top of the bread with olive oil. Cool for 10 minutes before serving. Cut the focaccia with a serrated knife.

STORING **The focaccia will keep at room temperature, covered with plastic wrap, for 2 days. Reheat in a 375°F oven for 10 minutes. To freeze focaccia, cut it in pieces, wrap each piece in plastic wrap, place in a resealable plastic freezer bag, and freeze for up to 1 month. Thaw for 1 hour and reheat as directed above.**

OLD-FASHIONED DINNER ROLLS

MAKES 9 TO 10 ROLLS Bread bakers have been using potatoes (and potato cooking water) for many years. Yeast love the starchy carbohydrates in potatoes, and their lumpy texture adds not only flavor and moisture, but also a chewy softness that is ideal in dinner rolls. Serve these at a family dinner and watch them disappear. The recipe can be doubled for a holiday dinner.

INGREDIENTS

1 small (5 ounce) russet potato, peeled and quartered

1½ teaspoons active dry yeast, or 1 teaspoon instant yeast

¼ cup (1¾ ounces) sugar

½ stick (2 ounces) unsalted butter, very soft

½ cup (4 ounces) warm whole milk (110° to 115°F)

1 large egg, at room temperature

2½ cups (12½ ounces) bread flour or unbleached all-purpose flour, plus more as needed

½ teaspoon salt

EQUIPMENT

Small Saucepan, Paring Knife, Potato Masher or Fork, Stand Mixer Fitted with a Dough Hook Attachment, Whisk, 10- to 12-inch Straight-Sided Translucent Plastic Tub or Mixing Bowl, Bowl Scraper, Baking Sheet, Parchment Paper or Silicone Mat, Instant-Read Thermometer, Cooling Rack

1 COOK THE POTATO: Put the quartered potato in the small saucepan, cover with water, and set over medium heat. Bring to a simmer and cook for 15 to 20 minutes, until the tip of a paring knife slides in and out easily. Drain well, reserving ¼ cup of the cooking water. Return the potato to the pan and mash using the potato masher or fork. Set aside to cool to room temperature.

2 MIX AND KNEAD THE DOUGH: Warm the reserved potato water to 110° to 115°F and pour into the bowl of the stand mixer. Add the yeast and 1 teaspoon of the sugar and whisk by hand to blend. Allow the mixture to sit for 10 minutes, or until the yeast is activated and foamy or bubbling. Measure ½ cup (3½ ounces) mashed potatoes and add to the bowl. Add the remaining sugar, butter, milk, and egg and whisk by hand until well blended. Add the flour and salt and knead on low speed for 2 to 3 minutes, until the dough begins to come together. It will seem sticky. With the mixer on low, add additional flour, a tablespoon at a time, until the dough begins to pull away from the sides of the bowl. Turn the speed to medium-low and continue to knead until the dough feels firm, dense, and springy, 5 to 6 minutes. Note: This dough is soft and sticky and will not pull away from the sides completely. Do not overknead or the starch from the potato will break down and make the dough gooey.

3 RISE THE DOUGH (FIRST RISE): Lightly butter or oil the tub or bowl, scrape the dough into the tub, and lightly coat the surface of the dough with a little butter or oil. Cover with plastic wrap or a damp lint-free cotton towel and let the dough rise until doubled in size, 45 to 60 minutes (longer if the room is cold). If you are using a tub, be sure to mark the starting level of the dough with a pencil or piece of tape so it's easy to tell when the dough has doubled.

4 PUNCH DOWN AND CHILL THE DOUGH: Turn the dough out onto a lightly floured work surface. Press down on the dough firmly to expel some of the air bubbles. Chill, covered, for at least 2 hours and up to overnight, or until the dough is very cold.

The dough is sticky and you may be tempted to add more flour than the recipe calls for, but don't—the extra flour will make the rolls tough and dry. The sticky problem is solved by chilling the dough thoroughly (up to 24 hours) before shaping. When cold, the dough is a breeze to work with.

GETTING AHEAD **The dough can be prepared through Step 4 and refrigerated overnight (the dough is easier to shape while it is cold, so shape immediately after removing from the refrigerator). The dough can also be shaped and risen through Step 6 and refrigerated for a day. To do this, let the rolls rise for 20 minutes, cover loosely with plastic wrap, and refrigerate overnight. The next day, let the rolls sit at room temperature for 30 minutes before baking. They may take a few extra minutes to bake—take their internal temperature to be sure they are cooked through.**

5 SHAPE THE DOUGH: Cut the dough into 3-ounce portions (about ⅓ cup) and shape each into a taut, round ball according to the directions on page 69. Line the baking sheet with parchment paper or a silicone mat and position the rolls on the sheet about 3 inches apart. For additional shaping suggestions, see the variations below.

6 PROOF THE DOUGH (SECOND RISE): Cover the rolls loosely with plastic wrap or a damp lint-free cotton towel and let rise until almost doubled in size, 35 to 45 minutes (longer if the room is cold). They should look like they have taken a deep breath and should pass the "thumb test" (page 70).

7 BAKE THE ROLLS: Preheat the oven to 375°F and position an oven rack in the center of the oven. Bake the rolls for 10 minutes. Rotate the pan and continue to bake for 10 to 15 minutes longer, until the rolls are golden brown and their internal temperature registers 200°F on the instant-read thermometer. Transfer to a cooling rack. Serve warm or at room temperature.

STORING **The rolls will keep, uncovered at room temperature, for 1 day. For longer storage, double-wrap each in plastic, put in a large resealable plastic freezer bag, and freeze for up to 3 weeks. Thaw on the counter for 1½ hours, or until they reach room temperature. To reheat, return to a 375°F oven for 5 to 7 minutes, until warmed through.**

Cloverleaf Rolls
Butter a standard muffin tin. After dividing the dough into portions, cut each portion into 3 equal pieces. Form each piece into a ball and nestle 3 balls into each muffin cup. Proof and bake as directed.

Dinner Roll Twists
After dividing the dough into portions, roll each one on the table under outstretched fingers until you form a rope 10 to 12 inches long and tapered at the ends. Fold the rope in half and gently twist the dough 2 or 3 times. Gently pinch the ends together. Proof and bake as directed.

CHALLAH

MAKES 1 LOAF This striking braided loaf is traditionally enjoyed at Friday night dinner in Jewish households. Kosher law forbids the serving of dairy with meat, so the classic challah is made with water instead of milk, and the crumb is tenderized with oil instead of butter. If you're not worried about keeping kosher, the dairy variation that follows has a more tender crumb. Leftover challah of either type is great for French toast or bread pudding.

INGREDIENTS

¾ cup (6 ounces) warm water (110° to 115°F)

2 tablespoons (1½ ounces) honey

1½ teaspoons active dry yeast, or 1⅛ teaspoons instant yeast

2 large eggs, at room temperature

3 tablespoons (1½ ounces) neutral oil, such as canola or safflower

2½ cups (12½ ounces) bread flour or unbleached all-purpose flour, plus more if needed

¾ teaspoons salt

1 large egg, lightly beaten

2 teaspoons poppy seeds (optional)

EQUIPMENT

Stand Mixer Fitted with a Dough Hook Attachment, Whisk, Bowl Scraper, 10- to 12-inch Straight-Sided Translucent Plastic Tub or Mixing Bowl, Baking Sheet, Parchment Paper or a Silicone Mat, Pastry Brush, Instant-Read Thermometer, Cooling Rack, Serrated Knife

1 MIX AND KNEAD THE DOUGH: Combine the warm water and honey in the bowl of the stand mixer and sprinkle the yeast over the top. Whisk by hand to blend well. Let the mixture sit for 5 to 10 minutes, until the yeast is activated and foamy or bubbling. Add the eggs and oil and whisk by hand until well blended. Stir in the flour and salt. Attach the dough hook and knead on low speed for 2 minutes, scraping down the bowl as necessary, until the dough begins to come together. Turn the speed to medium and knead for 6 to 8 minutes, until the dough is smooth, silky, and elastic. You may need to add a little extra flour, a tablespoon at a time, toward the end. The dough should begin to pull away from the sides of the bowl but still be slightly tacky.

2 RISE THE DOUGH (FIRST RISE): Lightly oil the tub or bowl, scrape the dough into the tub, and brush the surface of the dough with a little oil. Cover with plastic wrap or a damp lint-free cotton towel and let the dough rise until doubled in size, 45 to 60 minutes. If you are using a tub, be sure to mark the starting level of the dough with a pencil or piece of tape so it's easy to tell when the dough has doubled.

3 PUNCH DOWN AND SHAPE THE DOUGH: Turn the dough out onto a lightly floured work surface. Press down on the dough firmly to expel some of the air bubbles, but don't knead the dough again or it will be too springy and difficult to shape (if this happens, simply cover the dough with plastic wrap or a lint-free cotton towel and let it rest for 10 to 15 minutes to give the gluten some time to relax). Divide the dough into 3 equal pieces (about 8½ ounces each). Work with one piece at a time and keep the others covered to prevent a skin from forming. Using flattened hands, roll each piece back and forth, forming a rope about 15 inches long with tapered ends. You may not be able to stretch each piece to the

full length the first time; if that's the case, cover it and continue with another piece. Return to the first piece when you've finished the others and try stretching it a little more.

4 Line the baking sheet with parchment paper or a silicone mat and lay the 3 ropes on the sheet with the ends facing you. Pinch together the three ends furthest from you. Braid the dough, pinching the loose ends together at the bottom. Gently stretch the ends outward so the center is plump while the ends are tapered. Tuck the ends under just slightly.

5 PROOF THE DOUGH (SECOND RISE): Cover the braid loosely with plastic wrap or a damp lint-free cotton towel. Allow the braid to rise until it is almost double in size and looks like it has taken a deep breath, 40 to 50 minutes.

6 GLAZE AND BAKE THE CHALLAH: Preheat the oven to 375°F and position an oven rack in the center. Gently brush the entire surface of the braid with a light wash of beaten egg. (You will not use all the egg.) Take care that there are no pools or drips of glaze. Sprinkle with the poppy seeds, if you like. Bake for 20 to 25 minutes, until the top and bottom are golden brown and the internal temperature registers 190°F on an instant-read thermometer. Transfer to a rack to cool completely. To serve, slice with a serrated knife.

STORING **Challah is at its best the same day it is baked. But, you can store the bread, wrapped in plastic, at room temperature for 2 days. For longer storage, double-wrap in plastic and freeze in a resealable plastic freezer bag for up to 1 month. Thaw on the counter for 1½ to 2 hours, until it reaches room temperature. Reheat in a 375°F oven for 10 to 15 minutes, until the bread is warmed through.**

Dairy Challah This version of challah is more tender than the pareve challah above, because it contains milk and butter. Replace the water with the same amount of milk and the oil with the same amount of very soft butter.

RICH BREAKFAST DOUGH

MAKES ABOUT 1½ POUNDS A leaner version of brioche dough, this can be used for all those wonderful, yeasted breakfast breads you love, like sticky buns and coffee cake. Classic brioche, while delicious, is unnecessarily rich when paired with flavor-packed fillings and toppings. Despite the reduced amount of eggs and butter, this dough is still soft and easy to work with, and it bakes into a tender, flavorful partner for all manner of fillings, both sweet and savory.

INGREDIENTS

½ cup (4 ounces) warm whole milk (110° to 115°F)

¼ cup (1¾ ounces) sugar

1½ teaspoons active dry yeast, or 1⅛ teaspoons instant yeast

1 large egg plus 1 egg yolk, at room temperature

2½ cups (12½ ounces) bread flour or unbleached all-purpose flour

½ teaspoon salt

1 stick (4 ounces) unsalted butter, very soft (not melted)

EQUIPMENT
Stand Mixer Fitted with a Dough Hook Attachment, Whisk, Silicone or Rubber Spatula, 10- to 12-inch Straight-Sided Translucent Plastic Tub or Mixing Bowl, Bowl Scraper

what the pros know

Be sure the butter is very soft before beginning, or you'll have cold lumps of butter in the dough. If this happens, cover the dough and let it sit at room temperature for 20 to 30 minutes, until the butter has softened, then continue kneading.

GETTING AHEAD **You can freeze the dough for up to 1 month. Punch the dough down, wrap in plastic and place in a resealable plastic freezer bag. To thaw, refrigerate overnight, or place on the counter for 2 hours, or until room temperature. Continue with your recipe of choice.**

1 MIX AND KNEAD THE DOUGH: Combine the warm milk and sugar in the bowl of the stand mixer and sprinkle the yeast over the top. Whisk by hand to blend well. Let the mixture sit for 5 to 10 minutes, until the yeast is activated and foamy or bubbling. Add the egg and yolk and whisk by hand until well blended. Stir in the flour and salt with a silicone or rubber spatula. Attach the dough hook and knead on low speed for 2 minutes. The dough may look ragged at this point, but don't worry—the addition of butter will smooth it out. Increase the speed to medium and knead for 1 minute. With the mixer running, add the soft butter, 1 tablespoon at a time, allowing each addition to blend in before adding the next. Once all the butter has been added, decrease the speed to medium-low and continue to knead for 5 to 6 minutes longer, until the dough looks soft and silky.

2 RISE THE DOUGH (FIRST RISE): Lightly butter or oil the tub or bowl, scrape the dough into the tub, and brush the surface of the dough with a little butter or oil. Cover with plastic wrap or a damp lint-free cotton towel and let the dough rise until doubled, 1 to 1½ hours. If you are using a tub, be sure to mark the starting level of the dough with a pencil or piece of tape so it's easy to tell when the dough has doubled. At this point, the dough is ready to be punched down and used in your recipe of choice.

STORING **The dough can be punched down and refrigerated overnight. Wrap in plastic, leaving a bit of wiggle room for when the dough continues to expand in the refrigerator, or place in a bowl large enough to allow it to expand; cover with plastic wrap. (If you don't leave room for expansion, the dough will burst through the plastic wrap.)**

APRICOT, ALMOND, AND CHOCOLATE SPIRALED COFFEE CAKE

SERVES 10 TO 12 This gorgeous length of woven, glistening rolls deserves to be the centerpiece at a special brunch or morning gathering. The filling is an almond paste mixture topped with chocolate chips and tart dried apricots soaked in almond liqueur. It's a large coffee cake, and you can serve up to 16 guests by cutting slices rather than letting guests break off rolls. Don't worry about leftovers—there won't be any unless you hide some. If you've baked this ahead and plan to freeze it, add the drizzle of sugar glaze only after the coffee cake has been thawed and reheated, or the glaze will soak into the pastry.

INGREDIENTS

1 recipe Rich Breakfast Dough (page 93)

FILLING

8 ounces dried California apricots

3 tablespoons (1½ ounces) water

3 tablespoons (1½ ounces) amaretto (almond liqueur)

7 ounces almond paste, at room temperature

½ cup (3½ ounces) granulated sugar

¾ stick (3 ounces) unsalted butter, softened (65° to 68°F)

½ cup (3½ ounces) mini semisweet chocolate chips

APRICOT GLAZE

3 tablespoons (1½ ounces) apricot jam

1 tablespoon (½ ounce) water

SUGAR GLAZE

½ cup (1¾ ounces) unsifted confectioners' sugar

1 teaspoon warm water

EQUIPMENT

Food Processor Fitted with a Metal Blade, Small Saucepan, Silicone or Rubber Spatula, Medium Bowl, Rolling Pin, Pastry Brush, Chef's Knife, Baking Sheet, Silicone Mat, Large Metal Spatula, Cooling Rack, Two Spatulas or a Cake Lifter, Serrated Knife (Optional)

1 PLUMP THE APRICOTS FOR THE FILLING: Place the apricots in the bowl of the food processor and process until they are chopped into tiny pieces (or use an oiled chef's knife to chop them very finely). In the small saucepan, heat the water and amaretto over medium heat just until it begins to simmer. Remove from the heat and add the chopped apricots. Let the mixture sit for about 5 minutes, stirring several times with a spatula, until the liquid has been completely absorbed. Transfer to the medium bowl to cool while you prepare the rest of the filling.

2 MAKE THE FILLING: Cut or break the almond paste into 12 to 15 pieces. Place the almond paste and granulated sugar in the bowl of the food processor and process for 10 to 15 seconds, until the almond paste is cut into tiny pieces. Add the softened butter and process for 25 to 30 seconds, until the mixture is blended and smooth and forms a large ball. The filling will be very thick.

3 SHAPE THE DOUGH: Turn the dough out of the rising tub or bowl onto a work surface dusted with flour. Press down firmly to expel some of the air bubbles, but don't knead the dough again. Dust the dough with flour and roll into an 11 by 15-inch rectangle. Position the dough so that one of its long sides is parallel to the edge of your work surface. Brush any remaining flour from the surface and underside of the dough. Spread the almond filling in a thin layer over the dough, leaving a 1-inch border along the long side

GETTING AHEAD Prepare the coffee cake through Step 4, then cover loosely with plastic wrap and refrigerate overnight. The coffee cake will continue to rise slowly through the night. The next day, let it sit at room temperature for 1 hour before baking.

The baked and cooled coffee cake can be frozen, wrapped tightly in 2 layers of plastic wrap, for up to 2 weeks—do not add the sugar glaze until the day you serve the coffee cake. To thaw, set on the counter until it reaches room temperature, about 2 hours. Reheat as directed above.

of the dough opposite you. Sprinkle the plumped apricot pieces over the filling as evenly as possible. Do the same with the mini chocolate chips.

4 ROLL UP THE DOUGH: Beginning with the long edge closest to you, roll the dough into a cylinder, gently tucking and tightening as you go. Wet your fingers and rub a thin film of water along the empty border. Finish rolling the dough onto the border. Roll the dough backwards so that the seam is facing upward and pinch all along it to seal the dough. Turn the seam to face away from you and, using the tip of the chef's knife, cut the dough into slices at 1½-inch intervals, cutting only ¾ of the way across the roll so the seam is still intact—all the slices should be attached along a "spine." Gently lift the log of dough and center it on the prepared baking sheet, seam or "spine" down. Gently twist each slice away from the spine and lay it nearly flat on the sheet (the slices will overlap slightly and won't lie completely flat). Alternate the direction of the twists, one slice to the right, one slice to the left, until you reach the end. At first it will seem as though the roll is too long for the pan, but keep overlapping and you'll find you have room at the top and bottom of the coffee cake.

5 PROOF THE DOUGH (SECOND RISE): Cover the dough loosely with plastic wrap or a damp lint-free towel and allow to rise until it is almost doubled in size and looks like it has taken a deep breath, 40 to 60 minutes.

6 BAKE THE COFFEE CAKE: Preheat the oven to 375°F and position an oven rack in the center. Bake the coffee cake for 20 to 25 minutes, until golden brown on the top and bottom (check the bottom by lifting the coffee cake slightly with a large metal spatula). Transfer to a cooling rack.

7 WHILE THE PASTRY IS BAKING, MAKE THE APRICOT GLAZE: Heat the apricot jam and water in the cleaned small saucepan over medium-low heat, stirring with a silicone or rubber spatula to blend, until hot and fluid. When the cake is out of the oven and on the rack, rewarm the glaze and brush it over the cake. Cool for 15 minutes, then apply another layer of the glaze. Allow the coffeecake to cool an additional 20 minutes before adding the sugar glaze.

8 MAKE THE SUGAR GLAZE: In the cleaned medium bowl, stir the confectioners' sugar and warm water vigorously with a silicone or rubber spatula until there are no lumps remaining, adding a few more drops of water if needed. Use a fork to drizzle the glaze over the pastry, or transfer the glaze to a resealable plastic bag and squeeze it into one corner. Snip off the corner with a pair of scissors and pipe lines decoratively across the coffee cake. Use two spatulas or a cake lifter to transfer the coffee cake to a serving platter. Serve warm or room temperature. Let guests tear off rolls, or slice with a serrated knife.

STORING The coffee cake can be stored, uncovered at room temperature, for 1 day. For longer storage, cover with plastic wrap and leave at room temperature for another day, or store in the refrigerator for up to 3 days. Reheat in a 375°F oven for 8 to 10 minutes, until warmed through.

CINNAMON-CURRANT BREAD

MAKES 1 LOAF The technique here is a little unusual, but the rustic, cobblestone look of this version of cinnamon bread is very enticing. The rolled cylinder of dough is sliced down the center lengthwise, chopped up crosswise, and transferred to the pan in a jumble. Be sure to use a 9 by 5-inch pan. The bread won't dome as high as it would in a smaller pan, but you don't end up with currants and cinnamon sugar dripping onto the bottom of your oven.

INGREDIENTS

1 recipe Rich Breakfast Dough (page 93)

1 large egg, lightly beaten

½ cup (4 ounces) firmly packed light brown sugar

2 teaspoons ground cinnamon

½ cup (2¾ ounces) currants

EQUIPMENT

Rolling Pin, Pastry Brush, Small Bowl, Chef's Knife, 9 by 5-inch Loaf Pan, Instant-Read Thermometer, Cooling Rack

GETTING AHEAD **The bread can be prepared through Step 4 a day ahead. After the dough has risen half way, lightly butter or oil the top to keep it moist, cover loosely with plastic wrap, and refrigerate overnight. The dough will continue to rise slowly through the night. In the morning, let the bread sit at room temperature for 1 hour before baking. It may take a few extra minutes to bake—take the internal temperature to be sure it is cooked through.**

1 ROLL THE DOUGH: Turn the dough onto a work surface dusted with flour. Press down firmly to expel some of the air bubbles, but don't knead the dough. Dust with flour and roll into a 12 by 15-inch rectangle. Position the dough so that one of the long sides is parallel to the edge of your work surface. Brush any flour from the surface and underside of the dough.

2 FILL THE DOUGH: Brush the dough evenly with a thin film of beaten egg, leaving a 1-inch border along the long edge of the dough opposite you. In the small bowl, mix the brown sugar and cinnamon. Sprinkle this mixture over the egg glaze, then spread it with your fingers into an even layer. Scatter the currants evenly over the top.

3 SHAPE THE LOAF: Beginning with the long edge closest to you, roll the dough into a tight cylinder, gently tucking and tightening as you roll. Wet your fingers and rub a thin film of water along the empty border. Finish rolling the dough onto the border. Roll the dough backwards so that the seam is facing upward and pinch all along it to seal the dough. Use the chef's knife to slice the cylinder in half lengthwise, then crosswise into about 12 pieces. Generously butter the loaf plan and transfer the pieces to the pan. Try to arrange the bottom layer dough-side down to make it easier to remove the bread from the pan after baking and to prevent the sugar from burning on the bottom of the pan. Otherwise, just toss them in every which way. Level the top the best you can, but a rugged look is fine.

4 PROOF THE DOUGH (SECOND RISE): Cover the pan loosely with plastic wrap or a damp lint-free cotton towel and allow to rise until the dough reaches about ¼ inch below the rim of the pan, 1 to 1½ hours (longer if the room is cold).

5 BAKE THE BREAD: Preheat the oven to 350°F and position an oven rack in the center. Bake the loaf for 35 to 45 minutes, until an instant-read thermometer inserted into the center of the bread registers 190°F. Transfer to a rack and cool for 15 minutes, then turn the loaf out of the pan onto a piece of parchment paper to cool completely.

STORING **This bread will keep for 4 days at room temperature, wrapped in plastic. For longer storage, see page 86.**

MAPLE-PECAN STICKY BUNS

MAKES 10 BUNS Sticky buns are a favorite throughout the country, and each region seems to have its own variation. You'll like this one, with the deep, caramel-tinged flavor of real maple syrup paired with its finest dance partner–pecans. Be sure to turn these out of their baking pan while they are still quite warm, or the topping will stick to the pan and the dough to the topping. But if this does happen, set the pan on a burner turned to medium and, wearing an oven mitt, rotate the pan for 20 to 30 seconds, until the butter and sugar mixture is melted again. Turn out as directed.

INGREDIENTS

1 recipe Rich Breakfast Dough (page 93)

TOPPING

¾ stick (3 ounces) unsalted butter, softened (65° to 68°F)

⅓ cup (2½ ounces) firmly packed light brown sugar

⅓ cup (3¾ ounces) maple syrup (preferably Grade B; see page 99)

1 cup (4 ounces) chopped pecans

FILLING

½ stick (2 ounces) unsalted butter, softened

⅓ cup (2½ ounces) firmly packed light brown sugar

½ teaspoon ground cinnamon

EQUIPMENT

Stand Mixer Fitted with a Paddle Attachment or a Hand Mixer and a Medium Bowl, Bowl Scraper, 10-inch Round Cake Pan, Rolling Pin, Pastry Brush, Silicone or Rubber Spatula, Chef's Knife, Instant-Read Thermometer, Cooling Rack, Thin Knife or Small Spatula

1 MAKE THE TOPPING: Place the butter and brown sugar in the bowl of the stand mixer and blend on medium speed until the mixture is smooth and slightly lightened, 2 to 3 minutes. You can also use a hand mixer and a medium bowl, though you may need to beat the mixture a little longer to achieve the same results. Scrape down the bowl. With the mixer running on medium, pour the maple syrup in a thin stream down the side of the bowl and blend until smooth and homogenous. Scrape the topping into the cake pan and spread evenly. Scatter the chopped pecans over the top. Set aside while you make the buns.

2 ROLL THE DOUGH: Dust your work surface with flour. Turn the risen dough out of the tub and onto the flour. Press down firmly with your hands to expel as much of the gas as possible, but don't knead the dough or the gluten will be too developed for the dough to roll easily. Dust the top of the dough with flour. Roll the dough into a 10- by 16-inch rectangle. Position the dough so that one of the long sides is parallel to the edge of your work surface. Brush any remaining flour from the surface and underside of the dough.

3 MAKE THE FILLING: Place the butter, brown sugar, and cinnamon in the bowl of the stand mixer and blend on medium speed until the mixture is smooth and slightly lightened, 2 to 3 minutes. Scrape down the bowl. Use a silicone or rubber spatula to spread the filling over the dough, leaving a 1-inch border along the long side opposite you.

4 SHAPE THE BUNS: Beginning with the long edge closest to you, roll the dough into a cylinder, gently tucking and tightening as you roll. Wet your fingers and rub a thin film of water along the empty border. Finish rolling the dough onto the border. Roll the dough

GETTING AHEAD The sticky buns can be prepared through Step 5 one day ahead. Let the dough rise for 20 minutes, then cover the pan with plastic wrap and refrigerate overnight. The sticky buns will continue to rise slowly through the night. In the morning, let them sit at room temperature for 30 minutes to 1 hour, until they look fully risen, before baking. They may take a few extra minutes to bake—take the internal temperature to be sure they are cooked through.

backwards so that the seam is facing upward and pinch all along it to seal the dough. Turn the seam side down and use a chef's knife to cut the roll into 10 equal pieces. Set each bun with a cut side up on your work surface and gently flatten it slightly with the palm of your hand. Place the buns into the prepared cake pan, spacing them evenly.

5 PROOF THE DOUGH (SECOND RISE): Cover the pan loosely with plastic wrap or a damp lint-free cotton towel and set aside to rise until the rolls have almost doubled in size, 45 to 60 minutes (longer if the room is cold).

6 BAKE THE STICKY BUNS: Preheat the oven to 350°F and position an oven rack in the center. Bake the buns for 30 to 35 minutes, until the buns are deep golden brown and the centers register 185°F on an instant-read thermometer. Transfer to a cooling rack for 5 minutes, then turn the buns out of the pan. To do this, run a thin knife or small spatula around the edge of the pan to loosen the buns. Place a large plate or rimmed baking sheet upside down on top of the cake pan. Wearing oven mitts, hold the cake pan against the plate and invert it. The sticky buns will fall out of the pan onto the plate, along with their syrup and nuts. Serve the sticky buns warm or room temperature.

STORING The sticky buns are at their best the same day they are made, but will keep, covered with a cake dome at room temperature, for 2 days. For longer storage, cover and refrigerate for up to 4 days. Reheat in a 350°F oven for 7 to 10 minutes, until warmed through.

Layered pastries are some of the most impressive in a baker's repertoire, for it takes patience and attention to detail to construct these miracles of dough leavened by thin sheets of butter. Light and flaky, layered pastries satisfy our cravings for crunchy texture and buttery flavor, and can either stand on their own—like croissants—or pair beautifully with myriad fillings and toppings to create such popular treats as cheese Danish, coffee cake, and napoleons. Making croissants, Danish, or puff pastry is time-consuming, though much of that time is spent chilling the dough, and none of it is very difficult. The rewards of creating homemade versions of your favorite bakery pastries are, quite literally, mouthwatering.

This chapter includes recipes for classic croissants and Danish, as well as for "quick" puff pastry, which is virtually indistinguishable from puff pastry made the slow way and much easier to prepare. You'll also find some tips and recipes for working with phyllo, paper-thin sheets of dough that are brushed with melted butter and stacked to form multi-layered pastries such as baklava.

A Primer on Laminated Doughs

Puff pastry, croissant, and Danish doughs are referred to collectively as laminated, or layered, doughs. If you consider a piece of laminated paper, encased between two layers of plastic, you'll understand the theory behind the construction of these doughs. Butter is encased in dough and the combination is rolled out and folded over and over again to create hundreds of layers in the final product. The protein in the flour combines with the liquid in the dough to form gluten, and then, as the dough is rolled and folded, the gluten strands are developed, or elongated, giving the pastry structure, while the layers of butter separate the dough, creating flakiness and rich flavor. In the heat of the oven, the butter melts and the water in the butter turns to steam. The steam pushes against the dough layer above, creating an empty space where the butter used to be. These spaces in the dough are flakes. Meanwhile, the elasticity of the dough (made possible by gluten development) allows the layers to rise and separate with the expanding steam, creating a puffed, as well as a flaky dough. Here's a closer look at how laminated doughs are constructed.

THE DOUGH BLOCK (*DÉTREMPE*)

The dough block, or *détrempe,* is a simple combination of flour, water (or milk), and a small amount of cold butter. Unbleached all-purpose flour is perfect for laminated doughs because it has enough protein to form the structure that allows a high rise and a flaky texture, though some chefs prefer a combination of bread and cake flour. The butter is cut into the flour until it is in tiny pieces and the mixture resembles bread crumbs, similar to those in a mealy pie dough (see page 168). The fat coats the proteins in the flour, preventing the gluten strands from bonding together too firmly and lengthening, which could toughen the dough.

Once the butter is cut into the flour, liquid is added. Puff pastry is made with water. Croissants, which are basically a yeasted version of puff pastry, are made with milk instead, and they contain a bit of sugar along with the yeast. The additional fat from the milk helps keep the croissant dough tender and aids in browning. Danish dough is like croissant dough with eggs added, making it the most tender and cakelike of all the laminated doughs.

After the liquid goes in, the dough is mixed only until it forms a rough mass. Once the *détrempe* is formed, it is wrapped in plastic and refrigerated to allow time for the gluten strands to relax (even the brief mixing has lengthened and strengthened them a little, but they loosen when left alone for a while).

THE BUTTER BLOCK (*BEURRAGE*)

The butter block is simply cold butter combined with a small quantity of flour, which will absorb any water that may leak out of the butter during lamination. The butter is beaten while very cold until it is malleable. Some recipes call for beating the butter with a wooden dowel-like rolling pin, but it's faster and easier to cut the cold butter into pieces, toss it with the flour in the bowl of a stand mixer, and beat it with the paddle on medium speed for 1 to 2 minutes, just until smooth and blended. This technique produces butter that is cold but flexible, a consistency known to pastry professionals as "plastic."

Once the butter is plastic, it is ready to be incorporated into the dough. Laminated doughs require that the butter layers be kept in this plastic state for the best possible results. The butter must stay cold to prevent it from blending into the dough during the rolling process. It must also be flexible so it will effortlessly expand into a longer and thinner layer when rolled, rather than breaking into little butter pieces. The chilling time in each recipe will help you maintain the right temperature and consistency, but remember, if the butter gets warm and sticky at any time during the rolling process, stop and refrigerate the dough for 20 to 30 minutes before continuing.

INCORPORATING THE BUTTER BLOCK

There are several methods of incorporating the butter into the dough. The most efficient, the letter fold, not only incorporates the butter, but also creates the first fold of the dough, combining two steps into one. It involves rolling the dough into a long rectangle, then dividing it lengthwise into three equal sections and smearing two of the adjacent sections with the plastic butter. To encase the butter, the empty third folds up over the buttered center. Then the remaining third is folded over the center, buttered side down, as if you were folding a business letter. The butter is now incorporated and you've also completed one turn. The dough is ready to be rolled out again, and you'll finish your second turn in a matter of minutes. Now that's efficient!

TURNING THE BUTTER-FILLED DOUGH

The technique of rolling and folding the dough is known as *turning* the dough. There are two types of folds, and both require you to first roll the butter-filled dough out into a large rectangle. The recipes in this book will always specify which type of fold to use.

THE LETTER FOLD (ALSO KNOWN AS A SINGLE FOLD) Once you've rolled the butter-filled dough into a rectangle, divide it lengthwise into thirds and fold it in thirds as if you were folding a business letter.

THE BOOK FOLD (ALSO KNOWN AS A DOUBLE FOLD) This fold creates more layers than a letter fold. Starting with the butter-filled dough rectangle, fold the two short edges in toward the center, leaving a bit of space between them. To finish, fold one side over the other, just like closing a book.

what the
pros
know

As you incorporate the butter block for your first turn, if the butter is too cold to easily smear over the dough, you can place the butter between two sheets of plastic and roll it into a 9½ by 11-inch rectangle. Peel off one sheet of plastic, invert the buttered rectangle over the dough rectangle, center it, and peel off the other sheet of plastic.

Making Butter-Filled Dough

The technique of rolling and folding the dough is known as "turning" the dough. There are two types of folds, and both require you to first roll the butter-filled dough out into a large rectangle. The recipes in this book always specify which type of fold to use.

INCORPORATING THE BUTTER WITH A LETTER FOLD

LEFT: Roll the dough into a 15 by 12-inch rectangle. Visually divide the dough into 3 equal, 5-inch-wide sections and spread the cold pliable butter over the top two sections of dough, leaving the bottom third empty and leaving a ½-inch border around the edges of the buttered portion.

RIGHT: Begin a letter fold by folding the empty bottom third of the dough up over the center third of the dough.

FINISHED LETTER FOLD

LEFT: Fold the top third of the dough over the center and pinch the seams to finish the letter fold. Refrigerate the dough for 1 hour before rolling it out for the second turn.

FINISHED BOOK FOLD

RIGHT: For the second turn, use the book-fold method. Roll the dough into a 20 by 12-inch rectangle. Fold the two short edges toward the center of the dough, leaving a ¼-inch crevice between them. Make sure all the edges are lined up precisely. Then, fold one side of the dough over the other, as though you were closing a book.

1. **Don't overwork the dough block**—it will get plenty of exercise during the rolling and folding process. If there is too much gluten development the dough will be difficult to roll.

2. **When folding the dough,** brush off any flour left on the surface so it doesn't become incorporated. Extra flour can dry and toughen the dough and prevent the layers from adhering to one another.

3. **Keep the butter cold at all times,** and don't be afraid to return the dough to the refrigerator for 20 minutes at any point if it gets soft or butter oozes out.

4. **Wrap the dough in plastic wrap** when refrigerating it to keep a hardened "skin" from forming.

5. **Keep track of your turns.** Write the number on the plastic wrap so you don't forget. Too few turns results in scanty layers, whereas too many turns fuses the butter into the dough, preventing the layers from rising.

6. **When folding the dough,** take care to line up the edges precisely and square off the corners by gently pulling or stretching them as you fold them into the center. This attention to detail results in perfectly even layers, which create a high rise and flaky texture when the dough is baked.

7. **Whenever you begin a turn,** arrange the dough with its long folded side to the left and the short side parallel to the edge of your work surface. This helps to ensure consistent layering and a finer end product. You can position the dough in different directions while you are rolling, but begin the rolling and the folding in the proper position.

8. **When you roll,** always lift the rolling pin when you reach the edge of the dough. If you roll off the edge onto the work surface, you'll smash the layers at the edge, ruining the lamination there and causing the thinner, softer edges to stick to the work surface.

9. **There is a point during the process** at which the laminated dough may be refrigerated overnight. But make sure that the dough spends no more than 24 hours in the refrigerator or the yeast will contribute an unpleasant flavor to the dough. If you won't be using the dough within 24 hours, shape the dough, wrap it tightly in plastic, and freeze for up to 1 month.

10. **When proofing croissants or Danish,** go by the look of the dough rather than the clock. Rising times for croissants or Danish are approximate, since they depend entirely upon the temperature in the room. It's best to proof these pastries in a cool (65° to 75°F) part of the kitchen. If the air is too warm, either the butter will melt and leak out of the dough or the pastry's exterior will rise much more quickly than its interior, resulting in a gummy texture.

11. **Pastries made with puff pastry and croissant dough** are always brushed with an egg wash (usually whole egg beaten with a little cream) before baking to help them brown beautifully. Danish do not need an egg wash—the eggs in the dough help the pastries to brown. However, Danish are brushed with a sugar or jam glaze as soon as they're removed from the oven to give the pastry a glistening finish.

12. **Always chill laminated dough before baking.** Repeat the mantra "cold butter, hot oven." Cold butter produces the best rise and ensures flakiness. A hot oven begins to set the structure of the pastry quickly, before the butter has a chance to fully melt. Once the butter melts in the semi-solid structure, its disappearance creates holes or flakes, and the steam that is released from the butter forces the pastry upward to great heights.

A Primer on Phyllo

Phyllo is a paper-thin dough that is layered with melted butter to produce crisp, flaky pastries. It has been used for hundreds of years around the Mediterranean, and is an ancestor of puff pastry and other laminated doughs. Luckily, you can find good quality phyllo in the frozen section of the supermarket. Phyllo has a reputation for being tricky to work with, but if you understand how to defrost and work with it, you'll have success with this easy-to-use dough.

TYPES OF PHYLLO

Sheet (or leaf) phyllo is the type familiar to most Westerners. These thin, rectangular sheets of dough are brushed with melted butter, layered, and used to make baklava, spanakopita, *tiropetes,* and strudel, to name just a few pastries. Sheet phyllo is made with a simple dough similar in texture to fresh pasta dough. Although they're still painstakingly rolled and stretched out by hand in some traditional kitchens, most often the paper-thin sheets are formed by extruding the dough through a machine—much like rolling pasta. All the phyllo recipes in this chapter use sheet phyllo.

Shredded phyllo, also known as *kataif,* looks like shredded wheat or vermicelli, and is made from a thin batter that is drizzled in fine streams onto a hot griddle from a device resembling a potato ricer. Just as the strands set, they are scooped off and packaged. Whereas sheet phyllo is thin and delicate, prone to cracking and tearing, shredded phyllo is flexible, wiry, and virtually indestructible. It is, however, much harder to find, although if you shop in a market that has an Eastern Mediterranean clientele, it will almost certainly be in the frozen section next to the sheet phyllo. Shredded phyllo is not layered with butter like sheet phyllo. Instead, it is tossed with melted butter to coat the strands, then shaped and baked. If you find some shredded phyllo at the market, try your hand at Lemon Meringue Tartlets with Shredded Phyllo, page 236.

HOW TO BUY AND THAW SHEET PHYLLO

Choose phyllo packages from the back of the freezer case, where the temperature is more consistent. Phyllo sheets that have been thawed and refrozen will stick together and tear unmercifully. Always buy an extra box, just in case you get one that has thawing damage.

Thaw frozen phyllo in the refrigerator for 24 hours before use. If you try to thaw it quickly on the counter, condensation will form, the dough will get sticky, and you won't be able to pry the sheets apart. After it has thawed in the refrigerator, place the box on the kitchen counter for 1 to 2 hours and allow the dough to warm to room temperature. Cold phyllo is prone to cracking, whereas room temperature phyllo is more supple and easier to work with.

tips for success Phyllo

1. **Phyllo dries out quickly when exposed to air.** To prevent this from happening, cover the phyllo sheets not in use with a piece of plastic wrap large enough to extend over the sides of the phyllo stack. Top the plastic with a kitchen towel that has been dampened and wrung out.

2. **Brush the butter over the phyllo** with a soft bristle brush. Stiff bristles will tear the delicate dough.

3. **Apply melted butter sparingly.** Each layer of phyllo needs only the barest touch of butter, so work quickly and with a light hand. A common mistake is to coat each sheet heavily, which results in a leaden, greasy pastry rather than a light, crispy one.

4. **If you are layering many sheets of phyllo in a pan,** be sure to rotate the pan every few sheets. Most people are creatures of habit and will always begin buttering the pastry in the same corner each time. That corner ends up with a pool of butter. When you rotate the pan, the butter will be more evenly distributed.

5. **Bake phyllo at a medium temperature,** about 350°F, and watch the color closely. Although deep golden brown is perfect for most pastries, phyllo cooked until it's that hue will be bitter. What you want is a beautiful golden color instead. If the phyllo is browning too quickly, reduce the oven temperature by 25°F.

CLASSIC CROISSANTS

MAKES 24 CROISSANTS Layer upon layer of butter and dough produce the ultimate French breakfast treats, but you needn't limit yourself to croissants and their flavored variations. For example, try Morning Buns (page 113), a San Francisco twist on the classic cinnamon roll. Be sure to give yourself the time and counter space you'll need to enjoy the process of making the dough. There are tips at the end of the recipe for fitting the dough into your schedule (see "Getting Ahead," page 110). Be sure to read "A Primer on Laminated Doughs" (page 102), for tips that will help you turn out beautiful croissants.

INGREDIENTS

DOUGH BLOCK (*DÉTREMPE*)

½ cup (4 ounces) warm whole milk (110° to 115°F)

1 teaspoon plus 2 tablespoons (1 ounce) sugar

4 teaspoons (⅜ ounce) active dry yeast, or 1 tablespoon instant yeast

4 cups (20 ounces) unbleached all-purpose flour

2 teaspoons salt

½ stick (2 ounces) cold unsalted butter, cut into small pieces

1 cup (8 ounces) cold milk

BUTTER BLOCK (*BEURRAGE*)

3½ sticks (14 ounces) cold unsalted butter

2 tablespoons (1 ounce) unbleached all-purpose flour

1 large egg

1 tablespoon whole milk or cream

EQUIPMENT

Small Bowl, Whisk, Stand Mixer with Dough Hook and Paddle Attachments, Bowl Scraper, Rolling Pin, Pastry Brush, Ruler, Paring Knife or Pizza Cutter (Optional), Pastry Brush, Two Baking Sheets, Parchment Paper or Two Silicone Mats, Cooling Rack

1 MAKE THE DOUGH BLOCK: Pour the warm milk into a small bowl and whisk in 1 teaspoon of the sugar. Whisk in the yeast and set aside for 10 minutes, or until the yeast is activated and the mixture is bubbling.

2 In the bowl of a stand mixer fitted with the paddle attachment, combine the flour, remaining 2 tablespoons of sugar, the salt, and cold butter pieces. Blend on medium speed until the butter is cut into tiny pieces and the mixture resembles bread crumbs. Add the yeast mixture and the cold milk. Switch to the dough hook and mix on lowest speed for 1½ to 2 minutes, until the liquid is absorbed and has formed a very rough mass. Dust a work surface lightly with flour and turn the dough out onto it. Knead the dough 3 to 5 times, just to finish bringing it together. The dough will not be smooth or elastic; it will become fully kneaded and smooth during the rolling and turning process ahead. Don't overwork the dough now or you'll have trouble rolling it later. Wrap the dough loosely in plastic wrap (to allow a little room for expansion) and refrigerate for 30 to 60 minutes.

3 MAKE THE BUTTER BLOCK: Cut the butter into ½-inch pieces, toss with the flour, and refrigerate for 20 minutes. In the cleaned stand mixer fitted with the paddle attachment, beat the floured butter on medium speed, scraping down the bowl once or twice with a bowl scraper, for 1 to 2 minutes, until the butter and flour form a smooth mass. You are not trying to beat air into the mixture, just make it pliable and smooth while keeping it cold. Scrape the butter onto a piece of parchment paper or plastic wrap, wrap it up, and refrigerate while you roll out the dough.

what the pros know

Once the dough is made and shaped, pay attention to the proofing process. During this last rise, the many layers of butter in the dough should remain cool. If the room is too warm, the butter will melt, and instead of forming flaky layers in the oven, it will leak out of the dough, covering the baking sheet in a pool of liquid butter and "frying" the bottoms of the croissants in the process. To prevent this, pick a cool room temperature spot for proofing the croissants, preferably 65° to 75°F. Once they have risen, chill in the freezer for 10 minutes or in the refrigerator for 15 minutes just prior to baking. This will firm the butter, ensuring beautifully flaky croissants.

4 INCORPORATE THE BUTTER INTO THE DOUGH: Dust the work surface with flour. Set the dough in the center and dust the top with flour. Roll the dough into a 15 by 12-inch rectangle with a short side parallel to the edge of your work surface. Gently pull or stretch the dough to form straight edges and sharp corners. Brush any flour from the surface. Visually divide the dough crosswise into 3 equal, 5-inch-wide sections (you can lightly mark the dough with a ruler or the back of a knife if you wish). Spread the cold but pliable butter evenly over the top two sections of dough, leaving the bottom third empty and leaving a ½-inch border around the edges of the buttered sections. This is best done with your fingers, since the butter isn't quite warm enough to spread easily with a spatula. Alternatively, you can place the butter between two sheets of plastic and roll it into a 9½ by 11-inch rectangle. Peel off one sheet of plastic, invert the buttered rectangle over the dough rectangle, center it, and peel off the other sheet of plastic.

5 USE A LETTER FOLD TO ENCASE THE BUTTER: Fold the empty bottom third up over the center third of the dough. Then fold the top third down over the center. Pinch together the seams along the bottom and sides of the dough. Roll your rolling pin across the top briefly and gently 3 or 4 times to help seal the seams. This completes both the incorporation of the butter and your first turn of the dough. If the butter has become warm and squishy, wrap the dough in plastic and refrigerate for 1 hour before continuing with the second turn. If you have worked quickly and the butter is still cold yet pliable, continue with the next turn.

6 Position the dough with the short side parallel to your work surface and the long fold on your left. Dust the dough with flour and roll it into a 20 by 12-inch rectangle. Brush any flour from the surface of the dough. Fold the dough using the book-fold method: Fold the two short edges into the center of the dough, leaving a ¼-inch crevice between them. Line up the edges precisely and square the corners as you fold. Now fold one side over the other, as though you were closing a book. Roll your pin across the top of the dough briefly and gently 3 or 4 times to seal the seams. This completes your second turn. Wrap the dough in plastic and refrigerate for 1 hour.

7 Remove the dough from the refrigerator, dust with flour, and roll again into a 20 by 12-inch rectangle. Brush any flour from the surface of the dough. Fold the dough using the letter-fold method: Visually divide the dough lengthwise into 3 equal, 5-inch-wide sections (you can lightly mark the dough with a ruler or the back of a knife if you wish). Fold the bottom third up over the center of the dough, and then fold the top third down over the center, making sure to square the corners and fold as neatly and precisely as possible. Roll your rolling pin across the top of the dough again briefly to help seal the seams. This completes your third turn. The croissant dough is finished. Wrap in plastic wrap and refrigerate for at least 2 hours and up to 24 hours before cutting, shaping, and baking the dough.

8 CUT THE DOUGH: Roll the dough on a floured surface into a 26 by 14 by ¼-inch-thick rectangle. Cut the rectangle in half lengthwise to form two pieces that each measure 26 by 7 inches. Position the rectangles so the long edges are parallel to the edge of your work surface. On each piece, use a ruler and paring knife or pizza cutter to make nicks along the top edge of the dough every 4 inches. Along the bottom edge, measure 2 inches in from the left side and make a nick; then add a nick every 4 inches.

9 NOW CUT THE DOUGH INTO TRIANGLES: Line up your ruler with the top left corner and the first bottom nick (2 inches in from the left side of the dough). Cut along

You can spread the process of making croissants over 2 days. On the first day, finish making the dough (through Step 7). Wrap the dough loosely in plastic (it will expand slightly) and refrigerate overnight. The next day, roll, cut, shape, proof, and bake the croissants. You can also freeze the croissants already shaped (through Step 10). Place the croissants on a baking sheet and freeze until firm, then transfer them to resealable plastic freezer bags. They will keep for 4 to 6 weeks. To bake, transfer the frozen croissants directly to prepared baking sheets and let them defrost and proof at room temperature. Apply the egg wash after a couple of hours. The croissants should be ready for Step 12 after about 3 hours.

this line. This first skinny triangle is not a full croissant. You can use these "scrap" triangles to make baby croissants or simply sprinkle the surface with sugar and bake as a snack. Next, line up the ruler with the first nick on the top edge and the left corner bottom, and cut along that line, forming a full-size triangle. Then cut a line from the first nick on top to the first nick on the bottom to form the second triangle. Continue lining up the nicks and cutting until the whole sheet has been cut into 12 triangles. Mark and cut the second half of dough in the same way.

10 SHAPE THE DOUGH: Line the baking sheets with parchment paper or silicone mats. Line up all the triangles so that their bottom (4-inch) sides are parallel with the edge of your work surface. Make a 1-inch vertical slit in the center of the bottom edge of each triangle. To shape, grasp a triangle and, with the wide end in one hand and the point in the other, very gently stretch the dough until it is a couple inches longer. Set it back on the table (notice how it resembles the Eiffel Tower!). Pull the slit in the bottom apart slightly and roll the corners upward and outward, widening the slit. Now roll the entire triangle toward the tip, pulling gently on the tip to stretch the dough slightly. Tuck the tip under the roll (so it doesn't pull out during baking) and place the roll on one of the prepared baking sheets. Curve the ends in toward each other to form a crescent shape. Continue stretching and rolling the dough triangles until you have shaped all the croissants and placed them 2 inches apart on the baking sheets.

11 WASH WITH EGG AND PROOF: In the cleaned small bowl, lightly beat the eggs and milk. Brush each croissant evenly with the egg wash. Cover the remaining egg wash and refrigerate to use later. Allow the croissants to rise in a cool room-temperature spot until they are nearly doubled in size and look like they have taken a deep breath, 1 to 2 hours, depending on the warmth of the room. If you squeeze one gently, it should feel soft and marshmallow-like. Don't try to rush the rise by warming the croissants—you don't want the butter to melt.

12 BAKE THE CROISSANTS: Preheat the oven to 400°F and position a rack in the center. Chill the croissants in the freezer for 10 minutes or in the refrigerator for 15 minutes. This will firm the butter, creating a flakier texture. Brush the croissants once more with the egg wash. Bake one baking sheet at a time, rotating it halfway through, for 17 to 22 minutes, until the croissants are a deep golden brown. Transfer the croissants to a rack to cool.

STORING **Baked croissants keep, unwrapped at room temperature, for 1 day. For longer storage, wrap each croissant in plastic wrap and slip into a resealable plastic freezer bag. Freeze for up to 1 month. Thaw at room temperature for 30 minutes, then reheat in a 350°F oven for 7 to 8 minutes, until the crust is crisped and the center is warmed through.**

Almond Croissants

INGREDIENTS

1 recipe Classic Croissants (page 108), prepared through Step 9

1 recipe Almond Filling (page 119)

1 cup (3 ounces) raw sliced almonds (natural or blanched)

2 tablespoons confectioners' sugar (optional)

1   Begin Step 10 of Croissants recipe, but don't slit the dough triangles as described in the second sentence. Place 1 tablespoon of almond filling ½ inch from the bottom of each triangle. Use your finger or a spoon to gently smear the filling in a small triangle, keeping it centered on the dough and away from the edges.

2   Roll the dough as described in Step 10, rolling the bottoms of the stretched triangles (without slits) toward the tips. Brush with egg wash and proof as in Step 11. After brushing with egg wash for the second time in Step 12, sprinkle sliced almonds over the top of each croissant. Bake as directed.

3   If desired, dust lightly with confectioners' sugar just before serving.

Ham and Cheese Croissants

MAKES 24 CROISSANTS

INGREDIENTS

1 recipe Classic Croissants (page 108), prepared through Step 9

6 thin slices ham, each quartered

1½ cups (6 ounces) Swiss or Cheddar cheese, grated

1   Begin Step 10 of Classic Croissants recipe, but don't slit the dough triangles as described in the second sentence. For each triangle, roll or fold a piece of ham so that it is slightly smaller than the width of the croissant base. Place the ham about ½ inch from the bottom of the triangle. Sprinkle 1 scant tablespoon of grated cheese on top.

2   Roll the dough as described in Step 10, rolling the bottoms of the stretched triangles (without slits) toward the tips. Brush with egg wash and proof as in Step 11. After brushing with egg wash for the second time in Step 12, sprinkle a little grated cheese over the top of each croissant. Bake as directed.

Chocolate Croissants

MAKES 24 CROISSANTS

INGREDIENTS

1 recipe Classic Croissants (page 108), prepared through Step 9

1 cup (6 ounces) finely grated semisweet or bittersweet chocolate

2 tablespoons confectioners' sugar

2 ounces finely chopped semisweet or bittersweet chocolate (any cacao percentage)

EQUIPMENT

Fine-Mesh Strainer

1   Begin Step 10 of Croissants recipe, but don't slit the dough triangles as described in the second sentence. Place 2 teaspoons of grated chocolate ½ inch from the bottom of each triangle. Use your finger or a spoon to gently push the chocolate into the shape of a small triangle, keeping it centered on the dough and away from the edges.

2   Roll the dough as described in Step 10, rolling the bottoms of the stretched triangles (without slits) toward the tips. Brush with egg wash and proof as in Step 11. Bake as directed in Step 12. Let the croissants cool completely.

3   With a fine-mesh strainer, dust the top of the croissants with the confectioners' sugar. Melt the chopped chocolate (see page 43) until smooth and liquid. Transfer to a resealable plastic sandwich bag and squeeze the chocolate into one corner. Use a pair of scissors to snip off the corner of the bag, making a small hole. Pipe the melted chocolate over the croissants.

MORNING BUNS

MAKES 12 A classic start to the San Francisco Bay Area day, morning buns are an amped-up version of cinnamon rolls made with flaky croissant dough. The buns are baked in a muffin tin so the outside of each one gets deeply browned and caramelized. Then, as soon as they emerge from the oven, they are tossed in granulated sugar, giving them a sparkling finish.

INGREDIENTS

½ recipe (about 1½ pounds) Classic Croissants dough (page 108), prepared through Step 7

1 large egg

⅔ cup (5¼ ounces) firmly packed light brown sugar

2½ teaspoons ground cinnamon

½ cup (3½ ounces) granulated sugar

EQUIPMENT

Rolling Pin, Pastry Brush, Whisk, Two Medium Bowls, Chef's Knife or Bench Scraper, Standard 12-Cup Muffin Tin, Tongs, Silicone Mat or Parchment Paper

GETTING AHEAD The buns may be prepared through Step 3 a day ahead. Cover the pan loosely with plastic wrap and refrigerate overnight. The buns will rise slowly through the night. In the morning, let the buns sit at room temperature for 1 hour, or until fully risen before continuing with Step 5.

1 ROLL AND FILL THE DOUGH: On a lightly floured surface, roll the dough into an 18 by 11 by ¼-inch rectangle. Position the dough with a long side parallel to the edge of your work surface. Brush any flour from the surface of the dough. Whisk the egg in the small bowl just to break it up, then brush the entire surface of the dough lightly with the egg.

2 In a medium bowl, stir together the brown sugar and cinnamon until thoroughly blended. Sprinkle evenly over the dough, leaving a 1-inch border along the long edge of the dough farthest from you.

3 SHAPE THE DOUGH: Beginning with the long side closest to you, roll the dough into a cylinder, gently tucking and tightening as you roll. Finish rolling the dough onto the border. Roll the dough cylinder backward so that the seam is facing upward and pinch all along it to seal the dough. It should be 18 inches long. If not, roll it gently back and forth until it lengthens. Cut the cylinder into 12 equal pieces, each about 1½ inches wide. Generously butter the muffin pan and place each piece cut side up in a muffin cup.

4 PROOF THE DOUGH: Cover the pan loosely with plastic wrap and allow the buns to rise in a cool room-temperature spot until they have almost doubled in size (they will be slightly higher than the top of the muffin tin), 45 to 60 minutes. Don't try to rush the rise by warming the croissants—you don't want the butter to melt.

5 BAKE THE BUNS: Preheat the oven to 375°F and position a rack in the center. Chill the buns in the freezer for 10 minutes or in the refrigerator for 15 minutes. This will firm the butter and create a flakier texture. Bake for 25 minutes, or until the buns are deep golden brown. Place the granulated sugar in a medium bowl. Remove the tin from the oven and set it on a towel next to the bowl. Gently remove each bun with the tongs and drop it in the sugar, turning it to coat all sides. Then transfer each bun to the silicone mat or parchment paper to cool. Serve warm or at room temperature.

STORING The buns are at their best the same day they are made. They may be stored under a cake dome at room temperature for 2 days. Before serving, reheat in a 375°F oven for 6 to 7 minutes.

DANISH DOUGH

MAKES ABOUT 3 POUNDS, ENOUGH FOR 24 INDIVIDUAL PASTRIES Though similar to croissant dough, Danish dough includes eggs in the détrempe, which makes it the softest of all the laminated doughs. It is a bit stickier and more cakelike because of the eggs, but the extra fat they contribute coats the gluten strands and reduces gluten development. This dough is a pleasure to roll and shape and produces a flaky, blistered crust that is beautifully tender.

INGREDIENTS

DOUGH BLOCK (DÉTREMPE)

½ cup (4 ounces) warm whole milk (110° to 115°F)

1 teaspoon, plus 2 tablespoons (1 ounce), sugar

4 teaspoons active dry yeast, or 1 tablespoon instant yeast

2 cold large eggs

¾ cup (6 ounces) cold whole milk

3½ cups (17½ ounces) unbleached all-purpose flour

1 teaspoon salt

½ teaspoon ground cardamom

BUTTER BLOCK (BEURRAGE)

3 sticks (12 ounces) cold unsalted butter, cut into ½-inch pieces

¼ cup (1¼ ounces) unbleached all-purpose flour

EQUIPMENT

Small Bowl, Whisk, Stand Mixer with Dough Hook and Paddle Attachments, Silicone or Rubber Spatula, Medium Bowl, Parchment Paper, Rolling Pin, Ruler, Pastry Brush

1 MAKE THE DOUGH BLOCK: Pour the warm milk into a small bowl and whisk in 1 teaspoon of the sugar. Whisk in the yeast and set aside for 10 minutes, or until the yeast is activated and the mixture is bubbling.

2 In the bowl of a stand mixer, whisk together the remaining 2 tablespoons of sugar, the eggs, and cold milk. Whisk the yeast mixture into the egg mixture. In a separate, medium bowl, whisk together the flour, salt, and cardamom until well blended. Add the flour mixture to the egg mixture, attach the dough hook, and mix on lowest speed for 1½ to 2 minutes, until the liquid is absorbed and has formed a very rough mass. Dust a work surface lightly with flour and turn the dough out onto it. Knead the dough 3 to 5 times, just to finish bringing it together. The dough will not be smooth or elastic; it will become fully kneaded and smooth during the rolling and turning process ahead. Don't overwork the dough now or you'll have trouble rolling it later. Wrap the dough in plastic wrap and refrigerate for 30 to 60 minutes.

3 MAKE THE BUTTER BLOCK: Toss the butter pieces with the flour and refrigerate for 20 minutes. In the cleaned stand mixer fitted with the paddle attachment, beat the floured butter on medium speed, scraping down the bowl once or twice with a silicone spatula, for 1 to 2 minutes, until the butter and flour form a smooth mass. You are not trying to beat air into the mixture, just make it pliable and smooth while keeping it cold. Scrape the butter onto a piece of parchment paper or plastic wrap, wrap it up, and refrigerate while you roll out the dough.

Curiously enough, in Denmark, Danish pastry is known as *wienerbrod,* or Vienna bread. It was introduced to the Danes by Viennese bakers and quickly became a favorite in bakeries across the country. Cardamom, a spice popular in Scandinavia for sweets, often flavors the dough. If you don't have it on hand, you may leave it out or substitute another spice. For another layer of flavor, add the grated zest of 2 oranges—or 1 lemon and 1 orange—to the dough.

GETTING AHEAD **The dough can be completed the day before you shape and bake it. Wrap the dough loosely in plastic wrap (it will expand slightly) and refrigerate overnight. If you will only be using half the dough, wrap the other half in plastic and slip it into a resealable plastic freezer bag. Freeze for 4 to 6 weeks. Thaw the dough on a baking sheet, covered with plastic, overnight in the refrigerator.**

4 INCORPORATE THE BUTTER AND TURN THE DOUGH: Lightly dust the work surface with flour. Set the dough in the center and dust the top with flour. Roll the dough into a 15 by 12-inch rectangle with a short side parallel to the edge of your work surface. Gently pull or stretch the dough to form straight edges and sharp corners. Brush any flour from the surface. Visually divide the dough crosswise into 3 equal, 5-inch-wide sections (you can lightly mark the dough with a ruler or the back of a knife if you wish). Spread the cold but pliable butter evenly over the top two sections of dough, leaving the bottom third empty and leaving a ½-inch border around the edges of the buttered sections. This is best done with your fingers, since the butter isn't quite warm enough to spread easily with a spatula. Alternatively, you can place the butter between two sheets of plastic and roll it into a 9½ by 11-inch rectangle. Peel off one sheet of plastic, invert the buttered rectangle over the dough rectangle, center it, and peel off the other sheet of plastic.

5 USE A LETTER FOLD TO ENCASE THE BUTTER: Fold the empty bottom third up over the center third of the dough. Then fold the top third down over the center. Pinch together the seams along the bottom and sides of the dough. Roll your rolling pin across the top of the dough briefly and gently 3 or 4 times to help seal the seams. This completes both the incorporation of the butter and your first turn of the dough. If the butter has become warm and squishy, wrap the dough in plastic and refrigerate for 1 hour before continuing with the second turn. If you have worked quickly and the butter is still cold yet pliable, continue with the next turn.

6 Position the dough with the short side parallel to your work surface and the long fold on your left. Dust the dough with flour and roll it into a 20 by 12-inch rectangle. Brush any flour from the surface of the dough. Fold the dough using the book fold method: Fold the two short edges into the center of the dough, leaving a ¼-inch crevice between them. Line up the edges precisely and square the corners as you fold. Now fold one side over the other, as though you were closing a book. Roll your pin across the top of the dough briefly and gently 3 or 4 times to seal the seams. This completes your second turn. Wrap the dough in plastic and refrigerate it for 1 hour.

7 Remove the dough from the refrigerator, dust with flour, and roll again into a 20 by 12-inch rectangle. Brush any flour from the surface of the dough. Fold the dough using the letter-fold method: Visually divide the dough lengthwise into 3 equal, 5-inch-wide sections (you can lightly mark the dough with a ruler or the back of a knife if you wish). Fold the bottom third up over the center of the dough, and then fold the top third down over the center, making sure to square the corners and fold as neatly and precisely as possible. Roll your rolling pin across the top of the dough again briefly to help seal the seams. This completes your third turn. The Danish dough is finished.

STORING **Wrap the dough in plastic wrap and refrigerate for at least 2 hours or up to 24 hours before cutting, shaping, and baking the dough.**

CHEESE DANISH

MAKES 12 DANISH   There are two camps of Danish eaters—those who relish Bear Claws (page 118), and those who reach for the cheese Danish. The filling here is a lightly sweetened cream cheese, similar to cheesecake filling, which may be left plain and simple or paired with fruit or jam.

INGREDIENTS

½ recipe (about 1½ pounds)
Danish Dough (page 114)

½ recipe Cream Cheese Filling (page 119)
1 recipe Apricot Glaze (page 119)

Jam or fruit (optional)
Confectioners' sugar, for dusting

EQUIPMENT

Rolling Pin, Ruler, Chef's Knife, Two Baking Sheets, Parchment Paper or Two Silicone Mats, Cooling Rack, Pastry Brush, Fine-Mesh Strainer

GETTING AHEAD **You can spread the process of making the Danish dough and baking the shapes over 2 days, as described in the "Getting Ahead" notes for making croissants, page 110. You can also freeze the cheese Danish already shaped (through Step 2), but omit any fruit or jam until the pastries have thawed. Freeze as described for croissants for 4 to 6 weeks. To bake, transfer the frozen pastries directly to prepared baking sheets and let them defrost and proof at room temperature. Add the fruit or jam, if using, after 1 hour. They should be ready for Step 4 in about 2 to 3 hours.**

1   Dust your work surface with flour. Place the dough in the center and dust the top with flour. Roll into a 16 by 12 by ¼-inch rectangle. Position the dough so that one of the long edges is parallel to the edge of your work surface. Using a ruler and a chef's knife, mark the dough at 4-inch intervals along all four sides of the dough. Using the ruler to connect the marks on opposite sides, cut the dough into 12 (4-inch) squares.

2   Place a tablespoon of cream cheese filling in the center of each square, spreading it slightly into an oval toward two of the diagonal corners. Fold one of the other corners over the filling. Moisten its top with a touch of water. Bring the opposite corner over the first and press to seal. Line the baking sheets with parchment paper or silicone mats and transfer the pastries to the sheets. If you want to add a bit more flavor and color, place about ½ teaspoon of jam on each side of the exposed filling, or a quarter of an apricot, or a berry or two. Keep it spare, because both dough and filling will spread as the Danish bakes.

3   Cover the sheets loosely with plastic wrap and let the pastries rise in a cool room-temperature spot until the pastries are nearly doubled in size and look like they have taken a deep breath, about 1 hour depending on the warmth of the room. If you squeeze one gently, it should feel soft and marshmallow-like. Don't try to rush the rise by warming the Danish—you don't want the butter to melt.

4   Preheat the oven to 400°F and position a rack in the center. Chill the Danish in the freezer for 10 minutes or in the refrigerator for 15 minutes. This will firm the butter and create a flakier texture. Bake one sheet of Danish at a time (keep the second one chilled), rotating the sheet halfway through, for 14 to 16 minutes, until golden brown. Transfer Danish to a cooling rack and immediately brush with a thin layer of the apricot glaze. Bake and glaze the second pan of Danish the same way. Cool completely and use a fine-mesh strainer to dust with confectioners' sugar before serving.

STORING **Cheese Danish will keep, unwrapped at room temperature, for 1 day. For longer storage, wrap each one in plastic wrap and slip into a resealable plastic freezer bag. Freeze for up to 1 month. Thaw at room temperature for 30 minutes, then reheat in a 350°F oven for 7 to 8 minutes, until the crust is crisped and the center is warmed through.**

SPICED CARDAMOM TWISTS

MAKES 16 TWISTS These are crispy twists of dough sandwiching a filling of cardamom-scented sugar and chopped almonds. Cardamom is a fragrant relative of ginger and native to India. You can create variations on the theme by using a different nut or replacing the cardamom with cinnamon, ginger, or your own special spice blend.

INGREDIENTS

½ recipe (about 1½ pounds)
Danish Dough (page 114)

½ cup (3½ ounces) sugar

1½ teaspoons ground cardamom

1 large egg

½ cup (2½ ounces) finely chopped raw almonds (natural or blanched)

EQUIPMENT

Two Baking Sheets, Parchment Paper or Two Silicone Mats, Rolling Pin, Pastry Brush, Two Small Bowls, Ruler, Chef's Knife, Cooling Rack

GETTING AHEAD **You can spread the process of making the Danish dough and baking the twists over 2 days, as described in the "Getting Ahead" notes for making croissants, page 110. You can also freeze twists already shaped (through Step 2) as described for croissants, for 4 to 6 weeks. Thaw and proof directly on baking sheets at room temperature, covered loosely with plastic wrap. They should be ready for Step 4 in 2 to 3 hours.**

1 Line the baking sheets with parchment paper or silicone mats. Dust your work surface with flour. Place the dough in the center and dust the top with flour. Roll into a 16 by 12 by ¼-inch rectangle. Position the dough so that one of the long edges is parallel to the edge of your work surface. Brush any flour from the surface of the dough.

2 Place the sugar and cardamom in a small bowl and blend well. Place the egg in a separate small bowl and beat with a fork until blended. Brush the entire surface of the dough with a thin film of the egg. Spread the sugar mixture over the lower half of the dough, leaving a ½-inch border along the bottom. Sprinkle the almonds evenly over the sugar. Fold the top half of the dough down over the filling and press along the bottom edge to seal the dough. Using a rolling pin, roll over the dough 2 or 3 times to seal and slightly embed the filling in the dough. Using a ruler and a chef's knife, cut the rectangle into 16 1-inch-wide strips. Grasp a strip and twist the ends in opposite directions 4 times, then transfer to a prepared baking sheet. Repeat until all the strips have been shaped and set on the baking sheets 2 inches apart. Scoop up any fallen filling and sprinkle it over the tops of the twists.

3 Cover the twists and baking sheets loosely with plastic wrap and let the twists rise in a cool room-temperature spot until they are nearly doubled in size and look like they have taken a deep breath, about 1 hour. Don't try to rush the rise by warming the twists—you don't want the butter to melt.

4 Preheat the oven to 400°F and position a rack in the center. Chill the twists in the freezer for 10 minutes or in the refrigerator for 15 minutes. This will firm the butter and create a flakier texture. Bake one batch of twists at a time (keep the second one chilled), rotating the baking sheet halfway through, for 14 to 16 minutes, until golden brown. Transfer the twists to a cooling rack. Bake the second pan of twists the same way.

STORING **Danish twists will keep, unwrapped, at room temperature for 1 day. For longer storage, wrap each in plastic wrap and slip into a resealable plastic freezer bag. Freeze for 4 to 6 weeks. Thaw at room temperature for 30 minutes, then reheat in a 375°F oven for 7 to 8 minutes, until the crust is crisped and the center is warmed through.**

BEAR CLAWS

MAKES 12 CLAWS Almond lovers, here is your breakfast pastry. Bear claws are a classic shape, with golden brown "paws" hiding a ribbon of rich almond filling. For an extra layer of sweetness, drizzle some Confectioners' Sugar Icing (page 415) over the top, or simply dust lightly with confectioners' sugar.

INGREDIENTS

½ recipe (about 1½ pounds) Danish Dough (page 114)

½ recipe (about ¾ cup) Almond Filling (page 119)

1 recipe Apricot Glaze (page 119)

½ cup (1½ ounces) sliced almonds

Confectioners' sugar (for dusting)

Egg wash: 1 large egg beaten with 1 tablespoon milk or cream

EQUIPMENT

Rolling Pin, Ruler, Chef's Knife, Pastry Bag Fitted with a ½-inch Plain Tip, Pastry Brush, Two Baking Sheets, Parchment Paper or Two Silicone Mats, Small Bowl, Cooling Rack

GETTING AHEAD You can spread the process of making the Danish dough and baking the shapes over 2 days, as described in the "Getting Ahead" notes for making croissants, page 110. You can also freeze the bear claws already shaped (through Step 2). Freeze as described for croissants for 4 to 6 weeks. To bake, transfer the frozen bear claws directly to prepared baking sheets and let them defrost and proof at room temperature, covered loosely with plastic wrap. They should be ready for Step 4 in 2 to 3 hours.

1 Dust your work surface with flour. Place the dough in the center and dust the top with flour. Roll into a 16 by 12 by ¼-inch rectangle. Position the dough so that one of the long edges is parallel to the edge of your work surface. Using the ruler and a chef's knife, mark the dough at 4-inch intervals along all four sides of the dough. Use the ruler to connect the marks on opposite sides and cut the dough into 12 (4-inch) squares.

2 Place the almond filling in the pastry bag and pipe a 3-inch-long line of filling in the center of each square, leaving a ½-inch border at the edges. Brush the edges with a thin film of water, then fold the dough over the filling to meet the bottom edge. Press the edges to seal them. Use a chef's knife to cut 4 (½-inch-long) slits through the bottom sealed edge of each pastry. Line the baking sheets with parchment paper or silicone mats and transfer the pastries to the sheets. Curve the pastries into a smile so the slits along the sealed edge open and each toe of the "claw" separates.

3 Cover the pans loosely with plastic wrap and let the bear claws rise in a cool room-temperature spot until they are nearly doubled in size and look like they have taken a deep breath, about 1 hour. If you squeeze one gently, it should feel soft and marshmallow-like. Don't try to rush the rise by warming the Danish—you don't want the butter to melt.

4 Preheat the oven to 400°F and position a rack in the center. Chill the bear claws in the freezer for 10 minutes or in the refrigerator for 15 minutes. This will firm the butter and create a flakier texture. In a small bowl, lightly beat the egg and milk. Brush the bear claws with the egg wash and sprinkle each one with sliced almonds, or place a single sliced almond on each "toe." Bake one sheet of bear claws at a time (keep the second one chilled), rotating the sheet halfway through, for 14 to 16 minutes, until golden brown. Transfer the bear claws to a cooling rack and immediately brush with a thin layer of the apricot glaze. Bake and glaze the second pan of bear claws the same way. Cool completely and dust with confectioners' sugar before serving.

STORING Bear claws keep, unwrapped, at room temperature for 1 day. For longer storage, wrap each one in plastic wrap and slip into a resealable plastic freezer bag. Freeze for up to 1 month. Thaw at room temperature for 30 minutes, then reheat in a 350°F oven for 7 to 8 minutes, until the crust is crisped and the center is warmed through.

Almond Filling

MAKES ABOUT 1½ CUPS This filling is divine in Danish and croissants, and takes a mere 5 minutes to make in the food processor.

INGREDIENTS

4 ounces almond paste
2 tablespoons (1 ounce) sugar
1 stick (4 ounces) unsalted butter, softened (65° to 68°F)
1 large egg
Finely grated zest of ½ lemon
1 teaspoon pure vanilla extract
3 tablespoons (1½ ounces) unbleached all-purpose flour

EQUIPMENT

Food Processor Fitted with a Metal Blade or Stand Mixer Fitted with a Paddle Attachment, Silicone or Rubber Spatula

Break or cut the almond paste into 10 to 12 pieces and put them in the bowl of the food processor or stand mixer. Add the sugar and process or mix until the almond paste is cut into tiny pieces, 20 to 30 seconds. Add the butter and process or mix until well blended, 20 to 30 seconds longer. Scrape down the bowl. Add the egg, lemon zest, and vanilla extract and process or mix for about 10 seconds. Add the flour and process or mix for 10 seconds. Scrape down the bowl with a spatula and make sure everything is evenly mixed.

STORING The filling will keep, refrigerated in an airtight container, for up to 5 days. Let the filling come to room temperature before using, or it will be too stiff to spread easily.

Cream Cheese Filling

MAKES 1⅓ CUPS As luscious and tangy as cheesecake, this is the perfect filling for individual Danish or a coffee cake. Create other flavors by substituting orange or lime zest, or changing the flavor of the extract.

INGREDIENTS

8 ounces cream cheese
6 tablespoons (2½ ounces) sugar
1 large egg yolk
1½ tablespoons (½ ounce) unbleached all-purpose flour
Finely grated zest of ½ lemon
½ teaspoon pure vanilla extract

EQUIPMENT

Food Processor Fitted with a Metal Blade, Silicone or Rubber Spatula

Cut the cream cheese into 8 to 10 pieces and put in the bowl of a food processor. Add the sugar and process until the mixture is smooth, 20 to 30 seconds, scraping down the bowl with a spatula halfway through. Add the egg yolk and process for 5 seconds; scrape down the bowl. Add the flour, lemon zest, and vanilla extract and blend well, about 10 seconds. Scrape down the bowl and make sure everything is evenly mixed.

STORING The filling may be kept, refrigerated in an airtight container, for up to 5 days.

Apricot Glaze

MAKES SCANT ½ CUP

INGREDIENTS

¼ cup (2½ ounces) apricot jam
2 to 3 tablespoons water

EQUIPMENT

Small Saucepan, Fine-Mesh Strainer, Small Bowl

Combine the jam in the small saucepan with 2 tablespoons water. Warm over low heat until melted and fluid. If the glaze seems very thick, add another tablespoon of water. Strain through the fine-mesh strainer into the small bowl to remove any thick chunks of fruit. Use while warm and fluid.

STORING The glaze will keep, refrigerated in an airtight container, for 1 month. Reheat before using.

BRAIDED DANISH COFFEE CAKE

SERVES 6 TO 8 This beautiful coffee cake, woven in a braid, never fails to bring a gasp of delight. If you use half the recipe of the Danish dough, you can put together two coffee cakes at a time—one to bake today and the other for the freezer, ready to be thawed and baked for an easy weekend surprise. The filling can be either Almond or Cream Cheese Filling (page 119). If you assemble two coffee cakes at a time, you might want to try a different filling in each coffee cake. For an extra layer of flavor, sprinkle the top of the filling with finely chopped dark chocolate, and/or a ½-inch-wide length of raspberry or apricot jam. In the summer, use fresh raspberries, blueberries, or sliced plums instead of jam.

INGREDIENTS

¼ recipe (about ¾ pound) Danish Dough (page 114)

½ recipe (about ¾ cup) Almond or Cream Cheese Filling (page 119)

1 recipe Apricot Glaze (page 119)

1 large egg

1 tablespoon milk or cream

3 tablespoons (½ ounce) raw sliced almonds (if using almond filling)

Confectioners' sugar (for dusting), or Confectioners' Sugar Icing (page 415), for garnish

EQUIPMENT

Rolling Pin, Pastry Brush, Parchment Paper, Ruler, Chef's Knife, Silicone or Offset Spatula, Baking Sheet, Small Bowl, Cooling Rack

1 ROLL AND SHAPE THE DOUGH: Lightly dust your work surface with flour. Place the dough in the center and dust with flour. Roll into an 8 by 12 by ¼-inch rectangle. (If you are using half the Danish dough and making two coffee cakes, roll the dough to 16 by 12 inches, then cut in half to form two 8 by 12-inch rectangles.) Brush any flour from the surface of the dough. Cut a piece of parchment paper large enough to fit the baking sheet, transfer the dough to the paper, and position so that a short edge is parallel to the edge of your work surface.

2 Using the ruler and the back of a chef's knife, mark a 2-inch-wide strip down the center of the dough, from top to bottom. This is where the filling will go. On either side of the filling area, make diagonal cuts in the dough, 3 inches long and 1 inch apart. Use a silicone or offset spatula to spread the filling down the center strip of the dough. Braid the dough by crossing alternating strips of dough over the filling from the right and left, working from the top down. When you reach the bottom, press the dough to seal it, then tuck it under slightly. If you are making two coffee cakes, braid the second rectangle of dough the same way, then freeze to bake another day (see "Getting Ahead," page 122). Transfer the coffee cake, still on the parchment paper, to the baking sheet.

3 PROOF THE DOUGH: Cover the braid and baking sheet loosely with plastic wrap and let the coffee cake rise in a cool room-temperature spot until it has nearly doubled in size and looks like it has taken a deep breath, about 1 hour. Don't try to rush the rise by warming the coffee cake—you don't want the butter to melt.

GETTING AHEAD You can spread the process of making the Danish dough and baking the coffeecake over 2 days, as described in the "Getting Ahead" notes for making croissants, page 110. You can also freeze the coffeecake already shaped (through Step 2). Freeze on the baking sheet until firm, then wrap twice with plastic wrap. Freeze for 4 to 6 weeks. To bake, transfer the coffeecake directly to a prepared baking sheet and let it defrost and proof at room temperature, covered loosely with plastic wrap. It should be ready for Step 4 in 2 to 3 hours.

4 WASH WITH EGG AND BAKE: Preheat the oven to 400°F and position a rack in the center. Chill the coffee cake in the freezer for 10 minutes or in the refrigerator for 15 minutes. This will firm the butter and create a flakier texture. In a small bowl, lightly beat the egg and milk, and brush the top with the egg wash. Sprinkle with sliced almonds, if using almond filling. Bake the coffee cake, rotating the baking sheet halfway through, for 22 to 25 minutes, until golden brown. Transfer to a cooling rack and immediately brush with a thin layer of apricot glaze. Use a fine-mesh strainer to dust the coffee cake with the confectioners' sugar, or drizzle with icing. Cut slices with a serrated knife.

STORING The coffee cake will keep, unwrapped at room temperature, for 1 day. For longer storage, double-wrap in plastic and freeze for up to 1 month. Thaw at room temperature for 1 hour, then reheat in a 350°F oven for 9 to 12 minutes, until the crust is crisped and the center is warmed through.

QUICK PUFF PASTRY

MAKES 2¼ POUNDS Puff pastry is one of the most versatile doughs in the pastry kitchen. And while traditional puff pastry can be daunting, with its layering of butter and dough, this quick version—akin to a butter-laden pie dough—is relatively simple. Yes, there are still turns to be made, but the process is quicker and results in a light, flaky, layered dough almost indistinguishable from the classic. And the flavor is far superior to any frozen product from the supermarket.

INGREDIENTS

4½ sticks (18 ounces) cold unsalted butter

3 cups (15 ounces) unbleached all-purpose flour

¾ teaspoon salt

6 tablespoons (3 ounces) very cold water

1½ teaspoons cider vinegar

EQUIPMENT

Chef's Knife, Stand Mixer Fitted with a Paddle Attachment, Rolling Pin, Pastry Brush

what the pros know

None of the recipes in this chapter call for an entire recipe of puff pastry, so you'll have enough to make a pastry today, as well as freeze some for another day. Professionals always freeze their puff pastry in rolled-out sheets, and this is certainly an idea worth copying. Since puff pastry is always rolled out before use, you can roll half the dough into an 11 by 15-inch rectangle before freezing. Transfer to a parchment-lined baking sheet and wrap the entire pan in two different directions with plastic wrap. When you need the dough, it will thaw quickly since it's so thin, and you won't need to spend any time rolling.

1 Use a chef's knife to cut the cold butter into ¾-inch cubes. Transfer to the bowl of the stand mixer. Add the flour and salt and toss with your hands until the butter is coated. Chill the bowl in the refrigerator for 20 minutes. Combine the water and vinegar and refrigerate for 20 minutes as well.

2 Fit the bowl with the butter onto the stand mixer and blend with the paddle attachment on low speed for 1 to 1½ minutes. The butter will break into pieces of various sizes, the largest about ½ inch square—too big for pie dough, but perfect for quick puff pastry. (Don't overblend, as the butter will break into pieces too small to form the flaky layers you want in puff pastry.)

3 With the mixer on low, slowly add the water-vinegar mixture, drizzling it in at different points around the bowl. In about 10 seconds, the dough will begin to come together in large chunks and feel slightly moist, but it will not look smooth or finished. Turn the dough and any dry bits at the bottom onto a work surface that has been dusted with flour.

4 Shape the dough into a rough rectangle about 6 by 8 inches and about 1½ inches thick. Dust the top with flour and roll the dough into a 14 by 16-inch rectangle. Brush any flour from the surface of the dough. Make a letter fold (page 103) using a board scraper or offset spatula to help lift the "dough." Brush off any excess flour as you fold. It will look shaggy—have faith. Roll your pin across the top of the dough briefly and gently 1 or 2 times, just to fuse the dough. Wrap in plastic and refrigerate for 30 minutes. Repeat this turning step two times, chilling the dough for 30 minutes between each turn. Wrap the dough in plastic wrap and refrigerate for 1 hour or up to 48 hours before using.

STORING The dough can be double-wrapped in plastic and frozen for 4 to 6 weeks (see "What the Pros Know," left). Thaw overnight in the refrigerator before using. If the dough is still very cold, let it sit on the counter for 10 to 15 minutes, then check to see if it is flexible enough to roll.

PALMIERS

MAKES ABOUT 35 PALMIERS Palmiers are beautiful, addictive, easy to make, and loved by everyone. What more could you want from a cookie? Named (in French) for their resemblance to a palm frond, they are also called elephant ears or butterfly wings. They are simply puff pastry that is rolled out in sugar rather than flour, then folded with additional sugar, thinly sliced, and baked. Because they are sliced and laid cut side down on the baking sheet, they expand sideways instead of upward, resulting in "ears" that showcase the many layers contained in the dough. For a savory version with Parmesan and smoked paprika, see the variations at right.

INGREDIENTS

½ recipe (18 ounces) Quick
Puff Pastry (page 123)

1 cup (7 ounces) sugar, plus more if needed

EQUIPMENT

Rolling Pin, Ruler, Chef's Knife, Two Baking Sheets, Parchment Paper or Two Silicone Mats, Small Bowl, Small Metal Offset Spatula, Cooling Rack

1 Generously dust your work surface with sugar. Place the dough in the center and sprinkle the top with sugar, covering it completely. Roll into a 16 by 10-inch rectangle, using additional sugar as needed to keep the dough from sticking to the work surface. Position the dough so that one of the long edges is parallel to the edge of your work surface.

2 Using the ruler and the back of a chef's knife, mark a line dividing the dough in half vertically, each half 8 x 10 inches. Using the ruler and knife again, mark each half vertically into quarters (every 2 inches). Fold the two short edges toward the center, bending them at the first mark and lining up the edges at the second mark in each half. Repeat until the folded edges reach the center mark. Tighten each side to leave a ¼-inch space down the center of the dough. Fold one side on top of the other, forming a 10-inch-long cylinder. If you look at an end of the cylinder, you'll see the shape of a heart. Wrap in plastic and refrigerate for 30 minutes.

3 Line the baking sheets with parchment paper or silicone mats. Preheat the oven to 375°F and position an oven rack in the center. Place the remaining sugar in a small bowl. Trim the ends of the cylinder if they are uneven or cracked, then cut twelve ¼-inch-thick slices from the chilled cylinder, dip each side in sugar, and place 2 inches apart on the baking sheet. Rewrap and return the cylinder to the refrigerator. Bake the cookies for 7 to 10 minutes, or until golden at the edges. With a small metal offset spatula, flip each cookie over. Return to the oven and bake for 9 to 12 minutes longer, until they are a beautiful golden brown. Transfer to a rack and cool completely. Slice and bake the additional cookies, or freeze the remaining dough for another day. Serve alone, or with ice cream, sorbet, mousse, or a good cup of tea.

STORING **Palmiers will keep for 2 weeks in an airtight container at room temperature.**

GETTING AHEAD The palmiers may be rolled and shaped into a cylinder and refrigerated overnight before slicing and baking.

You can also freeze the dough, doubled-wrapped in plastic and tucked into a resealable plastic freezer bag, for up to 6 weeks. To use the frozen dough, thaw on the counter for 15 minutes, or until still quite cold but soft enough to slice safely. Slice the number of cookies you desire, then rewrap and return the remaining dough to the freezer.

Parmesan and Smoked Paprika Palmiers

This savory version of palmiers makes a wonderful, crisp appetizer. Omit the sugar and roll the dough on a work surface dusted with flour to the same dimensions as in Step 1. Mark the dough as described. Warm 2 tablespoons unsalted butter over low heat until melted but not hot. In a bowl, blend 6 tablespoons grated Parmesan cheese, ¾ teaspoon smoked paprika, ¼ teaspoon salt, and ⅛ teaspoon black pepper. Brush the dough with the melted butter and sprinkle with 4 tablespoons of the cheese mixture. Fold the short edges inward, as described in Step 2. Brush the newly folded edges of dough with butter and sprinkle with a bit of the remaining cheese mixture. Repeat, until the folded edges reach the center mark. Fold again so that the halves of the dough meet in the center. Brush the top with butter, then fold one side on top of the other, chill, and cut as described in Step 3. Bake each pan for 11 to 13 minutes, until golden, rotating the sheet halfway through the baking time.

Spiced Palmiers

For an extra layer of flavor, add a teaspoon of spice to the sugar used for rolling the dough. Try ground cardamom, cinnamon, ginger, nutmeg, or a combination of spices.

Vanilla Palmiers

For a subtle hint of vanilla in the caramelized cookies, use Vanilla Sugar (page 45) to roll the dough.

CHOCOLATE NAPOLEONS WITH PORT-BRAISED PEARS

SERVES 8 These elegant napoleons will bring your fall or winter menu to a sophisticated finish. A sensuously rich sabayon made with port and blended with melted chocolate fills the pastry and is accompanied by pears cooked in port. There are three components to this recipe, but they can all be made in advance for relaxed entertaining. The napoleons will need to be assembled just prior to serving, though, to ensure the pastry stays crisp. Luckily, this takes only a few minutes when everything is prepared ahead.

INGREDIENTS

½ recipe (18 ounces) Quick Puff Pastry (page 123)

4 teaspoons (scant ½ ounce), plus 5 tablespoons (2¼ ounces), granulated sugar

3 ounces finely chopped semisweet chocolate (up to 64 percent cacao)

1 cup (8 ounces) heavy whipping cream

Pinch of salt

3 large egg yolks

½ cup (4 ounces) ruby port

1 tablespoon (½ ounce) water

1 recipe Port-Braised Pears (page 263)

Confectioners' sugar, for dusting

EQUIPMENT

Four Baking Sheets, Parchment Paper, Rolling Pin, Pastry Brush, Dough Docker, Ruler, Chef's Knife, Cooling Rack, Double Boiler, Medium Bowl, Silicone or Rubber Spatula, Large Bowl, Whisk

1 ROLL AND CUT THE DOUGH: Line two baking sheets with parchment paper. Dust your work surface with flour. Place the dough in the center and dust the top with flour. Roll into an 11 by 17-inch rectangle. Position the dough so that one of the long edges is parallel to the edge of your work surface. Use a dough docker or 2 forks to poke holes all over the surface of the dough. These holes will inhibit the rise of the dough, creating a compact layered pastry more able to stand up to the weight of the napoleon filling. Brush any flour from the surface of the dough. Using the ruler and the back of a chef's knife, trim the dough to a 10 by 16-inch rectangle. Mark the dough at 2½-inch intervals along both short sides and draw lines connecting the marks. Mark the dough at 4-inch intervals along both long sides and connect those marks as well. Cut the dough into 16 (2½ by 4-inch) rectangles. Transfer 8 rectangles to each prepared baking sheet, being careful to keep their shape intact. Sprinkle each piece of dough with ¼ teaspoon granulated sugar and chill while you preheat the oven.

2 BAKE THE PASTRIES: Preheat the oven to 375°F and position 2 racks in the bottom and top thirds of the oven. Cover each sheet of dough rectangles with a piece of parchment paper and top with a second baking sheet. (If you only have 2 baking sheets and must bake one batch at a time, make sure to cool the pans completely before using them to bake the second batch of dough.) Bake for 15 minutes, then switch the pans between the racks and rotate each 180 degrees. Bake for 8 to 10 minutes longer, until golden brown, checking after 8 minutes to be sure dough is not getting too brown (which would make it taste bitter). Set the sheets on a cooling rack and immediately remove the top baking sheet and parchment and allow the rectangles to cool completely. Once cool, wrap in plastic or store airtight at room temperature until needed.

The puff pastry for napoleons is docked and weighted to prevent its full rise. This seems counterintuitive since you invested so much time and attention to create all those layers. But just because it's weighted doesn't mean it's not flaky. The resulting pastry is compact rather than airy, but still full of wonderfully crispy layers that are an appealing contrast to the soft and silky filling.

GETTING AHEAD **The puff pastry rectangles can be stored, airtight, at room temperature for 2 days. The braised pears can be stored in the refrigerator for up to 3 days. The sabayon can be refrigerated, airtight, for 24 hours.**

4 MAKE THE CHOCOLATE SABAYON: Bring 2 inches of water to a boil in the bottom of the double boiler. Place the chocolate, 2 tablespoons of the cream, and the salt in a medium bowl just large enough to fit over double boiler. Turn off the heat and place the chocolate-cream mixture over the steaming water. Stir occasionally with the spatula until the chocolate is melted and smooth and blended with the cream. Remove the bowl and set aside in a warm spot to keep the chocolate fluid. Whip the remaining cream until it holds soft peaks; refrigerate while you finish cooking the sabayon.

5 Fill the large bowl halfway with ice and water and set it aside. Return the water in the bottom of the double boiler to a boil, then reduce it to a simmer. Place the egg yolks and 5 tablespoons granulated sugar in the top of the double boiler (off the heat) and whisk until well blended and slightly lightened in color. Add the port and water and blend well. Set the top of the double boiler with the egg mixture over the simmering water. Cook, whisking constantly, until light and fluffy, resembling whipped cream in texture, and registers 160°F on an instant-read thermometer. Do not exceed 165°F or the eggs could scramble. This may take anywhere from 5 to 8 minutes, depending upon on the heat of the water and your whisking vigor. Remove from the heat and add the melted chocolate mixture to the sabayon. Whisk to blend completely. Set the sabayon into the bowl with ice water and whisk constantly until the mixture is just cool to the touch—don't let it get too cold; you don't want the chocolate to set. Remove from the ice bath and fold in the whipped cream. The sabayon may be made up to 24 hours in advance and kept, airtight, in the refrigerator.

6 ASSEMBLE THE NAPOLEONS: Just before serving, set a rectangle of pastry on each of eight plates. Top with 3 or 4 pieces of braised pear. Spoon the sabayon over the pear pieces, dividing evenly. Generously dust each remaining rectangle with confectioners' sugar and place on top of a sabayon-and-pear-topped rectangle. Spoon additional braised pears around the napoleons. Serve immediately.

STORING **This dessert must be served as soon as it is assembled, because eventually the pastry softens from the pear juices and the dessert loses the lovely contrast of textures.**

Napoleons with Vanilla Bean Pastry Cream **This version is closer to the classic pastry cream–filled bakery favorite. Prepare the puff pastry rectangles as directed above. Prepare 1 recipe Vanilla Bean Pastry Cream (page 419). Spoon 2 tablespoons seedless raspberry jam into a resealable plastic bag and snip off one of the corners to form a ¼-inch hole. Pipe a thick line of jam down the center of each of 8 rectangles, leaving a ½-inch border at both ends. Whip ½ cup heavy whipping cream into firm peaks and fold it into the pastry cream. Transfer this filling to a pastry bag fitted with a ½-inch plain tip. Pipe a thick layer of filling over each jam-lined rectangle, completely covering the pastry. Generously dust the remaining 8 rectangles with confectioners' sugar and set each on top of a pastry cream–topped rectangle. Serve immediately.**

PITHIVIER WITH FRESH APRICOTS

SERVES 8 A pithivier is a classic French pastry featuring a rich almond filling encased in two rounds of puff pastry. It's one of those sweets that is often forgotten in the rush for new desserts, but one slice and you'll wonder how you lived without it. A layer of sliced apricots provides a lively, tart counterpoint to the richness of the dessert. When apricots are out of season, canned apricots may be used.

INGREDIENTS

½ recipe (18 ounces) Quick
Puff Pastry (page 123)

1 recipe Almond Filling (page 119)
2 large, fresh apricots, halved and pitted,
or 4 to 5 canned apricot halves

1 large egg

EQUIPMENT

**Rolling Pin, Pastry Brush, 7- and 8-inch
Round Templates, Paring Knife, Baking
Sheet, Parchment Paper or a Silicone
Mat, Silicone or Rubber Spatula, Whisk,
Small Bowl, Cooling Rack, Serrated Knife**

GETTING AHEAD **The pithivier may
be assembled and frozen, double-
wrapped in plastic, for up to 2 weeks.
Thaw overnight in the refrigerator, then
bake as directed.**

1 Dust your work surface with flour. Place the dough in the center and dust the top with flour. Roll into an 11 by 15-inch rectangle. Brush any flour from the dough and position it so that one of the long edges is parallel to the edge of your work surface. Using the templates (such as cake cardboards or pot lids) and a paring knife, cut out one 7-inch and one 8-inch circle of dough.

2 Line the baking sheet with parchment paper or a silicone mat and place the 7-inch circle in the center of the sheet. Use a spatula to spread the almond filling in an even layer over the top, leaving a ½-inch border around the edge. Slice each apricot half into quarters. Arrange the apricot pieces over the top of the almond filling. Moisten the edge of the dough with a thin film of water. Center the 8-inch circle on top and press the edges together to seal.

3 Use the back of a paring knife and gently indent at 1½-inch intervals all around the edge of the pastry to create a scalloped edge. Whisk the egg in a small bowl to break it up. Brush a thin film of the egg over the top of the pastry, taking care that no drips roll over the edges of the dough, as this would seal the layers and prevent them from rising. Cut a small hole in the center of the pastry to allow steam to escape during baking. Using the back of a paring knife, draw a curved line from the steam vent to every other indentation along the edge. This slight marking of the egg wash will create a two-tone pattern as the pastry bakes.

4 Preheat the oven to 400°F and position an oven rack in the center. Chill the pithivier in the refrigerator while the oven preheats. Bake the pithivier for 40 minutes, or until deep golden brown. Transfer the pithivier to a rack and cool completely. Serve at room temperature, cutting the pastry with a serrated knife.

STORING **The pithivier keeps well at room temperature, covered with a cake dome,
for 3 to 4 days. For longer storage, double wrap in plastic and freeze for up to
1 month. To serve, thaw for 1 hour at room temperature, then reheat in a 375°F oven
for 10 to 15 minutes, until the crust is crisped and the center is warmed through.**

SAVORY JALOUSIE WITH SAUTÉED WILD MUSHROOMS

SERVES 8 TO 10 **A** jalousie is a classic French pastry featuring two long rectangles of puff pastry encasing a fruit filling. The top layer of pastry has slats cut in the dough so it resembles a Venetian blind and allows guests a glimpse of the filling inside. Here's a savory version filled with wild mushrooms, herbs, and cheese. A warm slice of jalousie accompanied by a green salad is a delightful vegetarian meal. For a party, you might want to center this striking pastry on the buffet table and let guests help themselves.

INGREDIENTS

½ recipe (18 ounces) Quick
Puff Pastry (page 123)

1 pound wild mushrooms such as portobello, shiitake, chanterelle, morel, or a combination of 8 ounces wild and 8 ounces button mushrooms

1 tablespoon (½ ounce) olive oil

1 tablespoon (½ ounce) unsalted butter

¼ teaspoon salt

4 grinds black pepper

¼ cup (2 ounces) heavy whipping cream

2 large cloves garlic, very finely chopped

2 tablespoons finely chopped fresh Italian parsley leaves

1 tablespoon snipped fresh chives

1 teaspoon finely chopped fresh thyme leaves

2 ounces Gruyère or other mild melting cheese

2 ounces Stilton or other good-quality blue cheese

1 large egg

EQUIPMENT

Large Sauté Pan, Two Baking Sheets, Parchment Paper or a Silicone Mat, Rolling Pin, Paring Knife, Pastry Brush, Dough Docker, Box Grater, Silicone or Rubber Spatula, Small Bowl, Cooling Rack, Serrated Knife

1 PREPARE THE FILLING: Clean and thinly slice the mushrooms. Heat the olive oil and butter in a large sauté pan over high heat. Add the mushrooms, salt, and pepper and cook, stirring occasionally, until all the liquid has evaporated and the mushrooms are lightly browned, 10 to 12 minutes. Decrease the heat to medium and add the cream, garlic, parsley, chives, and thyme. Simmer, stirring frequently, until the liquid has been absorbed, 1 to 2 minutes. Taste and adjust seasoning, if needed. Spread the mushrooms on an unlined baking sheet to cool completely before assembling the pastry.

2 ROLL AND CUT THE DOUGH: Line the second baking sheet with parchment paper or a silicone mat. Dust your work surface with flour. Place the dough in the center and dust the top with flour. Roll into a 10 by 15-inch rectangle. Use a paring knife to cut the dough in half so that you have two rectangles, each 5 inches wide and 15 inches long. Brush flour from the top and underside of one rectangle, fold in half, gently transfer to the center of the prepared baking sheet, and unfold into a rectangle again. Use a dough docker or 2 forks to prick holes in the dough.

3 The remaining rectangle of dough should have a little flour left on top. If not, dust it lightly before proceeding. Fold the remaining rectangle in half lengthwise, but don't press down or seal the dough. The little bit of flour that remains should prevent the two halves from sticking together. To form the slats, make 2-inch-long cuts at 1-inch intervals along the long folded side of the pastry. Unfold and reserve.

4 ASSEMBLE THE JALOUSIE: Grate the Gruyère and stir into the cooled mushrooms. Use a spatula to spread the filling in an even layer over the dough on the baking sheet, leaving a ½-inch border all the way around. Crumble the blue cheese over the top of the filling. Moisten the edges of the dough with a thin film of water. Carefully lift the folded dough and lay it lengthwise over half the filling with its long folded side down the center, then unfold, lining up all the corners and edges. Press firmly all along the edges to seal. Beat the egg in a small bowl just to break it up. Brush a thin film of the egg over the top of the pastry, taking care that no drips roll over the edges of the dough, as this would seal the layers and prevent them from rising.

5 BAKE THE JALOUSIE: Preheat the oven to 400°F and position an oven rack in the center. Chill the pastry in the refrigerator while you preheat the oven. Bake the jalousie for 25 to 28 minutes, until the pastry is a deep golden brown, rotating the sheet on the shelf halfway through the baking time. Transfer to a cooling rack. Serve warm or at room temperature with a simple green salad, or as an appetizer with a glass of wine. Slice using a serrated knife.

STORING **The jalousie may be stored, uncovered, at room temperature for 1 day. For longer storage, cover with plastic wrap and refrigerate for up to 3 days. Reheat in a 375°F oven for 10 to 12 minutes, until the crust is crispy and the center is warmed through.**

CLASSIC BAKLAVA WITH PISTACHIOS AND CARDAMOM

MAKES ONE 9 BY 13-INCH PAN (ABOUT 35 PIECES) Baklava, when made well, is a light, delicate, and flaky pastry, richly flavored with nuts and spices. In the traditional recipe, layers of phyllo are brushed with clarified butter, which is butter that has been cooked until all the water is evaporated, then strained to remove the milk solids. The advantage to clarified butter is that it has a long shelf life, which means baklava does, too, especially important in the hot areas where this pastry is traditionally served. Frankly, homemade baklava tends to disappear inside of a week, so you probably don't need to worry about taking the time to clarify butter, a process just cumbersome enough to keep most home bakers from making this truly delicious pastry. If you'd like to purchase clarified butter, it is available in Indian markets, labeled as "ghee." Orange flower water is available in many Greek and Italian delis, as well as markets catering to a Middle Eastern clientele.

INGREDIENTS

1 pound prepared phyllo dough (two 8-ounce twin packs, 20 sheets each), thawed for 24 hours in the refrigerator, then warmed to room temperature on counter for 1½ to 2 hours

FILLING

1 pound raw shelled pistachios

½ cup (3½ ounces) sugar

1 teaspoon ground cinnamon

1 teaspoon ground cardamom

2½ sticks (10 ounces) unsalted butter

SYRUP

⅔ cup (5¼ ounces) water

1½ cups (10½ ounces) sugar

1½ teaspoons orange flower water

EQUIPMENT

Food Processor Fitted with a Metal Blade, Medium Bowl, Small Saucepan, Pastry Brush, 9 by 13-inch Metal Baking Pan, Silicone or Rubber Spatula, Serrated Knife or Electric Carving Knife, Cooling Rack

1 MAKE THE FILLING: Place the pistachios, sugar, cinnamon, and cardamom in the bowl of the food processor and process for 15 to 20 seconds, until the nuts are finely chopped (the largest should be the size of mini chocolate chips). Transfer to the medium bowl and set aside. Melt the butter in the small saucepan and set aside.

2 PREPARE THE PHYLLO: Remove the phyllo from the packaging, unfold the sheets, and stack them so that they lie flat on your work surface. Cover the stack with plastic wrap, letting wrap fall over all four edges. Dampen and wring out a kitchen towel and place it on top of the plastic wrap to hold it in place and prevent the phyllo from drying out.

3 ASSEMBLE THE BAKLAVA: Brush the bottom of the baking pan with a thin layer of melted butter. Take out a sheet of phyllo and re-cover the rest (be sure to cover the remaining sheets each time you remove a new one). Place the sheet of phyllo on the bottom of the pan and brush the top with a thin coating of the butter. It's okay if you don't completely cover every spot with butter. You don't want to soak it—you'll have 40 layers of

Cutting the assembled pan of baklava prior to baking is challenging, since the layers of freshly buttered phyllo tend to bounce around and separate as the knife saws through the pastry. The best solution is to chill the baklava (preferably in the freezer) for 30 minutes while the oven preheats. Chilling solidifies the butter, which in turn holds the phyllo in place, making cutting a breeze. A serrated knife with a sharp tip (such as a steak knife) is a good tool for cutting the pastry. If you have an electric carving knife, it's even easier.

GETTING AHEAD **The assembled and cut baklava can be covered tightly with plastic wrap and refrigerated overnight or frozen for up to 4 weeks. To freeze, wrap the entire pan twice with plastic wrap so the pastry will not dry out or pick up any odors. Refrigerated baklava will bake in the specified period of time, but allow 7 to 10 extra minutes in the oven for baklava that has been frozen.**

buttered phyllo by the time you're done and too much butter will make the pastry greasy and heavy. Lay a second sheet of phyllo over the first and butter it the same way. Repeat until you have buttered and layered 10 sheets of phyllo in the pan. Use a spatula to spread about one-third of the pistachio filling evenly over the phyllo. Layer another 10 sheets of phyllo as described above, and top with another one-third of the nut filling. Repeat the layering again, topping with the remaining filling. Layer another 10 sheets of phyllo on top to finish the pastry. Cover the pan with plastic wrap and freeze for 30 minutes. Meanwhile, preheat the oven to 350°F and position an oven rack in the center.

4 CUT AND BAKE THE BAKLAVA: You'll need to cut the baklava before it goes in the oven for two reasons. First, you need to create pathways for the syrup at the end of the recipe to reach every part of the baklava. Second, the pastry will be so crisp after baking that it would simply shatter if you tried to cut it at that point. Using a thin sharp serrated knife or an electric carving knife, cut the baklava on the diagonal at 2-inch intervals, creating a diamond pattern. Use a gentle sawing motion and try not to compress the pastry by pressing down on it too hard with while cutting. Be sure to cut the pastry all the way to the bottom of the pan. Bake the baklava for 40 to 45 minutes, until golden in color. Transfer the pan to a rack and cool completely.

5 MAKE AND ADD THE SYRUP: Pour the water and sugar into the cleaned small saucepan and heat over medium heat until the sugar is dissolved and the liquid is clear. Bring to a simmer, then lower the heat to maintain a steady simmer; cook for about 5 minutes. Remove the pan from the heat and stir in the orange flower water. Immediately pour the syrup evenly over the entire surface of the baklava, allowing it to run down into the cut marks and along the sides of the pan.

6 Let the baklava cool to room temperature before serving. It is at its best about 24 hours after the syrup is added. Serve with tea or coffee.

STORING **Baklava will keep, covered with plastic wrap, at room temperature for up to 7 days, though the texture changes from flaky and crisp to more solid and crystallized as time goes by—both textures have their fans and are delicious.**

Hazelnut-Spice Baklava with Honey
Substitute hazelnuts for the pistachios and omit the cardamom. Increase the cinnamon to 1½ teaspoons and add ½ teaspoon ground cloves. Reduce the sugar in the syrup to ½ cup and add ¼ cup honey. Stir in 2 tablespoons Frangelico (hazelnut liqueur) just before pouring the syrup over the pastry.

ROASTED PEAR STRUDEL WITH CRANBERRIES AND GOLDEN RAISINS

SERVES 8 The jewel colors in each slice of this strudel create a gorgeous fall fruit mosaic. Crispy on the outside, soft and sweet inside, the strudel is easy to make and uses ingredients readily available from the supermarket. Common ingredients, perhaps, but the combination of flavors makes this an uncommonly good dessert. Good accompaniments include Vanilla Custard Sauce (page 424), or Softly Whipped Cream (page 416) and Caramel Sauce (page 426). You'll only need 5 sheets of phyllo for the recipe (the rest of the thawed box of dough will keep in the refrigerator for up to a week). Use the remaining dough another day to make Moroccan-Spiced Sweet-Potato Tiropetes (page 136).

INGREDIENTS

½ pound prepared phyllo dough (one 8-ounce twin pack, with 20 sheets included), thawed for 24 hours in the refrigerator, then warmed to room temperature on counter for 1½ to 2 hours

FILLING

⅓ cup (1½ ounces) dried cranberries

3 tablespoons (1¼ ounces) golden raisins

2 large (16 ounces) firm-ripe pears, such as Bosc, peeled, cored, and cut into ½-inch cubes

1 tablespoon freshly squeezed lemon juice

1 tablespoon Poire Williams liqueur (pear brandy), optional

¼ cup (2 ounces) firmly packed light brown sugar

1 teaspoon finely grated orange zest

¾ teaspoon ground cinnamon

3 tablespoons (1½ ounces) water

PHYLLO LAYERS

½ cup (1¾ ounces) walnuts, toasted and cooled

2 teaspoons granulated sugar

½ teaspoon ground cinnamon

5 sheets phyllo

½ stick (2 ounces) unsalted butter

EQUIPMENT

Baking Sheet, Parchment Paper or a Silicone Mat, Small Saucepan, Fine-Mesh Strainer, Silicone or Rubber Spatula, Medium Bowl, 9 by 9-inch Square Baking Pan, Cooling Rack, Slotted Spoon, Food Processor Fitted with a Metal Blade, Small Bowl, Pastry Brush, Paring Knife

1 Preheat the oven to 350°F and position an oven rack in the center. Line the baking sheet with parchment paper or a silicone mat.

2 MAKE THE FILLING: Combine the cranberries and raisins in the small saucepan and cover with water. Bring to a simmer, then remove from the heat and allow the mixture to stand for 5 minutes. Drain through the strainer, pressing any excess water out of the fruit with a spatula. Pat the fruit dry with paper towels. Transfer to a medium bowl.

3 Place the cubed pears in the bowl with the cranberries and raisins. Add the lemon juice, Poire Williams, brown sugar, orange zest, and cinnamon and gently stir with a spatula until the pears are evenly coated. Transfer to the baking pan and spread the fruit in a single layer. Add the water to the pan. Cover the pan tightly with foil and bake for 20 minutes, or until the pears are barely tender and still resist slightly when pierced with a skewer or the tip of a small knife. Transfer to a cooling rack and, using a slotted spoon, transfer the filling from the pan to a plate and let cool to room temperature. Increase the oven temperature to 375°F.

GETTING AHEAD **The filling may be made in advance and stored, airtight, in the refrigerator for 2 days. The walnut mixture may be made up to 1 week in advance and stored, airtight, at room temperature. The strudel should be baked within 1 hour of assembly.**

4 ASSEMBLE THE STRUDEL: Combine the walnuts, granulated sugar, and cinnamon in the bowl of the food processor and process for 10 to 15 seconds, until the nuts are finely chopped. Transfer to the small bowl. Remove the phyllo from the packaging, unfold 5 sheets and stack them so that they lie flat on your work surface. Cover the stack with plastic wrap, letting wrap fall over all four edges. Dampen and wring out a kitchen towel and place it on top of the plastic wrap to hold it in place and prevent the phyllo from drying out. Refold the remaining phyllo sheets, wrap tightly in plastic, return to the box, and refrigerate (use within 1 week).

5 Melt the butter in the cleaned small saucepan. Take out a sheet of phyllo and re-cover the rest (be sure to cover the remaining sheets each time you remove a new one). Place the sheet on your work surface so that one of its long edges is parallel with the edge of the work surface. Brush the top of the sheet with a thin coating of melted butter. Place a second sheet of phyllo on top, positioning a short end in the center of the first sheet to increase the overall length by ½ sheet. Brush the surface of the second sheet with melted butter. Scatter one-third of the walnut mixture over the surface of both sheets. Repeat the layering with 2 more sheets of phyllo and another one-third of the walnut mixture. Center the last sheet of phyllo on top, brush with butter, and sprinkle the remaining walnut mixture along the long side of the dough closest to you, leaving a 2-inch border along the long edge and at each of the short sides.

6 Spoon the fruit filling on top of the walnut mixture. Roll the phyllo around the filling, starting with the bottom edge and folding in the sides as you go. When you get to the end, gently lift the roll and place it diagonally and seam side down on the prepared baking sheet. The roll will be about 18 inches long. Brush all the exposed surfaces of the strudel lightly with the last of the melted butter. Use a paring knife to score the top, cutting just through the top layers of phyllo, at 1-inch intervals.

7 BAKE THE STRUDEL: Bake the strudel for 40 minutes, or until the phyllo is a beautiful golden color. Transfer to a cooling rack. Serve warm, using a serrated knife to slice into 1-inch-thick rounds. Since the strudel is small, serve two slices per person, slightly overlapping them.

STORING **The baked strudel may be stored at room temperature, covered with plastic wrap, for 1 day. Reheat in a 350°F oven for 10 to 15 minutes, until warmed through. For longer storage, cover with plastic wrap and refrigerate for up to 3 days. Reheat before serving.**

Roasted Apple Strudel with Cranberries and Golden Raisins
Substitute 2 large, firm baking apples for the pears. Substitute Calvados (Apple Brandy) for the Poire Williams liqueur.

MOROCCAN-SPICED SWEET-POTATO TIROPETES

MAKES 20 TO 24 TIROPETES Tiropetes are classic Greek filled pastries made with phyllo folded into little triangles. Often they are filled with spinach and feta, though nearly any filling you like, sweet or savory, makes a charming little appetizer-size package. In this version, sweet potatoes are combined with onion, garlic, cilantro, and a fragrant Moroccan spice blend. If you like, set a bowl of Greek yogurt alongside as a dipping sauce. The spice blend makes more than you'll need for the tiropetes because it's difficult for a coffee or spice grinder to grind a smaller amount. But you'll likely find all kinds of creative culinary uses for the leftover blend once you taste it (a pinch in scrambled eggs, flavoring fougasse (page 84) or other breads, as a rub on roasted pork loin). Store the extra spice blend in an airtight container in a cool, dark location with your other spices.

INGREDIENTS

1 pound prepared phyllo dough (two 8-ounce twin packs, 20 sheets each), thawed for 24 hours in the refrigerator, then warmed to room temperature on counter for 1½ to 2 hours

FILLING

1 large (1¼ pounds) sweet potato

2 tablespoons (1 ounce) olive oil

1 cup (4 ounces) finely chopped onion (about ½ large onion)

2 large cloves garlic, minced

1½ teaspoons Moroccan Spice Blend (see below)

1½ tablespoons chopped fresh cilantro

1 teaspoon salt

MOROCCAN SPICE BLEND

1½ teaspoons fennel seeds

1½ teaspoons cumin seeds

1½ teaspoons coriander seeds

1 tablespoon black peppercorns

1½ teaspoons ground ginger

2 tablespoons ground paprika

¼ to ½ teaspoon ground cayenne

PHYLLO LAYERS

12 sheets phyllo

1 stick (4 ounces) unsalted butter, cut into ½-inch pieces

EQUIPMENT

Paring Knife, Medium Sauté Pan or Skillet, Coffee or Spice Grinder, Small Bowl, Whisk, Medium Bowl, Potato Masher, Silicone or Rubber Spatula, Two Baking Sheets, Parchment Paper or Two Silicone Mats, Small Saucepan, Pastry Brush, Ruler, Cooling Rack

1 BAKE THE SWEET POTATO: Preheat the oven to 375°F and position an oven rack in the center. Pierce the potato in several spots with a fork. Place it on a piece of foil set directly on the oven rack and bake for 1 hour, or until tender when pierced with the tip of a paring knife. Transfer to a rack to cool completely. Use a paring knife to peel the potato and cut the flesh into 1½-inch-thick slices.

2 MEANWHILE, PREPARE THE SPICE BLEND: Heat the sauté pan or skillet over high heat until quite hot. Add the fennel, cumin, and coriander seeds, and black peppercorns and cook, shaking the pan constantly, until they are toasted, fragrant, and just beginning to smoke, about 30 seconds (do not let them burn or you will need to begin again). Immediately pour the spices onto a plate to cool. Once cooled, transfer to a coffee or spice grinder and grind until powdery. Pour into the small bowl and add the ginger, paprika, and cayenne. Whisk until the mixture is thoroughly blended. Set aside. Wipe out the sauté pan.

GETTING AHEAD The filling can
be made 1 day in advance—keep
refrigerated. The assembled *tiropetes*
can be frozen up to 3 weeks ahead
and stored inside a resealable plastic
freezer bag. Do not thaw before
baking, but do allow a few extra
minutes for the pastries to bake.

3 MAKE THE FILLING: Heat the olive oil in the sauté pan over medium heat. Add the onion and cook over medium-low heat for 5 to 6 minutes, stirring every minute or so, until the onions are translucent and soft. Add the garlic and continue to cook for 1 to 2 minutes, until softened (do not let it brown). Add 1½ teaspoons of the spice blend and heat until warmed and fragrant. Transfer to a medium bowl. Add the sweet potato slices, cilantro, and salt. Use a potato masher to crush the potatoes into the onion mixture, but leave some chunks of potato for an interesting texture in the filling—it shouldn't be completely smooth. Finish blending everything, if needed, with a spatula. Let the filling mixture sit for half an hour to allow the flavors time to meld.

4 ASSEMBLE THE *TIROPETES:* Line the baking sheets with parchment paper or silicone mats. Remove the phyllo from the packaging, unfold the sheets, and stack 12 of them so that they lie flat on your work surface. Cover the stack with plastic wrap, letting some excess wrap fall over all four edges. Dampen and wring out a kitchen towel and spread it over the top of the plastic wrap to hold it in place and prevent the phyllo from drying out. Refold the remaining phyllo sheets, wrap tightly in plastic, return to the box, and refrigerate (use within 1 week).

5 Melt the butter in the small saucepan. Take out a sheet of phyllo and re-cover the rest (be sure to cover the remaining sheets each time you remove a new one). Place the sheet on your work surface so that one of its long edges is parallel with the edge of the work surface. Brush the top of the sheet with a thin coating of the melted butter. Lay a second sheet of phyllo on top of the first and butter it the same way. Repeat once more, so that you layer and butter 3 sheets of phyllo. Using a paring knife and a ruler, mark the bottom long edge of the dough into six equal pieces. Do the same along the top long edge. Connect the markings and cut the dough into six strips. Place 1 tablespoon of the filling at the end of a strip, then fold the dough over the filling, forming a triangle, and continue to fold the dough as though you were folding a flag. When you reach the end of the strip, tuck the edge of the phyllo under the triangle. Set the *tiropete* on one of the prepared baking sheets and brush the top lightly with butter. Continue until you have filled and shaped all the *tiropetes,* dividing them evenly between the baking sheets.

6 BAKE THE *TIROPETES:* Preheat the oven to 375°F and position an oven rack in the center. Bake the *tiropetes,* one sheet at a time, for 20 to 22 minutes, until golden. Transfer the pan to a cooling rack. Let the *tiropetes* cool for at least 15 minutes before serving—the filling holds a lot of heat, and you don't want guests to burn their mouths. To serve, pile them on a platter and let guests help themselves.

STORING *Tiropetes* can be baked up to 1 hour in advance and kept, uncovered, at room temperature. If the phyllo softens, simply rewarm and recrisp them by heating in a 375°F oven for 5 minutes.

QUICK BREADS

Quick breads are the day-to-day workhorses of the baking kitchen, recipes for fast and easy favorites ranging from tea loaves to muffins to scones to biscuits, and those wonders of simplicity, popovers. Often the first recipes a beginning baker makes, they are well loved, easy to make, and quick to bake. The time span from measuring to table-top can be less than an hour—in some cases far less. And most quick breads are based on ingredients already in your pantry: flour, sugar, butter or oil, eggs, baking powder or soda, and buttermilk or cream.

These quick breads are not only tasty, they also give you the opportunity to hone your skills before attempting a more intimidating pie dough or a fancy cake, since many of the techniques used in this chapter are similar to those needed for more advanced baked goods. Once you feel comfortable whipping up a batch of scones or muffins, pie doughs and cake batters will seem much more approachable.

A Primer on Quick Breads

The baked goods in this chapter differ from those in the first two chapters because they do not rely upon yeast for their rise. These are called "quick" breads because they don't need the long fermentation time that traditional yeast-risen breads require. Instead, quick bread recipes rely upon chemical leaveners—baking soda and baking powder—for their rise, and once the batter is mixed, it goes directly into the oven. In fact, quick breads are not so much bread as a type of cake or biscuit. Baking soda is used in batters that include acidic ingredients, such as buttermilk, sour cream, natural cocoa powder, and molasses. Baking powder is used in recipes calling for milk, cream, vanilla, and other neutral ingredients—and sometimes in acidic recipes as well, where it supports the baking soda and enhances the rise. A word of warning, though: These two leaveners are not interchangeable. Always check their expiration dates if you haven't baked in a while, as they lose their potency over time. For a review of chemical leaveners, their specific properties, and how they make baked goods rise, please refer to page 35.

MIXING METHODS FOR QUICK BREADS

Three basic methods are used for making quick breads, and each one produces a specific texture in the final product. The key to mixing any quick bread, regardless of which method you choose, is to use a light hand. Remember that once liquid is combined with flour, gluten begins to form. Whereas yeast breads rely upon lengthy mixing or kneading to produce the strong gluten network needed for their structure, quick breads are just the opposite. Their gluten needs are minimal, and overmixing will quickly produce a tough, dense, unevenly textured product, so heed the instructions for mixing in each recipe.

THE MUFFIN METHOD

Sometimes called the quick-bread method, this technique involves blending the dry ingredients in one bowl, the liquid ingredients in another, and then combining the two just until moistened. You want to mix until no streaks of flour or pools of liquid remain, but don't worry too much about lumps remaining in the batter; they'll disappear during the baking process. Do you know how pancake batter is full of little flour lumps after mixing? Remember how those lumps disappear during cooking? Well, pancakes are actually a type of quick bread that is baked on a griddle instead of in the oven. Keep this in mind as you're chasing little lumps around the bowl in your batch of muffins: Stop mixing and get them in the oven. If you overmix, the muffins or quick bread will be tough and chewy, and you may also see some tunneling in the crumb (referred to as *worm holes* by some bakers)—a sure sign that too much gluten was developed during mixing.

Good muffins have a slightly uneven, coarse texture. Like the inside of an English muffin that's been torn in half, they have lots of nooks and crannies for butter and jam. If you prefer a fine-grained, cakelike texture, be sure to look for quick breads made using the creaming method of mixing. For instance, the Herb Corn Bread and Pumpkin Walnut Bread are both made using the muffin method, while the Chocolate-Banana Marble Bread and the Cinnamon-Streusel Sour Cream Coffee Cake have a closer-grained, finer crumb produced by the creaming method.

BAKING THE MUFFINS It's nice to dispense with the paper or foil cupcake liners and put the batter directly into the pan. A golden crust forms when the batter is in direct contact with the pan (and you don't lose half the muffin when you peel off the paper). Just be sure to thoroughly butter the pan or spray it with high-heat canola-oil spray so the muffins will pop out easily after baking. Try portioning the batter into the muffin cups using an ice cream scoop (professionals call them *dishers*), since it's precise and much less messy than a spoon. In general, fill muffin cups two-thirds to three-quarters full of batter, although if you like huge crowns on your muffins, go ahead and fill them to the top of the cup. (You will need to thoroughly butter the surface of the muffin pan, or spray it with high-heat canola-oil spray, so that your crowns don't stick.) If any cups are left empty, fill them halfway with water to keep the muffin pan from overheating (and overcooking the adjacent muffins). For best results, bake muffins in a hot oven, about 400°F. This ensures a fast rise, nicely rounded crowns, and a quick bake time. However, if you are baking miniature muffins or giant muffins, it's best to turn the oven down to 375° or 350°F.

IMPROVISING FLAVORS IN MUFFINS One of the reasons bakers love muffins is because they adapt so easily to so many flavors. Bakeries make one huge batch of muffin batter and then portion it out into smaller batches (enough, say, for 2 or 3 dozen muffins), adding different flavorings to each batch to get ten different muffins for the display case. You can follow their lead—hopefully on a much smaller scale—in your own kitchen. A standard 12-cup

tips for success   Why Fruit Can Turn Muffins Blue

Many fruits that are popular for muffins and quick breads contain water-soluble pigments called *anthocyanins*. Apples, blueberries, blackberries, cherries, some figs, nectarines, peaches, plums, raspberries, rhubarb, and strawberries all contain anthocyanins. Some of these fruits have more of the pigments than others (and some, like peaches, have them only in their skin and not in their flesh). Sometimes (as with blueberries) the pigments can leach out of the fruit and color the batter blue or purple as you are mixing. Other times the color change occurs during baking. When there is not enough acidity in the batter, you'll see a ring of blue around the fruit pieces when you break open your muffin. However, if the batter is made with an acidic liquid, such as buttermilk, the problem is averted. This is one of the reasons that muffin batters often contain buttermilk instead of milk (the other is the wonderful flavor the buttermilk adds to quick breads).

Mixing Muffin Batter

Bring all the liquid ingredients to room temperature before beginning. Milk and eggs are often whisked together with melted butter, and if the milk and/or eggs are chilled, the melted butter will congeal upon contact and form pockets of butter in the batter rather than blending in evenly. To prevent this from happening, melt the butter in a skillet, then turn off the heat and pour in the milk. Wait a couple of minutes for the residual heat from the pan to warm the milk to a perfect tepid temperature for combining with the eggs (either in the pan or in a medium bowl). Once you've combined the liquid ingredients, whisk the dry ingredients together in a separate bowl to blend them thoroughly and aerate them slightly. Pour the liquid mixture on top of the dry ingredients and mix with a rubber spatula, wooden spoon, or whisk. Mix until the batter is evenly moistened, with no dry spots or pools of liquid. You will see a spattering of small lumps throughout the batter, and this is fine. Once the batter is mixed, transfer it to the baking pan and get it in the oven. This is especially true of batters that contain baking soda, because it leavens immediately upon contact with liquid and acid.

muffin tin recipe will hold about 1 cup of add-ins (fresh fruit, dried fruit, chocolate chips, chopped toasted nuts) in addition to the batter. Fold these into the batter after mixing and just before you portion it into the muffin pan. You can add an extra layer of flavor by stirring a spice, extract, or oil into the batter. To add spice, stir 1 to 1½ teaspoons of it to the dry ingredients. For extract or oil, add ½ to 1 teaspoon of extract (such as almond) or ¼ to ½ teaspoon oil (such as peppermint) to the liquid ingredients. (Oils are much stronger than extracts, so you use only half as much.) The zest of a lemon or orange is a wonderful background flavor and moves to the front when the zest of two or more are added. If the recipe calls for melted butter, add the zest to the warm butter. If the recipe calls for oil instead of butter, add the zest to the dry ingredients.

THE CREAMING METHOD

Commonly used when making cakes, this technique produces a fine-grained, tender crumb and always begins with the beating together of butter and sugar. You can find an in-depth explanation of how and why this method works on page 301. The key points are to begin with butter that is slightly softened (65° to 68°F)—not squishy or greasy—and to beat it with the sugar on medium-high speed for a full 5 minutes, or until very light in color, nearly white. This fills the batter with thousands of minuscule air bubbles that will expand in the oven, creating a beautifully light and tender cake crumb. Your eggs and liquid should be room temperature when you add them to the batter, and be careful to keep the mixing to a minimum once you've added the dry ingredients.

THE CUT-IN METHOD

Used in this chapter for making biscuits and scones, this method relies on cold butter that is cut into small pieces that remain distinct from the dough around them. It is similar to the technique used for pie dough. Begin with a bowl of dry ingredients into which pieces of cold butter are added. The butter is then cut or broken, using fingers or a pastry blender, into smaller and smaller pieces, until the texture of the mixture looks like crushed crackers and peas (peas being the largest bits of butter). This is the same method used to produce flaky pie dough, but there is a key difference in the amount of liquid in the dough. Pie dough requires just enough to hold the mixture together, whereas biscuits and scones demand quite a bit of liquid to create the soft, tender interior you expect.

BISCUITS VERSUS SCONES

The difference between biscuits and scones sometimes depends upon whom you ask. Both rely on the same basic method for making the dough. Southerners often prefer shortening or lard in their biscuits; others love the flavor that butter imparts. Southern biscuits are often made from very wet doughs that are sticky and difficult to handle but result in soft, fluffy interiors. Scones, in general, are made from a slightly drier dough that is easier to handle, and are a tad more dense than they are fluffy. Scones are always sweetened, whereas biscuits are usually savory, made to accompany a meal rather than a cup of coffee. In the end, the recipes in this chapter titled Cream Scones and Buttermilk Scones could just as easily be called Cream Biscuits and Buttermilk Biscuits if their sugar and sweet flavorings were omitted and you will find variations for just such biscuits at the end of these recipes. In this book, lightly sweetened, richer doughs are called scones, and lighter, fluffier, savory doughs are biscuits. You can decide for yourself, for in the end, a scone or biscuit by any name would taste just as delicious.

tips
for success Why Fruit and Nuts Sink to the Bottom of Muffin Batter

It's simple—the batter is too thin to support them and/or the add-ins are too large. Many recipes tell you to toss the add-ins in a little flour to keep them from sinking, but the reality is that no amount of flour-tossing will help to suspend add-ins if the batter can't support them in the first place. If you make sure the pieces of fruit or nuts are no larger than blueberries, they should not sink.

THE TEXTURE OF BISCUITS AND SCONES—HOW AND WHY

Both biscuits and scones get their flaky, tender interior from a combination of the "crushed crackers" and the "peas." "Crushed crackers" are the smaller bits of butter, those that are starting to blend with the flour. As butter coats flour particles, it discourages gluten strands from forming, resulting in a tender dough. (Note: overmixing and over-kneading can counteract the tenderizing action of those "crushed crackers.") The "peas," on the other hand, stay distinct from the dough that forms around them when the liquid is added; each "pea" is like a little butter cocoon surrounded by dough. In the heat of the oven, the butter "peas" melt, leaving behind an empty cocoon—a space in the dough—otherwise known as a flake.

To achieve these spaces in the dough, the oven must be very hot (which is why most biscuits in this chapter are baked between 400° and 425°F). The high heat causes the proteins and starches in the dough to set quickly, firming the dough around the cocoon before the butter "peas" have melted and the little spaces disappear with them. Without the "peas," you don't have flakes, so keep in mind that you'll need some larger pieces of butter scattered throughout the dough. This is also why it is always important that the butter in the dough is cold before it is baked—to ensure the dough sets before the butter melts. If you feel the butter in your dough has warmed during the mixing process, refrigerate the scones or biscuits for 30 minutes to firm the butter again before baking.

Okay, so now you know that cold butter is one key to making biscuits and scones. The other key is minimal handling of the dough. More handling means more gluten and warmer butter. The perfect way to keep the butter cold and finish the dough quickly is to make the dough in the food processor. The speed and efficiency of the machine means that you don't need to worry about inadvertently warming the butter with your hands or overworking the dough. However, if you don't have a food processor or you delight in using your hands, here is the method for making biscuits or scones by hand.

MIXING THE DOUGH BY HAND

Cut your butter into ½ inch pieces and refrigerate for 30 minutes before beginning. Place all the dry ingredients in a large bowl and whisk to blend them thoroughly and aerate them slightly. Add the cold butter pieces and then immediately begin to break them into smaller pieces using one of these three methods: First, use your fingers to pinch pieces of butter between your thumbs and fingers and break them in half, letting the broken pieces fall back into the flour. Second, use a pastry blender (page 15) to break up the butter. This is a good choice if you have warm hands. Press the pastry blender into pieces of butter to split them. Some of the pieces will stick to the blender and you will eventually need to scrape them off with a dinner knife, then start again. Third, use two dinner knives and literally cut the butter into smaller pieces by making quick cutting motions through the flour. Whichever method you use, continue cutting until the mixture resembles a bowl of crushed crackers and peas. If at any point you feel the butter becoming soft and squishy, stop and put the bowl in the freezer for 10 or 15 minutes, then begin again.

Once the correct texture is reached, pour the liquid into the bowl all at once and stir with a fork until the mass forms shaggy clumps and begins to hold together. It will still look dusty on the bottom of the bowl and may look drier than you think wise, but don't worry. Turn the mixture out onto a work surface and gently squeeze or knead the dough until it holds together as a single mass. Don't go crazy here—it's not bread and you don't want to create a ball of gluten. Just gently fold it over until it is cohesive and barely smooth. Again, if the butter is quite soft, wrap the dough in plastic and refrigerate it. Otherwise, pat the dough into the shape required by the recipe and cut it as directed. Chill for 30 minutes or up to 24 hours, if desired, or pop the scones or biscuits straight into the oven.

ROLLING AND CUTTING BISCUITS AND SCONES

Most biscuits and scones will need to be rolled or patted into shape and then cut. (Patting the dough compresses it less than does a rolling pin, so many bakers prefer to pat.) First, lightly flour your work surface (*lightly* being the key word here). If the dough is very sticky, flour the top lightly, then pat or roll the dough into the size and shape described in the recipe. Dough rolled a second time is always a bit tougher. To avoid creating scraps you'll have to reroll, cut wedges from a circle of dough or square shapes from a rectangle of dough. Use a sharp chef's knife and cut straight down without dragging the knife, which can smash edges. If you want to use biscuit or cookie cutters, be sure they are stainless steel, with nice sharp edges. Your grandmother may have cut biscuits with a drinking glass, but those rounded edges will smash the dough and adversely affect the rise and shape of your biscuits or scones in the oven. Once cut, brush any remaining flour from the surface and underside of the dough and place the biscuits or scones on a prepared baking sheet. If you do have dough scraps, brush the flour from them and then gently knead them back together, press or roll out, and finish cutting your shapes.

BAKING BISCUITS AND SCONES

Biscuits and scones are baked in a hot oven (400° to 425°F, depending on the recipe). Due to the relatively small size of biscuits and scones, it is important to bake them quickly, before their interiors dry out. Baking sheets lined with parchment paper create golden brown, crispy bottoms, but you could line the pan with a thin silicone mat if you prefer. The biscuits and scones are done when they are fully risen (about twice their original size), nicely browned, and just firm to the touch in the center.

If a scone contains flavorings that melt into soft pools of liquid when hot, such as toffee or chocolate chips, the center may never feel firm—in which case it's better to judge by timing and other indicators. When baking at these high temperatures, it's important to have an accurate oven. If you're unsure, get an oven thermometer (see page 3) and some peace of mind.

MIXING QUICK BREADS NOW, BAKING LATER

As mentioned earlier, once the batter or dough for quick breads is mixed, it's best to bake it immediately. Baking soda and baking powder begin their leavening upon contact with liquids, so if you wait, you'll lose some volume in the final product. However, if you don't mind a decrease in rise, many quick breads can be mixed in advance. Muffin batter, for instance, will generally hold overnight in the refrigerator, but remember that the leaveners have already worked some rising magic, and the dough will be full of air bubbles ready to expand in the oven. Be careful—don't stir the batter around before you scoop it into the muffin cups or you'll burst those bubbles and your moderate decrease in rise will turn into a major flop. A better idea would be to scoop the batter into the prepared pan(s) as soon as it is mixed, then pop the pans into the refrigerator for their overnight stay.

In general, scones and biscuits may be mixed, shaped, and cut in advance and held overnight in the refrigerator, although their rise will be compromised, too. Since they are all baked at the same time, and you have no "original" baked scones or biscuits to compare them to, they will look and taste wonderful. Be forewarned—one day in the refrigerator is the maximum.

However, you can freeze the shaped and cut dough for 4 to 6 weeks. To do this, place the scones on a baking sheet and freeze until hard, about 1 hour. Transfer to a resealable plastic freezer bag. To bake, you have several options. Thaw them overnight in the refrigerator, then place them on the prepared baking sheet, brush with egg, top with sugar (if using), and bake. Or, thaw them at room temperature on the prepared baking sheet for about 20 minutes, until cool to the touch but no longer hard in the center, before baking. Or, bake them from their frozen state and add about 5 minutes of extra baking time (to allow for defrosting).

PARMESAN-HERB POPOVERS

MAKES 12 POPOVERS Popovers are culinary sleight of hand. Their simple ingredients and mixing method belie the great heights to which they rise during baking, puffing up like crispy brown balloons. A popover pan is designed to optimize that rise, with tall narrow cups that force the batter upward. The recipe here gives instructions for baking popovers in a regular muffin pan; the variation uses a popover pan.

Although they don't rise as high when baked in a muffin pan, they develop a rounded depression at the bottom that, when turned upside down, is the perfect spot for some sautéed mushrooms or a generous spoonful of soft-scrambled eggs. If you like, leave out the cheese and rosemary and fill the depression with your favorite jam.

INGREDIENTS

1 cup (8 ounces) whole milk

2 large eggs

2 tablespoons (1 ounce) unsalted butter, melted

1 cup (5 ounces) unbleached all-purpose flour

¼ teaspoon salt

¼ cup (1 ounce) freshly grated Parmesan cheese

1 teaspoon finely chopped fresh rosemary

EQUIPMENT

Standard 12-Cup Muffin Pan, Medium Bowl, Whisk, Silicone or Rubber Spatula, 2-Cup Liquid Measuring Cup, Cooling Rack, Small Offset Spatula (Optional)

GETTING AHEAD All of the ingredients may be measured in advance, but do not combine them until you are ready to bake the popovers.

1 Preheat the oven to 450°F and position an oven rack in the center. Lightly coat the muffin pan with melted butter, oil, or high heat canola oil spray. Once the oven is fully heated, heat the prepared muffin pan in the oven for 7 minutes.

2 In the medium bowl, whisk together the milk, eggs, melted butter, flour, and salt until well blended. Add the cheese and rosemary and blend well.

3 Use a spatula to scrape the batter into the measuring cup. Remove the pan from the oven and close the oven door. Divide the batter evenly among the prepared cups. Return the pan to the oven and bake for 15 minutes. Turn the oven down to 400°F and continue to bake for 15 minutes longer, until the popovers are puffed and deep golden brown. Cool the pan on a rack for a couple of minutes. Remove from the pan with a spoon or small offset spatula and serve hot.

STORING Popovers do not hold or store well, so plan on enjoying them when they are fresh from the oven. If they have cooled, reheat them briefly in a 350°F oven for 5 to 10 minutes, until warm.

Classic Popovers
This variation uses the classic popover pan. The deep wells in the pan need more batter, so you'll need to double the recipe above. Omit the Parmesan cheese and rosemary and increase the salt to ½ teaspoon. Bake for 20 minutes at 450°F, then lower the oven temperature to 350°F and continue to bake for 15 to 18 minutes, until the popovers are a deep golden brown. Serve immediately.

EASY MORNING MUFFINS WITH RASPBERRIES

MAKES 12 MUFFINS Soft-crumbed and as comforting as a hug when warm from the oven, these muffins call for the muffin method, making them perfect for home bakers who are too sleepy to pull out an electric mixer in the morning. Simply combine the dry ingredients in one bowl, the liquid in another, then mix the two and fold in the raspberries. If you measure out everything the night before, these can be tossed together in no time, even on a weekday morning (a great project for kids). A couple of tips: Don't mix the batter until perfectly smooth—it should still have a few small lumps in it; and remove the muffins from the tin after 5 to 10 minutes out of the oven, or condensation will build up and the bottoms will get soggy. And, of course, you can customize this recipe by leaving out the lemon zest and raspberries and adding fruit and flavorings of your choice, or see the variations at right.

INGREDIENTS

2 cups (10 ounces) unbleached
all-purpose flour

⅔ cup (4¾ ounces) plus 1 tablespoon sugar

2 teaspoons baking powder

½ teaspoon baking soda

Pinch of salt

¾ stick (3 ounces) butter

Finely grated zest of 1 lemon

⅔ cup (5¾ ounces) buttermilk

2 large eggs, at room temperature

1½ teaspoons pure vanilla extract

1 half-pint basket (6 ounces) fresh raspberries
or 1¼ cups frozen (do not defrost)

¼ teaspoon ground cinnamon

EQUIPMENT

Standard 12-Cup Muffin Tin, Large Bowl, Whisk, Medium Skillet, Medium Bowl, Silicone or Rubber Spatula, Large Ice Cream Scoop or Two Soup Spoons, Thin Knife or Spatula, Cooling Rack

1 Preheat the oven to 400°F and position an oven rack in the center. Lightly coat the muffin tin with melted butter, oil, or high-heat canola-oil spray. Place the flour, ⅔ cup of the sugar, the baking powder, baking soda, and salt in the large bowl. Whisk to blend thoroughly. In the medium skillet, melt the butter with the lemon zest (this will help to bring out the flavor of the zest and distribute it evenly in the batter). Turn off the heat. Add the buttermilk to the melted butter and let the mixture sit for 1 to 2 minutes, just until it is tepid. Pour the butter mixture into the medium bowl, add the eggs and vanilla, and whisk until well blended.

2 Make a well in the center of the dry ingredients. Pour the butter mixture into the well and stir gently with the rubber spatula. Mix only until there are no more streaks of flour or pools of liquid and the batter looks fairly smooth. A few small lumps scattered throughout are fine—they will disappear during baking. Gently fold in the raspberries until evenly distributed in the batter.

3 Use the large ice cream scoop or 2 soup spoons to divide the batter evenly among the prepared muffin cups. Stir together the remaining 1 tablespoon sugar and the cinnamon and sprinkle it over the tops of the muffins.

Muffins crowns (the name for the domed portion of the muffin) are everyone's favorite part. If you love big, billowing muffin crowns, fill each muffin cup all the way to the top edge. Be sure to thoroughly butter the top of the muffin pan so they don't stick there. Take note that large crowns will mean a smaller yield—you'll probably only get 9 muffins or so. Be sure to fill any empty muffin cups in the pan halfway with water to ensure the pan (and muffins) bake evenly. There are even special "muffin top" pans available, with wide, shallow cups that result in very little "stem" attached to the huge, crispy-edged crowns you crave.

4 Bake the muffins for 18 to 20 minutes, until the tops feel firm and a skewer inserted into the centers comes out clean. Transfer the muffin tin to a rack and let cool for 5 minutes. Gently run a thin knife or spatula around each muffin to free it from the pan, lift the muffins out, and transfer them to the rack to finish cooling (careful, these are tender while hot). Serve warm or at room temperature.

STORING When completely cool, the muffins can be stored, wrapped in plastic or sealed in a resealable plastic bag, at room temperature for 2 days. Reheat, wrapped in foil, in a 325°F oven for 8 to 10 minutes, until warmed through.

The muffins can also be frozen for up to 1 month, wrapped tightly in plastic wrap and then sealed in a resealable plastic freezer bag. Thaw, still wrapped, for 30 minutes before reheating. Note: The upside-down variations below can be kept in the refrigerator for 1 or 2 days but should not be frozen.

Streusel-Topped Muffins

To make the streusel, whisk together ¼ cup (2 ounces) firmly packed light brown sugar, ¼ cup (1 ounce) toasted and chopped almonds (or other nuts), ¼ cup (1¼ ounces) unbleached all-purpose flour, and 1 teaspoon ground cinnamon in a medium bowl. Melt 2 tablespoons (1 ounce) unsalted butter and pour it over the dry mixture. Stir with a spoon until the mixture is evenly damp and forms small clumps. Prepare the muffins as directed, but omit the sugar and cinnamon finish and instead sprinkle a tablespoon of streusel over each muffin. Bake as directed.

Rhubarb, Orange, and Ginger Muffins

Prepare the muffins as directed, but add ¾ teaspoon ground ginger plus 2 tablespoons finely chopped crystallized (candied) ginger to the dry ingredients. Substitute the zest of 1 large orange for the lemon zest. Omit the raspberries and add 6 ounces (generous 1 cup) cleaned rhubarb cut into ¼ inch pieces. Add an additional 1 tablespoon finely chopped crystallized ginger to the cinnamon/sugar topping. Bake as directed.

Plum-Cardamom Upside-Down Muffins

Generously butter the muffin tin, then pat 1½ teaspoons light brown sugar evenly over the bottom of each cup. Cover with 2 or 3 thin slices of a tart plum, arranged in an overlapping layer atop the sugar (you'll need about 2 to 3 plums total). Prepare the muffin batter as directed, omitting the raspberries, substituting orange zest for the lemon zest, and adding 1 teaspoon ground cardamom to the dry ingredients. Omit the sugar and cinnamon finish. Place a piece of foil on the bottom shelf of the oven to catch any drips and bake as directed. To remove the muffins from the tin, place a platter or baking sheet on top of the muffins and then flip the pans over. (Be careful, the juices will be quite hot.) Serve warm.

Blueberry Upside-Down Muffins

Generously butter the muffin tin, then pat 1½ teaspoons light brown sugar evenly over the bottom of each. Sprinkle ½ teaspoon freshly squeezed lemon juice over the sugar in each cup (you'll need a total of 2 tablespoons lemon juice). Cover the bottom of each cup with a single layer of blueberries (you will need a half-pint or 1 cup—6 ounces—of blueberries). Prepare the muffin batter as directed, omitting the raspberries, doubling the lemon zest, and adding ½ teaspoon ground nutmeg to the dry ingredients. Omit the sugar and cinnamon finish. Place a piece of foil on the bottom shelf of the oven to catch any drips and bake as directed. Cool and unmold as directed for Plum-Cardamom Upside-Down Muffins.

FETA, ROASTED PEPPER, AND BASIL MUFFINS

MAKES 12 MUFFINS Who says muffins have to be sweet? These are a great savory accompaniment to eggs or bacon on the breakfast table, and just as good alongside soup, salad, or roasted chicken. Do not substitute dried basil, because it just doesn't have the punch of flavor these muffins require. If fresh basil is unavailable, substitute a tablespoon of fresh thyme or a teaspoon of dried thyme instead.

INGREDIENTS

2 cups (10 ounces) unbleached all-purpose flour

2 teaspoons baking powder

½ teaspoon baking soda

½ teaspoon salt

¾ cup (3 ounces) crumbled feta cheese

½ cup (4 ounces) jarred roasted red bell pepper, patted dry and chopped into ¼-inch dice

3 tablespoons finely chopped fresh basil

1 cup (8 ounces) buttermilk

¼ cup (2 ounces) olive oil

1 large egg

EQUIPMENT

Standard 12-Cup Muffin Tin, Whisk, Large Bowl, Medium Bowl, 2-Cup Liquid Measuring Cup, Silicone or Rubber Spatula, Large Ice Cream Scoop or Two Soup Spoons, Parchment Paper, Thin Knife or Spatula, Cooling Rack

1 Preheat the oven to 375°F and position an oven rack in the center. Lightly coat the muffin tin with melted buter, oil, or high-heat canola-oil spray. Whisk the flour, baking powder, baking soda, and salt in the large mixing bowl. Set aside. In the medium bowl, stir together the feta cheese, roasted bell pepper, and chopped basil. Set aside.

2 Pour the buttermilk into the measuring cup. Add the olive oil and the egg and whisk together until well blended. Make a well in the center of the dry ingredients. Pour the buttermilk mixture into the well and stir gently with a spatula. Mix only until there are no more streaks of flour or pools of liquid and the batter looks fairly smooth. A few small lumps scattered throughout are fine—they will disappear during baking. Gently fold in the feta cheese mixture until evenly distributed in the batter.

3 Use the large ice cream scoop or 2 soup spoons to divide the batter evenly among the prepared muffin cups. Bake for 18 to 20 minutes, until the tops feel firm and a skewer inserted into the centers comes out clean. Transfer the muffin tin to a rack and let cool for 5 minutes. Gently run a thin knife or spatula around each muffin to free it from the pan, lift out the muffins, and transfer them to a rack to finish cooling (careful, these are tender while hot). Serve warm.

STORING When completely cool, the muffins can be stored at room temperature, wrapped in plastic or sealed in a resealable plastic bag, for 2 days. Reheat, wrapped in foil, in a 325°F oven for 8 to 10 minutes, until warmed through.

The muffins can also be frozen for up to 1 month, wrapped tightly in plastic wrap and then sealed in a resealable plastic freezer bag. Thaw, still wrapped, for 30 minutes before reheating.

what the pros know

To use parchment in the muffin pan instead of the traditional pleated paper muffin liners, cut twelve 5 by 5-inch squares of parchment. Fit one into each muffin cup in the pan, pleating the sides slightly where they overlap so they lay flat against the pan walls. The parchment will extend above the top of the muffin cup. Put a spoonful of muffin batter into each liner to anchor it in the pan. Adjust each paper, as necessary so they are centered and even. Finish filling with the muffin batter. Bake as directed.

CREAM SCONES

MAKES 8 SCONES Classic teatime accompaniments, these tender scones are flaky and just slightly sweet, which makes them an ideal starting point for the luscious Classic Strawberry Shortcake (page 255). Feeling adventurous? You can adapt these scones to your taste by adding flavorings to the dough, such as citrus zest, spices, chopped and toasted nuts, flavoring extracts or oils, and dried fruit (you'll find a few variations at the end of the recipe to get you started).

Make sure your butter and cream are quite cold and handle the dough just enough to bring it together and pat it into shape. The food processor method used below (and in all the scone recipes in this chapter) ensures that your scones will be flaky and tender. If you don't have a food processor, you can make the scones by hand following the directions at the beginning of the chapter (page 145).

INGREDIENTS

2 cups (10 ounces) unbleached all-purpose flour

¼ cup (1¾ ounces) sugar

2½ teaspoons baking powder

¼ teaspoon salt

1 stick (4 ounces) cold unsalted butter, cut into ½-inch cubes

1 cup (8 ounces) chilled heavy whipping cream

1 egg, lightly beaten

1 tablespoon sugar, or for more crunch and a touch of brown sugar flavor, 2 tablespoons turbinado or raw sugar

EQUIPMENT

Baking Sheet, Parchment Paper or a Thin Silicone Mat, Food Processor, Silicone or Rubber Spatula, Chef's Knife, Pastry Brush, Cooling Rack

1 Preheat the oven to 425°F and position an oven rack in the center. Line the baking sheet with parchment paper or a thin silicone mat. Place the flour, sugar, baking powder, and salt in the bowl of the food processor and process for 10 seconds to blend well. Add the cold butter pieces and pulse 5 times at 1-second intervals, or until the butter is cut into medium pieces. Add the cream and pulse another 20 times, or until the dough holds together in small, thick clumps. Use a spatula to scrape the dough out onto a lightly floured work surface. Gently squeeze the clumps together until they form a cohesive dough.

2 Pat the dough into a circle 7 inches in diameter and about 1 inch thick. Use a chef's knife to cut the dough into 8 equal wedges and transfer to the prepared baking sheet, spacing them about 2 inches apart.

3 Brush the tops with a thin coating of the lightly beaten egg (you will not use all the egg). Sprinkle evenly with the sugar. Bake the scones for 14 to 16 minutes, until firm to the touch and golden brown. Transfer to a rack and let cool for 5 minutes. Serve the scones warm or at room temperature.

STORING Once baked, serve the scones within 2 hours, when they are at their freshest and most appealing. Keep them uncovered at room temperature until serving time.

Chocolate Cream Scones
Use only 1¾ cups (8¾ ounces) unbleached all-purpose flour and add ¼ cup (1 ounce) unsweetened Dutch-process cocoa powder to the flour mixture. Increase the sugar to ⅓ cup plus 1 tablespoon (2¾ ounces).

Lemon-Poppy Seed Scones
Add ¼ cup (1¼ ounces) poppy seeds and the finely grated zest of 2 large lemons to the flour and sugar mixture. Bake for 17 to 20 minutes (this dough is a bit thicker than the original so it will take a couple extra minutes to bake).

Cream Scones with Currants
Another teatime classic. Add ½ cup (2½ ounces) dried currants after the butter has been cut into medium pieces the size of large peas, and just before adding the cream. (Make sure the dried fruit is moist and pliable. If it isn't, pour boiling water over the currants and let them soak for 5 minutes. Drain them, pressing out any excess moisture; then pat dry and let cool before adding to the dough.) Bake scones for 17 to 20 minutes (this dough is a bit thicker than the original so it will take longer to bake).

Cream Biscuits
This is a savory version, perfect for the dinner table. Omit the sugar and follow the recipe as directed for light, tender biscuits.

Chile, Cheddar, and Cornmeal Biscuits
Great all on their own, these can also be cut into 1-inch rounds and filled with thinly sliced ham, sweet-hot mustard and watercress, or other small greens for a fun, crowd-friendly hors d'oeuvre. To vary the flavor of the biscuits, add a handful of chopped fresh herbs, fresh corn kernels, crispy bacon bits, several finely chopped scallions, or flavorings of your choice (add just after you finish cutting in the butter and right before you add the cream).

Reduce the flour to 1⅔ cups (8¼ ounces) and add ⅓ cup (2 ounces) of fine yellow cornmeal. Omit the sugar. Increase the baking powder to 1 tablespoon, the salt to ½ teaspoon, and add 10 grinds of black pepper. Decrease butter to ¾ stick (3 ounces). Add ⅔ cup (2½ ounces) grated sharp cheddar cheese and 2 tablespoons diced roasted poblano chiles (fresh or canned). Pat into an 8 by 4-inch rectangle, about 1-inch thick. Cut in half lengthwise and then into quarters crosswise to form eight 2-inch squares. Just before baking, brush the top with egg and sprinkle an additional ⅓ cup (1½ ounces) grated cheese over the top. Bake 15 to 18 minutes.

CHOCOLATE TOFFEE SCONES

MAKES 8 SCONES For those who like their breakfast, tea, or snack time treats to be outrageously over the top, these decadent scones, filled with miniature chocolate and toffee chips, are just the ticket. They are especially moist due to the inclusion of eggs in the dough rather than the usual cream or buttermilk. You could dress them up with the grated zest of an orange or a handful of toasted and finely chopped walnuts or almonds, but the extra sprinkling of toffee chips already gilds these lilies. The toffee melts, then cools into a crunchy, golden brown topping. Oh yeah.

INGREDIENTS

2 cups (10 ounces) unbleached all-purpose flour

¼ cup (1¾ ounces) sugar

1 tablespoon baking powder

¼ teaspoon salt

1 stick (4 ounces) cold unsalted butter, cut into ½-inch cubes

½ cup (3½ ounces) mini chocolate chips

½ cup (2½ ounces) plus ⅓ cup (1¾ ounces) toffee baking bits

2 large eggs

2 tablespoons (1 ounce) milk

1 tablespoon pure vanilla extract

EQUIPMENT

Baking Sheet, Parchment Paper or a Thin Silicone Mat, Food Processor Fitted with a Metal Blade, Small Bowl, Whisk, Silicone or Rubber Spatula, Chef's Knife, Cooling Rack

GETTING AHEAD **Once the dough is prepared and cut (through Step 2), the wedges can be covered with plastic wrap and refrigerated for up to 24 hours.**

   The scone dough can also be cut and frozen for up to 1 month. Place the wedges on the baking sheet and freeze until hard, about 1 hour. Transfer to a resealable plastic freezer bag. Thaw overnight in the refrigerator before baking. Or, thaw at room temperature on the prepared baking sheet for about 20 minutes before baking.

1 Preheat the oven to 400°F and position an oven rack in the center. Line the baking sheet with parchment paper or a thin silicone mat. Place the flour, sugar, baking powder, and salt in the bowl of the food processor and process for 10 seconds to blend well. Add the cold butter pieces and pulse 5 times at 1-second intervals, or until the butter is cut into medium pieces. Add the mini chocolate chips and the ½ cup toffee baking bits but do not blend them in. In the small bowl, whisk together the eggs, milk, and vanilla until well blended. Pour the egg mixture into the processor and pulse another 25 times, or until the dough holds together in large, thick clumps.

2 Use a spatula to scrape the dough out onto a lightly floured work surface. Gently squeeze or knead the clumps together until they form a cohesive dough—it may seem a bit dry at first, but will come together with a few kneads. Pat the dough into a circle 7 inches in diameter and about 1 inch thick. Use a chef's knife to cut the dough into 8 equal wedges and transfer to the prepared baking sheet, spacing them about 2 inches apart.

3 Lightly press the remaining ⅓ cup toffee chips onto the tops of the scones, dividing evenly. Bake for 14 to 17 minutes, until fully risen and golden brown, especially around the bottom edges. Transfer to a rack and let cool for 5 to 10 minutes. Serve the scones warm or at room temperature.

STORING **Once baked, serve the scones within 6 hours, when they are at their freshest and most appealing. Store uncovered at room temperature until serving time.**

BUTTERMILK SCONES WITH DRIED CHERRIES AND ORANGE

MAKES 8 SCONES Buttermilk does wonders for baked goods, adding a touch of acidity and an appealingly homey taste whenever it is included. Buttermilk scones are a classic—these are perfumed with orange zest and flavored with chewy nuggets of dried sour cherries. And they're easily adapted. Omit the sugar and you've got warm dinner biscuits. Change the flavorings and you change the scone—try dried blueberries and lemon zest, dried cranberries and ginger, or dried apricots and toasted hazelnuts. If you love the flavor of gingerbread, try the variation at the end of the recipe, which is the base for Gingerbread Shortcakes with Caramelized Apples and Cider Sabayon (page 259).

INGREDIENTS

2 cups (10 ounces) unbleached all-purpose flour

¼ cup (1¾ ounces) sugar, plus 1 tablespoon for sprinkling

Finely grated zest of 1 large orange

1¾ teaspoons baking powder

½ teaspoon baking soda

¼ teaspoon salt

1 stick (4 ounces) cold unsalted butter, cut into ½-inch cubes

½ cup (3 ounces) dried sour cherries

¾ cup (6 ounces) cold buttermilk

1 egg, lightly beaten

EQUIPMENT

Baking Sheet, Parchment Paper or a Thin Silicone Mat, Food Processor Fitted with a Metal Blade, Silicone or Rubber Spatula, Chef's Knife, Pastry Brush, Cooling Rack

1 Preheat the oven to 425°F and position an oven rack in the center. Line the baking sheet with parchment paper or a thin silicone mat. Place the flour, ¼ cup sugar, orange zest, baking powder, baking soda, and salt in the bowl of the food processor and process for 10 seconds to blend well. Add the cold butter pieces and pulse 5 times at 1-second intervals, or until the butter is cut into medium pieces. Add the dried cherries, but don't blend them in. Pour in the buttermilk and pulse another 20 times, or until the dough holds together in large, thick clumps. Use a spatula to scrape the dough out onto a lightly floured work surface. Gently squeeze or knead the clumps together until they form a cohesive dough.

2 If the dough seems sticky, lightly dust your work surface with flour. Pat the dough into a circle 7 inches in diameter and about 1 inch thick. Use a chef's knife to cut the dough into 8 equal wedges and transfer to the prepared baking sheet, spacing them about 2 inches apart.

3 Brush the tops with a thin coating of the beaten egg (you will not use all the egg). Sprinkle evenly with the remaining 1 tablespoon sugar. Bake for 14 to 17 minutes, until firm to the touch and golden brown. Transfer to a rack and let cool for 5 minutes. Serve the scones warm or at room temperature.

tips for success   Improvising Flavors

Biscuits and scones are a blank canvas upon which you can work your culinary creativity. You can add a wide variety of dried fruits and nuts to the recipes here, as long as you keep the amount to about ½ cup per recipe (you can add up to 1 cup, but the scones will be thicker and will take a few extra minutes to bake). Add your flavorings after the butter is cut into the desired size and right before you stir in the liquid.

Zests, spices (½ to 1 teaspoon for each recipe here), extracts (½ to ¾ teaspoon for each recipe here), and oils (a few drops to ¼ teaspoon for each recipe here) may also be used to flavor the dough, as may chocolate and other flavored chips. Zests should be added with the dry ingredients, whereas extracts and oils should be added with the liquid in the recipe. You may also incorporate specialty or whole-grain flours into the biscuits or scones by substituting them for one-fourth of the total amount of flour in the recipe (for example, if the recipe calls for 2 cups of white flour, use ½ cup of whole wheat flour and 1½ cups of white flour).

GETTING AHEAD Once the dough is prepared and cut (through Step 2), the wedges can be covered with plastic wrap and refrigerated for up to 24 hours. They will not rise quite as high as when freshly mixed, but they will be attractive and tasty. To bake, proceed with Step 3.

The dough can also be cut and frozen for up to 1 month. Place the wedges on a baking sheet and freeze until hard, about 1 hour. Transfer to a resealable plastic freezer bag. To bake, thaw overnight in the refrigerator, then place on the prepared baking sheet and proceed with Step 3. Or, thaw at room temperature on the prepared baking sheet for about 20 minutes, or until cool to the touch but no longer hard in the center. Bake as directed.

STORING Once the scones are baked, serve them within 2 hours, when they are at their freshest and most appealing. Store uncovered at room temperature until serving time.

Gingerbread Scones
Omit the orange zest and dried sour cherries. Substitute ⅓ cup (2½ ounces) firmly packed light brown sugar for the sugar. Add 2½ teaspoons ground ginger, 1½ teaspoons ground cinnamon, and ½ teaspoon ground cloves to the flour mixture. Decrease the buttermilk to ½ cup plus 2 tablespoons (5 ounces) and combine with 2 tablespoons light, unsulfured molasses before adding.

Buttermilk Biscuits
This is a savory version, perfect for the dinner table. Omit the sugar, orange zest, and dried cherries and follow the recipe as directed for light, tender biscuits.

CANDIED GINGER SCONES

MAKES 8 SCONES These scones are light in texture with a crunchy brown sugar topping and an invigorating burst of ginger. The method for making them is unusual because there is no butter required—instead, cream is whipped to soft peaks and folded into the flour mixture, resulting in a fluffy, rather than flaky, interior. Great for breakfast or tea, they also make superb shortcakes (think plum, apricot, peach . . .).

INGREDIENTS

2 ounces crystallized ginger

¼ cup (1¾ ounces) granulated sugar

2 cups (10 ounces) unbleached all-purpose flour

1 tablespoon baking powder

½ teaspoon ground ginger

¼ teaspoon salt

1¼ cups (10 ounces) chilled heavy whipping cream

1 egg, lightly beaten

¼ cup (1¾ ounces) turbinado or raw sugar (light brown sugar may be substituted—it will be very tasty, but not quite as crunchy)

EQUIPMENT

Baking Sheet, Parchment Paper or a Thin Silicone Mat, Food Processor Fitted with a Metal Blade, Large Bowl, Whisk, Stand Mixer Fitted with a Whisk Attachment or a Hand Mixer and a Medium Bowl, Silicone or Rubber Spatula, Chef's Knife, Pastry Brush, Cooling Rack

GETTING AHEAD **Once the dough is prepared and cut (through Step 2), the wedges can be covered with plastic wrap and refrigerated for up to 24 hours.**

The scone dough can also be cut and frozen for up to 1 month. Place the wedges on the baking sheet and freeze until hard, about 1 hour. Transfer to a resealable plastic freezer bag. Thaw overnight in the refrigerator before baking. Or, thaw at room temperature on the prepared baking sheet for about 20 minutes before baking.

1 Preheat the oven to 375°F and position an oven rack in the center. Line the baking sheet with parchment paper or a thin silicone mat. Place the crystallized ginger and granulated sugar in the bowl of the food processor and process until very finely chopped—the mixture should resemble damp sand. Transfer to the large bowl and add the flour, baking powder, ground ginger, and salt. Whisk to blend well.

2 In the bowl of the stand mixer, or with a hand mixer and a medium bowl, whip the cream to soft peaks, with tips that fold over and barely hold their shape. Use a silicone or rubber spatula to scrape half of the whipped cream into the flour mixture and gently fold in with the spatula. Add the remaining whipped cream and continue to fold until there are no longer any obvious streaks of cream or patches of flour. The dough may seem a little dry at this point—don't worry.

3 Turn the dough out onto a work surface and knead gently a few times to finish bringing the dough together. If the dough seems very wet and sticky, sprinkle it with a little flour to keep it from sticking to your hands and the work surface. Pat the dough into a 7-inch circle. Use a chef's knife to cut the dough into 8 equal wedges. Place the scones on the prepared baking sheet, spacing them about 2 inches apart.

4 Brush the tops with a thin layer of the beaten egg. Top each scone with a generous layer of turbinado sugar. Bake for 18 to 20 minutes, until firm and golden brown. Transfer to a rack. Serve warm or at room temperature.

STORING **Once baked, serve the scones within 12 hours, when they are at their freshest and most appealing. Store uncovered at room temperature until serving time.**

PUMPKIN WALNUT BREAD

MAKES 1 LOAF This is the loaf you want on that gorgeous fall day, when it's too beautiful outdoors to fuss in the kitchen for long. It takes no time at all to whip this up because it is made using the muffin method, meaning you simply stir everything together by hand. The hardest part is measuring out all the spices. It freezes beautifully, so you might want to double the recipe and tuck one away for another day. Want to dress it up a bit? Add a generous layer of cream cheese frosting on top (and maybe in the middle as well) and try to resist cutting another slice.

INGREDIENTS

2 cups (10 ounces) unbleached all-purpose flour

¾ teaspoon baking soda

½ teaspoon ground cinnamon

¼ teaspoon allspice

¼ teaspoon ground cloves

¼ teaspoon ground ginger

¼ teaspoon salt

2 large eggs, at room temperature

⅓ cup (2¾ ounces) water

1½ cups (10½ ounces) sugar

1 cup (9 ounces) canned pumpkin puree

½ cup neutral-flavor vegetable oil (such as canola)

1 teaspoon pure vanilla extract

1 cup (4 ounces) chopped toasted walnuts

EQUIPMENT

9 by 5-inch Loaf Pan, Parchment Paper, Large Bowl, Whisk, Medium Bowl, Silicone or Rubber Spatula, Cooling Rack, Serrated Knife

GETTING AHEAD Pumpkin Walnut Bread freezes beautifully for up to 8 weeks when double-wrapped in plastic and placed inside a resealable plastic freezer bag. Defrost, still wrapped in plastic to avoid condensation on the cake, for at least 2 hours before serving.

1 Preheat the oven to 350°F and position an oven rack in the center. Lightly coat the loaf pan with melted butter or high-heat canola-oil spray and line it with a piece of parchment paper that extends 1 inch beyond the edge of both sides of the pan. In the large bowl, whisk together the flour, baking soda, cinnamon, allspice, cloves, ginger, and salt until thoroughly blended. In the medium bowl, whisk together the eggs and water. Add the sugar and blend well. Add the pumpkin puree, vegetable oil, and vanilla extract and blend well.

2 Add the pumpkin mixture to the dry ingredients and whisk until blended and smooth. Add the walnuts and stir until they are evenly distributed. Use a spatula to scrape the batter into the prepared loaf pan and level the top.

3 Bake for 55 to 65 minutes, until the bread is firm to the touch and a toothpick inserted into the center comes out clean. Transfer to a rack to cool completely. To serve, cut into ½-inch thick slices by sawing gently with a serrated knife. Any leftovers should be wrapped in plastic and stored at room temperature for up to 2 days, or in the refrigerator for up to 4 days.

Pumpkin Walnut Bread with Cream Cheese Frosting

Make the pumpkin bread as directed in the above recipe and let it cool. Generously spread ½ recipe Cream Cheese Frosting (page 414) over the top. If you *really* like frosting, split the cake in half horizontally and spread a layer of frosting in the center as well (do this first, before you frost the top). Serve within 4 hours; otherwise, refrigerate until serving. Some people love this bread ice cold, but if you'd like to take the chill off, remove it from the refrigerator about 30 minutes before serving.

CHOCOLATE-BANANA MARBLE BREAD

MAKES 1 LOAF Here's a banana bread that's soft, tender, and bursting with bananas, yet not overly sweet as so many versions are. The key is an intensely bitter cocoa-powder paste added to half of the batter, resulting in a deep, rich chocolate flavor that pairs perfectly with the sweetness of the bananas. The two batters are marbled together, producing a beautiful pattern and adding a sophisticated note to this all-American favorite. Because of the moisture that the bananas add, the loaf keeps well for at least 4 to 5 days at room temperature, and it freezes so well that you can put a couple of them away for unexpected visitors. Be sure the bananas are ripe and soft, with plenty of black spots speckling their skins, or you won't have the burst of banana flavor you want. Whirl them in the food processor for an ultra-smooth puree, or mash thoroughly with a fork if you prefer.

INGREDIENTS

2 large or 3 medium very ripe bananas, at room temperature

¼ cup (2 ounces) buttermilk, at room temperature

2 teaspoons pure vanilla extract

2 cups (7 ounces) sifted cake flour

1 teaspoon baking soda

¾ teaspoon baking powder

¼ cup (1 ounce) unsifted unsweetened Dutch-process cocoa powder

3 tablespoons (1½ ounces) boiling water, plus more if needed

1½ sticks (6 ounces) unsalted butter, softened (65° to 68°F)

1 cup (7 ounces) sugar

2 large eggs at room temperature, lightly beaten

EQUIPMENT

9 by 5-inch Loaf Pan, Food Processor Fitted with a Metal Blade (Optional), Two Medium Bowls, Fine-Mesh Strainer, Small Bowl, Whisk, Stand Mixer Fitted with a Paddle Attachment, Silicone or Rubber Spatula, Cooling Rack

1 Preheat the oven to 350°F and position an oven rack in the center. Lightly coat the loaf pan with melted butter or high-heat canola-oil spray and line it with a piece of parchment paper that extends 1 inch beyond the long edge of both sides of the pan. Peel the bananas and place them in the bowl of the food processor. Process to a smooth puree. (Alternately, mash them in a bowl using a fork.) Measure out 1 cup of the puree and transfer it to a medium bowl, discarding the rest of the puree or saving it for another use. Add the buttermilk and vanilla and whisk just until blended. Set aside.

2 Use a fine-mesh strainer to sift the cake flour, baking soda, and baking powder together into a medium bowl. Whisk to blend well. Set aside. Place the cocoa powder in the small bowl. Pour the boiling water over the cocoa and stir until it forms a smooth paste—it should run thickly off the spoon. If it is too thick, add another tablespoon of boiling water and stir again. Set aside.

3 Place the butter and sugar in the bowl of the stand mixer. Beat on medium-high speed until the butter is very light, almost white in color, 4 to 5 minutes. Scrape down the bowl with a spatula. Turn the mixer to medium speed and add the eggs, 1 tablespoon at a time, completely blending in each addition before adding the next. About halfway through

the eggs, turn off the mixer and scrape down the bowl with the spatula, then continue adding the rest of the eggs. Scrape down the bowl again.

4 With the mixer running on the lowest speed, add one-third of the flour mixture. Just as it is barely blended and you can still see a few patches of flour, add half the banana mixture. Repeat with the remaining flour and banana mixtures ending with the flour. Scrape down the bowl and finish blending the batter by hand.

5 Transfer half of the batter to the second medium bowl. Add the cocoa paste and, using the rubber spatula, gently but thoroughly blend it into the batter.

6 Drop alternating spoonfuls of dark and light batters into the prepared pan, then marbleize by using a spoon to gently turn the batter over in 3 places down the length of the pan.

7 Bake the banana bread for 55 to 65 minutes, until firm to the touch and a toothpick inserted into the center of the loaf comes out clean. Transfer to a rack to cool completely. When cool, remove from the pan, peel off the parchment paper, and cut slices by sawing gently with a serrated knife.

HERB CORN BREAD

MAKES 1 LOAF This is a very simple quick bread made using the muffin method, but the addition of fresh herbs and summer corn takes it to a whole new level. Don't substitute dried herbs here–they won't give you the dynamic flavor that fresh ones offer. This recipe can be baked in muffin tins, yielding a dozen tempting corn muffins (see the variation below).

INGREDIENTS

1 cup (5 ounces) unbleached all-purpose flour

1 cup (4½ ounces) medium-grind cornmeal (yellow or white)

¼ cup plus 1 tablespoon (2 ounces) sugar

1¼ teaspoons baking powder

1 teaspoon salt

½ teaspoon freshly ground pepper

1 large shallot, very finely chopped

¾ cup (4 ounces) fresh or frozen corn kernels

⅓ cup finely chopped fresh thyme leaves (about 2 bunches)

¼ cup finely chopped fresh sage leaves (1½ to 2 bunches)

2 tablespoons finely chopped fresh Italian parsley leaves

1 cup (8 ounces) half-and-half

2 large eggs

1 stick (4 ounces) unsalted butter, melted

EQUIPMENT

Two Medium Bowls, Whisk, Silicone or Rubber Spatula, 9 by 5-inch Loaf Pan, Cooling Rack, Serrated Knife

what the **pros** know For individual muffins, pre-heat the oven to 375°F. Mix the batter as directed above, then divide it evenly among 12 standard muffin cups that have been well buttered or oiled. Be sure to butter the top of the muffin tin to prevent the muffin crowns from sticking there. Bake for 20 minutes, or until firm to the touch and a skewer inserted into the center comes out clean.

1 Preheat the oven to 350°F and position an oven rack in the center. Lightly coat the loaf pan with melted butter or high-heat canola-oil spray and line it with a piece of parchment paper that extends 1 inch beyond the edge of both sides of the pan. In a medium bowl, whisk the flour, cornmeal, sugar, baking powder, salt, and pepper to blend well. Add the shallot, corn kernels, thyme, sage, and parsley. Whisk again to blend everything thoroughly.

2 In the second medium bowl (or large measuring cup), whisk together the half-and-half and eggs. Make a well in the dry ingredients and pour the egg mixture into the well, then add the melted butter. Use the whisk to gently combine the ingredients, stirring just until the batter is homogenous and there are no patches of egg or flour. Don't overmix or the corn bread may be tunneled with holes.

3 Use a spatula to scrape the batter into the prepared loaf pan. Bake for 40 to 50 minutes, until the center of the bread feels firm to the touch and a skewer inserted into the center comes out clean. Transfer to a rack and let cool 10 to 15 minutes before turning out of the pan (it may also be left in the pan to cool completely). Peel off the parchment paper and cut into slices with a serrated knife.

STORING When the corn bread is completely cool, tightly wrap in plastic wrap and store at room temperature for up to 3 days. Reheat wrapped in foil in a 325°F oven for 10 to 15 minutes, until warmed through.

To freeze, place inside a resealable plastic freezer bag and freeze for up to 1 month. To serve, thaw at room temperature—still in the bag to avoid condensation—for 1½ hours; then reheat as directed above.

CINNAMON-STREUSEL SOUR CREAM COFFEE CAKE

MAKES 1 LOAF There's a reason this coffee cake is an American classic. Its velvet crumb and generous layers of cinnamon streusel both inside and out make it a supreme indulgence on a lazy weekend morning. The touch of cocoa powder in the streusel tempers the sweetness and adds a subtle depth of flavor—you won't notice it's there, but it gives the topping a little extra oomph. Standing tall and beautifully brown, the cake's striking presence on the brunch table is like a magnet for family and friends. Also, it's a real "keeper" because it will be delicious and moist for at least 3 or 4 days after baking. Cakes like this one freeze beautifully, so you can even make it up to a month in advance. The best accompaniments are a bowl of fresh fruit and a cup of good coffee. Oh, and don't forget the Sunday paper.

INGREDIENTS

STREUSEL

½ cup (4 ounces) firmly packed light brown sugar

2 teaspoons ground cinnamon

2 teaspoons unsweetened cocoa powder

1 cup (4 ounces) pecans, toasted and chopped

CAKE

3 cups (15 ounces) unbleached all-purpose flour

2 teaspoons baking powder

½ teaspoon baking soda

½ teaspoon salt

2 sticks (8 ounces) unsalted butter, softened (65° to 68°F)

2 cups (14 ounces) granulated sugar

4 large eggs, at room temperature

1 tablespoon pure vanilla extract

1 (16-ounce) container sour cream, at room temperature

EQUIPMENT

10-inch Tube Pan with a Removable Bottom, Two Medium Bowls, Whisk, Stand Mixer Fitted with a Paddle Attachment or a Hand Mixer and a Medium Bowl, Silicone or Rubber Spatula, Small Bowl, Cooling Rack, Thin Knife or Spatula, Serrated Knife

1 Preheat the oven to 350°F and position an oven rack in the lower third. Lightly coat the pan with melted butter, oil, or high-heat canola-oil spray, dust it with flour, and tap out the excess.

2 MAKE THE STREUSEL: Place the brown sugar, cinnamon, and cocoa powder in a medium bowl and stir with a spoon until well blended. Smash any lumps of brown sugar or cocoa so the mixture is even in texture. Add the pecans and stir to blend. Set aside.

3 MIX THE CAKE BATTER: Place the flour, baking powder, baking soda, and salt in the second medium bowl and whisk to blend thoroughly. Set aside.

4 Place the butter and granulated sugar in the bowl of the stand mixer and beat on medium-high speed until the mixture is very light, almost white in color, 4 to 5 minutes. You can also use a hand mixer and a medium bowl, though you may need to beat the mixture a little longer to achieve the same results. Scrape down the bowl with a spatula.

what the pros know

Though this cake is striking in size and stature, sometimes it's more fun to offer an individual indulgence. In those cases, bake the batter in paper-lined muffin tins, filling each cup ⅔ full. Bake for 25 to 30 minutes, or until a skewer inserted into the center comes out clean. You'll need the paper liners to ensure the muffins release easily, since the streusel filling and topping can caramelize and stick to the pan. And the last thing you want to do with this type of cake (or muffin) is turn it upside down to remove it from the pan. If you do, the topping will fall off and make a mess. With paper liners, you just lift each treat out of the pan and serve. Makes about 2 dozen muffins.

5 Crack the eggs into the small bowl and beat with a fork to blend. Add the vanilla and beat well. With the mixer running on medium, add the eggs to the butter mixture about 1 tablespoon at a time, blending well after each addition. About halfway through, turn off the mixer and use the spatula to scrape down the bowl; then continue adding the rest of the eggs. Scrape down the bowl again.

6 With the mixer running on the lowest speed, add one-third of the flour mixture. Just as it is barely blended and you can still see a few patches of flour, add half of the sour cream. Repeat with the remaining flour and sour cream, ending with the flour. Scrape down the bowl and finish blending the batter by hand.

7 Spoon half of the batter into the prepared pan and smooth the top. Sprinkle half of the streusel evenly over the batter. Spoon the remaining batter into the pan and level and smooth the top. Sprinkle the remaining streusel over the top. Bake for 65 to 75 minutes, until the cake is firm to the touch and a skewer inserted into the center comes out clean. Transfer to a rack to cool for at least 30 minutes if you want to serve it warm, or about 1½ hours to cool completely. Run a thin knife or spatula around the edge and the inner tube of the pan to loosen the cake. Lift the center portion of the pan, with the cake, out of the ring. Run a thin knife or spatula around the bottom of the cake to release it from the bottom of the pan. Hold the cake firmly with your hands on both sides. Gently lift the cake, sliding it up the tube portion until it comes completely off the pan. Set it on a serving plate. Cut slices by gently sawing with a serrated knife.

STORING The cake will keep at room temperature for up to 4 days covered with plastic wrap or a cake dome. Once it has been cut, press a piece of plastic wrap against the cut edges to keep the interior fresh. The cake can be frozen, double-wrapped in plastic, for up to 4 weeks. Thaw, still wrapped in plastic to avoid condensation, for 3 hours before serving. Reheat, wrapped in foil, in a 325°F oven for 20 minutes, or until warmed through.

If there were a culinary flag, pie would be the central emblem, for no other dessert embodies good old-fashioned home baking more than pie. It peppers our language ("humble pie," "easy as pie") and serves as a link to our baking heritage. A picture of a golden pie cooling on a windowsill evokes nostalgia for our rural past. It may not be a glamorous dessert, but pie delivers more satisfaction per bite than any fancy five-star creation. Just watch the faces of family and friends when offered a piece still warm from the oven and you'll see the proof—people practically swoon in the presence of pie. Supermarket bakeries and big-box stores now offer huge, tempting pies, packaged and ready to take home, but they're a pale imitation of the real, handcrafted thing.

So why aren't homemade pies more common? Unfortunately, many home bakers are so intimidated by flaky crusts that they avoid making pies altogether. That's a shame, since pie crust is much easier to make than its reputation would have you believe. The primer below explains how pie dough works and will give you the confidence to make a wonderfully flaky crust on your first try. Still intimidated? As great as classic pie crust is, there are other options. You can make a mealy crust (described below), which is just as tasty, with less stress. Also offered are recipes for two alternatives that are even simpler, nearly foolproof, and still deliver great flavor—a tender, tangy cream cheese crust and a crunchy cookie crumb crust.

A Primer on Pie Crust

There are two types of basic pie crust: flaky and mealy. Dough for a flaky crust has pockets of butter in it and, when baked, breaks like shale, exposing the air spaces within where the butter has melted. A mealy crust (this is not a pejorative term, but a professional one that describes texture) is more tender and cookielike, shatters easily, and dissolves quickly in the mouth. Mealy crusts and flaky crusts can be made from the same recipe—the only difference is how the butter is cut into the flour before the water is added.

The cut-in butter for flaky dough resembles a mixture of crushed crackers and peas, whereas the butter for mealy dough is much finer, resembling bread crumbs. The tiny pieces of butter in mealy dough coat the protein strands, preventing them from bonding and forming gluten, and results in a very tender crust. Flaky dough needs a bit more gluten development to provide the structure necessary for flakes to occur. The larger pieces of butter in this dough do not coat the gluten strands as fully, resulting in a sturdier dough. Many beginners set out to make flaky dough and wind up with mealy dough by accident when they cut the butter pieces too small. The reality is, most bakeries use mealy dough instead of flaky dough, since it is easier to make and requires less attention. Mealy dough is quite delicious in its own right, so if you make it by accident, don't worry. Serve it with a smile and try for flaky another day. In the panoply of the home baker's repertoire, flaky pie crust is the Holy Grail, so let's explore it further.

Flaky Pie Crust

Flaky dough is a member of the "cut-in" family of pastries, requiring a technique similar to that for the biscuits and scones in "Quick Breads." This method of mixing cuts the butter into pieces that remain separate from the flour around them. Once liquid is added to the mixture, a dough forms, surrounding and enveloping the butter pieces, which remain distinct within the dough. As the dough is rolled, the butter pieces are flattened into flakes. During baking, the dough sets around these flakes. Then, as the flakes melt, they leave behind an empty space in the hardening dough, creating the texture associated with a flaky crust. Simple enough, yes, but lots can go wrong if you don't understand the role that each ingredient plays. Once you do, you'll be making fabulously flaky pie crust in no time.

THE BUILDING BLOCKS OF FLAKY PIE CRUST

FLOUR

For pie dough, the two key attributes of flour are protein and water absorption. Protein, when combined with liquid (such as the water in pie dough) and agitation (such as stirring, kneading, and rolling) forms strands of gluten. In bread, you want lots of gluten structure; in cakes, very little; and in pie dough, you want just enough. Enough to provide shape, flakiness, and strength to your dough without making it tough.

Cake flour has a very low protein content and will not produce enough gluten to form sufficient structure. Pastry flour has a bit more protein than cake flour and has long been used for pie dough, but is now very difficult to find. Bread flour, which contains a high level of protein, forms strong gluten strands too quickly to be of value in pie making and produces dry, tough pie crusts. All-purpose flour, because it's easy to use and available in every supermarket in this country, is the choice for this book's flaky pie crust recipe. Look for unbleached all-purpose flour, which produces pie dough that is full of flavor. The protein content should be between 10.5 percent and 11 percent (not every all-purpose flour has the same amount of protein; for more on this, see page 20).

Bleached flour, though it usually has a lower protein content than unbleached and thus might seem more well suited to the task at hand, provides little flavor and does not absorb as much water as unbleached, throwing off the ratio in the recipe here. If you make this recipe with bleached flour, the dough will be too wet, resulting in excessive shrinking during baking (not to mention the difficulties of working with a wet, sticky dough). For best results with pie dough, as with any baking, weigh your ingredients. If you don't have a scale, be sure to measure by the dip and sweep method described in "Measuring 101," page 3.

BUTTER

Butter not only adds the best flavor possible to your pie crust, it also browns and crisps the crust better than other fats. Many people swear by shortening in their crust because its high melting point means there is more time for the dough to set around the flakes of fat, ensuring a very flaky crust. But proper technique with the butter dough will produce a flaky crust with a much better flavor. After all, would you dip lobster in melted shortening? Then why put it in your pie crust?

When choosing butter, quality counts. Purchase a name-brand unsalted butter, which is usually of higher quality than the store's brand. Avoid salted butter, which will make your crust too salty.

The most important thing to remember when making all-butter pie dough is to keep the butter cold. The one drawback to butter is its low melting point (about 94°F), which means that the heat from your fingers can easily soften or melt the butter, allowing it to blend with the flour during the mixing and rolling stages rather than remaining separate. If there's no separation, there are no flakes. So keep it cold. Cut the butter into pieces and freeze them for 20 minutes before beginning the dough and use a food processor to cut in the butter quickly. Both work wonders to keep the butter cold. If at any time during the pie making process you notice that the butter is getting soft or squishy, immediately stop what you are doing and transfer the mixture to the refrigerator or freezer for 15 minutes to firm it up again.

SUGAR

Sugar, added to this dough in very small amounts, contributes a subtle sweetness and helps give the dough a lovely golden brown color. It is optional, and should be omitted if you are making a savory pie.

SALT

Salt enhances flavor. Without it, your crust will taste flat. When it's there, you don't notice it, but when it's missing, the crust is not nearly as delicious.

WATER

Water blends with the flour, activating its proteins and helping to create the gluten strands necessary for proper structure. Most recipes give a range for the amount of water needed, say, from 4 to 5 tablespoons. Experienced pie makers know when the dough feels like it has just the right amount of moisture, but this type of measurement can be confusing to baking novices. Since flours vary in their protein and moisture content, it can be difficult to specify an exact amount of water that will work across all circumstances. For instance, a bag of flour in Louisiana in July will contain more moisture than a bag in Phoenix, since flours absorb moisture from the air around them. And bleached flour will absorb less water than unbleached. The key is to add enough water to form a cohesive dough, but not so much that the dough is sticky and difficult to work with. Always add the lowest measurement of water first, then test the dough using the method described below, adding more if needed, about a teaspoon at a time, until the dough is finished.

Most recipes call for ice water, because icy cold water helps keep butter firm—one of the keys to a successful dough. If you like, you can measure your water and refrigerate it until needed.

ACID

Sometimes a recipe calls for the addition of a small amount of acid to the dough, such as a teaspoon of lemon juice or vinegar in flaky pie crust recipes. The theory is that the acid breaks up the long gluten strands and guards against toughness caused by the development of too much gluten during mixing and kneading. While it's true that acid can help to reduce gluten formation, unfortunately a teaspoon or two is not enough to do the job. In fact, you would need to add so much lemon juice or vinegar that the dough would be inedible. Proper technique will get you a lot further than a bit of acid in the dough.

HOW TO MAKE FLAKY PIE CRUST

Rule Number One: Don't panic!!! The more anxious you become, the less fun you have. Besides, the dough can smell fear (or at least it seems that way).

Rule Number Two: Get ready to bake. Read the recipe before you begin and measure out your ingredients. And remember, it's food, not world peace. Even less-than-perfect pies are still delicious, especially served warm with plenty of ice cream.

MIXING THE DRY INGREDIENTS

Measure the flour, sugar, and salt into the bowl of a food processor and blend well. You don't have to use a processor to make the dough, but it is a fast and efficient way to cut the butter into the flour, producing perfect-size butter pieces in seconds.

CUTTING IN THE BUTTER

Add the frozen butter pieces to the processor and pulse (1 second each) until the mixture looks like crushed crackers and peas. It's easy to go too far, so check the texture every 3 or 4 pulses. Another reason to use the processor is that its speed means the butter stays cold as long as possible. You can certainly cut the butter into the flour by hand using your fingers or a pastry blender, but remember to work quickly and set the bowl in the refrigerator if the

what the pros know

If a crack or hole forms while rolling, you will need to patch it. Your patch will not hold if you simply pinch the dough back together. You need to use a little water as glue. Brush any flour from the problem area. Then use your finger to lightly rub a thin film of cold water over it. To repair a crack, gently lift one side and position it so that it overlaps the other side and press together. To repair a hole, pinch a small piece of dough off the outer edge and lay it over the moistened area and press together. Once you have patched the crack or hole, tap the patched area firmly with the heel of your hand to seal it. Then dust with flour so it won't stick to your rolling pin. Continue rolling the dough to the desired size, chilling whenever necessary.

butter softens. Some pie makers even freeze the dry ingredients along with the butter, just to make sure everything stays cold. Once you reach the desired texture in the processor, transfer the ingredients to a bowl, add the water, and finish bringing the dough together by hand; it's the best way to ensure your crust turns out flaky.

ADDING THE WATER

It's not a good idea to add water while the dough is in the processor. As you pulse in the water, you also continue to cut the butter into smaller and smaller pieces, resulting in a mealy rather than a flaky crust. Instead, transfer the mixture to a mixing bowl.

Sprinkle a tablespoon of water over the mixture and "fluff" it in, then add another, and so on until the minimum amount of water has been added. Check for moisture content before you continue. Too little water and the dough will be crumbly, dry, and impossible to roll out. Too much water and the dough will be sticky and messy and shrink dramatically in the oven.

TESTING THE DOUGH

Grab a handful of the shaggy crumbs and clumps and squeeze them briefly. When you open your hand, they should hold together in a moist, but not sticky, mass. The dough should release easily from your hand, leaving very little residue. If clumps of dough or patches of flour fall through your fingers, the dough needs water. If, on the other hand, the dough tests too wet and sticky, there is little recourse but to begin again. By the time you knead enough flour into the dough to achieve the right consistency, the gluten will have strengthened to the point of toughening the dough. Because you can always add more water, and because wet dough is nearly impossible to rescue, it is always better to err on the side of dryness when you begin, adding water as needed. You may need to add even more water than the recipe states, depending on your measuring method and the dryness of your flour.

KNEADING THE DOUGH

Turn the dough clumps out onto a lightly floured work surface and gently knead them together. It will take between 3 and 6 kneads to bring the clumps into a cohesive dough. If it crumbles or falls apart, it's still too dry. Return it to the bowl and add additional cold water.

CHILLING THE DOUGH

Wrap the finished dough in parchment or plastic and refrigerate for 30 minutes. This resting time allows the gluten strands to relax and the dough to finish hydrating. Plus, it firms up the butter. If you are making a double-crust or lattice-top pie, be sure to divide the dough in half and wrap each half separately. Shape the dough into a round and flatten to about ¾ inch thick—this will make rolling the dough easier. If you have a square or rectangular pan, shape the dough into a square rather than a circle. It sounds elementary, but the correct beginning shape ensures that you'll roll to the desired finished shape.

ROLLING THE DOUGH

If the dough is chilled for longer than 30 minutes, it can become very firm. If this happens, let it sit on the counter for 10 to 20 minutes, until cool but malleable. You should be able to gently bend the dough without breaking it. Dust your work surface with flour, then dust the top of the dough as well. Don't be afraid of adding too much flour—many home bakers use so little that their dough sticks to the surface and tears. As long as your dough is cold, it will not absorb the flour. If the dough warms during the rolling process, transfer it to a baking sheet (described below) and return to the refrigerator to chill for 15 minutes before continuing.

To roll a circle, think of your dough as a clock face, with 12 o'clock at the top. Roll away from yourself and then back a couple of times, then turn the dough so 2 o'clock is at the top. As you roll, always lift the rolling pin at the edge of the dough so you don't smash the edge of the dough into the table. Continue to roll, turning the dough in 2-hour increments. Turning the dough keeps it rounded (so you don't end up with a square), and alerts you

Making Flaky Pie Crust

LEFT: Cut the butter into the dry ingredients until the mixture has the texture of "crushed crackers and peas."

RIGHT: Add the water until the dough is moist enough to hold together in large, shaggy clumps.

LEFT: Turn the dough clumps onto a lightly floured surface and gently knead them until a cohesive dough is formed. Flatten into a disk, then wrap in parchment or plastic, and chill for 30 minutes.

RIGHT: Roll the dough on a surface dusted with flour, or between two sheets of parchment or wax paper.

Sometimes the thought of making a pie from beginning to end in one stretch is too daunting. Here's a tip from pastry chefs that adapts well to the home kitchen: Make a double or triple batch of dough, divide it into portions, and roll it out, layering the rounds between sheets of parchment paper on a baking sheet. Wrap the entire sheet in plastic and refrigerate for up to 2 days, or double-wrap and store in the freezer for 4 to 6 weeks. Any time you want to make pie, you'll only need to prepare the filling. Simply remove a round (or two for a double-crust pie) of rolled dough from the refrigerator or freezer, let it sit on the counter until malleable, and transfer into a pie pan. Trim and crimp the edges, then chill while you prepare the filling. If you have plenty of freezer room and several pie pans, you could even freeze the dough in pie pans. If the pie pans are freezer-to-oven safe, they'll be ready to bake at a moment's notice.

immediately if it is sticking to the work surface. If it sticks, fold the dough back to expose the stuck area, loosen it with a small spatula, dust with flour and keep rolling. You don't need to roll a perfect circle, as you'll be trimming the edges once the dough is in the pie pan.

If you prefer, you can roll the flakey dough between two pieces of parchment or waxed paper. To do this, follow the instructions for rolling and transferring dough into a pan that are included under tart dough on page 210.

TRANSFERRING THE DOUGH

Fold the dough round into quarters, brushing any excess flour from the dough each time you fold. If the rolled-out round has been stored in the refrigerator or freezer for a length of time, you may need to let it sit at room temperature for 5 minutes or longer, until it is malleable enough to fold without cracking.

Put the point of the folded dough in the center of the pie or tart pan and unfold the dough, lifting it slightly as necessary to ease it into the crevices of the pan. Do not stretch or pull the dough; this can cause thin spots, holes, and/or shrinkage during baking. If you are making a double batch for a double-crust pie, keep the rolled-out dough for the top crust on a baking sheet in the refrigerator until you have filled the pie shell.

FINISHING THE DOUGH IN THE PIE PAN

For a single-crust pie, use a pair of kitchen scissors to trim the dough so it overhangs the edge of the pan by 1 inch. Fold the overhanging dough under itself around the pan edge, then crimp or form a decorative border (see below).

For a double-crust pie, roll out two batches of dough. Fit one round into the pie plate and chill the other on a baking sheet until needed. With a pair of kitchen scissors, trim the bottom dough so it is even with the rim of the pie pan. Spoon filling into the pie shell. Top with the remaining round of dough (folding and unfolding it as described above) and trim the dough so it overhangs the edge of the pan by 1 inch. Fold this overhang under the bottom crust around the pan edge, then crimp or form a decorative border (see below).

MAKING A LATTICE TOP

For a lattice-top pie, use a pair of kitchen scissors to trim the dough so it overhangs the edge of the pan by 1 inch. Chill while you cut the lattice strips. Firmly shape the dough into a small rectangle, then roll it into a large ⅛-inch-wide rectangle. Trim to a 14 by 12-inch rectangle. Use a pastry wheel, pizza cutter, or kitchen knife to cut the dough into fourteen 1-inch wide strips. If the strips of dough are warm and difficult to move, chill them on a baking sheet for 10 minutes. Spoon the filling into the pie shell.

Lay 7 of the lattice strips, evenly spaced, horizontally across the filling. Working from the right side, fold back every other strip (4 strips total) so that they are doubled back on themselves. Lay a vertical strip of dough down the center next to the folds in the strips. Unfold the horizontal folded strips back over this strip. Again working from the right side, fold the other 3 horizontal strips back on themselves. Lay a second vertical strip of dough next to this new fold. The new strip should be parallel to, and ½ inch from, the first vertical strip. Repeat twice more, until half of the pie has been latticed. Turn the pie so the unlatticed side faces you and continue weaving in the same manner until all the strips have been used. With a pair of kitchen scissors, trim any lattice ends even with the overhanging bottom crust. Fold the overhang under and crimp or form a decorative border (see below).

CRIMPING OR DECORATING THE EDGES

Some professionals like to leave a lot of overhang, 1½ to 2 inches, then roll it toward the center of the pie, forming a thick rope along the edge for a tall, prominent, decorative edge. Most commonly, though, the overhanging dough is trimmed to 1 inch, then folded under at the edge of the pan. To crimp the edges, use the first two fingers of your right hand on the inside and a knuckle of your left hand on the outside and press firmly to form a pattern. Or simply press the edges together with the tines of a fork. Trimmed dough scraps may be used to make a decorative border instead of crimping or using a fork. Cut shapes out of the trimmings using tiny cookie cutters, then fix them to the edge of the pie, using a bit of water as glue.

CHILLING THE PIE

No matter how fast you work, pie dough always needs to be chilled before baking. Repeat the mantra, "cold pastry, hot oven." To create flakes, the dough needs to cook before the butter completely melts, and to keep that butter as cold as possible, it must be chilled. Thirty minutes in the refrigerator is usually long enough. Do not chill a filled pie longer than 1 hour, as the sugar in the filling will turn to liquid and soak the bottom crust, making it soft and soggy.

GLAZING AND VENTING THE PIE

Double-crusted or lattice-top pies are at their most beautiful when brushed with the sheerest egg wash, usually a combination of egg yolk and milk or cream. You won't use all of the wash—you want a thin layer, with no gloppy drips or pools of egg along the edge. Don't brush the edges of pies, which will get plenty brown all on their own, but do cover every inch of the top crust or lattice with a thin coating of the wash. You might want to sprinkle the top with a dusting of sugar for color and a crispy contrast to the soft filling within. Always make a few vents in the top crust before baking (unless you have a lattice top). Simmering fruit creates a lot of steam, and if you don't provide an escape hatch, it will create one on its own, ruining the look of the pie. Three to four vents are adequate and may be cut with the tip of a paring knife, or you can create decorative vents with a tiny cookie cutter.

PREBAKING THE CRUST

For some single-crust pies and tarts, the crust must be baked before the filling is added. This technique is known as *blind baking* or *baking with a false filling*. Sometimes the crust is fully baked and sometimes only partially. Fully baked crusts are used with very wet fillings, such as custard for pumpkin pie, or fillings that will not be baked at all, such as pastry cream or lemon curd. Partially baked crusts suit fillings that need some oven time, but not quite as much as the crust does. For these fillings, give the crust a head start by partially baking it before adding the filling; that way both parts of the pie will be done at the same time.

Both fully baked and partially baked crusts start out the same way: A chilled uncooked crust is lined with heavy-duty foil, filled with weights to simulate a filling, then baked until the crust has set enough to release the foil easily, about 20 minutes. The weights are removed and the crust returned to the oven to continue baking. The partially baked crust is cooked only until it is lightly golden and dry across the bottom of the pan, while the fully baked crust is cooked until a golden brown.

Why use a false filling—why not just chill the crust and bake empty? As it softens in the heat of the oven, two things happen to an unfilled crust: The bottom puffs up, and the side shrinks or falls toward the center. The pie weights keep everything in place until the dough is set. Once set, the weights are removed so the crust can dry and crisp in direct contact with the oven's hot air.

The weights used for blind baking are ceramic or steel pellets sold as "pie weights." You can use dried rice or beans in their place. If you do, though, be sure to store them in a container marked "pie weights" and don't cook them, as the oven dries them out too much to be tasty. After a number of uses, they will begin to smell burned—at this point replace them. Ceramic and steel pie weights last forever and may be used repeatedly with no ill effects. Always use heavy-duty foil when lining pie or tart shells, as regular strength foil tears easily under the weight of the false filling. The last thing you want is burning hot pie weights raining onto the floor, your feet, or into the pie shell, where you'll have to pick them out of the dough with a spoon and tweezers. A few extra pennies for the heavy-duty foil can save a lot of heartache. The foil pie liner may be saved with the weights and reused several times.

BAKING THE PIE

Whether single or double-crust, bake the chilled pie in a hot oven, about 400°F. The dramatic contrast in temperatures between the cold dough and the hot air is what insures a flaky, crispy crust. The heat sets the crust quickly, creating the firm structure that allows the melting butter to leave behind an empty space. If the oven temperature is too low or the dough insufficiently chilled, the crust will simply collapse on top of itself as each piece of butter melts, resulting in a dense rather than a flaky dough. For best flavor and texture, cook the pie until the crust is a deep, dark golden brown.

COOLING THE PIE

Although cutting into a hot, fragrant pie is tempting, let it cool for at least 30 to 60 minutes before serving or the filling will be too warm to hold its shape. Fruit pies especially benefit from this cooling period, as the fruit reabsorbs some of the juices that would otherwise gush in every direction.

A FEW WORDS ABOUT FRUIT FILLINGS

WHAT TO LOOK FOR WHEN CHOOSING YOUR FRUIT

The most popular filling for pies by far is fruit. Once you've made a beautiful crust, make sure the fruit is just as flavorful. Keep the season in mind, as ripe fruit is much tastier than tired specimens flown in from around the world. Eating in season will keep your taste buds sharp for new fruits arriving with the turn of a calendar page. Frozen fruit can be of excellent quality, but is not great for making pies because the cells ruptured by ice crystals during freezing release too much liquid once thawed, making the pie watery and the crust soggy. If you do use frozen fruit, you'll need to increase the thickener in the pie to absorb the extra liquid, and it may take a little experimentation to get it right.

WAYS TO THICKEN A FRUIT FILLING

Fruit pies nearly always have a thickener in the filling along with sugar, lemon juice, and spices. Fruit releases water when cooked, and though some of this liquid will evaporate in the heat of the oven, if there is too much left in the bottom of the pie, the crust will be sodden. Thickeners are added to bind the liquid and keep it suspended in the fruit, rather than pooling below. Although there are many choices, flour or cornstarch are the thickeners most bakers prefer. Flour clouds the filling slightly, but is always on hand and easy to use. Cornstarch results in a shiny filling. Tapioca flour, not granules, gives a clear, natural look but it can be difficult to find so it's not called for in the recipes here. (Do give it a try if you run across it.) The three can be substituted for one another as long as you keep in mind that unbleached all-purpose flour has only about half of the thickening ability of cornstarch or tapioca flour, which means you'll need to use twice as much when using it in place of cornstarch or tapioca flour.

FLAKY PIE OR TART DOUGH

MAKES 1 (9- OR 10-INCH) PIE SHELL Many bakers are so intimidated by the idea of making flaky pie crust that they either settle for the prepared dough from the grocery store or don't make pie at all. But, like all baking, pie crust is quite straightforward once you know how the ingredients work together. If you're new to pie dough, be sure to read the primer (page 168); then take a deep breath and follow the steps below for a beautifully crisp, golden brown, flaky pie crust. This recipe doesn't call for shortening, as the flavor, aroma, and color of an all-butter crust can't be beat. The drawback to butter is that it can soften quickly at room temperature, which is why it's best to use the food processor to ensure great results every time. Weigh your dry ingredients if you can, but if you don't have a scale, you can measure by the dip-and-sweep method (page 4).

INGREDIENTS

1 stick (4 ounces) cold unsalted butter, cut into ½-inch pieces

3 to 4 tablespoons cold water

1¼ cups (6¼ ounces) unbleached all-purpose flour

1½ teaspoons sugar (omit for a savory crust)

¼ teaspoon salt

EQUIPMENT

Small Measuring Cup, Food Processor Fitted with a Metal Blade, Large Bowl, Rolling Pin, Pastry Brush, 9- or 10-inch Pie or Tart Pan, Kitchen Scissors

1 Place the butter pieces in a bowl or on a plate and freeze for at least 20 minutes. Refrigerate the water in a small measuring cup until needed.

2 MIX THE DOUGH: Place the flour, sugar, and salt in the bowl of the food processor. Process for 10 seconds to blend the ingredients. Add the frozen butter pieces and pulse 6 to 10 times (in 1-second bursts), until the butter and flour mixture looks like crushed crackers and peas.

3 Immediately transfer the butter-flour mixture to the large bowl. Sprinkle a tablespoon of the cold water over the mixture and "fluff" it in, then add another, and another, until 3 tablespoons have been added. Continue to fluff and stir 10 or 12 times. It will not be a cohesive dough at this point but a bowl of shaggy crumbs and clumps of dough. Before bringing the dough together, you need to test it for the correct moisture content. Take a handful of the mixture and squeeze firmly. Open your hand. If the clump falls apart and looks dry, remove any large, moist clumps from the bowl then add more water, one teaspoon at a time, sprinkling it over the top of the mixture and immediately stirring or mixing it in. Test again before adding any more water. Repeat, if needed. The dough is done when it holds together (even if a few small pieces fall off). If the butter feels soft and squishy, refrigerate before continuing. If the butter is still cold and firm, continue to the next step. (Note: Adding the liquid may also be done on low speed in a stand mixer fitted with

what the pros know

When doubling or tripling a batch of pie dough, whether for a double-crusted pie or simply to have some extra dough in the freezer for another day, it can be difficult to fit all the ingredients into your food processor (unless you have a large model). No problem. Take a tip from pastry chefs who have to make 20 times the recipe—use your stand mixer for the whole process. Simply chop the butter and freeze it for a couple of hours, then cut it into the dry ingredients, using the low speed and paddle attachment. Add the cold water just as the butter pieces reach the "peas and crushed crackers" stage, and continue to mix on low until the dough holds together in large, shaggy clumps. Once you've finished the dough, divide it into equal pieces, wrap in plastic, and refrigerate for 30 minutes. Roll each piece into a ⅛-inch-thick round and layer between sheets of parchment paper on a baking sheet. Wrap the entire sheet in plastic, then refrigerate or freeze until needed.

the paddle attachment—add three-fourths of the liquid, test for moistness, then add the remaining liquid if needed.)

4 KNEAD AND CHILL THE DOUGH: Turn the dough onto a work surface and knead gently 3 to 6 times. If it won't come together and looks very dry, return it to the bowl and add another teaspoon or two of water (one at a time), mixing in as above, and try again. Flatten the dough into a 6- or 7-inch disk, wrap in plastic or parchment paper, and refrigerate for 30 minutes. This allows time for the dough to hydrate fully and for the butter to firm up again.

5 ROLL THE DOUGH: If the dough has been refrigerated for more than 30 minutes, it may be very firm and hard and will crack if you try to roll it. Let it sit on the counter for 10 to 15 minutes until it is malleable but still cold. Dust your work surface generously with flour and set the disk on the flour. Dust the top with flour. Roll, turning the dough and following the directions on page 171, until you've got a 14- to 15-inch circle about ⅛ inch thick. If at any point the dough becomes warm and sticky, gently fold it into quarters, unfold it onto a baking sheet and refrigerate for 15 minutes, or until the butter is firm again.

6 If a crack or hole forms while rolling, brush any flour away and patch the area according to the instructions on page 171.

7 TRANSFER THE DOUGH: Fold the dough circle into quarters, brushing off any excess flour as you fold. Put the point of the folded dough in the center of the pie pan, tart pan, or baking sheet and unfold the dough, lifting it slightly as necessary to ease it into the crevices of the pan. Do not stretch or pull the dough, which can cause thin spots, holes, and/or shrinkage during baking.

8 TRIM THE DOUGH: Use a pair of kitchen scissors to trim the dough so it overhangs the edge of the pan by 1 inch. Fold the overhanging dough under itself around the pan edge, then crimp or form a decorative border (page 174). Chill for 30 minutes before baking.

STORING **The dough can be wrapped in plastic and refrigerated for up to 2 days, or double-wrapped in plastic, slipped into a freezer bag, and frozen for up to 1 month.**

EASY CREAM CHEESE PIE DOUGH

MAKES ENOUGH DOUGH FOR 9 TURNOVERS OR 8 DUMPLINGS, OR 1 (9- OR 10-INCH) PIE SHELL A nearly foolproof alternative to flaky dough, cream cheese dough can be made in the food processor in a couple of minutes. Rich cream cheese takes the place of water and helps to bring the dough together. The high proportion of fat means it's practically impossible to toughen the pastry. The dough's tangy flavor and flaky texture accent the fruit fillings in turnovers, though you could also use the dough for pies, either sweet or savory.

INGREDIENTS

1½ cups (7½ ounces) unbleached all-purpose flour

1 teaspoon sugar (omit for savory pastry)

Pinch of salt

1 stick (4 ounces) cold unsalted butter, cut into ½-inch pieces

1 (8-ounce) package cold cream cheese, cut into 9 pieces

EQUIPMENT

Food Processor Fitted with a Metal Blade, Rolling Pin, Chef's Knife, Ruler

GETTING AHEAD **The dough can be prepared through Step 2 and refrigerated for up to 2 days or slipped inside a resealable plastic freezer bag and frozen for up to 2 months (thaw overnight in the refrigerator before rolling).**

1 Place the flour, sugar, and salt in the bowl of the food processor and process for 10 seconds to blend. Add the cold butter pieces and process for 8 to 10 seconds, until the mixture looks like bread crumbs. Add the cream cheese and pulse 30 times (1-second pulses), or until large, shaggy clumps of dough form.

2 Turn the shaggy mass out onto a work surface and knead gently 2 or 3 times to create a cohesive dough. If you are making turnovers or dumplings, flatten into a 7-inch square (about ¾ inch thick) and wrap in plastic. (For a pie, shape the dough into a ¾-inch thick round.) Chill for 30 minutes.

3 Place the dough on a lightly floured surface. If you are making turnovers or dumplings, roll into a square about ⅛ inch thick (for rolling tips, see page 171). Use a chef's knife to trim to a 15-inch square. Use the ruler to mark 5-inch increments along all sides of the dough. With the ruler as a guide, cut the dough into 9 (5-inch) squares. (For a pie, follow the instructions for rolling and shaping on page 171.)

STORING **Place rolled-out squares between sheets of parchment or wax paper on a baking sheet, wrap in plastic, and refrigerate for up to 2 days. You may also freeze them, layered between sheets of parchment, wrapped in plastic and sealed in a resealable plastic freezer bag or airtight container, for up to 2 months.**

GRAHAM CRACKER CRUMB PIE CRUST

MAKES 1 (9-INCH) PIE CRUST This easy crust is kid-friendly to make and pairs well with any chilled, pudding-style filling or cheesecake. A scale will give you the most precise measurement. If you don't own one, be sure to finely grind or crush your cookies before you measure them. A food processor makes quick work of this, or you can place the cookies in a resealable plastic bag and powder them with a rolling pin. Lots of cookies work well here; just make sure they are dry and crispy. Gingersnaps, chocolate wafer cookies, and shortbread are fine. Big, chewy cookies with chocolate chips or dried fruit will not work and should be avoided.

INGREDIENTS

1½ cups (7 ounces) finely ground graham cracker cookie crumbs

1 tablespoon (½ ounce) sugar
¾ stick (3 ounces) unsalted butter, melted

EQUIPMENT

Medium Bowl, Silicone or Rubber Spatula, 9-inch Pie Pan, Cooling Rack

GETTING AHEAD **The baked crust can be prepared up to 1 week in advance, wrapped tightly in plastic, and stored at room temperature. If the crust softens during storage, re-crisp in a 350°F oven for 6 to 8 minutes.**

1 Preheat the oven to 350°F and position an oven rack in the center. Put the cookie crumbs and the sugar in the medium bowl and stir well with a spatula to blend. Add the melted butter and stir until all the crumbs are evenly moistened. Transfer the buttered crumbs to the pie pan. Use the heel of your hand, a tart tamper, or the bottom of a drinking glass to press the crumbs from the center outward into an even layer across the bottom of the pan. Use your thumbs to press the crumbs up the side of the pan and level them at the rim.

2 Bake for 8 to 10 minutes, until lightly colored and fragrant. Transfer to a rack to cool completely.

STORING **Store at room temperature covered in plastic wrap.**

Chocolate Cookie Pie Crust Substitute 1½ cups (7 ounces) finely ground chocolate cookie crumbs for the graham cracker crumbs. Omit the sugar.

Gingersnap Pie Crust Substitute 1½ cups (7 ounces) finely ground gingersnap cookie crumbs for the graham cracker crumbs.

Chocolate Sandwich Cookie Pie Crust Substitute 1½ cups (7 ounces) finely ground chocolate sandwich cookies (about 20 original-style Oreo cookies) for the graham cracker crumbs. Omit the sugar.

ALL-AMERICAN APPLE PIE

MAKES 1 (9-INCH) PIE, SERVING 8 TO 10 When choosing baking apples, look for firm, sturdy apples that will hold their shape in the oven. Otherwise you'll end up with applesauce pie. Tart apples are particularly good, since they balance the sweet ice cream that accompanies this pie like a well-loved sidekick. Tart Granny Smiths are reliable and available in every market in the country, but try seeking out local varieties at the farmers' market or roadside stands during apple season. Don't be afraid to mix and match apples. A few tart and sturdy ones with a few sweet can be a great combination (see page 244).

INGREDIENTS

2 recipes Flaky Pie or Tart Dough (page 177), prepared through Step 5

6 to 7 (2½ pounds) medium to large Granny Smith or other tart apples, peeled, cored, and cut into ¼-inch-thick slices

⅓ cup (2¼ ounces) or more sugar, either granulated or firmly packed brown sugar, plus 1 to 2 teaspoons granulated sugar for sprinkling

1 tablespoon freshly squeezed lemon juice

½ teaspoon ground cinnamon

⅛ teaspoon allspice

1 large egg yolk

1 tablespoon milk or cream

Good-quality vanilla ice cream, for serving

EQUIPMENT

9-inch Pie Pan, Baking Sheet, Large Bowl, Kitchen Scissors, Silicone or Rubber Spatula, Small Bowl, Pastry Brush, Paring Knife or Mini Cookie Cutter (Optional), Cooling Rack

GETTING AHEAD You can make the pie crust up to 2 days ahead and keep it chilled and covered. You can cut and toss the apples with the lemon juice up to 1 day in advance (they will brown, but they turn brown during baking anyway, so don't worry).

The pie may be completely assembled and refrigerated for up to 1 hour before baking, but if held longer, the sugar melts into a syrup, pools in the bottom of the pie shell, and makes the bottom crust soggy.

1 Preheat the oven to 400°F and position an oven rack in the lower third. Following the instructions in Step 7 on page 178, transfer one rolled-out circle of pie or tart dough to a 9-inch pie pan and the other to a baking sheet. Chill them until ready to use.

2 Taste the apples; if they are very tart, you may want to increase the sugar by 2 to 4 tablespoons. In the large bowl, gently toss the apples with the ⅓ cup sugar (or more), the lemon juice, cinnamon, and allspice until evenly coated.

3 Use the scissors to trim the dough in the pie pan so it is flush with the rim. Transfer the filling to the pie shell and press down firmly on the apples with the spatula to eliminate some of the air pockets. Scrape any sugar or spices left in the bottom of the bowl over the top of the apples. Top with the other dough half, again following instructions for transferring dough and decoratively crimping the edges on page 174. Chill for 30 minutes.

4 In a small bowl, beat the egg yolk with the milk to create an egg wash and use the pastry brush to lightly glaze the surface of the pie. Sprinkle the pie with 1 to 2 teaspoons sugar. Use a paring knife to cut 3 or 4 decorative slits in the pie to allow steam to escape (or use a mini cookie cutter to make cuts in the dough). Bake the pie for 50 to 60 minutes, until the crust is a lovely golden brown and the apples are bubbling and tender when pierced with the tip of a paring knife. Transfer to a cooling rack and let cool for 40 to 60 minutes. Serve warm or at room temperature with a scoop of ice cream.

STORING The pie will keep at room temperature under a cake dome for up to 2 days. For longer storage, cover with plastic wrap and refrigerate. Reheat in a 375°F oven for 15 to 20 minutes to warm the filling and re-crisp the crust.

LATTICE-TOP NECTARINE-BLACKBERRY PIE

MAKES 1 (9-INCH) PIE, SERVING 8 TO 10 A carefully woven lattice is the crowning glory of a summer pie, providing a tempting glimpse of the sweet fruit within through the slatted golden brown crust. For a different fruit filling, begin by substituting the fillings from All-American Apple Pie, or Apricot, Plum, and Ginger Pie. Then, as your confidence grows, create your own.

INGREDIENTS

2 recipes Flaky Pie and Tart Dough (page 177), prepared through Step 4

6 medium (2¼ pounds) nectarines

1 half-pint basket (6 ounces) blackberries

⅓ cup (2½ ounces) sugar, plus 1 to 2 teaspoons for sprinkling

3 tablespoons (1½ ounces) unbleached all-purpose flour

1 tablespoon (½ ounce) freshly squeezed lemon juice

1 large egg yolk

2 tablespoons milk or cream

Vanilla Crème Fraîche (page 420), Almond Cream (page 417), or vanilla ice cream, for serving

EQUIPMENT

9-inch Pie Pan, Two Baking Sheets, Paring Knife, Large Bowl, Silicone or Rubber Spatula, Small Bowl, Pastry Brush, Cooling Rack

GETTING AHEAD The pie dough may be prepared and rolled out, then layered between sheets of parchment paper on a baking sheet and wrapped in plastic. Refrigerate for up to 2 days or freeze for up to 1 month. Cut the dough into strips and weave the lattice on the day you assemble the pie.

1 Roll out one recipe of the pie or tart dough (Step 5). Transfer to a 9-inch pie pan (Step 7) and chill until ready to use. Firmly shape the other recipe of dough into a small rectangle, then roll it into a 14 by 12-inch rectangle that is about ⅛ inch thick, trimming if necessary to reach the right dimensions. Carefully fold the dough rectangle into quarters, transfer it to a baking sheet, unfold, and chill until ready to use.

2 Rinse the nectarines and pat dry. Use a paring knife to cut each in half, remove the pit, and cut each half into 4 or 5 slices. Transfer to the large bowl. Pour the blackberries out onto a baking sheet. Pick through them and discard any debris or molded berries. (Do not wash, or they will absorb the water and turn to mush.) Add the berries to the nectarine slices. Add the sugar, flour, and lemon juice and gently toss with a spatula until the fruit is evenly coated.

3 Scrape the filling into the chilled pie shell. From the chilled rectangle of dough, create a lattice (page 174). Refrigerate the pie for 30 minutes but no longer than 1 hour.

4 Preheat the oven to 400°F and position a rack in the bottom third of the oven. In a small bowl, beat the egg yolk with the milk or cream to create an egg wash, then use the pastry brush to lightly glaze the lattice and outside edge of the pie crust. Sprinkle the top with the 1 to 2 teaspoons sugar. Bake for 50 to 60 minutes, until the crust is golden brown and the fruit is bubbling and tender (test with the tip of a paring knife). Transfer to a cooling rack and allow the pie to cool for 40 to 60 minutes. Serve warm or at room temperature with crème fraîche, almond cream, or vanilla ice cream.

STORING The pie will keep at room temperature under a cake dome for up to 2 days. For longer storage, cover with plastic wrap and refrigerate. Reheat in a 375°F oven for 15 to 20 minutes to warm the filling and re-crisp the crust.

APRICOT, PLUM, AND GINGER PIE WITH ALMOND CRUMBLE TOPPING

MAKES 1 (9-INCH) PIE, SERVING 8 TO 10 Apricots have a short but sweet season, and this pie celebrates their arrival by pairing them with another summer favorite, plums. The crunchy almond topping is related to sugar cookies and is so addictive you'll have to keep friends and family from sneaking bits of it while the pie is cooling. You can make this pie using just apricots or just plums, but the festive jumble of colors and flavors of the combined fruits is especially appealing.

INGREDIENTS

1 recipe Flaky Pie or Tart Dough (page 177)

ALMOND CRUMBLE TOPPING

1 stick (4 ounces) unsalted butter, softened (65° to 68°F)

¼ cup (1¾ ounces) granulated sugar

¼ teaspoon pure vanilla extract

¼ teaspoon pure almond extract

⅛ teaspoon salt

1 cup (5 ounces) unbleached all-purpose flour

¼ cup (1 ounce) almond meal (ground almonds)

FILLING

4 large (12 ounces) apricots

3 large (12 ounces) plums

2 tablespoons plus 1 teaspoon (1 ounce) finely chopped crystallized (candied) ginger

¼ cup (2 ounces) firmly packed light brown sugar

1 tablespoon cornstarch

¼ cup (¾ ounce) raw sliced almonds

1 tablespoon turbinado sugar

Vanilla Crème Fraîche (page 420), Honeyed Yogurt (page 420), Almond Cream (page 417), or vanilla ice cream, for serving

EQUIPMENT

Stand Mixer Fitted with a Paddle Attachment or a Hand Mixer and a Medium Bowl, Silicone or Rubber Spatula, Large Bowl, Paring Knife, Cooling Rack

1 Preheat the oven to 375°F and position an oven rack in the lower third.

2 MAKE THE TOPPING: Place the butter and granulated sugar in the bowl of the mixer and beat on medium speed until very light in color, nearly white, about 5 minutes. You may also use a hand mixer and a medium bowl, though you may need to beat the mixture a little longer to achieve the same results. Scrape down the bowl with a spatula. Add the vanilla and almond extracts and the salt and blend well. Scrape down the bowl. Add the flour and almond meal all at once and turn the speed to low. Blend for 15 to 20 seconds, until the mixture forms small clumps about the size of small peas. Chill the topping in bowl, covered, while you make the filling.

3 MAKE THE FILLING: Use a paring knife to cut each apricot and plum in half and remove the pit. Slice each half into 3 pieces. Transfer to the large bowl, add the ginger, brown sugar, and cornstarch, and toss gently to evenly coat the fruit.

4 BAKE THE PIE: Scrape the filling into the chilled pie shell. Scatter the topping evenly over the top. Sprinkle the almonds over the topping, then the turbinado sugar. Bake for 55 to 65 minutes, until the pie shell is golden brown and the fruit juices are bubbling and thickened. Transfer to a cooling rack and allow the pie to cool for 40 to 60 minutes so some of the juices are reabsorbed. Serve warm or at room temperature, preferably with crème fraîche, honeyed yogurt, almond cream, or vanilla ice cream.

pros

Chopping crystallized ginger can turn into a sticky situation. The best way to prevent the ginger from sticking to the knife is to oil the blade of the knife before beginning. Another option is to combine the sugar and ginger in the bowl of a food processor and chop them together. The sugar coats the ginger and keeps the pieces from sticking together as they are chopped smaller and smaller.

GETTING AHEAD The almond crumble topping can be prepared in advance and stored in an airtight container in the refrigerator for up to 4 days, or up to 1 month in the freezer.

The pie crust can be prepared up to 2 days before assembling the pie, wrapped in plastic, and refrigerated, or it may be frozen for up to 1 month.

The pie can be completely assembled and refrigerated for up to 1 hour before baking. If held longer, the sugar melts into a syrup, pools in the bottom of the pie shell, and makes the bottom crust soggy.

STORING Store the pie under a cake dome at room temperature for up to 2 days. For longer storage, cover with plastic wrap and refrigerate. Reheat in a 375°F oven for 15 to 20 minutes to warm the filling and re-crisp the crust and topping.

Peach-Ginger Pie with Almond Crumble Topping
Pit 2½ pounds of firm-ripe peaches (peeled or not according to your taste) and cut into ¼-inch slices. Use to substitute for the apricots and plums.

Strawberry, Rhubarb, and Ginger Pie with Almond Crumble Topping
For the filling, use 1¼ pounds of rhubarb, rinsed and patted dry, ends trimmed, and cut into ½-inch pieces (about 5 cups), and a 1-pint basket (16 ounces) strawberries, rinsed, patted dry, hulled, and quartered. Combine the fruit with 1 cup (7 ounces) sugar, 3 tablespoons cornstarch, 2 tablespoons finely chopped crystallized (candied) ginger, and the finely grated zest of 1 large orange. Follow the recipe as directed, reducing the baking time to 40 to 50 minutes.

GREAT PUMPKIN PIE

MAKES 1 (10-INCH) REGULAR PIE OR 1 (9-INCH) DEEP-DISH PIE, SERVING 10 TO 12 Thanksgiving just may be everyone's favorite holiday. After all, what's better than a day completely devoted to a delicious feast shared by family and friends, all giving thanks for their blessings? This recipe takes an American classic to celebration status with a careful blend of spices and heavy cream, outshining the stale spice mix and evaporated milk of less enchanting recipes. Ever notice how spices clump up and don't blend well when added to a custard? The trick is to blend them first with the eggs, whose fat helps the clumps disperse evenly, before adding any liquid to the custard mixture.

INGREDIENTS

1 recipe Flaky Pie or Tart Dough (page 177), prepared through Step 8

3 large eggs

1½ teaspoons ground cinnamon

¾ teaspoon ground ginger

¼ teaspoon nutmeg (about 20 grates on a whole nutmeg)

¼ teaspoon ground cloves

¼ teaspoon ground allspice

⅛ teaspoon salt

1½ cups (12 ounces) heavy whipping cream

½ cup (4 ounces) firmly packed light brown sugar

¼ cup (1¾ ounces) granulated sugar

2 cups (16 ounces) canned pumpkin puree (not pumpkin pie filling)

Softly Whipped Cream (page 416), for serving

EQUIPMENT

10-inch Regular or 9-inch Deep Dish Pie Pan, Pie Weights, Cooling Rack, Whisk, Large Bowl, Fine-Mesh Strainer, Medium Saucepan, Silicone or Rubber Spatula, Thin and Sharp Knife

1 BAKE THE SHELL: Preheat the oven to 375°F and position an oven rack in the bottom third. Line the chilled pie shell with heavy-duty foil, pressing the foil firmly and smoothly into the crevices of the pan. Fill the pan with pie weights (page 175). Make sure the weights reach up the sides to the rim of the pan (the center does not need to be filled quite as full). Bake the shell for 20 to 22 minutes, until the foil comes away from the dough easily (if it doesn't, then bake another 5 to 6 minutes and check again). Remove the pan from the oven, close the oven door, and lift out the foil and weights from the shell; set them aside to cool. Return the pan to the oven to continue baking the shell for about 10 minutes, then remove the pan from the oven, close the oven door, and check to see if any cracks have formed. If you see a crack, very gently smear a tiny bit of reserved dough over the crack to patch it (page 171)—you need only enough to seal the opening. Return the pan to the oven and bake 10 to 15 minutes longer, until the crust is a nice golden brown all over. Transfer to a rack and cool slightly. Lower the oven temperature to 350°F.

2 WHILE THE PIE CRUST IS BAKING, MAKE THE FILLING: Whisk the eggs in the large bowl to break them up. Add the cinnamon, ginger, nutmeg, cloves, allspice, and salt and whisk well to blend evenly. Whisk in the cream, brown sugar, and granulated sugar and blend well. Strain the mixture through the strainer into the medium saucepan, pressing on the strainer with the spatula to push through any lumps of brown sugar. Add the pumpkin puree and whisk until the custard mixture is thoroughly blended. Cook over medium-low heat, stirring constantly with the spatula and scraping all over the bottom

what the

what the
pros
know

There's a trick to making pumpkin pie that keeps the prebaked crust crisp against the liquid custard filling, and it defies logic. You've probably always heard that a prebaked pie crust should be cooled before being filled with custard and sent back to the oven. Not here. The crust should be hot from the oven (or reheated until hot) and then filled with hot custard. It's crazy, but it works beautifully. The bonus is that hot crust plus hot custard equals a shorter baking time. While pumpkin pies usually take an hour or more to bake, this one is finished in about 30 minutes. Now that's a reason to be thankful.

GETTING AHEAD **The pie crust can be rolled, fitted into the pie pan, and trimmed up to 2 days before baking the pie and refrigerated, or it may be frozen for up to 1 month.**

The crust can be baked up to 3 days in advance and stored, wrapped in plastic, at room temperature.

The ingredients for the custard can be combined 1 day in advance and kept, airtight, in the refrigerator. Do not warm the custard on the stovetop until just before you bake it.

of the pan to prevent the eggs from scrambling, for 7 to 9 minutes, until the mixture feels lightly thickened and registers 150°F on an instant-read thermometer. Do not let the mixture scramble or you'll have to begin again. Remove from the heat.

3 If the pie crust has cooled, reheat it in the oven for 5 minutes. Scrape the hot custard into the hot pie shell and bake for 30 to 40 minutes, until the custard is set. Test by tapping the side of the pie pan—the center of the pie should look firm and move as one piece (professionals call this the *Jell-O jiggle*). Transfer the pie to a rack and cool completely, about 2 hours.

4 To serve, slice the pie with a thin and sharp knife and use a pie server to transfer each slice to a plate. Serve with whipped cream.

STORING **Store at room temperature for up to 8 hours. For longer storage, cover with plastic and refrigerate. Remove the pie from the refrigerator 1 hour before serving. Pumpkin pie is best the first or second day, as the crust begins to soften over time. It will keep, covered with plastic wrap, in the refrigerator for up to 4 days.**

ROASTED BUTTERNUT SQUASH-ONION PIE

MAKES 1 (9-INCH) PIE, SERVING 8 This fall pie is a sumptuous vegetarian option for the holiday table. But don't be surprised if even the omnivores clamor for a slice, since the sweet caramelized squash and onion paired with the salty, rich pecorino cheese is an irresistible combination. Serve it any time with a simple salad and a glass of wine for a very special dinner.

INGREDIENTS

1 recipe Flaky Pie or Tart Dough (page 177), prepared through Step 8

SQUASH

10 ounces butternut squash, peeled and cut into 1-inch cubes (about 1½ cups)

1 tablespoon olive oil

1½ teaspoons light brown sugar

¼ teaspoon salt

⅛ teaspoon black pepper

ONION

1 tablespoon olive oil

1 tablespoon unsalted butter

1 large (10 to 12 ounces) onion, cut into ¼-inch-thick slices

Salt

CUSTARD

¾ cup (6 ounces) whole milk

2 large eggs

½ cup (4 ounces) heavy whipping cream

½ cup (1½ ounces) plus ½ cup (1½ ounces) finely grated pecorino cheese

1 tablespoon snipped fresh chives

1½ teaspoons finely chopped fresh thyme

1½ teaspoons finely chopped fresh sage

1 teaspoon finely grated lemon zest

⅛ teaspoon salt

8 grinds black pepper

EQUIPMENT

9-inch Pie Pan, Pie Weights, Cooling Rack, Baking Sheet with ½-inch Sides, Silicone Mat (Optional), Medium Bowl, Silicone or Rubber Spatula, Thin and Sharp Knife, 10-inch Sauté Pan, Large Bowl, Whisk

1 BAKE THE SHELL: Preheat the oven to 375°F and position 2 oven racks in the top and bottom thirds. Line the chilled pie shell with heavy-duty foil, pressing the foil firmly and smoothly into the crevices of the pan. Fill the pan with pie weights (page 175). Make sure the weights reach up the sides to the rim of the pan (the center does not need to be filled quite as full). Bake the shell for 20 to 22 minutes, until the foil comes away from the dough easily (if it doesn't, then bake another 5 to 6 minutes and check again). Remove the pan from the oven, close the oven door, and lift out the foil and weights from the shell; set them aside to cool. Return the pan to the oven to continue baking the shell for about 10 minutes, then remove the pan from the oven, close the oven door, and check to see if any cracks have formed. If you see a crack, very gently smear a tiny bit of reserved dough over the crack to patch it (page 171)—you need only enough to seal the opening. Return the pan to the oven and bake 10 to 15 minutes longer, until the crust is a nice golden brown all over. Transfer to a rack and cool completely.

2 ROAST THE SQUASH WHILE THE PIE CRUST IS BAKING: Line the baking sheet with a silicone mat or lightly coat it with high-heat canola-oil spray. In the medium bowl, use a spatula to toss the squash cubes with the olive oil, brown sugar, salt, and pepper until all the squash is evenly coated. Scrape onto the prepared baking sheet and spread apart slightly. Roast on the top oven rack for 20 to 25 minutes, until deep golden and tender when pierced with the tip of a thin, sharp knife. Let cool on a rack. Decrease the oven temperature to 350°F.

GETTING AHEAD The crust can be baked up to 3 days in advance and stored at room temperature, wrapped in plastic.

The squash, onion, and custard can be prepared up to 1 day in advance and stored, in separate airtight containers, in the refrigerator.

3 CARAMELIZE THE ONION: Heat the olive oil and butter in a sauté pan over medium heat until the butter melts. Add the onion and cook, stirring occasionally, until deep golden, 20 to 25 minutes. Season with salt and set aside to cool.

4 PREPARE THE CUSTARD: In the large bowl, whisk together the milk and eggs until well blended. Whisk in the cream, ½ cup of the cheese, the chives, thyme, sage, lemon zest, salt, and pepper.

5 ASSEMBLE THE PIE: Spread the caramelized onion in the bottom of the cooled pie crust. Scrape the squash into the pie shell and spread into an even layer on top of the onion. Slowly pour the custard over the squash in a circular pattern. Sprinkle the remaining ½ cup cheese over the top.

6 BAKE THE PIE: Bake for 40 to 45 minutes, until the edge of the custard puffs and the center is set. To test, tap the side of the pie pan and watch the center of the custard. It should not look like liquid, but should move as one piece (the *Jell-O jiggle*). Transfer to a rack and let cool for about 30 minutes. Serve the pie warm, cutting it with a thin and sharp knife and using a pie server to transfer a slice to each plate.

STORING The pie will keep at room temperature for 4 hours. For longer storage, refrigerate, covered with plastic wrap, for up to 3 days. Reheat in a 375°F oven for 15 to 20 minutes to warm the filling and re-crisp the crust.

HERBED CHICKEN POT PIE

MAKES 1 (9-INCH) DEEP-DISH PIE, SERVING 8 The announcement "chicken pot pie for dinner!" is always greeted with cheers, and who doesn't need a few extra cheers? This savory favorite is easier than ever to make thanks to the roasted chicken and chopped vegetables available in most markets. The recipe can be made in individual pie pans or bowls as well, though you may need to prepare a double recipe of dough to ensure you have enough to top each serving. After Thanksgiving, use leftover turkey instead of chicken.

INGREDIENTS

1 recipe Flaky Pie or Tart Dough (page 177), prepared through Step 5

¾ stick (3 ounces) unsalted butter

1 cup (5½ ounces) diced onion, about 1 medium

½ cup (2½ ounces) diced celery, about 2 stalks

6 tablespoons (3 ounces) unbleached all-purpose flour

4 cups (1 quart) homemade chicken stock or canned low-sodium chicken broth

½ cup (3 ounces) peeled and diced carrot, about 1 medium

1 tablespoon olive oil

10 ounces sliced mushrooms

1 pound cooked chicken meat, diced

1 cup (5 ounces) frozen peas

1 tablespoon snipped fresh chives

1½ tablespoons finely chopped fresh parsley

1½ teaspoons finely chopped fresh thyme

Salt

Black pepper

1 large egg yolk

2 tablespoons milk or cream

EQUIPMENT

One Baking Sheet, Medium Saucepan, Silicone or Rubber Spatula, Whisk, Large Bowl, 10-inch Sauté Pan, Pastry Brush, 9-inch Deep-Dish Pie Pan or Other 8-Cup Baking Dish, Small Bowl, Cooling Rack

1 Transfer the circle of pie or tart dough to a baking sheet and chill until ready to use.

2 Melt the butter over medium heat in the saucepan. Add the onion and celery and cook, stirring occasionally with the spatula, for 5 to 7 minutes, until softened. Remove the pan from the heat and whisk in the flour. Whisk vigorously to blend the flour with the vegetables and butter. Return to the heat and cook, whisking, for 2 to 3 minutes (do not let the flour brown). Remove the pan from the heat. Add about 1 cup of the stock and whisk until the mixture is smooth and pastelike. This is your only chance to remove any lumps of flour, so whisk thoroughly. Once the paste is smooth, whisk in the remaining stock. Return the pan to the heat and bring to a boil, whisking frequently. Add the carrots. Reduce the heat and simmer for 5 minutes. Remove from the heat.

3 Fill the large bowl halfway with ice and water and set it aside. Heat the olive oil in the sauté pan over high heat. Add the mushrooms and cook, stirring every 2 to 3 minutes, until deep golden brown, 10 to 12 minutes. Add the mushrooms to the filling along with the chicken, peas, chives, parsley, and thyme. Season to taste with salt and pepper. Set the saucepan into the bowl of ice water. Stir occasionally until the filling is cool. (Chilling the filling prevents the flaky pastry from melting when it's placed on top of the pie.) Scrape the filling into the pie pan.

4 Preheat the oven to 375°F and position an oven rack in the center. Brush the edge of the pie pan with a thin film of water. Transfer the dough to the pan, roll the edges to

GETTING AHEAD The pie crust can be prepared, rolled, covered in plastic, and refrigerated for up to 2 days before assembling the pie.

The filling may be prepared 2 days in advance and stored, airtight, in the refrigerator.

The pie may be assembled, double-wrapped in plastic, and frozen for up to 1 month. When baking a frozen pie, allow an extra 10 to 15 minutes for the pie to bake through.

form a thick rope along the edge of the pan, then crimp or form a decorative border (page 174) as desired. Any leftover pie dough can be used to make decorative designs, such as a chicken, on top of the pie crust. In a small bowl, beat the egg yolk with the milk or cream and use the pastry brush to lightly glaze the surface of the pie.

5 Bake for 40 to 45 minutes, until the filling is bubbling and the crust is golden brown and crisp. Transfer to a rack and let cool for 15 to 20 minutes. Serve hot, spooning filling and crust into wide, shallow bowls.

STORING Any leftovers may be covered with plastic wrap and refrigerated for up to 4 days. Reheat in a 375°F oven for 15 to 20 minutes before serving.

BUTTERSCOTCH PIE

MAKES 1 (9-INCH) PIE, SERVING 8 TO 10 Butterscotch, a blend of brown sugar and butter, is not for the faint of sweet tooth, but if you love the rich flavor, with its subtle underpinnings of molasses and vanilla, you'll flip for this pie. A velvety pudding pie is especially welcome on a hot summer day when the cool filling sends shivers of delight through a heat-exhausted palate. The easy crust is another bonus—just cookie crumbs baked for 10 minutes and cooled, and it's ready for the filling. If you don't have a vanilla bean, increase the vanilla extract to 2 teaspoons.

INGREDIENTS

1 Graham Cracker Crumb Pie Crust (page 180)

1½ cups (12 ounces) whole milk

1 cup (8 ounces) plus 1¼ cups (10 ounces) heavy whipping cream

½ vanilla bean

5 tablespoons (1¼ ounces) cornstarch

¼ teaspoon salt

4 large egg yolks

½ stick (2 ounces) unsalted butter, cut into ½-inch pieces

¾ cup plus 2 tablespoons (7 ounces) firmly packed light brown sugar

1 teaspoon pure vanilla extract

1 tablespoon (½ ounce) granulated sugar

Caramel Sauce (page 426), for serving

EQUIPMENT

Small Saucepan, Whisk, Medium Bowl, Small Bowl, Medium-Mesh Strainer, Medium Saucepan, Stand Mixer Fitted with a Whisk Attachment or a Hand Mixer and a Medium Bowl, Silicone or Rubber Spatula, Small Offset Spatula, Pastry Bag Fitted with a ½-inch Star Tip (Optional), Thin and Sharp Knife, Pie Server

1 FLAVOR THE MILK AND CREAM: Pour the milk and 1 cup cream into the small saucepan. Use a paring knife to split the vanilla bean lengthwise. Turn the knife over and use the dull side to scrape out the seeds. Add them to the pan, along with the pod. Whisk well to break up the clumps of seeds. Place over medium heat and heat until the mixture just begins to simmer. Turn off the heat, cover, and let steep for 20 minutes.

2 FINISH THE PUDDING: Stir together the cornstarch and salt in the medium bowl. Place the yolks in the small bowl. Have the strainer and the cooled pie shell ready.

3 Melt the butter in the medium saucepan over medium heat. Add the brown sugar and begin whisking, slowly at first. When the sugar melts, whisk vigorously to form a smooth butterscotch paste. Let the paste boil, whisking constantly, for 1 minute. Pour the milk mixture into the butterscotch, whisking all the while. Bring the mixture back to a simmer. Remove from the heat (keep the burner on) and pour about ⅓ cup of the mixture into the bowl with the cornstarch. You'll need to whisk as you pour, so it's a good idea to twist a dampened kitchen towel into a rope and wrap it around the bottom of the bowl to stabilize it while your hands are occupied with other tasks. Whisk vigorously to blend the cornstarch and dissolve any lumps. Pour the cornstarch mixture back into the saucepan, whisking constantly. Return to the heat and bring the pudding back to a boil. Boil, whisking, for 1 minute to thicken.

4 Remove from the heat and pour about ⅓ cup of the mixture into the bowl with the yolks. Again, use the damp towel for stabilizing and whisk vigorously to blend. Pour the yolk mixture back into the saucepan and return the pudding to a boil, whisking constantly.

what the pros know

A couple of tips to remember when using cornstarch as a thickener: First, make sure there are no lumps of cornstarch left when you blend it with the first ½ cup of pudding—they will never dissolve once combined with the larger body of the pudding. Second, when it comes to boiling cornstarch-thickened puddings, more is definitely not better. It's important to bring the pudding to a boil to thicken the mixture, but, unlike flour, cornstarch does not continue to thicken with longer boiling. Instead, it loses some of its thickening ability after a few minutes of boiling. If you boil it for too long the pudding will thin out and run when the pie is cut.

GETTING AHEAD **The cookie crust may be prepared up to 1 week in advance, wrapped tightly in plastic, and stored at room temperature. If the crust softens during storage, re-crisp in a 350°F oven for 6 to 8 minutes.**

Once the pudding has boiled for about 30 seconds, remove it from the heat, stir in the vanilla extract, and pour through the strainer into the prepared pie crust. Press a piece of plastic wrap directly against the surface of the pudding to prevent a skin from forming. Refrigerate until cold, about 3 hours.

5 MAKE THE TOPPING: Place the 1¼ cups cream and the granulated sugar in the bowl of the stand mixer and whip on medium speed until soft peaks form. You can also use a hand mixer and a medium bowl. Remove the plastic wrap from the pie. Use the silicone or rubber spatula to scrape the topping onto the cooled butterscotch filling and use the offset spatula or the back of a spoon to spread it evenly all the way to the edge. The filling should be completely covered. Alternatively, pipe the topping over the filling in a decorative pattern, using a pastry bag fitted with a ½-inch star tip (but increase the cream by ½ cup, as piping requires a little more cream).

6 To serve, slice the chilled pie with a thin, sharp knife and transfer to plates with a pie server. Drizzle each slice with a spoonful of caramel sauce.

STORING **Butterscotch pie is best served the day it's made or the day after. It will keep, refrigerated, for up to 4 days, though the crust will begin to soften after 2 days and the whipped cream topping may begin to break down after a day or two depending upon the fat content of the cream (a higher fat content stabilizes the cream). Store in an airtight container or cover loosely with plastic wrap so the cream won't absorb odors from the refrigerator.**

BANANA CREAM PIE WITH CHOCOLATE AND CINNAMON

MAKES 1 (9-INCH) PIE, SERVING 8 TO 10 The old-fashioned favorite gets a new twist when paired with two of banana's best flavor companions: chocolate and cinnamon. Chocolate, in the form of a thin layer of ganache spread over the crust, forms a barrier against the moist filling, keeping the crust crisp for days longer than usual. Here's a trick to prevent the bananas from browning: As soon as the bananas are sliced, stir them into the pastry cream, which will seal the surface of the bananas and keep them fresh-looking for days.

INGREDIENTS

1 Chocolate Cookie Pie Crust (page 180)

1 recipe Cinnamon Pastry Cream (page 419)

1½ ounces semisweet or bittersweet chocolate (up to 60 percent cacao)

1 tablespoon (½ ounce) plus 1¼ cups (10 ounces) heavy whipping cream

3 large (1½ pounds) firm-ripe bananas

1 tablespoon (½ ounce) sugar

½ teaspoon pure vanilla extract

Chocolate curls (page 428) or additional chocolate cookie crumbs, for garnish

Caramel Sauce (page 426) and/or Dark Chocolate Sauce (page 427), for serving

EQUIPMENT

Small Microwave-Safe Bowl, Small Offset Spatula, Paring Knife, Silicone or Rubber Spatula, Stand Mixer Fitted with a Whisk Attachment or a Hand Mixer and a Medium Bowl, Pastry Bag Fitted with a ½-inch Star Tip (Optional)

1 Place the chocolate and 1 tablespoon cream in the microwave-safe bowl and microwave on high for 1 minute. Stir to blend. If there are any lumps, heat for 15 to 20 seconds longer and stir again. Pour the chocolate into the cooled pie shell and use the offset spatula or back of a spoon to spread in a thin layer across the bottom of the shell and as far up the sides as it will go. Chill for 10 minutes to set the ganache.

2 Use a paring knife to cut the bananas into ¼-inch-thick slices and gently stir into the chilled pastry cream until they are completely coated. Scrape the filling into the prepared pie crust and spread evenly to the edge. Chill while you make the topping.

3 Place the 1¼ cups cream, the sugar, and vanilla in the bowl of the stand mixer and whip on medium speed until soft peaks form. You can also use a hand mixer and a medium bowl. Scrape the topping onto the banana filling and use the cleaned offset spatula or the back of a spoon to spread it evenly all the way to the edge. The filling should be completely covered. Alternatively, use a pastry bag with a ½-inch star tip to decoratively pipe the topping (but increase the cream by ½ cup, as piping requires a little extra cream). Sprinkle with cookie crumbs or chocolate curls. Refrigerate 30 minutes before serving.

Bananas are one of those supermarket staples that are rarely given a second thought. But did you know there is a whole variety of bananas beyond the standard yellow favorite? Look for the following in specialty produce sections and give one of them a try in your next dessert. Manzano is the most popular dessert banana around the world, with dry, firm flesh and an apple flavor. Blue java or ice cream bananas have a beautiful silver-blue color before they ripen to yellow. When barely ripened, the fruit has a tart pineapple-cherimoya flavor, but if allowed to mature fully, it takes on a rich, almost liqueurlike flavor. The Brazilian banana is also known as the ladyfinger in Australia or the apple banana in Hawaii, and is very sweet yet balanced by an undertone of tartness. The mysore, also called ladyfinger, has a wonderful strawberry-citrus flavor and creamy flesh that is a beautiful orange color. And the iholena is a Hawaiian banana with salmon-pink flesh and a lovely, exotic flavor.

GETTING AHEAD **The crust may be prepared up to 1 week in advance, wrapped tightly in plastic, and stored at room temperature. If the crust softens as it sits, re-crisp in a 350°F oven for 6 to 8 minutes.**

The pastry cream (without bananas) may be prepared up to 2 days in advance and stored in an airtight container in the refrigerator.

STORING **This pie is best the same day it is made, but will keep, refrigerated, for up to 4 days, though the whipped cream topping may begin to break down after a couple of days (a higher fat content stabilizes the cream, page 33).**

Dulce de Leche Banana Cream Pie If you've ever tried bananas and caramel, you'll know that the sultry, bittersweet edge of caramel is a great complement to the sweet creaminess of bananas. For a luscious caramel version of this pie, make a Graham Cracker Crumb Crust (page 180) instead of chocolate, then substitute 2 ounces milk chocolate for the dark chocolate in the ganache layer. Make the Dulce de Leche Pastry Cream (page 419) and stir the bananas in as directed. *Dulce de leche*, a Latin American favorite, is a golden caramel cream made by boiling down milk with a bit of sugar until it is rich, thick, and insanely good. It is available in cans in the Latin American section of the supermarket.

Raspberry and Vanilla Cream Pie Make the chocolate cookie pie crust and spread the chocolate ganache in the shell as directed. Pour two half-pint baskets (12 ounces) fresh raspberries onto a baking sheet. Pick through them and discard any debris or molded berries. Do not wash them—they will absorb the water and turn to mush. Transfer the berries to the prepared pie crust and spread them in an even layer across the bottom. Prepare Vanilla Bean Pastry Cream (page 419). Once chilled, scrape it into the pie shell on top of the berries, and spread it into an even layer. Top with whipped cream and garnish as directed.

CHOCOLATE SILK PIE

MAKES 1 (9-INCH) PIE, SERVING 8 TO 10 Here's an update to a classic pie that takes full advantage of the richly flavored, high-quality chocolates that are readily available today. Satiny smooth and decadently rich, this is unbridled indulgence. The filling is a dense, almost trufflelike mousse that perfectly complements the crispy cookie pie shell. Although classic silk pie calls for a generous amount of butter, raw eggs, and run-of-the-mill chocolate, this version cuts down on the butter, takes modern egg safety concerns into account, and encourages you to use your favorite high-quality chocolate. Since the filling is not baked—which can change the flavor of chocolate—every lovely nuance in your chocolate will shine through.

INGREDIENTS

1 Chocolate Sandwich Cookie Pie Crust (page 180)

FILLING

3 large eggs

6 tablespoons (3 ounces) sugar

¾ stick (3 ounces) unsalted butter, cut into small pieces

⅓ cup (2¾ ounces) heavy whipping cream

10 ounces bittersweet chocolate (up to 70 percent cacao), finely chopped

1½ teaspoons pure vanilla extract

TOPPING

1¼ cups (10 ounces) heavy whipping cream

1½ tablespoons (¾ ounce) sugar

Dark chocolate curls (page 428) or additional cookie crumbs (optional), for garnish

Dark Chocolate Sauce (page 427) and/or Caramel Sauce (page 426), for serving

EQUIPMENT

Medium Saucepan, Stand Mixer Fitted with a Whisk Attachment, Whisk, Instant-Read Thermometer, Small Offset Spatula, Medium Bowl, Silicone or Rubber Spatula, Pastry Bag Fitted with a ½-inch Star Tip (Optional), Thin and Sharp Knife

1 MAKE THE FILLING: Bring 2 inches of water to a low boil over medium-low heat in the medium saucepan. Place the eggs and sugar in the bowl of the stand mixer and whisk by hand to blend. Place the bowl over the simmering water (the bottom of the bowl must not touch the water) and whisk constantly to prevent the eggs from scrambling. Heat until the mixture reaches 160°F on the instant-read thermometer and the eggs look light in color and texture. To check the temperature, remove the bowl from the heat so the mixture doesn't overcook while you are waiting for the thermometer to register. If the mixture has not yet reached 160°F, wash the thermometer—so any possible bacteria will not contaminate the eggs during your next check—dry it, and then put the bowl back over the water and continue to whisk. This step can take anywhere from 5 to 10 minutes—the more often you check the temperature, the longer it takes, so be patient. When the eggs reach 160°F, remove the bowl from the saucepan (keep burner on) and beat on high speed for 3 minutes.

2 While the eggs are beating, place the butter, cream, and chocolate in a medium bowl and set the bowl in the saucepan over the simmering water. Let it sit for 1 minute, then gently stir with the silicone or rubber spatula until the chocolate is melted and the mixture is smooth. Remove from the heat and wipe the bottom of the bowl dry. Add the chocolate

GETTING AHEAD **The pie crust may be prepared up to 1 week in advance, wrapped tightly in plastic, and stored at room temperature. If the crust softens during storage, re-crisp in a 350°F oven for 6 to 8 minutes. The filling must be made the day you assemble the pie.**

mixture to the eggs, lower the speed to medium, and beat until there are no streaks of egg visible. Scrape down the bowl and beat in the vanilla extract. Remove the bowl from the mixer and scrape down the side and bottom of the bowl, making sure that any streaks of egg are blended into the chocolate. Scrape the filling into the prepared pie crust and smooth the top. Refrigerate until cold, about 30 minutes.

3 MAKE THE TOPPING: In the cleaned mixer bowl, whip the cream and sugar into firm peaks. You may also use a hand mixer and a medium bowl. Use the silicone or rubber spatula to scrape the cream into the center of the pie, then use the offset spatula or back of a spoon to spread it all the way to the edge, making swirls as you go. For a more elegant version, pipe the cream over the filling, using a ½-inch star tip fitted into a pastry bag (but increase the cream to 1¾ cups and the sugar to 2 tablespoons, as piping requires a little more cream). Sprinkle the top with chocolate curls or a dusting of extra cookie crumbs if desired. Refrigerate for 30 minutes before serving.

4 To serve, cut slices with a thin, sharp knife, wiping with a moist, hot towel between slices. Serve each slice with a spoonful of chocolate and/or caramel sauce.

STORING **The pie will keep, refrigerated, for up to 5 days, though the whipped cream topping may begin to break down after a day or two depending upon the fat content of the cream (a higher fat content stabilizes the cream, page 33). Store in an airtight container or cover loosely with plastic wrap so the cream won't absorb odors from the refrigerator.**

Orange-Chocolate Silk Pie
Orange and chocolate are one of the great flavor pairings in the world of baking. To bring a sophisticated hint of orange to this pie, replace the vanilla extract with 1 to 2 tablespoons of Grand Marnier, the king of orange liqueurs. Other liqueurs, such as amaretto, Frangelico, or Kahlúa may be substituted to create further variations.

SUMMER BERRY TURNOVERS

MAKES 9 TURNOVERS There is an endearing charm about turnovers. Perhaps it's their appearance: Fat and sassy, they would never be mistaken for elegant pastries. Or maybe it's their particular talent for being desirable any time of day. They're great for breakfast, snacking, or dessert, and can even be made with savory fillings for a take-along lunch or dinner. A slightly tart fruit filling will balance the richness of the cream cheese dough, and dusting the tops with sugar before baking gives the turnovers a wonderful crunch and an extra layer of sweetness.

INGREDIENTS

1 recipe Easy Cream Cheese Pie Dough, prepared for turnovers and dumplings (page 179)

1 half-pint basket (6 ounces) raspberries

1 half-pint basket (6 ounces) blackberries

¼ cup (1¾ ounces) granulated sugar

2 tablespoons (1 ounce) unbleached all-purpose flour

2 teaspoons freshly squeezed lemon juice

1 large egg yolk

2 tablespoons milk or cream

1½ to 2 tablespoons sanding sugar, turbinado sugar, or granulated sugar

Softly Whipped Cream (page 416), Vanilla Crème Fraîche (page 420), Honeyed Yogurt (page 420), or vanilla ice cream, for serving

EQUIPMENT

Two Baking Sheets, Parchment Paper or Two Silicone Mats, Medium Bowl, Ruler, Small Bowl, Pastry Brush, Paring Knife, Cooling Rack

1 Preheat the oven to 375°F and position two racks in the lower and upper thirds of the oven. Line the baking sheets with parchment paper or silicone mats.

2 MAKE THE FILLING: Pour the raspberries and blackberries out onto a baking sheet. Pick through them and discard any debris or molded berries. Do not wash them—they will absorb the water and turn to mush. Transfer the berries to the medium bowl. Add the sugar, flour, and lemon juice and toss until the berries are evenly coated.

3 ASSEMBLE THE TURNOVERS: Lay the 5-inch squares of cream cheese dough in front of you. On each square, use a ruler or the back of a paring knife to mark a diagonal dividing line where you will fold the square in half to shape the turnover. (Be careful to mark the dough, not cut through it.) Divide the berry filling evenly among the squares, keeping it on one side of the dividing line and leaving a ½-inch border at the edges. In a small bowl, lightly beat the egg yolk with the milk or cream to create an egg wash. For each turnover, use a pastry brush to brush the border around the fruit with a thin film of the egg wash (set the rest of wash aside). Fold the dough in half over the fruit and press the edges with the tines of a fork to seal them. Transfer all the turnovers to one of the prepared baking sheets and refrigerate for 20 minutes before baking.

4 GLAZE AND BAKE THE TURNOVERS: Divide the turnovers between the baking sheets, 5 on one and 4 on the other. Brush the top of each turnover with a thin coating of egg wash and sprinkle with the sanding sugar. Use the tip of a paring knife to cut several slits in the top of each to allow steam to escape during baking. Bake the turnovers for 15 minutes, then rotate the sheets from front to back and switch the sheets between

GETTING AHEAD The turnovers may be assembled through Step 3 up to 1 hour before baking and chilled. Any longer, and the sugar melts and blends with the fruit juices, causing the dough to become soggy.

They may also be assembled through Step 3 and frozen, double-wrapped in plastic, for up to 1 month. Apply the egg wash and sugar just before baking. To bake, arrange on baking sheets while still frozen and bake as directed, adding 5 to 10 minutes to the baking time.

the racks. Bake for 10 to 15 minutes longer, until the pastry is golden brown. Transfer to a cooling rack. Serve the turnovers warm or at room temperature, with whipped cream, crème fraîche, honeyed yogurt, or vanilla ice cream.

STORING The turnovers keep at room temperature, wrapped in plastic, for 2 days. The plastic may soften the crust so to re-crisp and rewarm, heat in a 375°F oven for 10 minutes, or until warmed through. For longer storage, wrap airtight and refrigerate for up to 5 days. Reheat before serving.

Lemon-Blueberry Turnovers

You will need a generous ½ cup (4½ ounces) Lemon Curd (page 421 or store-bought) and a 1-pint basket (11 ounces) blueberries. For each turnover, place a tablespoon of lemon curd on each dough square. Top with 2 tablespoons of blueberries. Fold, seal, glaze, vent, and bake the turnover as described.

Cherry-Balsamic Turnovers

Simmer 3 tablespoons balsamic vinegar in a small saucepan over low heat until reduced to 1 tablespoon. Keep the heat low, or you will burn the vinegar and the mixture will be bitter. Transfer to a bowl. Wash, pat dry, and pit 12 ounces fresh sweet cherries, then cut them into quarters. Add to the bowl with the vinegar. Add ¼ cup (2 ounces) firmly packed light brown sugar, 2 teaspoons cornstarch, and ⅛ teaspoon ground cloves and stir well to coat all the fruit evenly. Divide the mixture among the 9 dough squares. Fold, seal, glaze, vent, and bake the turnovers as described.

Rhubarb Turnovers with Orange and Cinnamon

You will need 8 ounces rhubarb, rinsed, patted dry, and cut into ½-inch pieces (2 cups). Transfer to a bowl and add 6 tablespoons (3 ounces) sugar, 1½ teaspoons finely grated orange zest (from about half of a large orange), and ¼ teaspoon ground cinnamon. Stir well to coat all the fruit evenly. Divide the mixture among the 9 dough squares. Fold, seal, glaze, vent, and bake the turnovers as described.

PEACH-GINGERBREAD DUMPLINGS

MAKES 8 DUMPLINGS Fruit dumplings, related to turnovers, are often whole or halved fruit encased in pastry. The pit cavities of the fruit can be filled with dried fruit or sugar, but in this recipe the filling is soft, sweet almond paste blended with the same spices and molasses that make gingerbread so good. Though they look charmingly homespun, the flavor combination is sophisticated enough for a special dinner.

INGREDIENTS

1 recipe Easy Cream Cheese Pie Dough, prepared for turnovers or dumplings (page 179)

7 ounces almond paste, at room temperature

2 tablespoons (1 ounce) mild, unsulfured molasses

1½ teaspoons ground ginger

½ teaspoon ground cinnamon

¼ teaspoon ground cloves

4 large (7 to 8 ounces each) firm-ripe peaches

1 egg yolk

1 tablespoon milk or cream

1½ tablespoons sugar

Vanilla Custard Sauce (page 424) or vanilla ice cream, for serving

EQUIPMENT

Medium Bowl, Serrated Tomato Peeler or Very Sharp Vegetable Peeler, Small Spoon or Melon Baller, Small Bowl, Pastry Brush, Baking Sheet, Parchment Paper or a Silicone Mat, Chef's Knife or Small Round Cutter, Cooling Rack

GETTING AHEAD **The filling may be prepared up to 1 week in advance and stored, airtight, in the refrigerator. The dumplings may be assembled up to 4 hours in advance and stored in the refrigerator before baking.**

1 Preheat the oven to 375°F and position an oven rack in the lower third.

2 MAKE THE FILLING: Crumble the almond paste into the medium bowl. Add the molasses, ginger, cinnamon, and cloves. Use your fingers to knead the spices and molasses into the almond paste. If the mixture is too sticky, run your hands under cold water, shake off the excess, and continue—the thin film of water on your hands will prevent the mixture from sticking to your fingers. Once the mixture is well blended, divide it into 8 equal pieces (about 1 ounce each) and roll into balls.

3 FILL THE PEACH HALVES: Use the serrated tomato peeler to peel the peaches. Cut them in half, remove the pits, and use a small spoon or melon baller to remove the pit marks from the peach, enlarging the cavity slightly. Press a ball of almond paste into each cavity and flatten it level with the cut side of the peach. Spread the excess from the ball of almond paste along the cut surface of the peach. This thin film of almond paste will serve as a barrier to prevent the juices of the peach from soaking the pastry underneath.

4 ASSEMBLE THE DUMPLINGS: Spread 8 of the dough squares out in front of you. Place a peach half, cut side down, in the center of each square. In a small bowl, beat the egg yolk with the milk to create an egg wash. For each dumpling, use a pastry brush to brush a thin film of egg wash along all four edges of the square. Bring the four corners of each square to the center, over the rounded portion of the peach, and pinch the seams together. (You may need to stretch the dough slightly if you have large peaches.) Line the baking sheet with parchment paper or a silicone mat and set the dumplings, evenly spaced, on the sheet. Brush each dumpling lightly with egg wash. Use a chef's knife to cut the remaining square of dough into nine small squares, or use a small round cutter (about the size of a quarter) to cut eight small circles. Place one of the squares or circles at the top of each dumpling, hiding

the point where the four corners come together. Brush these with egg wash. Sprinkle the dumplings with the sugar. Chill for 15 minutes.

5 BAKE THE DUMPLINGS: Bake for 15 minutes, then rotate the baking sheet front to back on the rack. Bake for 15 to 18 minutes longer, until the pastry is golden brown and the peaches are tender when pierced through the crust with the tip of a paring knife. Transfer to a rack and let cool slightly. Serve warm dumplings in shallow bowls, each set in a pool of custard sauce, or with a scoop of vanilla ice cream.

STORING **The dumplings are at their best the same day they are baked. They may be stored overnight in the refrigerator in an airtight container or covered with plastic wrap. Reheat before serving in a 375°F oven for 10 to 15 minutes, until warmed through.**

Apple-Gingerbread Dumplings Substitute firm, peeled baking apples, such as Granny Smith, for the peaches.

Spread 8 of the dough squares out in front of you. Place a peach half, cut side down, in the center of each square. For each dumpling, brush a thin film of egg wash along all four edges of the square.

Bring the four corners of each square to the center, over the rounded portion of the peach, and pinch the seams together. (You may need to stretch the dough slightly if you have large peaches.)

If American pies embody the old-fashioned goodness of country baking, then tarts are their sophisticated big-city cousins. A tart's low profile and precise, vertical sides seem to seductively suggest that less is more. Filled to the brim with velvety rich pastry cream or chocolate ganache, and topped with glistening fresh fruit or a touch of gold leaf, tarts are, hands down, the most striking presence in a French pastry shop window. And the best news is that yours can look just as beautiful, since tarts are really more about attention to detail than any difficult-to-master technique. There's even an easy chocolate tart dough in this chapter that you simply press into the pan with your fingertips, but which delivers deep satisfying chocolate flavor.

Tarts are great for entertaining, since most steps can be done days, or even weeks, in advance. And no matter what the occasion, there's a tart flavor and size to match. Tiers of individual tartlets replete with chocolate curls and spun sugar can be served in lieu of a wedding cake. A classic fresh fruit tart, with rows of colorful fruit or a jumble of berries can be the centerpiece of any buffet or dessert table. And mini tartlets, tiny jewels of sweetness, are breathtaking when served at a tea, baby or wedding shower, or elegant evening fête. In fact, you get more oohs and aahs for time invested in a pretty tart than nearly any other pastry you can bake (and nobody needs to know how easy it was). Let's look at the differences between pies and tarts and learn the techniques that make tarts tick.

A Primer on Tarts

PIES VERSUS TARTS

Though pies and tarts are related, and may use some of the same doughs and fillings, some major differences set them apart from each other. Pies are baked in deep, slope-sided pans and require much more filling than tarts, which rarely have sides more than an inch tall. Because of the sheer volume of filling, the side of a pie would collapse if it were removed from the pan. For this reason, pies are usually presented in and served from their baking pans. In contrast, a tart pan has short, straight sides, which means the ratio of filling to crust is much lower. This, coupled with a tart pan's removable bottom, makes unmolding the tart a breeze, with no worries about the side collapsing. Like pies, tarts may be single- or double-crusted, though they usually have only a bottom crust. And since they are only an inch or so in height, eating a tart is a very different textural experience than eating a pie—one in which the crust plays a more prominent role in the dining experience. With only an inch or so of filling inside, the crust for tarts is an almost-equal partner to the filling. This means it had better be tasty. The recipes in this chapter offer the best crust/filling pairings in terms of texture and flavor, though you can certainly mix and match to satisfy your own taste.

TYPES OF TART CRUSTS

FLAKY PIE AND TART CRUST

Discussed in depth on page 169, flaky pie crust is wonderful for tarts with fruit fillings that are baked in the crust (as opposed to fresh, unbaked fruit that is sliced and arranged on top of a pastry cream or other filling), such as the Warm Cranberry Crumble Tart (page 218), and for savory tarts like the Fromage Blanc, Tomato, and Herb Tart (page 234).

COOKIE CRUST

Most often used for pies and cheesecakes, cookie crusts are an easy alternative crust for tarts and can be made in the same infinite variety of flavors to match any filling. The cookie crusts in "Pies, Turnovers, and Dumplings" (page 180) could be used in place of the Easy Chocolate Press-In Dough in the recipes for Malted Milk Chocolate Tart (page 223) and Mini Chocolate-Raspberry Tartlets (page 225).

SHORTCRUST

Called *pâte sucrée* in French, shortcrust has a higher proportion of butter and sugar to flour than does flaky dough, resulting in a more cookielike flavor and a crisp texture that shatters into crumbs. The complex flavor of shortcrust is well suited to many French-style fillings such as frangipane (a cakelike almond filling) and pastry cream, the silken, puddinglike base for those gorgeous fresh fruit tarts. It is a low-stress, high-flavor dough that comes together in minutes, and is also the most versatile and popular base for dessert tarts.

The name *shortcrust* is derived from a description of the butter's role in the dough. As the butter is cut into smaller and smaller pieces, it coats the gluten strands, preventing them from combining with other strands to form long, tight bonds (such as those needed in bread making). In this way, the butter "shortens" the gluten strands, creating a dough that is tender and crumbly, rather than flaky. Professionals often use the word "short" to describe pastries tenderized by an extra measure of butter. For instance, you've probably heard of shortbread cookies; they are tender and crumbly because of the high proportion of butter in the dough. Shortcrust usually has one or two egg yolks added, and perhaps a bit of water along with vanilla or other flavorings. Yolks, which are mostly fat, contribute to the shortening of the dough, as does the extra sugar, which also helps tenderize the dough.

What all this means to the home baker is that not only is shortcrust delicious, but it is also virtually impossible to ruin by overworking, which will be a relief if you've ever had a disaster with flaky dough. However, the extra butter means that this dough will soften as you work with it. When that happens, just refrigerate for 10 to 20 minutes to firm it up and make it easier to handle.

ROLLING SHORTCRUST DOUGH The extra butter and sugar that create a tender, delicious shortcrust dough also make the dough softer and more delicate than a flaky-style dough. For this reason, eschew rolling shortcrust on a flour-dusted countertop in favor of rolling it between two sheets of parchment paper, waxed paper, or plastic wrap. The dough can also be pressed into the tart pan by hand, but rolling ensures an even thickness. Both options are offered in the recipe here, so you can choose the method you like best.

CHILLING THE TART SHELL Always chill the unbaked shell for at least 1 hour in the refrigerator or 30 minutes in the freezer before baking. Chilling solidifies the butter, allowing more

what the pros know It's usually not necessary to grease or flour tart pans, as the tart doughs contain enough butter to release easily from the removable-bottom pans. The exception in this book: Mini Chocolate-Raspberry Tartlets (page 225), whose rich and crumbly chocolate press-in dough needs a thin layer of butter or a light coating of high-heat canola-oil spray to help the tartlets release from their one-piece cups. If you make tartlets with the shortcrust dough, which is firmer and crisper, there is no need to grease the pans. The major causes of sticking are rusty or damaged tart pans or undercooked dough, so take care of your pans, make sure your oven is accurate, and allow the dough to bake thoroughly.

About halfway through the baking time, you'll want to open the oven door and check to see if the tart shell has formed any cracks. Usually, the crust is just fine. But, if a crack has formed in the shell during baking, it will need to be patched. To do this, pull the tart shell from the oven and close the oven door. Take a small piece of the reserved dough and gently smear it over the crack. It should be a very thin layer, just enough to seal the surface. (A thick patch may not bake in the remaining oven time, and someone would get a mouthful of raw dough.) Return the tart to the oven and finish baking; the patch will only take about 5 minutes to cook through.

time for the structure of the tart to set before the heat of the oven melts the butter. One hour in the refrigerator means a better shape for your tart and a crust that is not greasy.

PREBAKING THE TART SHELL In nearly every case, the tart shell will need to be prebaked, also known as *blind baking* or *baking with a false filling*. Partially baked crusts are used in tarts that will be returned to the oven with a filling that needs a long baking; fully baked crusts are for tarts whose fillings are either exceedingly juicy (such as the Warm Cranberry Crumble Tart) or whose filling requires little or no baking at all (such as the Classic French Fruit Tart). For more information on prebaking pie and tart shells, please see the instructions on page 175.

POSITIONING THE OVEN SHELVES Tart shells are usually baked in the lower third of the oven, near the heat source, to help the bottoms cook and crisp quickly. Filled tarts are often baked in the lower third as well, to keep that bottom crust crisp, although custard-filled tarts should be baked in the center of the oven, away from a top or bottom heat source, so the custard bakes evenly and does not scramble because of proximity to a heating element. Deeply browned crusts are delicious, but if the edges of a tart are browning too fast, you'll want to shield them with thin strips of foil, an overturned tart ring (without the removable bottom) that is an inch larger than the pan you are baking in, or an edge guard, available in some cookware stores.

tips for success   Tart Fillings

- **Pastry cream** (page 419), also known as *crème pâtissière,* is a vanilla custard cooked on the stove, bound with flour or cornstarch, and boiled until thickened. Pastry cream, like other custards, may be flavored in many different ways by infusing the milk with whole spices, loose tea, coconut, and more (for details, see page 343). This method is preferred for the pure, clean flavor it delivers. Sometimes, in the interest of saving time, or if the infused milk needs an extra punch of flavor, you can add flavor by simply stirring flavoring oils, such as lemon or peppermint, or pure extracts, such as almond, directly

  into the cooked pastry cream. Add the flavorings to taste, starting with just a few drops. Once cooled, pastry cream is spread over the fully baked crust, then topped with fresh fruit. Occasionally, the fruit is folded into the pastry cream (as in a banana cream tart).

- **Frangipane** (page 216) is a dense, flavorful, cakelike filling that may be used one of two ways. It may be spread over the partially baked crust, baked until set, and then topped with fresh fruit once the tart has cooled, or it may be used as the base in a baked fruit tart, where the fruit is nestled into the raw frangipane before baking.

- **Lemon, lime, or passion fruit curd** (page 421) is wonderfully refreshing in a fully baked tart shell, whether alone or topped with fresh fruit.

- **Jam** is a simple—and delicious—filling, and a favorite throughout Italy. Be sure to use a high-quality jam, though, for there are no other flavors to mask a less-than-stellar product.

- **Cream, crème fraîche, and mascarpone** may also be used as fillings in a fully baked tart shell, when sweetened, flavored, and whipped until thickened.

VANILLA SHORTCRUST DOUGH

MAKES 1 (9- OR 9½-INCH) TART SHELL The wonderfully crisp and crumbly texture of this easy-to-use tart dough resembles a vanilla shortbread cookie, suitable to many types of fillings. There are different ways to make a shortcrust shell. This recipe offers two options for mixing the dough, with a food processor or by hand. There are also two options for forming the shell, by rolling out the dough or pressing it directly in the pan.

INGREDIENTS

1¼ cups (6¼ ounces) unbleached all-purpose flour

¼ cup (1¾ ounces) sugar

¼ teaspoon salt

1 stick (4 ounces) cold unsalted butter, cut into ½-inch pieces

2 large egg yolks

2 teaspoons pure vanilla extract

1 to 3 teaspoons water

EQUIPMENT

Food Processor Fitted with a Metal Blade or a Medium Bowl and Pastry Blender, Small Bowl, Whisk, Rolling Pin (Optional), 9- or 9½-inch Fluted Tart Pan with Removable Bottom

1 TO MIX THE DOUGH USING A FOOD PROCESSOR: Place the flour, sugar, and salt in the bowl of a food processor. Pulse 5 times to blend. Add the cold butter pieces and pulse 6 to 8 times, just until the butter is the size of large peas. In the small bowl, whisk together the egg yolks, vanilla, and 1 teaspoon water. Add to the butter mixture, then process just until the dough begins to form small clumps, 5 to 10 seconds. Do not let the dough form a ball. Test the dough by squeezing a handful of clumps—when you open your hand, they should hold together. If they are crumbly and fall apart, sprinkle 1 teaspoon water over the dough and pulse several times, then test again. Repeat, if necessary.

TO MIX THE DOUGH BY HAND: Place the flour, sugar, and salt in the medium bowl and blend well with the whisk. Add the cold butter pieces and toss until they are lightly coated with the flour. Use the pastry blender or your fingertips to cut the butter into the flour until the mixture resembles bread crumbs or crushed crackers. If at any time during this process the butter softens and becomes warm, place the bowl in the freezer for 10 minutes before continuing. In the small bowl, whisk together the egg yolks, vanilla, and 1 teaspoon water. Add to the dry ingredients and toss between your fingertips or with a fork 20 to 30 times to evenly distribute the moisture. The dough will still look very crumbly, but if the mixture is squeezed in your hand, it should hold together. If not, sprinkle another teaspoon of water over the top and toss to blend. Repeat, if necessary.

2 FINISH THE DOUGH: Turn the dough out on a lightly floured work surface and knead gently 2 or 3 times, just to finish bringing it together. Shape it into a disk about 6 inches in diameter. If the dough is still cool to the touch, continue on to the next step. If the dough is soft and sticky, wrap it in plastic and refrigerate for 30 minutes before continuing.

3 TO MAKE THE TART SHELL BY ROLLING THE DOUGH: Make sure the dough is cool but malleable. If it has been refrigerated or frozen and is quite hard, let it sit on the counter for 10 to 12 minutes before rolling; otherwise, the dough will crack under the

pros

Professionals have to keep one step ahead, and you can follow their lead. Both this shortcrust dough and Easy Chocolate Press-In Dough (page 212) may be refrigerated, wrapped in plastic, for up to 3 days, and they also freeze beautifully for up to 6 weeks. So, when preparing tart dough, think about doubling or tripling the recipe and refrigerating or freezing the extra batches.

To freeze made-ahead doughs, flatten each batch of dough into a 6- or 7-inch disk, double-wrap in plastic, and slip into a resealable plastic freezer bag. Thaw overnight in the refrigerator or on the counter for 1 hour before using. To make life even easier, roll or press the dough into the tart pan(s) immediately, then wrap the entire pan in plastic wrap and freeze in a resealable plastic bag. Be sure to include a nub of dough left over from trimming, to patch any cracks that form during baking. Then, when you want a tart, all you need to do is unwrap and pop it the preheated oven, allowing 3 to 5 extra minutes for baking.

pressure of the rolling pin. Since it's difficult to remove this dough from the work surface without tearing it unmercifully, place the dough disk between two 14-inch pieces of waxed paper, parchment paper, or plastic wrap. Roll it into an 11-inch round, rotating it (and the paper) clockwise slightly after each roll to create an even round. Remember to roll from the center outward and to lift the rolling pin at the edge to avoid smashing the edge into the paper, which will make removing the paper difficult.

As you roll, the paper or plastic wrap will get wrinkled into the dough. When this happens, peel it off, smooth out the wrinkles and lay it back on the dough. Flip the dough over and repeat, if necessary, with the top piece. Continue to roll, flipping and smoothing wrinkles as necessary, until the dough is 11 inches across and between ⅛ and ¼ inch thick. If the dough is soft and sticky, transfer it to a baking sheet and chill it for 30 minutes.

Peel off the top piece of paper or plastic. Leave the bottom piece attached—this will hold the dough together while you transfer it to the pan. Lift the dough by the exposed paper or plastic and flip it over and center it over the tart pan as best you can. Peel off the paper or plastic. (If it sticks and won't come off, place everything on a baking sheet and chill for 30 minutes—the paper will then peel off easily.) Ease the dough across the bottom of the pan and up the sides, pressing it into the corners of the pan with your fingertips. If the dough breaks or cracks, just press it together again. Once the dough is even in the pan, fold the excess dough at the edge inward to create a double layer of dough along the wall. Press firmly with your thumbs to fuse the two layers of dough, then roll your thumb over the rim of the pan to remove any excess dough there. Save the excess dough in case a crack forms in the crust during baking. Refrigerate for 1 hour or freeze for 30 minutes before baking.

TO MAKE THE TART SHELL BY PRESSING THE DOUGH INTO THE PAN BY HAND: First, chill the dough for 30 minutes. Break the cold dough into small pieces roughly an inch or two in diameter and scatter them evenly over the bottom of the tart pan. Use the heel of your hand to press the pieces of dough flat, connecting them into a smooth, even layer. Press from the center of the pan outward, building up some extra dough where the bottom meets the side. Using your thumbs, press this excess up the sides of the pan to form the walls, making sure they are the same thickness as the dough on the bottom of the pan. Roll your thumb over the rim of the pan to remove any excess dough (save this for patching any cracks that might form during baking). Refrigerate for 1 hour, or freeze for 30 minutes before baking.

The Laying-in Method for Tart Dough

Lift the dough by the exposed edge of the bottom sheet and flip it over and center it over the tart pan as best you can. Peel off the paper or plastic.

Ease the dough across the bottom of the pan and up the sides, pressing it into the corners of the pan with your fingertips. If the dough breaks or cracks, just press it together again.

EASY CHOCOLATE PRESS-IN DOUGH

MAKES 1 (9- OR 9½-INCH) TART SHELL This is a quick, easy tart dough with a deep chocolate flavor. No scary stuff—no cutting in the butter, no rolling out the dough, no blind-baking with foil and pie weights. The keys to success with this dough are chilling it before you bake it and an accurate oven temperature. It's difficult to know when a chocolate tart shell has finished baking because the dark dough obscures the "golden brown" color that is the usual visual clue. This is when a good oven thermometer saves the day. Heat your oven to the correct temperature, set a timer, and you'll be just fine.

INGREDIENTS

1 stick (4 ounces) unsalted butter, softened (65° to 68°F)

⅓ cup (2¼ ounces) sugar

1 large egg yolk

1 cup (5 ounces) unbleached all-purpose flour

2½ tablespoons unsweetened cocoa powder, preferably Dutch-process

EQUIPMENT

Stand Mixer Fitted with a Paddle Attachment, Silicone or Rubber Spatula, Medium Bowl, Whisk, 9 or 9-½-inch Fluted Tart Pan with Removable Bottom

what the pros know

Doughs rich in butter can be sticky and messy if the butter is too warm. If you're having trouble pressing the dough into the tart pan, place the pan (with the dough) in the refrigerator for 20 to 30 minutes before continuing. If you have very warm hands, you may want to roll the dough out between two sheets of parchment paper, waxed paper, or plastic wrap according to the directions on page 210.

1 Place the butter and sugar in the bowl of the stand mixer and beat on medium speed for 3 minutes. The mixture should be smooth and creamy. Scrape down the bowl with the spatula. If there are any lumps of hard butter still visible, beat for another minute to completely blend them into the mixture. Add the egg yolk and beat well. Scrape down the bowl.

2 In a the medium bowl, whisk together the flour and cocoa powder. Add to the butter mixture all at once. Turn the mixer to the lowest speed and blend just until the dough comes together (it should still have medium and small clumps) and looks moist, with a dark, uniform color. Scrape down the bowl. If there are any patches of flour or unincorporated butter, finish mixing the dough by hand with the spatula. If you beat too long or too vigorously on the mixer, you will have a smooth, batterlike dough, which will be harder to press into the pan because it is sticky. If this happens, chill the dough for 15 minutes before continuing.

3 Scrape the dough clumps into the tart pan. Use the heel of your hand to press the dough into an even layer across the bottom and up the side of the pan. Press from the center of the pan outward, building up some extra dough where the bottom meets the side. Using your thumbs, press this excess up the sides of the pan to form the walls, making sure the dough is level with the pan at the rim. Save any small bits of extra dough in case you need to patch a crack during the baking process. Make sure there are no cracks or thin spots—if there are, just press the dough to bring it together. Chill in the refrigerator for 1 hour or in the freezer for 30 minutes.

STORING **The dough keeps for 3 days in the refrigerator and up to 6 weeks frozen; see "What the Pros Know" (page 210) for details.**

The Pressing-in Method for Tart Dough

Use the heel of your hand to press the dough into an even layer across the bottom and up the side of the pan. Press from the center of the pan outward, building up some extra dough where the bottom meets the side. Using your thumbs, press this excess up the sides of the pan to form the walls, making sure the dough is level with the pan at the rim. Save any small bits of extra dough in case you need to patch a crack during the baking process. Make sure there are no cracks or thin spots—if there are, just press the dough to bring it together.

CLASSIC FRENCH FRUIT TART

MAKES 1 (9- OR 9½-INCH) TART, SERVING 8 TO 10 This French patisserie favorite has become a standard on this side of the Atlantic as well, though the mass-produced ones sold in many bakeries are often less than stellar. When homemade, this dessert is a revelation. A thin layer of melted white or semisweet chocolate helps the crust stay crisp by preventing the moisture in the velvety pastry cream from soaking into the cookielike crust. Finish the top with the ripest, most luscious fruit you can find: The summer berries here are an obvious choice, but also try slices of nectarines and plums, poached pears, pineapple, mango, or kiwi, depending upon the season. With berries, the "tumbled from the garden onto the tart" look is nice, but often the fruit for this tart is carefully arranged in precise, compact rows. Choose your style but, either way, make sure to place the fruit close enough together so that you cover as much of the pastry cream as possible.

INGREDIENTS

1 recipe Vanilla Shortcrust Dough (page 209), prepared through Step 3

1½ ounces white or semisweet chocolate, finely chopped

1 recipe Vanilla Bean Pastry Cream (page 419)

1 half-pint basket (6 ounces) raspberries

1 half-pint basket (6 ounces) blackberries

1 half-pint basket (5½ ounces) blueberries

2 tablespoons seedless raspberry jam

2 teaspoons water

Fresh Raspberry Sauce (page 427), for serving

EQUIPMENT

9- or 9½-inch Fluted Tart Pan with a Removable Bottom, Pie Weights, Cooling Rack, Double Boiler, Silicone or Rubber Spatula, Small Offset Spatula, Baking Sheet, Medium-Mesh Strainer, Medium Bowl, Small Saucepan or Small Microwave-Safe Bowl, Pastry Brush, Large Metal Spatula (Optional), Thin and Sharp Knife

1 BAKE THE SHELL: Preheat the oven to 375°F and position a rack in the bottom third. Line the chilled tart shell with heavy-duty foil, pressing the foil firmly and smoothly into the crevices of the pan. Fill the pan with pie weights (page 175). Make sure the weights reach up the sides to the rim of the pan (the center does not need to be filled quite as full). Bake the shell for 20 to 22 minutes, until the foil comes away from the dough easily (if it doesn't, bake another 5 to 6 minutes and check again). Remove the pan from the oven (hold the pan by the sides and not the bottom), close the oven door, and lift out the foil and weights from the shell; set them aside to cool. Return the pan to the oven to continue baking the shell for about 10 minutes, then remove the pan from the oven, close the oven door, and check to see if any cracks have formed. If you see a crack, very gently smear a tiny bit of reserved dough over the crack to patch it (page 208)—you need only enough to seal the opening. Return the pan to the oven and bake 10 to 15 minutes longer, until the crust is a nice golden brown all over. Transfer to a rack and cool completely.

2 MOISTURE-PROOF THE CRUST: Bring an inch of water to a boil in the bottom of the double boiler. Place the chocolate in the top of the double boiler off the heat. Then place the chocolate over the steaming water. Stir occasionally with the silicone or rubber spatula until the chocolate is melted and smooth. (Or, melt the chocolate in the microwave-safe bowl; see page 43.) Scrape the melted chocolate into the cooled tart shell and use the

GETTING AHEAD Once the crust has
been baked and cooled, it can be stored,
wrapped in plastic, at room temperature
for up to 3 days. The crust may soften
during this time, but can be re-crisped
by heating it in a 375°F oven for 8 to 10
minutes.

offset spatula to spread it into a thin layer across the bottom and about ½ inch up the side. Chill for 10 minutes to firm the chocolate.

3 FILL THE TART: Spoon the pastry cream into the tart crust and spread into an even layer. Refrigerate while you prepare the fruit. Pour the raspberries and blackberries onto the baking sheet and pick out and discard any moldy berries or debris. These berries are usually not washed, as they absorb water quickly and turn to mush. Rinse the blueberries in the strainer under cold water and pat dry. In the medium bowl, gently mix all of the berries together. Transfer to the tart, making sure there is a nice balance of all the berries in each area of the tart.

4 FINISH THE TART: Heat the raspberry jam and water in the small saucepan over low heat until melted, hot, and fluid or, microwave on low in the microwave-safe bowl. Do not let it boil or it will caramelize. Brush just enough of the melted jam over the tops of the berries to glaze them a bit. You don't want to overdo it; simply touch the brush to the berries to give them a shiny look. Refrigerate the tart until ready to serve.

5 Place the tart pan on top of a large can (the 28-ounce tomato cans are good) so that the bottom balances midair as the rim falls to the counter. Use the metal spatula to transfer the tart to a serving plate, or simply leave the bottom of the tart pan under the tart for support. Slice the tart with a thin and sharp knife, cutting down in one quick motion rather than sawing. This tart is lovely all by itself, though a spoonful of raspberry sauce is a good accompaniment.

STORING The tart holds beautifully for 2 days, but is at its prettiest the day it is made. Cover with plastic and refrigerate. After a couple of days the juices from the fruit begin to seep into the pastry cream, though the tart still tastes delicious.

DATE TART WITH SESAME-ALMOND FRANGIPANE

MAKES 1 (9- OR 9½-INCH) TART, SERVING 8 TO 10 Classic meets the casbah in this Moroccan version of a French tart. Frangipane, a building block of French pastry, is a dense, cakelike filling of butter, sugar, ground almonds, and eggs, often baked with sliced fruit nestled into the batter. In this case, some of the almonds have been replaced with toasted sesame seeds, adding an exotic and earthy flavor note that complements the luscious Medjool dates (see page 50 for more on these dates). Once baked, the top is brushed with a sheer glaze of honey and the tart is served accompanied by softly whipped cream flavored with orange blossom water. For a more classic French version of this recipe, see the apricot variation at the end.

INGREDIENTS

1 recipe Vanilla Shortcrust Dough (page 209), prepared through Step 3

½ cup (2½ ounces) whole natural almonds, toasted and cooled (page 46)

¼ cup (1¼ ounces) sesame seeds, lightly toasted and cooled (page 58)

½ cup (3½ ounces) sugar

½ stick (2 ounces) unsalted butter, softened (65° to 68°F)

2 large eggs

2 tablespoons unbleached all-purpose flour

¼ teaspoon almond extract

15 to 18 (about 10 ounces) Medjool dates

1 tablespoon light-flavored honey (such as orange blossom or clover)

Orange Blossom Cream (page 417), for serving

EQUIPMENT

9- or 9½-inch Fluted Tart Pan with a Removable Bottom, Pie Weights, Cooling Rack, Food Processor Fitted with a Metal Blade, Silicone or Rubber Spatula, Small Offset Spatula or Spoon, Paring Knife, Small Saucepan or Microwave-Safe Bowl, Pastry Brush, Large Metal Spatula (Optional)

1 BAKE THE SHELL: Preheat the oven to 375°F and position an oven rack in the lower third. Line the chilled tart shell with heavy-duty foil, pressing the foil firmly and smoothly into the crevices of the pan. Fill the pan with pie weights (page 175). Make sure the weights reach up the sides to the rim of the pan (the center does not need to be filled quite as full). Bake the shell for 20 to 22 minutes, until the foil comes away from the dough easily (if it doesn't, bake another 5 to 6 minutes and check again). Remove the pan from the oven (hold the pan by the sides and not the bottom), close the oven door, and lift out the foil and weights from the shell; set them aside to cool. Return the pan to the oven to continue baking the shell for about 10 minutes, then remove the pan from the oven, close the oven door, and check to see if any cracks have formed. If you see a crack, very gently smear a tiny bit of reserved dough over the crack to patch it (page 208)—you need only enough to seal the opening. Return the pan to the oven and bake 10 to 15 minutes longer, until the crust is a nice golden brown all over. Transfer to a rack and cool completely.

2 MAKE THE FILLING: Place the almonds, sesame seeds, and sugar in the bowl of the food processor and process for 30 to 60 seconds, until the nuts and seeds are finely ground. Add the softened butter and process until well blended, about 20 seconds. Add the eggs, flour, and almond extract and process to mix thoroughly, about 30 seconds, scraping down the bowl with the silicone or rubber spatula halfway through. Pour the filling

Frangipane is quite versatile in the professional pastry kitchen. Here it is used as the base for a baked fruit tart, but it can also be used as a filling in turnovers, Danish, and croissants. Sometimes pastry chefs bake it in baking sheets and use it for the cake layers in petits fours or other pastries. Its versatility extends to the nuts used as well. Nearly any toasted nut may be used in place of the traditional almonds, from macadamias to pistachios to hazelnuts, allowing the chef to match flavors in the frangipane to other components of the dessert.

GETTING AHEAD **The shell can be baked up to 2 days in advance, wrapped, and kept at room temperature. For longer storage, double-wrap in plastic and freeze for up to 1 month.**

The frangipane filling can be prepared and refrigerated in an airtight container up to 3 days in advance. Remove from the refrigerator 1 hour before assembling the tart so it will be soft enough to spread easily in the crust.

into the cooled tart shell and use the offset spatula or the back of a spoon to level and smooth the surface.

3 Use a paring knife to slit each date lengthwise and pluck out the seed. Finish cutting each date in half, then place two halves in the center of the tart, cut sides down. Arrange the remaining date halves in a circular pattern in two concentric rows. For the first row, rest one end of each date on the two in the center, like the spokes of a wheel meeting in the center. One end will rest on the center dates, while the other end will dip down into the frangipane. Once you've arranged the first ring of date halves, begin the second ring at the outer edge of the tart, placing each date about ½ inch apart, allowing a little frangipane to show through. You can lean the dates on those in the inner ring, or just lay them flat, depending upon the size of your dates.

4 Bake the tart for 22 to 28 minutes, until the filling is firm in the center and lightly browned. Transfer to a cooling rack, making sure you hold the pan by the sides and not the bottom (remember, it's a two-piece pan and can come apart!). Cool completely.

5 Heat the honey in the small saucepan over low heat until melted and very fluid. (Or, warm in a microwave-safe bowl in the microwave for a few seconds.) Brush the tart with a shimmer of the warm honey, making sure to lightly coat the filling and dates but not the edge of the tart shell.

6 Place the tart pan on top of a large can from your pantry (the 28-ounce tomato cans are good) so that the bottom balances midair as the rim falls to the counter. Use the metal spatula to transfer the tart to a serving plate or simply leave the bottom of the tart pan under the tart for support. Slice the tart with a thin sharp knife, cutting down in one quick motion rather than sawing. Serve the tart at room temperature, accompanied by a spoonful of orange blossom cream.

STORING **The tart will keep, plastic wrap pressed against the cut areas, at room temperature for 2 days and refrigerated for up to 4 days (be sure to bring the tart to room temperature before serving).**

Apricot-Frangipane Tart with Orange Blossom Glaze

Substitute ¾ cup (4 ounces) toasted and cooled whole natural almonds for the combination of almonds and sesame seeds. Increase the almond extract to ½ teaspoon. Substitute 1 pound fresh apricots, each one pitted and cut into 8 wedges, for the dates, arranging them in a circular pattern on the tart. A tart with fresh fruit will take a little longer to bake. Bake for 30 to 40 minutes, or until firm and lightly browned.

WARM CRANBERRY CRUMBLE TART

MAKES 1 (9- OR 9½-INCH) TART, SERVING 8 TO 10 **When the crisp fall air brings fresh cranberries to market, this tart will celebrate the season. Dressy enough for company, comforting enough for a night in front of the fire, it should be served warm with a generous scoop of vanilla ice cream alongside. The sweet crumble topping is a fine partner to the tart cranberries within. If you'd like to add a little more crunch, stir ⅓ cup coarsely chopped nuts into the crumble topping (walnuts and almonds would be especially good). If you're looking for a summer version, check out the blueberry variation at the end.**

INGREDIENTS

1 recipe Flaky Pie or Tart Dough (page 177), prepared through Step 7

FILLING

5 cups (20 ounces) fresh cranberries

¾ cup (5¼ ounces) sugar

Finely grated zest of 1 medium orange

4 teaspoons unbleached all-purpose flour

¼ teaspoon ground cinnamon

TOPPING

1 cup (5 ounces) unbleached all-purpose flour

¾ cup (5¼ ounces) sugar

¼ teaspoon salt

1 stick (4 ounces) cold unsalted butter, cut into ½-inch pieces

Vanilla ice cream, for serving

EQUIPMENT

9- or 9½-inch Fluted Tart Pan with a Removable Bottom, Kitchen Scissors, Pie Weights, Cooling Rack, Chef's Knife or Food Processor Fitted with a Metal Blade, Medium Bowl, Silicone or Rubber Spatula, Stand Mixer Fitted with a Paddle Attachment or a Pastry Blender, Large Metal Spatula (Optional)

1 TRIM AND FINISH THE TART DOUGH: Use the scissors to trim the dough so it overhangs the edge of the tart pan by 1 inch. Moisten the inside wall of dough with your finger dipped in cool water. Fold the overhanging dough inward to form a sturdy double-layered edge. Press firmly with your thumbs to fuse the two layers of dough, then roll your thumb over the rim of the tart to remove any excess dough there. Chill while the oven preheats.

2 BAKE THE SHELL: Preheat the oven to 375°F and position an oven rack in the lower third. Line the chilled tart shell with heavy-duty foil, pressing the foil firmly and smoothly into the crevices of the pan. Fill the pan with pie weights (page 175). Make sure the weights reach up the sides to the rim of the pan (the center does not need to be filled quite as full). Bake the shell for 20 to 22 minutes, until the foil comes away from the dough easily (if it doesn't, bake another 5 to 6 minutes and check again). Remove the pan from the oven (hold the pan by the sides and not the bottom), close the oven door, and lift out the foil and weights from the shell; set them aside to cool. Return the pan to the oven to continue baking the shell for about 10 minutes, then remove the pan from the oven, close the oven door, and check to see if any cracks have formed. If you see a crack, very gently smear a tiny bit of reserved dough over the crack to patch it (page 171)—you need only enough to seal the opening. Return the pan to the oven and bake 10 to 15 minutes longer, until the crust is a nice golden brown all over. Transfer to a rack and cool completely.

3 MIX THE FILLING: Coarsely chop half of the cranberries by hand with a chef's knife or with a few pulses in the bowl of the food processor. In the medium bowl, combine the chopped cranberries, whole cranberries, sugar, orange zest, flour, and cinnamon and stir to blend well. Use a silicone or rubber spatula to scrape the filling into the cooled tart shell.

4 MIX THE TOPPING: Place the flour, sugar, and salt in the bowl of the stand mixer. Add the cold butter and mix on medium-low speed until the mixture begins to form clumps the size of small peas (some will still look a little sandy, which is fine). This step may also be done by hand in the cleaned medium bowl, pinching the butter between your fingers, or cutting it with a pastry blender, until small clumps form. Cover the filling evenly with the topping.

5 Reduce the oven temperature to 350°F and bake the tart for 40 minutes, until the fruit is soft and bubbling and the topping is golden brown. Transfer to a cooling rack, making sure you hold the pan by the sides and not the bottom (remember, it's a two-piece pan and can come apart!). Cool for 20 minutes before serving. Or, cool completely, then reheat just before serving.

6 Place the tart pan on top of a large can from your pantry (the 28-ounce tomato cans are good) so that the bottom balances midair as the rim falls to the counter. Use the large metal spatula to transfer the tart to a serving plate or simply leave the bottom of the tart pan under the tart for support. Slice the tart with a thin, sharp knife and serve warm, with vanilla ice cream.

STORING **The tart keeps for 1 day at room temperature. For longer storage, cover with plastic wrap and refrigerate for up to 3 days. Allow 1 hour for the tart to come to room temperature, or reheat in a 350°F oven for 12 to 15 minutes.**

Warm Blueberry Crumble Tart Substitute 3 (1-pint) baskets (5 cups or 24 ounces) fresh blueberries for the cranberries and leave all of them whole. Reduce the sugar to ½ cup. Substitute finely grated zest of 1 large lemon for the orange zest. Omit the cinnamon.

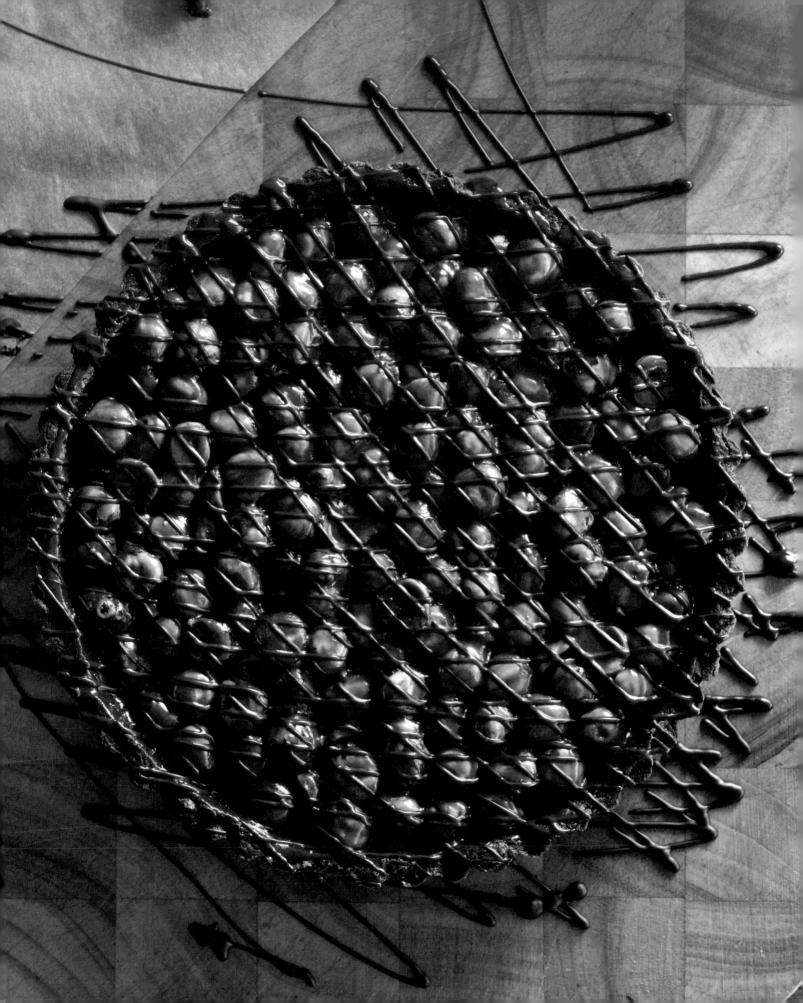

BACI TART WITH FRANGELICO CREAM

MAKES 1 (9- OR 9½-INCH) TART, SERVING 8 TO 10 Baci are popular Italian candies featuring the inspired trio of chocolate, caramel, and hazelnuts. This dessert translates the candies into tart form, with a chocolate crust cradling a chewy filling of caramel and toasted hazelnuts and topped with a drizzle of dark chocolate. A spoonful of whipped cream scented with Frangelico–the Italian hazelnut liqueur–sends this over the top. To truly gild the lily, add a touch of gold leaf, which stands in gorgeous, glittering contrast to the deep browns of the tart. Note: If you've never made caramel before, you'll want to familiarize yourself with the process (page 26) before beginning the recipe.

INGREDIENTS

1 recipe Easy Chocolate Press-In Dough (page 212), prepared through Step 3

½ cup (4 ounces) heavy whipping cream

½ stick (2 ounces) unsalted butter, cut into small pieces

¼ cup (2 ounces) water

2 tablespoons (1 ounce) light corn syrup

¾ cup (5¼ ounces) sugar

1½ cups (7 ounces) hazelnuts, toasted and skinned (page 52)

1½ ounces semisweet or bittersweet chocolate, finely chopped

Gold petals or gold leaf (page 436), optional

Frangelico Cream (page 417), for serving

EQUIPMENT

9- or 9½-inch Fluted Tart Pan with a Removable Bottom, Cooling Rack, Small Saucepan, Medium Saucepan, Heatproof Silicone Spatula, White Plate, Double Boiler, Kitchen Scissors or Sharp Knife, Large Metal Spatula, Thin and Sharp Knife

1 BAKE THE SHELL: Preheat the oven to 350°F and position an oven rack in the center. Bake the tart shell for 15 minutes. Remove the pan from the oven (hold the pan by the sides and not the bottom), close the oven door, check for cracks, and repair any with a bit of reserved dough. Return the pan to the oven and bake 15 to 17 minutes longer. Remove pan (again, holding by the sides) and place on a rack to cool while you prepare the filling. Leave the oven on.

2 MAKE THE FILLING: Combine the cream and butter in the small saucepan and heat just until the cream begins to simmer and the butter is fully melted. Remove from the heat and let the mixture sit while you make the caramel.

3 Combine the water and syrup in the medium saucepan. Sprinkle the sugar over the top. Cook over medium heat, stirring occasionally with a heatproof silicone spatula, until the sugar is dissolved and the liquid is clear. Turn the heat to high and boil rapidly, swirling the pan occasionally (do not stir) to cook the sugar evenly, until it turns a golden honey color. Watch carefully here and keep a white plate and spoon nearby so that you can tell the exact color by dropping a bit of caramel onto the plate. When it is honey-colored (think of the amber-colored honey at the supermarket), remove from the heat and immediately add the warm cream and butter mixture. Be careful! The caramel will rise dramatically in the pan and sputter, so you may want to wear an oven mitt on the hand pouring in the cream.

4 Stir with the spatula or wooden spoon to blend the caramel and cream. If there are any bits of hardened caramel floating around, put the pan over the lowest possible

While this tart is wonderful with hazelnuts, you can substitute other nuts for variations on them. Try macadamias, almonds, pecans, or walnuts, all of which pair well with chocolate and caramel. Toast the nuts first to bring out their flavor, and ensure they stay crispy within the soft caramel filling.

GETTING AHEAD The crust can be baked a day or two ahead of time. Wrap in plastic and store at room temperature.

heat and stir gently until the caramel melts. Add the hazelnuts to the caramel and cook over medium heat, stirring constantly, until the caramel turns a light golden brown, 1 to 2 minutes. It should be the color of those chewy square caramel candies in the supermarket. Immediately pour the filling into the cooled tart shell.

5 Bake at 350°F for 17 to 20 minutes, until golden brown and bubbling. Transfer to a cooling rack, making sure you hold the pan by the sides. Cool completely.

6 FINISH THE TART: Bring an inch of water to boil in the bottom of the double boiler. Turn off the heat. Place the chopped chocolate in the top of the double boiler and place over the steaming water. Stir occasionally with the spatula until the chocolate is melted and smooth. (Or, melt the chocolate in a microwave-safe bowl; see page 43). Place a resealable plastic sandwich bag in a cup and fold the top of the bag over the rim of the cup to hold the bag in place. Scrape the melted chocolate into the bag, then use your hand to squeeze the chocolate into one corner. Use the scissors or sharp knife to cut off the very tip of the corner, making a small hole. Squeeze the chocolate through the hole and stripe it over the entire surface of the tart in any pattern you like. If you like, sprinkle gold leaf petals sparingly over the top of the tart, or accent with small pieces of gold leaf sheets (page 436).

7 Place the tart pan on top of a large can from your pantry (the 28-ounce tomato cans are good) so that the bottom balances midair as the rim falls to the counter. Use the metal spatula to transfer the tart to a serving plate or simply leave the bottom of the tart pan under the tart for support. Serve at room temperature, using a thin, sharp knife to cut slices (for cleaner slicing, wipe the knife occasionally with a towel that's been rinsed in hot water and wrung out).

STORING **The tart keeps at room temperature, covered with plastic wrap, for 3 to 4 days.**

MALTED MILK CHOCOLATE TART

MAKES 1 (9- OR 9½-INCH) TART, SERVING 8 TO 10 Gorgeous, sophisticated, yet oh-so-easy to make, this tart features a filling that is nothing more than ganache (melted chocolate and cream) and malt powder, finished with a topping of voluptuously whipped cream piped into elegant ridges. The piping tip used to create this beautiful pattern is cut with a deep V in the end and is called the St. Honoré tip, named after the patron saint of French pastry chefs. Once you're comfortable with the up-and-down motion this tip requires (like making a bevy of small rainbows), you'll find yourself turning to it again and again. If you can't find a St. Honoré tip, simply use a large ½-inch star tip to pipe a decorative pattern over the surface of the tart. Don't skimp on the 70 percent dark chocolate, as its deep, dark flavor balances the milk chocolate and malt powder perfectly and guarantees that the filling won't ooze once the tart is cut.

INGREDIENTS

1 recipe Easy Chocolate Press-In Dough (page 212), prepared through Step 3

FILLING

10 ounces milk chocolate, finely chopped

2 ounces 70 percent cacao bittersweet chocolate, finely chopped

1 cup (8 ounces) heavy whipping cream

¼ cup plus 2 tablespoons (¾ ounce) malted milk powder, such as Ovaltine original (yellow label, not chocolate-flavored)

TO FINISH

1½ cups (12 ounces) heavy whipping cream

1 tablespoon malted milk powder

1 tablespoon sugar

½ teaspoon cocoa powder, for dusting (optional)

EQUIPMENT

9- or 9½-inch Fluted Tart Pan with a Removable Bottom, Cooling Rack, Medium Bowl, Small Saucepan, Whisk, Silicone or Rubber Spatula, Stand Mixer Fitted with a Whisk Attachment or a Hand Mixer and a Medium Bowl, Pastry Bag Fitted with a St. Honoré Tip or a ¾-inch Star Tip, Large Metal Spatula (Optional), Fine-Mesh Strainer (Optional), Thin and Sharp Knife

1 BAKE THE SHELL: Preheat the oven to 350°F and position an oven rack in the center. Bake the tart shell for 15 minutes. Remove the pan from the oven (hold the pan by the sides and not the bottom), close the oven door, check the crust for cracks, and repair any with a bit of reserved dough (page 208). Return the pan to the oven and bake 15 to 17 minutes longer. Remove the pan (again, holding by the sides) and place on a rack to cool completely.

2 PREPARE THE FILLING: Combine the milk chocolate and bittersweet chocolate in the medium bowl. In the small saucepan, heat the cream just until it begins to boil. Remove from the heat and whisk in the malted milk powder until dissolved. Immediately pour the cream over the chocolates and let the mixture sit for 1 minute; then whisk to blend. If any lumps of unmelted chocolate remain, heat the mixture gently by placing it over a saucepan with an inch of simmering water in the bottom. Stir gently with a silicone or rubber spatula until the lumps have melted. Scrape the filling into the cooled tart crust. Chill for 1 hour, or until the filling is set and firm.

what the pros know

A classic ganache contains equal parts dark chocolate and cream. The cacao (cocoa solids) in dark chocolate thickens the mixture upon cooling, ensuring the ganache sets up firm and sliceable. Because milk chocolate contains mostly sugar and milk powder (both of which turn to liquid when combined with hot cream) and very little cacao (less than 15 percent in most milk chocolates), milk chocolate ganache made with an equal part of cream cannot firm enough upon cooling to slice. This type of ganache requires a lot of milk chocolate (to bump up the cacao presence) and very little cream; otherwise, the cooled consistency will be more of a sauce than a tart filling. The addition of a few ounces of 70 percent dark chocolate ensures the filling is firm enough to hold its shape when cut, yet still full of the caramelly sweetness that milk chocolate lovers crave.

GETTING AHEAD **The crust can be baked a day or two ahead of time. Wrap in plastic and store at room temperature. You can fill the tart several days ahead, but do not pipe the whipped cream on top—simply wrap the filled tart shell with plastic and refrigerate until needed. Then, on the day you serve the tart, whip the cream and pipe as directed above.**

3 FINISH THE TART: In a stand mixer fitted with a whisk attachment (or, with a hand mixer in a medium bowl), whip the cream, sugar, and malted milk powder to medium peaks. (Do not whip into stiff peaks or the cream will be overwhipped and grainy by the time you pipe it. If this happens, simply stir in a tablespoon or two of extra cream until it smoothes out.) Transfer the whipped cream to the pastry bag fitted with the St. Honoré tip. With the point of the V in the piping tip facing upwards, practice making a few ridges on a plate or piece of parchment paper. To do this, move the bag in a slight arc as you squeeze. Each ridge is like piping a small rainbow—higher in the center than at the ends, where the tip almost touches the tart surface. Once you are comfortable with the technique, start at one edge and pipe straight lines of ridges across the tart. Alternatively, pipe shells or rosettes over the surface using a ½-inch star tip. Refrigerate for 30 minutes.

4 Place the tart pan on top of a large can from your pantry (the 28-ounce tomato cans are good) so that the bottom balances midair as the rim falls to the counter. Use the large metal spatula to transfer the tart to a serving plate or simply leave the bottom of the tart pan under the tart for support. To serve, use a fine-mesh sieve to dust the top of the tart lightly with cocoa powder, if desired. Cut the tart with a thin, sharp knife that has been warmed in hot water and wiped dry. Clean the knife with a warm towel between each slice to keep the whipped cream free of crumbs from the crust.

STORING **The tart may be kept in the refrigerator for 3 days, but the whipped cream may start to break down after several days.**

MINI CHOCOLATE-RASPBERRY TARTLETS

MAKES 15 (2½-INCH) MINI TARTLETS This is a great recipe for those occasions when you want something special but don't have a lot of hands-on time. Most of the time spent here is waiting for the crust to bake or the filling to chill, leaving you free to turn your attention elsewhere. The filling is ganache–a simple mixture of equal parts dark chocolate and cream that sets up rich and velvety, and is fabulous with fresh raspberries. No raspberries? No worries. Leave them out and give the ganache filling an extra spark of flavor with a tablespoon or two of liqueur (think Kahlúa, Grand Marnier, or amaretto) or ¼ teaspoon of extract (try mint, ginger, or almond) and then top with a matching garnish, such as a chocolate-covered coffee bean with the Kahlúa ganache. No flavorings? Still no worries–a bit of softly whipped cream on each tartlet is perfect simplicity. You can also use slightly smaller or larger tartlet pans, but the yield will change.

INGREDIENTS

1 recipe Easy Chocolate Press-In Dough (page 212), prepared through Step 2 and chilled for 30 to 60 minutes

2½ tablespoons plus 2 tablespoons seedless raspberry jam

4 ounces semisweet or bittersweet chocolate (up to 60 percent cacao), finely chopped

½ cup (4 ounces) heavy whipping cream

1 half-pint basket (6 ounces) fresh raspberries

1 teaspoon water

Confectioners' sugar, for dusting (optional)

EQUIPMENT

Fifteen (2½-inch) Mini Tartlet Pans, Two Baking Sheets, Wooden Spoon, Medium Bowl, Small Saucepan, Whisk, Microwave-Safe Bowl (Optional), Pastry Brush, Fine-Mesh Strainer (Optional)

1 SHAPE THE SHELLS: Lightly coat the tartlet pans with high-heat canola-oil spray. Break off a piece of the chilled dough about the size of a large cherry and press it into a tartlet pan, using your thumbs to create an even, ⅛-inch-thick layer of dough. Level it at the rim of the pan by rolling your thumb over the edge to remove any excess. Make sure there are no cracks or thin spots—if there are, just press the dough to bring it together. Repeat with the remaining dough and tartlet pans. Save any small bits of extra dough in case you need to patch a crack during the baking process. Transfer the tartlet pans to a baking sheet and chill for 30 minutes.

2 BAKE THE SHELLS: Preheat the oven to 350°F and position an oven rack in the lower third. Bake the shells on the baking sheet for 15 minutes. Remove the baking sheet from the oven, close the oven door, check the crusts for cracks, and repair any with a bit of reserved dough (page 208). Return the tartlet pans to the oven and bake 8 minutes longer. Transfer to a cooling rack and, using the rounded end of the wooden spoon, gently press down the center of each tartlet to make more room for the filling. Let cool completely.

3 FILL THE TARTLETS: Spoon ½ teaspoon of jam in the bottom of each tartlet. Set the tartlets aside, still on the baking sheet. Place the chocolate in the medium bowl. In the small saucepan, heat the cream just until it begins to boil. Immediately pour over the chocolate and let sit for 1 minute. Whisk gently to blend completely. If any lumps of

unmelted chocolate remain, heat the mixture gently by placing it over a saucepan with an inch of simmering water. Stir gently until the lumps have melted. Spoon a tablespoon of warm ganache into each tartlet (to within ⅛ inch of the top). Refrigerate the tartlets for 1 hour on the baking sheet, or until the filling is set and firm.

4 Turn each tartlet over and firmly tap it against your palm to remove it from its pan. Return the unmolded tartlets to the baking sheet.

5 FINISH THE TARTLETS: Pour the raspberries onto a baking sheet and sort through them to pick out and discard any moldy berries or debris. Raspberries are usually not washed, as they absorb water quickly and turn to mush. Arrange a few raspberries on the top of each tartlet. Melt the remaining 2 tablespoons raspberry jam with the water in the cleaned small saucepan over low heat until hot and fluid (do not let it boil or it will caramelize), or warm in the microwave-safe bowl. Brush just enough of the melted jam over the top of the berries to glaze them a bit. You don't want to overdo it; simply touch the brush to the berries to give them a shiny look. Serve immediately or refrigerate the tartlets until needed. Remove the tartlets from the refrigerator 1 hour before serving to allow the chocolate filling to soften slightly. Arrange on a platter and use a fine-mesh strainer to dust lightly with confectioners' sugar if desired.

STORING **The finished tartlets can be kept in an airtight container in the refrigerator for up to 3 days, though eventually the crust will soften.**

SOUR CHERRY LINZER TART

MAKES 1 (9 OR 9½-INCH) TART, SERVING 8 TO 10 A linzer tart is a lattice-topped Austrian specialty featuring a crust rich with butter, spices, and ground nuts enveloping a filling of raspberry jam. While a good-quality seedless raspberry jam would be delicious as the filling, you'll love the way dried sour cherries add their bright, tart flavor to this modern take on the classic favorite. Feel free to substitute 1¼ cups raspberry jam for the filling if you'd like to make the traditional tart. Good any time of year, this dessert is especially welcome during the holidays, when the fragrance of cinnamon and cloves fills the house with the irresistible scent of winter baking.

INGREDIENTS

DOUGH

1½ sticks (6 ounces) unsalted butter, softened (65° to 68°F)

¾ cup (5¼ ounces) sugar

1 large egg

1 large egg yolk

¾ teaspoon pure vanilla extract

Finely grated zest of 1 large orange

Finely grated zest of 1 large lemon

1⅓ cups (6½ ounces) unbleached all-purpose flour

⅓ cup (1½ ounces) whole natural almonds

¼ cup (1 ounce) whole hazelnuts

1¼ teaspoons ground cinnamon

¼ teaspoon ground cloves

½ teaspoon baking powder

¼ teaspoon salt

FILLING

2 cups (16 ounces) cherry or berry juice

¼ cup (1¾ ounces) sugar

2 (3-inch) cinnamon sticks

½ vanilla bean

1 cup (8 ounces) firmly packed dried sour cherries

1 tablespoon cornstarch

1 tablespoon water

Softly Whipped Cream (page 416) or vanilla ice cream, for serving

EQUIPMENT

Stand Mixer Fitted with a Paddle Attachment or a Hand Mixer and a Medium Bowl, Silicone or Rubber Spatula, Food Processor Fitted with a Metal Blade, Pastry Bag Fitted with a ⅜-inch Plain Round Tip, Small Saucepan, Fine-Mesh Strainer, Medium Bowl, Small Bowl, Whisk, Large Bowl, 9- or 9½-inch Fluted Tart Pan with a Removable Bottom, Cooling Rack, Large Metal Spatula (Optional)

1 MIX THE DOUGH: Place the butter and sugar in the bowl of the stand mixer and beat on medium speed until smooth and creamy looking, 2 to 3 minutes. You can also use a hand mixer and a medium bowl, though you may need to beat the mixture a little longer to achieve the same results. Scrape down the bowl with a spatula. Add the egg and egg yolk and blend well. Scrape down the bowl again. Add the vanilla, orange zest, and lemon zest and blend well; scrape down the bowl once more.

2 Place the flour, almonds, hazelnuts, cinnamon, cloves, baking powder, and salt in the bowl of the food processor and process until the nuts are finely ground, about 45 seconds. Add to the butter mixture and blend on low just until the ingredients are thoroughly mixed.

3 DIVIDE THE DOUGH: Split the dough into two portions, one slightly larger than the other. (The larger piece will line the tart pan, while the smaller portion will be piped in a lattice pattern over the top of the tart.) Wrap the larger portion in plastic and refrigerate for 30 to 45 minutes, until firm enough to press into the tart pan without it sticking to your hands. Spoon the smaller portion of dough into the pastry bag fitted with the ⅜-inch plain round tip and set aside at room temperature.

Grinding the nuts with the flour keeps the nuts from getting pasty or turning into nut butter. The flour absorbs the oils that are released when the nuts are ground fine, resulting in feathery nut pieces without oily residue. If you purchase ground nuts, simply skip this step and stir them into the other dry ingredients.

GETTING AHEAD **The dough can be wrapped tightly and frozen for up to 6 weeks.**

You can also press the bottom layer of dough into the tart pan, double-wrap tightly with plastic wrap, and freeze for 1 month (freeze lattice dough separately). When you want to bake it, unwrap, add the filling, pipe the lattice (soften the dough quickly in the microwave on the defrost setting). Transfer directly to the preheated oven (add 3 to 4 minutes to the baking time).

The cherry filling can be made up to 3 days in advance and kept in an airtight container in the refrigerator.

4 MAKE THE FILLING: Combine the juice, sugar, and cinnamon sticks in the small saucepan. Split the vanilla bean and scrape the seeds into the pan, adding the pod as well. Add the dried cherries. Bring to a simmer over medium heat. Reduce the heat to low and simmer until the cherries are plump and soft, 15 to 20 minutes. Pour the mixture through the fine-mesh strainer into the medium bowl. Return the juices to the saucepan and place the cherries in the medium bowl. Discard the cinnamon stick and vanilla bean pod. Bring the juices to a simmer. In the small bowl, whisk together the cornstarch and water until smooth. Pour the cornstarch mixture into the simmering juice, whisking constantly. Cook until the liquid thickens, 30 to 60 seconds, then immediately pour over the cherries and stir to blend. Cool completely (to speed cooling, place the bowl of cherries in a larger bowl of ice and cold water and stir occasionally).

5 Press the larger portion of chilled dough evenly across the bottom and up the sides of the tart pan. Chill in the refrigerator or freezer for 20 minutes. Preheat the oven to 350°F and position an oven rack in the lower third.

6 Spread the cherry filling evenly in the chilled shell. Using the dough in the pastry bag, create an angled lattice: Pipe straight lines of dough about 1 inch apart across the surface of the filling. Then, pipe slanted lines of dough over the straight lines, crossing them at an angle to create a diamond pattern. (Note: You won't need all the dough in the bag—you can roll and cut the leftover dough into shapes with a cookie cutter and make linzer cookies.)

7 Bake the tart for 40 to 45 minutes, until the filling is bubbling and the dough is nicely browned. Transfer to a cooling rack, making sure you hold the pan by the sides and not the bottom (remember, it's a two-piece pan and can come apart!).

8 Place the tart pan on top of a large can from your pantry (the 28-ounce tomato cans are good) so that the bottom balances midair as the rim falls to the counter. Use the metal spatula to transfer the tart to a serving plate or simply leave the bottom of the tart pan under the tart for support. Serve warm or at room temperature with a spoonful of whipped cream or a scoop of vanilla ice cream.

STORING **The linzer tart keeps, covered with plastic wrap, at room temperature for up to 3 days or in the refrigerator for up to 5 days. Allow the tart to come to room temperature before serving, or warm in a 350°F oven for 8 to 10 minutes.**

APRICOT-CHERRY GALETTE WITH ALMOND CREAM

MAKES 1 (10-INCH) GALETTE, SERVING 8 TO 10 A galette is a free-form tart that is shaped on a baking sheet–no tart pan needed. Known as a crostata in Italy, these hand-formed tarts are beautifully rustic and easy to shape. The tart dough is rolled into a large circle and centered on a baking sheet lined with parchment paper or a silicone mat. The sweet or savory filling is either mounded or carefully arranged in the center of the dough (depending on one's sense of style), leaving a border at the edge. The edge is then folded or pleated around the filling, leaving the center open to show the filling within. Galettes work best when made with a flaky-style dough, which has enough strength to hold its shape and remain crisp in contact with warm fruit juices. You can fill this tart with virtually any fruit that entices you at the market. For a savory version, see the Potato, Onion, and Gruyère Galette on page 232.

INGREDIENTS

1 recipe Flaky Pie or Tart Dough (page 177), prepared through Step 4

1½ pounds firm-ripe apricots

10 ounces ripe, sweet cherries

⅓ cup (2¼ ounces) granulated sugar, plus ½ teaspoon sugar (or 1 teaspoon turbinado or sanding sugar) for sprinkling

1½ tablespoons unbleached all-purpose flour

1 tablespoon (½ ounce) unsalted butter, melted

Almond Cream (page 417) or vanilla ice cream, for serving

EQUIPMENT

Rolling Pin, Baking Sheet, Parchment Paper or a Silicone Mat, Paring Knife, Cherry Pitter, Medium Bowl, Pastry Brush, Metal Spatula, Cooling Rack, Cake Lifter or Two Metal Spatulas or a Tart Pan Bottom

1 Preheat the oven to 400°F and position an oven rack in the lower third. Line the baking sheet with parchment paper or a silicone mat. Following the general instructions in Steps 5 through 7 on page 178, roll the dough into a 13-inch round and transfer it to the baking sheet. Chill for 1 hour.

2 Use a paring knife to cut and pit the apricots and slice them into ½-inch-thick wedges. Pit the cherries with the cherry pitter (or cut in half with the paring knife and pluck out the pits). Place the prepared fruit in the medium bowl and sprinkle the ⅓ cup sugar and the flour over the top. Use your hands to toss the fruit until it is evenly coated.

3 Mound the fruit mixture in the center of the chilled dough round, leaving a 1½-inch border at the edge. Fold that border up around the fruit, pleating it to make a pretty, circular enclosure and leaving the center open. Brush the top of the pleated dough with the melted butter and sprinkle with the ½ teaspoon sugar.

4 Bake the galette for 40 to 45 minutes, until a deep golden brown and the fruit is juicy and bubbling. Use the metal spatula to lift the galette slightly and check underneath. The crust should be a beautiful brown color. Transfer to a rack to cool for 15 minutes.

While a round galette is traditional, try a square or rectangular version if you like. Simply roll the dough into the shape you want, and then pleat as directed. If you're feeding a crowd, shape a large rectangular galette using a double recipe of the flaky dough for a gorgeous, rustic centerpiece. For an extra layer of flavor, spread a ¼-inch thick layer of almond filling (page 112) over the center of the dough and arrange the fruit on top. The almond filling not only lends flavor, but also absorbs fruit juices, helping to keep the crust dry and flaky.

GETTING AHEAD **The dough can be rolled out up to 2 days ahead, covered with plastic wrap, and refrigerated. The fruit can be pitted and sliced up to 4 hours ahead.**

5 Transfer the galette to a serving plate with the cake lifter, 2 spatulas, or a tart pan bottom, supporting the bottom as you move it. Slice and serve warm, accompanied by a spoonful of almond cream or vanilla ice cream.

STORING **The galette is best when eaten the same day it is baked, preferably while still warm. The juices will eventually cause the crust to become soft and then soggy. Store it, uncovered, at room temperature for 2 to 3 hours. For longer storage, cover with plastic wrap and refrigerate. To serve, reheat on the baking sheet in a 400°F oven for 10 to 15 minutes, until warmed through.**

Nectarine-Plum Galette
Substitute 1 pound firm-ripe nectarines and 1 pound firm-ripe plums for the apricots and cherries. Pit and cut the fruit into ½-inch slices. You may need additional sugar (up to ½ cup), depending on the tartness of your fruit. Increase the flour to 2½ tablespoons. Add ¼ teaspoon ground nutmeg and a pinch of cardamom with the sugar and flour.

POTATO, ONION, AND GRUYÈRE GALETTE

MAKES 1 (10-INCH) GALETTE, SERVING 8 TO 10 Here is a savory version of the free-form fruit tart known in France as a galette. Onions, sautéed until soft and sweet, are combined with sliced potatoes and grated Gruyère, an aged, wonderfully nutty cheese from Switzerland, for a comforting, all-season tart that is as welcome at the brunch table as it is at dinner.

INGREDIENTS

1 recipe Flaky Pie or Tart Dough (page 177), prepared through Step 4

1½ tablespoons olive oil, plus 1 tablespoon for drizzling

1 large onion (12 ounces), thinly sliced

½ teaspoon finely chopped fresh thyme or rosemary

¼ teaspoon plus 1 pinch kosher salt

Black pepper

4 ounces Gruyère cheese, coarsely grated

1 pound red potatoes, washed (left unpeeled) and cut into ¼-inch-thick slices

1 egg, lightly beaten

Crème fraîche, for serving (optional)

Golden caviar, for serving (optional)

EQUIPMENT

Rolling Pin, Baking Sheet, Parchment Paper or a Silicone Mat, Medium Sauté Pan, Large Bowl, Pastry Brush, Paring Knife, Metal Spatula, Cooling Rack, Cake Lifter or Two Metal Spatulas or Tart Pan Bottom, Chef's Knife

GETTING AHEAD The dough can be rolled out up to 2 days ahead, covered with plastic wrap, and refrigerated.

1 Preheat the oven to 400°F and position an oven rack in the lower third. Line the baking sheet with parchment paper or a silicone mat. Following the general instructions in Steps 5 through 7 on page 178, roll the dough into a 13-inch round and transfer it to the baking sheet. Chill for 1 hour.

2 Heat the 1½ tablespoons olive oil in the medium sauté pan over medium-high heat. Add the onion and cook, stirring occasionally, until soft and lightly colored, 8 to 10 minutes. Stir in the thyme, ¼ teaspoon salt, and 5 grinds pepper and blend well. Transfer to a plate and set aside to cool.

3 Combine the cooled onion mixture, cheese, and potatoes in the large bowl. Mound the filling in the center of the chilled tart shell, leaving a 1½-inch border at the edge. Fold that border up around the filling, pleating it to make a pretty, circular enclosure and leaving the center open. Drizzle the filling with the remaining 1 tablespoon olive oil and sprinkle lightly with salt and 3 grinds of pepper. Lightly brush the pleated dough with the beaten egg to give it shine and help it brown in the oven.

4 Bake the galette for 45 to 50 minutes, until the pastry is golden brown and the potatoes are soft when tested with a paring knife or skewer. Use the metal spatula to lift the edge of the galette slightly and check underneath. The bottom crust should be a beautiful brown color. Transfer to a rack to cool for 5 to 10 minutes.

5 Transfer the galette to a serving plate with the cake lifter, 2 spatulas, or a tart pan bottom supporting the bottom as you move it. Slice with a chef's knife and serve warm. If you like, serve with dollops of crème fraîche and spoonfuls of caviar.

STORING Store uncovered at room temperature for up to 6 hours. Or cover with plastic wrap and refrigerate for up to 2 days. Reheat in a 400°F oven for 10 to 15 minutes before serving.

FROMAGE BLANC, TOMATO, AND HERB TART

MAKES 1 (9- OR 9½-INCH) TART, SERVING 8 Fromage blanc, a fresh, soft, spreadable goat cheese with a texture similar to that of ricotta cheese, is a beautiful match for ripe tomatoes. If you cannot find it, simply substitute a log of your favorite mild, young goat cheese, broken into small pieces. This is best during the summer when the farmers' market is full of juicy heirloom tomatoes and fresh herbs. When tomato season is over and flavorful tomatoes are no longer available, substitute ½ cup of plump, coarsely chopped, sun-dried tomatoes for an intense burst of flavor.

INGREDIENTS

1 recipe Flaky Pie or Tart Dough (page 177), prepared through Step 7

2 medium, ripe tomatoes, cored

4 ounces fromage blanc

½ cup (8 ounces) heavy whipping cream or whole milk

2 large eggs

1 clove garlic, finely chopped or pushed through a press

1 tablespoon chopped or snipped fresh chives

1 teaspoon finely chopped fresh thyme, or 2 teaspoons chopped fresh basil

Pinch of salt

3 or 4 grinds of black pepper

EQUIPMENT

9- or 9½-inch Fluted Tart Pan with a Removable Bottom, Kitchen Scissors, Pie Weights, Serrated Knife, Medium Bowl, Whisk, Cooling Rack, Large Metal Spatula (Optional), Thin and Sharp Knife

1 TRIM AND FINISH THE TART DOUGH: Use the scissors to trim the dough so it overhangs the edge of the pan by 1 inch. Moisten the inside wall of dough with your finger dipped in cool water. Fold the overhanging dough inward to form a sturdy double-layered edge. Press firmly with your thumbs to fuse the two layers of dough, then roll your thumb over the rim of the tart to remove any excess dough there. Chill while the oven preheats.

2 BAKE THE SHELL: Preheat the oven to 375°F and position an oven rack in the bottom third. Line the chilled tart shell with heavy-duty foil, pressing the foil firmly and smoothly into the crevices of the pan. Fill the pan with pie weights (page 175). Make sure the weights reach up the sides to the rim of the pan (the center does not need to be filled quite as full). Bake the shell for 20 to 22 minutes, until the foil comes away from the dough easily (if it doesn't, bake another 5 to 6 minutes and check again). Remove the pan from the oven (hold the pan by the sides and not the bottom), close the oven door, and lift out the foil and weights from the shell; set them aside to cool. Return the pan to the oven to continue baking the shell for about 10 minutes, then remove the pan from the oven, close the oven door, and check to see if any cracks have formed. If you see a crack, very gently smear a tiny bit of reserved dough over the crack to patch it (page 171)—you need only enough to seal the opening. Return the pan to the oven and bake 10 to 15 minutes longer, until the crust is a nice golden brown all over. Transfer to a rack and cool completely. Leave the oven on.

what the
pros
know

The custard filling can be used to make myriad variations on this savory tart. The ratio of ½ cup cream or milk to 2 eggs to 4 ounces of cheese can be combined with about 1 to 1½ cups sautéed asparagus and lemon zest; sautéed mushrooms, garlic, and herbs; roasted peppers and olives; spinach and onion; corn and crispy bacon...you get the idea. If you don't have lots of bulk, such as vegetables, you'll want to add another ¼ to ½ cup cream or milk to the custard so the tart shell is full.

GETTING AHEAD **The dough can be rolled out up to 2 days ahead, covered with plastic wrap, and refrigerated.**

3 MAKE THE FILLING: Use the serrated knife to slice the tomatoes into ¼-inch-thick rounds. Place them in the bottom of the cooled tart shell in a single layer. Place the *fromage blanc* in the medium bowl and add the cream slowly, whisking all the while to blend the two together. Whisk in the eggs, one at a time, and blend thoroughly. Add the garlic, chives, thyme, salt, and pepper and blend well. Pour the filling over the sliced tomatoes in the tart shell. Fill the shell to no more than ¼ inch from the top or it may overflow while baking.

4 Bake the tart for 25 to 30 minutes, until the custard is set in the center—give the tart a gentle shake to check. Transfer the tart to a cooling rack, making sure you hold the pan by the sides and not the bottom (remember, it's a two-piece pan and can come apart!).

5 Place the tart pan on top of a large can from your pantry (the 28-ounce tomato cans are good) so that the bottom balances midair as the rim falls to the counter. Use the metal spatula to transfer the tart to a serving plate, or simply leave the bottom of the tart pan under the tart for support. Serve the tart warm or at room temperature. Cut it with a thin, sharp knife, slicing down in one quick, even motion rather than sawing.

STORING **The tart can be held at room temperature for up to 3 hours. For longer storage, cover with plastic wrap and refrigerate for up to 2 days (it will last for up to 4 days but the crust will become soggy). To serve, allow 1 hour for the tart to come to room temperature, or reheat in a 350°F oven for 10 to 12 minutes, until warmed through.**

LEMON MERINGUE TARTLETS WITH SHREDDED PHYLLO

MAKES 8 TARTLETS A new twist on an old favorite, this recipe features easy tartlet shells made of crispy shredded phyllo that are filled with a satiny lemon curd and topped with toasted meringue. If you've been intimidated by the fragile, fussy nature of phyllo sheets, you'll be amazed by how easy it is to use shredded phyllo. It can be found next to the sheet phyllo in the frozen food section of supermarkets that have a Middle Eastern clientele. If shredded phyllo is unavailable, the lemon curd and meringue used here will fit nicely into a 9-inch Vanilla Shortcrust (page 209) shell, fully baked and cooled. Follow the directions for baking the Classic French Fruit Tart shell on page 214.

INGREDIENTS

8 ounces thawed shredded phyllo (page 237)

1 recipe Lemon Curd (page 421)

1 stick (4 ounces) unsalted butter, melted

2 tablespoons sugar, plus 10 tablespoons (4½ ounces) for the meringue

4 large egg whites

EQUIPMENT

Standard 12-Cup Muffin Pan, Medium Bowl, Baking Sheet, Double Boiler, Whisk, Instant-Read Thermometer, Stand Mixer Fitted with a Whisk Attachment or a Hand Mixer and a Medium Bowl, Pastry Bag Fitted with a Large (½-inch or larger) Star Tip, Butane or Propane Chef's Torch

1 MAKE AND BAKE THE TARTLET SHELLS: Preheat the oven to 350°F and position an oven rack in the lower third. Lightly coat the muffin cups with melted butter, oil, or high-heat canola-oil spray. Place the phyllo in the medium bowl and use your hands to gently separate the fluff of strands, discarding any hard pieces or clumps of dough that refuse to separate. Pour the melted butter over the phyllo and sprinkle the 2 tablespoons sugar over the top. Toss gently with your hands until the phyllo is evenly coated with the butter and sugar.

2 Divide the buttered phyllo into 14 equal portions. Press 1 portion into each buttered muffin cup. Press firmly on the phyllo to compact the pastry and mold it to make room for the filling. (You'll have 2 portions left over—if you like, spread out on a small parchment-lined baking sheet and bake after the cups are finished as yummy snacks for the chef and any helpers.)

3 Bake the shells for 17 to 20 minutes, until the edges and bottoms are golden brown. The centers will still be light, but will crisp upon cooling. If the entire shell is golden brown, the phyllo will taste bitter. Transfer to a rack to cool completely.

4 FILL THE SHELLS: Remove the phyllo shells from the pan and set on the baking sheet. Place a generous spoonful of lemon curd in the center of each tartlet shell, mounding it slightly. (You will use about two-thirds of the lemon curd—save the rest for spreading on toast, as a topping for fresh berries, or enjoying on the extra baked phyllo.) Refrigerate the filled shells on the baking sheet until the meringue is ready to pipe.

Shredded phyllo is not sheets of phyllo that have been mechanically shredded, but instead a distant relative of sheet phyllo, with the texture of shredded wheat. In countries where it's widely consumed, the pastry is known as *kataifi* or *konafa*. It is made with a liquid batter rather than a dough, and is thrown out over a hot griddle in thin ribbons about the size of angel hair pasta. The batter is cooked for a few seconds, until firm but still pliable, then scooped up and set aside while the next batch is cooked. Tossed with a little melted butter (or oil) to help it crisp and brown while baking, shredded phyllo can be used for both sweet and savory dishes. For an easy yet impressive appetizer or side dish, bake into cups as described here (without sugar) and fill with sautéed vegetables and crumbled feta or goat cheese.

GETTING AHEAD **The tartlet shells can be baked up to 3 days in advance and held, wrapped airtight, at room temperature. If they seem soft when unwrapped, simply re-crisp in a 350°F oven for 8 to 10 minutes. Let cool before continuing with the recipe.**

5 MAKE THE MERINGUE: Bring an inch of water to a boil in the bottom of the double boiler. Place the egg whites and 10 tablespoons of sugar in the top of the double boiler off the heat. Set on top of the simmering water and whisk constantly (not vigorously, just enough to keep the whites moving) for 4 to 5 minutes, until the egg whites are hot to the touch and the mixture reaches 160°F on the instant-read thermometer (the mixture will look frothy, but not whipped). Remove the whites from the heat each time you test their temperature. When they are on the heat, keep whisking, as they may scramble. If that happens, there is no recourse but to begin again, so watch carefully.

6 Transfer the hot egg whites to the bowl of the stand mixer. You can also use a hand mixer and a medium bowl. Whip on high speed until the whites have cooled to room temperature, increased in volume, and resemble marshmallow fluff. Spoon the meringue into the pastry bag. Pipe a mound of meringue onto each tartlet, starting at the outside edge of the tartlet and circling inward, then upward, covering the entire surface.

7 TOAST THE MERINGUE: Be sure your tartlets are evenly spaced on the baking sheet and that nothing nearby might catch fire. Ignite your torch and lightly graze the meringue of each tartlet with the tip of the flame, rotating the baking sheet to toast all sides. The meringue will brown instantly, so move quickly; don't hold the flame in one place for long. Serve immediately or refrigerate until serving time.

NOTE: **To make measuring easier, the recipe calls for half a box of shredded phyllo, but you'll have more than you need to fill 12 muffin cups. Just bake this extra phyllo alongside and enjoy a delicious snack while you're working. The remaining half of the package can be wrapped in plastic, returned to the box, and refrigerated for up to 1 week or frozen for up to 2 months.**

STORING **The tartlets are at their best the same day they are assembled, but will hold in the refrigerator for up to 2 days.**

Fresh Strawberry Tartlets with Shredded Phyllo Use Vanilla

Bean Pastry Cream (page 419) instead of the lemon curd. If you can find tiny *fraises des bois* (highly perfumed wild strawberries) at the market, use them whole. Otherwise, wash, dry, and hull a pint (16 ounces) strawberries. Quarter each berry and set the quarters into the pastry cream around the edge of each tartlet, hulled side down and tips meeting in the center of the tartlet like a little tepee. You will need 6 to 8 strawberry quarters for each tartlet, slightly less if the berries are huge. Glaze by brushing the strawberries with a tablespoon of seedless raspberry jam warmed with a teaspoon of water until fluid.

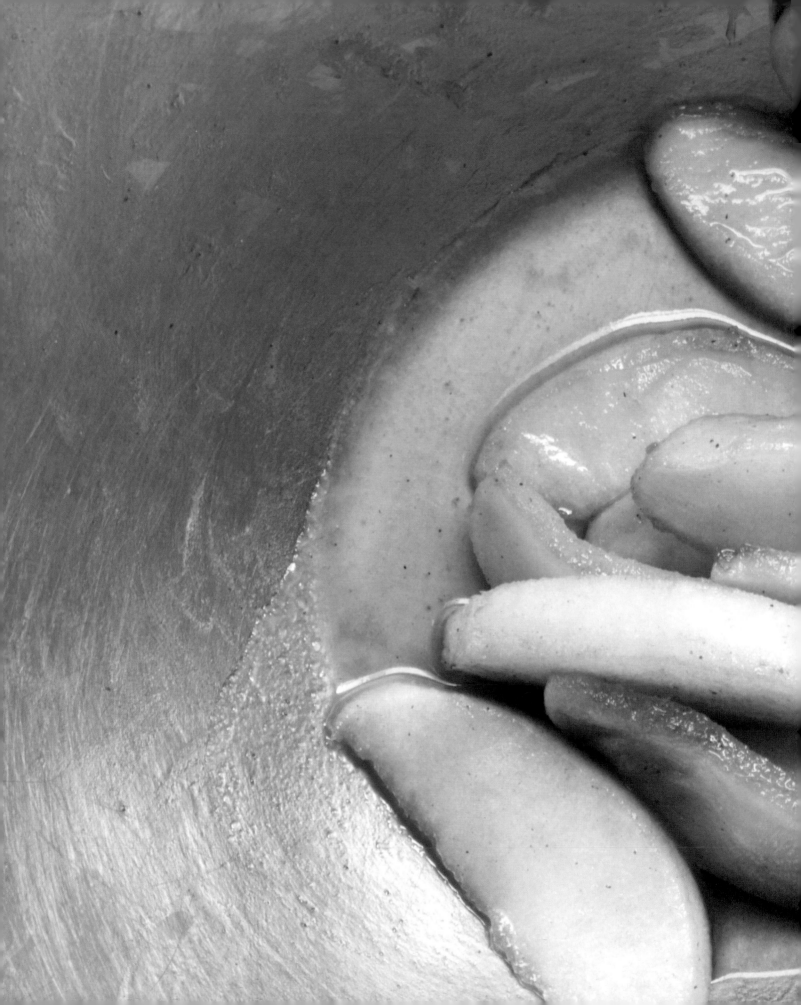

Sweet, bubbling fruit under a crisp, buttery topping fills the kitchen with an irresistibly enticing aroma that speaks of home and comfort. The desserts in this chapter are a pleasure to make because they're simple, easy to prepare, and connect you directly to the season at hand. A couple of pounds of fruit paired with a topping made from pantry staples adds up to an ending that is so much more than the sum of its parts. As the seasons change, so do the fruits at their peak of ripeness and flavor, and a trip to the farmers' market or produce stand is all the inspiration you'll need to get started. Whichever fruit you choose, it's good to know that nearly every recipe here can be adapted to the fragrant fruit in your grocery sack.

A Primer on Fruit Desserts

The tried-and-true motto for fruit desserts is: Keep it simple and keep it seasonal. Fruit chosen during a local growing season will always taste better than that shipped in from around the world. Think about it—faraway fruit needs to be pretty darn hard to survive the knocks it receives on the way from the field to packing house to truck to airport and beyond. The outside package may look pretty, but what's under that expensive, perfect skin is often an unripe, tasteless shadow of the real thing. Fruits grown locally, in season, can be allowed to ripen fully, so they arrive at your table with a luscious melting texture, sweet juices, and maximum flavor. The bonus is that locally grown ripe fruit is also less expensive than the stuff flown in from another country. For more information on fruits, their seasons, and tips for choosing the sweetest fruit, see "The Baker's Pantry."

Okay, your counter is laden with fruit and you're ready to go. This chapter is full of simple, easy recipes to showcase your bounty. These are American favorites that are as welcome at a more formal dinner as they are at midnight, spooned from the baking dish straight to your mouth. Crisps, cobblers, shortcakes, and simply cooked fruits fill the house with the irresistible aromas of spiced simmering fruit, buttery biscuits, and brown sugar. What's more, many of the basic components of these desserts can be prepared days or even weeks ahead of time, waiting patiently in the refrigerator or freezer for the whim to strike and the fruit to ripen—and then put together in the time it takes to slice the fruit and prepare the baking pan. Let's look at the various types of fruit desserts and the differences among them.

CRISPS AND CRUMBLES

This style of dessert consists of a deep dish of fruit topped with a streusel-style mixture, often containing nuts, that is served directly from its baking dish. Crisps are also sometimes referred to as crumbles, since the topping resembles clumps of bread or cookie crumbs. Crisps traditionally contain nuts whereas crumbles have oatmeal, but increasingly the lines are blurred. Apple-Cranberry Crisp with Oatmeal Topping (page 243) is classic, while the Pineapple, Kumquat, and Ginger Crisp with Coconut Topping (page 247) bridges boundaries. The filling in crisps and crumbles is a mixture of sliced or chunked fruit tossed with a bit of sugar, lemon juice, perhaps some spice, and maybe a little thickener such as flour, cornstarch, or tapioca flour (for more on these thickeners and their differences, see page 176). Truth be told, sometimes you don't even need thickener, since there is no bottom crust for the juices to turn soggy, like there is in pie.

MIXING CRISPS AND CRUMBLES

Both crisps and crumbles use the cut-in method for mixing dough, similar to the one for pie dough, some tart doughs, biscuits, and scones. All of the dry ingredients are placed in a bowl and cold butter is cut into the mixture with your fingers or pastry blender, food processor blade, or a mixer's paddle attachment. The recipes in this chapter call for a stand mixer, but feel free to mix the toppings using any of the other tools. The difference between crisps and other cut-in-method pastries is the final texture. Whereas the other pastries are always brought together into a cohesive dough with a bit of liquid, the topping for a crisp is left loose and crumbly. In fact, there is definitely some room for opinion as to when the crisp topping is finished—some like their toppings rather loose, or "dusty," with lots of tiny bits of butter and flour resembling damp sand. Others let the topping mix a bit further, until the butter and flour mixture starts to form definitive clumps about the size of peas or even small grapes, resulting in less sandy, more cookielike clumps of dough. Try both ways and see which you prefer.

COBBLERS

This is another fruit-on-the-bottom, served-from-the-baking-dish dessert, though the topping has a decidedly different texture. There are two schools of thought when it comes to cobbler topping. One prefers a wet, batterlike mixture that is spooned over the fruit. The other thinks the only proper topping is a biscuit-like dough, either rolled, then cut with a cookie cutter and arranged on top of the fruit or woven into a beautiful lattice. Both styles are delicious, quick to make, and sure to bring a smile. With either style, just be careful to make sure the topping is thin. If it's too thick, it will either sink into the fruit, creating soggy dumplings, or soak up too much juice and never fully cook through. For cakelike toppings, a thickness of ¼ inch works well. For biscuit toppings, a thickness of about ⅛ inch is perfect.

tips for success Individual Crisps and Cobblers

Crisps and cobblers can be baked in one large dish like the recipes in this chapter, or divided into individual ramekins, coffee cups, or custard cups for an all-your-own dessert. If you would like to change the baking dish, feel free. Most of these recipes, which are baked in 6-cup pans, will make 8 to 10 individual servings. Don't forget to leave enough room at the top of the baking dish for the topping, and be sure to set all the dishes on a baking sheet to make transferring in and out of the oven safe and easy. Also, the baking times will change because the fruit in a small container will heat up and cook faster than that in a larger pan. Don't rely on the times listed in each recipe for doneness. Instead, use the visual clues—golden brown topping and bubbling fruit that is tender when poked with the tip of a knife or skewer.

SHORTCAKES

Tender, flaky scones share equal billing with fruit in irresistible shortcake desserts. The scones may be made with cream, milk, or buttermilk and flavored with citrus zest, spices, chocolate, and more. But to make spectacular shortcakes, they should be assembled and served while the scones are still warm from the oven. Another key is to toss the fruit with sugar at least an hour in advance (but no more than two), to allow time for the sugar to pull some of the liquid out of the fruit, creating a sweet syrup that is perfect for spooning onto the scone. Gently split, lightly buttered (if you dare), then covered with fruit and softly whipped cream, warm-from-the-oven scones offer an immediate pleasure that no restaurant can match. The technique for making great scones is the cut-in method, covered at length in "Quick Breads" (page 144), which also includes the scone recipes for the short-cakes in this chapter.

Don't be intimidated by shortcakes. You can make the most delicious and tender scones in less than 5 minutes when you use a food processor, although it takes hardly any longer by hand, and homemade scones are much tastier than anything you can purchase.

USING FRESH FRUIT

There are times when the simplicity of unadorned fruit, served with only a knife, is the perfect after-dinner sweet. When you want just a little bit more, add a bit of fire to the fruit. Roasting concentrates the flavors and softens the flesh (as in Roasted Summer Fruit with Late Harvest Riesling, page 262). Some fruits benefit greatly from a slow, gentle cooking in liquid (poaching). Quince is a perfect example; when poached (as in the Rosy Quince, page 251), it turns from an unpalatably bitter and hard fruit to a sweet, soft, deep-coral colored indulgence. Pears also benefit from a slow cooking in liquid, and Port-Braised Pears (page 263) are imbued with both a rich wine flavor and a gorgeous ruby color.

tips
for success
Serving Crisps and Cobblers

Crisps and cobblers are best served warm from the oven, when the fruit is fragrant and juicy and the topping is crispy. The classic partner, and one that is hard to beat, is a scoop of vanilla ice cream, but there are other options. A pitcher of cold cream passed at the table to be poured over the warm dessert is decadent and fun. Softly Whipped Cream (page 416) is always welcome. A cool and silken Custard Sauce (page 424) is wonderful when spooned around the fruit and can be made in many flavors to complement both fruit and topping. Vanilla Crème Fraîche (page 420) and Honeyed Yogurt (page 420) add elegant, slightly acidic notes. Sabayon Cream (page 418) adds not only an airy richness and a touch of alcohol, but a definite touch of elegance as well.

APPLE-CRANBERRY CRISP WITH OATMEAL TOPPING

SERVES 6 TO 8 The ultimate comfort food on a cold fall or winter night, this dessert fills the house with the aroma of warm apples, butter, brown sugar, and cinnamon. If this crisp were a person, it would be your best friend. Granny Smith is a reliably tart and firm baking apple available in all supermarkets—but don't hesitate to use local varieties found in your area. Always taste the fruit; if it is quite sweet, you might want to reduce the sugar slightly. You can substitute quick oats for the old-fashioned, but don't use instant or you'll end up with soggy mush.

INGREDIENTS

TOPPING

½ cup (2½ ounces) unbleached all-purpose flour

½ cup (1½ ounces) old-fashioned oats (do not use instant)

½ cup (4 ounces) firmly packed light brown sugar

½ teaspoon ground cinnamon

¼ teaspoon salt

1 stick (4 ounces) cold unsalted butter, cut into ½-inch pieces

½ cup (2 ounces) pecans, toasted and chopped (optional)

FILLING

1½ pounds firm, tart baking apples (such as Granny Smith), peeled, cored, and cut into ¼-inch-thick slices

1 bag (12 ounces) cranberries, picked through, rinsed, and patted dry

¾ cup (6 ounces) firmly packed light brown sugar

1 tablespoon cornstarch or tapioca flour, or 2 tablespoons unbleached all-purpose flour

2 teaspoons freshly squeezed lemon juice

¾ teaspoon ground cinnamon

Vanilla ice cream, for serving

EQUIPMENT

Stand Mixer Fitted with a Paddle Attachment, Large Bowl, Silicone or Rubber Spatula, 9-inch Ceramic Pie Plate or Other Wide 6-Cup Baking Dish, Baking Sheet (Optional), Paring Knife

1 Preheat the oven to 350°F and position an oven rack in the center.

2 MAKE THE TOPPING: Place the flour, oats, brown sugar, cinnamon, and salt in the bowl of the stand mixer and mix on low speed until blended evenly, about 10 seconds. Add the cold butter pieces and mix on low for 3 to 4 minutes. At first the mixture will look dry, but eventually it will begin to look like wet sand, and finally it will form small clumps about the size of peas. Add the nuts, if using, and mix for a few more seconds to evenly disperse them.

3 MAKE THE FILLING: In the large bowl, use the spatula to toss together the apple slices, cranberries, brown sugar, lemon juice, cornstarch, and cinnamon until all the fruit is coated evenly. Scrape into the baking dish and spread in an even layer. Sprinkle the topping in an even layer over the fruit (do not press down).

4 BAKE AND SERVE THE CRISP: You may want to place a baking sheet or a piece of foil under the crisp to catch any juices that may bubble over. Bake for 45 to 55 minutes, until the topping is nicely browned and the fruit is bubbling and soft (the tip of a

Just because you see apples in the market all year doesn't mean they're always in season. Apples are a fruit known as a *good keeper*, which means they retain their texture and flavor longer than other varieties of fruit such as peaches or strawberries. They still deteriorate over time, however, especially without refrigeration (and when was the last time you saw supermarket apples in the refrigerated case?). Although usually associated with autumn, new crop apples begin ripening in summer and continue through fall, depending upon the variety. By spring, even the firm "baking" apples dissolve into applesauce with prolonged heat. For best results, bake with apples midsummer through winter, and choose other seasonal fruit during the remaining months.

GETTING AHEAD **The topping can be refrigerated in an airtight container for up to 1 week or frozen for up to 2 months. Do not defrost before using; simply sprinkle over the top of the fruit and bake. Frozen topping will increase the baking time by only a couple of minutes.**

paring knife should easily slide in and out of the apple slices). Spoon the warm crisp into bowls and place a scoop of ice cream next to each serving.

STORING **Store any leftovers in the refrigerator, covered with plastic wrap, for 2 to 3 days. Reheat, covered loosely with foil, in a 350°F oven for 10 to 15 minutes, until warmed through.**

Mixed Plum Crisp with Oatmeal Topping **Substitute 3 pounds of sliced plums for the apples and cranberries in the filling and add 1 teaspoon finely grated orange zest. Reduce the cinnamon to ½ teaspoon and add ½ teaspoon ground ginger. Plums tend to be tart, but if you have a sweet variety (always taste the fruit) you may want to reduce the amount of brown sugar to ½ cup.**

STRAWBERRY-RHUBARB CRISP WITH AMARETTI TOPPING

SERVES 6 TO 8 There's a reason strawberries are so often paired with rhubarb in pies, crisps, and other baked desserts: The sweetness of the strawberries perfectly complements the tartness of the rhubarb. Plus, the combination is a gorgeous tumble of red and pink. Crushed amaretti cookies add a deep almond flavor and crunchy texture to the crisp.

INGREDIENTS

TOPPING

1⅔ cups (3¾ ounces) coarsely crushed amaretti cookies (about 20 cookies)

½ cup (2½ ounces) unbleached all-purpose flour

¼ cup (1¾ ounces) sugar

7 tablespoons (3½ ounces) cold unsalted butter, cut into ½-inch pieces

½ cup (2½ ounces) chopped toasted natural (skin-on) almonds

FILLING

1 pound cleaned rhubarb, cut into ½-inch pieces

2 (1-pint) baskets (2 pounds) ripe strawberries, washed, dried, hulled, and quartered

½ cup (3½ ounces) sugar

2 teaspoons freshly squeezed lemon juice

1 tablespoon cornstarch or tapioca flour, or 2 tablespoons unbleached all-purpose flour

¾ teaspoon ground cinnamon

Vanilla ice cream, Softly Whipped Cream (page 416), or heavy cream, for serving

EQUIPMENT

Rolling Pin, Stand Mixer Fitted with a Paddle Attachment, Large Bowl, Silicone or Rubber Spatula, 9½-inch Deep-Dish Pie Pan or Other Wide 6-Cup Baking Dish, Baking Sheet (Optional), Paring Knife

1 Preheat the oven to 350°F and position an oven rack in the center.

2 MAKE THE TOPPING: Place the amaretti cookies in a resealable plastic bag and coarsely crush by rolling over them once or twice with the rolling pin. You do not want fine crumbs here, but little chunks of crushed cookie. Set aside. Place the flour and sugar in the bowl of the stand mixer and mix on low speed until blended evenly, about 10 seconds.

3 Add the cold butter pieces and mix on low for 3 to 4 minutes. The butter will break down into very small pieces, then the mixture will look like wet sand, and finally it will begin to form small clumps about the size of small peas. Add the crushed amaretti cookies and the almonds and mix for a few more seconds, just until they are evenly dispersed.

4 MAKE THE FILLING: In the large bowl, use the spatula to toss together the rhubarb, strawberries, sugar, lemon juice, cornstarch, and cinnamon until all the fruit is coated evenly. Scrape into the baking dish and spread in an even layer. Sprinkle the topping over the fruit in an even layer (do not press down).

5 BAKE AND SERVE THE CRISP: You may want to place a baking sheet or a piece of foil under the crisp to catch any juices that may bubble over. Bake for 40 to 50 minutes, until the topping is nicely browned and the fruit is bubbling and soft (the tip of a paring knife should easily slide in and out of the rhubarb pieces). Spoon some of the warm crisp into serving bowls and serve with ice cream, whipped cream, or a pitcher of heavy cream to pour around the bowl.

Rhubarb looks
like pink celery,
and indeed, it
is a vegetable. But traditional recipes
treat this native American plant like a
fruit, and it is lovely in baked goods.
Its acidic flavor adds a tart punch to
any dessert, balancing the sweetness
and heightening the textural and flavor
interest. In addition, its lovely pink hue
adds a bright color to desserts, which
makes rhubarb especially welcome
as one of the first arrivals of spring.

GETTING AHEAD **The amaretti
topping can be refrigerated in an airtight
container for up to 1 week or frozen for
up to 2 months. Do not defrost before
using; simply sprinkle over the top
of the fruit and bake. Frozen topping
will increase the baking time by only a
couple of minutes.**

STORING **Keep any leftovers in the refrigerator, covered with plastic wrap, for 2 to 3 days.
Reheat, covered loosely with foil, in a 350°F oven for 10 to 15 minutes, until warmed through.**

Blueberry-Nectarine Crisp with Amaretti Topping
**Substitute 2¼ pounds nectarines, cut into ½-inch slices, and 1 pint (11½ ounces)
blueberries for the strawberries and rhubarb. Substitute a generous pinch of freshly grated
nutmeg for the cinnamon.**

Cherry-Plum Crisp with Amaretti Topping **Substitute 2
pounds of sliced plums and 12 ounces of sweet pitted cherries for the strawberries and
rhubarb. Increase the sugar in the filling to ¾ cup (5¼ ounces) if the plums are tart. Add
1½ teaspoons kirsch (cherry brandy) to the mixture if you like.**

PINEAPPLE, KUMQUAT, AND GINGER CRISP WITH COCONUT TOPPING

SERVES 6 TO 8 If you haven't considered tropical fruit in a crisp, you've got to try this combination of warm, sweet pineapple paired with tart kumquats and spicy ginger, all under a crunchy coconut topping. It's perfect for winter and early spring, when tropical fruits and citrus are at their best and we crave big bold flavors. And the apricot variation that follows is luscious on a hot summer night. The brilliant yellow and orange filling looks like sunshine spilling onto the plate. Think wide, sandy beaches, a hammock between two palm trees, the soothing crash of the surf . . .

INGREDIENTS

TOPPING

½ cup plus 2 tablespoons (3 ounces) unbleached all-purpose flour

1 cup (3½ ounces) gently packed sweetened flaked coconut

⅓ cup (1½ ounces) chopped unsalted macadamia nuts

¼ cup (2 ounces) firmly packed light brown sugar

¼ cup (1¾ ounces) granulated sugar

Pinch of salt

1 stick (4 ounces) cold unsalted butter, cut into ½-inch pieces

FILLING

1 medium (about 3½ pounds) ripe pineapple

15 kumquats (about 4 ounces)

¼ cup (1 ounce) finely chopped candied ginger

3 tablespoons (1½ ounces) granulated sugar

2 tablespoons unbleached all-purpose flour

Coconut or vanilla ice cream, for serving

EQUIPMENT

Stand Mixer Fitted with a Paddle Attachment, Chef's Knife, Pineapple Slicer (Optional), Large Bowl, Paring Knife, Silicone or Rubber Spatula, 9-inch Ceramic Pie Pan or Other Wide 6-Cup Baking Dish, Baking Sheet (Optional)

1 Preheat the oven to 350°F and position an oven rack in the center.

2 MAKE THE TOPPING: Place the flour, coconut, nuts, brown sugar, granulated sugar, and salt in the bowl of the stand mixer and blend on low speed for 10 or 15 seconds. Add the cold butter pieces and continue to blend on low for 3 to 4 minutes until the butter is cut into small pieces about the size of peas.

3 MAKE THE FILLING: Use a chef's knife to slice the ends off the pineapple so it stands solidly on your cutting board. Remove the skin by slicing just under it from top to bottom. Remove any remaining "eyes" with the tip of your knife. Use a pineapple slicer to core the pineapple and quarter it lengthwise. Alternatively, use the chef's knife to slice the pineapple into quarters lengthwise and make an angled lengthwise cut along each quarter to remove the core. Cut each quarter lengthwise in half or thirds, depending on the size of the pineapple, then crosswise into 1-inch pieces. Transfer to the large bowl.

4 Rub off and discard the tiny, hard stem piece on the end of each kumquat (some may not have this). Use a paring knife to cut each fruit in half crosswise, then use the tip of your knife to pick out any seeds. Cut each half in two, then add to the bowl with the pineapple.

Choosing a ripe, sweet pineapple can be tricky. The best way to tell the ripeness of a pineapple is to smell it—if it has a wonderfully heady pineapple smell, then it's ready to use. Look for skin that is more yellow than green, and beware of soft spots or a slightly fermented odor, indicating that the fruit is past its prime. Many people like to test a pineapple by pulling out one of its green leaves at the top—the theory is that if the leaf separates easily from the fruit, then it's ripe—but this is actually the least accurate way to test your fruit. The new Gold variety is reliably candy-sweet and ready to use, but is often smaller than other types of pineapples. You may need to purchase an extra one to yield enough fruit for this recipe.

GETTING AHEAD **The crumble topping can be refrigerated in an airtight container for up to 1 week or frozen for up to 2 months. Do not defrost before using; simply sprinkle over the top of the fruit and bake. Frozen topping will increase the baking time by only a couple of minutes.**

5 Chop the candied ginger, if necessary, into rice-size pieces (you can leave them larger if you like big chunks). Add the ginger, granulated sugar, and flour to the fruit and toss well with the spatula. Scrape into the baking dish and spread in an even layer. Sprinkle the topping in an even layer over the fruit.

6 BAKE AND SERVE THE CRISP: You may want to place a baking sheet or a piece of foil under the crisp to catch any juices that may bubble over. Bake for 45 to 55 minutes, until the topping is golden brown and the fruit juices are bubbling and thickened. Serve warm or at room temperature with coconut or vanilla ice cream.

STORING **Keep any leftovers in the refrigerator, covered with plastic wrap, for 2 to 3 days. Reheat, covered loosely with foil, in a 350°F oven for 10 to 15 minutes, until warmed through.**

Pineapple, Apricot, and Ginger Crisp with Coconut Topping
Omit the kumquats and add 4 medium apricots, each half sliced into 4 pieces. If fresh apricots are not available, use 1 cup (about 4 ounces) quartered dried apricots in their place. (Try to find California dried apricots, which offer a more complex flavor than Mediterranean apricots.)

APRICOT-CHERRY ALMOND COBBLER

SERVES 6 TO 8 Apricots, cherries, and almonds are all members of the same botanical family, prunus, which accounts for the natural way their flavors support and enhance each other. There is a double dose of almond here to accent the fruit filling within. The cakelike topping bursts with the rich presence of almond paste, while almond liqueur gives a hint of flavor when tossed with the sliced fruit.

INGREDIENTS

FILLING

1 pound firm-ripe tart apricots, halved, pitted, and each half cut into 4 or 5 slices

1 pound sweet, firm-ripe cherries, pitted

½ cup (3½ ounces) sugar

1 teaspoon amaretto (almond liqueur)

TOPPING

¼ cup (1¾ ounces) sugar

2½ ounces almond paste (page 46), at room temperature

¾ stick (3 ounces) unsalted butter, softened (65° to 68°F)

1 large egg, at room temperature

½ teaspoon pure vanilla extract

1¼ cups (6¼ ounces) unbleached all-purpose flour

1½ teaspoons baking powder

¼ teaspoon salt

½ cup (4 ounces) whole milk, at room temperature

Vanilla or dulce de leche ice cream, or Almond Cream (page 417), for serving

EQUIPMENT

Large Bowl, Silicone or Rubber Spatula, 9-inch Ceramic Pie Pan or Other Wide 6-Cup Baking Dish, Stand Mixer Fitted with a Paddle Attachment, Medium Bowl, Whisk, Baking Sheet (Optional)

1 Preheat the oven to 350°F and position an oven rack in the center.

2 MAKE THE FILLING: In the large bowl, toss together the apricot slices, cherries, sugar, and amaretto until all the fruit is coated evenly. Use the spatula to scrape into the baking dish and spread in an even layer.

3 MAKE THE TOPPING: Place the sugar and almond paste in the bowl of the stand mixer and beat on medium speed until the almond paste is broken into tiny pieces. Add the softened butter and beat on medium-high until the mixture is very light in color, almost white, 4 to 5 minutes. Scrape down the bowl. Add the egg and vanilla and blend well. Scrape down the bowl. In the medium bowl, whisk together the flour, baking powder, and salt. With the mixer on lowest speed, add the flour mixture and milk alternately to the butter (page 302). Scrape down the bowl, and finish blending by hand with the spatula. Cover the fruit by letting the batter fall off the spatula in long bands over the fruit (don't try to spread it or it will sink into the fruit). Use the spatula to gently blend the bands of batter together until it covers the fruit in a single layer.

4 BAKE AND SERVE THE COBBLER: You may want to place a baking sheet or a piece of foil under the cobbler to catch any juices that may bubble over. Bake for 50 to 60 minutes, until the topping is nicely browned and a toothpick or skewer inserted into the topping comes out clean. The fruit should be bubbling and soft. Serve warm, accompanied by vanilla or *dulce de leche* ice cream, or softly whipped almond cream.

STORING **Keep any leftovers in the refrigerator, covered with plastic wrap, for 2 to 3 days. Reheat, covered loosely with foil, in a 350°F oven for 10 to 15 minutes, until warmed through.**

ROSY QUINCE

SERVES 6 Looking like it fell out of an old-world still life painting, the quince has an ageless, slightly off-kilter beauty that is unmistakable. Once it is cooked, it has a luscious apple-pineapple-citrus flavor, and a gorgeous color ranging from deep rose to pinkish orange. You can find quinces in the late fall and winter at farmer's markets and in the specialty produce section of the market. You'll love this as is, served simply with a bit of Vanilla Crème Fraîche or Honeyed Yogurt, but the poached quince slices can also be tucked into fall and winter crisps, pies, or other fruit-based desserts.

INGREDIENTS

2 pounds quinces, washed and patted dry

2 cups (16 ounces) white wine, such as Sauvignon Blanc

2 cups (16 ounces) water

1 cup (7 ounces) sugar

Zest of ½ orange, in strips

1 (3- or 4-inch) cinnamon stick

1 teaspoon cardamom seeds

Honeyed Yogurt (page 420) or Vanilla Crème Fraîche (page 420), for serving

EQUIPMENT

Vegetable Peeler, Chef's Knife, Melon Baller, Medium Nonaluminum Saucepan, Medium-Mesh Strainer, Large Bowl

GETTING AHEAD The poached quinces in their cooking liquid will keep, covered in the refrigerator, for up to a week.

1 Use a sharp vegetable peeler to remove the quince skin. Cut in half with a chef's knife (be careful here—the flesh is very hard). Use a melon baller to scoop out the center core and seeds. Reserve the peels and cores. Slice the fruit into ½-inch thick slices. Put the slices in the medium bowl, cover with plastic wrap, and set aside until needed. The fruit will turn brown, but don't worry—once fully cooked, it will turn pink.

2 Place the peels and cores in the medium saucepan and add the wine, water, sugar, orange zest, cinnamon stick, and cardamom seeds. Warm over medium heat until the mixture begins to simmer and the sugar dissolves. Reduce the heat, cover, and cook at a gentle boil for 30 minutes. The peels and cores are very flavorful and, with the other flavorings, will make a quince "stock" in which to poach the fruit. Strain the mixture through a medium-mesh strainer and return the liquid to the pan.

3 Add the quince slices to the pan and bring the mixture back to a boil over medium heat. Reduce the heat to very low, cover, and cook at the lowest possible simmer. Continue to cook, gently stirring the fruit once or twice to ensure that it cooks evenly, for 1½ to 2 hours, until the fruit is very tender and a beautiful deep rose to orange color. The fruit will be tender long before it has turned the beautiful color you want, so don't be tempted to remove it from the heat too early. Quinces have the amazing ability to hold their shape long after they are cooked through, so be patient.

4 Gently pour the contents of the pan into the large bowl and set aside to cool. If you would like the poaching liquid to be a bit thicker and deeper in color, return the liquid to the pan and boil over medium heat until reduced to 1¼ to 1½ cups. Cool the reduced poaching liquid and pour it over the quince slices. Spoon the quinces into compote dishes and top each one with a spoonful of vanilla crème fraîche, honeyed yogurt, or almond cream.

PEACH-VANILLA BEAN COBBLER WITH SUGAR CRUNCH LATTICE

SERVES 6 TO 8 This is an example of the biscuit-topped variety of cobbler, with a tender yet crunchy lattice covering warm, vanilla-scented peaches. Remember that the biscuit dough needs to be rolled thinly, about ⅛ inch, or the underside of the lattice will remain gooey rather than cooking through. The technique for weaving the beautiful lattice top may seem a bit intimidating, but it's one of those techniques that is easier to do than it is to describe. An alternative is to roll the dough as described, then use a 2-inch cookie cutter to cut as many shapes as possible (hearts or stars are two favorites). Arrange those shapes on the fruit in concentric circles, starting at the outer edge and working inward, slightly overlapping each row of dough.

INGREDIENTS

1 recipe Cream Scones (page 152), prepared through Step 2

2¼ pounds ripe peaches, peeled (see page 54) or not according to your taste

¼ to ½ cup (1¾ to 3½ ounces) sugar, plus 2 tablespoons for the lattice

1 vanilla bean, or 2 teaspoons pure vanilla extract

2 teaspoons freshly squeezed lemon juice

2 teaspoons cornstarch or tapioca flour, or 4 teaspoons unbleached all-purpose flour

Vanilla ice cream or Vanilla Crème Fraîche (page 420), for serving

EQUIPMENT

Paring Knife, Large Bowl, Small Bowl, Silicone or Rubber Spatula, 9-inch Ceramic Pie Pan or Other Wide 6-cup Baking Dish, Rolling Pin, Bench Scraper (Optional), Pastry Brush, Baking Sheet (Optional)

1 MAKE THE FILLING: Use a paring knife to halve and pit the peaches, then cut into ½-inch-thick slices. Transfer to the large bowl. Taste a peach slice—if it is sweet and ripe, use only ¼ cup sugar (or even less, if it is very sweet). If it's tart or slightly under-ripe, use up to an additional ¼ cup. Place the sugar in the small bowl. Use the tip of the paring knife to split the vanilla bean in half lengthwise. Turn the knife over and use the dull side to scrape out all the seeds into the sugar. Rub the mixture together with your fingers until the seeds are evenly dispersed. Pour over the fruit. Add the lemon juice and cornstarch (and the vanilla extract or paste, if using) and gently toss with the spatula until all the fruit is evenly coated. Press the fruit into the baking dish in an even layer.

2 MAKE THE LATTICE: Dust your work surface and the top of the dough with flour. Roll the dough into a 16-inch circle about ⅛ inch thick. Rotate the dough slightly each time you roll—this will help you roll the dough into an even circle and will alert you immediately when the dough is sticking to the surface. If it does stick, gently use a bench scraper to release the dough, lifting it off the surface and adding a bit more flour to the surface to prevent further sticking.

3 Cut the dough into 1½-inch wide strips. The strips toward the center of the circle will be longer than the strips toward the edges and this is fine. You will use the longer strips in the center of your baking dish when weaving the lattice, and the shorter strips near the edges of the dish.

what the pros know

All the crisps and cobblers in this chapter are baked in a wide, 6-cup baking dish. This means that the fillings and toppings are all interchangeable. There's a recipe for apple-cranberry crisp, but what if you want to make an apple-cranberry cobbler? Just team the filling from the first recipe with the topping from the second. Craving apricot and cherry crisp with amaretti topping? Pair the fruit from page 250 with the topping on page 245. There are many possible combinations in this chapter, each one offering a warm, sweet taste of the season.

4 WEAVE THE LATTICE: Brush any excess flour from the surface of the dough. Gently lift the strips and place half of them about ½-inch apart across the top of the fruit, letting any excess dough fall over the edge of the dish for the moment. Fold every other strip back halfway, exposing the fruit underneath. Precisely at that halfway point, place a strip of dough perpendicular, laying it over the unfolded strips. Unfold the folded strips, laying them over the new strip of dough. Fold back the strips that were left flat the first time, and place another new strip of dough over the fruit and flat strips of dough. Straighten and tighten the dough each time you do this so your lattice looks even. Continue in this manner until you reach the edge of the pan, then turn the pan and weave the other half of the lattice, beginning at the center and working outward. Once the lattice is finished, use the paring knife to trim any overhanging dough flush with the pan. Chill for 20 minutes.

5 BAKE AND SERVE THE COBBLER: Preheat the oven to 350°F and position an oven rack in the center. Sprinkle the lattice evenly with the remaining 2 tablespoons of sugar. You may want to place a baking sheet or a piece of foil under the cobbler to catch any juices that may bubble over. Bake for 40 to 50 minutes, until the topping is nicely browned and the fruit is bubbling and soft (the tip of the paring knife should easily slide in and out of the peach slices). Serve warm or at room temperature, accompanied by ice cream or crème fraîche.

STORING This cobbler is at its best immediately after baking. Store any leftovers in the refrigerator, covered with plastic wrap, for 2 to 3 days. Reheat, covered loosely with foil, in a 350°F oven for 10 to 15 minutes, until warmed through.

Peach-Raspberry Cobbler with Sugar Crunch Lattice
Pour ½ pint of raspberries out onto a baking sheet. Pick through them and discard any debris and molded berries. Do not wash, or they will absorb the water and turn to mush. Add the raspberries to the bowl with the peaches and continue with the recipe as directed above.

Individual Lattice-Topped Cobblers
Make and roll the biscuit dough as directed above, but cut the strips of dough 1 inch wide rather than 1½ inches. Weave the dough directly on your work surface rather than on the individual baking dishes. Divide the fruit among the baking dishes (you will need six 1½-cup dishes or eight 1-cup dishes). With a round cutter that is the same size as the top of the baking dishes, cut rounds of woven lattice. Place each round on top of the fruit, sprinkle with sugar, and bake as directed above, reducing the baking time to 25 to 35 minutes.

CLASSIC STRAWBERRY SHORTCAKE

SERVES 8 There's no surer sign of spring than sweet, red strawberries, and there's no better way to enjoy them than in this timeless classic. Here, a tender cream scone, warm from the oven, is split and lightly buttered, then topped with softly whipped cream and a bevy of dead-ripe strawberries. In this instance, a restaurant can't begin to match the goodness of your own kitchen (plus, you can eat it in your pajamas!). Don't even think of making strawberry shortcake unless you have fragrant, juicy strawberries at the peak of the season, for this recipe will do nothing to hide the lackluster flavor of unripe or out-of-season fruit. Yes, you can skip buttering the warm scones, but do make sure you sugar the berries at least an hour in advance so there are plenty of juices to spoon over the scones.

INGREDIENTS

1 recipe Cream Scones (page 152), prepared through Step 2

STRAWBERRIES

3 pints (3 pounds) ripe strawberries, rinsed and patted dry

2 to 4 tablespoons sugar

WHIPPED CREAM

1½ cups (12 ounces) heavy whipping cream

1 tablespoon sugar

1 teaspoon pure vanilla extract

FOR THE SCONES

2 tablespoons milk or heavy whipping cream

1 tablespoon sugar

4 teaspoons unsalted butter, softened (optional)

EQUIPMENT

Strawberry Huller or Paring Knife, Silicone or Rubber Spatula, Stand Mixer Fitted with a Whisk Attachment or a Hand Mixer and a Medium Bowl, Chef's Knife, Pastry Brush, Baking Sheet, Parchment Paper, Cooling Rack

1 PREPARE THE BERRIES: Hull the strawberries using the strawberry huller or the tip of the paring knife. If the berries are quite small, you can quarter them; otherwise, cut into ⅛- to ¼-inch-thick slices. Use the spatula to toss the berries with 2 tablespoons of sugar, then taste. If they need more sugar, add another tablespoon or two and toss well. Set aside for up to 2 hours. The sugar will draw juices from of the berries, which is a vital part of strawberry shortcake. Do not combine the berries and sugar more than 2 hours ahead or they will become mushy.

2 Place the cream, sugar, and vanilla in the bowl of the stand mixer (you can also use a medium bowl and a hand mixer). Whip until the mixture holds soft peaks. Be careful not to overwhip or it will become grainy and look curdled. If this happens, use a clean spatula to gently stir in several additional tablespoons of cream, just until the mixture has smoothed out.

3 CUT AND BAKE THE SCONES: Preheat the oven to 425°F and position an oven rack in the center. Lightly dust the work surface with flour and pat the scone dough into an 8 by 4-inch rectangle. Use the chef's knife to cut it in half lengthwise and into quarters crosswise, making eight 2-inch squares. Brush off any excess flour. Line the baking sheet with parchment paper and space the squares evenly on the baking sheet. Brush the top of each scone with a little milk or cream. Sprinkle the 1 tablespoon of sugar evenly over the

GETTING AHEAD The scone dough can be cut and placed on the baking sheet, covered with plastic wrap, and refrigerated for up to 24 hours before baking. The cut dough can also be wrapped airtight on the baking sheet and frozen for up to 6 weeks—do not defrost before baking. In either case, the scones will not rise quite as high as when the dough is freshly made, but they will be delicious nonetheless.

The whipped cream can be prepared up to 6 hours ahead and stored, covered, in the refrigerator. If it softens, use a whisk to whip it back to the desired firmness just before serving.

tops. Bake for 13 to 15 minutes, until golden brown. Transfer to a cooling rack for 5 to 10 minutes. These are best served while still warm, though they can also be served at room temperature.

4 ASSEMBLE THE SHORTCAKES: Split the warm scones in half and place a bottom half on each plate. Butter very lightly with about ½ teaspoon per scone (if the scones are room temperature, do not butter them). Spoon a little of the strawberry juice onto each scone bottom. Top with a generous spoonful of strawberries, letting some fall off the scones and onto the plate. Top with a spoonful of whipped cream and place the scone tops on the cream. Spoon any additional berries and their juices around the shortcakes.

Strawberry Shortcake with Rose Cream Substitute 1 teaspoon rose water for the vanilla extract.

Peach and Strawberry Shortcake Use only 2 pints strawberries and add 3 large, ripe peaches (peeled, see page 54, or not, according to your taste), pitted and sliced into ½-inch wedges. Add ¼ cup (2 ounces) freshly squeezed orange juice to the bowl of prepared fruit.

PISTACHIO-RASPBERRY CHOCOLATE SHORTCAKES WITH WHITE CHOCOLATE CREAM

SERVES 8 Chocolate and raspberries are a heavenly dessert match. In this shortcake, plump raspberries are paired with two kinds of chocolate—a midnight-dark chocolate scone and white chocolate-sweetened whipped cream. Except for the actual baking of the scones, everything can be prepared ahead of time, so you can relax, enjoy dinner with your guests, and assemble these at the last minute, when the scones are warm from the oven. Be sure to use real white chocolate here—read the ingredient label and make sure it lists cocoa butter as the main fat (there will be a bit of milk fat as well).

INGREDIENTS

1 recipe Chocolate Cream Scones (page 153), prepared through Step 2

WHITE CHOCOLATE CREAM

5 ounces good-quality white chocolate, finely chopped

3 tablespoons (1½ ounces) water

1⅓ cups (10½ ounces) heavy whipping cream

FOR THE SCONES

2 tablespoons heavy whipping cream

1 tablespoon sugar

¼ cup (1 ounce) unsalted pistachios, finely chopped

3 half-pint baskets (18 ounces) fresh raspberries

EQUIPMENT

Double Boiler, Silicone or Rubber Spatula, Stand Mixer Fitted with a Whisk Attachment or a Hand Mixer and a Medium Bowl, Chef's Knife, Pastry Brush, Two Baking Sheets, Parchment Paper, Cooling Rack

1 MAKE THE WHITE CHOCOLATE CREAM: Place 1 inch of water in the bottom of the double boiler and bring to a full boil. Place the chocolate and water in the top of the double boiler. Turn off the heat and set the chocolate over the steaming water. Let the mixture rest for 1 minute, then stir with the spatula until the chocolate is melted and smooth. Remove from the heat and set aside until completely cool to the touch but still fluid. Warm chocolate will cause the whipped cream to break down and become watery.

2 In the bowl of the stand mixer, or in a medium bowl with a hand mixer, whip the cream to soft peaks. Add the white chocolate to the cream and continue to whip until the white chocolate has blended completely with the cream and the mixture is thick and velvety-looking. Be careful not to over-whip the cream or it will become grainy and look curdled. If this happens, use the spatula to gently stir in several additional tablespoons of cream until the mixture has smoothed out.

3 CUT AND BAKE THE SCONES: Preheat the oven to 400°F and position an oven rack in the center. Lightly dust the work surface with flour and pat the scone dough into an 8 by 4-inch rectangle. Use the chef's knife to cut it in half lengthwise and into quarters crosswise, making eight 2-inch squares. Brush off any excess flour. Line one of the baking sheets and space the squares evenly on the sheet. Brush the tops with the 2 tablespoons of cream, sprinkle evenly with the tablespoon of sugar, and top with the pistachios, gently pressing into the surfaces. Bake for 14 to 16 minutes, until firm to the touch when lightly pressed in the center. Transfer to a rack to cool for 5 to 10 minutes. These are best served while still warm, though they can also be served at room temperature.

White chocolate not only sweetens and flavors the whipped cream, but adds stability as well. When the melted and cooled chocolate is combined with the cold whipped cream, the cocoa butter in the chocolate hardens, holding the air bubbles in the whipped cream in suspension much longer than otherwise possible. The boon for the baker is not just wonderful flavor, but the ability to make the cream 24 hours in advance, with no loss of volume. Just be sure the white chocolate is cool to the touch, for if warm, it can cause the whipped cream to separate and deflate.

GETTING AHEAD **The scone dough can be cut and placed on the baking sheet, covered with plastic wrap, and refrigerated for up to 24 hours before baking. The cut dough can also be wrapped airtight on the baking sheet and frozen for up to 6 weeks—do not defrost before baking. In either case, the scones will not rise quite as high as when the dough is freshly made, but they will be delicious nonetheless.**

   The white chocolate cream can be prepared up to 24 hours ahead and kept, covered, in the refrigerator.

4 PREPARE THE FRUIT: Pour the raspberries out onto the other baking sheet. Pick through them and discard any debris or molded berries. Do not wash, or they will absorb the water and turn to mush.

5 ASSEMBLE AND SERVE THE SHORTCAKES: Split the warm scones in half and place a bottom half on each plate. Top with a generous spoonful of white chocolate cream. Divide the raspberries among the plates, dropping some in the cream and some around the scones. Place the scone tops slightly askew on the berries and cream and serve immediately.

GINGERBREAD SHORTCAKES WITH CARAMELIZED APPLES AND CIDER SABAYON

SERVES 8 A very special ending to a celebratory autumn dinner (even if all you're celebrating is falling leaves), these shortcakes offer layer after layer of favorite cold-weather flavors. And the apple, cinnamon, and caramel bring to mind those other seasonal favorites: wood smoke curling from the fireplace, big plaid blankets, and trees ablaze with color.

INGREDIENTS

1 recipe Gingerbread Scones (page 157), prepared through Step 2

CIDER SABAYON

6 large egg yolks

6 tablespoons (3 ounces) granulated sugar

6 tablespoons (3 ounces) Calvados or other apple brandy

6 tablespoons (3 ounces) apple juice

¾ cup (6 ounces) heavy whipping cream

FOR THE SCONES

3 tablespoons turbinado (page 25) or Hawaiian washed raw sugar

APPLES

6 large, tart baking apples (such as Granny Smith), peeled, cored, and cut into ½-inch-thick slices

½ cup (3½ ounces) granulated sugar

¾ teaspoon ground cinnamon

1 tablespoon plus 1 tablespoon unsalted butter

EQUIPMENT

Large Bowl, Double Boiler, Whisk or Hand Mixer, Instant-Read Thermometer, Silicone or Rubber Spatula, Chef's Knife, Pastry Brush, Baking Sheet, Parchment Paper, Cooling Rack, Large Sauté Pan or Skillet, Paring Knife

1 MAKE THE SABAYON: Fill the large bowl halfway with ice and water and set it aside. Place 2 inches of water in the bottom of the double boiler and bring to a rolling boil. Reduce to a simmer. Place the egg yolks and sugar in the top of the double boiler off the heat and whisk briefly, just until well blended and slightly lightened in color. Add the Calvados and apple juice and blend well. Place the egg mixture over the simmering water and whisk constantly for about 5 minutes (a hand mixer can be used here), or until it becomes very light and fluffy, resembling softly whipped cream in texture, and registers 160°F on an instant-read thermometer. Do not exceed 165°F or the eggs could scramble. If you see the sauce beginning to scramble around the edges, quickly remove the top of the double boiler from the heat and whisk vigorously. This will usually save the sauce, but if it still looks flat and broken, or there are large pieces of scrambled egg in the sauce, there is no recourse but to begin again with new ingredients. As soon as the sauce is finished, remove it from the heat. Place immediately in the bowl of ice water. Stir occasionally with the spatula until cold to the touch.

2 In the bowl of the stand mixer, or with a hand mixer and a medium bowl, whip the cream to soft peaks. Use a clean spatula to fold the whipped cream into the cooled sauce.

3 CUT AND BAKE THE SCONES: Preheat the oven to 425°F and position an oven rack in the center. Lightly dust the work surface with flour and pat the dough into an 8 by 4-inch rectangle. Use the chef's knife to cut the dough in half lengthwise and into quarters crosswise, making eight 2-inch squares. Line the baking sheet with parchment paper. Brush off any excess flour and space them evenly on the prepared baking sheet.

The scone dough can be cut, placed on the baking sheet, covered with plastic wrap, and refrigerated for up to 24 hours before baking. The cut dough can also be wrapped airtight on the baking sheet and frozen for up to 6 weeks—do not defrost before baking. In either case, the scones will not rise quite as high as when the dough is freshly made, but they will be delicious nonetheless.

The sabayon can be prepared up to 8 hours ahead and refrigerated, covered. If it softens, use a whisk to whip it back to the desired firmness just before serving.

The apples can be cooked up to 8 hours in advance and kept, covered, in the refrigerator. Undercook the apples slightly, as they will continue to cook when you reheat them in a sauté pan just before serving.

Sprinkle the turbinado sugar generously over the tops and press lightly into the surfaces. Bake for 14 to 15 minutes, until firm to the touch and golden in color. Transfer to a rack to cool for 5 to 10 minutes. These are best served while still warm, although they may be served cool.

4 CARAMELIZE THE APPLES: While the scones are baking, toss the apple slices with the sugar and cinnamon until evenly coated. You might think that there are too many apple slices, but they shrink quite a bit during the cooking process. Melt 1 tablespoon butter in a large sauté pan or skillet over medium heat. When it has melted, swirl the pan to coat it with the melted butter, turn the heat to high, add half of the apple slices, and spread in a single layer. (Note: Don't try to cook the apples all at once—if you crowd them, they'll poach in their own juices rather than caramelize.) Cook, without stirring, for 2 minutes. Gently toss or stir the apples. Cook for 2 minutes longer, then toss or stir again. Continue in this manner until the apples are golden brown and cooked through (the tip of a paring knife should slide easily in and out of the slices), yet still hold their shape, 8 to 10 minutes total. Transfer to a large plate. Repeat with the 1 remaining tablespoon of butter and the rest of the apple slices.

5 ASSEMBLE AND SERVE THE SCONES: Split the warm scones in half and place a bottom half on each plate. Spoon the apples onto the scone bottoms, allowing some to fall onto the plate. Top with a generous spoonful of cider sabayon. Place the scone tops slightly askew and serve immediately.

ROASTED SUMMER FRUIT WITH LATE HARVEST RIESLING

SERVES 4 TO 6 This easy and sophisticated ending is just the ticket when you want something a little dressier after dinner than a piece of fresh-from-the-farm fruit. The heat highlights the flavors, the dessert wine adds complexity and sweetness, and the vanilla brings it all together. Serve with a bit of crème fraîche and a glass of the same dessert wine, then lean back and relax in the warm summer air. A crispy cookie is a wonderful accompaniment—try Tuiles (page 284) or Classic Sugar Cookies (page 282).

INGREDIENTS

4 medium firm-ripe apricots (about 8 ounces), washed and patted dry

4 Black Mission figs (or other sweet, thin-skinned figs), washed and patted dry

2 large firm-ripe nectarines or peaches (about 10 ounces), washed and patted dry

2 large firm-ripe plums (about 12 ounces), washed and patted dry

3 tablespoons (1½ ounces) sugar

1 vanilla bean

½ (750-milliliter) bottle (1½ cups) late-harvest Riesling or Muscat wine

Vanilla Crème Fraîche (page 420) or Honeyed Yogurt (page 420), for serving

EQUIPMENT

Chef's Knife, Large bowl, Small Bowl, Paring Knife, Silicone or Rubber Spatula, 9 by 13-inch Nonaluminum Roasting or Baking Pan, Small Saucepan

GETTING AHEAD The roasted fruit can be prepared up to 4 hours ahead of time and stored, covered with plastic, at room temperature. The fruit can be sliced and tossed with the vanilla sugar up to 2 hours ahead of roasting and stored in the refrigerator.

1 Preheat the oven to 400°F and position an oven rack in the center. Use the chef's knife to cut the apricots in half, remove the pits, and slice each half in two. Trim the stems from the figs and cut each in half. Cut the nectarines or peaches in half, remove the pits, and slice each half into thirds or quarters—you want all the fruit wedges to be about the same size. Cut the plums in half, remove the pits, and slice each half into thirds or quarters. Transfer all the fruit to the large bowl.

2 Put the sugar in the small bowl. Use the tip of the paring knife to slice the vanilla bean in half lengthwise. Turn the knife over and use the dull side to scrape the seeds into the sugar. Rub the mixture together with your fingers or a small spoon until the seeds are evenly dispersed in the sugar. Pour the sugar over the fruit and toss gently with the spatula until the fruit is evenly coated. Transfer to the roasting pan and spread in a single layer. Cut the vanilla bean into several pieces and tuck them in among the fruit. Add the wine to the pan.

3 Roast the fruit for 10 minutes. Gently stir and roast for 10 minutes longer, or until a skewer or knife slides in and out of the fruit easily.

4 Transfer the fruit to a serving bowl or compote dish. Pour the wine, juices, and vanilla bean from the roasting pan into a small saucepan and bring to a simmer. Cook for several minutes, or until slightly thickened and glossy looking. Pour over the fruit and stir to blend.

5 Just before serving, remove the pieces of vanilla bean. Serve the fruit warm or at room temperature in glass compote bowls or small martini glasses with a spoonful of vanilla crème fraîche or honeyed yogurt.

PORT-BRAISED PEARS

SERVES 8 These ruby-colored pear slices are lovely served with a bit of Cocoa Nib Cream (page 417) and a silken spoonful of their reduced braising syrup. They are also an integral part of Chocolate Napoleons with Port-Braised Pears (page 127), and an inspired accompaniment to Stilton Cheesecake (page 369). The pears can be prepared up to 3 days in advance, and it's a good idea to do so, for their color deepens while they wait in their syrup, taking on a beautiful garnet hue.

INGREDIENTS

1 cup (8 ounces) ruby port
¼ cup (1¾ ounces) sugar

2 tablespoons (1½ ounces) honey
1 three-inch long strip of lemon zest

4 Bosc pears

EQUIPMENT

12-inch Sauté Pan or Skillet with Lid, Silicone or Rubber Spatula, Vegetable Peeler, Chef's Knife, Melon Baller, Paring Knife, Slotted Spoon

GETTING AHEAD The pears can be prepared up to 3 days in advance and stored, covered, in the refrigerator. Remove the pears 1 hour before serving so they have time to warm to room temperature.

1 PREPARE THE BRAISING SYRUP: In a large sauté pan, bring the port, sugar, honey, and lemon zest to a simmer over medium-low heat. Stir several times with the spatula to make sure the sugar is dissolved. Simmer for 5 minutes to blend the flavors.

2 ADD THE PEARS: Peel, halve, and core the pears, using the melon baller to scoop out the core. Slice each pear half lengthwise into quarters. Add the pears to the braising syrup and stir gently to coat them with the liquid.

3 COOK THE PEARS: Cover the pan and cook the pears in the simmering syrup for 15 to 20 minutes, or until the pears are tender when pierced with the tip of a paring knife. Every 5 minutes, remove the lid and gently stir the pears to completely coat them again with the syrup. When tender, use a slotted spoon to transfer the pears to a bowl or storage container.

4 REDUCE THE SYRUP: Raise the heat to high and boil the syrup remaining in the pan for 2 to 3 minutes, or until it coats the back of a spoon and is thickened. Pour the reduced syrup over the pear slices and let the mixture cool to room temperature. Serve immediately or cover and refrigerate.

Cookies are perhaps the most versatile, approachable, and universally loved category of baking. Even people who might be intimidated by baking think nothing of whipping up a batch of their favorite cookies. And there are few occasions in life when a cookie is not a happy match for the moment, especially since there are so many flavors and textures to choose from.

Chocolate lovers can choose from the chewy, extra-chocolaty Classic Fudgy Brownies, the crisp and sophisticated Chocolate–Earl Grey Shortbread Coins, or the always comforting Chocolate Chip Cookies. Those who crave nuts in their cookies will enjoy the crunchy Cappuccino Biscotti with Hazelnuts and Chocolate, the beautifully piped Almond and Chocolate Spritz Cookies, and the Peanut Butter Thumbprints, sporting a new shape for an old favorite, with a lusciously chewy caramel-nut filling. If fruit is your favorite, try the Raspberry-Cherry Crumble Bars with buttery shortbread sandwiching an easy, delicious filling, or the refreshingly tart Classic Lemon Bars, wearing their topcoat of confectioners' sugar.

Baking cookies is considered easy and fun—child's play, really. Simply mix up the dough, drop it on a pan, pop it in the oven, and in no time you're happily devouring little bites of heaven. Unless something went wrong and you've pulled from the oven flat little pancakes or little burned rocks. Luckily, over time a set of guidelines and tips have emerged to help even a beginning baker produce the best possible cookies—those that are reliably delicious, uniformly shaped, and perfect every time.

If you're new to baking, or just want to improve your cookie-making prowess, take a few minutes to read through the introductory material below before you begin to bake.

A Primer on Cookies

TYPES OF COOKIES

Cookies are categorized either by their mixing method or the technique used to shape them.

MIXING METHODS

THE CREAMING METHOD By far the most commonly used mixing method, the creaming of butter and sugar is the beginning step for many cookies, bar cookies, and brownies. Butter and sugar are beaten until creamy, followed by the slow addition of eggs, then the brief blending in of the dry ingredients at the end.

It's important that you do not overbeat the butter and sugar; if you do, your cookies will spread and flatten in the oven. Why does this happen? Remember that creaming builds a vast network of air bubbles that will expand on contact with chemical leavening and the heat of the oven. The multitude of bubbles works wonders with batters in a cake pan, where the expanding batter has no choice but to rise straight up the sides of the pan. Cookies, however, are baked "free-form" on a baking sheet, and if the batter is full of air bubbles there is only one way the cookies can "rise" when the bubbles expand—outward in every direction, thereby creating flat cookies.

To avoid overcreaming, beat for only 1 to 2 minutes, until the butter and sugar are smooth and lump-free but not lightened in color. The eggs are then added one at a time and blended fully with the butter and sugar. Whisk together the dry ingredients in a separate bowl. (There is no need to sift unless the ingredients are quite lumpy, such as confectioners' sugar, cocoa powder, baking soda, and the like.) Turn the mixer off, scrape down the bowl, and add all the dry ingredients at once (if it's a very large amount of flour, you may need to add it in several batches). With the mixer on the lowest speed, beat the mixture just until it's smooth and homogenous. Now it's ready to be formed into cookies.

THE SPONGE METHOD This approach involves whipping the eggs, usually with the sugar, for at least 3 to 5 minutes until they are very light and thick enough to hold a 3-second "ribbon" (see page 303). It creates a fine-grained, open crumb in the cookie. This same method is used for creating the light and airy texture in a classic sponge cake, hence the name. The sponge method is used here to make Mexican Chocolate Crackle Cookies (page 286), where the air in the whipped eggs causes a dramatic rise and the equally dramatic cracks that are characteristic of this confectioners' sugar–dusted cookie.

THE ONE-STEP METHOD All the ingredients are added to the mixing bowl and blended until the correct consistency is reached. This method is most commonly used for shortbread (page 280), particularly the famous shortbread cookie in France known as *sablée* or "sandy"—a name that succinctly describes its texture. For shortbread, cold butter, cut into small cubes, is combined with the other ingredients, then mixed on medium speed with the paddle attachment. The butter pieces become smaller and smaller and eventually completely blend with the dry ingredients. At that precise moment, the dough is formed. This method may be adapted to the food processor with quick and easy results. Simply place all of the ingredients in the bowl of a food processor, then let it run until a dough forms.

SHAPING TECHNIQUES

Once the dough has been made, cookies can be further categorized based on how the dough is shaped and baked.

DROPPED Cookies are pushed from a spoon (or, in the case of professional bakers, from an ice cream scoop) onto the baking sheet, as in Chocolate Chip Cookies (page 273) and Cherry Oatmeal Cookies (page 274).

MOLDED OR SHAPED Cookies shaped by hand or rolled into balls include Mexican Chocolate Crackle Cookies (page 286) and Peanut Butter Thumbprints with Peanut Caramel (page 275). If the cookie is to be rolled into a ball shape, sometimes a small ice cream scoop is used instead of rolling by hand.

PIPED OR SPRITZ Cookies are shaped by forcing the dough through a cookie press or the tip of a piping bag, as with the Almond-Chocolate Spritz Cookies with Orange Blossom Water (page 278).

ROLLED OR CUTOUT Cookie dough is rolled thinly, then cut into shapes using cookie cutters or a sharp knife; see Classic Sugar Cookies (page 282).

ICEBOX OR SLICE-AND-BAKE Cookies are shaped into logs, chilled until firm, then sliced and baked, as in Chocolate–Earl Grey Shortbread Coins (page 280).

FILLED Cookies can be pressed with a thumb or the rounded end of a kitchen utensil to create a depression that can hold a filling. They can also be sandwiched with filling either before or after baking. Peanut Butter Thumbprints with Peanut Caramel (page 275) and Classic Sugar Sandwich Cookies (page 283) are filled cookies.

BAR OR SHEET These cookies are baked as a single large piece, then cut into smaller pieces later. Classic Fudgy Brownies (page 290), Cappuccino Biscotti with Hazelnuts and Chocolate (page 288), Peanut Butter and Chocolate Marble Brownies (page 292), Classic Lemon Bars (page 295), and Raspberry-Cherry Crumble Bars (page 296) all fall into this category.

STENCIL The batter is spread thinly through a stencil before baking, as with Tuiles (page 284), though they can also be baked free-form.

Shaping Spritz Cookies

Piped or pressed rosettes are elegant, but they are only one of many shapes spritz dough can take. Simply change the shape by changing the design disk in your cookie press. If you are piping the cookies by hand, take comfort in knowing you are following in the tradition of the original spritz cookies. When they're piped by hand, you have the opportunity to shape the cookies into all sorts of fanciful forms, from elegant scrolls to letters of the alphabet. As long as the various shapes are the same thickness and similar in size, they will all bake in the same amount of time.

Pipe rosettes (see page 310) on a prepared baking sheet, spacing the cookies about 1 inch apart. The rosettes should be about 1¾ inches in diameter.

A cookie press allows you to create a variety of shapes depending on the design disk you use, and it is easier to make your cookies a consistent size. Follow the manufacturer's instructions for your model for best results.

THE BUILDING BLOCKS OF COOKIES

BUTTER

There is no substitute for the wonderful flavor of butter in cookies. Butter also adds fat, which creates tenderness by coating the strands of protein in the flour and therefore preventing gluten from forming (gluten development can cause tough cookies). Butter makes cookies crisp and helps hold the air bubbles, formed during creaming, that expand in the heat of the oven. Butter also helps cookies to brown beautifully because of the milk solids in its fat.

The drawback to butter is its low melting point, which can make cookies lose their shape in the oven. Butter melts almost immediately upon contact with heat. If the butter melts before the starches and proteins in the flour have a chance to set enough to provide a solid structure, the cookie can't hold its shape and will flatten. This is why it's important to always chill butter cookie dough before baking. The few extra minutes it takes for cold butter to melt is usually enough time for the structure of the cookie to set, retaining the shape of the cookie.

Many people avoid this melting-butter issue by using shortening in their cookies. Because shortening has a much higher melting point, the cookie structure has plenty of time to set before the shortening melts. In fact, you've probably seen pictures showing the difference between bakery-perfect cookies made with shortening and flat cookies made with butter, in an effort to convince you that shortening is better for cookies. Don't believe it. Yes, made with the same recipe and baked when the dough is room temperature, the butter cookies will flatten, but this can be corrected by simply chilling the dough before baking. Using shortening in cookies means a big trade-off in flavor. All the recipes in this chapter were tested using butter. One note: Be sure to use unsalted butter, or your cookies will be too salty.

SUGAR

The choice of sweetener can dramatically affect both the flavor and appearance of cookies. White granulated sugar is most commonly used because it sweetens without adding extra flavor, browns beautifully, and helps cookies to stay crisp. Brown sugar, which is basically white sugar blended with molasses, acts differently in cookies because it brings in an additional layer of flavor. The acidic nature of molasses helps the eggs in cookie dough to set up quickly, which means cookies are more likely to keep their shape in the oven heat. The presence of molasses also makes brown sugar more hygroscopic than white sugar, which means it absorbs more moisture—great for keeping cookies moist and soft. (So don't use brown sugar in cookies that should stay crisp.)

Some people like to sweeten with honey, which, like brown sugar, contributes moistness while adding its own flavor. Remember that honey is sweeter than sugar, so you will need to use less when substituting for sugar. Honey is even more hygroscopic than brown sugar and cookies made with it will always become quite soft upon standing. Corn syrup, in contrast, helps cookies stay crisp and has an amazing ability to make baked goods brown. So, if your cookies are not brown enough but you like the flavor, try replacing 1 or 2 tablespoons of sugar with light corn syrup—you'll be amazed by the results (keep in mind, though, that the cookies will also be crisper than your original).

EGGS

Because they are able to trap air bubbles during the beating process, which then expand in the heat of oven, eggs aid in the rise of cookies. In addition, the protein in eggs act as glue, preventing cookies from crumbling. That same protein also aids in the browning of cookies. If the cookies contain acidic ingredients, such as brown sugar, molasses, cocoa powder, or chocolate, the proteins in the egg will set quickly, helping to preserve the domed shape of the cookies.

FLOUR

Nearly every cookie recipe calls for all-purpose flour. But, as discussed in "The Baker's Pantry" (page 21), not every all-purpose flour is the same. Be sure to use unbleached all-purpose flour for the cookies here, both for its environmental kindness (no bleaching) as well as its higher protein content. That protein combines with the liquid ingredients to form gluten, lengthened strands of protein that provide the structure for baked goods and prevent crumbly cookies. Protein also contributes to browning and chewiness.

Nearly every cookie recipe can be doubled, tripled, or increased to your heart's content with no ill effects. Good to know when preparing for the busy holiday season or a big event such as a wedding or graduation party. The only restriction you might run into is the size of your mixer (most stand mixers will only be able to hold a double batch) or your largest mixing bowl if you use a hand mixer.

Bleached all-purpose flours, which have a much lower protein content, create very tender cookies, though they are paler in color and puffier. By using different types of flour in your cookies you can get dramatically different results, all with the same recipe. For best results with the recipes in this book, though, stick to unbleached all-purpose flour.

LEAVENER

Cookies are tiny little baked goods and don't need much leavening. Baking powder is often used in cookies without acidic ingredients, whereas baking soda is used in doughs that contain acidic components such as molasses, cocoa, lemon juice, and chocolate. Beyond this basic difference, baking soda, which is alkaline and a powerful browning agent, is often added to cookie batters to ensure a golden brown color. Too much, though, and the cookies are not only brown but also bitter because of excess chemical leavening.

FLAVORINGS

Most cookie doughs accept changes in flavorings or additions quite well, allowing you to give a recipe your personal touch. There is never a problem with just adding a bit of extract or citrus zest to a plain recipe. Begin with ½ teaspoon extract (such as almond, peppermint, or coconut), then taste and add more if needed. Remember to use pure extracts for best flavor, and if you have a wonderful flavored oil, don't use more than ¼ teaspoon, as oils have very intense flavors.

You can change the "add-ins" (such as chocolate chips and nuts) to most drop cookies at will; just keep the proportions the same. Don't want semisweet chocolate chips? Substitute white chocolate chips. Or use half milk chocolate and half white chips. Or butterscotch chips, or—well, you decide. Or simply add a handful of dried fruit in addition to the chips (a little extra won't hurt). Same with toasted chopped nuts. Change raisins to dried cranberries, dried cherries, chopped apricots, or any other plump delicious dried fruit. If the fruit seems leathery, which can ruin a cookie, put it in a bowl, cover with boiling water and let it sit for 5 minutes. Drain and pat dry with paper towels. Add chopped candied ginger chunks for a bit of zing. Or a teaspoon or two of instant espresso powder for a bit of kick.

TIPS FOR BAKING COOKIES

CHILLING THE DOUGH It's a good idea to chill the dough for most cookies before baking. Chilling helps to prevent the cookies from flattening and encourages a nice shape with a rounded center. Refrigerate the dough for 30 minutes or up to 2 days before baking.

PREPARING THE BAKING SHEETS Heavy-duty aluminum baking sheets with ½-inch sides (otherwise known as *half-sheet pans*) bake evenly and are used by all professional bakers, and there's no reason you can't use them as well. Rimless cookie sheets are fine if you own them, but are not necessary for successful cookie-baking. If you absolutely need one, simply turn a rimmed baking sheet upside down and use the bottom for baking.

Line each baking sheet with parchment paper—this ensures quick and easy removal and makes cleanup a breeze—no more greasy, stained pans or worry that cookies will stick tenaciously. If you don't have parchment paper, silicone mats do the same trick. Make sure, however, that the ones you use for cookies are very thin, as the thicker silicone liners insulate the bottom of the cookies from heat and prevent them from acquiring caramelized, golden, crispy bottoms. If you don't have either parchment or thin silicone liners, very lightly coat the pan with flavorless vegetable oil or high-heat canola-oil spray (too heavy a hand will cause the cookies to spread). Avoid butter because it burns.

PORTIONING THE DOUGH All the cookies should be the same size and shape so that they bake in the same amount of time. The best way to do this with drop cookie dough (and some shaped doughs) is to use a spring-loaded ice cream scoop. Fill the scoop to overflowing, then use your thumb (or the side of the bowl) to scrape off the excess dough until it is level with the edge of the scoop. These scoops come in all sizes, from a couple of teaspoons to

½ cup for monster cookies, so choose the size you use most often. A tablespoon-size scoop is a good size to start with, producing cookies 2 to 3 bites in size. If the dough sticks to the scoop, dip the scoop into a cup of cold water after 3 or 4 uses, shake off excess water, and continue.

If you are slicing cookies from an icebox cookie log, turning the log one-eighth of a full roll each time you slice will keep the log rounded. Make sure each slice is the same width—you may want to use a ruler to guide you. Or, simply cut the first cookie to the correct thickness, then use that one as the model while you cut the rest. This same logic applies to cookies that are rolled and cut into shapes with cookie cutters. Make sure they are the same thickness and about the same size. If you have a variety of sizes, put similar sizes together on a baking sheet—larger sizes might take an extra couple of minutes in the oven. Likewise with cookies that may be a bit thicker or thinner than the average cookie.

SPACING THE COOKIES Be sure to leave room between cookies for the dough to expand. Unless otherwise indicated, 2 inches is a safe rule of thumb.

BAKING TWO SHEETS AT A TIME Most cookies bake best if there is only one baking sheet in the oven at a time. However, if you want to bake two sheets of cookies at a time (and sometimes it's necessary), position oven racks in the top and lower thirds of the oven. Once the cookies are in the oven, set your timer for half the total baking time. When it goes off, switch the sheets' positions in the oven and rotate them front to back. If you have only one sheet, rotate it front to back. Every oven has hot spots (yes, even convection ovens), and this rotation of the baking sheets—a practice borrowed from professional bakers—ensures that all your cookies will bake evenly.

COOLING THE COOKIES Once the cookies are done, transfer the baking sheet to a cooling rack. Leave the cookies on the sheet to cool. Because so many problems occur when home bakers try to transfer warm, fragile cookies to cooling racks, it's best to allow the cookies to cool completely on the baking sheet. Professional bakers don't have the time or space to transfer 500 cookies onto cooling racks, and their cookies turn out just fine. Of course, if the cookies need to be removed while warm for shaping (as with Tuiles, page 284), then do follow those cooling instructions precisely.

REUSING BAKING SHEETS If you are baking in batches and need to reuse baking sheets, you'll have to remove the warm cookies. Let the cookies cool on the baking sheet for 5 minutes, then transfer them to a cooling rack, using a large pancake spatula. If you've baked on parchment paper it is even easier. Simply slide the sheet of parchment paper onto the cooling rack, bringing the cookies with it. Rinse the baking sheets under cold water until cool and wipe dry before baking your next batch of cookies. Hot pans will melt the butter in the cookie dough before the pan even reaches the oven, causing flat and misshapen cookies.

HOW TO STORE COOKIES

Store each type of cookie separately in airtight containers. If cookies of various types and flavors are mixed, two problems occur. First, they absorb each other's flavors and all end up tasting the same. Second, crisp cookies absorb moisture from the soft cookies and become soft and stale-tasting. Lidded tin or stainless-steel containers are the best for storage, though plastic containers can work well provided they are airtight and fragrance free (many absorb odors and your cookies can end up tasting like last week's spaghetti sauce). Hard, clear plastic seems to resist odors better than opaque plastic. Resealable plastic bags are also great for storing cookies; just be sure to press the air out of the bag before sealing it. Always layer cookies between sheets of parchment or waxed paper to prevent them from sticking together.

HOW TO FREEZE DOUGH AND COOKIES

A frozen and thawed baked cookie never provides the same satisfaction as a just-baked, warm-from-the-oven one. A much better idea is to bake only what you need, storing the rest of the dough in the freezer for fresh cookies on another day. Luckily, most cookie doughs can be portioned in advance and then frozen, ready to be baked at a moment's notice, except for stencil cookie dough, which doesn't freeze well.

Scoop or otherwise portion the cookie dough onto a parchment-lined baking sheet, placing the cookies very close together. Set the sheet in the freezer. Once the cookies are frozen solid (usually 30 to 60 minutes), transfer them to an airtight container and layer between sheets of parchment—or throw them in a resealable plastic freezer bag—and return to the freezer. Be sure to write the name of the cookies and the date you packaged them on the outside of the container. Frozen cookie dough will keep for up to 3 months. Anytime you want cookies, you need only remove the desired amount, place on parchment-lined baking sheets, and pop in the oven. The frozen dough will need a few extra minutes of baking time, so pay attention to the visual clues provided by each recipe. In some instances, you'll need to let the dough thaw at room temperature for 10 to 15 minutes (follow directions in each recipe).

Rolls of slice-and-bake cookie dough also freeze well. Simply wrap the roll in plastic, twist the ends of the plastic like a candy wrapper, and tape them against the dough so they don't unravel in the freezer. If available, slip the roll inside a cardboard paper towel tube to help the dough keep its round shape. To slice a dozen cookies, let the roll sit at room temperature for about 15 minutes, or until the roll is cold yet soft enough to slice safely.

SOME ADDITIONAL TIPS

TASTING YOUR INGREDIENTS Many cookie recipes call for chocolate, nuts, dried fruits, jams, and spices; sample these before you add them. Baking will do nothing to improve the flavor of chocolate, especially chocolate that's gone rancid (white and milk chocolates are particularly susceptible to spoiling). The same is true of unsalted butter. Make sure you use fresh, unsalted butter that is no more than a couple of weeks old (rancid butter tastes acidic, as though lemon juice has been added). Dried fruit should be moist and pliable. Nuts should taste fresh. Always toast and cool nuts completely before using them in cookie recipes. Jams should have a nice balance of sweet and tart. Spices should be replaced every 6 months for the freshest, brightest flavor.

MEASURING PRECISELY Remember that cookies are like little cakes—too much flour makes them dry, too much sugar makes them wet, too much leavener makes them bitter. While a tablespoon of flour may not affect a cake batter much, it can make a world of difference in a cookie, turning it from lusciously chewy to dry and crumbly. A digital scale is recommended for all your bulk measuring—if you use dry cup measures, be as precise as possible (see page 3 for more measuring help).

TIMING PRECISELY A timer is indispensable. Just an extra minute or two in the oven can transform cookies from done to overdone. A timer keeps you on track, even in the midst of day-to-day household chaos.

CHOCOLATE CHIP COOKIES

MAKES ABOUT 60 COOKIES There's a reason Realtors like to bake these cookies when showing a house to potential buyers. Few among us can resist the mouthwatering aroma of butter, brown sugar, and chocolate that reminds us of all things warm and wonderful. There are many versions of this American classic–this is a favorite, bursting with chunks of both semisweet and milk chocolate, with an extra splash of vanilla added for a deep, round flavor.

INGREDIENTS

1½ sticks (6 ounces) unsalted butter, softened (65° to 68°F)

¾ cup (5¼ ounces) granulated sugar

¾ cup (6 ounces) firmly packed light brown sugar

2 large eggs, at room temperature

2 teaspoons pure vanilla extract

2¼ cups (11¼ ounces) unbleached all-purpose flour

1 teaspoon baking soda

1 teaspoon salt

6 ounces good-quality semisweet or bittersweet chocolate, chopped into ¼-inch chunks, or 1 cup (7 ounces) dark chocolate chips

6 ounces good-quality milk chocolate, chopped into ¼-inch chunks, or 1 cup (7 ounces) milk chocolate chips

½ cup (2¼ ounces) chopped nuts (walnuts, almonds, pecans, or hazelnuts), chopped, toasted, and completely cooled (optional)

EQUIPMENT

Two or Three Baking Sheets, Parchment Paper, Stand Mixer Fitted with a Paddle Attachment or a Hand Mixer and a Medium Bowl, Silicone or Rubber Spatula, Medium Bowl, Small Ice Cream Scoop, Cooling Rack

GETTING AHEAD You can make the dough up to 3 days ahead and refrigerate it in an airtight container. For nearly-spur-of-the-moment cookies, portion the dough onto a baking sheet lined with parchment paper, putting the scoops right next to each other to fit all of them on one sheet. Place the pan in the freezer for 30 to 60 minutes, until the balls of dough are frozen. Transfer the cookie dough balls to a resealable plastic freezer bag and freeze until needed, up to 3 months. To bake, take out as many cookies as you need, space them on a parchment-lined baking sheet, and bake as directed, adding a couple of minutes to the baking time.

1 Preheat the oven to 350°F and position an oven rack in the center. Line the baking sheets with parchment paper.

2 Place the butter, granulated sugar, and brown sugar in the bowl of the stand mixer and beat on medium-low speed until smooth and blended, about 2 minutes. You can also use a hand mixer and a medium bowl, although you may need to beat the mixture a little longer to achieve the same results. Scrape down the bowl with a spatula. Add the eggs one at a time and beat just until blended after each addition. Add the vanilla and blend well. Scrape down the bowl.

3 In a medium bowl, whisk together the flour, baking soda, and salt. Turn the mixer to the lowest speed and add the flour mixture all at once. Blend just until there are no more patches of flour. Scrape down the bowl.

4 Add the semisweet and milk chocolate chunks and the nuts (if using), and blend on low just until combined. Remove the bowl from the mixer and stir gently a few times with the spatula to make sure there are no more patches of unincorporated flour or butter lurking near the bottom of the bowl.

5 Using the small ice cream scoop or spoon, portion tablespoon-size mounds onto the prepared baking sheets, spacing them about 2 inches apart. Bake the cookies one sheet at a time, rotating the sheet halfway through, for 10 to 14 minutes, until the cookies are golden brown at the edges and still a bit pale in the center. If you want crisp cookies instead of chewy ones, bake for a couple of extra minutes. (To bake more than one sheet at a time, see page 271.) Transfer the cookies to a cooling rack and let them cool completely before serving.

STORING Keep the cooled cookies in an airtight container at room temperature for 3 to 4 days.

CHERRY OATMEAL COOKIES

MAKES ABOUT 50 COOKIES This variation on the classic oatmeal cookie is crisp at the edges, soft in the center, and plump with dried sour cherries. The tart cherries are the ideal contrast to the sweetly comforting dough, but you can substitute raisins, dried cranberries, or any other moist dried fruit you like.

INGREDIENTS

1 stick (4 ounces) unsalted butter, softened (65° to 68°F)

½ cup (4 ounces) firmly packed light brown sugar

¼ cup plus 1 tablespoon (2 ounces) granulated sugar

1 large egg

1 teaspoon pure vanilla extract

1 cup (5 ounces) unbleached all-purpose flour

¼ teaspoon baking soda

¼ teaspoon baking powder

¼ teaspoon salt

¾ cup (3¼ ounces) old-fashioned rolled oats

¾ cup (3½ ounces) dried sour cherries

EQUIPMENT

Two or Three Baking Sheets, Stand Mixer Fitted with a Paddle Attachment or a Hand Mixer and a Medium Bowl, Silicone or Rubber Spatula, Medium Bowl, Whisk, Small Ice Cream Scoop, Parchment Paper, Cooling Rack

GETTING AHEAD **You can make the dough up to 3 days ahead and refrigerate it in an airtight container. For nearly-spur-of-the-moment cookies, portion the dough onto a parchment-lined baking sheet, putting the scoops right next to each other to fit all of them on one sheet. Place in the freezer for 30 to 60 minutes, until the balls of dough are frozen. Transfer the cookie dough balls to a resealable plastic freezer bag and freeze until needed, up to 3 months. To bake, take out as many cookies as you need, space them on a parchment-lined baking sheet, and bake as directed, adding a couple of minutes to the baking time.**

1 Preheat the oven to 350°F and position an oven rack in the center of the oven. Line the baking sheets with parchment paper.

2 Place the butter, brown sugar, and granulated sugar in the bowl of the stand mixer and beat on medium speed until smooth and blended, about 2 minutes. You can also use a hand mixer and a medium bowl, although you may need to beat the mixture a little longer to achieve the same results. Scrape down the bowl with the spatula. Add the egg and vanilla and blend well.

3 In a medium bowl, whisk together the flour, baking soda, baking powder, and salt. Add to the butter mixture all at once. Turn the mixer to the lowest speed and blend slowly, just until there are no more patches of flour. Scrape down the bowl.

4 Add the oats and cherries and blend on low just until combined. Remove the bowl from the mixer and stir gently a few times with the spatula to make sure there are no more patches of unincorporated flour or butter lurking near the bottom of the bowl.

5 Using the small ice cream scoop or a spoon, portion tablespoon-size mounds onto the prepared baking sheets, spacing them about 2 inches apart. Bake the cookies one sheet at a time, rotating the sheet halfway through, for 13 to 16 minutes, until the cookies are golden brown at the edges and still a bit pale in the center. (To bake more than one sheet at a time, see page 271.) Transfer to a cooling rack and let the cookies cool completely.

STORING **Keep the cooled cookies in an airtight container at room temperature for 3 to 4 days.**

Cherry-Chocolate Chip Oatmeal Cookies Add ½ to ¾ cup chocolate chips (or your favorite eating chocolate cut into ¼-inch chunks) to the dough with the oatmeal and dried cherries. Milk chocolate or white chocolate chips may be substituted for dark chocolate if you like, or use a combination of all three. Bake as directed above.

PEANUT BUTTER THUMBPRINTS WITH PEANUT CARAMEL

MAKES ABOUT 50 COOKIES These are your favorite peanut butter cookies, all dressed up and ready for a party. Their centers are filled with a mixture of salted peanuts coated with caramel sauce, and their tops are drizzled with chocolate. You'll end up with more peanut caramel sauce than you need for this recipe, but it's hard to make it in a smaller quantity. Store any extra in the refrigerator (it keeps for several weeks) and use it whenever the mood strikes—for ice cream, fondue, toast . . . It won't hang around for long. Neither will the cookies.

INGREDIENTS

DOUGH

1 stick (4 ounces) unsalted butter, softened (65° to 68°F)

½ cup (4 ounces) firmly packed light brown sugar

½ cup (3½ ounces) granulated sugar

1 large egg

1 teaspoon pure vanilla extract

¾ cup (7½ ounces) creamy salted peanut butter (see page 276), at room temperature

1¾ cup (8¾ ounces) unbleached all-purpose flour

½ teaspoon baking soda

¼ teaspoon salt

PEANUT CARAMEL

1 cup (8 ounces) heavy whipping cream

½ cup (4 ounces) water

1 cup (7 ounces) granulated sugar

1 tablespoon light corn syrup

⅛ teaspoon salt

¾ cup (4 ounces) finely chopped roasted salted peanuts

4 ounces semisweet or bittersweet chocolate, finely chopped and melted (optional)

EQUIPMENT

Two Baking Sheets, Parchment Paper, Stand Mixer Fitted with a Paddle Attachment or a Hand Mixer and a Medium Bowl, Silicone or Rubber Spatula, Medium Bowl, Whisk, Small Ice Cream Scoop, Wooden Spoon, Cooling Rack, Small Microwave-Safe Bowl, Medium Saucepan, Heatproof Silicone Spatula, Medium Heatproof Bowl

1 Preheat the oven to 350°F and position two oven racks in the upper and lower thirds. Line the baking sheets with parchment paper.

2 MIX THE DOUGH: Place the butter, brown sugar, and granulated sugar in the bowl of the stand mixer and beat on medium speed until smooth and blended, about 2 minutes. You can also use a hand mixer and a medium bowl, although you may need to beat the mixture a little longer to achieve the same results. Scrape down the bowl with the spatula. Add the egg and vanilla and blend well. Scrape down the bowl again. Add the peanut butter, beat until well blended, and scrape down the bowl once more.

3 In the medium bowl, whisk together the flour, baking soda, and salt. Add to the butter mixture all at once. Turn the mixer to the lowest speed and blend slowly, just until there are no more patches of flour. Scrape down the bowl. Remove the bowl from the mixer and stir gently a few times with the spatula to make sure there are no patches of unincorporated flour or butter lurking near the bottom of the bowl.

4 Use the ice cream scoop to portion tablespoon-size mounds onto the prepared baking sheets, spacing them about 1½ inches apart. Or use a spoon to portion the dough, then roll each piece into a ball between your hands and place on the prepared sheets, about 20

While natural peanut butter is light years better in flavor than the commercial varieties, its delicious, earthy flavor doesn't translate well to cookies. Cookies made with it are usually disappointingly dry and crumbly. The addition of hydrogenated oils in the commercial peanut butters, along with the extra sugar they possess, gives the cookies just the right texture. You can adjust for the difference in textures between the two types of peanut butters, but it takes a bit of experimentation. In the meantime, stick with the commercial variety.

GETTING AHEAD You can make the dough up to 3 days ahead and refrigerate it in an airtight container. For nearly-spur-of-the-moment cookies, portion the dough onto a baking sheet lined with parchment paper, putting the scoops right next to each other to fit all of them on one pan. Place the pan in the freezer for 30 to 60 minutes, until the balls of dough are frozen. Transfer the balls to a resealable plastic freezer bag and freeze until needed, for up to 3 months. To bake, take out as many cookies as you need, space them on a parchment-lined baking sheet, and let them defrost for 30 minutes. Make the depression in the center of each one and fill and bake as directed.

cookies per sheet. Use the rounded handle end of the wooden spoon (or another kitchen utensil) to make a depression, about an inch in diameter, in the center of each cookie.

5 Bake the cookies, switching the sheets between the racks and rotating each front to back halfway through, for 13 to 16 minutes, until they are lightly golden brown all over and a bit darker at the edges. Transfer to a cooling rack. Immediately reinforce the depression in each cookie using the same kitchen utensil. Be careful not to push so hard that you crack the cookie or break through to the baking sheet below. Cool and reline one of the baking sheets, and bake the remaining cookie dough as directed. Let the cookies cool completely.

6 MAKE THE PEANUT CARAMEL: Microwave the cream in the small, microwave-safe bowl just until hot. Set aside. Place the water in the medium saucepan and add the sugar, corn syrup, and salt. (The pan will seem too large, but when the cream is added the mixture will rise dramatically.) Cook the sugar mixture over medium heat, stirring occasionally with the heatproof spatula, until the sugar dissolves. Set the hot cream on the counter next to the stovetop. Turn the heat to high and cook the sugar mixture, occasionally swirling the pan (not stirring) so that the sugar cooks evenly, until it turns a golden brown. Immediately turn off the heat and whisk in the cream, adding it in a slow, steady stream. Whisk to blend the caramel well. Pour into the heatproof bowl and let cool until warm and pourable (if it becomes cold and thick, simply reheat in the microwave until fluid again). Stir in the peanuts.

7 FILL THE COOKIES: Spoon peanut caramel into the depressions of each cookie. Allow the filling to cool and set for an hour before finishing with the chocolate (if using). Cover and refrigerate any leftover peanut caramel to use another day.

8 TOP WITH THE CHOCOLATE: Place the melted chocolate in a small resealable plastic bag. Snip a small hole in the corner of the bag and stripe the chocolate over the top of the cookies. Allow the chocolate to cool and harden completely before transferring the cookies to a storage container.

STORING **Keep the cooled cookies in an airtight container at room temperature for 3 to 4 days.**

Peanut Butter-Chocolate Thumbprints Make and bake the
cookies as directed above, but fill the centers with Dark Chocolate Ganache (page 412) instead of caramel. Allow the filling to cool and set completely before storing.

Classic Crosshatch Peanut Butter Cookies Make the cookie
dough as directed above (substitute crunchy peanut butter—not natural-style—if desired). Scoop tablespoon-size mounds onto parchment-lined baking sheets, spacing them about 1½ inches apart. Use the tines of a fork to press down firmly on the top of each cookie in two directions, forming the classic crosshatch pattern (dip the tines of the fork in sugar if they stick to the dough). Bake, switching the sheets between the racks and rotating each front to back halfway through, for 9 to 10 minutes, until golden brown around the edges. Cool and store in an airtight container at room temperature for up to 5 days.

AN ASSORTMENT OF COOKIES (CLOCKWISE): Cappuccino Biscotti with Hazelnuts and Chocolate; Almond Chocolate Spritz Cookies with Orange Blossom Water; Classic Sugar Cookies (Sandwich Cookie variation); Peanut Butter Thumbprints with Peanut Caramel

ALMOND-CHOCOLATE SPRITZ COOKIES WITH ORANGE BLOSSOM WATER

MAKES ABOUT 45 (2-INCH) COOKIES Buttery spritz cookies, the much-anticipated standard on the holiday cookie platter, deserve to be enjoyed all year-round. Instead of saving these for special occasions, why not make some to enjoy with a cup of tea, as an after-school snack, or with a bowl of ice cream? These are deeply almond due to the inclusion of almond paste, with a lovely tender crumb and enough structure to support a pool of dark chocolate in the center. The orange blossom water, with its delicate perfume of white citrus flowers, lends another subtle layer of flavor. If you can't find orange blossom water, substitute vanilla extract, which will impart its own unique floral notes to the dough.

INGREDIENTS

DOUGH

½ cup (5 ounces) firmly packed almond paste (do not substitute marzipan)

¾ cup (5¼ ounces) sugar

1¾ sticks (7 ounces) unsalted butter, softened (65° to 68°F)

1 large egg plus 1 yolk

1 teaspoon orange blossom water or pure vanilla extract

2 cups (10 ounces) unbleached all-purpose flour

Pinch of salt

CHOCOLATE FILLING

2 ounces semisweet or bittersweet chocolate (up to 56 percent cacao), finely chopped

1 tablespoon heavy whipping cream

EQUIPMENT

Stand Mixer Fitted with a Paddle Attachment or a Food Processor Fitted with a Metal Blade, Silicone or Rubber Spatula, Two Baking Sheets, Parchment Paper, Large Pastry Bag Fitted with a ½-inch Open Star Tip or a Cookie Press, Wooden Spoon, Small Microwave-Safe Bowl

1 MIX THE DOUGH: Place the almond paste and sugar in the bowl of the stand mixer (or in the food processor). Beat on medium speed for 1½ to 2 minutes (or process for 45 seconds), until the almond paste is broken into tiny pieces. Add the butter and continue to beat for another 2 minutes (or process for 1 minute), until the mixture is well blended and slightly lighter in color. Scrape down the sides of the bowl with the spatula.

2 Add the egg and yolk and blend well (or process for 15 seconds). Add the orange blossom water and beat another 15 seconds to blend (or process for 5 seconds). Scrape down the sides of the bowl. Add the flour and salt. Turn the mixer to the lowest speed and blend slowly (or process for 10 to 15 seconds), just until there are no more patches of flour. Remove the bowl and stir gently a few times with the spatula to make sure there are no patches of unincorporated flour or butter lurking near the bottom of the bowl.

3 SHAPE THE DOUGH: Line the baking sheets with parchment paper. Immediately spoon half of the dough into the pastry bag fitted with the star tip. Pipe rosettes (see page 310) on a prepared baking sheet, spacing the cookies about 1 inch apart. (Alternatively, use the cookie press according to the manufacturer's instructions.) The rosettes should be about ½ inch thick and about 1¾ inches in diameter. Repeat with the remaining dough. Chill the sheets in the refrigerator for 30 minutes.

4 Preheat the oven to 350°F and position two oven racks in the upper and lower thirds.

5 Bake the cookies, switching the sheets between the racks and rotating each front to back halfway through, for 15 to 20 minutes, until the cookies are rich, golden brown around the edges and across the bottom. Transfer to a cooling rack.

6 Immediately use the rounded handle end of the wooden spoon (or another kitchen utensil) to make a depression in the center of each cookie about ½ inch across. Be careful not to push so hard that you crack the cookie or break through to the baking sheet below. Let the cookies cool completely.

7 FILL THE COOKIES: Place the chopped chocolate and cream in the microwave-safe bowl and microwave on low for 30 seconds. Stir the mixture. Heat again for 30 seconds and stir until smooth. If there are still lumps, heat again for 30 seconds. Once smooth, spoon a little chocolate into each depression in the cookies. Allow the filling to cool and set completely.

STORING **These cookies are at their best the first or second day. Keep them in an airtight container, layered between sheets of parchment or waxed paper to keep them from sticking to each other, for up to 4 days.**

Almond Spritz Cookies with Apricot or Raspberry Jam

Make the cookie dough and bake as directed above, but instead of chocolate for the centers, use good-quality apricot or raspberry jam and fill the cookies while they are still warm. You'll need about ¼ cup (2¾ ounces) of jam (or a little bit more if there are seeds or chunks of fruit in the jam). Warm the jam in a small saucepan or in the microwave; then, to remove any large lumps or seeds, push it though a medium strainer into a bowl. Spoon the warm jam into the warm cookies and allow them to finish cooling together (this warm jam into warm cookies trick gives the jam a shiny, professional finish). Any leftover jam can be returned to the jar and used another day. For an extra layer of flavor and a beautiful finish, melt an ounce or two of dark chocolate and stripe it over the filled and cooled cookies.

CHOCOLATE-EARL GREY SHORTBREAD COINS

MAKES ABOUT 36 COOKIES Deeply chocolaty and delicately nubby from the texture of Earl Grey tea leaves, these are cookies for adults. Earl Grey, black tea flavored with bergamot oil (from a variety of bitter orange called bergamot), is an inspired match for dark chocolate. For the best flavor, use a top-quality bulk tea, which can often be purchased at your local coffee house. Serve the cookies with a cup of the tea—or any time you want a sophisticated cookie. Without tea leaves, they are a wonderful chocolate shortbread cookie that even children will love. The dough can also be rolled out and cut into shapes as directed in the variation at the end of the recipe.

INGREDIENTS

¼ cup (1¾ ounces) granulated sugar

1 tablespoon (¼ ounce) good-quality Earl Grey tea leaves

1 stick (4 ounces) cold unsalted butter, cut into ½-inch pieces

¾ cup (3¾ ounces) unbleached all-purpose flour

3 tablespoons (¾ ounce) unsweetened cocoa powder, either Dutch-process or natural

⅛ teaspoon salt

3 tablespoons sanding or decorator's sugar (optional) (page 25)

EQUIPMENT

Food Processor Fitted with a Metal Blade, Silicone or Rubber Spatula, Thin Knife, Baking Sheet, Parchment Paper, Cooling Rack

1 Place the granulated sugar and tea leaves in the bowl of the food processor and grind for 1 minute, or until the leaves are very finely chopped. Add the butter, flour, cocoa, and salt and process for about 45 seconds. Scrape down the bowl and break up any large clumps with the spatula. Process for another 15 to 30 seconds, until the dough looks uniformly dark and forms large, shaggy clumps. Dump the dough out onto a work surface and knead gently several times, just to bring it together.

2 Squeeze the dough into a log about 12 inches long and about 1 inch in diameter, and gently roll it back and forth until smooth. Don't add flour if the dough is sticky—simply refrigerate the dough for 15 or 20 minutes to firm up the butter, then try again.

3 If you like, sprinkle the sanding sugar on the work surface alongside the log and gently roll the log in the sugar, turning to coat evenly. Cut a piece of plastic wrap several inches longer than the log and center the log at one long edge of the wrap. Roll the log into the wrap so it is tightly bound by the plastic. Twist the ends of the wrap to secure the log and help to create a rounded shape. You can use a cardboard paper towel roll to keep the roll of dough nicely rounded during storage. Just slit the cardboard lengthwise and slip the log inside it to help keep the rounded shape. Refrigerate for 2 hours.

4 Preheat the oven to 300°F and position an oven rack in the center. Line the baking sheet with parchment paper.

5 Remove the cardboard and plastic wrap from the dough log and use a thin knife to slice it into ⅜-inch-thick rounds. Place about 18 cookies 1 inch apart on the prepared

GETTING AHEAD The dough can be held for 3 days in the refrigerator. For nearly-spur-of-the-moment cookies, bake only what you need for the day, then store the dough log (still in the cardboard tube) in the freezer for up to 2 months. To bake, thaw overnight in the refrigerator, or, if you're in a hurry, thaw on the counter for 10 to 15 minutes, just until soft enough to slice safely. Space them on a baking sheet and bake as directed.

baking sheet. Bake, rotating the sheet halfway through the baking time, for 30 minutes, or until the cookies are cooked through and look dry on top. (It's difficult to tell when dark chocolate cookies are done. This is when an oven thermometer and a timer are your best friends in the kitchen.) Transfer the cookies to a cooling rack and let them cool completely.

STORING Keep the cooled cookies in an airtight container at room temperature for up to 1 week.

Chocolate-Cocoa Nib Shortbread Cookies

Cocoa nibs are the cracked and roasted interior of cocoa beans—chocolate before it becomes chocolate. They are bitter (think coffee beans) and deeply flavored—and divine in this grown-up cookie. Omit the tea and make the dough as directed. Add an additional 2 tablespoons of flour to the dough (for a total of 1 cup minus 2 tablespoons, or 4¼ ounces). When the dough has finished mixing, add ¼ cup (1 ounce) roasted cocoa nibs to the processor and pulse 4 or 5 times to mix into the dough. Shape and bake as directed.

Cutout Shortbread Cookies

Shape the prepared dough into a flat disk, wrap in plastic, and refrigerate for 15 to 20 minutes to chill slightly. Lightly dust your work surface and the top of the dough with flour and roll the dough into a 10½-inch circle about ⅜-inch thick. Alternatively, roll the dough between two sheets of parchment or wax paper (see page 282, Step 3). Chill the dough for 30 minutes. Cut into shapes using the cookie cutter of your choice and transfer to parchment-lined baking sheets. To reroll scraps, brush any flour from the top and bottom of the dough, knead gently to bring together, and roll again. If the dough is sticky, chill it for 15 to 20 minutes and try again. Once all the cookies are cut, transfer the baking sheet(s) to the refrigerator and chill the cutout cookies for 30 minutes; then bake and store as directed. The size of your cookie cutter will affect the yield of the recipe—you may get only 1 to 2 dozen cookies.

CLASSIC SUGAR COOKIES

MAKES 40 TO 50 COOKIES Here's a deliciously crisp and tender sugar cookie that can assume many shapes and be served as is, or sandwiched with jam, chocolate, or your favorite filling. The cookies also make a great canvas for decorating at holiday times.

INGREDIENTS

2¼ cups (11¼ ounces) unbleached all-purpose flour

¾ cup (5¼ ounces) plus 2 tablespoons sugar

¼ teaspoon salt

2 sticks (8 ounces) cold unsalted butter, cut into ½-inch pieces

2 large egg yolks

2 teaspoons pure vanilla extract

EQUIPMENT

Stand Mixer Fitted with a Paddle Attachment or a Hand Mixer and a Medium Bowl, Small Bowl, Whisk, Parchment Paper, Rolling Pin, Three Baking Sheets, Cookie Cutters, Fine-Mesh Strainer, Cooling Rack

1 Place the flour, ¾ cup of the sugar, and the salt in the bowl of the stand mixer and beat on low speed for 15 seconds, just to blend the ingredients. You can also use a hand mixer and a medium bowl, though it may take a little longer to achieve the same results. Add the butter and mix on low until the butter is broken into tiny pieces, 2 to 3 minutes. Turn the mixer to medium-low and mix until the mixture forms small clumps about the size of peas, 2 to 3 minutes longer.

2 In the small bowl, whisk together the egg yolks and vanilla. Add the egg mixture to the butter mixture and blend on medium-low until the dough comes together to form several large clumps. Turn the dough out onto a work surface and knead several times, just to bring it together. Divide the dough in half and shape each half into a disk about ½ inch thick. Wrap the disks in plastic and refrigerate for about 30 minutes, or until cold but still pliable.

3 Place one disk of dough between two sheets of parchment or waxed paper and roll ⅛ inch thick. If the dough cracks when you start to roll, it may be too cold. Let it sit for 10 minutes, then try again—this dough rolls most easily when it is at cool room temperature. As you roll, the parchment will wrinkle, especially on the bottom. When this happens, peel off the top parchment paper, smooth out any wrinkles, and place it back on the dough. Flip the dough over and repeat with the paper on the other side. You may need to do this several times during the rolling process. Note: The dough may also be rolled out on a lightly floured work surface, but be sure to brush any excess flour from the top and bottom of the dough before chilling and baking (the parchment method is easier and cleaner). Place the rolled-out dough, with the parchment still attached, on a baking sheet and transfer to the refrigerator to chill for 30 minutes. Repeat with the remaining disk of dough.

4 Remove the parchment from top and bottom of one piece of rolled out dough and place the dough on your work surface. Line the baking sheet with new parchment paper. Use cookie cutters to cut the dough into desired shapes and transfer to the parchment-lined sheet, spacing the cookies about 1½ inches apart. Stack the cookies on the sheet pan with a piece of parchment paper between each layer. Scraps of dough can be gently kneaded and then rerolled, but the more they are rerolled, the less tender the cookies, so strategically place your cookie cutters to leave as few scraps as possible. Repeat with the remaining sheet of dough. Chill the cut shapes while the oven preheats.

GETTING AHEAD **At the end of Step 2, the dough can be wrapped airtight and chilled for up to 3 days, or frozen for up to 2 months. You may find it even more convenient to chill or freeze the cutout dough at the end of Step 4, wrapping the entire baking sheet. There is no need to thaw the frozen shapes before baking—simply add a minute or two to the baking time.**

5 Preheat the oven to 375°F and position an oven rack in the center. Sprinkle the cookies on each baking sheet with some of the remaining 2 tablespoons of sugar (you may not use it all) just before they go into the oven. Bake one pan at a time, rotating the sheet about halfway through, for 10 to 13 minutes, until light golden brown. Transfer to a rack to cool completely. Repeat with the remaining cookie shapes. Decorate the cookies as desired or leave them plain and simple.

STORING **The cookies can be stored in an airtight container, layered between sheets of parchment or waxed paper, at room temperature for up to 1 week.**

Sandwich Cookies

Cut the dough into shapes using a cutter with a simple shape, such as a square or circle. Leave half of the shapes solid, and transfer to baking sheets. Bake and cool as directed. Cut a hole in the center of the remaining cookies using a smaller cutter. For instance, if you used a 2-inch cutter for all your cookies, use a ¾-inch cutter to cut windows in half of the cookies. You can use a cutter of the same shape, or cut the window with a mini cookie cutter that matches the season or occasion (trees for Christmas, bunnies for Easter, houses for a housewarming party, flowers for a gardener, etc.). Again, bake and cool as directed. When the cookies have all cooled, spread about 1 teaspoon of jam (or ganache, page 412, Nutella, or your favorite spread) on the solid cookies, which will be the bottom of the sandwich. Dust the cut-out "window" cookies with confectioners' sugar. Carefully lift each window cookie and place it over the jam, lining it up with the edges of the bottom cookies. Makes 30 to 35 sandwich cookies.

Sugar Cookie Pillows

Scoop the prepared dough into tablespoon-size balls (a small ice cream scoop is handy here). Chill or freeze airtight until needed. Roll each ball in sugar and place about 2 inches apart on a parchment-lined baking sheet. Using the bottom of a juice glass, slightly flatten each ball to about ¼ inch thick. Bake at 375°F for 12 to 14 minutes, until lightly golden brown around the edges. Transfer to a rack to cool completely.

TUILES

MAKES 13 OR 14 LARGE (4-INCH) ROUND COOKIES, OR 20 TO 25 SMALLER ROUND OR VARIOUSLY SHAPED COOKIES

Thin and shatteringly crisp, a tuile (French for "tile") is a vanilla-scented wafer cookie baked into a thin round, then laid over a rolling pin while warm so that it cools into the gently curved shape of a terra-cotta roof tile. The batter is a snap to make and the cookies bake quickly, but do require your attention while shaping and cooling. Some tips: Bake them on a silicone mat to ensure their easy removal while still warm; watch them carefully so they don't burn; and store them absolutely airtight, as they soften quickly. Bake only a few at a time until you get the hang of shaping the warm cookies.

INGREDIENTS

½ cup plus 2 tablespoons (4¼ ounces) sugar

½ cup (1¾ ounces) sifted cake flour

2 large egg whites

¾ teaspoon pure vanilla extract

½ stick (2 ounces) unsalted butter, melted

EQUIPMENT

Medium Bowl, Whisk, Baking Sheet, Silicone Mat, Small Offset Spatula, Stencil (Optional), Cooling Rack, Small Spatula

what the pros know

The batter for these cookies can be spread through a stencil to give the cookies a specific shape, or it can be shaped free-form with a spatula, as shown here, but be careful to make each cookie an even thickness. You can make your own stencils by cutting a pattern with a sharp knife out of an upside-down lid of a plastic tub of ricotta (or something similar). Consider leaves, flowers, long thin rectangles (for wrapping around a pencil to form spirals), or even spoon shapes, for a crisp trompe l'oeil cookie to accompany ice cream or mousse.

1 Place the sugar and cake flour in the medium bowl and whisk to blend. Whisk in the egg whites and vanilla until well blended. Whisk in the melted butter until a smooth, thin batter is formed. Cover and refrigerate for 30 minutes.

2 Preheat the oven to 350°F and position an oven rack in the center. Line the baking sheet with the silicone mat. Drop about 1 tablespoon of batter onto the mat. With the offset spatula, spread the batter into a thin circle about 4 inches in diameter. Make 3 more circles, spacing them 3 to 4 inches apart. Alternately, set a stencil on the mat and use the spatula to fill the center, scraping off any excess, so the cookie is the same thickness as the stencil around it. Remove the stencil and repeat with more batter. Bake the tuiles for 7 to 9 minutes, until the edges are golden brown but the center is still pale.

3 Transfer the cookies to a rack and let cool for 1 to 2 minutes, until they can be loosened and lifted from the sheet without tearing. Use the small spatula to loosen the edges and help you lift each warm cookie off the pan and quickly shape them. For tuiles: Drape the warm cookies, smooth side down, over the top of a lightly sprayed or oiled rolling pin or dowel (at right). Let cool for 1 minute, then remove and set aside. Repeat until all the cookies are shaped. For bowls: Gently drape the warm cookies over on upside-down custard or coffee cup and use your fingers to press the warm cookie snugly against the mold. For cigarettes: Turn the warm cookies over so the smooth side is facing upward. Roll them loosely around a pencil, small dowel, or the handle of a wooden spoon or similar kitchen utensil that has been lightly sprayed or oiled (at right). Allow the cookies to cool completely before transferring them to an airtight container. Bake additional cookies on a silicone mat on a cool baking sheet (or reuse the same sheets by rinsing under cold water, then wiping dry).

GETTING AHEAD **The batter can be stored in a covered container in the refrigerator for up to 5 days.**

STORING The cookies will keep for several days in an airtight container at room temperature. However, because they are so sensitive to moisture, it's best to bake them the same day you want to serve them.

Two-Tone Tuiles

Transfer 3 tablespoons of cooled *tuile* batter to a small bowl. Stir in 1 teaspoon of cocoa powder. Transfer the chocolate batter to a resealable plastic bag or a disposable pastry bag. Snip a small hole in the corner of the bag. Use the plain batter to shape *tuiles* on the baking sheet. Pipe the chocolate batter over the top of the *tuiles,* drawing veins in leaves or detailing flowers or other shapes. To make a spider web, pipe a chocolate spiral on a round tuile from the center outward. Use a toothpick to gently draw a line through the spiral from the center to the edge, then move the toothpick over 1 inch and draw another line back toward the center. Continue in this manner until you have completed the web pattern.

Line the baking sheet with the silicone mat. To make a free-form cookie, drop about 1 tablespoon of batter onto the mat. With the offset spatula, spread the batter into a thin circle about 4 inches in diameter. Make 3 more circles, spacing them 3 to 4 inches apart.

A circle shape is not only great for making classic tuiles (shaped over a rolling pin) and "cigarettes" (loosely wrapped around the round handle of a kitchen utensil), but also for creating bowls for sorbet or mousse (cool the cookies over a custard cup) or for leaving flat to assemble into free-form napoleons, with round cookies separating layers of whipped cream and berries.

MEXICAN CHOCOLATE CRACKLE COOKIES

MAKES ABOUT 45 COOKIES This is a great place to use that extra-dark 70 percent cacao chocolate you've had your eye on. Because of how they are mixed, the cookies are very chocolaty, yet surprisingly light and delicate. The touch of chile powder adds an intriguing backnote—not heat exactly, but a sultry earthiness that enhances the chocolate flavor. You can find ancho chile powder in the Mexican spice section at the supermarket or specialty Mexican and Latin American markets. The dough is made using the sponge method—that is, the eggs and sugar are whipped together until very light in texture then the remaining ingredients are added. Before baking, each ball of dough is coated first in granulated sugar and then in a thick layer of confectioners' sugar. The granulated sugar creates a thin, crisp, outer shell during baking, while the confectioners' sugar adds a cooling sweetness to each bite. As the cookies rise, big chocolate cracks form in the white coating, creating the dramatic, two-tone look of the cookie.

INGREDIENTS

3 tablespoons (1½ ounces) unsalted butter, cut into ½-inch pieces

1 tablespoon coffee liqueur or cooled brewed coffee

6 ounces 70 percent cacao bittersweet chocolate, finely chopped

2 large eggs

½ cup (3½ ounces) plus ½ cup (3½ ounces) granulated sugar

¾ cup (3¾ ounces) unbleached all-purpose flour

½ cup (3 ounces) whole almonds, toasted and cooled completely

¾ teaspoon ground cinnamon

½ teaspoon baking powder

¼ teaspoon ancho chile powder (optional)

¾ cup (3 ounces) unsifted confectioners' sugar

EQUIPMENT

Double Boiler, Silicone or Rubber Spatula, Stand Mixer Fitted with a Whisk Attachment or a Hand Mixer and a Medium Bowl, Food Processor Fitted with a Metal Blade, Two or Three Baking Sheets, Parchment Paper, Small Ice Cream Scoop, Two Small Bowls, Cooling Rack

1 Bring 2 inches of water to a boil in the bottom of the double boiler. Place the butter, liqueur, and chocolate in the top of the double boiler (off the heat). Turn off the heat, then set the chocolate over the steaming water. Stir occasionally with the spatula until the chocolate is melted and the mixture is smooth. Remove and let cool slightly while you whip the eggs.

2 Place the eggs and ½ cup of the granulated sugar in the bowl of the mixer and whip on high speed until very light in color and thick, 5 to 6 minutes. You can also use a hand mixer and a medium bowl, though you may need to beat the mixture a little longer to achieve the same results. Scrape the melted chocolate mixture into the eggs and whip until blended, about 1 minute. Scrape down the sides of the bowl.

3 Place the flour, nuts, cinnamon, baking powder, and chile powder (if using) in the food processor and process until the nuts are very finely chopped, 60 to 90 seconds. Add the flour mixture to the egg mixture and beat on low speed just until combined. Stir gently

GETTING AHEAD **At the end of Step
3, the dough can be refrigerated in an
airtight container for up to 3 days. Or,
for nearly-spur-of-the-moment cookies,
portion the dough onto a baking sheet
lined with parchment paper, putting the
scoops of dough right next to each other
to fit all of them on one pan. (Do not roll
in the sugars, though). Place the pan in
the freezer for 30 to 60 minutes, until
the balls of dough are frozen. Transfer
to a resealable plastic freezer bag, then
freeze until needed, up to 3 months. To
bake, take out as many cookies as you
need, roll in the two types of sugar, and
space them on a parchment-lined baking
sheet. Bake as directed, adding a couple
of minutes to the baking time.**

a few times with the spatula to make sure there are no patches of unincorporated flour or butter lurking near the bottom of the bowl. Cover the dough with plastic and refrigerate for 1 to 2 hours, until firm.

4 Preheat the oven to 325°F and position an oven rack in the center. Line the baking sheets with parchment paper.

5 Scoop the chilled dough into tablespoon-size balls using the ice cream scoop or a spoon. Place the remaining ½ cup of granulated sugar in one small bowl and the confectioners' sugar in the other. Roll each dough ball in the granulated sugar and then in the confectioners' sugar. Be sure to coat the dough generously with the confectioners' sugar—in this instance, more is better. Space the cookies about 1½ inches apart on the prepared baking sheets.

6 Bake the cookies one sheet at a time, rotating the sheet halfway through the baking time, for 11 to 14 minutes, until the cookies are puffed and cracked. If you nudge a cookie, it should slide on the sheet rather than stick. It is better to slightly underbake these cookies than to go too far—when overbaked they are dry and unpalatable. Transfer to a cooling rack and let cool completely.

STORING **These cookies are best the same day they are baked. Any leftovers can be stored in an airtight container at room temperature for 3 to 4 days.**

CAPPUCCINO BISCOTTI WITH HAZELNUTS AND CHOCOLATE

MAKES ABOUT 45 BISCOTTI Biscotti—twice-baked, super-crunchy Italian favorites—are made for dunking into a steaming cup of coffee, tea, or hot chocolate. They can often be too hard to enjoy out of hand, though. This particular style of biscotti, with a bit of butter added for additional flavor and a softer texture, is great for snacking, whether dipped or dunked. They are good make-ahead cookies and keep well in an airtight container for weeks. Theoretically. You probably won't be able to keep them around long enough to find out. Many variations can be made from this recipe by leaving out the espresso powder, changing the nuts to almonds, walnuts, or pistachios, adding ½ cup of dried fruit (such as raisins or cranberries), and/or leaving out or changing the type of chocolate chips.

INGREDIENTS

1½ tablespoons instant espresso powder

2 teaspoons warm water

1 stick (4 ounces) unsalted butter, softened (65° to 68°F)

⅔ cup (4¾ ounces) granulated sugar

3 large eggs, at room temperature

2¾ cups (13¾ ounces) unbleached all-purpose flour

½ teaspoon baking powder

¼ teaspoon salt

1 cup (4½ ounces) chopped skinned (see page 52) toasted hazelnuts

5 ounces good-quality semisweet or bittersweet chocolate, cut into ¼-inch chunks, or 1 cup (6½ ounces) mini chocolate chips

½ cup (3½ ounces) superfine sugar (optional; to make your own, see page 24)

½ teaspoon ground cinnamon (optional)

EQUIPMENT

Small Bowl, Stand Mixer Fitted with a Paddle Attachment or a Hand Mixer and a Medium Bowl, Silicone or Rubber Spatula, Medium Bowl, Whisk, Two Baking Sheets, Parchment Paper, Cooling Rack, Serrated Knife

1 Preheat the oven to 350°F and position an oven rack in the center.

2 MIX THE DOUGH: In the small bowl, stir together the espresso powder and warm water until the powder is dissolved. Set aside.

3 Place the butter and granulated sugar in the bowl of the stand mixer and beat on medium speed until smooth and slightly lightened in color, 2 to 3 minutes. You can also use a hand mixer and a medium bowl, although you may need to beat the mixture a little longer to achieve the same results. Add the espresso mixture and blend well. Scrape down the bowl with the spatula. Add the eggs, one at a time, beating well (15 to 20 seconds) and scraping down the sides of the bowl after each addition.

4 In the medium bowl, whisk together the flour, baking powder, and salt. Add to the butter mixture all at once. Turn the mixer to the lowest speed and blend slowly, just until there are no more patches of flour. Turn off the mixer and scrape down the bowl.

The first baking of the biscotti (in logs) is important for the final appearance of the cookies. The dough must be baked thoroughly. If the dough is underdone, the cookies will have an unattractive raw dough line through their centers, which will not disappear during the second baking. Press gently on the top of the logs to make sure they are firm and set before removing them from the oven. Once cooled, slice into cookies with a sharp serrated knife using as few strokes as possible to prevent cracking and crumbling.

GETTING AHEAD **The cookie dough can be frozen for up to 2 months. Shape the dough into logs (Step 6), wrap tightly in plastic, and place on a baking sheet in the freezer. Once the logs are frozen, remove from the sheet and return to the freezer. To bake, remove the plastic wrap, place on a parchment-lined baking sheet, and thaw at room temperature for 1 hour before placing in the oven. Bake and toast as directed.**

5 Add the hazelnuts and chocolate chips and mix on low just until blended. Remove the bowl from the mixer and stir gently a few times with the spatula to make sure the nuts and chips are evenly distributed and there are no patches of unincorporated flour or butter lurking near the bottom of the bowl.

6 SHAPE AND BAKE THE DOUGH. Divide the dough in half. On a work surface lightly dusted with flour, gently squeeze and roll each piece to shape into logs about 13 inches long. Line one baking sheet with parchment paper. Place the logs on the sheet about 4 inches apart. Press down on the logs, flattening them slightly until they are each about 2 inches across the top. Place the second baking sheet under the first (to prevent the bottoms of the logs from browning too quickly). Bake for 30 to 35 minutes, until the logs are firm to the touch and lightly golden brown. Transfer the pan to a cooling rack and let the logs cool completely. (If you attempt to slice them while warm, the chocolate will smear and the cookies will look messy.)

7 CUT THE LOGS AND BAKE THEM A SECOND TIME: Turn the oven down to 275°F and position two racks in the top and bottom thirds of the oven. Carefully transfer the cookie logs to a cutting surface. Use the serrated knife to slice the logs on a slight diagonal into cookies ⅜ inch thick. Line the second baking sheet with parchment paper. Place the cookies, cut side down, on the parchment-lined sheets (you'll need both sheets to hold all the cookies). Toast the cookies in the oven, switching the sheets between the racks and rotating each front to back halfway through, for 30 to 40 minutes, until dry and lightly tinged with color. Transfer to a cooling rack.

8 While the cookies are toasting, prepare the finishing sugar if you like. Whisk together the superfine sugar and cinnamon in the cleaned medium bowl. As soon as the cookies are out of the oven and on the rack, immediately roll them in the cinnamon sugar and return to the baking sheet to cool completely.

STORING **The cookies will keep in an airtight container at room temperature for up to 2 months. If the cookies soften during storage, re-crisp them in a 300°F oven for 10 to 15 minutes, let cool, and return to storage container.**

Nutella Biscotti with Hazelnuts and Chocolate **If you can't get enough of this creamy, intensely flavored hazelnut-chocolate spread from Italy, you'll love it incorporated into a crisp biscotti. Omit the espresso and water mixture and add ½ cup (6 ounces) room temperature Nutella to the butter and sugar mixture. Add 2 teaspoons pure vanilla extract after the eggs.**

CLASSIC FUDGY BROWNIES

MAKES 16 (2-INCH) BROWNIES Rich, dark, fudgy, and slightly chewy, these homemade brownies are always a hit, so much better than anything you can buy. Serve cold with a glass of milk, or warm from the oven with a scoop of ice cream. Like a simple black dress, they can be accessorized to match any occasion. For a casual snack, serve them right out of the pan. For something a bit dressier, dust the brownies with a layer of confectioners' sugar, then use a stencil and cocoa powder for a contrasting design (see page 436). Inspired by Jackson Pollock? Drizzle melted dark chocolate (or dark, milk, and/or white chocolates) wildly over the top. For a very special occasion, paint a message or design right onto the brownies using gold luster dust (see page 436) or frost them with a layer of Dark Chocolate Ganache (page 412) accented with the elegance of gold leaf (page 436).

INGREDIENTS

1 stick (4 ounces) unsalted butter, cut into ½-inch pieces

4 ounces semisweet or bittersweet chocolate (up to 64 percent cacao), finely chopped

2 ounces unsweetened chocolate, finely chopped

1 cup (7 ounces) sugar

2 large eggs, at room temperature

1½ teaspoons pure vanilla extract

½ cup (2½ ounces) unbleached all-purpose flour

Pinch of salt

½ cup (about 3¾ ounces) chocolate chips or chunks (optional)

½ cup (2 ounces) chopped nuts, toasted and cooled completely (optional)

EQUIPMENT

8-inch Square Cake Pan, Parchment Paper, Double Boiler, Silicone or Rubber Spatula, Whisk, Cooling Rack, Thin Knife or Flexible Spatula, Chef's Knife

1 Preheat the oven to 350°F and position an oven rack in the center. Line the pan with foil or parchment paper across the bottom and up two of the sides, then lightly coat with unflavored oil or high-heat canola-oil spray.

2 Bring 2 inches of water to a boil in the bottom of a double boiler. Place the butter, semisweet chocolate, and unsweetened chocolate in the top of the double boiler (off the heat). Turn off the heat, then set the butter and chocolate over the steaming water. Stir occasionally with the spatula until the chocolate is melted and the mixture is smooth.

3 Remove the chocolate mixture from the heat and whisk in the sugar. Whisk in the eggs, one at a time, stirring well to incorporate each before adding the next. Stir in the vanilla extract. Whisk in the flour and salt. Continue to stir until the mixture changes from dull and broken-looking to smooth and shiny, about 1 minute. Whisk in the chocolate chips and chopped nuts, if using.

4 Scrape the batter into the prepared pan and spread evenly. Bake for 35 to 40 minutes, until a skewer inserted into the center of the brownies comes out with a few moist crumbs clinging to it (do not overbake). Transfer to a rack and cool completely.

There are two types of brownies—fudgy and cakey. Fudgy brownies always begin with butter and chocolate melted together, which creates a dense, chewy texture. Cakey brownies begin with butter and sugar creamed together, and the chocolate is added later. The creaming step fills the batter with air, lightening it and making it more cakelike in texture. You can change the style of your brownies by simply changing the mixing method to achieve the texture you want.

5 Run a thin knife or flexible spatula around the edges of the pan to loosen the brownies. To remove the brownies from the pan, grasp the foil or parchment paper extending up the sides and pull gently upward. Set the brownies on a cutting surface and use a chef's knife to cut into 16 equal pieces. Since these are fudgy, it's a good idea to keep a hot, wrung-out towel nearby so you can wipe the knife clean between slices. You could also serve the brownies right out of the pan, if you like, pressing a piece of plastic wrap against any cut surfaces and across the top to keep them fresh.

STORING **Tightly wrap the remaining brownies in plastic or place in an airtight container. They will keep well at room temperature for 2 to 3 days, or in the refrigerator for up to 5 days.**

Chocolate Mint Brownies with White Chocolate Chunks
Omit the vanilla extract and add ¾ teaspoon pure mint extract instead. Do not use nuts or dark chocolate chips at the end of Step 3, but instead add 4 ounces of good-quality white chocolate chopped into ¼-inch pieces. Bake and cool as directed above. Melt an additional 1½ ounces of white chocolate and pipe or stripe it over the top of the cooled brownies in any pattern you like (page 431). Let the white chocolate cool and harden before cutting the brownies.

Chocolate-Pecan Brownie Cookies
Use toasted pecans for the nuts and substitute mini chocolate chips for the larger chips or chunks. Use a spoon or small ice cream scoop to portion tablespoons of batter about 1 inch apart on parchment-lined baking sheets. Bake at 350°F for 8 to 10 minutes, rotating the sheet halfway through. The cookies won't seem done, but will firm up as they cool. The tops should look matte instead of shiny—you may want to bake a few to get the timing right before you commit to the entire batch. Makes about 45 cookies.

PEANUT BUTTER AND CHOCOLATE MARBLE BROWNIES

MAKES 12 LARGE OR 24 REASONABLY SIZED BROWNIES Chewy and boldly flavored, these brownies walk a thin line between sweet and salty, which is part of what makes them so addictive–eating them is like trying to have just one potato chip. This recipe needs a moderately sweet chocolate for the best texture, as the chocolates with higher percentages of cacao make the batter too dry and bitter. Save those for a recipe in which their intense flavor can shine.

INGREDIENTS

5 ounces semisweet chocolate (up to 56 percent cacao), finely chopped

1 stick (4 ounces) unsalted butter, softened (65° to 68°F)

2 cups (16 ounces) firmly packed light brown sugar

¾ cup (6¾ ounces) creamy salted peanut butter (see page 276), at room temperature

3 large eggs, at room temperature

2 teaspoons pure vanilla extract

1¼ cups (6 ounces) unbleached all-purpose flour

2 teaspoons baking powder

½ teaspoon salt

½ cup (2¾ ounces) unsalted peanuts, chopped

EQUIPMENT

9 by 13-inch Baking Pan, Parchment Paper, Double Boiler, Silicone or Rubber Spatula, Stand Mixer Fitted with a Paddle Attachment or a Hand Mixer and a Medium Bowl, Small Bowl, Medium Bowl, Whisk, Small Offset Spatula, Paring Knife, Cooling Rack, Thin Knife or Flexible Spatula

1 Preheat the oven to 350°F and position an oven rack in the center. Line the baking pan with parchment paper or foil across the bottom and up two long sides, then lightly coat with melted butter, oil, or high-heat canola-oil spray.

2 Bring 2 inches of water to a boil in the bottom of the double boiler. Place the chopped chocolate in the top of the double boiler (off the heat). Turn off the heat, then set the chocolate over the steaming water. While you are preparing the rest of the recipe, occasionally stir the chocolate with the spatula until it is smooth and melted. Let it sit over the warm water until needed.

3 In the bowl of the stand mixer, cream the butter and brown sugar on medium-high speed for 5 minutes, or until much lighter in color (the mixture will look clumpy and sandy even when fully creamed). You can also use a hand mixer and a medium bowl, although you may need to beat the mixture a little longer to achieve the same results. Scrape down the sides of the bowl with the cleaned spatula. Add the peanut butter and beat well on medium-high for 30 seconds. Scrape down the bowl again. Crack the eggs into the small bowl and beat with a fork to blend. With the mixer running on medium, add the eggs, about a tablespoon at a time, incorporating each addition fully before adding the next. Beat in the vanilla. Scrape down the bowl.

4 In the medium bowl, whisk together the flour, baking powder, and salt. Add to the peanut butter mixture all at once, then blend on the lowest speed just until you no longer see any streaks of flour and the batter is smooth. Scrape the sides and bottom of the bowl to make sure that any patches of flour or butter are blended into the batter.

5 Stir half of the batter into the melted chocolate (it may look slightly grainy, but this is fine). Stir the chopped peanuts into the remaining half of the batter.

6 Use a small offset spatula to spread a little more than half of the plain peanut batter in the bottom of the prepared pan. This layer will be very thin, and it will seem like there is not enough batter, but it will be fine. Top with all of the chocolate batter, spreading it into an even layer (this is easiest to do by dropping big dollops of batter around the pan, then merging them with the spatula). Drop the remaining peanut batter by the level tablespoon in 3 evenly spaced rows of 5 dollops each. If you have any batter left, drop it in wherever you like. Drag a toothpick or the tip of a paring knife through each dollop a couple of times, swirling it into the chocolate batter around it. The batter will look very rough and ragged—don't worry, it will smooth out as it bakes, and the slightly rugged look that remains is very appealing.

7 Bake the brownies for 30 to 40 minutes, until the top is golden brown and a toothpick inserted into the center comes out with a few moist crumbs clinging to it. Transfer to a rack to cool for 15 to 20 minutes. To remove the brownies from the pan, run a thin knife or flexible spatula around the two short edges to loosen them from the pan. Grasp the parchment paper along the two long edges and pull gently upward. Set the brownies on a cutting surface and cut as desired. Serve warm.

STORING **The brownies will keep, wrapped tightly in plastic, at room temperature for 2 to 3 days or in the refrigerator for 4 or 5 days. These brownies are at their best when warm. Reheat them for 15 to 20 seconds in the microwave to restore their chewiness and bring out their flavors.**

CLASSIC LEMON BARS

MAKES 36 (1½ INCH) SQUARES Eyes light up at the sight of these tart and refreshing favorites. A soft, puckery lemon filling atop a vanilla-scented shortcrust is just the ticket after a rich winter meal, and it is also a refreshing treat on a hot summer day. Okay, okay, it's great anytime. Surprisingly easy to make, these bars deliver a lot of satisfaction for the amount of elbow grease invested. Of course lemon is the classic, but you could substitute lime juice as well. Or, for a more exotic version, try an equal amount of passion fruit juice instead of the lemon juice.

INGREDIENTS

1 recipe Vanilla Shortcrust Dough (page 209), prepared through Step 2

4 large eggs

2 cups (14 ounces) granulated sugar

5 tablespoons (1¾ ounces) unbleached all-purpose flour

⅔ cup (5⅔ ounces) strained freshly squeezed lemon juice

Confectioners' sugar, for dusting (optional)

EQUIPMENT

9-inch Square Cake Pan, Silicone or Rubber Spatula, Cooling Rack, Whisk, Medium Bowl, Thin Knife or Small Spatula, Fine-Mesh Strainer

GETTING AHEAD The crust can be baked up to 3 days in advance and held, wrapped in plastic, at room temperature. Or freeze the baked crust, double wrapped in plastic, for up to 1 month. You don't need to defrost the crust before adding the filling and baking—just add a few minutes to the baking time.

1 Preheat the oven to 350°F and position an oven rack in the center.

2 Line the pan with foil across the bottom and up all four sides, then lightly coat with melted butter, oil, or high-heat canola-oil spray. With the spatula, scrape the dough into the prepared pan and press it into an even layer across the bottom of the pan. Chill for 30 minutes.

3 Bake the chilled crust for 35 to 45 minutes, until golden brown. Transfer to a rack and allow to cool for 20 minutes. Reduce the oven temperature to 300°F.

4 Whisk the eggs and granulated sugar together in the medium bowl. Whisk in the flour until there are no lumps. Whisk in the lemon juice. Pour the filling over the crust. Bake for 50 to 60 minutes, until the filling is set and does not jiggle when you tap the side of the pan. Transfer to a rack to cool completely. When cool, refrigerate for 1 hour.

5 To serve, grasp the foil and lift the cookies out of the pan. Set them on a cutting surface. Gently peel back the foil, using the tip of a thin knife or small spatula to help separate the bars from the foil if necessary. Cut into 1½-inch squares and transfer to a serving plate or storage container. Just before serving, use a fine-mesh strainer to dust confectioners' sugar over the tops. (Wait until the last minute to do this or the confectioners' sugar will soak into the filling and look blotchy.)

STORING The bars keep well at room temperature for 1 day. For longer storage, keep them airtight in the refrigerator for up to 3 days. The bars cannot be frozen, however, because the crust becomes soggy when defrosted.

RASPBERRY-CHERRY CRUMBLE BARS

MAKES 36 (3 BY 1-INCH) BARS These homey, irresistible bars can be put together in no time, will feed a crowd, and are loved by everyone. The brown sugar–oatmeal crust provides just the right sweetness and crunch against the soft, tart, lightly chewy filling in the center, which is simply a mixture of raspberry jam and dried sour cherries. Pack them in lunches, bring them to bake sales, or serve them warm with ice cream—this is a good recipe to have in your repertoire. Use old-fashioned oats when you want a hearty crunch, or quick oats for a more tender bite, but don't use instant oats or you'll have mush.

INGREDIENTS

1¾ cups (8¾ ounces) unbleached all-purpose flour

1¾ cups (6 ounces) old-fashioned or quick oats (not instant)

1 cup (8 ounces) firmly packed light brown sugar

¼ teaspoon salt

2 sticks (8 ounces) cold unsalted butter, cut into ½-inch pieces

1 (16-ounce) jar good-quality seedless raspberry jam

1 cup (5½ ounces) dried sour cherries

Confectioners' sugar, for dusting

EQUIPMENT

9 by 13-inch Baking Pan, Stand Mixer Fitted with a Paddle Attachment or a Food Processor Fitted with a Metal Blade, Silicone or Rubber Spatula, Cooling Rack, Medium Bowl, Thin Knife or Flexible Spatula, Fine-Mesh Strainer

1 Preheat the oven to 350°F and position an oven rack in the center. Line the baking pan with foil across the bottom and up the two long sides, then lightly coat with melted butter, oil, or high-heat canola-oil spray.

2 MIX THE CRUMBLE DOUGH: Place the flour, oats, brown sugar, and salt in the bowl of the stand mixer and beat on low speed until evenly mixed (or place in the food processor and process for 5 seconds). Add the cold butter and mix on low speed until the mixture looks like wet sand and starts to form clumps, 5 to 6 minutes (or process for 45 to 60 seconds, pausing to scrape down once with the spatula).

3 BAKE THE BOTTOM CRUST: Divide the dough in half. Pat one half into an even layer in the prepared pan. Set the other half aside. Bake for 20 to 25 minutes, until golden and crisp. Transfer to a rack and cool for 20 minutes. Leave the oven on.

4 MAKE THE FILLING: Empty the jar of jam into a medium bowl and stir well to break up any lumps. Add the cherries and stir until well mixed and all the cherries are coated with jam. Spread evenly over the cooled crust, all the way to the edges. Sprinkle the remaining dough evenly over the filling.

5 Bake for 35 to 40 minutes, until the topping is golden brown and the filling is bubbling. Transfer to a rack and cool completely, 1½ to 2 hours.

The bottom crust can be baked and the bars assembled (but not baked) and frozen in the pan for up to 6 weeks. Wrap tightly with two layers of plastic reaching all the way around the pan. To bake, do not defrost; simply unwrap the pan and bake for a few extra minutes.

6 UNMOLD THE COOKIES: To serve, run a thin knife or spatula around the edges of the pan to loosen any dough or filling. Lift the cookies out using the foil as handles and place on a cutting surface. Cut into 3 by 1-inch bars. Just before serving, use the fine-mesh strainer to lightly dust confectioners' sugar over the cookies.

STORING **Keep the bars in an airtight container between layers of parchment or waxed paper for up to 4 days at room temperature. Dust with confectioners' sugar just before serving.**

what the
pros
know

These bar cookies are a template for your creativity in the kitchen. While this recipe is sure to please, you can use the dough as a starting point, then change the filling flavors to suit your tastes and the occasion. Use only jam in the center, and leave out the dried fruit, filling it with your favorite preserve. Or try a layer of quince paste, fig spread, or poppy seed filling instead. Change the jam and fruit pairing to other tasty combinations such as apricot jam and snipped dried mango; orange marmalade with dried, sweet-tart cranberries; or cherry jam with snipped apricots. You can even flavor the dough to accent the filling, such as adding ½ teaspoon almond extract during mixing, then scattering a handful of sliced almonds over the top of the bars just before baking. Or leave the fruit out altogether and cover the dough with a layer of Nutella (hazelnut chocolate spread). A quick stop in the jams and jellies aisle is sure to spark some ideas.

There is no pastry more evocative of a special occasion than a cake. Birthday cakes, graduation cakes, wedding cakes—our milestones are often sweetened with a slice of cake. Whether you're toasting a grand occasion or savoring a moment of quiet in a hectic day, a homemade cake can turn any time into a celebration. If you've never made cake from scratch or have struggled to do so in the past, this chapter will guide you to success in your cake baking efforts. If you're a baking whiz, you'll find some fun ideas to add to your repertoire.

Baking a cake from scratch can be a supremely satisfying endeavor, but remember that each cake is really a little chemistry experiment, so for best results, take the time to read through this introductory section. Once you have some background information, you'll have a better idea of how, and why, to approach each recipe. Your cakes will improve, your confidence will grow, and cake making will become a fun and rewarding, as well as delicious, experience.

A Primer on Cakes

Let's look at the different types of cakes and their special qualities, the techniques used to create them, and how to make the most of the time you spend in the kitchen.

There are two main categories of cakes—butter cakes and sponge (or foam) cakes. Butter cakes rely on creaming—beating together butter and sugar to incorporate air bubbles—and chemical leavening (baking powder and/or baking soda) for their rise. Sponge cakes rely almost exclusively on foam—eggs filled with air bubbles—for their rise.

Various other types of cakes may not fit completely into either of these categories. For instance, combination cakes are neither true butter cakes nor true sponge cakes but include techniques from both, such as the upside-down cake on page 329. The batter starts off like a butter cake, but the egg whites are separated from the yolks, whipped, and folded in at the end. Tortes are dense cakes whose flour has been partially or completely replaced by finely chopped or ground nuts. They are leavened mainly by whipped egg whites, though sometimes a bit of chemical leavener is added as well. Chocolate tortes are similar, but they contain a measure of melted chocolate in their batter, and have a denser, almost fudgelike texture. Flourless chocolate cakes are a variation on the chocolate torte and contain a larger measure of melted chocolate for an almost truffle-like consistency. Cheesecakes are actually sensuously thick custards that happen to be baked in cake pans, and they can be found in the custard chapter (page 347).

Muffins and quick breads, covered in chapter 5, are also cakes. Although they sometimes use the butter cake creaming method, they are often distinguished from the cakes in this chapter because of the "muffin" style of mixing. This muffin method combines all the dry ingredients in one bowl, all the wet ingredients in another, then blends the two briefly to create a batter.

BUTTER CAKES

Instructions for butter cakes nearly always start with the words "cream the butter and sugar." The classic American favorite in this category is pound cake, although any cake recipe that calls for beaten butter and sugar and is moist, tender, and full of stand-alone flavor is almost certainly a butter cake. It is well worth your time to review the techniques for measuring (page 3), as this step is crucial to the light texture, fine crumb, and successful rise of your cake.

HOW BUTTER CAKES WORK

Butter cakes are an emulsion of butter, sugar, eggs, and flour. You may be familiar with another very common emulsion—vinaigrette dressing for your salad. A bit of mustard, a few tablespoons of vinegar, and a cup of oil will separate if haphazardly placed into a bowl together. But if the mustard and vinegar are blended first, and then the oil is added in a slow stream while you whisk constantly, the disparate ingredients will blend beautifully into a cohesive dressing.

Making a butter cake is the same idea—throw cold butter, sugar, eggs, and flour into a bowl and you'll have a mess. But if all the ingredients are brought to the correct temperature, then slowly combined in a prescribed order they will blend smoothly and create a beautifully risen cake. This method in cake making is called the *creaming method*.

Before you start, it is very important that the butter is at the correct temperature. Butter that is 65° to 68°F is perfect. At this temperature, it is cool to the touch, but pliable enough that, if you were possessed by a sudden artistic urge, you could sculpt the butter and it would hold the shape. It takes 30 to 40 minutes for butter sitting on the kitchen counter to reach the proper temperature. If you don't have time and need to mix the cake immediately, see "What the Pros Know" below. Many recipes use the words "room temperature" to describe the texture above, but do not allow the butter to reach room temperature—especially in the summer!—or it will be too soft. If it is squishy soft, separated, or beginning to lose its third dimension, measure out some new butter.

The consistency of butter at 65°F allows it to hold the maximum number of air bubbles during the beating process. These air bubbles are vital to the rising and texture of the cake because the only thing that chemical leaveners (either baking soda or baking powder) do is increase the size of the bubbles; they don't create new ones. As the bubbles get larger, the cake gets taller. If there are too few bubbles in the butter, your cake will be dense and heavy. Butter that is too cold (and therefore not elastic enough to hold bubbles) or too warm (and therefore too soft to keep bubbles in suspension) will result in cake that does not have the fine crumb and open texture you desire.

CREAMING THE BUTTER AND SUGAR Cut the butter into pieces and put them in the bowl of your mixer, then add the sugar. Beat on medium-high speed for 4 to 5 minutes (6 to 7 minutes with a hand mixer), until the mixture is very light, almost white in color. Scrape down the bowl a couple of times during the process so the mixture blends evenly. Remember, once you add any additional ingredients to the butter and sugar, the opportunity to create new air bubbles is over, so don't hurry it along. However, you can go too far here, beating so long that friction warms the butter to the point where it can no longer hold the bubbles in suspension, causing them to collapse. Just keep the time in mind, watch the color of your butter, and you'll do fine.

ADDING THE EGGS When the mixture is fully creamed, it's time to add the eggs. Your eggs must also be at room temperature. To warm refrigerated eggs to room temperature in 5 minutes, see page 302. Cold eggs chill the butter, making it seize into clumps and collapsing valuable air bubbles in the process. Crack the eggs into a small bowl and whisk with a fork to break them up thoroughly. The eggs need to be added to the butter mixture slowly, so it can absorb the eggs and hold them in suspension, just like the mustard and vinegar hold the oil in suspension for a vinaigrette. A whole egg plopping into the batter can cause the mixture to separate and deflate air bubbles, so it's best to break the egg up first.

what the pros know

If you decide to make a cake on the spur of the moment and must start with cold butter, don't use a microwave oven to soften it. Instead, cut the butter into tablespoon-size pieces, put it in the mixing bowl with the sugar, and begin beating. Start off on a low speed so the butter pieces don't fly out of the bowl and then increase the speed as the butter softens and smoothes out. It will take a couple of minutes longer for the mixture to become fully creamed, but it will make a fine cake batter. Note: Be sure your mixer's motor and beaters are powerful enough to mix cold butter before attempting this shortcut—a stand mixer with a paddle attachment handles it well.

If the mixture breaks while you are adding the eggs, don't panic. Total disasters are rare, and usually the basis for a new dessert creation! Hey, it's food, not world peace. No sense in throwing out the batch—it will probably still be quite edible, and you may be the only one who notices that the texture is a bit heavy.

ADDING ALTERNATELY Most butter cakes require two more batter components—a flour mixture and a liquid. Let's say you dumped in all of the dry ingredients at once. It would take quite a bit of mixing to blend them into the batter, leading to gluten development and, in turn, tunneling (humorously called *worm holes*) in the cake. Conversely, if all the liquid was added at once, the emulsion would break, and so would many air bubbles. With alternate adding, the liquid helps the flour portions to blend in more quickly, and the flour absorbs the liquid additions, preventing the mixture from breaking. The liquid in the recipe may be milk, buttermilk, sour cream, coffee, and so on, but the method used to add the dry and liquid components to the batter is always the same.

To add alternately, have all your dry ingredients in one bowl and whisk them to blend. Sifting separates and aerates the dry particles, but it does not mix them. When you whisk them before adding them to the batter, you ensure that each ingredient will be evenly dispersed. Have ready your room-temperature liquid in the measuring cup—remember, too cold will chill the butter and too hot will melt it, causing a loss of air bubbles. Turn the mixer to the lowest setting and add one-third of the dry ingredients (no need to measure—a guesstimate is fine). When they are almost completely blended and you see only a couple of small flour patches, pour in half of the liquid. Just as the liquid is almost completely blended, scrape down the bowl. Repeat with another third of the flour and the remaining liquid. Scrape down the bowl again. Add the remaining flour and beat just until blended and smooth. Your batter is now ready to be scraped into the prepared cake pan(s). Follow these steps and your cake will rise with a soft, tender, and open texture.

SPONGE (OR FOAM) CAKES

Sponge cakes are the airy, delicate cakes whose rise and texture depend upon air bubbles whipped into the eggs; the voluminous, bubble-filled eggs are called the *foam*. Angel food cake, chiffon cake, genoise, and separated egg sponge cake are the basic styles of sponge cake.

Angel food cake has no fat, containing only egg whites (and is thus often served on spa menus), but it does have plenty of sugar, which contributes not only sweetness but also moisture and tenderness. Meringue is a key component in sponge cakes, and sugar also keeps the egg whites supple, helping them expand fully in the heat of the oven. Chiffon cake also has a similar towering lightness, with egg yolks and oil for a more tender crumb and luxurious mouthfeel. Like angel food cake, chiffon cake relies on an egg white foam for rise, although it also con-

Bringing Cold Eggs to Room Temperature

To bring cold eggs still in their shells to room temperature quickly, place them in a bowl, cover with hot tap water, and let them sit for 5 minutes. If you have already cracked the eggs into a bowl and need to warm them, place the bowl into a larger bowl filled with hot tap water for 5 to 6 minutes, stirring occasionally. Don't use boiling water to speed things along—you're trying to take off the chill, not cook them.

To blend the eggs into the creamed butter and sugar, add them gradually. With the mixer running on medium speed, add the beaten egg a tablespoon at a time, allowing each addition to blend in before adding the next. You'll notice that as soon as you add a bit of egg, the mixture will loosen slightly, but in just a few seconds it will smooth out again—this is exactly the pattern you want. Every so often, scrape down the bowl so everything

blends evenly. If too much egg is added at once, the mixture may stay in a "broken" or curdled state, refusing to smooth out. If this happens, scrape down the bowl and continue to beat for 10 to 15 seconds, to see if it will smooth out. If not, just continue with the recipe. In some recipes, curdling may occur due to the sheer volume of eggs added and not because of a mistake on your part. Don't panic—it will smooth out when the flour is added.

tains a small amount of chemical leavener. Look for Tangerine–Poppy Seed Chiffon Cake on page 336. Genoise, the building block of classic European layer cakes (and the basis of Strawberry Rose Roulade, page 338), is a sponge cake in which whole eggs are warmed with sugar, then beaten until they form a thick, stable foam before being combined with the flour. Separated egg sponge cake (also known as *biscuit*) is true to its name—the egg yolks and egg whites are beaten separately, then folded together with flour. This type of sponge cake is featured in the Lemon Mascarpone Layer Cake on page 333. Sometimes, melted butter or a butter and milk mixture are folded into genoise or separated egg sponge for a moister, denser, and more substantial crumb.

Genoise and separated egg sponge cake are the basis of most fancy European layer cakes. These cakes differ from American layer cakes in their lack of butter and their inherent dryness. However, their sturdy, open structure means they can drink up moisture after they have cooled. Moisture and flavor are added to sponge cakes by lightly soaking each layer with a simple sugar syrup to match or complement the flavors in the filling and frosting. A simple syrup is nothing more than equal parts sugar and water brought to a boil, then removed from the heat and flavored with juice, liqueur, extracts, or oils.

HOW SPONGE CAKES WORK

Sponge cakes have a reputation for being tricky but, in fact, they are simpler to make than butter cakes. The keys to success are understanding how to create the various egg foams and how to fold the flour into the foam without deflating it.

Another critical factor is pan preparation. Always line the bottom of the pan with parchment paper so the cake easily releases every time. The sides of the pan, however, should not be greased or prepared in any way. The batter of these lean cakes needs to grip the sides and climb up the pan as the air bubbles expand. Any fat on the sides of the pan will inhibit the rise, and in the case of angel food and chiffon cakes will result in severely dense and gummy cakes.

Sponge-cake disasters are almost always a result of underwhipping (and the resulting lack of air bubbles), overwhipping (and the resulting breakdown of bubbles), or improper folding (and the physical destruction of air bubbles). Let's look at the basic steps in whipping eggs and combining them with other ingredients.

WHIPPING WHOLE EGGS To whip whole eggs for genoise, the eggs and sugar are warmed slightly over a simmering water bath. This warmth helps to dissolve the sugar and allows the mixture to whip higher, holding the maximum number of air bubbles in suspension. Once the eggs and sugar have warmed, beat them on high speed for 6 to 7 minutes (10 to 12 minutes if you use a hand mixer). Many recipes say "until tripled in volume," but that's a tricky call for most people. Make sure the foam is very light in color, thick, and billowy, like whipped cream. Use the ribbon test to check whether the foam is sufficiently thick before continuing with the recipe.

The ribbon test: Remove the bowl from the mixer and lift the beater out of the foam. Holding it an inch or two above the surface, draw the beater across the bowl, letting a "ribbon" or trail of batter drop from it onto the surface of the foam. When the eggs are properly beaten for genoise, that ribbon will hold its shape on top of the foam practically indefinitely.

You may run across a recipe that directs you to beat until you've created a ribbon with a specific time attached to it, such as a 3-second ribbon. In this case, whip the eggs on high for several minutes, then do the ribbon test. As the ribbon drops to the surface, pick a point on it and begin counting from the moment it hits the surface until it disappears from sight and sinks back into the body of foam. If you were able to count three "one thousands," then the eggs have sufficient volume for that particular recipe.

MERINGUE: EGG WHITES WHIPPED WITH SUGAR Sugar is like a little insurance policy for whipped whites, since one of its many roles is to add moisture to baked goods. When egg whites get over-whipped, they dry out, but the addition of sugar is like a spring shower, adding moistness and flexibility to the foam. It's best to add the sugar at the soft-peak stage of whipping (see page 304); added too early, the sugar may melt into a syrup and separate out to the bottom of the bowl. Added too late, the whites will already be too dry to be fully rescued. Add the sugar in a slow, steady stream to the softly peaked egg whites with the mixer running on medium. When the last bit of sugar

what the
pros
know

The step of adding the sugar in a slow stream is known to professionals as *raining in the sugar,* a phrase most descriptive, since the sugar falling into the whites looks like a gentle spring rain.

has been added, continue to beat for 15 to 20 seconds (or as the recipe directs) to fully disperse the sugar and create the maximum number of air bubbles.

WHIPPING EGG WHITES Be sure that the bowls you use to separate the whites from the yolks are very clean, and that your mixing bowl and whisk attachment are squeaky clean as well. Any fat (such as egg yolk or a bit of oil) or dirt inhibits the egg whites from whipping to their full volume. In fact, fat can prevent the egg whites from whipping at all, so give everything a quick wash before you start.

Room-temperature egg whites have slightly more volume when whipped, but not really enough to matter. More important is to separate the eggs while they are refrigerator-cold, since a warm egg yolk breaks easily and will ruin your egg whites. (For more, see page 27.) To retrieve little bits of egg yolk from egg whites, use a clean piece of egg shell as a scoop and put it next to the piece of yolk—it will glide right into your scoop.

Though a copper bowl is traditional for whipping egg whites, it is not necessary. There is a chemical reaction that occurs when whites are whipped in a copper bowl that makes the resulting foam very stable. For a similar stability without the copper, some recipes may call for a bit of cream or tartar or lemon juice in the whites. These both help to stabilize the whipped egg whites. Whip your egg whites on medium speed—not high—for a couple of reasons. A lower speed creates a more stable foam structure; those formed on high speed break down more quickly. A lower speed also allows you to monitor the progress of the egg whites more closely, which means you are less likely to overwhip them.

STAGES OF WHIPPED WHITES Nearly all recipes use whipped egg whites in one of two forms: soft peak or firm peak. To determine each stage, you'll need to watch the progress of the whites closely. The whites will change from yellowish and watery to frothy and loose looking, then turn white in color, resembling cappuccino foam. The whisk attachment will leave soft trail tracks in the foam. This is the soft peak stage. This can take from 1 to 3 minutes, depending upon the strength and speed of your mixer. To test the whites, remove the bowl from the mixer. Swirl the whisk attachment in the eggs, pull it straight out, then slowly turn it upright. Take note of the slope leading to the tip of the foam. At soft peak stage, the slope should lean to the side, barely holding its shape above the whip. If you want firm peaks, continue whipping briefly, then check again. The slope should be pointing straight up, or nearly so. Don't look at the tip to ascertain the stage of whipped whites—it may stand straight up, even when the whites are soft, and it may flop over, even when the whites are firm, especially if sugar has been added, which makes the tip heavy and prone to bending. Use the whipped whites immediately because they begin to break down as soon as they are removed from the mixer.

THE SCIENCE BEHIND WHIPPED WHITES As egg whites are whipped, their protein strands, which are coiled like party streamers, unwind and then join with other unwound protein strands to form a new, soft, flexible net of party streamers around the air bubbles. The elasticity of the net allows the bubbles trapped within to expand in the oven's heat, causing the cake to rise. The cake stops rising and is "set" when the proteins in the eggs are fully cooked and no longer flexible. The key, then, is to keep the proteins moist and flexible during the rising process. When egg whites are overwhipped, the net of party streamers coils so tightly together that the very moisture that keeps the net flexible is squeezed out. This is why it is always better to slightly underwhip egg whites than to overwhip them. When overwhipped, the foam looks lumpy, won't rise well, and cannot be folded smoothly into a batter. The clumps of dry foam simply break apart into smaller clumps, resembling tiny marshmallows dispersed throughout the batter. The only way to smoothly incorporate overwhipped egg whites is to smash them into the mixture with your spatula, which pretty much renders them useless for leavening the cake. Until you get the hang of whipping egg whites, check for soft and firm peaks early and often.

RESCUING OVERWHIPPED EGG WHITES If you overwhip your whites, you can rescue them with the following trick: Remove the bowl of beaten whites from the mixer. Add one additional egg white and stir gently with a silicone spatula (no more whipping!) until it is incorporated and the mass of whites has smoothed out. The whites will not be quite as stable, and your ratio of ingredients will be slightly off, but in most cases the cake will still be successful (this trick will not work for angel food cake).

Folding In Whipped Egg Whites

Folding is a smooth, gentle motion that blends two mixtures, and is used when one of them is very fragile or needs special care. Generally, the lighter mixture—the foam—is always folded into the heavier mixture, such as melted chocolate, to keep from deflating the egg whites. To fold, spoon the light mixture on top of the heavier one. Using the slim edge of your silicone spatula, cut through the center of the bowl from noon to six o'clock, then let the broad side of the spatula scoop under the heavy mixture and up the side of the bowl near the nine o'clock position. Once the spatula is out of the bowl, let the batter gently drop off into the center of the bowl. Turn the bowl one quarter and begin again. Continue until there are no more streaks and the two mixtures have been thoroughly combined. When flour is folded into a foam, the flour is sifted over the top of the foam, about one-third at a time, and gently folded in, using the same technique.

If the batter is very heavy, it may collapse the egg whites during the folding process. Professionals have a neat trick to avoid this problem. They "sacrifice" a quarter of the whipped whites by stirring them into the dense batter before folding begins. This will lighten the batter considerably, and make folding in the remaining whites easier and more successful.

Dividing cake batter between pans is not an exact science. Professionals weigh their batter, then set each cake pan on the scale and fill it with the correct amount of batter, but this technique can be a bit much for the home baker. Of course you can "eyeball" the amounts, but a better idea is to use a large spring-loaded ice cream scoop, portioning the same number of scoops into each cake pan. This will bring you very close to dividing the batter perfectly between the pans.

TIPS FOR SUCCESSFUL CAKE BAKING

CHOOSING THE RIGHT PAN SIZE For best results, always use the pan size called for in the recipe. If you must alter the pan size, be sure to consult the pan size chart (page 12) to help you do it efficiently. Never fill cake pans higher than two-thirds full, to allow plenty of room for expansion. To divide batter evenly between two or more pans, see the tips at left. Remember that once you have changed pan sizes, the cake will not bake in the original time allotted. If baked in a wider pan, the depth of the batter will decrease and the batter will finish more quickly; if baked in a narrower pan, the depth of the batter will increase and the batter will require more time. Usually, this works out well as long as you remember to watch your cake's progress in the oven and don't rely slavishly on exact baking times.

CONFIRMING YOUR OVEN'S TEMPERATURE Many people assume their oven's thermostat is accurate, but the reality is that the temperature of most home ovens, even brand new ones, is often off by 25 to 75 degrees. If the oven's temperature is too low, the cake will be heavy and coarse-grained. A too-hot oven will create an overbrowned crust and a volcano effect: The sides and top set before the center has finished rising; then, as the center completes its rise, it breaks through the top crust, making the cake resemble a small volcano. Purchase a good oven thermometer and allow your oven to fully preheat, a good 20 to 30 minutes, before baking. These simple steps are some of the easiest and quickest ways to improve anything you bake.

PLACING THE OVEN RACK CORRECTLY AND ROTATING THE PANS Cakes are best baked in the center of the oven, so be sure to adjust your oven rack before preheating. If the pan is too close to the walls of the oven, the batter will rise unevenly. Center the cake pan on the rack, so that there is plenty of room around it.

When baking two pans of batter at a time, position the racks in the top third and lower third of the oven. Place one cake pan on each rack, then halfway through the baking time, switch the pans, and rotate each pan from front to back on the rack. Do this as quickly and as gently as possible so you do not deflate the batter in the pans or cool down the oven. The cakes may need an extra minute or two of baking, since some oven heat will be lost during the rotation.

PREPARING YOUR INGREDIENTS Before you begin to bake, read through the recipe and make sure that you have all the ingredients needed. Then, measure each ingredient precisely and complete any advance preparation. For instance, nuts may need to be toasted and then cooled completely. Adding warm nuts can ruin a cake batter by melting the butter and collapsing the air bubbles contained within. Place all the measured ingredients—known as your *mise en place*—in front of you. This will allow you to proceed with the recipe calmly and efficiently.

PREPARING YOUR EQUIPMENT Part of *mise en place* is getting your tools ready, too. When baking cakes, always line the bottom of the pan with a piece of parchment paper—there is no better insurance policy for successfully removing a cake intact from its baking pan. Simply trace the pan bottom onto the parchment paper, then cut out the shape required. As for greasing and flouring, different cakes require different preparations, so follow the instructions accompanying each recipe.

In general, pans for butter cakes should be brushed with butter before the parchment paper is placed on the bottom of the pan, to keep the paper in place when the batter is added. Melted butter applied with a pastry brush is the most effective way of coating the pan, though a light but even coat of flavorless cooking spray also does the trick. Do make sure your cooking spray is fresh—rancid oil will lend its flavor to the outside of your cake.

Why are home bakers often encouraged to remove cakes from the pan while still warm? In most cases, it's just not necessary. The theory is that the bottom crust can become soggy from trapped steam if cooled in the pan—but cake crusts, when cooled in the pan on a cooling rack, are rarely soggy—just soft and moist. This warm-from-the-pan technique may have begun when home bakers had no access to parchment paper, and removing completely cooled cakes in one piece could be a dicey proposition. Professionals do not have the time or enough cooling racks to turn 20, 30, or even 100 cakes out of their pans at just the precise moment. Instead, all cakes are cooled in their pans on tall bakery rolling racks and unmolded as needed. Parchment paper and good bakeware make it all possible.

Parchment paper is one of the pastry chef's best friends, ensuring that cakes and pastries reliably release from their baking pans. Although many cookbook readers are encouraged to first butter and flour the bottom of the pan, then line it with parchment, and then butter and flour the parchment, the pastry chef would never waste precious time and ingredients unnecessarily. Parchment paper is a tool to take the place of greasing and flouring; however, a bit of grease underneath can keep paper from sliding in the pan as batter is added. Do butter the sides of the pan, though, if the recipe calls for it. And if the cake batter is particularly sticky (as with a traditional fruitcake), then a layer of butter and flour on top the parchment may be a good idea. Cutting a piece of parchment paper to fit a tube pan can be difficult. Specialty cookware stores often carry precut rounds for cake pans and tube pans to make the task easier.

Some recipes—especially those in Bundt or decorative pans—may need a more generous coating of butter or cooking spray as well as a dusting of flour or fine dry bread crumbs to prevent the cake from sticking. Always firmly tap out any excess flour. For chocolate butter cakes, use cocoa powder instead of flour, since flour often leaves a whitish cast on the dark cakes. For information on preparing pans for sponge cakes, see page 303.

TESTING FOR DONENESS There are several tests to determine when a cake is done, and it is always best to employ all of them. First, watch the clock or set the timer, although this is the least reliable of the tests, since differences in oven heat and pan materials can throw off baking times. It's a good idea to check a little early, since you can always bake the cake longer if needed. Once the cake is overbaked or burned, there's not much recourse than to start over. Second, look at the color and texture of the cake. Do they match the description of doneness in the recipe? The description is more important than the actual baking time, since ovens and pans may vary. Third, gently touch the top of the cake right in the center—is it firm but springy (done), or does it feel a bit soft and squishy? Fourth, insert a toothpick or skewer into the center of the cake. When you pull it out, is it clean, with perhaps just a few little crumbs clinging to it (done), or are there lots of crumbs or gooey batter (not done)? Fifth, trust your nose. Just as the cake finishes, the house is filled with an irresistible aroma.

Many people wait until they see the cake pulling away from the sides of the pan before they remove it from the oven, and while this can be a sign of doneness, bakers know that it is definitely not the best one. Many cakes don't fully shrink from the edges until they are overdone, and your cake may be dry if you employ this tactic. Also, sponge cakes must grip and stick to the edges of the pan to rise, so this method won't work with foam cakes. Instead, use a combination of the methods above.

COOLING THE CAKE PROPERLY Let cakes cool on a cooling rack. The rack allows air to circulate under and over the pan for faster and more efficient cooling. In most circumstances, there is no need to turn the cake out of the pan while still warm. The exception is a butter cake baked in one of those exquisitely shaped tube or Bundt pans, which is more likely to release the cake intact if still slightly warm. In fact, cakes are at their most tender and breakable state while warm, so why tempt fate? As long as you have parchment paper in the bottom of the pan there's no need to worry if the cake will release from the pan.

Angel food and chiffon cakes must cool upside down to set their airy structure. Some of the angel food tube pans are fitted with metal feet on the rim for just this purpose, but if yours doesn't have them, be sure you have a long-necked bottle (such as a wine or soda bottle) or several overturned juice glasses or coffee cups on which to set the upside-down pan, so the surface of the cake does not come in contact with the counter.

CAREFULLY UNMOLDING THE CAKE Run a thin, flexible knife or spatula around the edge of the pan to loosen the cooled cake. As you do this, press the knife into the side of the pan (flex it outward) so that it does not gouge or tear the cake. Place a cake cardboard (white side toward the cake), a tart pan bottom, or a plate on top of the cake pan. Holding the two together, flip them over so that the pan is on top. The cake will fall out of the pan. If it doesn't, there may be solidified butter holding the cake in the pan, in which case you'll need to warm the bottom of the pan slightly to melt the butter and release the cake. Turn a stove burner on medium and set the cake pan bottom on the flame for a few seconds, moving it in a circle until the bottom is hot to the touch. Remove from the flame and turn the cake out of the pan.

If you will use the cake immediately, peel off the parchment paper, set a serving plate on top of the cake, then grasp the cardboard and the plate and flip over so the cake is again rightside up. If you will be assembling a layer cake or wrapping and storing the cake for future use, leave the parchment paper attached. It will help to stabilize the cake and aid in moving it without breakage.

TIPS FOR SUCCESSFUL CAKE DECORATING

LEVELING AND SPLITTING THE CAKE First, make sure the parchment paper is still attached to the bottom of the cake. If not, cut a parchment round and set your cake on top—this will allow you to turn the cake easily. Place your cake right side up on your work surface. Lean over so you are at eye level, looking sideways at the cake. Spread your left hand (if you are right-handed) flat on top of the cake and use this hand to rotate the cake in a complete circle while you look at the top edge. If it's fairly level, move on to the next step. If it is quite uneven, pick the lowest point on the top edge, then set your serrated knife there. You must trim the top of the cake to this lowest point or the cake will be lopsided, perhaps dangerously so if there are several layers. Yes, you can compensate with extra frosting, but more than a half inch or so is just too much to enjoy. The good news is, the trimmings are snacks for the chef (or bribes for the chef's little helpers).

To slice the cake in half for two layers, first measure the cake's height. Halfway up its side, insert a toothpick sideways into the cake to a depth of about 1 inch. Continue, inserting additional toothpicks at 2-inch intervals around the cake. Set your serrated knife just above the toothpicks and place your left hand flat on top of the cake. Use a gentle sawing motion as you cut across the cake. Take your time, move slowly, and make sure your knife stays at the toothpick level. A nice long knife is helpful here, so that the end of the knife is always visible out the other side of the cake. Once the knife tip disappears inside the cake, it's easy to slice unevenly. Keep your hand on top, pressing down lightly to turn the cake—this also allows you to feel the position of the knife inside the cake. If you accidentally turn the knife upward or downward, you'll be able to feel that right away and correct the position. In a matter of moments, you'll have two even layers. Always save the bottom layer of cake, with the parchment attached, to use as the top of your layer cake. The parchment paper keeps the bottom even and free of crumbs, which is just what you want when frosting the top of your cake.

ASSEMBLING AND FILLING LAYER CAKES It is easiest and most efficient to assemble your layer cakes on a cake cardboard the same size as your cake pan. Cake cardboards are available in cake-supply, specialty cookware, and large craft stores. They make moving and storing the cake easier. Always use the white side of the board not the brown in contact with the food. If you don't have (or can't get) a cake cardboard, use a tart pan bottom or flat plate.

Brush each cake layer with a flavored soaking syrup if directed (or desired). Brush each layer on the cut side, if you have the option, which more readily soaks up the syrup. Scoop the filling onto the cake and use an offset spatula to spread it evenly to the edge. Use a second cake cardboard or tart pan bottom to move tender cake layers around and to help slide them into place on top of the filling. Repeat until all layers have been filled.

FROSTING TIPS

APPLYING A CRUMB COAT The crumb coat is a very thin, see-through layer of frosting that seals in any crumbs, fills cracks, and smoothes the outside of the cake in preparation for the final, thicker coat of frosting. It's like spackling a wall in preparation for painting. Cover the entire cake with a very thin coating of frosting. Once the crumb coat is finished, refrigerate the cake for 10 to 15 minutes, just to chill and set the crumb coat. If chilled for too long, the crumb coat becomes very hard and the final coat of frosting will slide off the cold, slick surface as you try to apply it.

APPLYING THE FINAL FROSTING Scoop a large mound of frosting and plop it into the center of the cake. Using an icing spatula (a straight spatula not offset is best here), spread the frosting back and forth, pushing it toward the edge of the cake in all directions. Try to get an even layer across the top of the cake first. If you can't tell whether the frosting is even, you can stick a very clean plastic ruler into the frosting at several points around the cake to see how you're doing.

A pastry chef trick for a perfectly straight sides on a frosted cake is to use a cake cardboard the same size as your cake pan to assemble the cake. The cake shrinks slightly during baking, so when placed in the center of the board, there will be a ¼-inch ring of exposed cardboard all around the cake. To frost the side, hold the cake up at eye level with one hand while you fill in that ¼-inch ring of space between the edge of the cardboard and the cake with frosting. Once it's filled in, smooth and straighten the sides by holding the edge of your icing spatula straight up and down, resting it against the cardboard edge while rotating the cake by twisting the wrist that is supporting the cake.

Once the top is even, work on the side of the cake. It is most efficient to lift the cake (on the cardboard) up on your left hand and hold it at eye level while you work with the spatula in your right hand (if you're right-handed). Twist your wrist to reach all sides of the cake. Otherwise, turn the cake frequently on your work surface to reach all sides evenly. Spread frosting around the side, working on about a 2-inch-wide area at time, until the side is evenly coated. Once the side is frosted, run the spatula a few more times over the top to smooth the edge.

If you can see the cake through the side, or if the frosting is a mess and you are frustrated, do what many bakeries do and cover the sides with chopped toasted nuts, chocolate sprinkles, chocolate shavings or curls, coconut, and so forth (see "Coating a Cake with Nuts," page 310).

DECORATING TIPS

USING A PASTRY BAG If you would like to pipe a top and/or bottom border, or decorate the surface of the cake, you'll need to use a pastry bag. Buy a pastry bag that is at least 14 inches long, as smaller bags are difficult to fill and keep clean as you work.

To fill a pastry bag, drop the tip, pointed end first, into the bag and adjust it so it's poking out from the bottom like the nose cone on a spaceship. Twist the bottom of the bag just above the pastry tip to push it down into the tip. This will prevent any filling from leaking out of the tip while you are filling the bag. Set the bag in a large drinking glass or measuring cup and fold down the top of the bag to make a collar, or cuff, at least 3 inches wide. This makes the bag easier to fill and also helps to keep the outside of the bag clean. The key is to keep the frosting in the bag or on the cake—once the outside of the bag gets dirty, then your hands get dirty and it goes on from there. You don't want to find frosting in your car, on your sofa, or on your dog, so keep it clean.

Scoop up some frosting with a silicone spatula, insert the spatula as far as possible into the bag, then scrape it off against the side of the bag. Repeat. Never fill the bag more than halfway, or you'll have problems with the frosting exiting the wrong end of the bag. Lift the bag out of the cup, unfold the cuff, and hold the top edges of the bag with one hand while you use the other to slide down the bag, pushing all the frosting toward the tip end (the twisted part near the tip will untwist on its own).

Grip the bag between the thumb and forefinger of your right hand if you're right-handed, just above the mound of frosting, and twist the bag twice to trap the frosting in the bottom of the bag. As you pipe, you'll need to occasionally squeeze down the frosting and twist the bag tight again. When decorating, always squeeze the bag from the top near the twist—use the fingers of your other hand to guide the tip at the bottom. Don't squeeze with the "guiding" hand near the tip or you'll force frosting up and out the wrong end of the bag.

For basic cake decorating, just a couple of piping tips will serve you well. A small, ⅛-inch plain tip for writing on cakes with frosting and a ½-inch open star tip for piping decorations and borders are all you need to get started. With the star tip, you can pipe shells and rosettes, to name just a few options. To learn about other types of tips and for more instruction on using them, look for a book or magazine that specializes in decorating and you'll find a wealth of ideas.

PIPING BASIC BORDERS

Shells: Fit the pastry bag with a star tip of desired size and fill no more than halfway with frosting. Hold the tip at a 45-degree angle to the surface of the cake. It should be about ½-inch above the surface. Press firmly and build a small mound of frosting, then slowly release the pressure as you pull the tip toward the surface of the cake and away from the mound. Stop the pressure and lift the tip from the cake. You should have a teardrop-shaped shell. Begin the next shell on the tail of the one before it. Continue until you have circled the top and/or bottom edge of the cake.

Rosettes: Fit the pastry bag with a star tip of desired size and fill no more than halfway with frosting. Hold the tip at a 90-degree angle to the surface of the cake. It should be about ½-inch above the surface. Your goal is to fill the space between the end of the tip and the surface of the cake. Press firmly and make a small, tight circle (no hole in the center like a doughnut). When you come around to the beginning point, stop the pressure and lift the tip away from the icing. You should have a closed round of icing. Continue until you have circled the top edge of the cake.

WRITING ON CAKES WITH CHOCOLATE You can use frosting and a tiny ¹⁄₁₆-inch plain tip in a pastry bag to write messages on cakes, but an easier method is to melt an ounce or two of dark chocolate (or white if the cake is chocolate) in a bowl set over hot—not boiling—water, stirring until melted and smooth. Dry the bottom of the bowl and scrape the chocolate into a disposable pastry bag or use a resealable plastic bag. Squeeze the chocolate into the bottom of the bag or one of the corners and cut a small hole in the end or corner. Practice writing on a scrap of paper, then write on the cake. If it's a disaster, chill the cake until the chocolate is set, then lift off the writing with the tip of a paring knife. Melt new chocolate and try again (the old will be contaminated with moisture—save it for use in a pudding cake or batter).

COATING A CAKE WITH NUTS Place the toasted, chopped, or sliced nuts on a dinner plate. Hold the cake (on its cardboard) in one hand over the plate and tilt it just slightly toward the plate. Use your other hand to pick up some nuts, open your palm, and press it flat against the cake. Move your hand away and let any excess nuts fall back onto the plate. Turn the cake and repeat until all the sides are coated evenly. This same technique can be used with shredded coconut, colored sugar, sprinkles and jimmies, or grated chocolate.

DECORATING IDEAS: BEYOND FROSTING While piping and nuts are very traditional, there are other ways of decorating cakes that produce beautiful results with simple techniques. Chocolate curls and decorations, gold leaf, sugared fresh flowers, stencil designs and spun sugar are some of these options that are covered in detail in the "Basic Recipes and Finishing Touches" chapter. Their presence can turn a delicious cake into a gorgeous show-stopper in just a few steps.

DOUBLE-VANILLA POUND CAKE

SERVES 6 TO 8 Pound cake gets its name from the classic ratio of one pound each of butter, sugar, flour, and eggs. This old-fashioned ratio has been modified slightly for today's tastes, resulting in a close-grained, tender, and buttery cake that is as welcome after school as it is at a dinner party. A double dose of vanilla—both extract and bean—gives this cake a delicious depth of true vanilla flavor.

INGREDIENTS

¾ cup (5¼ ounces) sugar

1 vanilla bean

1½ sticks (6 ounces) unsalted butter, softened (65° to 68°F)

3 large eggs, at room temperature

1 tablespoon pure vanilla extract

2 cups (7 ounces) sifted cake flour

½ teaspoon baking powder

¼ teaspoon salt

⅓ cup (3 ounces) sour cream, at room temperature

EQUIPMENT

8½ by 4½-inch Loaf Pan, Parchment Paper, Stand Mixer Fitted with a Paddle Attachment or a Hand Mixer and a Medium Bowl, Paring Knife, Silicone or Rubber Spatula, Small Bowl, Fine-Mesh Strainer, Medium Bowl, Whisk, Cooling Rack

1 Preheat the oven to 350°F and position an oven rack in the center. Lightly coat the pan with butter, oil, or high-heat canola-oil spray and fit it with parchment paper to extend up both long sides to the top of the pan.

2 CREAM THE BUTTER AND SUGAR: Place the sugar in the bowl of the stand mixer. You can also use a hand mixer and a medium bowl, although you may need to beat the mixture a little longer for each step to achieve the same results. Use a paring knife to split the vanilla bean lengthwise, then turn the knife over and use the dull edge to scrape the seeds into the sugar. (Save the vanilla pod for another use.) Blend on low speed until the seeds are evenly dispersed. Add the butter and beat on medium-high until the mixture is very light—almost white—in color, 4 to 5 minutes. Scrape down the bowl with the spatula.

3 ADD THE EGGS: Beat the eggs in the small bowl. With the mixer running on medium speed, add the eggs to the butter mixture about 1 tablespoon at a time, allowing each addition to completely blend in before adding the next. About halfway through, turn off the mixer and scrape down the bowl, then continue adding the eggs. Mix in the vanilla extract. Scrape down the bowl again.

4 ADD DRY AND WET INGREDIENTS ALTERNATELY: With the fine-mesh strainer, sift the cake flour, baking powder, and salt into the medium bowl and whisk together. With the mixer on the lowest speed, add the flour mixture and sour cream alternately, beginning with one-third of the flour mixture and half the sour cream; repeat, then finish with the flour mixture. Scrape down the bowl and finish blending the batter by hand.

5 BAKE THE CAKE: Scrape the batter into the prepared pan and smooth the top. Bake for 45 to 55 minutes, until firm to the touch and a toothpick inserted into the center comes out clean. Transfer to a rack to cool completely. When cool, remove from the pan, peel off the parchment paper, and serve.

what the pros know

The technique of poking holes in a hot-from-the-oven cake, then brushing it with a flavored syrup, is a time-honored tradition for adding another layer of both flavor and moistness to pound cakes. Feel free to try this method with any pound cake. While the cake is baking, make a simple syrup with ½ cup sugar and ½ cup water (or use a flavorful liquid, such as coffee, tea, lemon juice, etc.). Heat the syrup until the sugar has melted, then remove from the heat. You can infuse the syrup with the flavor of spices such as cinnamon sticks, whole cloves, cardamom seeds, or slices of fresh ginger as well; just be sure to strain them out once the syrup has cooled. Add additional flavorings to the syrup if you like, such as liqueur, extract, or flavoring oils. As soon as the cake is removed from the oven, use a toothpick or skewer to poke holes all over the top of the cake. Be sure the toothpick touches the bottom of the pan with each poke. Use a pastry brush to evenly coat the cake with the syrup. Do not neglect the edges of the cake—it's fine if some of the syrup goes down the sides of the pan. Continue to brush until all of the syrup has been used. Allow the cake to cool completely, then remove from the pan.

STORING The cake can be made several days ahead and kept at room temperature, wrapped in plastic wrap. Or double-wrap, put in a resealable plastic freezer bag, and freeze for up to 8 weeks.

Sour Cream–Spice Cake
Omit the vanilla bean and reduce the vanilla extract to 2 teaspoons. Add ½ teaspoon ground cinnamon, ¼ teaspoon ground cloves, and ¼ teaspoon ground nutmeg to the dry ingredients.

Orange-Cardamom Pound Cake
Omit the vanilla bean and reduce the vanilla extract to 1½ teaspoons. Add the finely grated zest of 1 large orange to the creamed butter and sugar and blend well. Add 1 teaspoon of ground cardamom to the dry ingredients.

Individual Bundt Cakes
This variation uses an individual-serving size Bundt cake pan, which has six 1-cup Bundt molds. Prepare the pan by buttering or oiling (with cooking spray) each mold thoroughly, then dusting with flour or fine dry bread crumbs and tapping out the excess. Spoon about ½ cup batter into each of the molds. Place the leftover batter (enough for one mini Bundt) in a small baking dish and bake in the oven on the same shelf—a nice chef's treat. Bake the individual Bundts for 16 to 19 minutes, until firm to the touch and a toothpick inserted into the center comes out clean. Do not overbake, as these small cakes dry out quickly. Transfer to a rack and let cool for 10 minutes, then turn the cakes out while they are still warm. Makes 6 individual Bundt cakes.

Mini Bundt Cakes
This variation uses a mini Bundt pan with twelve ¼-cup Bundt molds. Prepare the pan as directed in the individual Bundt cakes variation above. Spoon 3 tablespoons batter in each Bundt mold. Bake for 12 to 14 minutes, until firm to the touch and a toothpick inserted into the center comes out clean. Do not overbake, as these small cakes dry out quickly. Transfer to a rack and let cool for 10 minutes, then turn the cakes out while they are still warm. Rinse the baking pan under cold water until cool, dry thoroughly, prepare again and bake the remaining batter. Fill any unused molds halfway with water so the cakes bake evenly. Makes about 15 mini Bundt cakes.

CHOCOLATE VELVET POUND CAKE

SERVES 6 TO 8 This classic cake has a deep chocolate flavor and close-grained, velvety crumb. A great keeper, it's nice to have on hand in the freezer for that unexpected occasion. The cake can be dressed up with a little Dark Chocolate Ganache (page 412) spooned over the top and allowed to drip alluringly down the sides. Be sure to let the ganache cool to between 85° and 90°F before spooning it over the cake—at that temperature, it is cool enough to run in thick rivulets for a beautiful finish. For a stunning finish to a special occasion, bake the cake in individual or min bundt pans, glaze with chocolate ganache, then add a tophat of Spun Sugar (page 433).

INGREDIENTS

1½ sticks (6 ounces) unsalted butter, softened (65° to 68°F)

1¼ cups (8¾ ounces) sugar

1 teaspoon water, at room temperature

2 teaspoons instant espresso powder, such as Medaglia d'Oro

3 large eggs, at room temperature

1 cup (5 ounces) unbleached all-purpose flour

½ cup (2 ounces) unsifted unsweetened Dutch-process cocoa powder

¼ teaspoon baking powder

Pinch of salt

½ cup (4 ounces) buttermilk, at room temperature

EQUIPMENT

8½ by 4½-inch Loaf Pan, Parchment Paper, Stand Mixer Fitted with a Paddle Attachment or a Hand Mixer and a Medium Bowl, Silicone or Rubber Spatula, Small Bowl, Fine-Mesh Strainer, Medium Bowl, Whisk, Cooling Rack

1 Preheat the oven to 350°F and position an oven rack in the center. Lightly coat the pan with melted butter, oil, or high-heat canola-oil spray, and fit it with parchment paper to extend up both long sides to the top of the pan.

2 CREAM THE BUTTER AND SUGAR: Place the butter and sugar in the bowl of the stand mixer and beat on medium-high until light—almost white—in color, 4 to 5 minutes. You can also use a hand mixer and a medium bowl, although you may need to beat the mixture a little longer to achieve the same results. Scrape down the bowl with the spatula.

3 ADD THE EGGS: In the small bowl, stir together the water and espresso powder until smooth. Crack the eggs into the bowl and beat to blend. With the mixer running on medium, add the eggs to the butter mixture about 1 tablespoon at a time, allowing each addition to completely blend in before adding the next. About halfway through, turn off the mixer and scrape down the bowl, then continue adding the eggs. Scrape down the bowl again.

4 ADD THE DRY AND WET INGREDIENTS ALTERNATELY: With the fine-mesh strainer, sift the flour, cocoa powder, baking powder, and salt into the medium bowl and whisk to blend. With the mixer running on the lowest speed, add the flour mixture and the buttermilk alternately, beginning with one-third of the flour mixture and half of the buttermilk; repeat, then finish with flour mixture. Scrape down the bowl and finish blending the batter by hand, if necessary.

The addition of espresso here is not just an enticement for caffeine addicts. Full-bodied, bitter espresso is often paired with dark chocolate because it deepens and enhances the flavor, making it taste even more, well, chocolaty. You won't notice the coffee flavor, but if you leave it out, the cake will have a lighter chocolate profile. If you wish to omit the espresso, try adding 1 teaspoon pure chocolate extract, or 2 teaspoons pure vanilla extract.

5 BAKE THE CAKE: Scrape the batter into the prepared baking pan and smooth the top. Bake for 45 to 55 minutes, until firm to the touch and a toothpick inserted into the center comes out clean. Transfer to a rack to cool completely. When cool, remove from the pan, peel off the parchment paper, and serve.

STORING The cake can be made several days ahead and kept at room temperature, wrapped in plastic wrap. Or double-wrap it, put in a resealable plastic freezer bag, and freeze for up to 8 weeks.

Individual Chocolate Velvet Bundt Cakes Use an individual Bundt cake pan (with six 1-cup molds) and follow the instructions for the Individual Bundt Cakes variation (page 312), but bake for 16 to 19 minutes. See recipe introduction for finishing ideas. Makes 6 individual Bundt cakes.

Mini Chocolate Velvet Bundt Cakes Use a mini Bundt pan (with twelve ¼-cup molds) and follow the instructions for the Mini Bundt Cakes variation (page 312), baking for 13 to 15 minutes. See recipe introduction for finishing ideas. Makes about 18 mini Bundt cakes.

Mini Chocolate Velvet Pound Cake with Chocolate
Ganache Glaze and Spun Sugar

CLASSIC YELLOW LAYER CAKE

SERVES 8 TO 10 This buttery, vanilla-scented cake is a variation on pound cake (page 311), with a little extra leavener added to lighten the crumb. Although nearly any frosting pairs well with this celebration favorite, it is especially luscious filled and frosted with silken chocolate ganache for the two-toned birthday cake most of us remember from childhood. For a special party or tea, make the mini cupcakes variation at the end of the recipe (shown at left), then top them with swirls of Cream Cheese Frosting (page 414) and finish them with pretty Sugared Flowers (page 438) and/or touches of gold leaf (page 436).

INGREDIENTS

1 recipe Dark Chocolate Ganache (page 412), prepared at least 8 hours ahead, covered, and stored at room temperature

1½ sticks (6 ounces) unsalted butter, softened (65° to 68°F)

¾ cup (5¼ ounces) sugar

3 large eggs, at room temperature

1 tablespoon pure vanilla extract

2 cups (7 ounces) sifted cake flour

¾ teaspoon baking soda

¼ teaspoon salt

⅓ cup (3 ounces) sour cream, at room temperature

EQUIPMENT

9 by 1¾-inch Round Cake Pan, Parchment Paper, Stand Mixer Fitted with a Paddle Attachment or a Hand Mixer and a Medium Bowl, Silicone or Rubber Spatula, Small Bowl, Fine-Mesh Strainer, Medium Bowl, Whisk, Cooling Rack, Two (9-inch) Round Cake Cardboards or Tart Pan Bottoms, Thin and Flexible Knife or Spatula, Serrated Knife, Icing Spatula, Thin and Sharp Knife

Classic Yellow Mini Cupcakes Topped with Cream Cheese Frosting and Finished with Sugared Flowers and Gold Leaf

1 Preheat the oven to 350°F and position an oven rack in the center. Lightly coat the pan with melted butter, oil, or high-heat canola-oil spray and fit it with a round of parchment paper.

2 CREAM THE BUTTER WITH THE SUGAR: Place the butter and sugar in the bowl of the stand mixer and beat on medium until very light—almost white in color, 4 to 5 minutes. You can also use a hand mixer and a medium bowl, although you may need to beat the mixture a little longer to achieve the same results. Scrape down the bowl with the spatula.

3 ADD THE EGGS: Beat the eggs and vanilla in the small bowl to blend. With the mixer on medium, add the eggs to the butter mixture about 1 tablespoon at a time, allowing each addition to completely blend in before adding the next. About halfway through, turn off the mixer and scrape down the bowl, then resume adding the eggs. Scrape down the bowl again.

4 ADD THE DRY AND WET INGREDIENTS ALTERNATELY: With the fine-mesh strainer, sift the cake flour, baking soda, and salt into the medium bowl and whisk together. With the mixer on the lowest speed, add the flour mixture and the sour cream alternately, beginning with one-third of the flour mixture and half the sour cream; repeat, then finish with flour mixture. Scrape down the bowl and finish blending the batter by hand, if necessary.

5 BAKE THE CAKE: Scrape the batter into the prepared pan and smooth the top. Bake for 30 to 35 minutes, until firm to the touch and a toothpick inserted into the center comes out clean. Transfer to a rack to cool completely.

GETTING AHEAD The unfrosted cake can be held, wrapped in plastic, at room temperature for 1 day. It can also be frozen, double-wrapped in plastic and sealed in a resealable plastic freezer bag, for up to 4 weeks. Leave the parchment paper on the cake until you are ready to assemble.

6 UNMOLD THE CAKE: Run the thin and flexible knife or spatula around the edge of the pan to loosen the cake. Place the cardboard on top of the pan, hold both together, and flip over. Remove the pan, leaving the parchment on the cake. Flip again onto a second cake cardboard (or a plate) so the cake is right side up. Level the cake, if necessary (see page 308). Using a serrated knife, slice the cake horizontally into two layers (see page 308).

7 ASSEMBLE AND FROST THE CAKE: Place the cake cardboard (or plate) on your work surface. Flip the top layer of cake over and place it, cut side up, on the cardboard—this will be the bottom of the cake. With the icing spatula, spread 1 cup of ganache evenly over the surface of the cake, all the way to the edge. Flip the bottom layer and slide it, cut side down, into place on top of the ganache. Peel off the parchment paper. Voilà—a crumb-free surface for frosting. Spread a very thin layer of the frosting, known as a *crumb coat,* over the cake. Chill for 15 minutes, just to set the crumb coat. Use the remaining ganache to frost the top and side of the cake. Use a spoon to create swirls all over the top by gently pressing the tip of the spoon, rounded edge down, into the frosting in a back-and-forth motion. To serve, slice the cake with a thin and sharp knife.

STORING The cake can be stored at room temperature for 2 days or in the refrigerator for up to 4 days. Be sure to remove it from the refrigerator at least 1 hour before serving to allow the cake and frosting to soften to the perfect eating consistency. Once cut, there is no need to wrap the whole cake with plastic; simply press a piece of plastic wrap firmly against the cut surfaces to keep the cake fresh.

Classic White Layer Cake
Same delicious flavor, but with a soft white crumb that is especially appropriate for baby showers, weddings, and tea cakes. Follow the recipe, but substitute 4 large egg whites for the 3 whole eggs.

Yellow or White Cupcakes
Bake the yellow or white batter in a standard-size muffin tin lined with paper cupcake liners, filling each cup to ¼ inch from the top of the liner. Bake for 15 to 20 minutes, until firm to the touch and a toothpick inserted into the center comes out clean. You'll need just ½ recipe of the ganache to frost the cupcakes. Makes about 12 cupcakes.

Mini Yellow or White Cupcakes
Bake the yellow or white batter in a mini-muffin tin lined with mini-cupcake liners, filling each cup with 1 tablespoon of batter to ¼ inch from the top of the liner. Bake for 11 to 14 minutes, until firm to the touch and a toothpick inserted into the center comes out clean. Makes about 50 mini cupcakes.

DEVIL'S FOOD CAKE

MAKES 2 (9-INCH) CAKE LAYERS, SERVING 8 TO 12 The deep chocolate flavor of this cake comes from the technique of pouring boiling water over cocoa powder, which intensifies and releases all the chocolate notes within. Be sure to use unsweetened Dutch-process cocoa powder; natural cocoa powder will react unfavorably with the baking powder. If you're not sure which kind you have, check the ingredient label: Dutch-process cocoa powder contains alkali, whereas natural does not.

You can do so many things with this cake: Cover it with a satiny coat of Orange Sabayon Cream for a sophisticated ending. Or, layer it with silken chocolate ganache in a Mile-High Chocolate Layer Cake (page 321), and it's a chocolate lover's dream. Surprise your guests by serving them Retro Ringers with Silver Leaf (page 322), a grown-up version of the childhood lunchbox favorite. Or, treat the whole classroom to a big batch of cupcakes (see variations) topped with White-Chocolate Cream Cheese Frosting (page 414) or another frosting of your choice (see pages 408 to 415 for ideas).

INGREDIENTS

½ cup (2½ ounces) unsifted unsweetened Dutch-process cocoa powder

½ cup (4 ounces) plus 1 cup (8 ounces) water

1½ sticks (6 ounces) unsalted butter, softened (65° to 68°F)

1 cup (7 ounces) granulated sugar

¾ cup (6 ounces) firmly packed light brown sugar

3 large eggs, at room temperature

2 teaspoons pure vanilla extract

2 cups (7 ounces) sifted cake flour

¼ cup (1¼ ounces) unbleached all-purpose flour

2 teaspoons baking powder

¼ teaspoon salt

Orange Sabayon Cream (page 418)

EQUIPMENT

Two (9 by 1¾-inch) Round Cake Pans, Parchment Paper, Two Small Bowls, Small Saucepan, Whisk, Stand Mixer Fitted with a Paddle Attachment or a Hand Mixer and a Medium Bowl, Silicone or Rubber Spatula, Fine-Mesh Strainer, Medium Bowl, Cooling Rack, Thin and Flexible Knife or Spatula, Two (9-inch) Cake Cardboards or Tart Pan Bottoms

1 Preheat the oven to 350°F and position oven racks in the lower and upper thirds. Lightly coat the pans with butter, oil, or high-heat canola-oil spray and line the bottoms with rounds of parchment paper.

2 MIX THE COCOA POWDER: Place the cocoa powder in a small bowl. Heat ½ cup of the water in the small saucepan just until it begins to simmer. Pour it over the cocoa and whisk or stir until blended and smooth. Add the remaining 1 cup water and stir until the mixture is smooth. Set aside until the mixture cools to room temperature. If it is warm, it will melt the butter and ruin the texture of your cake.

3 CREAM THE BUTTER WITH THE SUGARS: Place the butter, granulated sugar, and brown sugar in the bowl of the stand mixer. Beat on medium-high speed until very light in color, 4 to 5 minutes. You can also use a hand mixer and a medium bowl, although you may need to beat the mixture a little longer to achieve the same results. Scrape down the bowl with the spatula.

4 **ADD THE EGGS:** Beat the eggs and vanilla in the other small bowl to blend. With the mixer on medium, add the eggs to the butter mixture about 1 tablespoon at a time, allowing each addition to completely blend in before adding the next. About halfway through, turn off the mixer and scrape down the bowl, then resume adding the eggs. Scrape down the bowl again.

5 **ADD THE DRY AND WET INGREDIENTS ALTERNATELY:** With the fine-mesh strainer, sift the cake flour, all-purpose flour, baking powder, and salt into the medium bowl and blend with the cleaned whisk. With the mixer on the lowest speed, add the flour mixture and the cocoa water alternately, beginning with one-third of the flour mixture and half the cocoa water. Repeat, then finish with flour mixture. Scrape down the bowl and finish blending the batter by hand, if necessary.

6 **BAKE THE CAKE:** Divide the batter evenly between the two prepared pans and smooth the tops. Bake for about 30 minutes, or until the tops are firm to the touch and a toothpick inserted into the centers comes out clean. Transfer to a rack to cool completely.

7 **UNMOLD THE CAKES:** Run the thin and flexible knife or spatula around the edge of a pan to loosen the cake. Place a cake cardboard on top of the pan, hold the two together, and flip over. Remove the pan, leaving the parchment on the cake. Set the second cake cardboard or plate on top, then flip again. The cake will now be right side up. Repeat with the remaining cake.

8 Level the cakes (see page 308). Turn one over onto a cake cardboard or serving plate, and remove the parchment paper. Spread a generous ¾ cup sabayon cream over the surface. Turn the second cake over onto the cream, cut side down. Peel off the parchment paper. Voila!—a crumb-free surface for frosting. Use the remaining frosting to cover the top and sides of the cake. Serve immediately or refrigerate until needed.

STORING **The unfrosted cakes can be wrapped in plastic and held at room temperature for 1 day. They can also be frozen, double-wrapped in plastic, each one inside a resealable plastic freezer bag, for up to 4 weeks. Leave the parchment paper intact. To thaw, unwrap the cakes and defrost at room temperature for about 1 hour. Once frosted, refrigerate for up to 3 days under a cake dome. If it has been cut, simply press a piece of plastic wrap firmly against the cut surfaces to keep it fresh.**

Devil's Food Sheet Cake
Position an oven rack in the center of the oven. **Lightly butter or oil a 9 by 13 by 2-inch baking pan and line the bottom with parchment paper. Scrape the batter into the pan and bake for 45 to 55 minutes, until firm to the touch and a toothpick inserted into the center comes out clean. Transfer to a rack to cool completely.**

Devil's Food Cupcakes
Line the cups of 2 standard-size cupcake tins with **paper cupcake liners for 20 cupcakes. Fill each liner half full with batter. Bake for 15 to 20 minutes, until the tops are firm to the touch and a toothpick inserted into the centers comes out clean. Transfer to a rack to cool completely. Makes 20 cupcakes.**

Mini Devil's Food Cupcakes
Prepare the oven as directed for cupcakes **above. Line the cups of mini-cupcake tins with mini-cupcake liners, filling each cup with 1 rounded tablespoon of batter to ¼ inch from the top of the liner. Bake for 12 to 15 minutes, until firm to the touch and a toothpick inserted into the centers comes out clean. Transfer to a rack to cool completely. Makes about 80 mini cupcakes.**

MILE-HIGH CHOCOLATE LAYER CAKE

SERVES 10 TO 12 Layer upon layer of deep, dark chocolate cake and ganache create a supremely decadent 8-layer celebration cake worthy of the most special occasion. For an extra layer of moisture and flavor, make a flavored sugar syrup by heating ½ cup water and ½ cup sugar just to a simmer and add 1 teaspoon instant espresso powder, a couple of tablespoons of your favorite liqueur, or 2 teaspoons pure vanilla extract. Brush a little on each layer before spreading the ganache. If you feel unsure of your piping skills, cover the top of the cake with easy chocolate curls (page 428), some Sugared Flowers (page 438), or a stencil pattern (page 436).

INGREDIENTS

1 recipe Devil's Food Cake (page 320), cooled completely

2 recipes Dark Chocolate Ganache (page 412), made at least 8 hours ahead and kept at room temperature

EQUIPMENT

Serrated Knife, Three (9-inch) Cake Cardboards or Tart Pan Bottoms, Icing Spatula, Pastry Bag Fitted with a ½-inch Star Tip

STORING The frosted cake can be made a day ahead of time and left, uncovered or under a cake dome, at room temperature. For longer storage, refrigerate for up to 4 days. This cake is best served at room temperature, so be sure to take it out of the refrigerator about 1½ hours before serving. Once cut, there is no need to wrap the whole cake with plastic; simply press a piece of plastic wrap firmly against the cut surfaces to keep it fresh.

1 Place the two cakes, parchment still attached, right side up on your work surface. The parchment will allow you to easily turn the cakes as you slice them. Level the cakes, if necessary (see page 308). Using the serrated knife, slice each cake horizontally into two layers (see page 308).

2 Place one of the cake cardboards (or a plate) on your work surface. Use the other two cardboards or tart pan bottoms to move the cake layers around (see page 308), and to flip the layers, if needed, to remove the parchment paper. Be sure to save one of the bottom layers, with the parchment still attached, for the top layer of the cake.

3 Place the first cake layer, cut side up, on the assembly cardboard or plate. (If desired, moisten each layer with flavored simple syrup as it is added.) With the icing spatula, spread a generous ½ cup of ganache evenly over the surface, all the way to the edge. It will seem a bit thin, but remember, this cake has 8 layers of cake and frosting! Top with a second layer, parchment removed and cut side up, and spread on another generous ½ cup of ganache. Repeat with the third cake layer, cut side up, and more ganache. Top with the final (bottom) layer of cake, cut side down, and remove the parchment paper. Voilà!—a crumb-free surface for frosting.

4 Set aside 1 cup of the remaining ganache for piping. With the icing spatula, spread a very thin layer (crumb coat) of the frosting over the cake. Chill for 15 minutes. Frost the top and sides of the cake with all but the reserved 1 cup of ganache.

5 Fill the pastry bag with the reserved ganache. Pipe a decorative border around the top edge. If the frosting is very soft, refrigerate for 30 minutes. Otherwise, serve immediately or leave at room temperature until serving time.

RETRO RINGERS WITH SILVER LEAF

MAKES 8 CAKES This version of a childhood lunchbox favorite is all grown up and ready for a party, with rounds of chocolate cake hiding a center of real cream and finished with a cloak of fine-quality bittersweet chocolate. Your friends will enjoy the sly wink the silver leaf gives to the shiny foil wrapping of the original snack cakes. This recipe is all about chocolate, so use the best quality possible in the glaze. Edible silver leaf can be purchased from Indian grocery stores and fine cookware shops.

INGREDIENTS

1 recipe Devil's Food Sheet Cake
(page 320), cooled completely

FILLING

⅓ cup (2¾ ounces) heavy whipping cream

1 teaspoon sugar

Scant ½ teaspoon pure vanilla extract

GLAZE

8 ounces bittersweet chocolate (up to 64 percent cacao), finely chopped

1 cup (8 ounces) heavy whipping cream (if using chocolate that is over 60 percent cacao, add an extra ¼ cup cream)

Edible silver leaf (page 436) or silver dragées

Fresh Raspberry Sauce (page 427)

1 half-pint basket (6 ounces) fresh raspberries

EQUIPMENT

3-inch Round Cookie Cutter, 2-inch Round Cookie Cutter, Paring Knife, Stand Mixer Fitted with a Whisk Attachment or a Hand Mixer and a Medium Bowl, Pastry Bag Fitted with a ½-inch Plain Tip, Medium Bowl, Small Saucepan, Whisk, Cooling Rack, Two Baking Sheets with Rimmed Edges, Parchment Paper, Mini Offset Spatula, Fine-Mesh Strainer (Optional), Silicone or Rubber Spatula (Optional), Icing Spatula

1 **CUT THE CAKES:** Use the 3-inch cutter to cut eight rounds from the cake. Save the scraps for snacking. Insert a small paring knife into the side of a round, ¼ inch from the bottom, and push the tip approximately two-thirds of the way through the cake. Push the 2-inch cutter down into the center of the cake until it hits the paring knife. Gently wiggle the knife and cutter until the cylinder of cake is cut free. Remove the knife and the cutter with the cake piece in it. Pop the cake out of the cutter and slice off a ¼-inch-thick round, which will become the "cover" for the opening, sealing in the cream filling. Set the cover aside and enjoy the remaining cake for yourself. Repeat with all the rounds.

2 **MAKE THE FILLING:** In the bowl of the stand mixer, whip the cream, sugar, and vanilla on medium speed into firm peaks. You can also use a hand mixer and a medium bowl. Transfer to the pastry bag (or a quart-size resealable plastic bag and snip off one of the corners). Pipe the cream to fill the hole in each cake. Press the round slices of reserved cake on the tops.

3 **MAKE THE GLAZE:** Place the chopped chocolate in the medium bowl. Warm the cream in the small saucepan just until it begins to boil. Immediately pour over the chocolate. Let the mixture sit for 1 or 2 minutes, then whisk gently until completely blended and smooth. If there are any lumps of chocolate left, place the bowl over a saucepan of gently simmering water and stir constantly until they melt. Remove the glaze from the heat and let cool slightly for 5 to 10 minutes. It should be pourable but slightly thickened, about the consistency of heavy cream or honey.

what the
pros
know

This is a recipe for which *mise en place* and a couple of kitchen towels for cleaning hands and workspace of chocolate are especially important. Nothing here is particularly difficult, but once you get started, it's best to proceed unimpeded to the finish. Read through the recipe, gather everything you need, and don't answer the phone. Being prepared allows you to enjoy baking and decorating.

4 GLAZE THE CAKES: Working with one cake at a time, place it on a cooling rack set on a parchment-lined baking sheet. Set the bowl of glaze next to the baking sheet. Pour 3 tablespoons of glaze onto the top of the cake, then use the offset spatula to gently push the glaze across the top, letting the excess run down the side to coat them. Dab glaze onto any exposed patches of cake. As you finish each cake, use the offset spatula to move it to the far end of the cooling rack so you won't accidentally drip glaze on it and mar its finish. Repeat with the remaining 7 cakes. (If the glaze becomes too thick to pour over the cakes, reheat it in the microwave oven or set over a bit of simmering water until fluid again. If you run out of glaze, reuse the excess on the parchment paper by scraping the ganache into a fine-mesh strainer (to remove any crumbs) set over the bowl of glaze and pushing it through with the silicone spatula, if necessary. Gently reheat the glaze to make it fluid again, and continue covering the cakes. Any leftover glaze can be used as an ice cream topping, rolled into truffles, or stirred into hot milk or coffee.

5 Use a pair of tweezers or the tip of a paring knife to break off a bit of silver leaf, if using, and touch it to the surface of each glazed cake. The moisture on the surface will cause the silver leaf to adhere instantly. If using a knife, work close to the cake, so the silver leaf does not break loose from the knife and disintegrate into the air. If you are garnishing with silver dragees, sprinkle them over the top now, while the glaze is still tacky and can hold them. To remove the cakes from the rack, carefully slide an offset spatula underneath each cake, releasing the chocolate glaze around the edges from the rack. Move the cakes by supporting them with an icing spatula while the glaze is still soft, but no longer dripping.

6 Refrigerate the cakes for at least 20 minutes or until serving time. To serve, spoon a bit of raspberry sauce on one side of each cake and scatter a few raspberries around.

STORING **The finished cakes can be stored on the parchment-lined pan wrapped in plastic in the refrigerator for up to 1 day.**

PUMPKIN SPICE CAKE WITH MAPLE-CREAM CHEESE FROSTING

SERVES 8 TO 10 When the leaves are falling and the air is crisp, this cake will warm the kitchen with the fragrance of fall. The comforting flavor of spiced pumpkin in a soft and tender cake is layered with a luscious cream cheese frosting sweetened with real maple syrup. Be sure to use the darkest, most flavorful maple syrup you can find–look for Grade C, which is not an indication of quality but of darkness and intensity of flavor. School party? Make the cupcake variation and top each one with a little candy pumpkin.

INGREDIENTS

CAKE

1 stick (4 ounces) unsalted butter, softened (65° to 68°F)

1½ cups (12 ounces) firmly packed light brown sugar

2 large eggs, at room temperature

1 teaspoon pure vanilla extract

1 cup (8 ounces) canned pumpkin puree (not spiced pumpkin pie filling)

2 cups (7 ounces) sifted cake flour

1 teaspoon baking soda

¼ teaspoon baking powder

¼ teaspoon salt

½ teaspoon ground cinnamon

¼ teaspoon ground allspice

¼ teaspoon ground nutmeg

⅛ teaspoon ground cloves

½ cup (4 ounces) buttermilk, at room temperature

FROSTING

12 ounces cream cheese, at room temperature

¾ stick (3 ounces) unsalted butter, at room temperature

½ cup plus 1 tablespoon (6½ ounces) pure maple syrup, preferably Grade C

1¾ cups (5¼ ounces) sifted confectioners' sugar

1 cup (4 ounces) pecan pieces, toasted (see page 56) and finely chopped, for garnish

EQUIPMENT

9 by 1¾-inch Round Cake Pan, Parchment Paper, Stand Mixer Fitted with a Paddle Attachment or a Hand Mixer and a Medium Bowl, Silicone or Rubber Spatula, Small Bowl, Fine-Mesh Strainer, Medium Bowl, Whisk, Cooling Rack, Food Processor (Optional), Thin and Flexible Knife or Spatula, Two (9-inch) Cake Cardboards or Tart Pan Bottoms, Serrated Knife, Icing Spatula, Thin and Sharp Knife

1 Preheat the oven to 350°F and position an oven rack in the center. Lightly coat the pan with melted butter, oil, or high-heat canola-oil spray and fit it with a round of parchment paper.

2 CREAM THE BUTTER WITH THE SUGAR: Beat the butter and brown sugar in the bowl of the stand mixer on medium-high until very light in color, 4 to 5 minutes. You can also use a hand mixer and a medium bowl, although you may need to beat the mixture a little longer to achieve the same results. Scrape down the bowl with the spatula.

3 ADD THE EGGS: Beat the eggs and vanilla in the small bowl to blend. With the mixer on medium, add the eggs to the butter mixture about 1 tablespoon at a time, allowing each addition to completely blend in before adding the next. About halfway through, turn off the mixer and scrape down the bowl, then resume adding the eggs. Scrape down the bowl again. Add the pumpkin and blend well.

4 ADD THE DRY AND WET INGREDIENTS ALTERNATELY: With the fine-mesh strainer, sift the cake flour, baking soda, baking powder, salt, cinnamon, allspice, nutmeg, and cloves into the medium bowl and whisk to blend. With the mixer on the lowest speed, add the flour mixture and the buttermilk alternately, beginning with one-third of the flour mixture and half of the buttermilk; repeat, then finish with the flour mixture. Scrape down the bowl and finish blending the batter by hand.

GETTING AHEAD The unfrosted cake can be frozen, double-wrapped in plastic and sealed in a resealable plastic freezer bag, for up to 4 weeks. To thaw, unwrap the cake and let it defrost at room temperature for about 1 hour. Make the frosting and frost the cake the day you wish to serve.

5 BAKE THE CAKE: Scrape the batter into the prepared pan and smooth the top. Bake for about 1 hour, or until the top is firm to the touch and a toothpick inserted into the center comes out clean. Transfer to a rack to cool completely.

6 MAKE THE FROSTING: Place the cream cheese and butter in the cleaned bowl of the mixer or a food processor. Blend until smooth. Add the maple syrup and confectioners' sugar and mix thoroughly. Scrape down the bowl with a clean spatula and blend again briefly.

7 UNMOLD THE CAKE: Run the thin, flexible knife or spatula around the edge of the pan to loosen the cake. Place a cake cardboard or tart pan bottom on top of the pan, hold the two together, and flip over. Lift the pan off the cake, leaving the parchment on the cake. Flip again so the cake is right side up. Level the cake, if necessary (see page 308). Using the serrated knife, slice the cake horizontally into two layers (see page 308).

8 ASSEMBLE AND FROST THE CAKE: Place a cake cardboard (or plate) on your work surface. Using the second cardboard or tart bottom, transfer the cake's top layer to the assembly cardboard, cut side up. With the icing spatula, spread a generous ½ cup of frosting evenly over the surface. Flip over the bottom layer of cake, slide it into place on top of the frosting, then remove the parchment paper. Voilà!—a crumb-free surface for frosting. Use the remaining frosting to cover the top and side of the cake. Use a spoon to create swirls all over the top by gently pressing the tip of the spoon, rounded edge down, into the frosting in a back-and-forth motion. Press the toasted pecans into the side of the cake (see page 55). Serve immediately, slicing with a thin, sharp knife, or refrigerate until needed.

STORING The cake will keep, refrigerated, for 3 days. It is best served at cool room temperature, so be sure to take it out of the refrigerator 30 to 45 minutes before serving. Once cut, there is no need to wrap the whole cake with plastic; simply press a piece of plastic wrap firmly against the cut surfaces to keep the cake fresh.

Pumpkin Spice Bundt Cake
Prepare a 10-inch Bundt pan (10- to 12-cup capacity) by lightly but thoroughly coating the pan with butter or high-heat canola oil spray, then dusting with flour (tap out any excess). Scrape the batter into the pan and smooth the top. Bake for 35 to 40 minutes, until firm to the touch and a toothpick inserted into the center comes out clean. Transfer to a rack and cool for 30 minutes. Then turn out onto a cake cardboard or serving platter while still warm. Omit the frosting. Let the cake finish cooling, then spoon Confectioners' Sugar Icing (page 415), Dark Chocolate Ganache (page 412), or chilled Caramel Sauce (page 426) over the top and let it drip down the sides. Or simply dust with confectioners' sugar and serve with Cider Sabayon (page 418).

Pumpkin Spice Cupcakes with Maple–Cream Cheese Frosting
Position the oven racks in the upper and lower thirds of the oven. Line 2 standard-size cupcake tins with paper liners. Fill each liner three-fourths full with batter. Bake for 15 to 20 minutes, until the tops are firm to the touch and a toothpick inserted into the centers comes out clean. Cool the cupcakes; frost the day you wish to serve them. Cut the frosting recipe in half, or you'll have a lot left over. Makes 18 cupcakes.

Pumpkin Spice Mini Cupcakes with Maple–Cream Cheese Frosting
Prepare the oven as directed for cupcakes. Spoon the batter into mini-muffin tins lined with paper liners, filling each cup with 1 tablespoon of batter to ¼ inch from the top of the liner. Bake for 12 to 14 minutes, until firm to the touch and a toothpick inserted into the centers. Transfer to a rack to cool completely. Makes about 65 mini cupcakes.

ALMOND, APRICOT, AND CHOCOLATE CHIP CAKE WITH AMARETTO GLAZE

SERVES 10 TO 12 This Bundt-style cake has an incredibly moist crumb and deep almond flavor, with tiny nuggets of tart dried apricots and miniature chocolate chips speckling each piece. The trio of flavors is an irresistible blend of sweet, tart, and bitter, made even better by the easy chocolate-amaretto glaze. Almond paste, a smooth, slightly sticky mixture of ground almonds and sugar, is the key to the cake's texture—don't substitute marzipan here, as it contains too much sugar.

INGREDIENTS

CAKE

1 cup (7 ounces) sugar

½ cup (5 ounces) packed almond paste, cut into ½-inch pieces, at room temperature

2 sticks (8 ounces) unsalted butter, softened (65° to 68°F)

5 large eggs, at room temperature

2 teaspoons amaretto (almond liqueur)

⅔ cup (3¼ ounces) plus ⅓ cup (1¾ ounces) unbleached all-purpose flour

1 teaspoon baking powder

Pinch of salt

1½ cups (6 ounces) dried apricots, preferably California or Blenheim, halved

½ cup (3 ounces) mini chocolate chips

GLAZE

2 ounces semisweet chocolate (60 percent or less cacao), finely chopped

¼ cup (2 ounces) heavy whipping cream

1½ tablespoons amaretto (almond liqueur)

EQUIPMENT

10-inch Bundt Pan (10- to 12-Cup Capacity), Stand Mixer Fitted with a Paddle Attachment or a Hand Mixer and a Medium Bowl, Small Bowl, Silicone or Rubber Spatula, Medium Microwave-Safe Bowl, Whisk, Food Processor Fitted with a Metal Blade, Cooling Rack, Baking Sheet with Rimmed Edges, Small Saucepan, Cake Lifter or Tart Pan Bottom, Serving Platter or 10-inch Cake Cardboard, Serrated Knife

1 Preheat the oven to 350°F and position an oven rack in the center. Lightly but thoroughly coat the pan with melted butter, oil, or high-heat canola-oil spray, then flour it and tap out any excess flour. (The almond paste makes this cake a bit sticky and it will adhere to any spots you have missed.)

2 MAKE THE BATTER: Beat the sugar and almond paste in the bowl of the stand mixer on medium speed until the almond paste is broken into tiny pieces, 2 to 3 minutes. You may also process the sugar and almond paste in a food processor and then transfer the mixture to a medium bowl to finish with a hand mixer. (If you try to blend the sugar and almond paste with a hand mixer alone, you'll have almond paste flying out of your mixing bowl.) Add the butter and continue to beat on medium until the mixture is very light—almost white—in color, about 5 minutes. If you're using a hand mixer, you'll need to beat the mixture a little longer to achieve the same results.

3 ADD THE EGGS: Beat the eggs in the small bowl to blend. With the mixer on medium speed, add the eggs about 1 tablespoon at a time, allowing each addition to completely blend in before adding the next. About halfway through, turn off the mixer and scrape down the bowl with the spatula, then continue adding the eggs. Add the amaretto and blend. Scrape down the bowl again.

4 In the medium bowl, whisk together the ⅔ cup flour, the baking powder, and salt. Add to the batter and beat well. Place the remaining ⅓ cup flour and the dried apricots in the bowl of the food processor and process until the apricots are chopped into small pieces

GETTING AHEAD The unglazed cake can be frozen, wrapped tightly in 2 layers of plastic, for up to 1 month. Do not apply the chocolate glaze until the day you thaw and serve the cake, as freezing causes the glaze to lose its shine and become blotchy. To defrost, set the cake—still inside the plastic—on the counter for a couple of hours, or until it reaches room temperature.

about the size of small peas or lentils (no smaller, or the pieces in contact with the pan will become very hard during baking). Add the apricots and the chocolate chips to the batter and blend well. Scrape down the bowl, making sure that any patches of flour or butter at the bottom are blended in. Scrape the batter into the prepared pan.

5 Bake the cake for 40 to 45 minutes, until the top is firm to the touch and a toothpick inserted into the center comes out clean or with just a few moist crumbs clinging to it. Transfer to a rack to cool until lukewarm. Set a small cooling rack on top of the pan, hold the pan and rack together, and flip over and set the rack on the counter. The cake should fall out of the pan. If it doesn't, tap it firmly against the rack. If it still doesn't come out, warm the pan briefly by moving it back and forth over a medium flame on the stove for 15 to 20 seconds. The cake should come out easily now. Set the rack with the cake on the rimmed baking sheet.

6 MAKE THE GLAZE: Place the chopped chocolate in the medium bowl. Heat the cream in the small saucepan just until it begins to boil. Immediately pour over the chocolate and let sit for 1 minute. Whisk gently until melted and blended completely. If you still have hard lumps of chocolate, set the bowl over simmering water and stir constantly until they melt—or heat in the microwave oven in 30-second bursts, stirring between each one, until melted. Add the amaretto and whisk to blend. Let the glaze cool slightly, until it is about 90°F and the thickness of honey.

7 GLAZE THE CAKE: Spoon the glaze over the cake, letting it drip down the sides. Any excess glaze on the baking sheet can be scooped up and poured over the cake again (or refrigerated and warmed up on another day to use as a topping for ice cream). To serve, use the cake lifter or tart pan bottom to transfer the cake to a serving dish or cake cardboard. Cut the cake with the serrated knife using a gentle sawing motion.

STORING The glazed cake holds well at room temperature for several days. Once it has been cut, keep it fresh by pressing a piece of plastic wrap against the cut edges.

APRICOT-RASPBERRY UPSIDE-DOWN CAKE

SERVES 8 TO 10 A simple, homey upside-down cake is always a welcome delight. These cakes have fallen a bit out of favor lately, perhaps because people are afraid they'll end up with a slice of cake topped with canned pineapple rings and a fluorescent pink cherry. That's a bad rap for a dessert that so beautifully melds fruit of the season with warm-from-the-oven cake. A couple of tips: Take a few extra minutes to arrange the fruit in a pretty pattern in the bottom of the pan, because when you unmold the cake, the fruit will be the top—and the decoration. Wait at least 30 minutes before turning it out of the pan to allow time for the juices to be reabsorbed and to ensure that the fruit will stay on top of the cake rather than sliding off in an avalanche of juice.

INGREDIENTS

TOPPING

½ stick (2 ounces) unsalted butter, cut into small pieces

½ cup (4 ounces) firmly packed light brown sugar

4 medium (8 ounces) apricots

1 half-pint basket (6 ounces) raspberries

CAKE

1 stick (4 ounces) unsalted butter, softened (65° to 68°F)

1 cup (7 ounces) granulated sugar

2 large eggs at room temperature, separated

1½ teaspoons pure vanilla extract

1 cup plus 2 tablespoons (6 ounces) unbleached all-purpose flour

¼ cup (1¼ ounces) fine cornmeal

½ teaspoon baking powder

¼ teaspoon salt

½ cup (4 ounces) whole milk, at room temperature

Almond Cream (page 417) or ice cream, for serving

EQUIPMENT

Medium Skillet or Sauté Pan, Whisk, Paring Knife, Baking Sheet, 9 by 1¾-inch Round Cake Pan (Not Springform), Stand Mixer with Paddle and Whisk Attachments or a Hand Mixer and a Medium Bowl, Silicone or Rubber Spatula, Small Bowl, Fine-Mesh Strainer, Medium Bowl, Whisk, Large Bowl, Cooling Rack, Thin and Flexible Knife or Spatula

1 Preheat the oven to 350°F and position an oven rack in the center.

2 PREPARE THE TOPPING: Melt the butter in the skillet over medium heat, then blend in the brown sugar. It will look grainy at first but will smooth out as the sugar melts. Whisk vigorously to blend the mixture—you do not want to see any pools of melted butter separating from the sugar. Once the mixture is melted and smooth, pour it into the bottom of the cake pan. Set aside to cool.

3 With a paring knife, halve and pit the apricots and slice each half into 4 wedges. Pour the raspberries out onto a baking sheet. Pick through them and discard any debris or molded berries. Do not wash, or they will absorb the water and turn to mush. Arrange a row of slightly overlapping apricot slices around the outer rim of the pan. Then arrange a double row of raspberries. Fill in the center of the cake pan with overlapping apricot slices. Set aside.

4 CREAM THE BUTTER WITH THE SUGAR: Beat the butter and granulated sugar in the stand mixer with the paddle on medium-high speed until very light—almost white—in color, 4 to 5 minutes. You can also use a hand mixer and a medium bowl, although you may need to beat the mixture a little longer to achieve the same results. Scrape down the bowl with the spatula.

5 **ADD THE EGGS:** Beat the egg yolks and vanilla in the small bowl to blend. With the mixer on medium, add the yolk mixture about 1 tablespoon at a time, allowing each addition to completely blend in before adding the next. Scrape down the bowl.

6 **ADD THE DRY AND WET INGREDIENTS ALTERNATELY:** With the fine-mesh strainer, sift the flour, cornmeal, baking powder, and salt into the medium bowl. If any cornmeal is left in the strainer, add it to the bowl. Whisk to blend. With the mixer on the lowest speed, add the flour mixture and milk alternately, beginning with one-third of the flour mixture and half the milk; repeat, then finish with the flour mixture. Scrape down the bowl. Transfer to the large bowl.

7 **FINISH THE BATTER AND BAKE THE CAKE:** In the cleaned mixer bowl with a clean whisk attachment, whip the egg whites on medium speed to firm peaks. You can also use the hand mixer. Gently fold into the batter until no streaks of white remain (it will be quite thick). Scrape the batter into the prepared pan and smooth the top. Bake for 50 to 60 minutes, until the top is golden, firm to the touch, and a toothpick inserted into the center comes out clean. Transfer the cake to a rack to cool for 30 minutes.

8 **UNMOLD THE CAKE:** Run the thin, flexible knife or spatula around the edge of the pan to loosen the cake. If the cake is very rounded, press down gently to level the top. Place a serving plate on top of the pan, hold the two together, and flip over. The cake should slide right out. If it doesn't, hold the pan over a medium flame on the stove for 15 to 20 seconds to melt the syrup in the bottom of the pan. Flip again. To serve, cut the cake with a thin, sharp knife and accompany with a spoonful of softly whipped almond cream or a small scoop of ice cream.

STORING **This cake is best served the day it is made, preferably warm from the oven. It will not look as pretty the second day (or even 8 hours later), although the flavor will still be good. Once cut, there is no need to wrap the whole cake with plastic; simply press a piece of plastic wrap firmly against the cut surfaces to keep it fresh and store it under a cake dome.**

Plum-Blackberry Upside-Down Cake Substitute blackberries for
the raspberries (if the blackberries are large, you may need 2 baskets), and freestone plums for apricots. If the plums are not freestone, you will need a few extra to compensate for the flesh left on the pit.

LEMON MASCARPONE LAYER CAKE

SERVES 10 TO 12 This soft, moist, towering cloud of a dessert lies somewhere between a cake and a trifle, its lemon syrup-soaked cake layers alternating with lemon mascarpone cream. Perfect for entertaining, the cake is at its best the day after you assemble it, when the flavors and textures have had a chance to blend and mellow. Meyer lemons are especially fragrant, but this cake is outstanding with supermarket Eureka lemons as well. There are a few steps here, but almost everything can be done ahead, which makes putting it together pretty easy—check the notes at the end of the recipe.

INGREDIENTS

1 recipe Lemon Curd (page 421)

SPONGE CAKES

6 large eggs, separated

7 tablespoons (3 ounces) plus 7 tablespoons (3 ounces) sugar

1¾ cups (6 ounces) sifted cake flour

LEMON SYRUP

½ cup (3½ ounces) sugar

½ cup water

¼ cup (2 ounces) freshly squeezed lemon juice

MASCARPONE FILLING

2½ cups (20 ounces) heavy whipping cream

7 tablespoons (3 ounces) sugar

1 pound mascarpone

EQUIPMENT

Two (9 by 1¾-inch) Round Cake Pans, Parchment Paper, Stand Mixer Fitted with a Whisk Attachment or a Hand Mixer and a Medium Bowl, Two Large Bowls, Silicone or Rubber Spatula, Fine-Mesh Strainer, Cooling Rack, Small Saucepan, Two Medium Bowls, Thin and Flexible Knife or Spatula, Serrated Knife, 9-inch Cake Cardboard or Serving Platter, Pastry Brush, Icing Spatula, Pastry Bag Fitted with a ½-inch Star Tip, Thin and Sharp Knife

1 Preheat the oven to 375°F and position oven racks in the lower and upper thirds. Fit each cake pan with a parchment round. Do not grease the pans.

2 MAKE THE CAKES: Whip the egg yolks and 7 tablespoons of the sugar in the bowl of the stand mixer on high speed until thick and very light in color, 4 to 5 minutes. You can also use a hand mixer and a medium bowl, although you may need to beat the mixture a little longer to achieve the same results. Transfer to a large bowl and set aside while you whip the egg whites.

3 In the cleaned mixer bowl with the cleaned whisk attachment, or in the cleaned medium bowl with clean beaters, whip the egg whites on medium speed to soft peaks. With the mixer running, gradually add the remaining 7 tablespoons of sugar; continue beating until the egg whites hold firm peaks. Fold one-third of the egg whites into the beaten yolks with the spatula, then use the fine-mesh strainer to sift half of the flour over the top and gently fold it in. Repeat. Fold in the last of the egg whites until no streaks of white remain.

4 Divide the batter evenly between the prepared pans. Bake for 18 to 22 minutes, until the tops are golden, firm to the touch, and a toothpick inserted into the centers comes out clean. Halfway through the baking time, switch the pans on the racks so they bake evenly. Transfer the cakes to a rack to cool completely.

5 MAKE THE LEMON SYRUP: Heat the sugar and water in the small saucepan, stirring occasionally, until the sugar has completely dissolved and the liquid is clear. Remove from the heat and cool completely. Stir in the lemon juice.

Blending mascarpone with the whipped cream filling adds not only flavor and a delightful richness, but also stability. Whipped cream alone can deteriorate quickly, becoming watery and losing volume as the hours tick by. But when mascarpone is combined with whipped cream, it stabilizes the mixture, allowing the cream to keep its shape and texture for days. And though this recipe uses a pound of mascarpone, even a small amount—a couple of tablespoons for each cup of cream—will have the same effect.

GETTING AHEAD The sponge cakes can be made up to 3 days in advance, wrapped in plastic, and stored at room temperature. Be sure to leave the parchment paper on (it will help stabilize the layers and aid in moving them without breakage). The cakes can be frozen, double-wrapped in plastic, each inside a resealable plastic freezer bag, for up to 8 weeks. To thaw, unwrap and defrost at room temperature for 1 hour. The lemon syrup can be made up to 1 week in advance. The lemon curd can be made up to 3 days in advance.

6 MAKE THE MASCARPONE FILLING: Place the cream and sugar in the cleaned mixer bowl and whip until soft peaks form. Place the mascarpone and 1 cup lemon curd in a large bowl and stir until blended—it should be the consistency of pudding. Gently fold in the whipped cream until the mixture is homogenous and thick. If the mixture becomes overworked, it will look grainy or separated. If this happens, stir in several tablespoons of cream with the spatula and stir just until the mixture has smoothed out again. Transfer 2¼ cups of filling to a medium bowl to use for piping decorations. Transfer half of the remaining filling to another medium bowl. Refrigerate all 3 bowls of mascarpone mixture. You may want to label the three bowls: one for piping, one for filling layers, and one for frosting.

7 UNMOLD THE CAKES: Run the thin, flexible knife or spatula around the edge of a pan to loosen a cake. Turn the pan upside down and give it a sharp rap on the table to release (don't worry, these cakes are very sturdy). Turn the cake right side up, leaving the parchment paper attached. Repeat with the remaining cake. Level the cakes, if necessary (see page 308). Using the serrated knife, slice each cake horizontally into two layers (see page 308). Set aside one of the bottom layers to use last, and remove the parchment from the other layer.

8 ASSEMBLE THE CAKE: Place a cake layer, cut side up, on the cake cardboard or serving plate. Brush the cake with ¼ of the lemon syrup. With the icing spatula, spread ⅓ of the mascarpone filling on top. Place 3 level tablespoons of the remaining lemon curd on top of the filling and spread evenly to the edge. Place a second cake layer on top, cut side up, and repeat with lemon syrup, mascarpone filling, and lemon curd. Place third layer on top, cut side up, and repeat.

9 Top with the last cake layer, placing it bottom up (cut side down). Remove the parchment paper. Voilà!—a crumb-free surface for frosting. Moisten it with the remaining lemon syrup. Use the cleaned icing spatula to spread the mascarpone reserved for frosting mixture over the cake, spreading it quite thinly on top with more on the side.

10 FINISH AND SERVE THE CAKE: Spoon the piping mascarpone into the pastry bag and pipe rosettes (page 310) over the entire top of the cake, starting around the outside edge and working your way to the center. Put a few tablespoons of the remaining curd into a resealable plastic sandwich bag and squeeze it into one of the corners. Snip off the corner and pipe a center of lemon curd into each of the rosettes. Refrigerate for at least 4 hours before serving, so the flavors and textures have a chance to meld. To serve, slice with a thin, sharp knife.

STORING The cake will keep, refrigerated, for 3 to 4 days. Once cut, there is no need to wrap the whole cake with plastic; simply press a piece of plastic wrap firmly against the cut surfaces to keep it fresh.

Passion Fruit Mascarpone Layer Cake Substitute Passion Fruit Curd (page 421) for the lemon curd.

FLOURLESS CHOCOLATE CAKE WITH CRÈME FRAÎCHE TOPPING

SERVES 8 TO 10 There's no simpler or better dessert to please a chocolate-lover (or the cook) than a flourless chocolate cake. The batter can be prepared and in the oven in less than 15 minutes. This cake is all about the chocolate, so use the best you can.

INGREDIENTS

CAKE

10 ounces semisweet or bittersweet chocolate (up to 70 percent cacao), finely chopped

1¼ sticks (5 ounces) unsalted butter, cut into small pieces

5 large eggs

½ cup (3½ ounces) sugar

TOPPING

1 (8-ounce) container crème fraîche

¼ cup (2 ounces) heavy whipping cream

1½ tablespoons sugar

1 teaspoon pure vanilla extract

1 teaspoon framboise (raspberry brandy) or Chambord (black raspberry liqueur) (optional)

2 half-pint baskets (12 ounces) raspberries

EQUIPMENT

9-inch Springform Pan, Double Boiler, Stand Mixer Fitted with a Whisk Attachment, Silicone or Rubber Spatula, Cooling Rack, Thin and Flexible Knife or Spatula, Icing Spatula, Thin and Sharp Knife

GETTING AHEAD The cake (without topping) can be wrapped in plastic and stored for 3 to 4 days at room temperature. You can also freeze the cake (without topping), double-wrapped in plastic and then in foil, for up to 2 weeks. Unwrap and thaw at room temperature. Add the topping just before serving.

1 Preheat the oven to 350°F and position an oven rack in the center. Lightly coat the pan with melted butter, oil, or high-heat canola-oil spray.

2 MAKE THE CAKE: Bring 2 inches of water to a boil in the bottom of the double boiler. Place the chocolate and butter in the top portion (off heat). Reduce the heat to a simmer and set the chocolate mixture on top. Heat gently, stirring frequently, until melted and smooth. Set aside.

3 Whip the eggs and sugar in the bowl of the stand mixer on high until the mixture holds a 3-second ribbon (see page 303). With the spatula, scrape the eggs on top of the chocolate mixture and gently but thoroughly fold in until no streaks of egg remain.

4 Scrape the batter into the prepared pan. Bake for 30 to 40 minutes, until firm to the touch and a toothpick inserted into the center comes out with a few moist crumbs clinging to it. Transfer to a rack to cool completely. It will fall in the center and look a bit uneven—this is normal.

5 Run the thin, flexible knife or spatula around the edge of the pan to loosen the cake and then pop off the side. Slide onto a serving plate.

6 MAKE THE TOPPING: Place the crème fraîche, cream, sugar, vanilla, and framboise in the cleaned mixer bowl and whip until firm peaks form. Be careful not to overwhip or it will become grainy. If this happens, add 2 tablespoons of cream and stir—the mixture should smooth out. If not, add a little more cream.

7 With the icing spatula, spread the crème fraîche evenly across the top of the cake. Pick through the raspberries and discard any debris or molded berries. Pile them on top of the cake. Cut the cake with a thin, sharp knife, wiping the knife with a hot, damp towel between each slice.

STORING Remove immediately or refrigerate until needed, up to 3 days. Remove the cake from the refrigerator at least 30 minutes before serving, so the texture has a chance to soften.

TANGERINE-POPPY SEED CHIFFON CAKE

SERVES 10 TO 12 Chiffon cake, like angel food cake, has a dramatically tall and impressive presence, and relies mainly on whipped egg whites for leavening. Unlike angel food cake, which is fat-free, chiffon cake has a beautifully tender and moist crumb from both oil and egg yolks. Big on flavor, yet light and refreshing, it's time for chiffon cake to make a fashionable return to the dessert table. This cake is perfumed with layers of tangerine juice, zest, and oil–then speckled and textured with the lovely crunch of poppy seeds. It's best to use a pan with metal "feet" attached to the rim, but if your pan does not have them, have ready a wine or soda bottle with a neck that the pan's center tube will fit over for cooling. When tangerines are out of season, substitute freshly squeezed tangerine juice from the supermarket, or use sweet-tart blood oranges or navel oranges.

INGREDIENTS

CAKE

1¾ cups (6 ounces) sifted cake flour

1 cup minus 2 tablespoons (6 ounces), plus ¼ cup (1¾ ounces) granulated sugar

1½ teaspoons baking powder

¼ teaspoon salt

½ cup (3¼ ounces) poppy seeds (optional)

¼ cup plus 2 tablespoons (3 ounces) flavorless vegetable oil, such as safflower or canola

6 large eggs, separated

Finely grated zest of 2 large tangerines

½ cup (4 ounces) strained freshly squeezed tangerine juice

1½ teaspoons pure vanilla extract

¼ teaspoon pure tangerine oil

¾ teaspoon cream of tartar

ICING

2 cups (6¾ ounces) confectioners' sugar

3 tablespoons strained freshly squeezed tangerine juice

⅛ teaspoon pure tangerine oil

Fresh, organic citrus blossoms, Sugared Flowers (page 438), or candied tangerine zest (page 352), for garnish

EQUIPMENT

Fine-Mesh Strainer, Large Bowl, Whisk, Stand Mixer Fitted with a Whisk Attachment or a Hand Mixer and a Medium Bowl, Silicone or Rubber Spatula, 10-inch Ungreased Tube Pan with a Removable Bottom, Skewer, Thin and Flexible Knife or Spatula, Medium Bowl, Serrated Knife

1 Preheat the oven to 325°F and position an oven rack in the lower third.

2 MAKE THE CAKE: With the fine-mesh strainer, sift the cake flour, the 1 cup minus 2 tablespoons granulated sugar, the baking powder, and salt into the large bowl. Add the poppy seeds and whisk to blend. Make a well in the center and pour in the oil, egg yolks, tangerine zest and juice, vanilla extract, and tangerine oil. Whisk vigorously until the mixture is very smooth. Set aside.

3 Make sure your whisk attachment (or beaters) and your mixing bowl are scrupulously clean. In the bowl of the stand mixer, whip the egg whites on medium just until frothy. You can also use a hand mixer and a medium bowl. Add the cream of tartar and whip on medium-high until soft peaks form. With the mixer on medium, slowly add the remaining ¼ cup of granulated sugar and whip until the whites hold very firm peaks. (This cake requires stiff egg whites for its height and open texture, so don't be afraid to beat a few seconds longer than you normally would for firm peaks.) To check for firm peaks, with a spoon scoop

Chiffon cake was invented in Los Angeles in the 1920s by an insurance salesman named Henry Baker. For years he kept the recipe secret while he supplied his catering clients and the legendary Brown Derby restaurant with his much-loved cakes. Finally, in 1947, he sold the recipe to General Mills, and it quickly became a favorite across America. The oil in chiffon cake produces a meltingly tender crumb, one that stays soft and sliceable even when refrigerated or frozen. This is why many pastry chefs think chiffon cake is the perfect base for ice cream cakes.

GETTING AHEAD **The unglazed cake can be wrapped in plastic and refrigerated for 1 week. To freeze, set the unglazed cake on a cake cardboard or plate and wrap in two layers of plastic wrap and freeze for up to 6 weeks. Thaw on the counter for 1½ hours, then apply the glaze and garnish before serving.**

out some whites—they should sit firmly on the spoon, and the peaks that formed in the bowl when the spoon was lifted should hold their shape.

4 Use the spatula to gently stir a mound of beaten whites into the bowl of batter. This step slightly lightens and loosens the mixture, making it easier to fold in the remaining whites without deflating them. Scrape the remaining egg whites into the bowl and gently but thoroughly fold them into the batter until no streaks of egg whites remain.

5 Scrape the batter into the pan and smooth the top. Bake for 50 to 60 minutes, until the cake has risen, the top is lightly golden and feels firm to the touch, and a skewer inserted into the center comes out clean. Immediately invert the pan onto its feet or over the wine or soda bottle. Allow to cool completely, at least 2 hours.

6 Invert the cake so it is right side up. Run the thin, flexible knife or spatula around the edges to loosen it from the pan. As you do this, gently press the knife into the side of the pan to avoid gouging the cake. Push the removable bottom upward to free the cake from the side. Run the same knife around the inside tube and along the bottom of the cake, if necessary, to finish loosening it. Place a plate on top of the cake and invert, removing the cake from the pan. Depending on the look you want, either leave the cake upside down on the plate or invert it again to set it right side up.

7 MAKE THE ICING: With the fine-mesh strainer, sift the confectioners' sugar into the medium bowl. Whisk in the tangerine juice and tangerine oil until the mixture is very smooth. Spoon over the top of the cake, directing some of the icing right onto the edges so that it cascades down the sides. Immediately garnish the top of the cake with the citrus blossoms, sugared flower petals, or candied zest. As the glaze hardens, it will anchor the garnishes to the cake. To serve, slice with the serrated knife using a gentle sawing motion.

STORING **The cake will keep well at room temperature, covered with plastic wrap or under a cake dome, for several days. Once cut, press a piece of plastic wrap firmly against the cut surfaces to help keep it fresh.**

STRAWBERRY ROSE ROULADE

SERVES 12 TO 14 This cake celebrates spring, highlighting two of the season's most anticipated offerings—gorgeous roses and sweet, juicy strawberries. Though strawberries are often available year-round, they are at their absolute best during the warm spring months. They pair beautifully with rose because both are members of the same botanical family.

The baking sheet used here is also known as a half-sheet pan or jelly roll pan. If your pan is a slightly different size, you can use it anyway—just check a bit early for doneness if the pan is a little larger, or add a few minutes to the baking time if it's a bit smaller.

INGREDIENTS

CAKE

6 large eggs

1 cup (7 ounces) granulated sugar

2 teaspoons pure vanilla extract

1 cup (3½ ounces) sifted cake flour

¼ teaspoon salt

¾ stick (3 ounces) unsalted butter, melted and cooled but still fluid

FROSTING AND FILLING

1 pint-basket (about 16 ounces) strawberries

2 cups (16 ounces) heavy whipping cream

2 tablespoons granulated sugar

2 teaspoons rose water

Confectioners' sugar, for dusting

Sugared rose petals (page 438), for garnish

EQUIPMENT

12 by 17-inch Baking Sheet with 1-inch Sides, Parchment Paper, Medium Saucepan, Stand Mixer Fitted with a Whisk Attachment or a Hand Mixer and a Medium Bowl, Whisk, Instant-Read Thermometer, Fine-Mesh Strainer, Medium Bowl, Silicone or Rubber Spatula, Offset Spatula, Cooling Rack, Strawberry Huller (Optional), Paring Knife, Thin and Flexible Knife or Spatula, Long Metal Spatula or Two Short Spatulas, Serrated Knife

1 Preheat the oven to 350°F and position an oven rack in the center. Line the pan with parchment paper.

2 MAKE THE CAKE: Bring 2 inches of water to a boil in the medium saucepan. Place the eggs and granulated sugar in the bowl of the stand mixer and set the bowl over the simmering water. If using a hand mixer, use a medium bowl. Whisking constantly to prevent the eggs from scrambling, heat the mixture to about 110°F on the instant-read thermometer, or just until the eggs are warm to the touch and the sugar has dissolved. You should not feel any graininess when you rub some between your fingers. Don't let the mixture get too hot—you're trying to dissolve the sugar and get maximum volume from the eggs, not cook them.

3 Whip the egg mixture on high speed until very light in color, voluminously thick, and resembling whipped cream, 7 to 10 minutes. If using a hand mixer, it will take 4 to 6 minutes longer. Be sure to use the ribbon test (see page 303) to check their thickness before proceeding—the ribbon of beaten egg should sit on top of the mixture practically indefinitely. Blend in the vanilla extract.

4 With the fine-mesh strainer, sift the flour and salt into the medium bowl. Sift half the flour over the egg mixture and gently fold in with the silicone or rubber spatula. Repeat with the remaining flour, folding gently until no streaks of flour remain. Stir a generous scoop of batter into the cooled melted butter and mix until the butter is completely blended. Scrape this mixture over the batter and gently but thoroughly fold it in. Immediately scrape the batter into the prepared pan and use the offset spatula to gently spread it into an even layer.

GETTING AHEAD **The cake may be baked up to 1 week ahead and frozen in its baking pan, wrapped twice with plastic wrap. Thaw at room temperature. Make the filling and assemble the cake on the day you wish to serve it.**

5 Bake the cake for about 15 minutes, or until the top is lightly golden, feels firm to the touch, and a toothpick inserted into the center comes out clean. Transfer to a rack to cool completely.

6 MAKE THE FROSTING AND FILLING: Wash the strawberries and pat dry, then use a strawberry huller or paring knife to hull them and slice thinly. Set aside. In the cleaned bowl of the stand mixer, whip the cream, granulated sugar, and rose water until soft peaks form. Transfer half of the whipped cream to the cleaned medium bowl, cover, and refrigerate (this will be used to frost the cake). Gently fold the strawberries into the remaining cream to make the filling.

7 Run the thin, flexible knife or spatula around the edges of the pan to loosen the cake. With the fine-mesh strainer, dust the top of the cake with confectioners' sugar and place a piece of parchment paper that is the size of the pan on top of the cake. Hold the paper and pan together, flip over, and set down on your work surface. Remove the pan and peel the parchment paper off the top—the easiest and least damaging way to do this is on the diagonal, from corner to corner. Position the cake so that one of the long sides is parallel to the edge of your work surface.

8 Use the offset spatula to spread the filling evenly over the cake, leaving a 1-inch border along the long edge opposite you. Starting at the long edge closest to you, fold the edge of the cake over the filling and then begin to carefully roll the cake into a log, pulling upward and slightly forward on the paper underneath and using the paper to help you roll the cake. When finished, the seam should be on the bottom.

9 Use the long metal spatula to carefully slide the roll onto a serving platter. If this step is too tricky, just cut the roll in half to make moving it easier and place them back together on the platter. Trim the ends with a serrated knife. Use the reserved whipped cream to frost all around the cake. Refrigerate at least 2 hours before serving.

10 GARNISH AND SERVE THE CAKE: Decorate the cake and serving platter with the sugared rose petals. Cut the cake into 2-inch-thick slices by sawing gently with the serrated knife on a slight diagonal.

STORING **The cake is best eaten the same day it is made. It will still taste good the second day, but the cream will start to break down and lose its volume and shape. Store in the refrigerator, covered loosely with plastic wrap.**

This chapter explores the world of soft, spoonable comfort food, those lusciously rich, smoothly sweet, and divinely simple desserts you all crave. From crème caramel to crème brûlée and from chocolate bread pudding to cheesecake, these desserts cheer and console you like no other sweet can. They are some of the simplest desserts to make. If you're new to custard-based desserts, however, read through the primer below before turning on the oven. Then choose from this selection of old- and new-fashioned desserts, put on your bunny slippers, and enjoy.

A Primer on Custards

BAKED CUSTARDS

All custards consist of the same basic ingredients—milk and/or cream, whole eggs or egg yolks, sugar, and flavoring. That's it. The texture and richness of custard is determined by whether you use milk or cream (or a combination of both) and whole eggs (firmer) or egg yolks only (softer). The classic continuum of custards begins on the lean side with crème caramel (also known as *crème renversée* or flan), which is traditionally made with whole milk and whole eggs—although flan is sometimes enriched with condensed or evaporated milk or extra egg yolks. In the center of the continuum is *pot de crème*, which uses both whole milk and heavy cream and both whole eggs and egg yolks. At the rich end is crème brûlée, which is traditionally made with heavy cream and egg yolks. These traditional categories are quite flexible today, and you may see many variations on the themes above, all called by different names as each baker expresses individual creativity.

Crème caramel is baked in a caramel-lined dish, then unmolded for serving. Because the custard has to stand on its own, it needs extra protein to be sturdy enough to keep from collapsing on the plate. Whole eggs provide plenty of that protein in the form of egg whites. Traditionally, milk is paired with the whole eggs, resulting in a firm but lean custard that holds its shape well when unmolded. To give the custard a more tender texture, most modern crème caramels substitute cream for part of the milk and/or a couple of egg yolks for one of the eggs.

Pot de crème, French for "pot of cream," gets its name from the small, decorative ceramic cup with matching lid that was once the traditional baking vessel. You can still find these charming cups in some secondhand and antique shops, although nowadays everyone bakes custards in ramekins or custard cups. *Pot de crème* contains both whole milk and heavy cream as well as whole eggs and egg yolks, giving it a lovely balance of structure and softness.

Crème brûlée is the ultimate in richness. Translated as "burned cream," this most popular of restaurant desserts is anything but burned. The custard is first baked and chilled, then topped with a sprinkling of sugar that is quickly caramelized just before serving. The shatteringly crisp surface of almost bitter sugar is the perfect contrast to the creamy custard underneath. Heavy cream and egg yolks, both rich in fat, give this custard its velvety smoothness. The yolks provide not only fat, but a natural emulsifier called *lecithin,* which contributes to the luxurious texture. Because of its richness, crème brûlée is usually served in small baking dishes that are also quite shallow, providing exactly the right ratio of creamy custard to crisp sugar topping. However, you need a very steady hand to remove a baking pan of these shallow dishes, surrounded by hot water, from the oven without tipping or splashing water into the custard. If you're just beginning to bake, you will probably want to use ramekins or custard cups. If you have the shallow dishes, do use them, but note that the baking time will be shorter than specified in these recipes, so be sure to rely on visual clues for doneness.

HOW TO MAKE BAKED CUSTARD

FLAVORING THE CUSTARD This is done using a technique called *infusion*, which is similar to the process of making tea. The milk and/or cream, sugar, and flavoring are gently heated to a simmer on the stove. The pot is removed from the heat, covered, and allowed to sit until the liquid has absorbed enough flavoring to permeate the custard. Then the flavorings are strained out and the eggs are added before baking. This technique ensures a perfectly smooth texture for the custard, which would otherwise be marred by the slight grittiness of powdered spices, zests, or other flavorings. The only noninfused flavorings that are added are perfectly smooth to begin with (or when melted), such as chocolate, extracts, and liqueurs.

Taste the infusion after the initial steeping and before you add the eggs. If the flavor is not strong enough, let it steep in the warm liquid 15 minutes longer, then check again. Keep in mind that you want the flavor to taste quite strong because custards are usually served chilled, and cold dulls our perception of flavor. Some flavors will be strong in 20 minutes, others release their flavors more slowly and may take up to an hour. Combine several flavorings for your own unique creation!

tips for success Some Ideas for Flavoring Custards

These suggestions will help get you started when choosing flavorings for your custards. Changing the flavor is as easy as changing the ingredient you steep in the milk/cream mixture. You can also combine flavors below for additional flavoring options, such as ginger-orange, coffee-cinnamon, or lavender-almond.

Citrus: Add the zest of 1 large orange or 2 lemons to the milk/cream mixture. Heat and allow to infuse for at least 25 minutes.

Coconut: Toast ¾ cup dried unsweetened shredded coconut (see page 49) and add it to the milk/cream mixture. Heat and allow to infuse for at least 45 minutes.

Coffee or tea: Add ⅓ cup whole coffee beans or aromatic tea leaves (any type, from black to green to herbal will work

well—if they are in a teabag, cut it open and add the contents) to the milk/cream mixture. Heat and allow to infuse for 15 to 20 minutes.

Herbs: Add ¼ cup packed fresh herb leaves (try lemon verbena, lemon balm, lavender, basil, mint, or tarragon) to the milk/cream mixture. Heat and allow to infuse for at least 20 minutes.

Spices: Always toast whole spices before using them for infusing. Heat a dry (not nonstick) skillet over medium heat. When hot, add the spices and shake the pan (so they toast evenly) for about 1 minute, or until they are warm to the touch and fragrant. Add them immediately to the milk/cream mixture. Heat and allow to infuse for at least 25 minutes.

Nuts: Toast ¾ cup chopped nuts of your choice (almonds, hazelnuts, pecans, or

pistachios work well) according to their directions in chapter 2. Add the warm nuts to the milk/cream mixture. Heat and allow to infuse for at least 45 minutes.

Ginger: The acid in fresh ginger can cause the milk mixture to curdle, so blanch the ginger before use. Slice five quarter-size pieces of fresh ginger. Bring a small saucepan of water to the boil. Add the ginger and cook for 1 minute. Transfer the ginger to the milk/cream mixture with a slotted spoon, heat, and allow to infuse for at least 30 minutes.

Extracts, flavored oils, and liqueurs: Add to the custard mixture after the eggs have been blended in. Add ¼ to ½ teaspoon of extract, or ⅛ to ¼ teaspoon of flavored oil, or 1 to 2 tablespoons of liqueur, according to your taste.

TEMPERING THE EGGS Once you have flavored the milk/cream mixture, it's time to add the eggs. Tempering is the process of slowly adding a hot liquid to eggs. Eggs, when shocked all at once with a wave of hot liquid, can easily scramble into a useless mess. However, when the hot liquid is added slowly, accompanied by constant whisking, the eggs increase in temperature without coagulating.

To temper, after the milk mixture has been infused with flavorings, reheat it to just below the boiling point. In a medium bowl, whisk the eggs until they are well blended. Twist a damp kitchen towel into a rope and wrap it around the bottom of the bowl to secure it while you temper the eggs. Slowly add about ½ cup of the hot milk mixture to the eggs, whisking constantly. Once the liquid is incorporated, add another ½ cup in the same manner. At this point, you can pour the rest of the hot liquid into the eggs in a slow stream, continuing to whisk constantly.

STRAINING THE CUSTARD AND FILLING THE CUPS Once you have added the eggs, strain the entire mixture through a fine-mesh strainer into a large liquid measuring cup or a pitcher with a pour spout. The straining serves two purposes. First, it removes any solid flavorings that were added (these should be discarded, except for vanilla beans; see page 44). Second, it removes the chalazae of the eggs (see page 27) that harden quickly in the heat of the oven and could mar the smooth texture of your custard. The pour spout makes it easy to portion the custard into each ramekin or custard cup without spilling it. Place the custard cups in the roasting/baking pan and make sure they are not touching each other or the sides of the pan. Divide the custard evenly among the cups.

BAKING IN A WATER BATH All baked custards are surrounded by warm water as they bake (the exceptions are bread puddings and cheesecakes, which may or may not use water baths, depending upon the recipe). This warm water is called a *water bath* or *bain-marie*. Because custards need to bake very gently, and fluctuations in heat—especially high heat—can cause the custard to become grainy or curdle, a water bath is used to ensure slow, gentle baking. All ovens have cycles, and at various times during the baking process the oven is cooler or hotter than the temperature you have set. The surrounding water moderates these fluctuations in temperature by absorbing the heat, then transferring it gently to the cups, keeping them at a constant, low temperature.

To prepare a hot water bath, pull out the oven rack halfway, so it is still level but easy to reach. Place the baking pan with the filled cups in the center of the rack. Remove one of the custard cups from the baking pan. Pour very hot tap water into that space until it reaches a level that is halfway up the sides of the cups. Do not use boiling water, as it can easily overcook the outside of the custards. Replace the missing cup.

COVERING THE CUSTARDS Custards are always covered during baking, because the dry heat of the oven in direct contact with the surface of the custard can cause a skin or crack to form. By lightly covering the custards with foil, some of the steam created by the water bath is trapped, creating a moist environment and preventing a skin from forming. The foil should lie across the tops of the custard cups, resting on their rims, but should not touch the custard itself. If you like, you can lay the foil across the entire pan, but don't crimp the edges so tightly that steam cannot escape—simply crimp in several places to hold the foil in place. If you create an airtight environment, the steam will build up and cook the custards very rapidly, quickly turning them into a curdled mess. Once the custards are covered, gently push the rack back into place in the oven and proceed with baking.

TESTING CUSTARDS FOR DONENESS There are two methods. The first is to remove the covering from the baking pan and tap the side of the pan firmly with a spoon or spatula while watching the surface of the custards. The second method is to use a pair of tongs to remove one of the cups from the baking pan, close the oven door, and give the custard cup a gentle shake on the counter. Choose the one you're most comfortable with. In either case, the surface of the custard should have what professionals light-heartedly refer to as the *"Jell-O jiggle."* That is, a warm custard will always jiggle a bit, but it should move as one piece, with just a small bit of custard in the very center—about the size of a dime—rippling like liquid. The custard will keep cooking for a bit once it's out of the oven (known as "carry-over" cooking), setting that liquid portion in the center. Chilling will also help the custard to finish firming. If you want to bake the custards until they are completely set across the center, you must watch them very closely as they can easily overbake and become grainy.

tips for success Why Baking Times Vary

Home bakers often wonder why recipes for baked custards give such a wide range of baking times—for instance, 45 to 60 minutes. This is due to a number of variables, such as how warm the custard was when it went into the oven, how long the oven door was open when adding the water bath and covering the cups, and how often the custard was checked. Remember that every time you open the oven door and check the custard, much of the oven heat is lost. When you close the door, it has to heat up again. This can create a cycle of frustration. You decide to give the custard "just 5 more minutes," then open the door to find nothing has progressed. In the meantime, your oven was just heating up to proper temperature when you opened the door again. If you check the custard and it is not done, don't open the door again for at least 10 minutes so that your baking can progress enough to make a difference between checks. Don't worry if your custard takes even longer to bake than the time stated; the times are only a guideline. Use visual clues to determine doneness.

COOLING AND STORING CUSTARDS To remove the custard cups from the hot water once they're out of the oven, use a pair of tongs (rubber or silicone-tipped ones are especially helpful here) or your hand protected by a kitchen towel. Place the cups on a rack and let them cool to room temperature, 40 to 60 minutes; then cover with plastic wrap and refrigerate. Covering the custards prevents them from picking up any odors in the refrigerator and keeps a skin from forming. Most custards can be held in the refrigerator for 1 to 2 days. In fact, crème caramel is best after an overnight stay in the refrigerator, as the caramel lining has plenty of time to absorb moisture from the custard and turn to liquid, resulting in more caramel "sauce" when the custard is turned out of the cup.

SERVING CUSTARDS Most custards are at their best chilled, although some chefs prefer to serve them after they have "warmed" to room temperature for 30 minutes. Crème brûlée and *pots de crème* are always served in their baking dishes, but crème caramel is always unmolded. To do this, run a thin, flexible paring knife or mini-spatula around the edges of each cup, taking care to press the knife into the cup so you don't gouge the custard. Place a serving plate upside down on top of the cup; then, holding them together, invert them. The custard should slide out of the cup and onto the plate. If the custard is a bit hesitant, pick up the plate, hold the cup in place on the plate, and give the two a firm but gentle shake once or twice.

HOW TO CARAMELIZE CRÈME BRÛLÉE Before crème brûlée can be served, it needs a thin topping of caramelized sugar. Always use pure cane sugar when caramelizing crème brûlée. Sugar made from sugarcane melts more easily and browns beautifully, whereas that made from sugar beets melts unevenly. Instead of browning, the beet sugar often just rolls up into little black sugar balls. For more information on sugars, see page 24.

Although many recipes tell you to caramelize under the broiler, that method makes it difficult to control the browning of the sugar, and the high heat often causes some of the custard to curdle. Try one of the two methods described here instead.

Caramelizing with a propane or butane torch: Professional pastry chefs use a torch to caramelize crème brûlée and, once you have used one, you'll wonder why you waited so long to try it. Most kitchenware stores now carry small, affordable, easy-to-use torches that aren't as intimidating as the large hardware store models, which work just as well (and last longer). The surface of each cold custard is sprinkled with sugar, which is then caramelized to a deep golden brown with the torch. The molten caramel solidifies into a crisp surface as it cools. (For detailed instructions on how to do this, see Vanilla Crème Brûlée, page 358.)

Making a Caramel Lattice

Instead of using a torch, some may decide to make caramel in a saucepan (see page 26), then pour it over the surface of the custard. This is a good idea in principle, but often causes one of two problems—either the custard curdles from the extreme heat of the caramel or the layer of caramel ends up too thick and nearly impossible to break with a spoon. One solution is to use a fork or spoon to drizzle hot caramel in lattice-style patterns over a silicone mat or a piece of parchment paper lightly coated with unflavored oil or high-heat canola-oil spray. The lattices can be made in advance, held in an airtight container between sheets of parchment paper, and set atop each custard just before serving. This method results in a delicate, crispy caramel topping.

BREAD PUDDING

Bread pudding is simply a basic custard poured over dried bread and baked, although its fans will say the result is definitely more than the sum of its parts. Whether sweet or savory, there are three keys to great bread pudding: a well-flavored custard, the correct custard-to-bread ratio, and bread with enough body to withstand the soaking of the custard and still contribute its own flavor and texture. Be sure to seek out well-crafted bread, dense and hearty, for the best texture in your bread pudding. Supermarket sliced bread makes terrible bread pudding because the bread turns to mush in the oven. Rustic breads with chewy texture and thick crusts don't absorb the custard properly. Challah, brioche, panettone, and bakery French bread loaves (even baguettes, in a pinch) make terrific bread puddings. For the best texture, trim the crusts so the custard can be absorbed evenly. And, although most bread puddings have custards flavored with vanilla extract, you can create your own unique custard recipe by following the flavoring guidelines on page 343 before you pour the custard over the bread.

HOW TO MAKE BREAD PUDDING

SOAKING THE BREAD CUBES Pour the custard over the bread and place a piece of plastic wrap on top to keep the bread submerged (a small plate on top will help as well). Allow enough time for the bread to become soft all the way through the center; otherwise, you'll have bread cubes that are moist on the outside and dry on the inside. To test, cut one of the cubes open and check the center.

BAKING BREAD PUDDING Although some recipes call for baking bread pudding in a water bath in the style of the classic baked custards above, it's really an unnecessary complication. With the correct ratio of custard to bread, the pudding comes out soft and custardy without a bain-marie. It is important, though, to keep the baking temperature low—at 325°F—to ensure that the eggs bake slowly, imparting that creamy texture that is the trademark of bread pudding. It can be difficult to tell when bread pudding is done. The best ways are to look for the *Jell-O jiggle*, as described above, and to gently press down in the center of the pudding using a spoon. If liquid custard pools around the spoon, the pudding needs a little more time. If the top is golden brown, the pudding moves as one when gently tapped, and there is no loose custard in the center, then the pudding is done. If you see the pudding rising up dramatically, remove it from the oven. The eggs are starting to "soufflé" and this indicates they are cooking beyond their soft and creamy state.

Bread pudding may also be baked in individual ramekins or custard cups, which will considerably shorten the baking and reheating times. Remember that baking times are only suggestions; judge the doneness of your bread pudding from the visual clues.

REHEATING BREAD PUDDING Most bread pudding is at its best served warm. However, it can be prepared ahead of time and simply reheated: Cover the top with foil and place in a 325°F oven for 20 to 30 minutes, until the pudding is warmed through. Warm bread pudding begs for accompaniment—Softly Whipped Cream (page 416), cold Custard Sauce (page 424), ice cream, or just heavy cream poured over the top.

CHEESECAKE

Cheesecake, although baked in a cake pan, is really a custard whose milk and/or cream has been replaced with cream cheese, ricotta cheese, or sour cream. The texture should be meltingly smooth and creamy, yet firm enough to hold its shape when chilled and cut. Because cream cheese is so dense, the infusion method cannot be used to add flavor. Flavoring is added in the form of extracts, juices, liqueurs, ground spices, chocolate chips, toffee bits, and so on.

HOW TO MAKE CHEESECAKE

CHOOSING THE RIGHT PAN A springform pan, a 2-piece pan that is deeper than a regular cake pan, is the best choice for most cheesecakes and is the one used for recipes in this book. It is 2½ to 3 inches deep and has sides that remove easily with the flip of a clip, allowing you to remove the cake from the pan without turning it upside down.

A cheesecake pan is a 3-inch-deep, one-piece pan. It is what you'll need if you bake cheesecakes in a water bath, since there is no possibility of water seeping into the cheesecake during baking, as it would with a springform pan.

Unmolding cheesecake from a cheesecake pan is a bit trickier than unmolding from a springform pan, since you'll need to turn it upside down to get it out. First, before baking, be sure to line the pan with a round of parchment paper in the bottom so you're assured of easy removal later. After baking, let it cool completely and chill for at least 4 hours. Dip the pan into a bowl or sink of very hot water that reaches about ¾ of the way to the rim. Hold in place for 10 to 15 seconds, then run a thin, flexible knife or icing spatula around the edges to loosen the cake from the pan. Dry the pan with a towel, then invert it onto a plate. If it doesn't come out, dip and try again. Once it drops out of the pan, quickly remove the parchment paper and re-invert it onto a clean plate, right side up.

MAKING THE CRUST The classic cheesecake crust is crushed graham cracker crumbs mixed with melted butter, and it remains the favorite. Some cooks like to add a tablespoon or two of sugar, a bit of cinnamon, or a handful of chopped toasted nuts, and none of these hurt the basic ratio of crumbs to butter. Other cookies, such as gingersnaps or chocolate wafers, can be substituted for the graham crackers—just be sure to use the same measurement of finely ground cookie crumbs.

Once the ingredients are blended, transfer the crust mixture to a lightly buttered or oiled baking pan, then press down on it firmly to create a solid mass, starting in the center and working in concentric circles until you reach the edge. You can use the heel of your hand or the bottom of a juice glass. If you want the crust to extend up the side of the pan, you'll need to use your fingertips to move it into place. Although it is not necessary, it's nice to bake the crust before adding the filling. This gives the crust a crisp texture to complement the smooth custard. If you prebake the crust, be sure to let it cool before pouring in the filling.

MAKING THE FILLING A food processor allows you to make a cheesecake on the spur of the moment, using ingredients cold from the refrigerator. The food processor incorporates less air than a mixer and blends the mixture beautifully. Cheesecakes can be made successfully with a mixer, but be sure to bring all the ingredients to room temperature before beginning. Either piece of equipment can give you a smooth, creamy cheesecake if the proper techniques are used. (See "Why Cheesecakes Crack," at right.)

To mix the batter, place the cream cheese and sugar in the bowl of the food processor and process until the mixture is very smooth, stopping to scrape down the sides 2 or 3 times. The sugar's sharp crystals aid in smoothing out the cream cheese. Once you add the eggs, the extra liquid in the eggs will prevent any lumps from dissolving, so be sure your cream cheese is very, very smooth before continuing. Add the eggs one at a time, fully incorporating each egg before adding the next. Sometimes additional liquid, in the form of sour cream, heavy cream, or juice is added at this point; blend it in well. Finally, mix in any flavorings. If you are adding chunks or chips of some sort, remove the bowl from the processor or mixer and fold them in by hand to keep them from being broken down into little pieces.

BAKING THE CHEESECAKE Pour the filling into the cooled crust, set the pan on a baking sheet with ½-inch sides (in case of leakage), and bake it in the center of the oven. The oven temperature should be low, about 325°F. You want the temperature low enough so that you don't need to add starch, such as flour or cornstarch, to prevent the eggs from scrambling. Starches mar the texture of a creamy cheesecake, and can compromise the flavor, as well. Be sure that your oven's temperature is correct (see page 8).

You don't necessarily need to use a water bath to bake cheesecakes, although some people swear by them. The water bath does keep the surface of the custard moist, helping to prevent cracks, but proper mixing, correct oven temperature, and removing the cheesecake when the center is still fairly liquid are easy to do and will reliably produce dense, creamy New York–style cheesecake. If you do use a water bath, be sure to use a cheesecake pan or completely wrap the bottom of your springform pan in two layers of foil to prevent any water from seeping into the cheesecake through the seams.

TESTING CHEESECAKE FOR DONENESS This is the most difficult part for home bakers, because cheesecake is finished when the edges are set but the center is still a 2- to 3-inch-wide pool of liquid batter. The truth is, it doesn't look finished or set. Even professionals have to remind themselves that it really will be firm and perfect once the cheesecake has chilled and cooled. Because of carry-over cooking, the cheesecake continues to set after removal from the oven, and firms further during a long chill in the refrigerator. To test for doneness, tap the side of the cheesecake pan and watch the center (as described for baked custards above). And just as with baked custards, allow at least 10 minutes between each test for doneness so that your oven can retain enough heat to finish baking the cheesecake. Treat the suggested baking times as a guide and use the visual clues as your true indicator of doneness.

COOLING AND CHILLING CHEESECAKE Immediately after removing the cheesecake from the oven, run a thin, flexible knife or spatula around the edges of the pan to loosen the cheesecake—this allows the cake to contract away from the sides as it cools, and prevents cracks (see "Why Cheesecakes Crack," below). Allow the cheesecake to cool at room temperature for 1 to 2 hours, until completely cool. Then cover with plastic wrap and refrigerate for at least 4 hours before serving.

SERVING CHEESECAKE To cut a cheesecake, use a thin, sharp knife, and dip it in hot water or wipe with a hot, wrung-out towel in between each slice. As you cut, pull the knife out from the bottom of the cake, to keep the surface beautifully smooth.

WHY CHEESECAKES CRACK There are several reasons cheesecakes crack, but yours will never have cracks again if you pay attention to several fine details that make all the difference.

OVERBEATING Most recipes call for making cheesecakes with a traditional mixer (either a stand mixer or a hand mixer). However, mixers were designed to beat air into batters, and one of the best ways to keep cheesecakes from cracking is to incorporate as little air as possible. Remember that air bubbles expand in the heat of the oven, causing baked goods to rise. In the case of cheesecake, too many air bubbles cause a dramatic rise, known to professionals as *souffléing*. This rise is good in cakes, but bad in cheesecakes, which have no flour to set the structure and hold the rise in place. Consequently, when the cheesecake is removed from the oven, it falls as dramatically as it rose, and cracks in the center.

That's why it's better to mix cheesecake batter in a food processor, a machine that blends quickly without incorporating much air, producing a smooth, dense batter. And because the processor mixes so efficiently, you can use all the ingredients straight from the refrigerator. If you use a mixer, you must let your ingredients warm to room temperature before beginning so that your mixer can blend the ingredients quickly, adding fewer air bubbles.

TOO HOT OVEN Cheesecakes need to be baked in a low oven—325°F is ideal. As the eggs bake, the proteins in the egg whites unwind, combine with other protein strands, and form new networks, winding tighter and tighter as the heat increases. If the oven temperature is too high, the proteins in the surface of the cheesecake, which are exposed directly to the high heat, will bind too tightly and dry out, forming cracks in the surface (these are generally small and concentric in nature).

IMPROPER COOLING We all know that everything contracts as it cools. The key is to control the direction of that contraction in a cooling cheesecake. If the cake is stuck to the side of the pan as it cools, it cannot contract away from it, so the cake contracts from the most vulnerable spot—the center of the cake—forming huge, Grand Canyon–style cracks. When you release the cake by running a spatula around the sides of the pan as soon as you remove it from the oven, you allow the cake to contract inward, keeping the center of the cake smooth and serene. You also need to allow plenty of time for your cake to cool. In fact, cheesecakes are great desserts to make a day ahead of time. If you rush the warm cheesecake into the refrigerator so you can serve it in an hour, the cake will contract dramatically, causing cracks. The cake should first cool to room temperature and then chill in the refrigerator for at least 4 hours before you unmold and serve it.

WHITE CHOCOLATE-LIME CRÈME CARAMEL

SERVES 6 Whether you call it flan, crème caramel, or crème renversée, it's hard to resist a creamy custard turned upside down and served in a pool of liquid caramel. The flavors of crème caramel are always more complex than regular custard because of the caramel that surrounds it during baking and chilling, which adds a layer of flavor beyond the custard itself. A measure of white chocolate gives this one a lovely texture, while the lime and caramel work in tandem to cut the sweetness of the chocolate. Though this is a classic crème caramel, with whole milk and eggs only, the white chocolate makes it taste richer and creamier.

INGREDIENTS

CUSTARD
2 cups (16 ounces) whole milk

3 tablespoons (1½ ounces) sugar

Grated zest of 3 limes

3 large eggs

6 ounces white chocolate, finely chopped

CARAMEL LINING
½ cup (4 ounces) water

1 cup (7 ounces) sugar

¼ teaspoon cream of tartar

Candied lime zest (page 352) and Softly Whipped Cream (page 416), for serving

EQUIPMENT
Medium Saucepan, Small Saucepan, Six (6-Ounce) Ceramic Ramekins or Custard Cups, Small Bowl (Optional), Large Roasting or Baking Pan, Whisk, Medium Bowl, Fine-Mesh Strainer, Pitcher or Large Measuring Cup with Spout, Tongs, Cooling Rack, Mini-Spatula

1 MAKE AND FLAVOR THE CUSTARD: Heat the milk, sugar, and lime zest in the medium saucepan over low heat just until the mixture begins to simmer. Remove from the heat, cover, and allow to steep for 1 to 1½ hours, until the lime flavor is strong. You can even leave the mixture to steep overnight in the refrigerator, if you like.

2 MAKE THE CARAMEL LINING: Pour the water into the small saucepan and add the sugar and cream of tartar. Cook over medium heat, stirring constantly, until the sugar has dissolved and the liquid is clear. Increase the heat to high and boil rapidly, swirling the pan occasionally (without stirring) to cook the sugar evenly, until the caramel turns a deep golden brown (for more on caramelizing sugar, see page 26). Remove from the heat and immediately divide the caramel among the custard cups, swirling each cup to distribute the still-liquid caramel evenly up the sides. Be careful to go only about halfway up the sides. The caramel is very hot and you don't want it to drip off the edge of a cup and onto your skin. You may want to keep a small bowl of ice water nearby in case a bit of caramel touches your skin. Set the caramel-lined cups in the roasting pan, making sure they don't touch, and let them cool for 10 minutes.

3 Preheat the oven to 325°F and position an oven rack in the center.

4 TEMPER THE EGGS: Place the saucepan with the lime-infused milk mixture back over medium heat, uncover, and reheat just until it begins to simmer. Whisk the eggs in the medium bowl. Twist a damp kitchen towel into a rope and wrap it around the bottom

GETTING AHEAD **The caramel-lined cups can be prepared a day in advance and kept at room temperature, covered with plastic wrap. The custards can be baked up to 2 days in advance and chilled, covered with plastic wrap. Unmold shortly before serving.**

of the bowl to secure it while you temper the eggs. Pour about ½ cup of the hot milk mixture into the eggs, whisking constantly. Once blended, whisk in another ½ cup. Then slowly pour the rest of the mixture into the eggs, whisking constantly. Add the white chocolate and whisk until melted and blended completely.

5 STRAIN AND BAKE THE CUSTARD: Pour the mixture through the strainer into the pitcher and discard the zest. Divide the warm custard among the cups in the pan. Pull out the oven rack and place the pan on the rack. Remove one of the cups, pour enough hot tap water (not boiling) into that area to come halfway up the sides of the cups, and replace the cup. Cut a piece of foil large enough to fit just inside the edges of the roasting pan, then lay the foil across the top of the cups, making sure it doesn't touch the custard. You may need to smooth and flatten the foil on the counter if any wrinkles touch the custard. Gently push the rack back into the oven, shut the oven door, and bake the custards for 30 to 40 minutes, until they are just set and their centers are no longer wobbly (test by gently tapping the side of the pan with a spoon).

6 Remove the foil and then the pan from the oven, being careful not to tilt the pan and splash water on top of the custards. Set the pan on a heatproof surface. Use a pair of tongs (or your hand protected by a kitchen towel) to immediately remove the cups from the water bath and place them on a rack to cool to room temperature, about 40 minutes. Cover with plastic wrap and refrigerate until cold, at least 4 hours or overnight.

7 UNMOLD THE CUSTARDS: Run a mini-spatula or a thin, flexible knife inside the edge of a cup, pressing the knife into the cup to avoid gouging the custard. Place a serving plate upside down on top of the cup, then, holding the two together, invert them. The custard should slide out of the cup and onto the plate. Candied lime zest is a lovely garnish here. Place a few strands on top of each custard and scatter a few more around each plate.

8 SERVE THE CUSTARDS: Crème caramel is at its best at room temperature, so let the custards, still in their cups, sit out for about 30 minutes before serving. If you like, place a small spoonful of softly whipped cream on top of each. Candied lime zest is a lovely garnish here. Place a few strands on top of each custard and scatter a few more around each plate.

TO MAKE CANDIED CITRUS ZEST: Zest 4 limes, lemons, oranges, tangerines, or grapefruits using a vegetable peeler. Scrape off any white pith with the tip of a knife and cut the zest into long thin strips. In a small saucepan, bring 1 cup of water and 1 cup of sugar to a boil. Stir briefly until the sugar has dissolved and the liquid is clear. Add 2 tablespoons of light corn syrup and the zest. Reduce the liquid to a simmer, cover, and cook for 20 to 30 minutes, or until the zest is translucent and tender. Use immediately or refrigerate the candied zest in the syrup in an airtight container for up to 1 month.

White Chocolate–Lemon Crème Caramel Substitute the zest of 2 lemons for the lime zest.

White Chocolate–Orange Crème Caramel Substitute the zest of 1 large orange for the lime zest.

COFFEE-CARDAMOM POTS DE CRÈME

SERVES 6 Coffee and cardamom is an intriguing and exotic flavor pairing from the eastern Mediterranean. The tradition comes from Turkey and Egypt, where cardamom seeds are sometimes boiled with the beans for coffee or ground along with the beans into powder. The roasted, bitter flavor of the coffee is a great match with the citrusy, floral qualities of cardamom, a member of the ginger family.

INGREDIENTS

1¼ cups (10 ounces) heavy whipping cream
1¼ cups (10 ounces) whole milk
⅓ cup (2⅓ ounces) plus 1 tablespoon sugar

½ cup (1¼ ounces) coffee or espresso beans (decaffeinated beans may be used)
2 teaspoons cardamom seeds

7 large egg yolks
Softly Whipped Cream (page 416) and chocolate-covered coffee beans, for serving

EQUIPMENT

Medium Saucepan, Whisk, Medium Bowl, Fine-Mesh Strainer, Pitcher or Large Measuring Cup with Spout, Six (6-Ounce) Custard Cups or Ceramic Ramekins or Coffee Cups, Large Roasting or Baking Pan, Tongs, Cooling Rack

1 MAKE AND FLAVOR THE CUSTARD: Combine the cream, milk, sugar, coffee beans, and cardamom seeds in the medium saucepan. Cook over medium heat, stirring to help the sugar dissolve, until the mixture is just below the boiling point (there will be a ring of bubbles around the edge of the pan and wisps of steam rising from the center, but bubbles will not be breaking the surface). The acid in the beans could cause the mixture to curdle if it boils, so watch closely. Remove from the heat, cover, and let steep for 15 minutes.

2 Preheat the oven to 325°F and position an oven rack in the center.

3 TEMPER THE EGGS: Place the milk mixture back over medium heat, uncover, and reheat to just below the boiling point. Whisk the egg yolks in the medium bowl. Twist a damp kitchen towel into a rope and wrap it around the bottom of the bowl to secure it while you temper the eggs. Pour about ½ cup of the hot milk mixture into the eggs, whisking constantly. Once blended, whisk in another ½ cup. Then slowly pour the rest of the mixture into the eggs, whisking constantly.

4 STRAIN AND BAKE THE CUSTARD: Pour the mixture through the strainer into the pitcher. Place the custard cups in the large roasting pan, making sure they don't touch, and divide the warm custard among them. Pull out the oven rack and place the pan on the rack; then remove one of the cups, pour enough hot tap water (not boiling) into that area to come halfway up the sides of the cups, and replace the cup. Cut a piece of foil large enough to fit just inside the edges of the roasting pan, then lay the foil across the top of the cups, making sure it doesn't touch the custard. You may need to smooth and flatten the foil on the counter if any wrinkles touch the custard. Gently push the rack back into the oven, shut the oven door, and bake the custards for 45 to 65 minutes, until they are almost set—there should still be a small liquid area in the very center of each custard, about the size of a dime (test by gently tapping the side of the pan).

There are a couple of ways to prevent custard cups from slipping out from between your tongs as you move them from baking dish to cooling rack. Silicone-tipped tongs provide a sticky grip surface that holds onto the ceramic or glass custard cups admirably. A quick alternative is to wrap each end of the tongs several times with a rubber band—this new-found gripping power will prevent the cups from tilting or falling during transfer.

GETTING AHEAD **The custards may be baked 1 or 2 days in advance and refrigerated, covered with plastic wrap.**

5 Remove the foil and then the pan from the oven, being careful not to tilt the pan and splash water on top of the custards. Set the pan on a heatproof surface. Use a pair of tongs (or your hand protected by a kitchen towel) to immediately remove the cups from the water bath and place them on a rack to cool to room temperature, about 40 minutes. Cover with plastic wrap and refrigerate until cold, at least 4 hours or overnight.

6 SERVE THE *POTS DE CRÈME*: Place each custard cup on a small dessert plate. Serve with a spoonful of whipped cream and a few chocolate-covered coffee beans.

Earl Grey Tea Pots de Crème Tea is a fragrant alternative to coffee when flavoring custards. Use Earl Grey or your favorite here. Omit the coffee beans and cardamom and replace with 3 tablespoons Earl Grey tea leaves. Steep for 15 to 20 minutes.

Varietal Honey Pots de Crème A fascinating variety of honeys are available across the country, from tupelo to lavender to chestnut and beyond. This custard is a luscious way to showcase their unique flavors. Omit the coffee beans and cardamom. Replace the sugar with 4 to 6 tablespoons of varietal honey (to taste).

DUO-TONE CHOCOLATE POTS DE CRÈME

SERVES 6 Milk chocolate is often overlooked in the quest for the newest and darkest offerings, but it's still a favorite—with kids and adults alike. Its presence is a surprise in this recipe, as the luscious milk chocolate custard is hidden under a thin layer of warm chocolate ganache. So although the spoon dips into a dark surface, it comes out with a lighter custard full of the malty, caramel-like qualities of milk chocolate. The interplay of cool, milky sweetness against warm, dark richness is sublime.

INGREDIENTS

CUSTARD

7 ounces good-quality milk chocolate, finely chopped

1 large egg

4 large egg yolks

1¼ cups (10 ounces) heavy whipping cream

1¼ cups (10 ounces) whole milk

¼ cup (1¾ ounces) sugar

GANACHE

1½ ounces semisweet or bittersweet chocolate (up to 64 percent cacao)

5 tablespoons (2½ ounces) heavy whipping cream

Softly Whipped Cream (page 416) and milk or dark chocolate curls (page 428), for serving

EQUIPMENT

Medium Bowl, Small Bowl, Medium Saucepan, Whisk, Fine-Mesh Strainer, Pitcher or Large Measuring Cup with Spout, Six (6-Ounce) Ceramic Ramekins or Custard Cups, Large Roasting or Baking Pan, Tongs, Cooling Rack, Small Saucepan, Silicone or Rubber Spatula

1 Preheat the oven to 325°F and position an oven rack in the center.

2 MAKE THE CUSTARD: Place the chopped chocolate in the medium bowl. Combine the egg and egg yolks in the small bowl. Heat the cream, milk, and sugar in the medium saucepan over medium heat until just before the mixture boils. Immediately pour it over the chopped chocolate. Let it sit for 1 minute, then whisk gently but thoroughly to completely blend the mixture. Add the whole egg and yolks, whisking to incorporate thoroughly.

3 STRAIN AND BAKE THE CUSTARD: Pour the custard through the strainer into the pitcher. Place the custard cups in the large roasting pan, making sure they don't touch, and divide the warm custard among them. Pull out the oven rack and place the pan on the rack; then remove one of the cups, pour enough hot tap water (not boiling) into that area to come halfway up the sides of the cups, and replace the cup. Cut a piece of foil large enough to fit just inside the edges of the pan, then lay the foil across the top of the cups, making sure it doesn't touch the custard. You may need to smooth and flatten the foil on the counter if any wrinkles touch the custard. Gently push the rack back into the oven, shut the oven door, and bake the custards for 50 to 60 minutes, just until the edges of the custards are set—there should still be a dime-size liquid area in the very center of the custard (test by gently tapping the side of the pan).

4 Remove the foil and then the pan from the oven, being careful not to tilt the pan and splash water on top of the custards. Set the pan on a heatproof surface. Use the tongs (or your hand protected by a kitchen towel) to immediately remove the cups from the water bath and place them on a rack to cool to room temperature, about 40 minutes. Cover with plastic wrap and refrigerate until cold, at least 4 hours or overnight.

GETTING AHEAD **The custards may be baked up to 2 days in advance and refrigerated, covered with plastic wrap. Cover with the warm ganache shortly before serving.**

5 ADD THE GANACHE LAYER: Place the chopped semisweet chocolate in the cleaned small bowl. Heat the cream in the small saucepan over medium heat just until it begins to simmer (do not allow the cream to boil and evaporate). Immediately pour the cream over the chocolate. Allow the mixture to sit undisturbed for 1 minute, then gently stir with the spatula until thoroughly blended and smooth. Spoon a tablespoon of ganache onto the surface of each custard, then gently swirl each cup until the dark chocolate completely covers the custard. (If the ganache seems too thick to spread easily, heat another tablespoon of cream and add it to the mixture).

6 Serve the custards immediately, while the ganache is still warm, or refrigerate up to 1 hour. As the ganache chills, it begins to harden and pull away from the sides of the cup, losing its silken texture and exposing the custard beneath, thereby spoiling the surprise. Serve each with a spoonful of whipped cream, topped with a scattering of chocolate curls if you like.

VANILLA CRÈME BRÛLÉE

SERVES 8 This is it—the ultimate in sweet, creamy richness, topped with a crisp crust of caramelized sugar. You'll surprise everyone by serving one of the most popular restaurant desserts ever, and no one needs to know how simple it is. The vanilla bean gives every bite a round, deep vanilla flavor as well as an unmistakable underpinning of spicy floral notes. You can substitute other flavorings—orange or lemon zest, coffee beans, spices, or a combination of these (see page 343)—to create a personalized crème brûlée. For a less rich, yet still delicious version, substitute whole milk for half of the cream. If you don't have a propane or butane torch for caramelizing the tops, see page 346 for an alternative method.

INGREDIENTS

3 cups (24 ounces) heavy whipping cream

½ cup (3½ ounces) plus 5 tablespoons (2¼ ounces) pure cane sugar

1 vanilla bean

9 large egg yolks

EQUIPMENT

Medium Saucepan, Paring Knife, Whisk, Medium Bowl, Fine-Mesh Strainer, Pitcher or Large Measuring Cup with Spout, Eight (6-Ounce) Ceramic Ramekins or Custard Cups, Large Roasting or Baking Pan, Tongs, Cooling Rack, Propane or Butane Torch

1 MAKE AND FLAVOR THE CUSTARD: Place the cream and ½ cup of the sugar in the medium saucepan. Use the tip of a paring knife to split the vanilla bean in half lengthwise. Turn the knife over and use the dull side to scrape out the seeds, and add both the seeds and the pod to the saucepan. Whisk well to break up the clumps of vanilla seeds. Cook over medium-low heat, stirring several times to dissolve the sugar, just until the mixture begins to simmer. Remove the pan from the heat, cover, and let steep for 30 minutes.

2 Preheat the oven to 325°F and position an oven rack in the center.

3 TEMPER THE EGGS: Reheat the mixture over medium heat, uncovered, until it begins to simmer. In the medium bowl, whisk the egg yolks. Twist a damp kitchen towel into a rope and wrap it around the bottom of the bowl to secure it while you temper the eggs. Pour about ½ cup of the hot milk mixture into the eggs, whisking constantly. Once blended, whisk in another ½ cup. Then slowly pour the rest of the mixture into the eggs, whisking constantly.

4 STRAIN AND BAKE THE CUSTARD: Pour the mixture through the strainer into the pitcher. Reserve the vanilla pod (rinse it under water and let it dry, then save it for use in vanilla sugar). Place the custard cups in the large roasting pan, making sure they don't touch, and divide the warm custard among them. Pull out the oven rack and place the pan on the rack. Remove one of the cups, pour enough hot tap water (not boiling) into that area to come halfway up the sides of the cups, and replace the cup. Cut a piece of foil large enough to fit just inside the edges of the roasting pan, then lay the foil across the top of the

Always use pure cane sugar for the caramelized sugar topping on crème brulee. Cane sugar melts and browns more evenly than beet sugar. Both granulated sugars are nearly identical and interchangeable in most recipes, but when it comes to caramelizing sugar, pure cane sugar is the hands-down winner for perfect crème brulée every time.

GETTING AHEAD **The custards can be baked 1 or 2 days ahead and refrigerated, covered with plastic wrap. Caramelize them shortly before serving. It may be possible to caramelize the custards up to 1 hour in advance and store them in the refrigerator, depending on the humidity within. The crisp sugar topping absorbs humidity and gradually turns soft and may even liquefy. If this happens, sprinkle another 2 teaspoons of sugar on top of the softened caramel and caramelize again.**

cups, making sure it doesn't touch the custard. You may need to smooth and flatten the foil on the counter if any wrinkles touch the custard. Gently push the rack back into the oven, shut the oven door, and bake the custards for 35 to 50 minutes, until edges of the custards are almost set—there should still be a small liquid area in the very center of the custard, about the size of a dime (test by gently tapping the side of the pan).

5 Remove the foil and then the pan from the oven, being careful not to tilt the pan and splash water on top of the custards. Set the pan on a heatproof surface. Use the tongs (or your hand protected by a kitchen towel) to immediately remove the cups from the water bath and place them on a rack to cool to room temperature, about 40 minutes. Cover with plastic wrap and refrigerate until cold, at least 4 hours or overnight.

6 CARAMELIZE THE CUSTARDS: Sprinkle the surface of each cold custard with 2 teaspoons of the remaining sugar (use a tablespoon for large, shallow crème brûlée dishes). Shake the cup gently to distribute the sugar evenly—make sure it covers the custard all the way to the edge (any exposed custard will blacken immediately under the torch's flame). Set the sugared custards on a flameproof surface, such as a metal baking sheet. Caramelize one custard at a time: Light the torch and, with the tip of the flame just touching the surface, move the flame over the sugar in a gentle circular motion until most of the sugar is melted and looks like tiny water droplets. Continue to heat, using the same circular motion, until the sugar turns a deep golden brown. The molten caramel will bubble and smoke—this is normal. Repeat until all the custards are caramelized. The molten caramel will solidify into a crisp surface as it cools. Refrigerate for 10 minutes before serving.

7 SERVE THE CRÈME BRÛLÉE: Place each custard cup on a small dessert plate. Crème brûlée needs no adornment or accompaniment, but if you'd like to gild the lily, place a crisp cookie, such as a *tuile* (page 284), on the side or top with a few fresh berries.

Crème Fraîche Crème Brûlée with Raspberries
Fresh raspberries float to the top of this custard as it bakes, breaking the surface with a jolt of red. The custard around each berry curdles just a bit from the acidity in the fruit—no matter, this is a divinely decadent treat. Substitute Crème Fraîche (page 420) for the heavy whipping cream. Sort through a half-pint basket (6 ounces) of fresh raspberries and discard any debris or moldy berries, but do not wash the berries or they will disintegrate. Divide the berries among the custard cups. Pour the custard on top and follow the recipe as directed.

BLUEBERRY CLAFOUTI

SERVES 8 *Clafouti is a simple fruit and custard combination based on crepe batter. The batter is poured over the fruit and baked at a high temperature to create a gorgeous brown top and crispy, caramelized edges all around. You may vary the fruit and flavorings to your heart's content. The French classic is cherries with their pits intact, lending a touch of bitter almond flavor to the dessert, but it's also delicious with sliced ripe pears, fresh figs, peaches, apricots, or blackberries.*

INGREDIENTS

1 half-pint basket (about 4½ ounces) fresh blueberries

4 large eggs

6 tablespoons (2½ ounces) granulated sugar

Finely grated zest of 1 lemon

1 teaspoon pure vanilla extract

5 tablespoons (2 ounces) unbleached all-purpose flour

Pinch of salt

¾ cup (6 ounces) whole milk

¼ cup (2 ounces) heavy whipping cream, crème fraîche, or sour cream

2 tablespoons limoncello (lemon liqueur) or amaretto (almond liqueur), optional

1 tablespoon confectioners' sugar

Softly Whipped Cream (page 416), for serving

EQUIPMENT

9- or 9½-inch Ceramic Tart Pan, Baking Sheet, Medium-Mesh Strainer, Medium Bowl, Whisk, Fine-Mesh Strainer

what the pros know

After all that talk about baking custards at a low temperature, why does this recipe call for a 400°F oven? The custard here contains flour, which prevents the eggs from turning into a scrambled mess. Not silky like crème brûlée, this custard has a soft sturdiness and a tender chewiness that pairs beautifully with fresh fruit.

1 Preheat the oven to 400°F and position an oven rack in the center. Lightly butter the pan and coat it with granulated sugar.

2 Pour the berries onto the baking sheet and pick through them, removing any stems or debris. Transfer them to the strainer and rinse under cold water. Pat dry and pour into the tart pan.

3 Place the eggs and granulated sugar in the medium bowl and whisk vigorously to blend. Add the lemon zest and vanilla extract and blend again. Add the flour and salt and whisk until most of the flour lumps have blended into the eggs. Add the milk and cream and whisk until the mixture is completely blended.

4 Pour the batter over the blueberries and move the berries around, if necessary, so they are distributed evenly. Bake for 35 to 40 minutes, until the clafouti is set and firm in the center, the top is browned, and the edges look crispy.

5 Sprinkle immediately with the liqueur if you like. Let cool for 5 to 10 minutes. Use the fine-mesh strainer to sift the confectioners' sugar over the top and serve warm, with spoonfuls of whipped cream.

STORING Clafouti is best served warm from the oven. For longer storage, refrigerate for up to three days. Reheat in a 400°F oven for 8 to 10 minutes before serving. The clafouti batter can be prepared 1 or 2 days in advance. Make the batter (through Step 3) and store in the refrigerator, covered with plastic wrap.

BITTERSWEET CHOCOLATE BREAD PUDDING

SERVES 8 TO 10 **Perhaps the darkest, most intense chocolate bread pudding you've ever experienced,** this recipe depends on ½ pound of top-quality chocolate and a long, leisurely soak of custard and bread before baking. For best results, start the day before you want to serve the pudding–the next day, simply slip it into the oven. To add even more chocolate flavor, stir a cup of milk chocolate or white chocolate chips or chopped bar chocolate into the custard and bread mixture before baking.

INGREDIENTS

1 loaf (1 to 1½ pounds) challah, brioche, or other rich, dense bread

1¾ cups (14 ounces) whole milk

1¾ cups (14 ounces) heavy whipping cream

8 ounces semisweet or bittersweet chocolate (up to 70 percent cacao), finely chopped

2 large eggs

2 large egg yolks

1¼ cups (8¾ ounces) sugar

Pinch of salt

Caramel Sauce (page 426), and Softly Whipped Cream (page 416) or vanilla ice cream, for serving

EQUIPMENT

9 by 2-inch Round Cake Pan or Ceramic Baking Dish, Serrated Knife, Baking Sheet with ½ inch Sides, Cooling Rack, Medium Saucepan, Whisk, Medium Bowl, Fine-Mesh Strainer

1 Preheat the oven to 325°F and position an oven rack in the center. Lightly butter the cake pan.

2 TOAST THE BREAD: Use the serrated knife to cut away the crust from all sides of the bread. If you are using challah, which is braided, just do the best you can and don't worry about the bits of crust in the crevices of the braid. Cut the bread into 1-inch cubes. Spread the cubes on the baking sheet and toast in the oven for 20 minutes. Transfer to a rack to cool. Measure out 4 cups of bread cubes and place them in the prepared cake pan. Transfer the remaining bread cubes to a resealable plastic bag and set aside (or freeze) for another use.

3 MAKE THE CUSTARD: Heat the milk and cream in the medium saucepan over medium heat just until the mixture simmers. Remove the pan from the heat and add the chopped chocolate. Let it sit for 1 minute, then whisk vigorously to blend the chocolate into the mixture.

4 TEMPER THE EGGS: Whisk the eggs, yolks, sugar, and salt in the medium bowl to blend thoroughly. Twist a damp kitchen towel into a rope and wrap it around the bottom of the bowl to secure it while you temper the eggs. Pour about ½ cup of the chocolate mixture into the eggs, whisking constantly. Once blended, whisk in another ½ cup. Then slowly pour the rest of the chocolate mixture into the eggs, whisking constantly.

5 SOAK THE BREAD CUBES: Pour the custard through the strainer over the bread in the baking dish. Cover the baking dish with plastic wrap and press down gently so that all the bread cubes are soaked with the custard. Refrigerate for at least 8 hours, preferably overnight. This gives the bread cubes plenty of time to soak up the chocolate

While this bread pudding will satisfy those with a craving for intense dark chocolate, it can be made to please those who prefer their chocolate lighter in flavor. Simply substitute 10 ounces of milk or white chocolate for the dark chocolate in the recipe. The slight increase in the amount of chocolate is needed to create the wonderfully strong presence of these milder chocolates—flavors that might otherwise be muted by the bread and custard.

GETTING AHEAD The bread pudding can be baked up to 2 days in advance. Cool to room temperature, then cover with plastic wrap and refrigerate. Reheat in a 325°F oven for 20 to 25 minutes, until heated through.

custard, turning them from white to a deep chocolate brown color throughout. Every once in a while, remove the plastic and gently stir the mixture, then return it to the refrigerator.

6 BAKE AND SERVE THE BREAD PUDDING: Preheat the oven to 325°F and position an oven rack in the center. Remove the plastic wrap from the pan and bake the pudding for 60 to 75 minutes, until the center is set. To check, use a spoon to press down firmly in the center of the pan. The pudding is done when the center feels firm and no loose custard bubbles up around the spoon. Transfer to a rack to cool for 15 to 20 minutes, then cut the warm pudding into wedges and serve. Top with a spoonful of whipped cream or ice cream and pour caramel sauce over the top.

STORING Bread pudding is at its best the first day or two, but it can be covered with plastic wrap and refrigerated for up to 4 days. Reheat in a 325°F oven for 20 to 25 minutes, until heated through.

Chocolate Bread Pudding with Dried Sour Cherries and Apricots
Cherries and apricots pair beautifully with chocolate, and here they deliver a burst of bright flavor in the midst of warm chocolate sweetness. For the best flavor, use California, or Blenheim, dried apricots rather than the Turkish variety. To the toasted bread cubes in the baking dish add ½ cup (3 ounces) dried sour cherries and ⅓ cup (1½ ounces) dried apricot halves, snipped into quarters with kitchen scissors that have been lightly oiled so they don't stick to the fruit.

BANANAS FOSTER BREAD PUDDING

SERVES 8 TO 10 **Bananas Foster**, a New Orleans invention, is a delightful concoction of sautéed bananas finished with a flambéed brown sugar and rum sauce over vanilla ice cream—a restaurant showstopper. Here, those favorite flavors and sense of fun are translated into a banana bread pudding, paired with a butterscotch-rum sauce that can be made ahead. This recipe is great for entertaining, since there's no last-minute prep or leaping flames to worry about. Serve it warm with a scoop of vanilla ice cream and you'll have your own showstopper. Airline-size bottles of banana liqueur can be found at most good liquor stores, but if they're unavailable, just add an extra tablespoon of rum instead.

INGREDIENTS

BREAD PUDDING

1 loaf (1 to 1½ pounds) challah, brioche, or other rich, dense bread

2 ripe bananas

2 large eggs

4 large egg yolks

⅔ cup (4¾ ounces) granulated sugar

2 teaspoons pure vanilla extract

2 cups (16 ounces) heavy whipping cream

2 cups (16 ounces) whole milk

BUTTERSCOTCH-RUM SAUCE

2 sticks (8 ounces) unsalted butter, cut into ½-inch pieces

1 cup (8 ounces) firmly packed light brown sugar

1 teaspoon ground cinnamon

3 tablespoons dark rum

1 tablespoon banana liqueur (or substitute additional rum)

1 tablespoon pure vanilla extract

Vanilla ice cream, for serving

EQUIPMENT

9 by 9 by 2-inch Square Cake Pan or Ceramic Baking Dish, Serrated Knife, Baking Sheet with ½-inch Sides, Food Processor Fitted with a Metal Blade, Silicone or Rubber Spatula, Medium Bowl, Whisk, Cooling Rack, Large Saucepan

1 Preheat the oven to 325°F and position an oven rack in the center. Lightly coat the cake pan with butter, oil, or high-heat canola-oil spray.

2 TOAST THE BREAD: Use the serrated knife to cut away the crust from all sides of the bread. If you are using challah, which is braided, just do the best you can and don't worry about the bits of crust in the crevices of the braid. Cut the bread into 1-inch cubes. Spread the cubes on the baking sheet and toast in the oven for 20 minutes. Transfer to a rack to cool. Measure out 6 cups of bread cubes and place them in the cake pan. Transfer the remaining bread cubes to a resealable plastic bag and set aside (or freeze) for another use. Leave the oven on.

3 MAKE THE CUSTARD: Peel the bananas and break or cut them into chunks. Place in the bowl of the food processor and process, scraping down the bowl once or twice with the spatula, until they are pureed and very smooth. In the medium bowl, whisk together the eggs, egg yolks, and granulated sugar until well blended. Add the banana puree and vanilla and whisk well. Add the cream and milk and whisk until well blended.

4 SOAK THE BREAD CUBES: Pour the custard over the bread cubes in the baking dish. Cover with plastic wrap and press down gently so that all the bread cubes are soaked with the custard. Set aside for 30 minutes to allow the bread to absorb the custard. Every few minutes, press down gently again so the bread cubes on top are covered with custard.

5 BAKE THE BREAD PUDDING: Remove the plastic wrap and bake the pudding for 45 to 60 minutes, until the top is nicely browned and the center is set. To check, use a spoon to press down firmly in the center of the pan. The pudding is done when the center feels firm and no loose custard bubbles up around the spoon. Remove from the oven and transfer to a rack to cool.

6 MAKE THE SAUCE: Melt the butter in the large saucepan over low heat. Add the brown sugar and cinnamon and raise the heat to medium. Bring to a boil, whisking frequently. Cook for 2 minutes at a boil, whisking constantly, until the mixture is thick and smooth. Remove from the heat and—away from the flame—add the rum, banana liqueur, and vanilla. Return to the heat and boil for 1 minute, whisking. Use the sauce while warm.

7 Serve the bread pudding warm, cut into squares, and topped with enough warm sauce to drip down the sides and pool on each plate. Set a scoop of vanilla ice cream on top of each serving.

STORING **The cooled bread pudding can be covered with plastic wrap and refrigerated for up to 4 days. Reheat in a 325°F oven for 20 to 25 minutes, until heated through.**

VANILLA BEAN CHEESECAKE

SERVES 10 TO 12 **Tall, dense, creamy, and silky smooth,** this is for those who love New York–style cheesecake. The vanilla seeds add a tiny, almost imperceptible crunch in addition to a floral sweetness. If you are worried about your cheesecake cracking, the guidelines for avoiding cracks (page 349) will put you at ease. For a pretty presentation, cover the top of the cheesecake with rows of neatly arranged raspberries, blackberries, or blueberries then make the berries glisten by brushing on a bit of warmed jam.

INGREDIENTS

2 cups (8 ounces) (14 full-size crackers) finely ground graham cracker crumbs (or chocolate cookie crumbs)

1 stick (4 ounces) unsalted butter, melted

1½ pounds cream cheese

1 cup plus 2 tablespoons (8 ounces) sugar

1 (16 ounce) container sour cream

3 large eggs

1 vanilla bean, or 1 tablespoon pure vanilla extract

Roasted Summer Fruit (page 262) or fresh berries, for serving

EQUIPMENT

9-inch Springform Pan, Medium Bowl, Silicone or Rubber Spatula, Cooling Rack, Food Processor Fitted with a Metal Blade, Paring Knife, Baking Sheet with ½-inch Sides, Thin and Flexible Knife or Spatula, Icing Spatula, Thin and Sharp Knife, 9-inch Cake Cardboard

1 Preheat the oven to 325°F and position an oven rack in the center. Lightly coat the pan with butter or high-heat canola-oil spray.

2 MAKE THE CRUST: Place the crumbs and melted butter in the medium bowl and stir with a fork to moisten the crumbs evenly. With the silicone or rubber spatula, scrape into the prepared pan. Press the crumbs into an even layer across the bottom and about halfway up the side of the pan, working outward from the center. Bake the crust for 16 to 18 minutes, until set and lightly browned. Transfer to a rack to cool. Leave the oven on.

3 MAKE THE FILLING: Place the cream cheese and sugar in the bowl of the food processor and process until smooth and creamy, about 1 minute, scraping the bowl down twice with a silicone or rubber spatula to ensure the mixture blends evenly and that there are no lumps (you won't be able to smooth them out later). Add the sour cream and process until incorporated and smooth, about 20 seconds, scraping down the bowl halfway through. Add the eggs one at a time, pulsing 3 to 5 seconds after each addition to blend them in thoroughly.

4 Use a paring knife to split the vanilla bean lengthwise. Turn the knife over and use the dull side to scrape out the seeds into the mixture. Reserve the vanilla pod for another use. Process for 8 to 10 seconds, until the seeds are evenly distributed. Scrape the mixture into the cooled crust.

5 BAKE THE CHEESECAKE: Set the cheesecake pan on the baking sheet (in case of leakage) and bake for 60 to 75 minutes, until the edge is set but the center is still a 2- to 3-inch-wide pool of liquid batter (it will firm up during cooling and chilling).

6 Transfer the cheesecake to a cooling rack and immediately run a thin, flexible knife or spatula around the edge of the cake, gently pressing into the side of the pan to avoid

For some people, cheesecake just isn't complete without a thin layer of velvety sour cream on top. The sour cream feels light and soft in your mouth against the dense, creamy texture of the cheesecake. If you'd like to give it a try, you'll need to wait for about an hour after the cheesecake is pulled from the oven. Heat the oven to 425°F and combine 1½ cups (12 ounces) sour cream with 2 tablespoons sugar in a small bowl. Spread it evenly over the surface of the cheesecake and return to the oven for 5 minutes. Remove and let cool completely.

GETTING AHEAD **The crust can be prepared up to 4 days in advance and stored, wrapped in plastic, at room temperature. The cheesecake can be prepared up to 2 days ahead. Cover with plastic wrap and refrigerate. It will still be delicious for an additional 2 to 3 days, but the crust will soften quite a bit.**

gouging the cake. This will release the cake from the side of the pan and prevent cracking as it cools. Let the cheesecake cool completely, 1 to 2 hours. When cool, cover with plastic wrap and chill for at least 4 hours before serving.

7 UNMOLD THE CHEESECAKE: Run the thin knife or spatula around the cake edge again as described above. Pop the side off the springform pan. Use an icing spatula to loosen the bottom of the cake from the pan and then slide it off the pan bottom onto a cake cardboard or serving plate.

8 SERVE THE CHEESECAKE: Cut the cheesecake into wedges with a thin, sharp knife, pulling the knife out at the bottom of the cake to keep the surface of the cake smooth and beautiful. Dip the knife in hot water and then wipe dry after each slice. Serve with a generous spoonful of Roasted Summer Fruit or a few fresh berries.

STORING **The cooled cheesecake can be covered with plastic wrap and refrigerated for up to 4 days.**

Chocolate Marble Cheesecake **Set aside 1 cup of the batter. Melt 4 ounces of semisweet or bittersweet chocolate in a double boiler and stir it into the cup of batter until completely blended. Pour half the remaining vanilla batter into the crust. Drizzle half of the chocolate batter over the top. Pour on the remaining vanilla batter and drizzle the remaining chocolate batter over the top. Run a knife through the batter in three figure-eight swirls, turning the cake pan as you go and taking care not to scrape up any of the crust. Bake as directed.**

CITRUS-GOAT CHEESE CHEESECAKE

SERVES 8 TO 10 This recipe is based on a classic ricotta cheesecake with a generous measure of goat cheese added. It lends a mellow, acidic flavor that makes guests sit up and take notice of what is often a plain-Jane, second-fiddle-to-New-York-cheesecake. Not any more. This is for those who like their cheesecake a little less creamy, a little bit lighter, and bursting with flavor. Serve with—what else?—the best fruit of the season. If you've ever eaten goat cheese paired with sweet, ripe fruit, you'll know it's a natural. Fresh berries are a simple and delicious accompaniment, or go all out and serve with Rosy Quince (page 251) or Roasted Summer Fruit (page 262).

INGREDIENTS

1 cup plus 2 tablespoons (4½ ounces) finely ground shortbread cookie crumbs

2 tablespoons (1 ounce) unsalted butter, melted

11 ounces fresh, mild goat cheese

⅔ cup (4¾ ounces) sugar

1 (15-ounce) container whole-milk ricotta cheese

2 large eggs

2 large egg yolks

1 teaspoon pure vanilla extract

Finely grated zest of 1 orange

Finely grated zest of 1 lemon

Sugared Flowers (page 438), for garnish

EQUIPMENT

8-inch Springform Pan, Medium Bowl, Food Processor Fitted with a Metal Blade, Silicone or Rubber Spatula, Cooling Rack, Baking Sheet with ½-inch Sides, Thin and Flexible Knife or Spatula, Icing Spatula, Thin and Sharp Knife, 8-inch Cake Cardboard or Serving Plate

1 Preheat the oven to 325°F and position an oven rack in the center. Lightly coat the pan with butter or high heat canola oil spray.

2 MAKE THE CRUST: Spoon about 2 tablespoons of crumbs into the prepared pan and rotate to coat the bottom and sides. They won't fill every spot on the pan, and may seem sparse—this is fine. Tap the excess crumbs into the medium bowl and add the remaining crumbs. Add the melted butter to the bowl and stir with a fork to blend until all the crumbs are evenly moistened. With a spatula, scrape the mixture into the pan. Press the crumbs into an even layer across the bottom (do not go up the sides). Bake the crust for 12 to 15 minutes, until set and lightly browned. Transfer to a rack to cool completely. Leave the oven on.

3 MAKE THE FILLING: Place the goat cheese and sugar in the bowl of the food processor and process until smooth and creamy, about 1 minute. Scrape down the bowl once with the spatula. Add the ricotta cheese and process until incorporated and smooth, 20 to 30 seconds, scraping down the bowl halfway through. Be sure there are no lumps left (you won't be able to smooth them out later). Add the eggs, egg yolks, vanilla, and orange and lemon zests and process until well blended, about 20 seconds. Scrape the mixture into the cooled crust.

4 BAKE THE CHEESECAKE: Set the cheesecake pan on the baking sheet (in case of leakage). Bake for 35 to 45 minutes, until the edge is set but the center still has a 1-inch-wide pool of liquid batter (it will firm up during cooling and chilling).

5 Transfer the cheesecake to a cooling rack and immediately run a thin, flexible knife or spatula around the edge of the cake, gently pressing into the side of the pan to avoid gouging the cake. This will release the cake from the side of the pan and prevent cracking as it cools. Let the cheesecake cool completely, 1 to 2 hours. When cool, cover with plastic wrap and chill for at least 4 hours before serving.

6 UNMOLD THE CHEESECAKE: Run a thin knife or spatula around the cake edge again, as described above. Pop the side off the pan. Use an icing spatula to loosen the bottom of the cake from the pan and then slide it off the pan bottom onto a cake cardboard or a serving plate. Garnish the cake with sugared flowers if desired.

7 SERVE THE CHEESECAKE: Cut the cheesecake into wedges with a thin, sharp knife, pulling the knife out at the bottom of the cake to keep the surface of the cake smooth and beautiful. Dip the knife in hot water and then wipe dry after each slice. Serve with a scattering of fresh berries or the fruit of your choice.

STORING The cooled cheesecake can be covered with plastic wrap and refrigerated for up to 4 days.

STILTON CHEESECAKE WITH PORT-BRAISED PEARS

SERVES 12 TO 14 AS A FIRST COURSE The world of cheesecakes encompasses more than just dessert. In this version, blue cheese lends its salty, pungent flavor to the creamy filling, creating a memorable make-ahead hors d'oeuvre or first course. Stilton, the king of big, complex, deeply flavorful blue cheeses, is especially good here, but it's not the only option. Choose a blue cheese you love, whether mild or aged, and the cheesecake will reflect that choice beautifully. Pears and walnuts—classic accompaniments to a wedge of blue cheese—appear here in the crust and as garnish. Set out with crackers or toasted baguette slices for a crowd, or serve thin slices with mixed greens and additional toasted walnuts for the first course of a special meal.

INGREDIENTS

½ cup (2 ounces) walnuts, toasted and cooled completely

½ cup (2½ ounces) unbleached all-purpose flour

3 tablespoons (1½ ounces) cold unsalted butter, cut into small pieces

1 large egg yolk

1 pound cream cheese

2 large eggs

¼ teaspoon freshly ground black pepper

8 ounces crumbled Stilton, or other good-quality blue cheese

1 recipe Port-Braised Pears (page 263)

Crackers, or toasted baguette or walnut bread slices, for serving

Lightly dressed salad greens and additional toasted walnuts, for serving as a plated first course (optional)

EQUIPMENT

8-inch Springform Pan, Food Processor Fitted with a Metal Blade, Silicone or Rubber Spatula, Cooling Rack, Medium Bowl, Baking Sheet with ½-inch Sides, Thin and Flexible Knife or Spatula, Icing Spatula, 8-inch Cake Cardboard or Serving Platter, Thin and Sharp Knife

1 Preheat the oven to 325°F and position an oven rack in the center. Lightly coat the pan with butter or high-heat canola-oil spray.

2 MAKE THE CRUST: Place the walnuts and flour in the bowl of the food processor and process for 15 seconds, or until the nuts are finely ground. Add the butter pieces and process another 10 seconds. Add the egg yolk and process for 10 to 15 seconds, until the mixture looks like wet sand and holds together in small clumps. With the spatula, scrape the mixture into the prepared pan and press the crumbs into an even layer across the bottom (do not go up the sides). Bake the crust for 20 minutes, until set and lightly browned. Transfer to a rack to cool completely.

3 MAKE THE FILLING: Place the cream cheese in the bowl of the food processor and process until smooth and creamy, about 1 minute. Scrape down the bowl twice to ensure the mixture blends evenly and that there are no lumps left (you will not be able to smooth them out later). Add the eggs, one at a time, pulsing 3 to 5 seconds after each addition to blend them in thoroughly. Add the black pepper and blend well. Transfer the mixture to the medium bowl and gently fold in the Stilton. Scrape the mixture into the cooled crust and spread evenly.

GETTING AHEAD The cheesecake can
be prepared 2 days ahead. Cover with
plastic and refrigerate. It will still be
delicious for an additional 2 to 3 days,
but the crust will soften quite a bit.

4 BAKE THE CHEESECAKE: Set the cheesecake pan on the baking sheet (in case of any leakage). Bake for 25 to 35 minutes, until the edge is set but the center still has a loose area about the size of a quarter (it will firm up during cooling and chilling).

5 Transfer the cheesecake to a cooling rack and immediately run a thin and flexible knife or spatula around the edge of the cake, gently pressing into the side of the pan to avoid gouging the cake. This will release the cake from the side of the pan and prevent cracking as it cools. Let the cheesecake cool completely, 1 to 2 hours. When cool, cover with plastic wrap and chill for at least 4 hours before serving.

6 UNMOLD THE CHEESECAKE: Run the thin knife or spatula around the cake edge again, as described above. Pop the side off the pan. Use an icing spatula to loosen the bottom of the cake from the pan and slide it off the pan bottom onto a cake cardboard or serving plate.

7 SERVE THE CHEESECAKE: Cut the cheesecake into wedges with a thin, sharp knife, pulling the knife out at the bottom of the cake to keep the surface of the cake smooth and beautiful. Dip the knife in hot water and then wipe dry after each slice.

8 To serve as hors d'oeuvres, set out on a platter surrounded by slices of the braised pears and crackers or toasted bread. To serve as a first course, place a thin slice of cheesecake next to a salad of mixed greens, along with slices of the braised pears and toasted walnuts. Try using a little of the pears braising liquid as part of the vinaigrette for the salad to tie the dish together. Accompany with a couple of slices of toasted baguette.

STORING The cooled cheesecake can be covered with plastic wrap and refrigerated for up to 4 days.

SOUFFLÉS, MERINGUES, *and* PÂTE À CHOUX

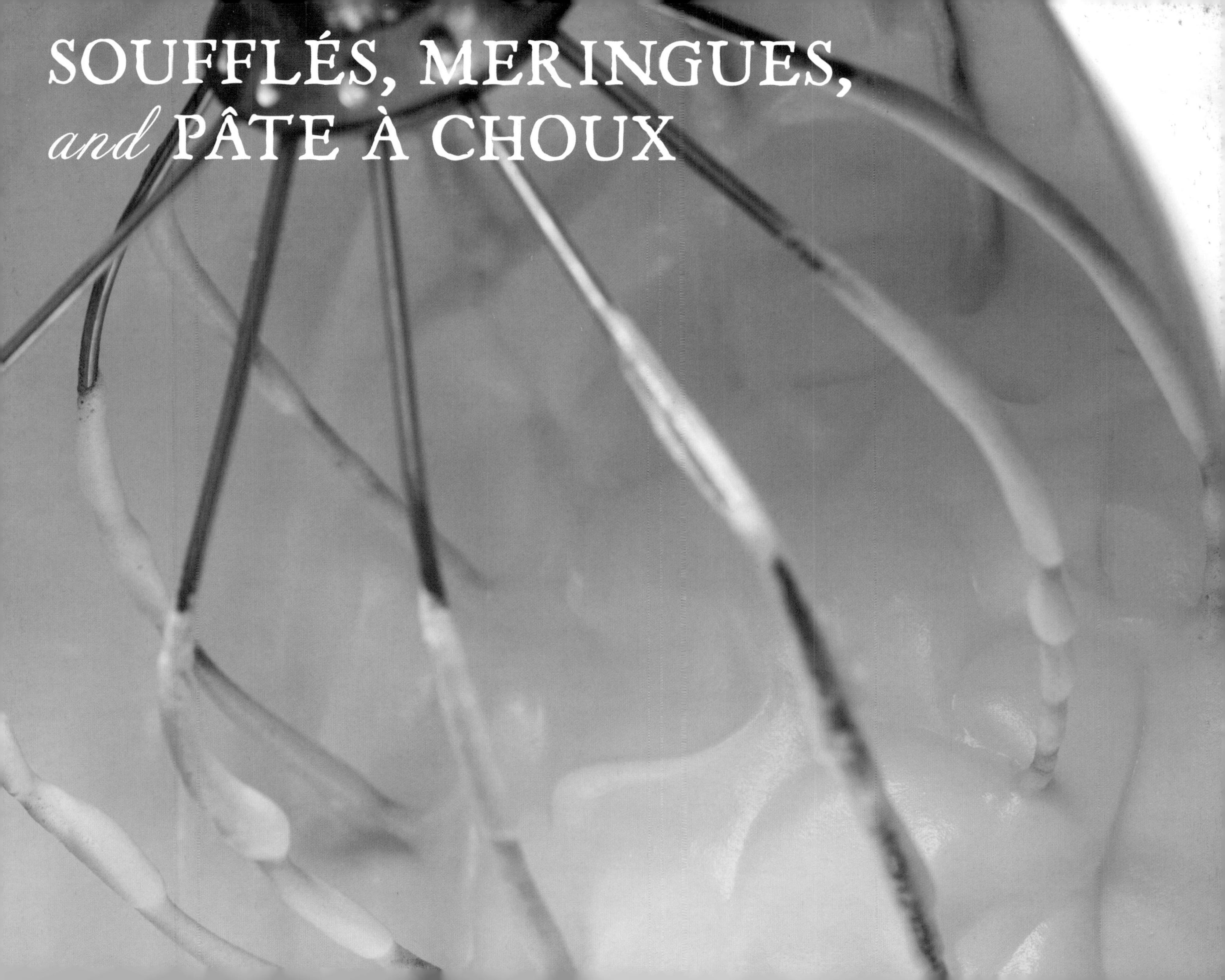

This chapter is all about the power of eggs. Each dessert and savory dish depends upon eggs for loft and light texture. Soufflés are nothing more than a simple sauce or fruit puree turned into dessert Cinderella by the addition of whipped egg whites. Meringues rely completely upon egg whites and sugar whipped together to a voluminous froth for their ethereal, melt-in-the-mouth texture. And pâte à choux, the dough used to create those crunchy-on-the-outside, hollow-on-the-inside favorites, éclairs and cream puffs, would not be able to puff or hollow without the eggs beaten into them that expand exponentially, stretching the dough to its very limits. What follows is an exploration of these three types of pastry and the culinary magic of the egg.

A Primer on Soufflés

Perhaps the most dramatic and eagerly anticipated of desserts, the soufflé is always rushed to the table at the last minute, its delicate, towering puff filling the room with a heady fragrance as it elicits oohs and aahs of appreciation for the chef's culinary prowess.

Although there is great mystery surrounding the soufflé, it is actually one of the easiest desserts to prepare. It's simply a white sauce, or béchamel, to which flavorings and whipped egg whites are added. The mixture is then turned into a mold and baked. That's it! Some dessert soufflés are even easier, with egg whites folded into a simple fruit puree rather than a cooked sauce, which results in a more intense fresh fruit flavor (with the bonus that it's fat free).

PREPARING SOUFFLÉ DISHES

A soufflé dish is a deep, straight-sided mold, usually made of ceramic. Certainly you can bake soufflé batter in a shallow pan with sloping sides—or any pan you like, for that matter—but only a soufflé dish's straight sides will produce a dramatic, puffy crown by forcing the rising batter up above the rim of the dish. You can use either a single large soufflé dish, spooning portions onto plates at the table, or serve each guest an individual soufflé. If you use individual dishes, place them on a baking sheet for easier transport in and out of the oven and keep a pair of tongs nearby to transfer the hot soufflés to serving plates.

Before you begin to make the soufflé, prepare your baking dish or dishes. The dish should be generously buttered, including the rim, to help the batter slip easily up the sides. Take your time and don't miss any spots during this preparation—either melt a bit of butter and brush it over the dish or use high-heat canola-oil spray. As the soufflé rises, it will stick to any bare spot and the batter there will not rise any further, so be thorough. If you are making a sweet soufflé, dust the buttered dish with granulated sugar and tap out the excess. For savory soufflés, use fine, dry bread crumbs or a finely grated hard cheese, such as Parmesan.

Many people believe that a parchment or foil collar must be tied around the soufflé dish or the soufflé will not rise properly. The fact is, if you need a collar, you're filling your dish too full. The collar supports the soufflé mixture that has risen way above where it could support itself naturally. All large soufflé dishes have a "fill line" inside, about ½ to ¾ inch from the rim. The soufflé mixture should not fill the dish beyond this line or it will rise too high and then collapse over the sides of the dish. If you have extra soufflé batter left after you've filled the dish, bake the remaining in a separate pan rather than risk a collapse. In most cases, small (4-ounce capacity or less) individual soufflé dishes can be filled all the way to the top, for their contents weigh so little that there is not much danger of collapse.

HOW TO MAKE A SOUFFLÉ

CREATING THE SAUCE BASE

Whether sweet or savory, the sauce base provides both the structure and flavor of the soufflé. Most savory soufflés, as well as some dessert ones, are based on béchamel, also known as white sauce, a blend of cooked flour and butter whisked with milk. Other dessert soufflés are based on pastry cream, a cornstarch or flour-thickened custard. Still others use citrus curd as their base. There is even a very simple dessert soufflé that combines fruit puree (such as raspberry, mango, or pear) with whipped egg whites. Whichever base you use, keep in mind that the flavor of the base will be diluted with the large volume of egg whites. This means that your base needs to be ultraflavorful. Fruit puree should be ripe and intense. Curd should be strong and tart. Both béchamel and pastry cream should really pack a wallop in the taste department. When you have added your flavorings to béchamel or pastry cream, it should almost taste too strong, so that by the time you fold in the egg whites the flavor will be just right.

Béchamel, the most common base, begins with a roux of butter and flour that is cooked briefly, then joined by milk and simmered to the consistency of thin pudding. Egg yolks and flavorings are added; then egg whites are whipped and folded in. Some flavorings for béchamel-based soufflés are stirred in at the end, but you can also infuse flavorings in the milk before you begin the sauce. For instance, steep cinnamon sticks or orange zest in the milk when making a chocolate soufflé, or garlic cloves when making a mushroom soufflé. For further information on infusing, see the introduction to "Custards, Bread Puddings, and Cheesecakes" on page 343.

WHIPPING THE EGG WHITES

Properly whipped egg whites are essential to the success of any soufflé. There is an in-depth discussion of eggs in "Cakes" (page 304) but here's a quick review: When whipping egg whites, make sure that your mixing bowl and whisk or beaters are perfectly clean. Begin whipping on low to medium-low until the whites look frothy, then turn the mixer to medium and beat until the whites hold soft peaks when the whisk is lifted from the bowl. If you are adding sugar, do so with the mixer running on medium, slowly raining in the sugar and continuing to beat until the whites form firm peaks (at this point, the eggs will stay put if the bowl is held upside down). If you are not adding sugar, be very cautious when whipping to firm peaks because it's easy to go too far without the added moisture and elasticity of sugar. You can save overbeaten whites by adding another egg white to the mixture and stirring it in until well incorporated, but since the ratio of ingredients is now out of whack and the whites are not at their optimum volume, your soufflé will have a denser texture and will not rise as high as expected.

BAKING THE SOUFFLÉ

BAKING TEMPERATURE AND TIME Many traditional soufflé recipes call for classic French baking temperatures of between 425° and 450°F, which result in a dramatic rise and a slightly undercooked, saucelike interior. Most Americans prefer their soufflés cooked all the way through, with sauce added at the table, so the baking temperatures here have been lowered to between 375° and 400°F, depending upon the dish size and ingredients included in the recipe. This lower temperature is still high enough to encourage an impressive rise, yet the slightly longer baking time that is required means the center is cooked all the way through.

ENCOURAGING THE SOUFFLÉ'S RISE To make sure the soufflé rises properly, use an oven thermometer to check that your oven's temperature is accurate. A soufflé might never rise in a too-cool oven. Also, keep the oven door closed while the soufflé is baking, so it has a constant temperature in which to complete its rise. Rather than opening the door, turn on the oven light to watch the magic. The soufflé should rise at least an inch or two above the rim of the pan. If you suspect the soufflé is finished, open the door, reach in, and touch the center of the soufflé lightly with your finger—if it feels firm and set, it's done. If it feels soft and squishy, check again in a few minutes. Once the soufflé is cooked, serve it immediately—it will begin to fall a couple of minutes after you remove it from the oven.

WHY A SOUFFLÉ FALLS IN THE OVEN There are several reasons why a soufflé might fall while it is still in the oven: improperly beaten egg whites; moving the soufflé around before it has finished cooking; and overcooking the soufflé. Overbeaten egg whites, whipped until they are broken and clumpy, will not rise properly and are very fragile, since they have already started to break down. If you overbeat your whites, it's better to whip some new ones than to expect a perfect soufflé (although you can probably have a passable one by beating in another egg white; see page 375). If you move the soufflé before it has fully baked and the structure of proteins is not yet set, it will probably fall. And if you overbake the soufflé, the egg whites wind too tightly, pull apart, release their moisture, and the whole thing collapses. The good news is...even if the soufflé falls, as long as it's not burned, it will still be tasty. Turn it out on a plate, slice it into wedges, and serve it like a cake.

PREPARING SOUFFLÉS AHEAD
Chocolate soufflé is the one soufflé that can be prepared up to 24 hours in advance, spooned or piped into its baking dish, and held in the refrigerator until baking time. This is possible because of the viscosity of the chocolate when cold—it holds the air bubbles in place and prevents them from deflating. This is not true of other soufflés, though any soufflés made with a béchamel base can be made up to 3 hours in advance. The crucial factors are a hot béchamel, which lightly "poaches" the egg whites and helps to set their structure; properly beaten egg whites; and correct storage. If you are going to bake the soufflé within an hour, cover the dish of prepared batter with an overturned bowl and let it sit on the counter. If the soufflé will be baked more than 1 hour after it is prepared, cover the dish with plastic wrap and chill it, then transfer it directly to the oven for baking. Soufflés made with just fruit puree and egg whites must be baked immediately. The fruit puree can be prepared in advance, of course, but the whites must be whipped just prior to baking. In restaurants, it is not possible to start each soufflé from scratch. The flavored béchamel or pastry cream is prepared up to 2 days in advance and refrigerated. When an order comes into the kitchen, the proper amount of sauce base is weighed out and warmed slightly, and the egg whites are whipped specifically for that order. You can do the same at home, warming the base in a double boiler, or on low in the microwave.

SAUCING THE SOUFFLÉ
The classic accompaniment to a dessert soufflé, vanilla custard sauce (page 424), can be flavored in many ways to complement any soufflé flavor. The chilled sauce is poured into the hot soufflé immediately upon serving. You might want to give each guest a mini pitcher of sauce, so they can pour as much—or as little—as they like. Softly Whipped Cream (page 416) and Vanilla Crème Fraîche (page 420) are other good options. A fruit sauce, such as Raspberry Sauce (page 427) can be stunning with a chocolate or light fruit soufflé. Caramel Sauce (page 426) and Dark Chocolate Sauce (page 427) are a bit heavier on the palate, but are excellent when paired with soufflés that can stand up to their strong flavors, such as a chocolate soufflé. One wonderful accompaniment to dessert soufflés is a tiny scoop of super-premium ice cream. Dropped into the center of an individual soufflé upon serving, the ice cream transforms into a cool and creamy sauce as it melts (try coffee ice cream in chocolate soufflé).

Savory soufflés don't always need a sauce, but some good accompaniments are (depending upon the flavors in the soufflé) roasted red bell pepper sauce (page 389) or tomato sauce. You might choose to serve the soufflé alongside salad instead of using a sauce, or with tapenade (a chopped olive mixture) or salsa, or even slices of good bread upon which to spread the warm soufflé.

A Primer on Meringues

Meringue is a combination of egg whites and sugar whipped to a marshmallowy froth. Once whipped, it can be used as frosting, pie topping, or—as in this chapter—shaped by piping or spreading on a baking sheet, then baking in a low oven to set and dry its structure. Meringue can be thought of as a solid form of cotton candy: It appears to have structure, yet it melts in your mouth to a soft, mellow sweetness.

Raw eggs may contain salmonella and should be avoided by the very young, the very old, or anyone with a compromised immune system. Note that all meringues included in recipes in this book are either baked or heated to a safe temperature so, as long as you follow the recipe guidelines, you'll be able to share your baked goods without worry.

TYPES OF MERINGUE

There are three basic types of meringue, defined by the proportions of egg whites to sugar and the method used to combine them.

FRENCH MERINGUE

Also called *common meringue,* French meringue is simply egg whites whipped into soft peaks, with sugar then "rained" into the whites while the mixer is running. When firm peaks form, the meringue is finished. French meringue is the least stable of the three types, and must be used immediately. It is usually used to leaven soufflés and cakes such as sponge cake and flourless chocolate cake, and may also be baked or turned into royal icing. It is the meringue of choice for most of the recipes in this book.

SWISS MERINGUE

Also called *warm meringue,* Swiss meringue is made by warming sugar and egg whites over simmering water until the sugar has melted, then whipping the mixture until it holds firm, glossy peaks. The recipes in this book always warm the eggs and sugar to 160°F before whipping, which kills any salmonella bacteria that might be present and makes the raw meringue safe for everyone. Swiss meringue can be used as a base for buttercream, in mousses, and to top pies, tarts such as Lemon Meringue Tartlets (page 236), cakes, and baked Alaska.

ITALIAN MERINGUE

Also referred to as *cooked meringue,* Italian meringue is the most stable of the three types. To make this meringue, egg whites are whipped into soft peaks while a sugar syrup is cooked to the soft ball stage. The cooked sugar is poured into the whipping egg whites and the mixture cools as it is beaten. The hot sugar cooks the egg whites and creates a sturdy meringue that is used as a base for buttercream, in mousses, for pies and frosting cakes, and for candies such as marshmallows.

SOFT VERSUS HARD MERINGUES

The texture of a meringue can be soft or hard, depending upon how much sugar is added. Soft meringues have less sugar, usually a ratio of 1 part sugar to 1 part egg whites. Hard meringues have at least twice that ratio, or 2 parts sugar to 1 part egg whites. Hard meringues are better for baking into crisp shells or disks or giving shape to buttercream or mousses, whereas soft meringues are better for items that don't need the meringue for structural support, such as cakes and cookie icing.

PROBLEMS WITH MERINGUES AND HOW TO FIX THEM

DRY, LUMPY, BROKEN EGG WHITES

Overbeating is the problem here. Whipping egg whites unwinds their proteins. Once unwound, the proteins begin to link together with other proteins, forming a network that traps air bubbles, which in turn allows the whites to increase in volume. The longer the whites are beaten, though, the more tightly the proteins wind together. When overbeaten, the proteins are wound so tightly that they squeeze out the moisture within, resulting in dry, lumpy, broken egg whites, which are of no value in a meringue that should be smooth and fluffy. Sugar added to the whipping whites serves as a moisturizer, keeping them smooth, moist, and flexible, and reduces the possibility of overbeating.

French Meringue

RIGHT: Make sure that your mixing bowl and whisk or beaters are perfectly clean. Begin whipping the egg whites on low to medium-low until the whites look frothy, then turn the mixer to medium and beat until the whites hold soft peaks when the whisk is lifted from the bowl.

BOTTOM LEFT: With the mixer running on medium speed, slowly rain in the sugar.

BOTTOM RIGHT: Continue to beat until the whites form firm peaks (at this point, the eggs will stay put if the bowl is held upside down).

WEEPING AND BEADING

Both are baking problems. Weeping refers to liquid leaking out from under the meringue, which happens when the meringue is underbaked and the proteins in the meringue don't get hot enough to solidify. The meringue deflates or collapses and the liquid surrounding the air bubbles separates from the mixture and forms a moist layer beneath the meringue. To prevent weeping, be sure to cook your meringue all the way through. Beading, which is also a release of liquid, is caused by too much heat. The proteins on the outside of the meringue harden quickly, tightening and squeezing out their moisture, which forms droplets, or beads, over the surface of the meringue. Often these droplets turn lightly brown, as the sugar in them caramelizes in the heat. If you're having a problem with beading, next time reduce the heat of your oven and/or remove the meringue from the oven sooner.

SHAPING MERINGUE

Once meringue has been whipped, use it immediately, because beaten egg whites begin to break down almost as soon as you create them. Shape or pipe the meringue as desired and get it in the oven quickly. Meringues can be shaped by hand or piped with a pastry bag; use the method you are most comfortable with. Piping gives you a precise shape and is also quicker. For tips on judging doneness, see page 395.

FLAVORING MERINGUE

Meringue is a blank canvas for flavor, but be careful how you add the flavoring. Extracts and alcohol can be added toward the end of the whipping process, but remember that oil inhibits egg whites from whipping, so flavored oils, nuts, chocolate, spices, zest, and anything with natural oils should not be added until the meringue has reached full volume. Either whip a flavoring in for a few seconds or fold it in after the meringue is removed from the mixer. Fold carefully to prevent the loss of air bubbles and the likelihood of flat meringue.

A Primer on Pâte à Choux

Pâte à choux, sometimes referred to as *cream puff dough,* is a simple, quick, versatile pastry to have in your repertoire. The dough, which can be prepared in under 15 minutes from common ingredients in your pantry, puffs dramatically and forms a hollow center (great for filling) and can be used for both sweet and savory filled pastries, such as éclairs, cream puffs, fritters, profiteroles, and *gougères* (a savory appetizer created by adding grated cheese to the dough). The baked pastries are easy to keep on hand, since they freeze beautifully. Just refresh for a few minutes in a hot oven and your pastries are ready to be filled and served.

Pâte à choux relies on two leaveners to achieve the crispy balloon effect for which it is famous. The first is, of course, eggs. But water is also an important part of the rise. The water trapped in the dough turns to steam in the heat of the oven, causing the dough to swell.

HOW TO MAKE PÂTE À CHOUX

Pâte à choux begins with water and butter brought to a boil. Be sure to catch it just as the butter is completely melted and the mixture begins to boil, for if left unattended, water could evaporate and throw off the proportions of the recipe. The just-boiling mixture is removed from the heat and flour is added and beaten until smooth. The flour immediately absorbs the hot water and the vigorous beating develops the gluten necessary for an elastic dough—one that will stretch and rise in the oven. The dough is put back over the heat to dry it slightly, then beaten until it forms a dull mass around the end of the spoon. Next, the eggs are added. You can transfer the dough to a standing mixer fitted with the paddle attachment at this point, but the eggs can also be incorporated by hand. Beat the dough 1 minute to cool it slightly—you don't want the eggs to scramble when added. Then add the eggs a little at a time, beating well between additions, until the dough is shiny and smooth. Because of variations among flours and eggs, the amount of egg needed is not precise. You'll want to add enough so that the dough becomes sticky and shiny, but not so much that the dough is slack, for it won't rise as high in the oven.

TESTING PÂTE À CHOUX A good way to test *pâte à choux* is with the "string test": Place a bit of dough between your thumb and index fingers—when you pull them apart, a string of dough about 1½ to 2 inches long will form between them. Once the correct consistency is reached, the dough is shaped, and baked until golden brown and crisp.

FLAVORING PÂTE À CHOUX This versatile dough adapts to many flavors. Both spiced and chocolate variations follow the master *pâte à choux* recipe. Feel free to create other flavors by adding citrus zest, or extracts to the dough (see page 399). You can also substitute juice, coffee, or wine for the water in the recipe. Occasionally, you even see milk substituted for the water, which creates a tasty variation—but because of the milk fat, the pastry is softer and not quite as crisp.

PIPING PÂTE À CHOUX To ensure that each portion is the same size and shape (and they all bake evenly), pipe the dough rather than shaping it by hand, except when making *gougères,* which are a rustic, country preparation portioned with spoons. Until you get the hang of piping shapes the same size, it helps to follow a form or template drawn on parchment. For instance, to shape éclairs, mark a rectangle on the paper about 4 inches long and 1 inch wide, so that each éclair is uniform. If you draw templates, be sure to turn the parchment sheet pen- or pencil-side down on the pan before piping, or the marks will transfer to your dough. Because pâte à choux is sticky, it can be difficult to stop the flow from the pastry bag at the end of each piped shape. Try using a lightly oiled dinner knife to help. Slice it across the opening of the pastry tip to both stop the flow from the pastry bag and disconnect it from the individual shape you just piped.

Before baking, brush the top of each pastry with a thin film of beaten egg, taking care that it doesn't drip down the sides and glue the pastry to the pan, which would prevent it from rising to its full potential.

BAKING PÂTE À CHOUX The dough should be baked in a 400°F oven for the best rise. When baked fully, the dough is a deep golden brown, with no bubbling moisture around the sides. Be sure to leave the shapes in long enough to dry and crisp. Many recipes start the baking at 400°F, then reduce the temperature to 350°F to dry the insides and crisp the outer shell without burning the crust.

Testing Pâte à Choux

BITTERSWEET CHOCOLATE SOUFFLÉS WITH VANILLA CUSTARD SAUCE

SERVES 8 This is the ultimate dessert soufflé. It delivers dark chocolate in an elegant party dress, and is also the only soufflé that can be prepared up to 24 hours in advance and held in the refrigerator before baking. Since the sauce can be made in advance as well, the combination is perfect for entertaining.

INGREDIENTS

8 ounces bittersweet chocolate (up to 70 percent cacao), finely chopped

1 tablespoon (½ ounce) unsalted butter, cut into ½-inch pieces

1 tablespoon (½ ounce) unbleached all-purpose flour

½ cup (4 ounces) whole milk

1 teaspoon pure vanilla extract

½ teaspoon instant espresso powder dissolved in ½ teaspoon water

Pinch of salt

3 large eggs, separated, plus 1 additional egg white

¼ cup (1¾ ounces) granulated sugar

Confectioners' sugar, for dusting

Vanilla Custard Sauce (page 424) or Caramel Sauce (page 426), Dark Chocolate Sauce (page 427), and Softly Whipped Cream (page 416), for serving (optional)

EQUIPMENT

Eight (5½- or 6-Ounce) Individual Soufflé Dishes, Double Boiler, Silicone or Rubber Spatula, Small Saucepan, Whisk, Large Bowl, Stand Mixer Fitted with a Whisk Attachment or a Hand Mixer and a Medium Bowl, Pastry Bag Fitted with a ½-inch Plain Tip, Baking Sheet, Fine-Mesh Strainer

1 Preheat the oven to 375°F and position an oven rack in the bottom third. Generously butter the soufflé dishes (including the rims), dust them with sugar, and tap out the excess.

2 MELT THE CHOCOLATE: Pour 2 inches of water in the bottom of the double boiler and bring to a rolling boil. Off the heat, place the chocolate in the top of the double boiler. Turn the heat off and set the chocolate over the steaming water. Stir occasionally with the spatula until the chocolate is melted and smooth. Leave over the warm water until needed. Alternately, melt the chocolate in the microwave (page 43) and set aside.

3 MAKE THE BÉCHAMEL: Melt the butter in the small saucepan over medium heat. Remove from the heat, add the flour, and whisk well to remove any lumps. Return to the heat and cook for 1 minute, whisking constantly. Remove the pan from the heat and add the milk slowly, whisking constantly to remove any lumps. Return the pan to the heat and bring to a boil, whisking constantly. Cook for 1 to 2 minutes, until thickened to the consistency of thin pudding. Remove from the heat and whisk in the vanilla. Whisk in the espresso powder and pinch of salt. With a clean spatula, scrape the melted chocolate into the large bowl. Add the béchamel sauce and whisk to blend. Whisk in the egg yolks. Cover and keep warm while you whip the egg whites.

4 WHIP THE EGG WHITES: In the very clean bowl of the stand mixer, whip the 4 egg whites on medium speed until they form soft peaks. With the mixer running, rain in the granulated sugar and beat until firm peaks form. You can also use a hand mixer and a medium bowl. With a spatula, gently stir one-fourth of the egg whites into the chocolate béchamel sauce to lighten the mixture. Fold in the remaining whites just until there are no more streaks of whites.

The chocolate really shines through in this recipe. There is nothing here to hide the off-notes and sugary sweetness of poor-quality chocolate. Similarly, the nuances of your favorite chocolate will emerge. If you use a sweet, mild dark chocolate, the finished soufflé will delight you and melt in your mouth like a puff of chocolate cotton candy. If you use extra-dark bittersweet chocolate with lots of complex, winelike flavors, your soufflé will reflect those qualities as well.

GETTING AHEAD **The soufflé batter can be piped into the dishes up to 24 hours before baking. Set them on the baking sheet, wrap with plastic so that the chocolate does not absorb flavors, and refrigerate. Unwrap and transfer the sheet of soufflés directly to the oven for baking.**

5 FILL THE DISHES AND BAKE: Transfer the soufflé batter to the pastry bag. Pipe the batter into each soufflé dish, filling it to ¼ inch below the rim. Transfer the dishes to the baking sheet. Bake for 14 to 18 minutes (higher percentage chocolates will bake more quickly), until the soufflés are set and firm to the touch in the center. Serve immediately, dusted with confectioners' sugar and accompanied by individual pitchers of custard sauce.

For an over-the-top dessert, break open the tops of the soufflés and, instead of the custard sauce, pour in caramel sauce and chocolate sauce, then top with generous spoonfuls of whipped cream. Pass additional sauce and cream around the table. Ooh-la-la!

Large Soufflés
You can also bake this in a 6-cup buttered and sugared soufflé dish. Bake for 32 to 38 minutes, until set and firm to the touch in the center. Serve immediately.

MEYER LEMON SOUFFLÉS WITH RASPBERRY SAUCE

SERVES 8 Lemon soufflé is the temperature opposite of icy cold lemonade, yet both provide the same powerful jolt of flavor and palate-tingling satisfaction. This is essentially lemon curd with meringue folded in—a light, refreshing dessert at any time of year. Meyer lemons, a cousin to the supermarket Eureka lemons, are not quite as acidic and have an exquisite floral perfume. They are available during the winter and spring, but if you can't find them, Eureka lemons are a fine substitute.

INGREDIENTS

4 large eggs, separated, plus
1 additional egg white

⅓ cup (2¼ ounces) plus ¼ cup
(1¾ ounces) granulated sugar

2 tablespoons (¾ ounce)
unbleached all-purpose flour

Finely grated zest of 2 lemons

½ cup (4 ounces) strained
fresh Meyer lemon juice

½ stick (2 ounces) unsalted butter,
cut into ½-inch cubes

Confectioners' sugar, for dusting

2 recipes Fresh Raspberry Sauce
(page 427), for serving

Softly Whipped Cream (page 416) for serving

EQUIPMENT

Eight (5½- or 6-Ounce) Individual Soufflé Dishes, Double Boiler, Whisk, Silicone or Rubber Spatula, Fine-Mesh Strainer, Large Bowl, Stand Mixer Fitted with a Whisk Attachment or a Hand Mixer and a Medium Bowl, Pastry Bag Fitted with a ½-inch Plain Tip, Baking Sheet

1 Preheat the oven to 375°F and position an oven rack in the bottom third. Generously butter the soufflé dishes (including the rims), dust them with sugar, and tap out the excess.

2 PREPARE THE LEMON CURD: Place the egg yolks, the ⅓ cup granulated sugar, and the flour in the top portion of the double boiler and whisk until well blended and slightly lightened in color, about 1 minute. Add the lemon zest and juice and whisk well. Bring 2 inches of water to a rolling boil into the bottom of the double boiler. Reduce the heat so the water is at a simmer and place the top of the double boiler over the water. Cook until the curd is very thick, 5 to 7 minutes, whisking constantly and scraping around the edges frequently so the eggs don't scramble. When the whisk is lifted and a bit of curd falls back into the mixture, it should hold its shape on the surface rather than just blending back into the mixture.

3 With the spatula, scrape the curd into the strainer set over the large bowl. Use the spatula to press the curd firmly through the strainer. Add the butter pieces to the curd, burying them so they begin to melt. Wait 1 minute, then whisk until the butter is completely melted and blended with the curd. Place a piece of plastic wrap directly on the surface of the curd to prevent a skin from forming.

4 WHIP THE EGG WHITES: In the very clean bowl of the stand mixer, whip the 5 egg whites on medium speed until they form soft peaks. With the mixer running, rain in the remaining ¼ cup granulated sugar and beat until firm peaks form. You can also use a hand mixer and a medium bowl. With the spatula, gently stir one-fourth of the egg whites

GETTING AHEAD The curd may be
prepared up to 3 days in advance and
refrigerated in an airtight container with
a piece of plastic wrap pressed against
its surface. Warm in a double boiler
before adding the whipped egg whites.

into the lemon curd to lighten the mixture. Fold in the remaining whites just until there are
no more streaks of whites.

5 FILL THE DISHES AND BAKE: Transfer the soufflé batter to the pastry bag. Pipe
batter into the soufflé dishes, filling each one to ¼ inch below the rim. Transfer the
dishes to the baking sheet. Bake for 9 to 12 minutes, until the soufflés are set and firm
to the touch in the center. Use a fine-mesh strainer to dust with confectioners' sugar, and
serve immediately with raspberry sauce. Pass a bowl of whipped cream to accent the
soufflé as well.

Passion Fruit Soufflés Substitute passion fruit juice for the lemon juice.
Serve with Dark Chocolate Sauce (page 427) and pass a bowl of Ginger Cream (page 417).

BLINTZ SOUFFLÉS WITH SUGARED STRAWBERRIES

SERVES 6 TO 8 A blintz is a crepe that enfolds lightly sweetened fresh cheese. This recipe takes the luscious filling and translates it to an easy soufflé that is especially good for breakfast. Baking this soufflé in individual gratin dishes reduces the baking time and provides extra room for strawberries on top of each serving. A champagne Mimosa on the side is all you need for a simple yet special brunch.

INGREDIENTS

2 pints (about 2 pounds) fresh strawberries

About 7 tablespoons sugar, divided

1 teaspoon freshly squeezed lemon juice

8 ounces cream cheese, softened

2 tablespoons (¾ ounce) unbleached, all-purpose flour

1 (15-ounce) container whole-milk ricotta cheese

¼ cup (2 ounces) crème fraîche or sour cream

Finely grated zest of 1 large orange

Finely grated zest of 1 large lemon

½ teaspoon pure vanilla extract

½ teaspoon ground cinnamon

4 large eggs, separated, plus 1 additional egg white

EQUIPMENT

Paring Knife, Medium Bowl, Six (12-Ounce) Individual Gratin Dishes or Eight (9- to 10-Ounce) Gratin Dishes or Shallow Soup Bowls, Stand Mixer with Paddle and Whisk Attachments, Large Bowl, Hand Mixer and a Medium Bowl (Optional), Silicone or Rubber Spatula, Baking Sheet

GETTING AHEAD The night before, you can prepare the baking dishes; prepare the soufflé base through Step 3 (refrigerate in an airtight container); and wash and dry the strawberries (but don't slice or sugar them until the morning or they'll begin to break down).

1 PREPARE THE STRAWBERRIES: Wash the berries and pat dry. Hull, then use a paring knife to quarter them if they are small to medium in size, or cut them into ¼-inch thick slices if they are large. Transfer to the medium bowl, sprinkle with 1 to 2 tablespoons sugar and the lemon juice, and gently stir to coat. Set aside. The sugar will draw the juices from the berries.

2 Preheat the oven to 375°F and position an oven rack in the lower third. Generously butter the dishes, dust them with sugar, and tap out the excess.

3 MAKE THE SOUFFLÉ BASE: In the bowl of the stand mixer fitted with the paddle, beat the cream cheese and 2 tablespoons of the sugar on medium speed until smooth. Add the flour and blend well. Add the ricotta and crème fraîche and blend well. Add the orange and lemon zests, vanilla, cinnamon, and egg yolks and blend well. Transfer to the large bowl.

4 WHIP THE EGG WHITES: In the very clean bowl of the stand mixer with the whisk attachment, whip the 5 egg whites on medium speed until they form soft peaks. With the mixer running, rain in the 3 tablespoons of the sugar and beat until firm peaks form. With a spatula, gently stir one-fourth of the egg whites into the soufflé base to lighten the mixture. Fold in the remaining whites just until there are no more streaks of whites.

5 FILL THE DISHES AND BAKE: Divide the batter among the prepared gratin dishes , filling each one to ½-inch below the rim, and set on the baking sheet. Bake for 15 to 20 minutes, until set and firm to the touch. Serve immediately, topped with a spoonful or two of the sugared strawberries and their juices. Pass the remaining strawberries in a bowl and let your guests help themselves to more.

RASPBERRY SOUFFLÉS WITH HIDDEN CHOCOLATE TRUFFLES

SERVES 10 This is an example of a fruit puree soufflé. There is no sauce base here; instead, the soufflé consists of meringue folded into raspberry puree. It has an intense fresh-fruit flavor and is just the ticket for a light and lively ending to a special meal. A chocolate truffle is hidden in the center of each soufflé, but you could just as easily tuck a couple of fresh berries inside, or let it stand alone. If you like, serve with a tiny scoop of mango or passion fruit sorbet instead of the crème fraîche.

INGREDIENTS

3 ounces semisweet or bittersweet chocolate (up to 70 percent cacao), finely chopped

6 tablespoons (3 ounces) heavy whipping cream

2 half-pints (12 ounces) fresh raspberries, or 12 ounces frozen raspberries

1 tablespoon plus ¼ cup (2 ounces) sugar

1 teaspoon framboise (raspberry brandy), optional

5 large egg whites

Vanilla Crème Fraîche (page 420) or Framboise Cream (page 417), for serving

EQUIPMENT

Ten (5½- or 6-Ounce) Individual Soufflé Dishes, Medium Microwave-Safe Bowl, Medium Bowl or Baking Sheet, Food Processor Fitted with a Metal Blade, Silicone or Rubber Spatula, Fine-Mesh Strainer, Stand Mixer Fitted with a Whisk Attachment or a Hand Mixer and a Medium Bowl, Pastry Bag Fitted with a ½-inch Plain Tip, Baking Sheet, Small Offset Spatula

1 PREPARE THE TRUFFLES: Place the chopped chocolate and cream in the microwave-safe bowl and heat in the microwave, stirring every 30 seconds, until the chocolate is melted and the mixture is smooth. If you are using a high-percentage chocolate and the mixture looks broken or curdled at this point, stir in an extra tablespoon or two of cream, just until the mixture smooths out again. Cover with plastic wrap and refrigerate for 30 minutes, or until cold enough to scoop. Use a small spoon to scrape ½ tablespoon of the ganache into a small round and set it on a plate. Repeat, making 10 small truffles. Cover with plastic wrap and refrigerate until needed.

2 Preheat the oven to 400°F and position an oven rack in the bottom third. Generously butter the soufflé dishes (including the rims), dust them with sugar, and tap out the excess.

3 MAKE THE RASPBERRY PUREE: If the raspberries are frozen, transfer to a medium bowl and defrost completely. If the berries are fresh, pour them onto a baking sheet and sort through them, discarding any debris or moldy berries—do not wash the berries or they will disintegrate. Place the raspberries (including any juices) in the bowl of the food processor and process until the berries are completely pureed. Use a spatula to scrape the puree into the strainer set over the medium bowl and press it through. You should have about 1 cup of puree. Discard the seeds in the strainer. Stir the 1 tablespoon sugar, and the framboise (if using), into the puree.

4 WHIP THE EGG WHITES: In the very clean bowl of the stand mixer, whip the egg whites on medium speed until they form soft peaks. You can also use a hand mixer and a medium bowl. With the mixer running, rain in the remaining ¼ cup sugar and beat until firm peaks form. With the spatula, gently stir one-fourth of the egg whites into the

You can bake a soufflé in any dish, from a gratin dish to a coffee cup, but keep these three things in mind when changing dishes: One, if the dish doesn't have straight sides, the soufflé won't rise dramatically over the top, though it will still be light and taste delicious. Two, if you change the dish, make sure it is exactly the same capacity as the one in the recipe, or you'll also change the yield, or number of servings. And three, if the dish is larger or smaller than the one called for in the recipe, the baking time will change. Deeper dishes will require more time, while shallow dishes will bake quickly. In this case, don't follow the time guidelines in the recipe, but instead look for a nice increase in volume and a center that is set when gently touched with a fingertip.

GETTING AHEAD **Prepare the chocolate truffles up to 4 days in advance and keep refrigerated in an airtight container. Prepare the raspberry puree up to 24 hours in advance and refrigerate in an airtight container until needed.**

raspberry puree to lighten the mixture. Fold in the remaining whites just until there are no more streaks of whites.

5 FILL THE DISHES AND BAKE: Transfer the soufflé batter to the pastry bag. Pipe batter into the soufflé dishes to fill halfway. Set a truffle on top of the batter in each dish. Finish filling the soufflé dishes all the way to the top. Set the dishes on the baking sheet. (You may have a little batter left over—if so, fill another soufflé dish or custard cup.) Run the offset spatula across the top of each soufflé dish, flattening the top and leveling it with the rim. Bake for 14 to 17 minutes, until set and firm to the touch in the center. Use a fine-mesh strainer to dust with confectioners' sugar, then top with a spoonful of crème fraîche or framboise cream. Serve immediately.

Blackberry Soufflés
Substitute blackberries for the raspberries (buy an extra half-pint of blackberries, or you may not have enough puree, since there are fewer blackberries in each basket because of their larger size).

CORN SOUFFLÉ WITH RED PEPPER SAUCE

SERVES 6 TO 7 Gorgeous, golden, and bursting with two kinds of corn–both fresh kernels and cornmeal–this soufflé makes a great main course for a light summer dinner. The smoked paprika adds an intriguing undercurrent of flavor, but if you don't have it on hand, simply leave it out or substitute a pinch of cayenne. You can make this soufflé during the winter and spring with frozen corn kernels, but don't use dried basil; it tastes dusty and tired compared to the vibrant flavor of fresh basil. If fresh is unavailable, omit it.

INGREDIENTS

RED PEPPER SAUCE

1 (15-ounce) jar roasted red bell peppers

1 tablespoon water

1 teaspoon olive oil

⅛ teaspoon salt

SOUFFLÉ

3 tablespoons (1 ounce) unbleached all-purpose flour

2 tablespoons (½ ounce) fine cornmeal

⅛ teaspoon smoked paprika

½ stick (2 ounces) unsalted butter, cut into pieces

1 teaspoon minced garlic (about 1 medium clove)

1⅓ cups (10½ ounces) whole milk

2 cups (11½ ounces) fresh corn kernels (about 3 ears)

¼ cup (1 ounce) finely grated Parmesan cheese

1 tablespoon chopped fresh basil

1 teaspoon salt

5 large eggs, separated, plus 1 additional egg white

¼ teaspoon cream of tartar

EQUIPMENT

Medium-Mesh Strainer, Blender, Large Bowl, Whisk, Medium Saucepan, Stand Mixer Fitted with a Whisk Attachment or a Hand Mixer and a Medium Bowl, Silicone or Rubber Spatula, 7½-cup Soufflé Dish, Baking Sheet, Small Saucepan

1. MAKE THE SAUCE: In the strainer, rinse the roasted peppers well under cold water. Pat dry with paper towels. Transfer to the bowl of the blender and add the water, olive oil, and salt. Blend until smooth, 20 to 30 seconds. Set aside.

2. MAKE THE BÉCHAMEL: In the large bowl, whisk together the flour, cornmeal, and paprika. Melt the butter in the medium saucepan over medium heat. Add the garlic and cook, stirring occasionally, until fragrant, about 1 minute. Remove from the heat, add the flour mixture, and whisk well to remove any lumps. Return to the heat and cook for 1 to 2 minutes, whisking constantly. Remove from the heat again and add the milk slowly, whisking constantly to remove any lumps. Return to the heat and bring to a boil, whisking constantly. Boil for 1 to 2 minutes, then add the corn kernels and continue to cook for 3 to 4 minutes, whisking until the sauce has thickened and the corn is cooked through. Remove from the heat and whisk in the Parmesan, basil, and salt. Whisk in the egg yolks and transfer to the large bowl. Set aside.

3. Preheat the oven to 400°F and position an oven rack in the bottom third. Generously butter the soufflé dish (including the rim), coat it with finely grated Parmesan, and tap out the excess.

4. WHIP THE EGG WHITES: In the very clean bowl of the stand mixer, whip the 6 egg whites and the cream of tartar on medium speed until they form firm peaks. You may also use a hand mixer and a medium bowl. Be careful not to overbeat. With the spatula,

You can get an even deeper corn flavor if you toast the cornmeal before beginning the recipe. Place a small dry skillet over high heat. When the pan is hot, add the cornmeal and toss or stir frequently until the cornmeal is very fragrant and has a golden toasted look, 3 to 4 minutes—don't let it brown. Immediately pour the cornmeal onto a plate to cool.

GETTING AHEAD **The red pepper sauce can be made up to 2 days ahead and refrigerated in an airtight container. The béchamel can be prepared through Step 2 and refrigerated, a piece of plastic wrap pressed directly against the surface of the sauce, up to 2 days in advance. Reheat in a double boiler (or the microwave) before continuing with the recipe.**

gently stir one-fourth of the egg whites into the béchamel to lighten the mixture. Fold in the remaining whites just until there are no more streaks of whites.

5 FILL THE DISH AND BAKE: Transfer the batter to the prepared baking dish and place on the baking sheet. Bake for 20 minutes. then reduce the oven temperature to 375°F and bake for 18 to 22 minutes longer, until set and firm to the touch. While the soufflé is baking, transfer the red pepper sauce to the small saucepan and heat through. Serve the soufflé immediately, accompanied by the sauce.

Individual Corn Soufflés
Prepare 7 (8-ounce) individual soufflé dishes with butter and Parmesan as described above. Place the dishes on a baking sheet and evenly divide the soufflé batter among them. Bake at 400°F for 15 minutes, then reduce the oven temperature to 375°F and bake for 7 to 10 minutes longer, until firm to the touch.

MUSHROOM AND FONTINA SOUFFLÉS

SERVES 8 This is your basic cheese soufflé embellished with mushrooms, shallots, and fresh thyme. The mushrooms are minced in a food processor, since larger slices would weigh down the soufflé and prevent it from rising. It's perfect for dinner, with a simple salad and toasted baguette slices on which to spread the earthy soufflé. While it's delicious with white button mushrooms, if you add some wild mushrooms to the mix it's even better.

INGREDIENTS

MUSHROOMS

1¼ cups (4 ounces) sliced mushrooms

1 tablespoon unsalted butter

1 shallot, very finely chopped

1 teaspoon minced fresh thyme

BÉCHAMEL AND EGG WHITES

½ stick (2 ounces) unsalted butter, cut into pieces

¼ cup (¼ ounce) unbleached all-purpose flour

1 cup (8 ounces) whole milk

¾ cup (3 ounces) grated fontina cheese

¼ cup (1 ounce) grated Parmesan cheese

½ teaspoon salt

4 grinds black pepper

Pinch of cayenne (optional)

4 large eggs, separated, plus 1 additional egg white

¼ teaspoon cream of tartar

EQUIPMENT

Eight (5½- 6-Ounce) Individual Soufflé Dishes, Food Processor Fitted with a Metal Blade, Medium Sauté Pan, Small Saucepan, Whisk, Large Bowl, Stand Mixer Fitted with a Whisk Attachment or a Hand Mixer and a Medium Bowl, Silicone or Rubber Spatula, Pastry Bag Fitted with ½-inch Plain Tip, Baking Sheet

1 Preheat the oven to 400°F and position an oven rack in the bottom third. Generously butter the soufflé dishes (including the rims), coat them with fine, dry bread crumbs or finely grated Parmesan cheese, and tap out the excess.

2 COOK THE MUSHROOMS: Process the mushrooms in the bowl of the food processor until very finely chopped, 20 to 30 seconds. Melt the butter in the medium sauté pan over high heat until hot and bubbling. Add the shallot and cook until translucent, about 1 minute. Add the mushrooms and cook until they have given up their liquid, it has evaporated, and the mushrooms look dry, about 5 to 6 minutes. Stir in the thyme and set aside.

3 MAKE THE BÉCHAMEL: Melt the butter in the small saucepan over medium heat. Remove from the heat, add the flour, and whisk well to remove any lumps. Return to the heat and cook for 1 minute, whisking constantly. Remove from the heat and add the milk slowly, whisking constantly to remove any lumps. Return to the heat and bring to a boil, whisking constantly. Boil for 1 to 2 minutes, whisking, until thickened to the consistency of thin pudding. Transfer the mixture to the large bowl and whisk in the mushroom mixture, fontina, Parmesan, salt, pepper, and cayenne. Whisk in the egg yolks and set aside.

4 WHIP THE EGG WHITES: In the very clean bowl of the stand mixer, whip the 5 egg whites and the cream of tartar on medium speed until they form firm peaks. You can also use a hand mixer and a medium bowl. Be careful not to overbeat. With the spatula, gently stir one-fourth of the egg whites into the béchamel to lighten the mixture. Fold in the remaining whites just until there are no more streaks of whites.

5 FILL THE DISHES AND BAKE: Transfer the soufflé batter to the pastry bag. Pipe the batter into the prepared soufflé dishes, filling each one to ¼ inch below the rim. Set the dishes on the baking sheet. Bake for 13 to 16 minutes, until the soufflés are set and firm to the touch in the center. Serve immediately.

Large Soufflés
Butter a 7½-cup soufflé dish and coat with bread crumbs or Parmesan as described above. Place on the baking sheet and gently scrape in the batter. Bake for 30 minutes, or until set and firm to the touch in the center.

Goat Cheese and Herb Soufflés
Omit the mushroom mixture. Substitute 6 ounces fresh, soft goat cheese for the fontina and Parmesan. Add 2 tablespoons chopped fresh chives, 1 teaspoon minced fresh thyme, and 1 teaspoon minced fresh parsley to the béchamel with the goat cheese.

Blue Cheese Soufflés
Omit the mushroom mixture. Substitute 5 ounces crumbled blue cheese, such as Stilton or Gorgonzola, for the fontina and Parmesan.

PEANUT BUTTER AND CHOCOLATE MARJOLAINE

SERVES 10 Marjolaine is a classic French dessert with layers of almond or hazelnut meringue, chocolate ganache, and hazelnut buttercream. The version here is a bit more fun—and definitely more American—because it uses peanuts in the meringue layers and peanut butter buttercream. The result is pretty enough for any special occasion, yet playful.

INGREDIENTS

GANACHE

7 ounces semisweet or bittersweet chocolate (up to 60 percent cacao), finely chopped

1 tablespoon unsalted butter, cut into 4 pieces

1 cup (8 ounces) heavy whipping cream

PEANUT MERINGUE

1½ cups (7½ ounces) unsalted roasted peanuts

¼ cup (1¾ ounces) plus 1¼ cups (8¾ ounces) granulated sugar

1 tablespoon (¼ ounce) cornstarch

8 large egg whites

¼ teaspoon cream of tartar

BUTTERCREAM

15 tablespoons (7½ ounces) unsalted butter, very soft, but not melted

1¼ cups (5 ounces) unsifted confectioners' sugar

1 cup minus 2 tablespoons (9 ounces) creamy salted peanut butter (see page 276), at room temperature

1 cup finely chopped store-bought peanut brittle, or finely chopped additional peanuts

EQUIPMENT

Medium Bowl, Small Saucepan, Whisk, 12 by 17-inch Rimmed Baking Sheet, Food Processor Fitted with a Metal Blade, Stand Mixer with Whisk and Paddle Attachments or a Hand Mixer and a Medium Bowl, Silicone or Rubber Spatula, Offset Spatula, Cooling Rack, Serrated Knife, Approximately 12 by 5-inch Cake Cardboard or Serving Platter, Pastry Bag Fitted with a ¼-inch Star Tip

1 MAKE THE GANACHE: Place the chocolate and butter in the medium bowl. Bring the cream to a boil in the small saucepan over medium heat. As soon as the cream boils, pour it over the chocolate. Let sit for 1 minute, then whisk until blended and smooth. If you are using a high-percentage chocolate and the mixture looks broken or curdled at this point, stir in an extra tablespoon or two of cream, just until the mixture smooths out again. Cover with plastic wrap and set aside for 2 to 3 hours or up to overnight, until the ganache has cooled completely and has the texture of frosting.

2 MAKE THE MERINGUE LAYERS: Preheat the oven to 350°F and position an oven rack in the center. Lightly coat the baking sheet with butter or high-heat canola-oil spray, line it with parchment paper, then lightly coat it with butter or spray again, dust it with flour, and tap off the excess. Place the peanuts, the ¼ cup granulated sugar, and the cornstarch in the bowl of the food processor and process until the nuts are finely ground, 20 to 30 seconds. Place the egg whites and cream of tartar in the bowl of the stand mixer with the whisk and whip on medium-high speed until soft peaks form, 1½ to 2 minutes. You can also use a hand mixer and a medium bowl, although you may need to beat the mixture a little longer to achieve the same results. With the mixer running, slowly rain in the remaining 1¼ cups granulated sugar, then turn the speed to high and whip until the meringue is very stiff, 30 to 45 seconds. Carefully fold the nut mixture into the meringue with the silicone or rubber spatula until no more patches of dry ingredients remain. Spread the meringue evenly in the prepared baking sheet using the offset spatula.

3 Bake the meringue for 25 minutes, or until it is golden in color, the center feels firm to the touch, and the edge begins to pull away from the side of the pan. Transfer to a rack and cool completely.

GETTING AHEAD **The meringue layers can be made up to 5 days in advance Wrap them airtight in plastic and store at room temperature. The ganache and peanut buttercream can be made up to 5 days in advance and kept, refrigerated, in separate airtight containers. Bring to room temperature (allow 2 hours) before using or both of them will be too firm to spread easily.**

4 MAKE THE BUTTERCREAM: Place the butter in the bowl of the stand mixer with the paddle and beat on medium-low until smooth, about 20 seconds. You can also use a hand mixer and a medium bowl, though you may need to beat the mixture a little longer at each step to achieve the same results. Add the confectioners' sugar and beat, using the cleaned silicone or rubber spatula to scrape down the bowl once halfway through, until smooth and blended, 2 to 3 minutes. Scrape down the bowl again. Add the peanut butter and beat until smooth, another minute or so. Scrape down the bowl and make sure everything is well blended. Set aside ½ cup for piping. The remaining buttercream will be used for filling the layers.

5 CUT THE MERINGUE: Run a knife around the edges of the baking sheet to loosen the meringue. Lift the meringue out of the pan, using the parchment paper as support, and transfer to a cutting surface. Position the meringue so that one of the long sides is parallel to the edge of your work surface. Use the serrated knife to cut the sheet crosswise through the parchment, into 4 pieces, each 11 by 3¼ inches. Leave each piece attached to the parchment.

6 ASSEMBLE THE MARJOLAINE: Transfer one piece of meringue to the cake cardboard or serving platter and place it top side down. Peel off the parchment paper. With the offset spatula, spread ½ of the buttercream in an even layer over the meringue. Top with another meringue layer, again peeling off the parchment, and on it spread $1/3$ of the ganache. Top with a third layer of meringue and spread with the remaining half of the buttercream, then place the final layer of meringue on top. Spread the remaining $2/3$ of the ganache in an even layer over the top and two long sides of the cake. Press the chopped peanut brittle or additional chopped peanuts onto the two long sides of the cake (see page 310). You will not use all the brittle; save the remainder to scatter on each plate (or as a treat for the chef). Spoon the reserved buttercream into the pastry bag and pipe a line of shells (see page 309) down the top edges of the long sides. Refrigerate for at least 1 hour and up to 24 hours.

7 While the cake is cold, trim the two short ends with a serrated knife to neaten the appearance and show off the layers inside. Let the cake sit at room temperature for at least 40 minutes before serving. Cut the cake with the serrated knife into 1-inch-thick slices.

STORING **The cake is at its best within 24 hours. It can be stored, plastic wrap pressed against the cut edges, in the refrigerator for up to 4 days, but the meringue will soften considerably from the moisture in the refrigerator and the fillings—and the peanut brittle will soften and begin to melt. Return to room temperature before serving.**

PAVLOVAS WITH HONEY-LAVENDER CREAM AND POACHED STRAWBERRIES

MAKES 8 PAVLOVAS Pavlova, the favorite dessert of Australia and New Zealand, consists of a meringue shell that is crispy on the outside and soft on the inside, cradling a filling of whipped cream and fruit. It was named in honor of the Russian ballerina Anna Pavlova, famous at the time for her beautiful dancing. Apparently the dessert was as light and lovely as Anna herself, who toured New Zealand in the late 1920s and Australia in the mid 1930s. This version features poached strawberries and whipped cream sweetened with lavender sugar, an easy-to-make combination of granulated sugar and dried lavender ground to a fine powder. You might wonder why anyone would bother to poach strawberries, since they are so delicate in their fresh state. The heat from the poaching syrup softens their flesh, making them meltingly tender so they practically dissolve in your mouth. The poached berries meld beautifully into the soft cream and marshmallow-like meringue in this very special dessert.

INGREDIENTS

MERINGUE
⅔ cup (4¾ ounces) sugar

1 tablespoon cornstarch

3 large egg whites

¼ teaspoon cream of tartar

Pinch of salt

¼ teaspoon pure vanilla extract

STRAWBERRIES
3 pint baskets (about 3 pounds) fresh strawberries

2 cups (16 ounces) water

1¼ cups (8¾ ounces) sugar

HONEY-LAVENDER CREAM
2 tablespoons (1 ounce) sugar

1 tablespoon dried lavender blossoms or 2 tablespoons fresh lavender blossoms

1½ cups (12 ounces) heavy whipping cream

1½ tablespoons mild-flavored honey, such as orange blossom

Fresh lavender, for garnish

EQUIPMENT
Fine-Mesh Strainer, Small Bowl, Stand Mixer Fitted with a Whisk Attachment or a Hand Mixer and a Medium Bowl, Silicone or Rubber Spatula, 12 by 17-inch Baking Sheet, Parchment Paper or Silicone Mat, ⅓-cup Dry Measuring Cup, Cooling Rack, Strawberry Huller or Paring Knife, Medium Saucepan, Spice or Coffee Grinder, Slotted Spoon

1 MAKE THE MERINGUES: Preheat the oven to 250°F and position an oven rack in the center. Use the fine-mesh strainer to sift 2 tablespoons of the sugar and all the cornstarch into the small bowl. Place the egg whites, cream of tartar, and salt in the bowl of the stand mixer and whip on medium-high speed for 1½ to 2 minutes, until soft peaks form. You can also use a hand mixer and a medium bowl, although you may need to beat the mixture a little longer at each step to achieve the same results. Add the vanilla and, with the mixer running, slowly rain in the remaining sugar. Turn the speed to high and whip until the meringue is very stiff, 30 to 45 seconds. Sift the sugar-cornstarch mixture over the meringue and gently fold it in with the spatula just until blended.

2 Line the baking sheet with parchment paper or a silicone mat. Gently spoon meringue into the ⅓-cup measuring cup, level the top, and use the spoon to help turn it out

what the pros know

Be sure you purchase dried lavender from a culinary source such as the bulk department of a health food store or a specialty herb supplier, so you can be sure the flowers were not treated with harmful chemicals. Flowers grown for commercial and potpourri use are laden with pesticides and should never be used in cooking or baking.

GETTING AHEAD **The meringues can be baked up to 3 days in advance and stored in an airtight container at room temperature. The strawberries can be poached up to 2 days in advance and refrigerated in the poaching syrup. The lavender sugar can be prepared up to 1 month in advance and stored airtight at room temperature. The honey-lavender cream can be prepared up to 3 hours in advance and chilled in an airtight container.**

onto the baking sheet. Create 7 more portions in this manner, spacing them evenly. Use the back of the spoon to make a well in each meringue. The finished meringues should be about 3 inches wide and 1 inch tall.

3 Bake the meringues for 50 to 55 minutes, until faintly golden and crispy on the outside. The interior will still be soft and fluffy. Transfer to a rack and cool completely.

4 POACH THE STRAWBERRIES: Wash the berries and pat dry. Hull each berry using a strawberry huller or the tip of a paring knife. If the strawberries are large, cut them into quarters or ¼-inch thick slices. Place the water and sugar in the medium saucepan and bring to a boil. Simmer for 1 to 2 minutes, until the sugar is completely dissolved. Carefully transfer the berries to the syrup and bring back to a simmer. As soon as the syrup begins to boil again, remove from the heat and cover the pot. Let the berries sit in the syrup until the mixture is room temperature, about 30 minutes—they will poach in the residual heat.

5 MAKE THE HONEY-LAVENDER CREAM: Place the sugar and lavender in the spice or coffee grinder and grind until the texture is very fine. Transfer to the small bowl. Place the cream, honey, and 1½ tablespoons of the lavender sugar in the cleaned bowl of the stand mixer and whip until the cream holds soft peaks (save the remaining lavender sugar for another use). You may also use the cleaned hand mixer and medium bowl here. Cover with plastic wrap and refrigerate for 30 minutes to allow the flavors to blend.

6 ASSEMBLE THE PAVLOVAS: Use the slotted spoon to scoop the strawberries from the poaching liquid and drain slightly on paper towels. (Save the poaching syrup for flavoring sparkling water or use it for a refreshing twist in your favorite cocktail.) Place a meringue on each serving plate. Fill the center of each meringue with honey lavender cream and top with 4 or 5 strawberries. Garnish with some fresh lavender and serve immediately.

PÂTE À CHOUX

MAKES ENOUGH DOUGH FOR 20 (4 BY 1-INCH) ÉCLAIRS, 20 (2½-INCH) CREAM PUFFS, OR 32 (1-INCH) GOUGÈRES This versatile dough is perfect for entertaining, since pâte à choux pastries can be made in advance and frozen, then re-crisped the day you wish to serve them. Even if you're intimidated by other pastry-making, pâte à choux is quick, easy, and low stress. It used to require strenuous beating by hand to blend the eggs into the dough, but now it's simple: The stand mixer does all the work.

INGREDIENTS

1 stick (4 ounces) unsalted butter, cut into ½-inch pieces

1 cup (8 ounces) water

¼ teaspoon salt

1 cup (5 ounces) unbleached all-purpose flour

4 large eggs, plus another tablespoon or two, if needed

EQUIPMENT

Medium Saucepan, Wooden Spoon, Stand Mixer Fitted with a Paddle Attachment, Medium Bowl

what the pros know

Additional flavors can be created by adding the grated zest of one large orange or lemon to the liquid. Or by adding ½ teaspoon extract or ¼ teaspoon flavoring oil with the eggs.

1 Cook the butter, water, and salt in the medium saucepan over low heat, stirring from time to time with the wooden spoon so the butter melts evenly. When the butter has melted, increase the heat and bring to a boil. Immediately remove the pan from the heat and add the flour all at once. Beat vigorously with the wooden spoon until the dough comes together in a mass around the spoon. Place the pan back over the medium heat and continue to cook, beating, for another minute or so to dry out the dough—the pan will have a thin film of dough on the bottom.

2 Transfer the dough to the bowl of the stand mixer. Beat on medium speed for 1 minute to slightly cool the dough and develop the gluten. In the medium bowl, beat the eggs together until you can't distinguish the yellow from the white. With the mixer on medium, add the eggs a couple tablespoons at a time, allowing each addition to blend completely into the dough before continuing. When all the eggs are incorporated, the mixture should be shiny and elastic and stick to the side of the bowl. It should also pass the "string test": Place a bit of dough between your thumb and forefinger and pull them apart. The dough should form a stretchy string about 1½ to 2 inches long (see page 380). If the dough has not reached this stage, beat another egg and continue adding it, a little at a time, until the dough is finished. To shape and bake, see individual recipes.

STORING The dough can be kept in the refrigerator in an airtight container for up to 3 days.

Spiced Pâte à Choux Add 1 teaspoon sugar, 1 teaspoon ground cinnamon, and ¼ teaspoon ground cloves to the flour. Whisk to combine, then add the flour mixture as directed.

Chocolate Pâte à Choux Sift 1 tablespoon sugar and 2 tablespoons cocoa powder (natural or Dutch-process) into the flour. Whisk to combine, then add the flour mixture as directed.

DULCE DE LECHE ÉCLAIRS WITH MILK CHOCOLATE GLAZE

MAKES 20 ÉCLAIRS If you haven't tried dulce de leche–condensed milk that has been cooked to a thick, golden brown caramel–now's the time. Cans can be found in gourmet shops, in the ethnic section of supermarkets, and in markets catering to a Latin American clientele. It has a wonderfully complex, creamy flavor that marries perfectly with the cinnamon and clove-scented pâte à choux and a sweet milk chocolate glaze.

INGREDIENTS

1 recipe Spiced Pâte à Choux (page 399)

1 recipe Dulce de Leche Pastry Cream (page 419)

1 large egg

4 ounces good-quality milk chocolate, finely chopped

½ cup (4 ounces) heavy whipping cream

EQUIPMENT

Two Baking Sheets, Parchment Paper, 1-inch-wide Ruler, Pastry Bag with a ½-inch Plain Round Tip and a Bismarck (see page 401) or ¼-inch Plain Round Tip, Two Small Bowls, Pastry Brush, Paring Knife, Cooling Rack, Small Saucepan, Whisk, Twenty Pleated Paper Éclair Cups (Optional)

1 Preheat the oven to 400°F and position two racks in the top and lower thirds of the oven. To make the templates, line the baking sheets with parchment paper, then remove the paper and use the ruler as a guide to draw twenty 4 by 1-inch rectangles with a pencil, dividing and spacing them evenly between the sheets. Turn the pieces of parchment paper over and return them to the baking sheets with the marks facing the sheets.

2 PIPE THE PÂTE À CHOUX: Spoon the dough into the pastry bag fitted with the ½-inch plain round tip. Pipe the dough into ½-inch-high rectangles to fill each template. (To stop the flow of dough from the pastry bag and disconnect it from the piped dough, slice a lightly oiled dinner knife across the opening of the tip.)

3 GLAZE AND BAKE THE PÂTE À CHOUX: In a small bowl, lightly beat the egg to blend thoroughly. Brush a light coating of egg over the tops of the piped dough, being careful that the egg does not drip down the sides (it will glue the éclairs to the parchment). You will not use all the egg. Bake both sheets of the éclairs for 20 minutes, then reduce the oven temperature to 350°F, switch the sheets between the racks, rotate the pans from front to back, and bake for 20 minutes longer. Reduce the temperature again, to 300°F, and bake 10 to 15 minutes longer (to dry out the interior). The éclairs should be a deep golden brown, with no more bubbling moisture visible around the sides. Transfer the éclairs to a rack to cool completely.

4 FILL THE ÉCLAIRS: Spoon the pastry cream into the cleaned and dried pastry bag fitted with the Bismarck or ¼-inch plain tip. If using the Bismarck tip, first make a little hole in one of the short ends of the éclair with the tip of a paring knife. Then, insert the end of the Bismark into the éclair as far as it will go. Squeeze firmly as you slowly pull the tip out of the pastry, filling the cavity with the pastry cream. If using the plain tip, make two evenly spaced small holes in the bottom of an éclair with the tip of a paring knife. Insert the plain tip into each one, squeezing firmly to fill the center of the pastry. Repeat to fill the remaining éclairs.

GETTING AHEAD **The unbaked piped rectangles can be refrigerated, covered with plastic wrap, for up to 4 hours before baking. You can freeze the unfilled baked éclairs, wrapped in plastic and sealed inside a resealable plastic freezer bag, for up to 1 month. Re-crisp the baked éclairs in a 375°F oven for 5 to 8 minutes. The chocolate glaze can be prepared up to 1 week in advance and refrigerated in an airtight container; reheat in a double boiler before use.**

5 MAKE THE GLAZE: Place the chocolate in a small bowl (which should be just large enough to accommodate an éclair, which is about 4 inches long). Bring the cream to a boil in the small saucepan. Immediately pour it over the chocolate and let the mixture sit for 1 minute. Whisk until the mixture is completely blended and smooth. Cool for 10 minutes.

6 GLAZE THE ÉCLAIRS: Turn the éclairs upside down, dip the top of each one halfway into the chocolate glaze, then lift it and let the excess glaze drip back into the bowl. Set right side up on a serving platter or parchment-lined baking sheet and allow 30 minutes for the glaze to set. Refrigerate until serving time. Reserve any leftover milk chocolate glaze for another use.

7 Éclairs are best when served the same day they are filled, and are good with a strong cup of coffee or tea. If you can find the long, thin pleated paper cups used to serve éclairs in bakeries (available in cake decorating shops), set an éclair in each one. Otherwise, serve them as they are, singly on small plates or all together on a platter for guests to help themselves.

STORING **You can store éclairs in the refrigerator, covered with plastic wrap, for up to 3 days. However, they are at their best the same day they are filled, as the pastry absorbs moisture from the pastry cream and eventually becomes soggy.**

CREAM PUFFS WITH COCOA NIB CREAM

MAKES 20 CREAM PUFFS Cream puffs are an example of the adage "less is more." There's something incredibly satisfying about the simplicity of a crisp pastry shell surrounding whipped cream, especially when served in a pool of Dark Chocolate Sauce. The chocolate ante is upped by adding a bit of cocoa powder to the pâte à choux and infusing the cream with the flavor of cocoa nibs. Alice Medrich was the first to flavor whipped cream with nibs and it is an inspired creation. Cocoa nibs, resembling little chocolate chips, are the roasted and chopped meat of the cocoa bean, in its final stage before being transformed into bar chocolate. They are very bitter, but when steeped in cream, they lend all the flavor of deep, dark chocolate without the dark color or heaviness that melted chocolate would contribute. It's a delightful surprise to bite into the cream puff and experience the full flavor of dark chocolate in a light and airy confection.

INGREDIENTS

2¼ cups (18 ounces) heavy whipping cream

¼ cup (1 ounce) roasted cocoa nibs

1 recipe Chocolate Pâte à Choux (page 399)

1 large egg

2 tablespoons plus 1 teaspoon (1 ounce) granulated sugar

Confectioners' sugar, for dusting

1 recipe Dark Chocolate Sauce (page 427), for serving

EQUIPMENT

Small Saucepan, Fine-Mesh Strainer, Small Heatproof Bowl, Silicone or Rubber Spatula, Two Baking Sheets, Parchment Paper, 2½-inch Round Biscuit Cutter, Pastry Bag with a ½-inch Plain Tip and a ½-inch Star Tip, Small Bowl, Pastry Brush, Cooling Rack, Stand Mixer Fitted with a Whisk Attachment or a Hand Mixer and a Medium Bowl, Serrated Knife

1 PREPARE THE COCOA NIB CREAM: Heat the cream and cocoa nibs in the small saucepan over medium heat until the cream begins to boil. Immediately remove from the heat, cover, and let steep for 20 minutes. (Set a timer for this; if the nibs are left in the cream for too long, it will become very bitter.) Strain through the strainer into the heatproof bowl (or storage container), pressing firmly on the nibs with the spatula to release as much cream as possible. Cover and refrigerate for at least 6 to 8 hours or overnight.

2 To make the templates, line the baking sheets with parchment paper, then remove the paper and use the biscuit cutter or another 2½-inch template as a guide and draw twenty 2½-inch circles, dividing and spacing them evenly between the sheets. Turn the pieces of parchment paper over and return to the sheets so that the marks are facing the sheets. Preheat the oven to 400°F and position two racks in the top and lower thirds of the oven.

3 PIPE THE PÂTE À CHOUX: Spoon the dough into the pastry bag fitted with the ½-inch plain tip. Pipe the dough into ½- to ¾-inch-high circles to fill each template. (To stop the flow of dough from the pastry bag and disconnect it from the piped dough, slice a lightly oiled dinner knife across the opening of the tip.)

Cream puffs are endlessly variable, and for more whipped cream flavoring ideas, see page 417. You can also fill the cream puffs with pastry cream or lemon curd, or make either of these more light and airy by folding in an equal amount of whipped cream. For a more sophisticated twist, spread a thin layer of Dark Chocolate Ganache (page 412) across the bottom of each puff, then fill with Orange Sabayon Cream (page 418). For a classic French ending, make profiteroles by filling the center of each puff with ice cream, then pouring Dark Chocolate Sauce (page 427) over the top.

GETTING AHEAD **Unbaked piped puffs can be made up to 4 hours ahead and refrigerated, covered with plastic wrap. You can freeze unfilled baked puffs, wrapped in plastic and sealed inside a resealable plastic freezer bag, for up to 1 month. Re-crisp in a 375°F oven for 5 to 8 minutes and let cool before filling with the whipped cocoa nib cream. The infused (unwhipped) cocoa nib cream can be stored airtight in the refrigerator for up to 3 days. Whip the cream the day you assemble the puffs.**

4 GLAZE AND BAKE THE PÂTE À CHOUX: In a small bowl, lightly beat the egg to blend thoroughly. Brush a light coating of egg over the tops of the piped dough, being careful that the egg does not drip down the sides (it will glue the puffs to the parchment). You will not use all the egg. Bake both sheets of the puffs for 20 minutes, then reduce the oven temperature to 350°F, switch the sheets between the racks, rotate the pans from front to back, and bake for 20 minutes longer. Reduce the temperature again, to 300°F, and bake 10 to 15 minutes longer (to dry out the interior). The cream puffs should be a deep golden brown, with no bubbling moisture visible around the sides. Transfer to a rack to cool completely.

5 WHIP THE CREAM: Pour the infused cream into the bowl of the stand mixer (or into the medium bowl if using the hand mixer). Add the granulated sugar and whip until firm peaks form. Refrigerate until needed.

6 FILL THE CREAM PUFFS: Use the serrated knife to slice each puff in half across its equator. Spoon the cocoa nib cream into the cleaned and dried pastry bag fitted with the ½-inch star tip. Pipe the cream in a circular motion in the bottom of each cream puff, making a couple of swirls, until the cream is about 1½ inches high. Place the cream puff lid on top. Repeat until all the cream puffs are filled. Refrigerate until needed.

7 The puffs are at their best the same day they are filled. Spoon some chocolate sauce onto each plate. Dust the top of the cream puffs with confectioners' sugar. Transfer a cream puff to each plate. Alternately, put them all on a platter and let guests help themselves, serving the sauce in a pitcher on the side. Serve immediately.

STORING **Keep filled cream puffs in the refrigerator, covered with plastic wrap, for up to 2 days. They are at their best the same day they are filled, as the whipped cream begins to break down and the pastry absorbs its moisture and eventually becomes soggy.**

CLASSIC GOUGÈRES

MAKES 32 GOUGÈRES Gougères are traditional cheese-laced pâte à choux appetizers from the Burgundy region of France, flavored with mustard, Gruyère cheese, and cracked black pepper–heavenly with a glass of red wine. Try different cheeses and flavorings and you will have a whole new hors d'oeuvre. Or, split the baked puffs in half and fill them with crab or lobster salad, or any filling you like. They aren't as flashy as some art-directed appetizers, but they always disappear first at a party.

INGREDIENTS

1 recipe Pâte à Choux (page 399)

1 cup (4 ounces) grated Gruyère cheese

2 teaspoons Dijon mustard

½ teaspoon ground or cracked black pepper

1 large egg

EQUIPMENT

Two Baking Sheets, Parchment Paper, Stand Mixer Fitted with a Whisk Attachment, Small Bowl, Pastry Brush, Cooling Rack

what the

Gougères are one of those versatile pastries that caterers love to have on hand. The *pâte à choux* is made plain, then divided into several bowls, and each portion gets its own flavorings—one becomes a classic version like the recipe here, another might be blended with goat cheese and herbs, or blue cheese and walnuts. Instant variety. Do try this at home.

GETTING AHEAD **Refrigerate or freeze as directed for eclairs (page 401).**

1 Preheat the oven to 400°F and position two racks in the top and lower thirds of the oven. Line the baking sheets with parchment paper.

2 In the bowl of the stand mixer, combine the dough, ¾ cup of the cheese, the mustard, and black pepper. Mix on low just until evenly blended.

3 Spoon 1-inch rounds of the dough onto the prepared baking sheets, about 1 inch apart. In a small bowl, lightly beat the egg to blend thoroughly. Brush a light coating of egg over the tops of the rounds, being careful that it does not drip down the sides (it will glue the dough to the parchment). You will not use all the egg. Sprinkle each round with a little of the remaining ¼ cup cheese.

4 Bake the *gougères* for 20 minutes, then reduce the oven temperature to 350°F, switch the sheets between the racks, rotate each pan from front to back, and bake for 10 to 15 minutes longer, until the *gougères* are a deep golden brown and no bubbling moisture is visible around the sides of each shape. Transfer to a rack to cool briefly. Serve the *gougères* warm, piled on a platter for guests to help themselves.

STORING **Baked *gougères* may be stored airtight at room temperature for up to 3 days. Before serving, warm and crisp them for 7 to 9 minutes in a 375°F oven, until the outside crust is crisp and the interior is heated through.**

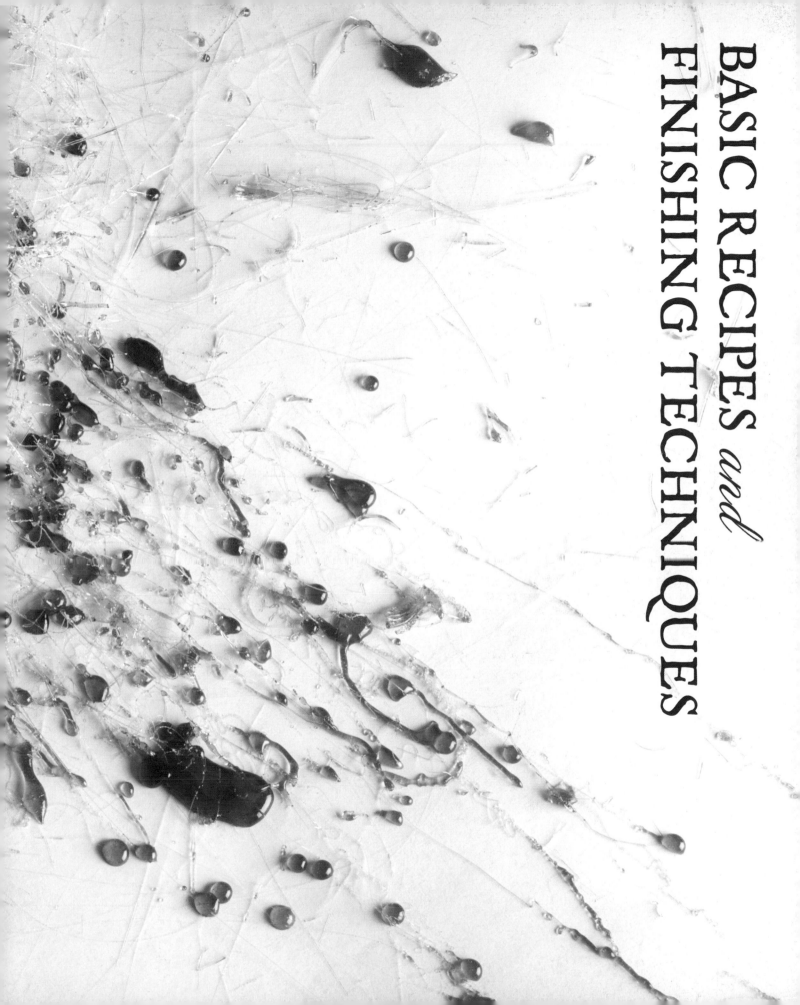

BASIC RECIPES *and* FINISHING TECHNIQUES

This chapter provides you with recipes you'll turn to again and again in your dessert-making. It also encourages you to express your personality and artistic creativity in your pastries. Contained within it are the basic recipes for frostings, fillings, and sauces referred to throughout the book. Most of them can be changed according to your taste. For instance, while custard sauce, pastry cream, and whipped cream—all infused with vanilla bean—are delightful on their own, with a simple change or two they can be transformed into Earl Grey custard sauce, dulce de leche pastry cream, and cocoa nib whipped cream. Each recipe comes with flavor ideas, in the hope that you'll be inspired to go even further as you develop your dessert skills.

There are also ideas for decorating and garnishing your desserts. Nothing here is difficult and all of it is fun. Try your hand at chocolate curls, decorate for a special occasion with a touch of gold leaf, or garnish with a few beautiful sugared flowers. Make a pretty dessert even prettier with a simple stencil finish. Set a piece of cake into a luscious pool of elegantly swirled sauces. Or surprise your guests by topping their dessert with a tangle of spun sugar, glinting in the candlelight. Whatever your inspiration, this chapter will help you to achieve it.

Frostings

MATCHING FROSTINGS WITH CAKES

There are plenty of frostings and flavors to choose from in this chapter, and you can feel free to mix and match with the cake recipes. Do keep in mind, however, the type of cake and frosting and make sure they are a good pairing before you get creative.

Butter cakes are best served at room temperature—their texture gets hard and dry in the refrigerator—so they should be paired with frostings that are also at their best at room temperature, such as a buttercream or ganache. If you want to pair a butter cake with whipped cream, it's best to assemble it at the last moment and serve it while the whipped cream is still cold and the butter cake is soft and tender.

Some fillings, frostings, and accompaniments, such as whipped cream, pastry cream, and sabayon cream, must be refrigerated for food safety issues. These are best when paired with sponge cakes, since their light texture and open crumb do not suffer under refrigeration. Sponge cakes are also wonderful served at room temperature, so you can pair them with buttercream or ganache, as well. Some people like cream-cheese frosting icy cold, and some appreciate its soft voluptuousness at room temperature, so serve it the way you like it, but do choose a cake to go with it that is tasty at your serving temperature of choice.

SILKY VANILLA BUTTERCREAM

MAKES ABOUT 5 CUPS (1¾ POUNDS), ENOUGH FOR A 2-LAYER, 8- OR 9-INCH CAKE WITH PIPED BORDERS, OR 24 CUPCAKES **Velvety** smooth and uniquely satisfying, buttercream is the king of cake frostings. This version is a Swiss meringue buttercream, which simply means that the egg whites and sugar are heated together before beating. The color is creamy white, so it takes food coloring well if you are so inclined. The buttercream can also be flavored in many ways, which makes it a versatile partner for nearly any type of cake. There are a few ideas at the end of the recipe to get you started in that direction. It may seem like a lot of frosting, but it's better to have a little buttercream left over than to be caught short in the middle of preparations for a special occasion. Any leftover frosting may be refrigerated or frozen and used another day.

INGREDIENTS

4 large egg whites

1½ cups (10½ ounces) sugar

1 pound unsalted butter, very soft, but not melted

2 teaspoons pure vanilla extract

EQUIPMENT

Stand Mixer Fitted with a Whisk Attachment or a Hand Mixer and a Medium Bowl, Whisk, Medium Saucepan, Instant-Read Thermometer, Silicone or Rubber Spatula

GETTING AHEAD **Buttercream may be refrigerated for up to 5 days or frozen for up to 2 months. To use, follow the directions under "What the Pros Know," page 410.**

1 Place the egg whites and sugar in the bowl of the mixer (or the medium bowl, if using a hand mixer) and hand-whisk to blend. Bring 2 inches of water to a gentle boil in the medium saucepan. Place the bowl over the simmering water and heat, whisking constantly so that the whites do not scramble, until the mixture reaches 160°F on the thermometer. Be sure to remove the bowl from the heat when taking the temperature so the eggs don't overheat while you set down the whisk and use the thermometer. If the temperature is not hot enough, rinse the thermometer under very hot water (so you don't contaminate the whites with any bacteria left on the thermometer when you test again), dry and set aside, then put the whites and sugar back over the heat.

2 Once the correct temperature is reached, immediately remove the mixture from the heat and whip with the mixer on high speed until it has cooled to room temperature, is light and billowing, and resembles marshmallow fluff. If the mixture is warm, it will melt the butter you'll be adding next, so touch the meringue and make sure it has cooled to room temperature before continuing.

3 With the mixer on medium-high speed, add the soft butter a couple of tablespoons at a time, allowing each addition to blend in fully before adding the next. Halfway through the butter, stop the mixer and use the spatula to scrape down the sides of the bowl thoroughly. Continue until all the butter has been added and the mixture resembles velvety mayonnaise. Add the vanilla extract and blend well. Note: There is nearly always a point in this process when you think the buttercream is ruined. It will look broken and awful. Just continue adding the butter and beating and all will be fine in the end. Use the buttercream immediately or refrigerate or freeze until needed.

To use butter-cream that has been refrigerated or frozen, you will need to return it to the velvety consistency it has when at room temperature. Remove it from the storage container and chop it into chunks using a bench scraper. If it is too hard to chop, soften it in the microwave for 15 to 20 seconds, or until you can break it apart. Place the chunks in the bowl of a stand mixer and set over simmering water until about ⅓ of the buttercream is melted. Alternatively, microwave the chunks for about 15 to 20 seconds at a time, or until it is still cool to touch but softened. Beat with the paddle attachment on low speed to blend the melted and cold pieces together, then gradually turn the mixer up and continue to beat until the buttercream is smooth and velvety. Don't be afraid to heat it a bit more if it is still too cold to blend smoothly. Professionals don't premelt any of the mixture, and you might want to try their technique. They add all the butter chunks to the mixer bowl, begin beating with the paddle attachment, and very lightly touch the sides of the metal bowl with the flame of a propane torch, just long enough to warm the butter enough to emulsify and smooth the buttercream. Keep the flame moving—if you hold it in one place for too long, it will burn the buttercream on the inside of the bowl.

STORING Buttercream may be stored in an airtight container in the refrigerator for up to 5 days.

Dark Chocolate, Milk Chocolate, or White Chocolate Buttercream
Melt 1 pound of finely chopped dark (up to 60 percent cacao), milk, or white chocolate with ½ cup water in a double boiler according to the directions on page 43. Remove and let it sit until cool to the touch—if you add it while it's warm, you'll melt the butter in the buttercream. Add the cooled chocolate at the end of Step 3 and stir it in thoroughly with a rubber spatula. If you whip it in, you will significantly lighten the color of the dark or milk chocolate frosting.

Espresso Buttercream
Omit the vanilla. Dissolve 1 tablespoon plus 1 teaspoon instant espresso powder in 2 teaspoons water and add at the end of Step 3.

Tangerine, Orange, or Lemon Buttercream
Omit the vanilla. Add ½ to 1 teaspoon tangerine, orange, or lemon oil and the finely grated zest of 2 tangerines, 1 large orange, or 2 large lemons at the end of Step 3.

Almond Buttercream
Omit the vanilla. Add 1 to 1½ teaspoons pure almond extract and 2 to 3 tablespoons amaretto (almond liqueur) at the end of Step 3 and blend well.

Nutella Buttercream
Omit the vanilla. Add ¾ cup (8¼ ounces) room temperature Nutella at the end of Step 3.

tips for success Broken Buttercream

Buttercream is an emulsion, and it will curdle or break if the temperatures of the ingredients are too disparate from one another. Don't worry; broken buttercream is easy to fix.

1. **If the buttercream breaks because of heat:** If the meringue is still warm when you begin to add the butter, or if you overheat buttercream that has been refrigerated, the butter will melt, resulting in a runny, soupy mess. If this happens, you need to cool the mixture. Slip a bowl of ice water under the bowl of the mixer (or hold a couple of packages of frozen vegetables against the sides) and continue to beat until the butter cools down enough to emulsify and smooth the mixture.

2. **If the buttercream breaks because of cold:** If the butter is too cold when you add it to the meringue, the texture will look like small curds of scrambled egg. If this happens, you need to warm the mixture. Professionals very lightly touch the sides of the metal bowl with the flame of a propane torch while the mixer is running, just until the butter warms up enough to emulsify and smooth the mixture. You can try this method, too; just be sure to keep the flame moving so you don't burn anything on the inside of the bowl. Another option is to place the bowl in a larger bowl of hot water (or over simmering water) for 30 to 60 seconds, then beat again. Repeat until the mixture is smooth.

3. **If the buttercream breaks because of time elapsing:** If the buttercream was beautiful when made, but has been sitting out for a while—either you got distracted with a phone call, or the cake is taking longer than anticipated—it may lose its smoothness when spread and may even look curdled. Simply grab a whisk and stir vigorously to bring it back together. If the room is very warm, you may need to follow Step 1.

Correct Buttercream   **Broken Buttercream**

DARK CHOCOLATE GANACHE

MAKES 3 CUPS (1½ POUNDS), ENOUGH FOR A 2-LAYER, 9-INCH CAKE OR 16 CUPCAKES **Voluptuously** smooth and rich, ganache is nothing more than the combination of chocolate and cream, but it is one of the most useful mixtures in the pastry kitchen. It can be used for frosting cakes, glazing cakes and éclairs, filling tarts and cookies, shaping into truffles, saucing desserts, and more. Take care to chop your chocolate finely–into about ¼-inch pieces–because big chunks won't melt completely when the hot cream is poured over the top, and your ganache will be dotted with chunks of hard chocolate. If this happens, strain out the chunks, melt them gently in a microwave oven (10 seconds at a time, stirring between each heating) until melted, then stir back into the ganache. For an in-depth discussion of chocolate and how to work with it, see page 37. Note: If you like to use dark chocolate with a high percentage of cacao, you'll need to add extra cream, or the ganache will break and take on a curdled look. If your chocolate is over 62 percent cacao, add an additional ¾ cup cream to the recipe below. If your chocolate is 70 percent or higher, add an extra 1 cup cream.

INGREDIENTS

12 ounces semisweet or bittersweet chocolate (up to 60 percent cacao), finely chopped

1½ cups (12 ounces) heavy whipping cream

EQUIPMENT

Medium Bowl, Small Saucepan, Whisk

Place the chocolate in the medium bowl. Heat the cream in the small saucepan over medium heat until it begins to boil. Immediately pour the cream over the chocolate. Let the mixture sit for 1 minute, then gently whisk until the ganache is completely smooth and blended. If you are using a high-percentage chocolate and the mixture looks broken or curdled at this point, stir in an extra tablespoon or two of cream, just until the mixture smooths out again. Use as directed.

TO USE AS FROSTING: Let the ganache cool for 1 hour, then cover with plastic wrap and set aside to finish cooling at room temperature until it has the consistency of frosting, 8 to 10 hours. If you make it the night before, it will be the perfect texture for frosting cakes and cupcakes in the morning.

TO USE AS A GLAZE: Set the ganache aside until it has cooled to the consistency of pourable honey, 15 to 20 minutes. Pour the ganache over the cake. You can also dip the tops of cupcakes, cream puffs, or éclairs into the ganache for a quick-and-easy icing.

TO USE AS A SAUCE: Spoon the ganache onto the dessert plates or over ice cream while still warm. If it has cooled and is too thick, heat gently over a double boiler until warm and fluid, or simply add additional cream (or water) until the desired sauce consistency is reached.

Ganache is an emulsion—a careful combination of two ingredients that would never blend otherwise, such as oil and vinegar. Chocolate and cream, if tossed into a bowl, would never result in ganache. But chop the chocolate finely, pour heated cream over it, gently whisk to combine the two in suspension, and—ganache. Once the chocolate is blended and smooth, stop whisking. Continuing to stir as the ganache cools will cause it to become grainy. If this happens, gently melt the mixture over a double boiler until fluid; then allow it to cool again.

Occasionally, the ganache will break while you are whisking the mixture together, either because the cocoa butter got too hot and separated from the chocolate or because there was not enough liquid. If your ganache is broken or curdled, pour an additional tablespoon of extra cream into the bowl and whisk it in. Continue adding a tablespoon at a time until the ganache smoothes out. Then continue with the recipe.

GETTING AHEAD **Ganache may be prepared up to 2 days ahead and stored, tightly covered, at room temperature. It will keep refrigerated for up to 2 weeks, and may be frozen for up to 6 weeks. Be sure to allow enough time for the ganache to return to room temperature (2 to 3 hours) before using it as frosting, or warming it for use as a glaze or filling.**

TO USE AS A TART OR THUMBPRINT COOKIE FILLING: As soon as the ganache is smooth and blended, pour it into a baked tart shell or spoon into the depressions of thumbprint cookies. Allow about 3 hours for the ganache to cool and set in the tart or cookies (to hurry the setting, place in the refrigerator—1 hour for the tart and 20 minutes for the cookies).

STORING **The ganache may be prepared up to 2 days ahead and kept at room temperature, covered. For longer storage, refrigerate in an airtight container for up to 2 weeks.**

Milk Chocolate or White Chocolate Ganache Substitute 18 ounces of milk chocolate or white chocolate for the dark chocolate.

CREAM CHEESE FROSTING

MAKES ABOUT 3 CUPS (1½ POUNDS), ENOUGH FOR A 2-LAYER 9-INCH CAKE OR 16 CUPCAKES Snowy white, velvety smooth, and sweet yet tangy, it's no wonder cream cheese frosting partners with everything from banana bread to pumpkin spice cake to chocolate cupcakes. It's easy to make, loved by everyone, takes color beautifully, and is a cinch to spread into gorgeous swirls. What more could you want from a frosting?

INGREDIENTS

12 ounces cream cheese, at room temperature

¾ stick (3 ounces) unsalted butter, at room temperature

Finely grated zest of 1 lemon

3 cups (9¾ ounces) unsifted confectioners' sugar

1½ teaspoons pure vanilla extract

EQUIPMENT

Stand Mixer Fitted with a Paddle Attachment or a Hand Mixer and a Medium Bowl, Silicone or Rubber Spatula, Fine-Mesh Strainer

1 Place the cream cheese, butter, and lemon zest in the bowl of the stand mixer and blend on medium speed until smooth, about 1 minute. You can also use a hand mixer and a medium bowl, although you may need to beat the mixture a little longer to achieve the same results. Scrape down the bowl with the spatula and beat again for 15 seconds.

2 Use the fine-mesh strainer to sift in the confectioners' sugar and blend on low for 15 seconds, then scrape down the bowl. Add the vanilla, turn the speed to medium, and beat for 1 minute. Use immediately or refrigerate until needed.

STORING Cream cheese frosting can be made up to 3 days ahead and kept refrigerated in an airtight container. If it's too stiff to spread easily, allow it to warm at room temperature for 30 minutes, stir well, and then use as desired.

Maple–Cream Cheese Frosting See Pumpkin Spice Cake with Maple–Cream Cheese Frosting (page 325).

White Chocolate–Cream Cheese Frosting Melt 7 ounces white chocolate (see page 43), then let it sit until cool to the touch but still fluid. Prepare the frosting as directed but decrease the confectioners' sugar to 2 cups (6½ ounces), then after you have added the confectioners' sugar, beat the chocolate into the frosting thoroughly.

CONFECTIONERS' SUGAR ICING

MAKES 1½ CUPS (9 OUNCES), ENOUGH FOR A 10- TO 12-INCH BUNDT CAKE OR 24 CUPCAKES Simple, yes. But that doesn't mean it's not perfect sometimes. After all, what would Bundt cake be without this icing? A bit less elegant, no doubt. Vary the thickness of the icing by reducing or adding liquid, but be judicious—the icing should look thicker than you think it should. If it is too thin, just whisk in some extra confectioners' sugar (you may need to adjust the flavorings, depending upon how much sugar you add).

INGREDIENTS

2 cups (8 ounces) unsifted confectioners' sugar

2 to 3 tablespoons water, or as needed

½ teaspoon pure vanilla extract

EQUIPMENT

Fine-Mesh Strainer, Medium Bowl, Whisk

Use the fine-mesh strainer to sift the confectioners' sugar into the medium bowl. Whisk the water and vanilla into the sugar until a smooth glaze forms. Use less water for a glaze that covers thickly and drips down the sides of cakes in big, slow-moving rivulets. Use a little more water for a thinner, more transparent glaze.

STORING If you will not be using the icing immediately, press a piece of plastic wrap directly on the surface of the icing to prevent a skin from forming and set aside at room temperature until needed.

Lemon or Tangerine Icing Substitute freshly squeezed lemon or tangerine juice for the water. Omit the vanilla and add ⅛ teaspoon lemon or tangerine oil. If you like, add the finely grated zest of 1 large lemon or tangerine.

SOFTLY WHIPPED CREAM

MAKES 2 CUPS The quintessential partner to nearly any dessert, whipped cream—which should be thick yet soft and smooth—can be flavored in a multitude of ways, though vanilla is the classic. Chill your bowl and whisk in the freezer for 10 minutes before you begin. Look for pasteurized cream (instead of ultra-pasteurized) or, if you can find it, use manufacturing cream, which contains a higher percentage of milk fat and whips up to be thicker, more luscious, and more stable than any other type. For more on types of cream, see page 33.

INGREDIENTS

1 cup (8 ounces) heavy whipping cream
2 teaspoons sugar

1 teaspoon pure vanilla extract

EQUIPMENT

Stand Mixer Fitted with a Whisk Attachment or a Hand Mixer and a Medium Bowl

Place the cream, sugar, and vanilla in the bowl of the mixer (or in a medium bowl, if using a hand mixer) and whip on medium speed until soft peaks form. Cream whipped on medium speed is more stable than one whipped on high speed. When used as an accompaniment, the cream should look smooth and satiny, and barely hold its shape. To use as a filling or frosting, whip for another 10 to 15 seconds, until firmer. Use immediately or refrigerate until needed.

STORING Whipped cream is at its best when used within 2 hours of preparation. However, it can be whipped up to 8 hours ahead and stored in an airtight container in the refrigerator. If the cream seems too soft when you're ready to use it, beat it lightly with a hand whisk to firm it up.

Almond Cream Substitute ¼ teaspoon pure almond extract for the vanilla.

Cocoa Nib Cream See Cream Puffs with Cocoa Nib Cream (page 402).

Framboise or Chambord Cream Substitute 1 to 2 teaspoons framboise or Chambord (raspberry brandies) for the vanilla.

Frangelico Cream Substitute 1 to 2 teaspoons Frangelico (hazelnut liqueur) for the vanilla.

Ginger Cream Substitute ⅛ teaspoon ground ginger for the vanilla. When the cream is whipped, fold in 1 tablespoon of very finely chopped candied ginger.

Orange Blossom Cream Substitute ½ teaspoon orange blossom water for the vanilla.

Poire Williams Cream Substitute 1 to 2 teaspoons Poire Williams (pear brandy) for the vanilla.

White Chocolate Cream See Pistachio-Raspberry Chocolate Shortcakes with White Chocolate Cream (page 257).

ORANGE SABAYON CREAM

SERVES 6 TO 8 Called zabaglione in Italy, its birthplace, sabayon is a mixture of egg yolks, sugar, and wine whisked over simmering water until thick and light, with the texture of whipped cream. While it is traditionally served warm immediately after cooking, some like it best when cooled and folded into whipped cream—the cream stabilizes and lightens the sabayon, creating a sophisticated make-ahead accompaniment to all manner of desserts, from cakes and tarts to napoleons and shortcakes.

INGREDIENTS

6 large egg yolks

6 tablespoons (3 ounces) sugar

¾ cup (6 ounces) Marsala

¾ cup (6 ounces) heavy whipping cream

Finely grated zest of 1 large orange

EQUIPMENT

Large Bowl, Double Boiler, Whisk, Instant-Read Thermometer, Stand Mixer Fitted with a Whisk Attachment or a Hand Mixer and a Medium Bowl, Silicone or Rubber Spatula

what the pros know

Fortified wines, such as Marsala and Madeira, are traditional in sabayon, but champagne or dessert wine can be substituted. Liquors such as brandy and rum, and liqueurs such as amaretto or Grand Marnier, can be used as well, but are problematic because their high alcohol content evaporates quickly over heat, resulting in a flat, broken sabayon. To use liquor or liqueur, substitute half of the amount with some juice or liquid. For instance, you might pair apple juice with Calvados (apple brandy), rum with water, or coffee with Kahlua.

1 Fill the large bowl halfway with ice and water and set it aside. Place 2 inches of water in the bottom of the double boiler and bring to a rolling boil. Reduce to a simmer. Place the egg yolks and sugar in the top of the double boiler (off the heat) and whisk briefly, just until well blended and slightly lightened in color. Add the Marsala and blend well. Place the egg mixture over the simmering water and whisk constantly for about 5 minutes (a hand mixer may be used here), or until very light and fluffy, with a texture resembling softly whipped cream, and registers 160°F on the thermometer. Do not exceed 165°F or the eggs could scramble. If you see the sauce beginning to scramble around the edges, quickly remove the top of the double boiler from the heat and whisk vigorously. This will usually save the mixture, but if it still looks flat and broken, or there are large pieces of scrambled egg in the sauce, there is no recourse but to begin again. As soon as the sauce is finished, immediately set the top of the double boiler in the bowl of ice water. Stir the sauce occasionally until cold to the touch.

2 In the bowl of the stand mixer (or in a medium bowl, if using a hand mixer), whip the cream and orange zest until soft peaks form. Use the spatula to fold the whipped cream into the cooled sauce. Cover and refrigerate until needed.

STORING **The sabayon may be held, airtight, in the refrigerator for up to 24 hours, though it is most fluffy during the first 4 hours.**

Chocolate Port Sabayon See Chocolate Napoleons with Port-Braised Pears (page 127).

Cider Sabayon See Gingerbread Shortcakes with Caramelized Apples and Cider Sabayon (page 259).

VANILLA BEAN PASTRY CREAM (CRÈME PÂTISSIÈRE)

MAKES ABOUT 2 CUPS A classic filling for fresh fruit tarts, éclairs, and cream pies, pastry cream is really just a flour-thickened custard sauce, which also means that it can take on a near-endless variety of flavorings, from spices and citrus to chocolates and liqueurs. Take a look at the Vanilla Custard Sauce recipe (page 424) for further flavoring ideas.

INGREDIENTS

1½ cups (12 ounces) whole milk

1 vanilla bean (or 1½ teaspoons pure vanilla extract)

1 large egg

2 large egg yolks

6 tablespoons (3 ounces) sugar

¼ cup (1¼ ounces) unbleached all-purpose flour

2 tablespoons (1 ounce) cold unsalted butter

EQUIPMENT

Large Bowl, Medium Saucepan, Paring Knife, Two Medium Bowls, Whisk, Fine-Mesh Strainer

GETTING AHEAD **Store the pastry cream for up to 5 days in the refrigerator in an airtight container with a piece of plastic wrap pressed directly on the surface to prevent a skin from forming.**

1 Fill the large bowl halfway with ice and water and set it aside. Pour the milk into the medium saucepan. Use the tip of a paring knife to cut the vanilla bean in half lengthwise. Turn the knife over and use the dull side to scrape the seeds into the saucepan, then add the pod. Heat until the mixture just begins to simmer. Remove from the heat and let steep for 30 minutes. (If using vanilla extract instead of a vanilla bean, skip this step and add the extract later.)

2 Heat the milk to just below the boiling point and remove from the heat. In a medium bowl, whisk together the egg, egg yolks, and sugar until well blended and smooth. Add the flour and whisk vigorously until the mixture is very smooth. Pour about ½ cup of the hot milk into the yolk mixture, whisking constantly to temper the yolks. Slowly pour the yolk mixture back into the hot milk, whisking all the while.

3 Heat the mixture, whisking constantly to prevent the flour from lumping, until it reaches a boil. Continue to cook and whisk for another minute, until the pastry cream is very thick. Remove from the heat and whisk in the butter (and vanilla extract, if using). Strain the pastry cream through the strainer set over a medium bowl to remove any lumps or tiny bits of egg. (Save the vanilla bean: Rinse it thoroughly, allow to dry, then use it to make vanilla sugar, page 45).

4 Press a piece of plastic wrap directly on the surface of the pastry cream, then set the bowl into the bowl of ice water. Once the pastry cream has completely cooled, use or store in the refrigerator until needed.

Cinnamon Pastry Cream
Omit the vanilla bean. Whisk ½ teaspoon ground cinnamon into the egg and sugar mixture in Step 2, before adding the flour.

Dulce de Leche Pastry Cream
Whisk 1 cup (11 ounces) room-temperature *dulce de leche* (page 51) into the strained pastry cream at the end of Step 3.

Crème Fraîche

MAKES 1 CUP

Crème fraîche is cultured cream (much like yogurt is cultured milk), and has a wonderfully nutty flavor. It is available in the dairy section of many supermarkets and specialty grocers. It is also very easy to make at home.

INGREDIENTS

1 cup (8 ounces) heavy whipping cream (do not use ultra-pasteurized)
2 tablespoons (1 ounce) buttermilk

EQUIPMENT

Small Saucepan, Instant-Read Thermometer, 12-Ounce Jar

Pour the cream into the small saucepan and warm over low heat until it reaches 100°F on the thermometer, stirring occasionally. Remove from the heat and stir in the buttermilk. Pour into the jar, cover the opening with the lid or plastic wrap, and let the mixture sit at room temperature for 24 to 48 hours. The mixture will thicken considerably and take on a slightly sour, nutty flavor. Keep tasting as it develops, and when it reaches the flavor you like, put the crème fraîche in the refrigerator. It will become more sour and nutty as time passes. If it looks a little watery or separated, don't worry—just stir until the mixture is homogenous again.

STORING Crème fraîche will keep, covered, in the refrigerator for up to 1 week.

Vanilla Crème Fraîche
Place 1 cup chilled crème fraîche—either store-bought or homemade—in a bowl and add 1 tablespoon sugar and ½ teaspoon pure vanilla extract or vanilla paste (page 44). Whisk until blended and then taste. Add a little extra sugar, if you like. Whisk until the mixture has the texture of softly whipped cream. If the crème fraîche is overwhipped, it will look broken or curdled. You can rescue it by gently stirring in 1 to 2 tablespoons additional crème fraîche with a silicone spatula. Refrigerate until needed.

Honeyed Yogurt

MAKES 1 CUP

Simple and chic, this accompaniment is easy to make with the readily available Greek-style yogurt now in supermarkets and gourmet stores across the country. Greek yogurt (regular yogurt drained of excess liquid) is very thick and luscious, and sweetening it with a bit of honey makes for a welcome alternative to whipped cream. You can vary the flavor by using different honey varietals or a teaspoon of your favorite liqueur.

INGREDIENTS

1 cup (9 ounces) plain Greek-style yogurt
2 tablespoons honey

EQUIPMENT

Medium Bowl

Place the yogurt and honey in the medium bowl and stir until blended and thick. Refrigerate until needed.

STORING Honeyed yogurt can be prepared up to 4 days in advance and stored in an airtight container in the refrigerator.

LEMON CURD

MAKES 2½ CUPS The pastry kitchen would be incomplete without the tart, tangy freshness of lemon curd. Use it to flavor soufflés; to fill thumbprint cookies, tarts, cakes, and turnovers; to dollop on scones and biscuits and alongside cake slices; to spoon over fresh berries; to fold into whipped cream; and even to spread on morning toast. One taste and you'll be starting your list as well.

INGREDIENTS

3 large eggs

3 large egg yolks

1 cup minus 1 tablespoon (6½ ounces) sugar

¾ cup (6 ounces) strained freshly squeezed lemon juice

6 tablespoons (3 ounces) cold unsalted butter, cut into ½-inch pieces

EQUIPMENT

Large Bowl, Double Boiler, Whisk, Instant-Read Thermometer, Fine-Mesh Strainer, Medium Bowl, Silicone or Rubber Spatula

what the pros know

Lemon curd is a custard, with lemon juice as the liquid instead of milk or cream. The same rules apply for cooking curd as for other stovetop cooked custards (such as custard sauce): Keep the heat medium-low, stir constantly to prevent the eggs from curdling, and don't overcook or you'll have lemon-flavored scrambled eggs. Keep an eye on the thickness of the curd and test with the instant-read thermometer if you're having trouble telling when it's done. Always pour curd through a fine strainer to remove any little bits of scrambled egg (there are always a few).

1 Fill the large bowl halfway with ice and water and set it aside. Fill the bottom of the double boiler with 2 inches of water and bring to a rolling boil. Check to see that the water is at least 2 inches below the top portion of the double boiler.

2 Place the eggs, egg yolks, and sugar into the top of the double boiler (off the heat) and whisk until blended. Add the lemon juice and mix well. Reduce the heat until the water is at a gentle boil. Place the egg mixture over the water and cook, whisking constantly but leisurely, and scraping the edges frequently so the eggs don't scramble there, until the curd is very thick, about 7 minutes. A finished curd should hold its shape; when the whisk is lifted and a bit of curd falls back into the bowl, it should remain distinct on the surface rather than blending back into the mixture, and should register about 180°F on the thermometer. Do not let the curd boil, or you will have bits of scrambled egg in your curd (if this happens, quickly remove the bowl from the heat and continue to the next step).

3 Immediately strain the curd through the strainer set over the medium bowl. Use the spatula to push the curd through the strainer, leaving behind any bits of scrambled egg. Add the cold butter pieces to the curd, burying them so they melt quickly. Wait 1 minute, then whisk until the butter is completely melted and blended with the curd. Press a piece of plastic wrap directly on the surface of the curd, then set the medium bowl in the large bowl of ice water. Once the curd has completely cooled, use or store in the refrigerator until needed.

STORING The lemon curd may be prepared up to 3 days in advance and should be consumed within 5 days. Keep the curd refrigerated in an airtight container with a piece of plastic wrap pressed directly on the surface to prevent a skin from forming.

Lime or Passion Fruit Curd
Substitute strained freshly squeezed lime juice or seedless passion fruit juice for the lemon juice.

Sauces

Although nearly every pastry in this book can stand on its own, the finishing touch of a sauce adds flavor, moisture, and texture to your desserts, elevating them from special to extraordinary.

DECORATING WITH SAUCES

In many cases, serving your dessert with a dollop of cream or a drizzle of sauce is just right. There are times, however, when you want to pull out all the stops to dazzle your guests, and that's where sauce designs come in. When serving individual plates of dessert, decorating the plate with a design created by interweaving two complementary sauces gives a beautiful, professional canvas on which to present your dessert. When creating designs with more than one sauce, keep in mind that the sauces should: (1) have flavors that complement and highlight the dessert, (2) be the same consistency or thickness, so one sauce doesn't sink under the other, and (3) have contrasting colors, so the design really pops.

CHOOSING SAUCES

Consider the flavors first. The sauces should complement the dessert and each other. Chocolate sauce is tasty, but can easily overwhelm the flavor of the dessert if used in large amounts. Caramel sauce is a great accent sauce because its creamy bittersweet flavor goes with nearly everything, and its color complements the range of brown tones in the baking world. Raspberry or other fruit sauces provide a bright acidity and fresh fruit flavor, but like chocolate can overwhelm in large amounts. Because of its versatility, many dessert designs begin with custard sauce.

Custard sauce is a favorite with pastry chefs because of its cold, creamy texture, its ability to take on nearly any flavor and thus complement any dessert, and its color—usually a neutral beige that is a wonderful contrast for darker accent sauces. For these reasons, it is often the first sauce that is spooned onto a plate, coating it like a blank canvas. Because it is difficult to re-cook custard sauce, the accent sauce will need to be adjusted, if necessary, to match the thickness of the custard sauce. For instance, chocolate, caramel, and raspberry sauces are sometimes heavier and more viscous than custard sauce, which would cause them to sink underneath the custard, obliterating any design. But a bit of water, cream, or milk added to the accent sauces can easily adjust their consistency. Always do a test plate first to make sure the sauces are compatible in texture and to try out your design.

Sauce designs should be prepared just before serving the dessert. Many sauces, including custard sauce, chocolate sauce, and caramel sauce, develop a skin when exposed to air over time, so while it may seem like a good idea to make your designs and refrigerate them until serving time, it's not recommended. Besides, your guests will be thrilled to see you flaunt your creative talent at dessert time.

EQUIPMENT FOR DESIGNING WITH SAUCES

Once you've chosen and prepared (or bought) your sauces, the fun begins. It is easiest to create designs if you pour each sauce into a squeeze bottle. Pastry chefs use these bottles to control the flow of sauces and to avoid the drips and mistakes that occur when using spoons. You'll also want a few skewers or toothpicks for marbleizing sauces. Follow the steps below to begin your foray into sauce designs, and then take off in your own creative direction.

CREATING DESIGNS WITH SAUCES

Spiderweb: Coat the plate with a light-colored sauce. On top of the light sauce, draw a spiral with a dark sauce, beginning in the center and spiraling outward to the edge of the plate. Use the tip of a toothpick and draw a line from the center to the edge of the plate. Repeat with another line, ending about 1 inch from the first. Always begin in the center and end at the edge, spacing the lines evenly.

Alternating Spiderweb: Follow the directions above, except begin every other line with the toothpick at the outer edge and draw into the center.

String of Hearts: Coat the plate with a light-colored sauce. Use a dark sauce in a squeeze bottle to pipe circles of sauce about ½ inch in diameter in a ring around the edge of the plate. The exact size of the circles doesn't matter— the smaller or larger the circles, the smaller or larger the hearts. Use the tip of a toothpick to draw a continuous line beginning just outside one of the circles, through the center of it, and onward to the next circle (do not lift the tip off the plate). As the toothpick runs through each circle, the circle will change into a heart shape.

Two-Tone Hearts: You'll need 3 sauces for this technique. Coat the plate with a light-colored sauce. Use a darker sauce in a squeeze bottle to make several circles about 1 inch in diameter. Use another dark or light sauce to pipe a circle about ½ inch in diameter into the center of the larger circles. Use the tip of a toothpick to draw a line through each circle, beginning outside the circle and finishing an inch or so below the circle. As you pull the toothpick through the circles, each one will form a multicolored heart.

Herringbone: Coat the plate with a light-colored sauce. Use a dark sauce in a squeeze bottle to pipe a series of parallel lines, about ½-inch apart, across the plate. Use the tip of a toothpick to draw parallel straight lines about ½ inch apart and at a 90-degree angle through the dark lines, creating a herringbone pattern. For a slight variation, drag every other line in the opposite direction, that is, begin one line at the left side of the plate, then rather than beginning at the left again for the next line, simply drag it back from the right side of the plate.

VANILLA CUSTARD SAUCE

MAKES 2⅓ CUPS Custard sauce, also known as crème anglaise, is a smooth, velvety sauce, a great companion for desserts that benefit from a pool of cool creaminess to highlight and complete their flavor and texture. Because it is a custard, it may be flavored in many ways by infusing spices, nuts, citrus zest, tea leaves, and more into the milk portion before beginning the cooking process. Some flavor variations at the end of this recipe will help get you started. Custard sauce is good to use when creating sauce designs on dessert plates, as its light color contrasts well with chocolate, caramel, or raspberry sauces.

INGREDIENTS

1 cup (8 ounces) whole milk

1 cup (8 ounces) heavy whipping cream

¼ cup (1¾ ounces) sugar

1 vanilla bean or 2 teaspoons
pure vanilla extract

5 large egg yolks

EQUIPMENT

Large Bowl, Medium Saucepan, Paring Knife, Small Bowl, Whisk, Silicone or Rubber Spatula, Instant-Read Thermometer, Fine-Mesh Strainer, Medium Bowl

1 Fill the large bowl halfway with ice and water and set it aside. Combine the milk, cream, and sugar in the medium saucepan and warm over medium heat, stirring occasionally, until the sugar is dissolved. (If you are using vanilla extract, proceed to Step 2.) Use the tip of a paring knife to cut the vanilla bean in half lengthwise. Turn the knife over and use the dull side to scrape out the seeds, and add both the seeds and the pod to the saucepan. Heat until the mixture just begins to simmer. Remove from the heat and let steep for 30 minutes, or until you like the flavor.

2 Heat the milk mixture to just below the boiling point. Remove the pan from the heat. In the small bowl, whisk the egg yolks together. Slowly pour about 1 cup of the hot milk into the yolk mixture, whisking constantly, to temper the yolks. Slowly pour the yolk mixture back into the hot milk in the saucepan, whisking all the while. Return to medium-low heat and cook, stirring constantly with the spatula, until the custard thickens and registers 178° to 180°F on the thermometer (see right).

3 Immediately strain the custard sauce through the strainer set over the medium bowl to remove any tiny bits of scrambled egg. (Save the vanilla bean: Rinse it thoroughly, allow to dry, then use it to make vanilla sugar, page 45.) If you're using vanilla extract instead of the vanilla bean, add it now and whisk to blend. Press a piece of plastic wrap directly on the surface of the sauce then set the bowl into the bowl of ice water. Once the custard sauce has completely cooled, use or store in the refrigerator until needed.

STORING **Keep the custard sauce for up to 5 days from the day it was made, refrigerated in an airtight container with a piece of plastic wrap pressed directly on the surface to prevent a skin from forming.**

Be very careful that you do not allow the mixture to boil once you have added the egg yolks, for they will scramble and cause the sauce to separate. If you have an instant-read thermometer, watch for a temperature of 178° to 180°F, a point—just under boiling—at which the egg yolks will thicken, but not scramble. When testing the temperature, remove the pan from the heat to prevent the eggs on the bottom of the pan from scrambling while the thermometer takes a few seconds to register. If the custard begins to boil, immediately strain it through a fine strainer, then smooth it out by pouring it into a blender and blending on "liquefy" for 10 to 15 seconds (be cautious with hot liquid in a blender—never fill it more than halfway, and remove the center portion of the lid to allow steam to escape). Strain again and cool as directed.

Coffee Custard Sauce
Decrease the vanilla to ½ bean or 1 teaspoon pure vanilla extract. Add ¼ cup (¾ ounce) coffee or espresso beans and steep them along with the vanilla bean. Strain the beans out at the end of step 1 and discard, then continue as directed.

Earl Grey Custard Sauce
Substitute 3 tablespoons Earl Grey tea leaves for the vanilla bean and steep for 15 to 20 minutes.

Brandy Custard Sauce
Omit the vanilla. Once the sauce has cooled completely, stir in 1 to 2 tablespoons brandy or other liquor or liqueur.

Cinnamon Custard Sauce
Substitute 2 (3-inch) cinnamon sticks for the vanilla and add ½ teaspoon ground cinnamon to the egg yolks.

Ginger Custard Sauce
Omit the vanilla. Slice a thumb-size length of fresh ginger into thin rounds (don't worry about peeling it). Drop into a small pan of boiling water and cook for 2 minutes. Drain and add to the milk mixture instead of the vanilla bean.

Raspberry Custard Sauce
Omit the vanilla. Once the sauce has cooled completely, stir in ¼ cup (2 ounces) strained raspberry puree and 1 teaspoon framboise or Chambord.

CARAMEL SAUCE

MAKES 2 CUPS Caramel sauce can partner with all manner of desserts, and with good reason: its smooth bittersweet flavor complements almost every ending. It keeps very well for at least 2 weeks in the refrigerator, so it's easy to make ahead and have on hand for spur-of-the-moment desserts. If you are a novice to caramelizing sugar, you'll want to familiarize yourself with the process by reading the notes on page 26. This sauce reaches pouring consistency when chilled. For a caramel sauce meant to be served warm, see the variation at the end.

INGREDIENTS

¼ cup (2 ounces) water

1 tablespoon light corn syrup

1 cup (7 ounces) sugar

1¾ cups (14 ounces) heavy whipping cream

EQUIPMENT

Medium Saucepan, Small Saucepan, Wooden Spoon or Silicone Spatula

what the **pros** know

For the best flavor and color, cook the caramel until it is deep golden brown tinged with red—this is the color right before it begins to blacken. Caramel that is too light will result in a sauce that is simply sweet, with none of the complex bitter notes that make caramel sauce so deliciously compelling. Use a white plate and a spoon to check the color, and have the warm cream nearby so that you can add it immediately when the correct color is reached. The cream will prevent the caramel from darkening any further.

1 Pour the water and corn syrup into the medium saucepan. Sprinkle the sugar over the top, 2 to 3 tablespoons at a time, allowing each addition to moisten before adding the next. In the small saucepan, heat the cream just until it begins to boil. Remove from the heat and set aside.

2 Place the sugar mixture over medium-low heat and stir with the wooden spoon or the spatula until the sugar is dissolved and the liquid is clear. Increase the heat to high and boil rapidly, swirling the pan occasionally (don't stir) so that the sugar cooks evenly. Cook until the caramel turns a deep golden brown. Test the color by dipping a clean spoon into the caramel and dripping a bit on a white plate.

3 Immediately turn off the heat and add the warmed cream. (Be careful here—the mixture will rise dramatically in the pan and sputter, so you may want to wear an oven mitt on the hand holding the pan.) Stir with the wooden spoon or the spatula to blend. If any bits of caramel have solidified, set the pan back over very low heat and stir gently until they melt. Cool the caramel to room temperature.

STORING Caramel sauce may be stored in the refrigerator in an airtight container for up to 2 weeks.

Warm Caramel Sauce
Decrease the cream to 10 tablespoons (5 ounces). Warm the sauce in the microwave or a double boiler before using. Makes 1 cup.

Dark Chocolate Sauce

MAKES 2 CUPS

Dark Chocolate Ganache (page 419) may be used as chocolate sauce, but this sauce with crème fraîche and brandy offers a twist on the classic. If you use a chocolate with more than 60 percent cacao, you'll need to add a little extra cream to achieve a pouring consistency. This sauce should be served warm. For a cold sauce, you'll need to add another ¼ to ½ cup cream or milk to thin it to a proper sauce consistency.

INGREDIENTS

8 ounces bittersweet chocolate (up to 70 percent cacao), finely chopped
1 cup (8 ounces) heavy whipping cream
½ cup (4 ounces) crème fraîche
1 to 2 tablespoons brandy

EQUIPMENT

Medium Bowl, Small Saucepan, Whisk

Place the chopped chocolate in the medium bowl. Bring the cream and crème fraîche just to a simmer in the small saucepan over medium heat. Immediately pour the cream mixture over the chocolate. Let sit for 1 minute. Gently whisk until the sauce is smooth and homogenous. Stir in the brandy. Serve warm.

STORING **The sauce keeps in the refrigerator, in an airtight container, for up to 1 week. Reheat in a double boiler or on low in the microwave.**

Fresh Raspberry Sauce

MAKES ½ CUP

A staple in dessert kitchens all across America, raspberry sauce is a bright, refreshing complement to any dessert that needs some tart fruit flavor. Make it the day you need it because it never tastes—or looks—as good the second day. Thanks to good-quality frozen raspberries, this sauce can be made all year long.

INGREDIENTS

1 half-pint basket (6 ounces) fresh raspberries or 1½ cups (6 ounces) frozen raspberries
1 teaspoon freshly squeezed lemon juice
1 teaspoon framboise or Chambord (optional)
1 to 2 tablespoons sugar

EQUIPMENT

Food Processor Fitted with a Metal Blade, Fine-Mesh Strainer, Small Bowl, Silicone or Rubber Spatula

1 If using fresh raspberries, pour the raspberries out onto a baking sheet. Pick through them and discard any debris and molded berries. Place fresh raspberries in the bowl of the food processor. If you are using frozen berries, first measure the berries, then thaw them and add (along with their juices) to the bowl of the food processor. Process for 15 to 20 seconds, until completely pureed.

2 Pour the puree through the strainer set over the bowl, using the spatula to press the puree through. Press firmly and repeatedly to extract as much puree as possible. Stir in the lemon juice and framboise. Add the sugar to taste. Refrigerate until needed.

STORING **The raspberry sauce should be used as a sauce the same day it is made. Keep leftovers (to stir into yogurt, sparkling water, or mixed drinks) refrigerated in an airtight container for up to 3 days.**

Fresh Blackberry Sauce Substitute blackberries for the raspberries.

Decorations and Garnishes

DECORATING WITH CHOCOLATE

Easy chocolate decorations allow you to give your chocolate desserts that extra touch of style and elegance. All of these techniques may be done with dark, milk, or white chocolate.

CHOCOLATE SHAVINGS

Shavings are thin shards of chocolate used for decorating or garnishing desserts. You will need a block or bar of chocolate that is at room temperature.

If using a bar of chocolate, hold the bar with a paper towel to prevent the heat in your fingers from melting the chocolate. Run a sharp vegetable peeler down the long thin edge of the chocolate, pressing firmly to create shavings.

If using a block of chocolate, set it on a parchment-lined baking sheet with the short end of the pan and chocolate block toward you. Place a small cake cardboard or cutting board between you and the edge of the work surface (to keep your clothes clean, and just in case the knife slips). Hold a chef's knife at an 85-degree angle, with the top of the knife bent toward you. Scrape the knife down the block toward you for long, thin shards.

For fine shavings, run the chocolate down the large holes of a box grater.

CHOCOLATE CURLS

To make curls from a bar of chocolate, have the bar at warm room temperature. To warm the chocolate, rub it between your hands briefly or set it on a baking pan in the oven with only the pilot light for 5 to 8 minutes, or place the chocolate under a table lamp and let the heat from the light bulb soften the chocolate slightly.

Hold the bar with a paper towel to prevent the heat in your fingers from melting the chocolate. Run a sharp vegetable peeler down the long, thin edge of the chocolate, pressing firmly as for making shavings. If the chocolate crumbles or makes shards, it is too cold for curls. Warm again as directed above, then give it another try.

To make curls from a block of chocolate, set it on a parchment-lined baking sheet as for making shavings (above). The chocolate must be slightly warmed (as above for making curls from a bar). Curls are easiest with a block of milk chocolate, but dark or white chocolate at the right temperature will also yield nice curls. Hold a chef's knife at an 85-degree angle, with the top of the knife bent toward yourself. Scrape slowly and very firmly down the block toward you, forming large loopy curls with jagged edges.

Transfer the shavings or curls to the dessert, serving plates, or a storage container with a spoon or bench scraper, as the warmth of your hands would melt the chocolate. If you won't be using the chocolate curls immediately, store them in the refrigerator indefinitely.

PIPED CHOCOLATE

Piped decorations can be used to celebrate an occasion (Happy Birthday), delineate portions on a cake, or create a whimsical finish for any number of desserts. The decorations can be as simple or as elaborate as you want. All you need is melted chocolate—dark, milk, or white are all fine—and a bag for piping.

Line a baking sheet with parchment, a silicone mat, waxed paper, or plastic wrap (smooth out any wrinkles). Melt the chocolate according to the directions on page 43 and spoon into a pastry bag fitted with the tiniest plain round tip, a nonpleated resealable plastic bag (squeeze the chocolate into one of the corners and then snip off the tip of the bag), or a disposable pastry bag. Take care to make sure the hole is very small—you can always enlarge it a bit, but chocolate looks the best, and is easier to control, when piped through a tiny opening.

For free-form shapes, let your imagination guide you. If you have a design you'd like to copy, slip it under the parchment paper and trace it with the chocolate.

You can also pipe words or greetings in chocolate, directly on top of a cake or dessert, or on a piece of parchment as described above and then very carefully transfer to the pastry using a spatula for support. For individual desserts, it's fun to pipe a design, greeting, or celebratory phrase on the rim of each plate. For the best success with writing, stand directly over the writing surface, with the bag held at a 90-degree angle. Shape the words and make each letter by slightly moving your whole body in the shape of the letter, rather than just the bag at the end of your hand—this creates a more fluid and controlled style of writing. Hold the tip of the bag at least ½ inch from the surface and let the chocolate fall out in a thin rope rather than smashing it against the surface, which will make your message messy.

For a little extra fun, sprinkle colored sprinkles, tiny silver dragées, gold petals, or luster dust over the piped shapes while still wet. Transfer the sheet to the refrigerator for 10 minutes, or until the decorations are hard enough to be removed from the pan, then gently pop or lift them off with an icing spatula or mini offset spatula. If you won't be using the shapes immediately, store them in the refrigerator indefinitely, layered between sheets of parchment in an airtight container.

CHOCOLATE CUTOUTS

For clean-edged, precise chocolate shapes, nothing beats cookie cutters. Use small or mini cookie cutters to cut shapes from a thin sheet of chocolate, then apply the shapes to the top (or sides) of cakes, cupcakes, and tarts. To create chocolate cutouts, line a baking sheet with parchment, a silicone mat, waxed paper, or plastic wrap (smooth out any wrinkles). Melt the chocolate according to the directions on page 43. Spread the melted chocolate in a thin layer across the sheet—it doesn't matter how much chocolate you use, but it should be about ⅛ inch thick. If you want a few shapes, then a few ounces of chocolate is enough; for lots of shapes, you'll need 8 ounces or more.

Let the chocolate cool until it is almost but not quite set. Use a small cookie cutter to cut chocolate shapes close together (like cutting cookies for decorating) Push the edges of the cutter to the baking sheet so that the shapes release easily. Once you've cut shapes in the chocolate, transfer the sheet to the refrigerator for 10 minutes, or until the chocolate is completely set and hard.

Use an icing spatula or mini offset spatula to gently pop or lift the cut shapes off the pan (leftover chocolate scraps can be reused for anything needing chocolate). If you like, you can decorate the cutouts by piping designs or details on them with chocolate in a contrasting color, or paint them with luster dust. If you won't be using the cutouts immediately, store them in the refrigerator indefinitely, layered between sheets of parchment in an airtight container.

Decorating with Chocolate

CHOCOLATE SHAVINGS

CHOCOLATE CURLS

PIPED CHOCOLATE

CHOCOLATE CUTOUTS

SPUN SUGAR

MAKES ENOUGH TO DRAPE AND TOP A 9-INCH CAKE, MAKE 8 INDIVIDUAL (3-INCH) NESTS OR 12 SMALL (1-INCH) NESTS, OR CREATE LOTS OF DRIZZLED DECORATIONS. While spun sugar is not hard to make, it does take a little time and attention to detail—mostly prepping your kitchen so you don't spend the next month scraping sticky caramel off your cabinets and floor. You can use two forks nestled together to fling the caramel across the spoon handles, but it is more efficient to use a wire cutter to snip off the rounded bottom of a metal sauce whisk to create plenty of tines to form more strands of caramel. Do not attempt to make any caramel decorations on a humid day; the caramel will be sticky and the spun sugar will collapse instead of staying light and airy. For a review of cooking sugar and making caramel, see the discussion on page 26.

INGREDIENTS

¼ cup (2 ounces) water

1 cup (7 ounces) sugar

¼ teaspoon cream of tartar, or 2 tablespoons light corn syrup

EQUIPMENT

Parchment Paper, Baking Sheet, Two Long-Handled Wooden Spoons or Dowels, Heavy Saucepan or Pasta Pot, Medium Bowl, Small Saucepan, Instant-Read Thermometer, White Plate, Trivet, Cut-Off Whisk or Two Forks

1 Cover the floor and cabinets with parchment paper or newspaper in a 3-foot area along the counter where you will be working. Line the baking sheet with parchment paper or a silicone mat. Lightly oil the wooden spoons or dowels and arrange them on your work surface so that their handles protrude from the edge of the surface by 7 or 8 inches. Position them 6 to 8 inches apart and set a heavy saucepan or pasta pot on them to hold them in place.

2 Fill the medium bowl halfway with ice and water and set it aside. Pour the water into the small saucepan. Sprinkle the sugar over the top 2 to 3 tablespoons at a time, allowing each addition to moisten before adding the next. Add the cream of tartar or corn syrup. Set the pan over medium-low heat and stir until the sugar is dissolved and the liquid is clear.

3 Increase the heat to high and boil rapidly, swirling the pan occasionally so that the sugar cooks evenly (do not stir). Cook until the sugar turns amber. Test the color by dipping a clean spoon into the caramel and dripping a bit on a white plate. This is one of the few instances where you do not want a dark golden brown color, so keep it light.

4 Immediately remove the caramel from the heat and set the bottom of the saucepan in the bowl of ice water. This will stop the caramel from cooking—and coloring—any further. Hold it in the ice water for about 5 seconds; then remove, dry the bottom of the pan, and set on the trivet or on a folded kitchen towel.

5 Let the caramel cool, testing it every minute or so, until it falls off the ends of the whisk in thin streams rather than drops. Dip the ends of the whisk into the caramel and fling

In a cool kitchen, the caramel in the pot can get cold quickly, making it hard and unusable. To avoid this problem, set the pot over a very low heat on top of a heat diffuser on the stove, or place the pot on a warming tray set to a low temperature. If you don't have either, you'll need to do it the old-fashioned way—reheating the caramel over a burner. Set the pan back over a low flame and give it a few minutes to melt again. Don't hurry it along over a high flame or the caramel will burn quickly. Reheated caramel will always be a bit darker, but as long as it is not too dark or burned, it will work just fine. If it gets too dark, you'll need to make some new caramel, for there is no way to save blackened sugar.

STORING Although spun-sugar decorations are best when fresh, you can place them in an airtight container and store at room temperature for up to 2 weeks. Be sure to put a paper cup of desiccant (available at craft and floral supply stores) inside with the spun sugar (don't let it touch the sugar), to absorb any moisture in the air and keep the decorations looking their best.

it quickly back and forth across the top of the spoon handles. The caramel should form thin, gossamer threads between the spoons. Repeat 2 or 3 times, then gather the spun sugar with your hands, pull it off the dowels, and shape it as desired, working quickly as the spun sugar becomes quite brittle as it cools. Set the shape on the prepared baking sheet. Repeat until you have used all the sugar or until you have enough spun sugar for your needs. If the caramel cools and becomes too thick to use, simply reheat over low heat until fluid again (don't boil or the caramel will darken too much).

6 Drape the spun sugar around a cake, on top of a tart, around a cream puff, or stack layer after layer of it to create a huge beehive for a dramatic presentation. Spun sugar is at its best the same day it is made, so serve the sugar or decorate with it within a couple of hours.

Spun Sugar Nests
Make little nests by gathering the warm spun sugar, swirling the strands, and tucking them into the indentation of a lightly oiled cupcake pan or a custard cup. Use a mini cupcake pan when shaping nests to garnish cupcakes or mini Bundt cakes. When the caramel nests have cooled, remove from the mold and store. Of course, you can shape the nests free-form as well.

Caramel Decorations
Prepare a baking sheet by lining it with lightly oiled parchment paper or a silicone mat. Cook the caramel as directed above, letting it turn a light golden brown color. Stop the cooking with the ice bath as directed. Use a small spoon to drizzle shapes and decorations onto the prepared sheet. You can also make cross-hatches and use them on top of custard for crème brûlée (for details, see page 346). As soon as the caramel decorations are cool, store them between pieces of parchment paper in an airtight container as described above.

Spun-Sugar Nests

Spun-sugar—threads of caramel gathered together—is one of the most dramatic dessert finishes ever. The thin, glistening, angel hair presence is one part delicious sugar, two parts fairy-tale gorgeous.

Dip the ends of the whisk into the caramel and fling it quickly back and forth across the top of the dowels.

Gather the spun sugar with your hands, pull it off the dowels, and shape it as desired.

DECORATING WITH GOLD OR SILVER LEAF, GOLD PETALS, AND LUSTER DUST

Gold adds an elegant touch to pastries, elevating them with a glint of precious metal from pretty to stunning. Be sure to purchase culinary gold leaf, which is 22 to 24 carats and completely edible. Culinary gold is available in fine cookware stores in both leaf and petal forms and can also be found in art supply stores.

Gold or silver leaf comes in small square packets with tissue-thin square sheets of gold or silver tucked between sheets of paper. Be careful when opening the packet, as the leaves are so thin they will practically dissolve in the air if you fling it open and allow them to fall out of their sheaves. To apply gold or silver leaf, you'll need something for it to stick to—a moist line of melted chocolate, a tiny bit of frosting, even a tiny drop of water will help the leaf adhere to your dessert. Gently peel back one of the sheaves, exposing some of the leaf within. Hold the packet in one hand close to the dessert with a paring knife in the other hand. With the tip of the knife, pick up a piece of the gold or silver leaf, tear it off, and transfer it to the pastry, touching it to the point on the pastry where you want the gold or silver to stick. The little pieces of leaf are at their most beautiful when standing up, waving in the air slightly, catching the light. You can also gently smooth them down to lie flat with the knife tip or a small brush.

Gold petals are gold leaves that have been broken into small pieces. They are more convenient than sheets if you like to apply little gold flecks to your pastries. They come in a boxlike shaker—you can shake out as few or as many as you like. You can also take the top off the box and pick up individual petals with a pair of tweezers, applying them more precisely.

Powdered gold is gold that has been ground to a fine powder and may be sprinkled over desserts for a shimmering finish. It can be more difficult to find than gold leaf and petals. You can substitute gold-colored luster dust.

Luster dust is edible mineral dust with a fine, sparkly finish. It is available in myriad colors, from aquamarine to pumpkin to sunflower to silver, as well as a whole range of gold tones, from bright and shiny to subdued and antique. Luster dust may be applied directly to desserts that have a dry surface by brushing it on with a fine artist's brush. More commonly, though, luster dust is combined with a bit of clear alcohol to create "paint" that can be brushed free-hand onto a dry dessert surface (such as chocolate cookies or mini tartlets) or used to paint designs on individual decorating components, such as chocolate cutouts (page 429). You can also paint fresh fruit and flowers to give them a shimmering, transparent gilding that can be beautiful in a centerpiece or as a garnish to individual plates of dessert. The alcohol may be lemon or almond extract, or you could use a clear, flavorless alcohol such as vodka. To mix up some "paint," tap ¼ teaspoon or so of luster dust into a small cup. Add a few drops of alcohol, just until the dust is liquid. Use immediately, before the alcohol evaporates. If it evaporates and you are left with dry color in the cup, simply add a few more drops of alcohol and continue.

DECORATING WITH STENCILS

Stencils are a quick and easy way to give your cake, tart, cookies, or brownies a great finish with very little effort. Stencils can be purchased from cookware stores or craft stores. Be sure they are made of sturdy plastic or heavy cardboard so they can be lifted without folding or crumpling and ruining your design.

You can make your own stencils, too, with a piece of sturdy cardstock, a cake cardboard, or foam core. Sketch or trace the design onto the stencil surface, keeping in mind the size of the cake or pastry you will be decorating. Cut out the design with a box cutter or craft knife. Use cookie cutters, wrapping paper, or pictures as inspiration, or simply draw a design freehand. Bold, graphic designs produce better-looking results than small intricate ones. Stencils can be reused numerous times—simply dust them off with a dry pastry brush after each use and store flat in a resealable plastic bag. You can even improvise stencils from objects around the house, placing them on the cake, dusting with cocoa or sugar, then removing them carefully with a pair of tweezers or your hands. Craft supplies, doilies, buttons, jar lids—the ideas are endless once you start.

It's a good idea to practice using a stencil on a piece of parchment paper to get a feel for how gently to tap the strainer, how much powder you'll need for coverage, and how to remove the stencil without damaging the design.

To use a stencil, place it on the pastry. If the top of the cake or pastry is moist, placing the stencil directly on it could damage the finish. In such a case, try dusting the top of the dessert with one of the stencil toppings to create

Confectioners' sugar is the classic medium for a stencil design, and it can be beautiful, but It's not the only option. Here are some ideas to get you started. All powders used with stencils need to be sieved through a very fine strainer over the stencil for a velvety-looking finish.

Natural cocoa powder for light brown

Dutch-process cocoa powder for dark brown

A mixture of cocoa powder and gold or silver luster dust for shimmery brown

A mixture of confectioners' sugar and cocoa for a light brown

A mixture of confectioners' sugar and luster dust for an iridescent color

A mixture of confectioners' sugar and spices for a light brown sugar that is flavored

Finely grated dark, milk, or white chocolate

a dry surface; then place the stencil and sieve a contrasting powder on top. Place the powder in the strainer and tap it gently over the surface of the pastry and/or stencil. You don't want gobs of powder that will cause your guests to cough when they take a bite, but you definitely want the design to show up clearly. Once you've added the powder, carefully lift the stencil straight up about an inch, then slowly move it to the side and away from the pastry. If you move quickly or tilt the stencil, some of the powder could fall from it onto your design.

Another fun idea is to layer designs and use several different powders to create a visually stunning yet easy finish. To do this, apply one color of powder all over the surface. Then set a stencil on top and sift a different color of powder over it. You could even use a third stencil to finish the design, being very careful to get the last layer of powder exactly where you want it, or covering the rest of the cake with cardstock or cardboard so you don't get powder from the third shape drifting over onto other parts of the cake. Gorgeous!

SUGARED FLOWERS

Almost any dessert is made more enticing by the presence of fresh flowers shimmering under a crystal sugar finish. The good news on the entertaining front is that these flowers can be prepared in advance—in fact, far, far in advance. If kept in an airtight container with desiccant (available in craft and floral supply stores) in a cool, dark location, they will last at least 3 months, and perhaps up to 6 months or more.

CHOOSING FLOWERS

The most important thing to remember when sugaring flowers is to make sure that the blossoms are edible. Check the list (page 439), which, though not comprehensive, covers the most commonly available varieties. If you're not sure whether a flower is edible, check with a local authority at a gardening or nursery supply store, or with an agent of a local university's cooperative extension, or a current botanical reference book. Some flowers may have edible petals but poisonous leaves or stems, and others are completely inedible, so be careful—a few nonedible types to avoid are delphinium, foxglove, and lily of the valley.

In addition to being edible, the flowers must also be free of pesticides. This means you should not buy from a florist shop, where the perfect blossoms are full of the stuff. Edible flowers are often available at farmers' markets, and many specialty markets and supermarkets carry small packages of edible flowers in the produce section. Of course, the best way to ensure a plentiful and untainted supply is to plan for such a harvest in your own garden, or borrow from a neighbor. If you grow edible flowers, the best time to pick the blooms is early in the day, just as they reach full bloom.

Once you purchase or pick your flowers, use them as quickly as possible, because fresh, firm blossoms turn out best. Small, delicate petals deteriorate rapidly, so don't let them sit around in the refrigerator for days—if you do, you'll be disappointed to find they have wilted.

SUGARED FLOWERS

Fresh flowers preserved under a glittering finish of sparkling sugar are a lovely way to finish any special-occasion dessert. Also called candied or crystallized flowers, this romantic garnish is beautiful on cakes and cupcakes, tarts, pies, and custards. In short, they make any dessert even more special by virtue of their presence. A tiny watercolor brush works well for applying the egg whites.

INGREDIENTS

1 cup (7 ounces) superfine sugar

1 to 2 tablespoons powdered pasteurized egg whites

Edible flowers (whole and/or petals)

EQUIPMENT

One or Two Baking Sheets, Parchment Paper or Two Silicone Mats, Small Bowl, Small Whisk or Fork, Tweezers, Small-Soft Bristle Brush

what the pros know

When sugared flowers are suspended and air is allowed to circulate around them, drying occurs more quickly and evenly. If you have a fine-mesh rack, or a piece of screening, this is a great time to use it. Just make sure any items from the garage or hardware store are washed well and completely dry before setting flowers on top.

1 Line the baking sheets with parchment paper or silicone mats. Pour the sugar onto a dinner plate and set aside. Place the powdered egg whites in the small bowl and add enough water to dilute them to the consistency of fresh egg whites. Mix gently with the small whisk or a fork until well blended (don't create froth).

2 Pick out the whole flowers and set them aside. Gently pull any petals you want to sugar off the remaining flowers. Make sure that both whole flowers and petals are clean and dry.

3 With the tweezers, hold a flower or petal. Dip the brush into the liquid egg whites and lightly paint the entire surface of the flower. You must cover every surface—front and back—with the whites, for any exposed surface will decompose. Hold the flower over the plate of sugar. Gently spoon the sugar over the flower, allowing the excess sugar to fall back onto the dish. Check both sides of the flower—if you missed a spot, simply touch it up with the brush and a little more sugar. Still holding the flower over the plate, gently tap the tweezers on the side of the plate (or with your finger) to knock off any excess sugar.

4 Set the flower on the prepared baking sheet and continue sugaring the remaining flowers and/or petals. When you have finished, go back through the sugared blooms and check again for any spots that may need touching up.

5 Set the baking sheet in a warm, dry place for several days, turning the flowers with the tweezers once a day to ensure that they dry evenly. This turning is especially important for whole flowers, as their heft and density can inhibit moisture from evaporating from the bottom of the flower. When the flowers are very dry, they will be crisp.

STORING **Keep the sugared flowers between layers of parchment paper in an airtight container. If possible, set a small cup of desiccant in the container with the blooms (but don't let it touch the flowers) to absorb any excess moisture. Stored in a cool, dry location (not the refrigerator), the sugared flowers will keep for 2 to 3 months, and perhaps 6 months or more.**

While all the flowers on this list are edible, some have a sweet flavor and some are savory. They may all be sugared and used as decoration.

Sweet Flowers

Almond blossoms (*Prunus* species)
Apple blossoms (*Malus* species)
Carnations (*Dianthus caryophyllus*)
Dianthus (*Dianthus* species)
Elderflowers (*Sambucus* species)
Gardenias (*Gardenia jasminoides*)
Geraniums (*Pelargonium* species—both the flowers and leaves are edible)

Honeysuckle (*Lonicera* species)
Jasmine (*Jasminum polyanthum*)
Lemon blossoms (*Citrus* species)
Lilac (*Syringa vulgaris*)
Orange blossoms (*Citrus* species)
Plum blossoms (*Prunus* species)
Roses (*Rosa* species)
Tulips (*Tulipa* species)
Violets (*Viola odorata*)

Neutral-Flavored Flowers

Borage blossoms (*Borago officinalis*)
Calendulas or pot marigolds (*Calendula officinalis*)

Cornflowers or bachelor's buttons (*Centaurea cyanous*)
Johnny jump-ups (*Viola tricolor*)

Savory and Bitter Flowers

Basil blossoms (*Ocimum basilicum*)
Chive blossoms (*Allium schoenoprasum*)
Chrysanthemums (*Chrysanthemum* species)
Iceland poppies (*Papaver nudicaule*)
Nasturtiums (*Tropaeolum majus*)
Rosemary blossoms (*Rosmarinus officinalis*)
Sweet marigolds (*Tagetes lucida*)
Thyme blossoms (*Thymus* species)

ACKNOWLEDGMENTS

Bakers have always been the heart of Sur La Table— creative scientists, enthusiastic about their craft and dedicated to sharing it with those they love. The process of this book has been organic, based on the foundation set by our customers' love of baking and grown out of Sur La Table's commitment to them by supplying the tools to fuel their passion. This book brings life to that passion, and Cindy Mushet, our resident creative scientist, was the perfect choice to communicate our commitment. Her nurturing style and solid technical skill, coupled with her teaching experience, has brought it all together.

She has not been alone in achieving that end. Under Kirsty Melville's guiding hand, Lane Butler jumped in to keep the ship on course while Jean Lucas took time off to breathe life into Kate. Sur La Table's own maverick, Doralece Dullaghan, with her unending dedication to every detail and passionate modus operandi, made our dreams of croissants, soufflés, and cookies come flavorfully alive. Along the way, without the support of Robb Ginter, Janis Donnaud, Kathy Grocott, Kimberley McBain, Rebecca Burgess, Cory Chandler, David Bauer, Tom Rafferty, Mark Beard, Barbara Dimas, John Walker, Will McCoy, Phillip Stevenson, Liz Paquette, and Nathan Slosser, there would have been no port in the storm.

Synergy for the visualization of this book was magically created by Alison Lew, Maren Caruso, Kim Konecny, Kerrie Sherrell Walsh, Joshua LaCunha, Stacy Ventura, Sarah Roseme, Christine Wolheim, and Lori Engels. Clearly, science was at work here, for the combined total was greater than the sum of the parts. They got our vision of baking and manifested it in the amazing design and mouthwatering photography in this book.

We especially want to thank Alice Medrich for her inspired foreword, and Peter Reinhart, Sherry Yard, David Lebovitz, Flo Braker, Dorie Greenspan, and Emily Luchetti for their kind words and support over the years—bakers without equals!

The real acknowledgment of this book will be the legacy and inspiration that it has created for the future bakers and customers of Sur La Table. Let no page go unstained from use and no crumb go uneaten . . .

—KATHY TIERNEY
CEO, Sur La Table

Thank you . . .

To the entire crew of Sur La Table, who strive to provide their clients with the finest and most beautiful equipment possible, and whose desire for a book that addressed the needs, wants, and questions of bakers everywhere resulted in the work within your hands. Special thanks to Doralece Dullaghan, who headed this project for Sur La Table. To Lane Butler, Jean Lucas, Kirsty Melville, and Chris Schillig at Andrews McMeel Publishing for their heartfelt enthusiasm, their incredible editorial precision, and their ability to laugh heartily in spite of the stress—you were the icing on the cake. To Margo True and Deri Reed for their amazing talents in arranging each tiny brushstroke into a masterful picture. To Maren Caruso, Kim Konecny, and Kerrie Sherrell Walsh for the gorgeous photographs that grace this book. To Alison Lew, whose beautiful design brings this book to life. To Doe Coover, for her kindness and wise counsel. To Kathi Saage for her keen editing skills, insightful testing (and testing . . .), and soft shoulder. To Michele Fagerroos for her true friendship, extraordinary pastry skills, and tales of Ozzie that brightened each day. To Theresa Maranzano, for everything, always. To John Warneke, for literally getting me back on my feet. To Patsy Firth-Trotter, Jennie Junio, Terry Paterson, Sara Rose, Barbara Stanforth, Ali Wanne, and the students in P&B II, all of whom embody the boundless giving of the human spirit. To my family, especially my parents, for everlasting love. To Miguel, for always believing in me. And to Bella, for love, patience, and late-night giggles—you are the cherry on top.

—CINDY MUSHET

INDEX

black pans, 9
bowls, 9
bowl scraper, 12
Bundt cake pans, 13
for cake baking, 306
cake pans, 10, 12–13
ceramic pans, 9, 11
cooling racks, 14
for designing with sauces, 422
digital scale, 5
double boiler, 14, 43
dowel rolling pins, 16
flan rings, 11
flexible silicone baking pans, 9
food processor, 9
glass pans, 9
graters, 14
hand mixer, 9
huller, 17
ice cream scoops, 14
juicer, 14
knives, 14–15
Kugelhopf pan, 13
loaf pans, 10, 12
measuring, 8
mixing, 9
muffin pans, 10, 12
nonstick pans, 9
offset spatulas, 17
pans, 9–13, 10, 306
parchment paper, 15, 151
pastry bags, 15, 309, 401
pastry blender, 15
pastry board, 15
pastry brushes, 15
pastry tips, 401
peeler, 15
pie pans, 10–11, 13
popover pan, 16
Pyrex, 10, 11
rolling pins, 16
ruler, 16
scissors, 16
silicone baking pans, 9
spatulas, 17
spoons, 17
springform pans, 10, 12–13
squeeze bottle, 16
stand mixer, 9
straight spatulas, 17
straight-sided tub, 17

strainer, 17
tart pans, 10–11, 13
thermometers, 8
timers, 17, 272
tongs, 354
torch, propane or butane, 16
tube pans, 10, 13
wire whisks, 17
wooden spoons, 17
espresso, 314
buttercream, 410
powder, 51
Espresso Buttercream, 410

F

false filling, baking with, 175
fats. *See also* butter; oils
equivalents, 7
gluten related to, 22
fennel seeds, 51
fermentation, 66, 68
feta cheese, 47
Feta, Roasted Pepper, and Basil
Muffins, 150–51
figs, 51
fillings
almond, 119
cream cheese, 119
fruit, 176
for tarts, 208
Flaky Pie Dough, 177–78
flan rings, 11
flexible silicone baking pans, 9
flour, 20–24
all-purpose, 21
in baking, 20–24
bleached v. unbleached, 22
bread, 21–22, 63
cake, 4, 21
choosing, 22
gluten in, 22
making, 21
measuring, 22
pastry, 21
self-rising, 21
specialty, 63
storing, 22
tapioca, 59
types of, 21
unbleached all-purpose, 4

Flourless Chocolate Cake with Crème
Fraîche Topping, 335
flowers
edible, 439
sugared, 437–38
food processor, 9
fougasse, 83–84
Framboise Cream, 51, 417
Frangelico Cream, 51, 417
frangipane, 208
apricot-, tart, 217
date tart with sesame-almond,
216–17
French meringue, 377, 378
Fresh Blackberry Sauce, 427
Fresh Raspberry Sauce, 427
Fresh Strawberry Tartlets with
Shredded Phyllo, 237
fromage blanc, 47
Fromage Blanc, Tomato, and Herb
Tart, 234–35
frostings, 408. *See also* buttercream;
icing
cream cheese, 414
maple–cream cheese, 325–26,
414
matching with cakes, 408
tips, 308–9
white chocolate–cream cheese,
414
fruit, 240–63. *See also specific fruit*
about, 240
classic French, tart, 214–15
cobblers, 241
crisps, 241
crumbles, 241
dried equivalents, 7
fillings, 176
fresh, 242
in muffins, 144
roasted summer, with late harvest
Riesling, 262
shortcakes, 242

G

galettes
apricot-cherry, 230–31
nectarine-plum, 231
potato, onion, and gruyère, 232
shapes for, 231